ROUTLEDGE HANDBOOK OF URBAN FOOD GOVERNANCE

AF888607

The *Routledge Handbook of Urban Food Governance* is the first collection to reflect on and compile the currently dispersed histories, concepts and practices involved in the increasingly popular field of urban food governance.

Unpacking the power of urban food governance and its capacity to affect lives through the transformation of cities and the global food system, the *Handbook* is structured into five parts. The first part focuses on histories of urban food governance to trace the historical roots of current dynamics and provide an impetus for the critical lens on urban food governance threaded through the *Handbook*. The second part presents a broad overview of the different frames, theories and concepts that have informed urban food governance scholarship. Drawing on the previous parts, part three engages with the practice of urban food governance by analysing plans, policies and programmes implemented in different contexts. Part four presents current knowledge on how urban food governance involves different agencies that operate across scales and sectors. The final part asks key figures in this field what the future holds for urban food governance in the midst of pressing societal and environmental challenges. Containing chapters written by emerging and established scholars, as well as practitioners, the *Handbook* provides a state of the art, global and diverse examination of the role of cities in delivering sustainable and secure food outcomes, as well as providing refreshed theoretical and practical tools to understand and transform urban food governance to enact more sustainable and just futures.

The *Routledge Handbook of Urban Food Governance* will be essential reading for students, scholars, practitioners and policymakers interested in food governance, urban studies, sustainable food and agriculture, and sustainable living more broadly.

Ana Moragues-Faus is a Senior Research Fellow in the School of Economics and Business at the University of Barcelona.

Jill K. Clark is Associate Professor in the John Glenn College of Public Affairs at Ohio State University.

Jane Battersby is a Senior Lecturer in Environmental and Geographical Science at the University of Cape Town.

Anna Davies is Professor of Geography, Environment and Society at Trinity College Dublin.

"Cities are emerging powerhouses of food systems transformation. The *Handbook of Urban Food Governance* takes readers on a journey through a plethora of examples, providing a diversity of ideas of how to govern cities for better food systems. Recommended for anyone looking for a sense of hope and possibility."

Professor Corinna Hawkes, *Director Centre for Food Policy, City, University of London*

"Anyone interested in urban development and food systems transformation will treasure this book, which is a unique resource for understanding the crucial issue of urban food governance, and get inspired from various practices and innovative and inclusive forms of collaborative food governance."

Cecilia Marocchino, *Urban Food Agenda Coordinator, FAO, Rome*

"The *Handbook of Urban Food Governance* provides readers with frameworks and examples of how cities around the globe are redefi ning food governance. Those interested in more equitable sub-national food policy – such as urban planners – will find the book especially useful in guiding professional practice."

Professor Samina Raja, *Urban and Regional Planning and Director, Food Systems Planning and Healthy Communities Lab*

ROUTLEDGE HANDBOOK OF URBAN FOOD GOVERNANCE

Edited by Ana Moragues-Faus, Jill K. Clark, Jane Battersby and Anna Davies

Routledge
Taylor & Francis Group
LONDON AND NEW YORK

earthscan
from Routledge

Cover image: Getty Images

First published 2023
by Routledge
4 Park Square, Milton Park, Abingdon, Oxon OX14 4RN

and by Routledge
605 Third Avenue, New York, NY 10158

Routledge is an imprint of the Taylor & Francis Group, an informa business

© 2023 selection and editorial matter, Ana Moragues-Faus, Jill K. Clark, Jane Battersby, and Anna Davies; individual chapters, the contributors

The right of Ana Moragues-Faus, Jill K. Clark, Jane Battersby, and Anna Davies to be identified as the authors of the editorial material, and of the authors for their individual chapters, has been asserted in accordance with sections 77 and 78 of the Copyright, Designs and Patents Act 1988.

All rights reserved. No part of this book may be reprinted or reproduced or utilised in any form or by any electronic, mechanical, or other means, now known or hereafter invented, including photocopying and recording, or in any information storage or retrieval system, without permission in writing from the publishers.

Trademark notice: Product or corporate names may be trademarks or registered trademarks, and are used only for identification and explanation without intent to infringe.

British Library Cataloguing-in-Publication Data
A catalogue record for this book is available from the British Library

Library of Congress Cataloging-in-Publication Data
Names: Moragues-Faus, Ana, editor. | Battersby, Jane, 1975– editor. |
Clark, Jill K., editor. | Davies, Anna, 1970– editor.
Title: Handbook of urban food governance / Ana Moragues-Faus,
Jane Battersby, Jill K. Clark, Anna Davies.
Description: New York, NY : Routledge, 2023. |
Includes bibliographical references and index.
Identifiers: LCCN 2022020863 (print) | LCCN 2022020864 (ebook) |
ISBN 9780367518004 (hardback) | ISBN 9780367519742 (paperback) |
ISBN 9781003055907 (ebook)
Subjects: LCSH: Food security. | Food supply–Government policy. | Urbanization.
Classification: LCC HD9000.5 .H3627 2023 (print) |
LCC HD9000.5 (ebook) | DDC 362.5/8–dc23/eng/20220831
LC record available at https://lccn.loc.gov/2022020863
LC ebook record available at https://lccn.loc.gov/2022020864

ISBN: 978-0-367-51800-4 (hbk)
ISBN: 978-0-367-51974-2 (pbk)
ISBN: 978-1-003-05590-7 (ebk)

DOI: 10.4324/9781003055907

Typeset in Bembo
by Newgen Publishing UK

This book is dedicated to foundational urban food governance thinkers and do-ers no longer with us: Marielle Dubbeling, Wayne Roberts and Vanessa Watson; and to current and future researchers, activists and practitioners working towards more equitable, just and sustainable urban food futures.

CONTENTS

FIGURES

TABLES

CONTRIBUTORS

Editors

Ana Moragues-Faus is a Senior Research Fellow in the School of Economics and Business at the University of Barcelona, Spain. She works closely with civil society organisations and policymakers to build sustainable and just food systems, mobilising critical analytical tools and co-productive practices.

Jill K. Clark is Associate Professor in the John Glenn College of Public Affairs at Ohio State University, USA. Her work focuses on community and state governance of food systems and inclusive and equitable public participation.

Jane Battersby is a Senior Lecturer in Environmental and Geographical Science at the University of Cape Town, South Africa. Her research and activism focuses on urban food and nutrition security, governance and planning in African cities. She works closely with civil society and local and provincial governments on urban food policy issues.

Anna Davies is Professor of Geography, Environment and Society at Trinity College Dublin, Ireland, where she directs the Environmental Governance Research Group. Her research explores the ways in which sociotechnical innovations and their governance in urban settings are transforming ancient practices of food sharing.

Contributors

Julian Agyeman is Professor of Urban and Environmental Policy and Planning at Tufts University, USA. His research centres on critical explorations of the complex and embodied relations between humans and the urban environment and their effects on public policy and planning processes and outcomes, particularly in relation to notions of justice and equity.

Alison Alkon is Professor of Sociology at the University of the Pacific, USA. Her research explores how racial and economic inequalities intersect with the ways we produce, distribute and consume various foods. Her most recent co-edited book examines the relationship between food and gentrification in North America.

Lauren Baker, PhD, has more than 20 years of experience leading cross-sectoral research, policy and advocacy for sustainable food systems in nonprofit, academic, business, policy and philanthropic contexts. She lectures and teaches in the Global Food Equity programme at the University of Toronto and at Ryerson University, Canada.

Karen Bassarab is a Senior Research Program Manager at the Johns Hopkins Center for a Livable Future in Baltimore, MD, USA, where she manages the Food Policy Networks project and works on research focused on community food systems and policy.

Viktor Bedö is a research designer with a focus on bodies, technologies and infrastructure in urban space. He is Visiting Professor at Critical Media Lab at FHNW Basel and visiting research fellow at the Centre for Urban and Community Research at Goldsmiths, University of London, UK.

Alison Blay-Palmer is Professor in Geography and Environmental Studies at Wilfrid Laurier University in Waterloo, Canada. She is the UNESCO Chair on Food, Biodiversity and Sustainability Studies as well as the Director of the Laurier Centre for Sustainable Food Systems.

Katrin Bohn is an architect and urban practitioner and a Senior Lecturer at the University of Brighton, UK. With André Viljoen, she has worked widely on their urban design concept Continuous Productive Urban Landscape (CPUL). Her practice centres around sustainable architecture and urban design with a focus on productive urban landscapes, urban agriculture and the urban food system.

Basil Bornemann is a Senior Researcher and Lecturer at the Social Research and Methodology Group and the Sustainability Research Group, University of Basel, Switzerland. His research focuses on sustainability-oriented governance transformations and their democratic implications in various areas such as energy and food.

Luciene Burlandy is a lead researcher on analysis of food and nutrition policies and programmes, and justice in food systems, in partnerships with Brazilian and international universities. She is currently a member of the State Council for Food and Nutrition Security of Rio de Janeiro.

Kirsten Valentine Cadieux is grateful to be in a community with a circle of learners and organisers growing and sharing food in the Twin Cities, including with the Twin Cities Community Agricultural Land Trust, and at her day job teaching community food systems and environmental justice and sustainability at Hamline University, USA.

Joy Carey is an independent Sustainable Food Systems Planning Consultant with a focus on cities. She has worked in sustainable food and farming with the UK and international food sectors since 1990, contributing to the development of the City Region Food Systems assessment methodology and the MUFPP monitoring framework.

Ruth Catlow is Artistic Director of Furtherfield, UK, the founder of DECAL Decentralised Arts Lab at Furtherfield, and networked cultures expert. Her artistic practice and curatorial work at Furtherfield has focused on critical investigations of digital and networked technologies and their emancipatory potential.

Paul Currie uses urban metabolism, resource nexus and political ecology as lenses for shaping sustainable, inclusive cities. At ICLEI Africa, he manages the Urban Systems Unit, supporting local governments to apply systems perspectives and facilitating the development of policies and plans appropriate to contexts of change and uncertainty.

Patricia Camacho Dias has been a member of the Municipal Food and Nutrition Security Council of Niterói and of the State Food and Nutrition Security Council of Rio de Janeiro. She currently coordinates the Collaborating Center for School Food and Nutrition (CECANE–UFF), a partnership between the Fluminense Federal University and the National Education Development Fund to support the National School Food Program (PNAE).

Scott Drimie has directed the Southern Africa Food Lab since 2013 and is Professor (Extraordinary) at the Department of Global Health, Stellenbosch University, South Africa. He has two decades of research, facilitation and teaching expertise related to food systems, livelihoods and vulnerability, with in-depth knowledge of food and nutrition security.

James Duminy is Lecturer in Human Geography at the University of Bristol, UK, and Honorary Research Associate at the African Centre for Cities, University of Cape Town. His research examines the historical and contemporary governance of urban change in the Global South.

Alexandra Duprey is currently a Climate Resilience Specialist working in Washington DC, USA. Her work lies at the intersection of urban planning, environmental policy and equity. She sees effective urban food governance as an important consideration for cities working to fill the gaps in food security and access.

Florence Egal is a medical doctor with experience on humanitarian work and a long career with FAO's Food and Nutrition Division. She co-led the technical team producing the Milan Urban Food Policy Pact, contributed to drafting the URL-GP, and engaged on territorial governance throughout the UN Food Systems Summit.

Thomas Forster is an educator/consultant active in civil society engagement with urban and territorial governance, alongside negotiations for the SDGs, the New Urban Agenda and the UNFSS. He has led key technical teams drafting the MUFPP or the Urban–Rural Linkages: Guiding Principles and Framework for Action to Advance Integrated Territorial Development (UN-Habitat).

Thierry Giordano is a researcher at CIRAD, Montpellier, France. From 2016 to 2018, he was a Decentralized Cooperation Advisor to the Director of the Partnership Division at FAO, supporting the development of collaborations between FAO, local governments and local government networks on food systems. He holds a PhD in Agricultural Economics from Montpellier Sup Agro.

Jess Halliday is a consultant and associate of the RUAF Global Partnership on Sustainable Urban Agriculture and Food Systems, based in France, specialising in governance of urban and city region food systems. She received her PhD in food policy from the Centre for Food Policy, City University London in 2015.

Gareth Haysom is a researcher at the African Centre for Cities at the University of Cape Town, South Africa. His work uses food as a lens to better understand urbanisation in cities of the Global South with a specific interest in African cities, working in a variety of countries and across city types.

Aniek Hebinck is a researcher of food system change at the Dutch Research Institute for Transitions, Erasmus University Rotterdam, the Netherlands. She has a PhD from the Stockholm Resilience Centre. In her work she combines a food systems perspective, foresight and transition thinking to explore the diverse pathways for change and innovation.

Jaz Hee-jeong Choi is the Director of the Care-full Design Lab and Vice-Chancellor's Principal Research Fellow in the School of Design at RMIT, Australia. Her transdisciplinary research and practice explore how design can be done care-fully in different cultural contexts, often through playful and participatory engagements.

Sara Heitlinger is a Lecturer in Computer Science at the Centre for Human Computer Interaction Design at City, University of London, UK. Drawing on methods from the arts and humanities, her research looks at the intersections between citizen-led innovation, sustainability and co-designing urban futures.

Lesli Hoey is Associate Professor of Urban and Regional Planning, University of Michigan, USA. Her research examines ways that planning mechanisms limit and build equitable, healthy and sustainable food systems. Her work is comparative, spanning sustainable diets in Kenya and Vietnam, governance in the United Nations Food Systems Summit, nutrition policy and food environments in Bolivia, and collective impact and state food charters in the USA.

Lara Houston is a researcher working at the intersection of Science and Technology Studies and Human–Computer Interaction. At the University of Sussex, UK, she is Research Fellow on the CreaTures project, investigating how citizen-led creative practice can inform sustainable transitions. She has previously held research positions at City, University of London, Goldsmiths and Cornell University.

Alice J. Hovorka is Professor and Dean at the Faculty of Environmental and Urban Change, York University, Canada. Her research programme broadly explores human–environment relationships with specialisations in animal geographies, gender and environment, urban geography and Southern Africa. She has long been interested in contemporary urban life in Botswana.

Aiden Irish, PhD, is a Research and Extension Project Manager at Ohio State University, USA. His research and work focuses on the role of community engagement and multi-stakeholder collaboration in local and regional food system planning.

Daniel Keech is a Senior Researcher at the Countryside and Community Research Institute (CCRI), University of Gloucestershire, UK. He joined CCRI in 2012 after 20 years of working with civil society organisations concerned with environmental and food issues. Research interests include urban food systems, European food cultures and cultural landscapes, and rural–urban spatial and functional relationships.

Luitfred Kissoly is a development economist working as a Lecturer cum Researcher at the Ardhi University in Dar es Salaam, Tanzania. Currently, his research focuses on diverse aspects of development economics, including food security, welfare analysis, agri-food systems, rural development and related aspects. His doctorate was obtained from Gottfried Wilhelm Leibniz University Hanover, Germany.

James Kuhns, MSc, has been active in policy and project development in food security and urban agriculture for the past 25 years. He is co-coordinator at Toronto Urban Growers and an associate of the Ryerson Centre for Studies in Food Security, Canada.

Roman Malec is resilience advisor at the Office of Emergency and Resilience of the Food and Agriculture Organization of the United Nations (FAO). He contributes to the Food for the Cities Programme, specifically as part of the City Region Food Systems project, currently being implemented in Antananarivo, Kigali and Colombo.

Astrid Mangnus is a Postdoctoral Researcher at the Copernicus Institute of Sustainable Development, Utrecht University, the Netherlands, working on creative practices aimed at sustainability transformations. The focus of her research is on breaking through sustainability deadlocks with art, play, community organisation and radically new ways of thinking and doing.

Damian Maye is Professor of Agri-Food Studies at the Countryside and Community Research Institute, University of Gloucestershire, UK. He has a long-standing research interest in the geography and sociology of agri-food restructuring. He is Associate Editor of the *Journal of Rural Studies* and has recently finished a major new textbook, *Geographies of Food*.

Steven R. McGreevy is Assistant Professor of institutional rurban sustainability studies, Department of Technology, Policy, and Society, Section of Governance and Technology for Sustainability, the Netherlands. His research interests include novel approaches to sustainable bioregional revitalisation, sustainable agri-food transitions and post-growth food systems, using simulation and serious gaming as a tool for education and governance.

Oona Morrow is a critical geographer at Wageningen University, the Netherlands, who explores how food provisioning in cities can become more circular, inclusive and shared. Through research on gender and household sustainability, urban agriculture, alternative food networks, urban commons, food sharing and community composting, she examines the relationship between grassroots innovation and urban policy.

Joe Nasr is a Toronto-based scholar, lecturer and consultant based at the Ryerson University Centre for Studies in Food Security, Canada, who has explored urban agriculture and food security issues for three decades. He co-curated the Carrot City initiative, co-founded the Toronto Urban Growers network, and co-edits the Springer Urban Agriculture Book Series.

Anne Palmer is the Director of Practice at the Johns Hopkins Center for a Livable Future and an associate scientist at the Bloomberg School of Public Health in Baltimore, MD, USA, where she conducts research on state and local food policy and food systems.

Serena Pollastri is a Lecturer in Urban Futures at Lancaster University, with previous experience in China (Tongji University and BJTU) and Italy (Politecnico di Milano). Her practice-based research explores visual design processes articulating pluralistic futures, with a focus on food and more-than-human environments.

Ana Puhac is an urban food system consultant at FAO's Food and Nutrition Division. She has supported the development of FAO's urban food system programmatic area since 2016 through coordination of global projects and implementation of technical areas on food system governance, food chains, food environments and public food procurement.

Matt Reed is Associate Professor of Food Citizenship and Director of the Countryside and Community Research Institute, University of Gloucestershire, UK. As a sociologist, he examines the interfaces of technology and the environment in the food system, spanning organic farming, local food provisioning, urban agriculture, agri-environmental schemes, emergent food technologies and commercial fishing.

Cecilia Rocha is the Director of the Centre for Studies in Food Security, Ryerson University, Canada, and a member of the International Panel of Experts on Sustainable Food Systems (IPES-Food). She is the author of a number of scholarly papers and reports on food policy and programmes in Brazil.

Marlyne Sahakian is Assistant Professor of Sociology at the University of Geneva, Switzerland. Her research interest is in understanding everyday practices in relation to environmental promotion, well-being and social change. She is a co-founder of SCORAI Europe, a network for sustainable consumption research and action, and a member of ENOUGH, a network focused on sufficiency.

Guido Santini is an Officer at FAO's Plant Production and Protection Division where he leads a global workstream on sustainable crop and agri-food systems in city regions. He has more than 20 years of work experience in international development cooperation in Sub-Saharan Africa, Asia, Latin America and Europe.

Raychel Santo is a Senior Research Program Coordinator at the Johns Hopkins Center for a Livable Future in Baltimore, MD, USA, where she supports food policy councils through the Food Policy Networks project and works on research related to urban agriculture and the relationship between diet and climate change.

Emma L. Sharp is a Lecturer in Te Kura Mātai Taiao/School of Environment at the University of Auckland, Aotearoa New Zealand. Her research focuses on food and soil politics, care, alternative economies and community engagement. She is a Primary Investigator with Te Pūnaha Matatini – Centre of Research Excellence hosted by the University of Auckland.

Tammara Soma is Assistant Professor at the School of Resource and Environmental Management (Planning Program) at Simon Fraser University and Research Director of the Food Systems Lab, Canada. Originally hailing from Indonesia, she conducts research on issues pertaining to food loss and waste, food system planning, food access and the circular economy.

Carolyn Steel is a London-based architect and academic and is a leading thinker on food and cities. Her award-winning books *Hungry City: How Food Shapes Our Lives* (2008) and *Sitopia: How Food Can Save the World* (2020) have established her concept of 'sitopia' (food-place) internationally. She is a director of Kilburn Nightingale Architects.

Cecilia Tacoli is a Senior Associate at the Institute for Environment and Development, UK. Her collaborative work with partners in the Global South like grassroots organisations, UN agencies and consortia of social and natural scientists, explores how urbanisation and rural–urban transformations shape food systems.

Makiko Taguchi is an Agricultural Officer with the Plant Production and Protection Division at the Food and Agriculture Organization of the United Nations. Her wide portfolio includes projects on city region food systems, urban agriculture, cereal cropping systems and agroforestry.

Alex Taylor is a Sociologist at the Centre for Human Centred Interaction Design, at City, University of London, UK. With a fascination for the entanglements between social life and machines, his research ranges from empirical studies of technology in everyday life to speculative design interventions.

René van Veenhuizen is Senior Programme Manager at Hivos in the Netherlands, and Coordinator of the Secretariat of the RUAF – Global Partnership on Sustainable Urban Agriculture and Food Systems, which is hosted by Hivos. He co-edits the Urban Agriculture Magazine and is co-author of several books on sustainable food systems and urban agriculture.

Joost Vervoort is Associate Professor for Foresight and Anticipatory Governance at the Copernicus Institute of Sustainable Development, Utrecht University, the Netherlands. He holds a PhD from Wageningen University and has led work on foresight and futures across Asia, Africa, the Americas and Europe in the context of climate change, food and sustainability.

André Viljoen is Professor of Architecture at the University of Brighton, UK, where he contributes to design teaching and research. He has a long-standing interest in the interplay between design and low environmental impact buildings and cities. With Katrin Bohn, in the 1990s, he developed the Continuous Productive Urban Landscape concept.

Stefan Wahlen is Professor of Food Sociology at Giessen University, Germany. His research and teaching concerns food consumption practices and food cultures as well as their political, organisational and institutional parameters. He earned his PhD in Consumer Economics from the University of Helsinki (Finland) with a thesis entitled 'Governing Everyday Consumption'.

Daniel N. Warshawsky is Associate Professor in the School of Public and International Affairs at Wright State University in Dayton, Ohio, USA, where he teaches courses in geography and public administration and conducts his research on urban food systems in North America and Africa.

Marc C. A. Wegerif is a Senior Lecturer and Development Studies Program Coordinator at the University of Pretoria in South Africa. His research focuses on agrarian transformation, land rights and food systems. He has over 30 years of development sector work experience from project level to national and international policy and advocacy.

Sabine Weiland is Associate Professor of Political Science at the European School of Political and Social Sciences (ESPOL) and Director of the ESPOL-LAB, Catholic University of Lille, France. Her research focuses on sustainable development and societal transformation, reflexive governance, food politics, environmental politics and the role of knowledge in political processes.

Miriam J. Williams is a Lecturer in Geography and Planning at Macquarie University, Australia. Her research focuses on care, commons, justice and food. She is a member of the International Community Economies Institute. Her research has been published in international journals such as Antipode, Urban Studies and Cities.

Gisèle Yasmeen is Senior Fellow at the Institute of Asian Research at the School of Public Policy and Global Affairs, University of British Columbia, Canada. She has published on foodscapes and food-systems in Asia since the early 1990s. She is a former federal government and not-for-profit executive and has advised numerous Canadian and international clients.

Laine Young is a PhD Candidate from Wilfrid Laurier University in the Geography and Environmental Studies programme. She works with the Laurier Centre for Sustainable Food Systems on her dissertation research exploring intersectional feminist analysis in urban agriculture projects in Quito, Ecuador.

ACKNOWLEDGEMENTS

We want to thank our respective families, friends and communities for their support throughout the elaboration of this *Handbook*. We feel extremely fortunate to have been able to engage with and learn from so many experts across the globe in developing this collective piece which constitutes a steppingstone in progressing the field of urban food governance. The writing and editing of the *Handbook of Urban Food Governance* mostly took place during the COVID-19 pandemic, when contributors were under much stress. We are very grateful for their commitment and generosity, as we are in debt to the reviewers of the chapters, specifically: Patrick Bresnihan; Chiara Certoma, Pay Drechsel, Scott Drimie; James Duminy; Jessica Duncan; Florence Egal, Louise Fitzgerald; Thomas Foster, Thierry Giordano, Mary Greene; Jess Halliday; Gareth Haysom, Lesli Hoey, Aiden Irish, Erika Lee; Sarah Lupolt, Sarah Martin, Alwynne McGeever; Oona Morrow; Dioniso Ortiz, Cecilia Rocha; Monika Rut; Raychel Santo; Charlotte Spring; Daniel Warshawsky; Marc Wegerif. The *Handbook* is ultimately a testimony of the global, vibrant and committed community working on urban food governance. We also want to thank our funders that allow us to continue developing engaged academic work.

1
TOWARDS URBAN FOOD GOVERNANCE FOR MORE SUSTAINABLE AND JUST FUTURES

Ana Moragues-Faus, Jill K. Clark, Jane Battersby and Anna Davies

Introduction

The last 20 years have seen a resurgence of academic and applied interest in governing urban food systems, exemplified by hundreds of cities developing urban food policies and engaging in such initiatives as the Milan Urban Food Policy Pact, as well as the growth of a vibrant community of academics and practitioners researching the field. As actors find their footing in the complex set of relationships that comprise urban food governance and engage in activities to guide, steer, control, or manage food system outcomes in specific urban areas (Moragues-Faus & Battersby, 2021, p. 5), we learn more about the possibilities and consequences of urban areas as sites of food governance. As this *Handbook* illustrates, urban food governance is conceptualised differently, takes on unique expressions, and has various transformational aims across the globe. The volume provides a unique collection that traverses dispersed histories, theories, concepts, practices of, and future visions for urban food governance, exploring the potential for urban food governance to transform lives, cities, and the planet.

Growing interest in urban food governance is the result of the intersection of a number of issues. First, there is a widespread dissatisfaction with the food system and its economic, health, ecological, and social impacts, which contribute to climate change and rising levels of malnutrition across the globe. Second, the political and symbolic power of cities has increased steadily, as captured by such concepts as "planetary urbanisation," which highlights how all of the earth's inhabitants and territories are involved in and affected by global urbanisation processes, or the notion of cultural and methodological "cityism," which champions a focus on urban spaces in lieu of more complex understandings of urbanisation processes and outcomes (Brenner, 2018; Connolly, 2019; Millington, 2016). In some contexts, these processes have been coupled with decentralisations of power, from national to local governments, which has shifted the attention of global development agencies and donors towards urban realities and

DOI: 10.4324/9781003055907-1

devolved austerity measures. This wave of decentralisation has also contributed to the rise of cities as key powers in transforming food systems. Following these developments, urban food policy pioneers signalled a lack of national leadership on food systems reform, which was a key driver for cities to develop food strategies and specific measures (Moragues-Faus & Morgan, 2015). Third, in some cities and municipalities where the state is closer to citizens, novel co-governance approaches to manage decentralisation, in which civil society and the public and private sector come together to, in this case, steer food system outcomes, have emerged. These co-governance approaches range from increased citizen participation and the development of new deliberation spaces, such as food policy councils, to the unfolding of a new municipalist movement with associated political parties. Finally, the rise of complex systems thinking, and particularly its application in the food realm, has blurred long-standing dichotomies around the roles of urban and rural spaces in understanding and shaping food system outcomes on local and global scales. In fact, integrated approaches to food policymaking have mostly been developed in cities, moving away from the dominant agricultural and rural focus of food-related interventions devised at national and international levels (Lang et al., 2009). These overlapping issues have led to a diversity of theoretical and practical approaches to study urban food governance, but they remain largely disconnected.

While there has been a recent upsurge in interest, urban food governance is not new. Historic governance of food systems has inevitably shaped urban form and dynamics. For example, historical control of urban space and urban populations is inherently and fundamentally linked to the control of food in the African context. These past processes have shaped how food is produced, transformed, distributed, consumed, and disposed of around the globe today, resulting in negative health, environmental, and socioeconomic impacts that affect people's lives and the future of our planet within and beyond urban boundaries. Indeed, cities and towns are largely responsible for resource depletion and climate change. They host the majority of overweight or obese adults, while one in three stunted children live in urban areas (IFPRI, 2017), with the changing nature of urban food environments driving dietary transitions and trends in malnutrition (e.g. Cooksey-Stowers et al., 2017; Demmler & Qaim, 2020).

Characteristics of food retail, dietary choices, and dietary outcomes are all profoundly shaped by their interactions with the urban, including access to adequate water, sanitation and energy for both retailers and consumers, housing quality, transport equity, urban livelihood, and income stability (Battersby & Haysom, 2018). However, conceptual models proposed to understand and intervene in urban food environments (e.g. Turner et al., 2018) largely omit the role of the urban in shaping food environments and their outcomes. This is a clear example of why the urban food governance lens needs to be sharpened and widened in its consideration of the interactions between urban, food, and governance dynamics.

In this context, the *Handbook of Urban Food Governance* aims to unpack the power of urban food governance and its capacity to affect lives through the transformation of cities and the global food system. It is the first collection to reflect and compile currently dispersed histories, concepts, and practices involved in this increasingly popular and important field. This critical and collective exercise contributes to the reassessment of the role of cities in delivering sustainability and food security outcomes, while also providing refreshed theoretical and practical tools to understand and transform urban food governance in order to enact more sustainable and just futures. The *Handbook* draws on the knowledge of both academics and practitioners and includes contributions from established and emerging scholars from a range of disciplines and locations. While it is impossible to represent a complete picture of urban food governance around the globe, this *Handbook* compiles key contributions to this rapidly evolving field and offers a range of critical concepts, tools, and examples that constitute an essential guide and source of inspiration to develop a transformative agenda at the intersection of cities, food, and governance.

In this introductory chapter, we first present the contents of the *Handbook*, synthesising the main contributions and describing how they relate to each other. The *Handbook* has five parts. Part I focuses on histories of urban food governance in order to trace the historical roots of current dynamics and provide an impetus for the critical lens on urban food governance threaded through the *Handbook*. Part II presents a broad overview of the different frames, theories, and concepts that have informed urban food governance scholarship. Part III engages with the practice of urban food governance by analysing governance arrangements and the plans, policies, and programmes implemented in different contexts. Part IV presents current knowledge on how urban food governance involves different agencies that operate across scales. Finally, Part V explores how urban food governance futures have been, and are being, incorporated into visioning exercises designed to meet the pressing global, societal, and environmental challenges we face. Based on an analysis of the chapters, we reflect on what urban food governance is, highlighting key common messages and gaps identified in the individual chapters. We then propose a series of principles that together constitute a framework for critical analysis of urban food governance dynamics and devise ways to build more sustainable and just urban food futures.

The Handbook of Urban Food Governance: histories, theories, practices, agencies, and futures of urban food governance

Part I Histories of Urban Food Governance

This part traces the historical roots of current urban food governance dynamics, with chapters exploring the historical metabolic relations of cities and how they have shaped current food systems. That is, they focus on the ways in which urban food planning has always been a response to both governance challenges of contemporary urban conditions and imagined and actualised visions of future food systems. The part can therefore be read as a complement to the final part of this volume, which deals with urban food futures. The chapters in Part I map the key actors, policies, and processes that have shaped urban food governance discourses at different scales and geographies. Being mindful of the impact of historical governance processes encourages us to think more critically about intended and unintended consequences of current governance approaches.

In the first chapter, **Carolyn Steel** (Chapter 2), writing about the role of food systems in shaping Western civilisation and using cases as far back as the emergence of cities in ancient Sumeria, argues for the centrality of food to the physical, economic, social, and political structure of urban settlements. She illustrates both how the governance of the provision of food for cities has increasingly shifted from the public to the private sector and the deleterious effects of state inaction in the governance of food (through planning, land reform, taxation, or environmental regulation). Drawing on these histories, she concludes by charting a hopeful path towards building resilient urban futures by re-acknowledging the centrality of food in urban and rural well-being.

Delving into the specific case of Kenya, in his chapter **James Duminy** (Chapter 3) argues that in order to understand contemporary urban food governance systems, it is essential to grasp the rationalities, practices, and legacies of historical governance. The governance of urban food systems in Kenya was informed by the politics of labour and political stability. In turn, the urban demand for food formed and reformed the national agricultural and development policy landscape. The history described in this chapter encourages us to situate our analysis of urban food governance within wider political, economic, and spatial governance considerations.

Gisèle Yasmeen's chapter (Chapter 4) on the history of food and urban governance in South East Asia closes this part by mapping the ways in which the economies, social lives, and geographies of cities in South East Asia are fundamentally shaped by histories of food trade and urban food governance. She points out that despite the centrality of food to these urban spaces, broader urban governance work has typically ignored the food system and its governance.

Part II Frames, theories, and concepts of urban food governance

This part provides an overview of the diverse organising structures – the frames, theories, and concepts – that have informed urban food governance scholarship. The chapters describe a suite of frames through which urban food has typically been examined, as well as broader theories and concepts of governance that have been applied to food in urban contexts. Particular attention is paid to how power in urban food governance is enacted and [re]distributed between multiple actors across different scales. The chapters also engage with the range of ways that social theories and concepts have been used to better understand urban food governance, from long-standing interactions with political economy to more emergent activities, such as utilising social practice theories and feminist ethics of care.

This part begins with a set of chapters mobilising different theories to understand urban food governance dynamics. First, **Marlyne Sahakian and Stefan Wahlen** (Chapter 5) identify how social practice theory research and action have been adopted by and adapted to food and urban studies because it offers an alternative to the individualistic drivers behind many of the attempts to reconfigure consumption onto more sustainable pathways. Instead, social practice approaches elevate the rules, tools, skills, and understandings that shape habits and routines around food, from growing and shopping, to cooking, eating, and divesting of food waste, as well as how these have changed and are likely to continue changing in the future. While the outputs of social practice analyses are often discursive rather than quantifiable, which can create challenges for policymakers to translate them into practical policy processes, changing a system ultimately requires a change in thinking. Adopting social practice approaches brings new frames and ultimately brings new solutions to the table.

In a similarly relational vein, **Miriam Williams and Emma Sharp** (Chapter 6) explore the potential of a feminist ethics of care approach to better understand urban food governance. The strengths of such an approach, they argue, centre around the attention it gives to the interdependencies and responsibilities existing within and beyond food systems. Drawing on case studies from Australia and Aotearoa (New Zealand), they explore how care has been used to make connections as well as create new forms of politics and materialities, while also exploring how governance can foster or discourage such care in an urban setting. Importantly, humans are decentred in these cases, replaced with more-than-human actors and influencing imaginaries of a more care-full and just urban food governance future.

The chapter by **Damian Maye, Daniel Keech, and Matt Reed** (Chapter 12) mobilises a different perspective by providing an overview of innovation and transition theory, with a particular focus on social innovation in urban food governance. It argues that innovation (institutional, technical, and especially social) is critical for sustainable urban food system transitions. The authors suggest that viewing governance as collaborative modes of action allows a shift from people being characterised as only consumers to more holistic citizens who can create new forms of social justice. The chapter then presents the living labs concept as a key epistemology and methodology to enact technical and social change.

Part II also includes two chapters that explore emerging connections being made by researchers and practitioners in the urban governance field with previously disconnected concepts and framings, such as food and democracy and commons in urban locations. In their chapter, **Basil Bornemann and Sabine Weiland** (Chapter 7) bring their long-standing interest in food democracy into the urban realm. Working through discussions of food democracy (which place food at the centre of democracy debates) and urban democracy (where the urban becomes the locus of attention), they outline the implications of bringing these concepts together. This requires both a narrow and a broad reading of urban food democracy, from enabling participation in the design and implementation of urban food systems (narrow) to examining the democratic credentials of all decisions around food in urban areas (broad), which extend far beyond urban administrative boundaries.

In a similar vein, **Oona Morrow** (Chapter 8) explores how the concept of the commons, which has long been a feature of debates about sustainable development, also resonates with urban food governance. She argues that reframing urban areas and food as commons fundamentally changes the ways we think about food governance, particularly in high-income democracies where food is predominantly governed as a privately owned and traded commodity. Morrow focuses on sites of commoning that span the food system, from community growing to community composting, and that take place in diverse settings. She shows how diverse sites, settings, and practices are themselves governed by those who are commoning and those who are charged with urban policy responsibilities. However, these sites, settings, and practices have rarely been examined as central to urban food governance.

The final set of chapters in Part II focus their attention on the role that power plays in the formation and implementation of urban food governance. While it is well-established that power is highly uneven within global food systems, **Julian Agyeman, Alison Alkon, and Alexandra Duprey** (Chapter 9) focus on the urban scale in their analysis of state-led urban agriculture interventions in Boston, Massachusetts in the United States. While assumed to bring positive benefits to urban dwellers, the lack of inclusion of local diverse populations in the planning process for the urban agriculture scheme stripped power from already disadvantaged communities. The authors illustrate how a lack of participatory planning reinforced uneven power differentials. Importantly, they also show that once planners recognised concerns from residents, they slowed the process and brought in the community. This culminated in a widely supported initiative.

There are parallels between the ideas expressed in Chapter 9 by Agyeman et al. and those articulated by **Alice Hovorka** (Chapter 11), who examines the contribution that feminist political ecology can bring to urban foodscapes, and in particular the emphasis on uneven access to, distribution, and control of resources. Hovorka offers empirical illustrations from research on gender and urban agriculture in Gaborone, Botswana, focusing on gender dynamics in the production of a feminist foodscapes conceptual frame to examine how food systems operate in urban areas to produce gendered relations of power. This feminist foodscapes concept pushes past simplistic readings of gender, identifying the inherent gender inequities embedded within ideological, institutional, and individual realms of society and, importantly, within urban food governance itself.

Finally, in her chapter on conceptualisations of urban governance, **Jess Halliday** (Chapter 10) provides an overview of six different conceptualisations that are relevant to urban food governance. She makes these theoretical framings accessible to a non-academic audience in order to provide inspiration and guidance for food-aware cities without them necessarily being dependent on consultants, academics, or civil society organisations. The chapter identifies and explains four different governance forms (multilevel, polycentric, collaborative, and networked governance) and two conceptualisations of governance practice (adaptive and reflexive governance). The chapter is motivated by action, with the intention that it be used to inform the design and review of food governance structures and processes.

Part III Practising Urban Food Governance

In Part I, Chapter 2 Steel describes the practices resulting from the historical shift from public to private governance of food systems, as well as the turn back towards food as a public concern. This public reappropriation of food, while uneven, has resulted in an increase in urban food governance practices characterised by diversity. This part includes nine chapters that review governance practices, including relational arrangements, processes of decision-making, tools used for implementation, and the intended impacts of those practices on certain aspects of the food system.

Two chapters concentrate on local governance arrangements and the relationship to local government. **Karen Bassarab, Rachel Santo, and Anne Palmer** (Chapter 13) start by reviewing urban food policy councils (FPCs) in the U.S. FPCs are considered governance mechanisms that increase public awareness about the food system, build cross-sector relationships, and advance policy solutions. The chapter documents the many arrangements between FPCs and urban local governments, including organisational relationships, membership of FPCs, and community and political engagement with FPCs. The chapter closes by raising critical questions about representation and voice in FPCs.

By providing the reader with an understanding of the interplay between Africa's urban transition and urban food governance, **Gareth Haysom and Paul Currie** (Chapter 14) make a case that Global North concepts of urban food governance (including FPCs) do not translate directly to the African experience. The chapter outlines who governs food and how in African cities, using four cases to illustrate nascent food governance, authority, agency, and the role of external players. The authors contend that while there is opportunity for urban food governance in African cities, wider urban system deficiencies, such as poverty and inequality, need to be integrated into governance strategies so they can have meaningful impacts.

Governance processes often aim to employ formal governance tools to effect change. The chapter by **Jill Clark and Aiden Irish** (Chapter 15) defines the range of food policy tools employed by urban areas in the U.S. The authors provide a framework based on the intersection of policy tools, stages in the supply chain, and policy priorities to better understand how cities can and do implement policy. Applying the framework, the authors show that policy is topically thin in important areas such as labour, the environment, and middle infrastructure; there is a narrow focus on authority tools; and more universal coverage of urban policy is likely needed to address equity. Finally, the authors note that a shift towards indirect governance tools poses managerial, accountability, and legitimacy challenges.

The chapter by **Lesli Hoey** (Chapter 16) dives into governance processes around one specific governance tool, city planning. Hoey first reviews the state of food system planning in cities, followed by employing policy process theories of incrementalism and windows of opportunity to illustrate how food systems planning is institutionalised in cities. By doing so, Hoey brings the political conditions that support food system transformation to the fore, with examples from around the globe to illustrate how "savvy" policy entrepreneurs can create conditions amenable to advancing their food system agendas.

The next two chapters focus on governance tools used in cities in Brazil. The chapter by **Luciene Burlandy, Cecilia Rocha, and Patricia Camacho Dias** (Chapter 17) focuses on public food procurement as a strategic tool in urban food governance. The authors provide detailed analyses of how cross-scalar and cross-sector governance arrangements and processes are expressed in Brazilian cities, including how rural smallholder producers are connected to urban initiatives within the national context of the Right to Food. They also address the challenges associated with implementing urban public procurement via federal policy, highlighting the role of civil society in the development, implementation, and maintenance of food programming that addresses the needs of its most vulnerable groups (including family farmers and smallholders).

Cecilia Rocha and Luciene Burlandy (Chapter 18) offer another chapter on innovations in governance tools, namely the use of participatory budgeting in cities. Their chapter describes the general structures and processes of participatory budgeting and its intended role in urban governance. As in the previous chapter, the authors detail some of the implementation challenges participatory budgeting has faced, including difficulties in scaling-up, and that the process can be overly controlled by government or captured by powerful interests. They conclude that participatory budgeting is only meaningful if the associated budget is meaningful. Finally, Rocha and Burlandy turn to Belo Horizonte, a city known as an innovative leader in food policy, to consider the potential of using participatory budgeting in food governance.

The final three chapters in the part use cases to illustrate governance practice around specific nodes in the food system: waste, food markets, and urban agriculture. **Daniel Warshawsky and Tammara Soma** (Chapter 19) use case studies in Dayton, Ohio, U.S. and Bogor, Indonesia to explore the formal and informal mechanisms employed to govern waste, and illustrate the differing impacts of waste in the Global North and South. The authors describe the roles of street vendors, households, and other local players as they engage in informal livelihood strategies, including sharing, gifting, scavenging, and reusing food. The diversity of strategies governing waste is highlighted, but the dominant model is to treat the poor as "food waste infrastructure," which Warshawsky and Soma argue results from a charity and a neoliberal market-based approach and an absence of focused governance.

Marc Wegerif and Luitfred Kissoly (Chapter 20) describe urban food market governance in African cities, using Dar es Salaam as a case. They outline three main sectors engaged in governance, in addition to "symbiotic" society. First, the corporate sector is composed of foreign ownership and influence in food governance. Second, the state role in food governance is "light" touch and low capacity. Third, the civil society role has limited capacity and low levels of representativeness. Finally, "symbiotic" society, which is not a formally recognised sector, is made up of socially embedded economic actors that govern most of the small-scale food markets and production. The more equality there is within this group, the greater the equality of the marketplace. The main sectors have little interaction with one another, and the authors question if they should, as symbiotic society would likely not be represented. The impacts of changes in governance on food security of urban residents and the livelihoods of farmers are woven into the chapter.

The final chapter by **Lauren Baker, James Kuhns, and Joe Nasr** (Chapter 21) focuses on one of the most common urban food system practices, urban agriculture, and examines cases from across the globe. The authors discuss three interrelated challenges in urban agriculture: land and space, financial resources, and equity. They also describe tensions within governance, including those around the implementation of regulations and the lack of implementation of other policy tools. These challenges and tensions are sometimes related to the unique nature of urban agricultural practice and its interface with existing governance structures, which are not designed to deal with it. The authors suggest tools (such as food strategies and action plans) and processes (such as multistakeholder engagement) to support urban agriculture.

Part IV Scales and Agencies in Urban Food Governance

As shown in the previous part on practices, urban food governance processes involve multiple actors associated with the food system, including civil society, public and private stakeholders, and a number of sectors, from food production to health or planning. In recent years, we have witnessed increased cross-scalar activity led by multiple initiatives and focused on connecting cities with their hinterlands while also creating trans-local alliances across regions and countries. The chapters in this part discuss the multiple agencies involved in urban food governance, as well as its cross-sectoral and cross-scalar character.

In order to consider this multiplicity of agencies, **Scott Drimie** (Chapter 22) analyses the role and diversity of the private sector in urban food governance. The chapter is a unique contribution, since private sector agencies are seldom explored in the study of urban food governance dynamics, despite their central role in shaping urban food practices and associated sustainability and justice outcomes. Drimie points to the importance of governance that not only enables coordination and coherence across sectors but also mediates power dynamics. One proposal is to adopt a human rights framework that supports the application of an inclusive political approach, which requires identifying different types of power, how they are exerted, and the tools that build a more pluralistic and rational approach to collaboration.

The roles of different agents and powers are also addressed in **Kirsten Valentine Cadieux**'s (Chapter 23) analysis of structural inequalities in urban food systems. She explores how community food land regimes help address the inequalities built into the organising principles of twentieth-century urban form. She argues that community food land initiatives challenge structural inequalities, which consider food and related elements to be commodities rather than rights. Cadieux contends that urban community food land activities support a model of economic development focused on the basic needs and livelihoods of residents, featuring community engagement and racial equity as the basis of wealth generation and collective learning processes.

A recurrent debate in urban food governance concerns the relationship between cities and rural areas. Two chapters address these linkages in this *Handbook*. First, **Cecilia Tacoli** (Chapter 24) reclaims a much more complex understanding of rural–urban linkages that embraces the diverse spatial, sectoral, and functional dimensions at play, breaking the food production–consumption dichotomy that pervades imaginaries and discourses. For that purpose, she argues that it is necessary to consider these linkages as framed by social relations and political and institutional contexts. According to Tacoli, the types of linkages that contribute to social, economic, and environmental sustainability occur mainly when the added value produced through functional linkages is retained and reinvested locally, with appropriate institutional support. She explores the contribution of small towns as market nodes and spaces for equitable sustainable development, including income-generating activities and poverty reduction.

Alison Blay-Palmer, Jess Halliday, Guido Santini, Joy Carey, Roman Malec, Makiko Taguchi, Rene van Veenhuizen, and Laine Young (Chapter 25) also address the relationship between urban and non-urban areas in shaping food system outcomes. For that purpose, they highlight territoriality and urban–rural relations and propose and mobilise the notion of city region food systems, which have gained international attention in the last decades. They argue that the potential benefits of the city region food system approach are manifold and include simultaneously delivering economic, social, environmental, and health impacts that range from closing material resource flows to alleviating poverty. Although these initiatives also face challenges, the authors identify key tools to overcome these limitations, including flexible resources to support city region governance processes; engagement of multiple actors to bridge sectors, policy silos, and scales; and a collective vision to steer the process.

Urban food governance is constantly reshaped by both spatial relationships and cross-scalar interactions. The final two chapters of the part engage directly with how urban food governance dynamics have re-scaled, with a particular focus on their international dimensions. **Thomas Forster, Florence Egal, and Ana Puhac** (Chapter 26) provide an overview of how urban food governance has become a key focus of different global policy agendas. They trace the convergence between global and local/urban/regional food governance since the 1970s and explore how urban food systems have been progressively integrated into the sustainable development agenda through such milestones as the 2030 Agenda for Sustainable Development (the Sustainable Development Goals), the New Urban Agenda, and the Milan Urban Food Policy Pact. The authors highlight opportunities to build good food governance by taking a systems approach to add value and operationalise current processes, seeking multi-actor participation and human rights.

Finally, **Thierry Giordano's** chapter (Chapter 27) focuses on the development of city food networks across the globe as they rescale the impact of urban food governance. Giordano explores the emergence and development of four key transnational networks: the Milan Urban Food Policy Pact (MUFPP), C40 Cities Climate Leadership Group (C40), ICLEI Local Governments for Sustainability (ICLEI), and United Cities and Local Governments (UCLG). His analysis allows him to identify their main functions of exchanging knowledge and practices, providing political support to anchor the role of cities in food system reform, and seeking financial resources, as well as their potential global advocacy role.

Part V Urban Food Governance Futures

Meta-societal issues like climate change, global pandemics, and technological innovation are changing our urban environments and the foods that residents acquire, consume, and dispose of. Both the food and urban arenas require management that considers not only current implications but also future trajectories, therefore bringing concepts of anticipatory governance into play. Such anticipatory governance seeks to manage technologies while such management is still possible (Guston, 2014), building capacities in such futuring techniques as foresight and backcasting, as well as emphasising the importance of wide engagement in imagining and creating futures. Despite critiques over the possibilities of effective anticipatory governance and concerns that such governance is a public relations exercise for unproven technologies, considering the future of urban food is a vital endeavour.

The enduring influence of visions and, importantly, the question of whose visions are admitted to futuring exercises that produce enduring visions are discussed in the chapter by **Jaz Hee-jeong Choi, Sara Heitlinger, Alex Taylor, and Viktor Bedö** (Chapter 28). Focusing on governance for open urban food futures, the authors explore the challenges and opportunities in redesigning ways of building and maintaining food systems, which have typically had agendas driven by technocapitalist practices. Calling for new ways and means, new sites and settings, and new structures and participants to think through urban food futures and their governance, they join with Morrow (Chapter 8) in demanding more open, commons-based systems of thinking. More than this, they focus on the multiple, always changing nature of food, with its vital materialities, and the need for governance to be flexible enough to work with this characteristic.

Embedding more diverse voices in thinking about the future of urban food governance is also a central pillar of the chapter by **Aniek Hebinck, Joost Vervoort, Astrid Mangnus, and**

Steven McGreevy (Chapter 29), who trace the evolution of participatory foresight activities in the contrasting contexts of Eindhoven in the Netherlands and Kyoto in Japan. The future orientation of these exercises is proposed as both a useful device to plan for more sustainable futures and a means to think about how to address challenges in the present. Providing a cautionary note, the authors identify a suite of prerequisite issues that must be considered if such future-oriented activities are to be just and effective. Further exploration of what constitutes fairer futuring (Fitzgerald & Davies, 2022) in urban food governance is required.

Adopting a different lens, **Sara Heitlinger, Lara Houston, Jaz Hee-jeong Choi, Alex Taylor, and Ruth Catlow** (Chapter 30) explore more-than-human computer interaction and its implications for urban food governance. They investigate the increasing visibility of digital technologies – from sensors to artificial intelligence – in global food chains and in urban areas due to smart city interventions. They raise concerns about the vagaries of algorithmic governance; issues of privacy, control, agency, and access; and who gets to benefit from the application of these innovations. Governance is present in these arenas, driven primarily through logics of efficiency in supply chains and traceability for food safety. However, while benefiting shareholders and reducing liability from food safety risks, such interventions currently do little to put urban food systems onto more sustainable pathways. Bringing an emergent, more-than-human perspective to bear on this issue, the authors explore ways that digital technologies might disrupt urban food governance more substantially and sustainably.

Serena Pollastri explores historical visions of the future and the role given to food and governance within them in her chapter (Chapter 31). Reviewing plans, films, artworks, and speculative urban design interventions featuring food that have emerged over the past century, Pollastri concludes that visions of the future are intimately connected to the present conditions in which they are formed. As such, they reveal important information about how issues were conceived and responses imagined from each historical perspective. Nonetheless, such interventions have not remained in the past due to their endurance, and they continue to exert influence over societal ideas and expectations about the future.

Certainly, as **Katrin Bohn and André Viljoen** emphasise in their chapter (Chapter 32), creating supportive urban food governance is crucial in cultivating more just and sustainable urban food futures. However, they find that matters of urban food production remain underrepresented in discussions and practices of urban food governance futures. Specifically, they identify a research and practice gap between food governance and urban spatial design. In response, they explore how the concept of continuous productive urban landscapes could bring these arenas into closer conversation, and they argue for planning policies that place food-focused activities at their core and provide spaces of food exchange, encounter, and experience.

Understanding and transforming urban food governance

The process of editing this *Handbook* has allowed us to scope the wide-ranging scholarship on and practice of urban food governance and reflect on what is being done, the current trends, and what aspects might be missing. This exercise has surfaced the complexity of defining urban food governance. Indeed, many contributors within the *Handbook* have developed their work in this field without providing a clear definition of the term. Recently, two of us have proposed defining urban food governance as all modes of governing encompassing activities carried out by different actors to guide, steer, control, or manage the pursuance of food system outcomes in a specific urban area (Moragues-Faus & Battersby, 2021, p. 5). While this definition is useful in helping to expand narrow conceptualisations of governance and clarifying how governance dynamics are related but differ from policy processes, it is difficult to implement given its all-encompassing character and, to date, lack of application to specific case studies. In the context of this *Handbook*, we want to expand this definition by building on an analysis of the *Handbook* chapters to develop a critical analytical framework in the form of a guide that will help readers understand urban food governance and provide pointers on how urban food governance can constitute a means of delivering sustainability, justice, and food security outcomes. Below, we present the main elements of this framework and the rationale for each element's importance. While we present them as separate principles, they clearly intersect in multiple ways to impact urban food governance practice.

Principle 1: Time matters

Adopting both historical and future-focused perspectives supports planning for uncertain and evolving urban food.

Urban food governance has *historical roots*, and we can recognise how food has shaped cities and vice versa through those global and local layers of history, with governance tools and dynamics playing a key role in connecting both domains. These rich understandings can be used to inform planning for more sustainable urban food futures. As the chapters of Part I show, urban food governance across centuries has not only shaped cities but also societies and ecologies at large. However, while it is important to take a historical approach to understanding current urban food governance dynamics, it is also urgent to revisit previous works, which on too many occasions are tainted by Western scholars' ethnocentric historical and geographical frames, as Yasmeen evidences in her historical account of Asian urban food governance (Chapter 4). Taking a historical approach can be an analytical exercise intertwined with designing effective urban food governance practices. For instance, the translation of practices across contexts must contend with historical relations between urban areas and national governance, confront colonial and racist histories present in urban areas, and deal centrally with power and politics.

Given differences in historical relations, there are no prescribed roles for urban actors in relation to either one another or other scales. For example, when instituting participatory budgeting, the Brazilian government considered cities as sites for democratic change, while in the United States cities are seen as actors within a vacuum created by a long trend of devolution. In Africa, cities can be seen as sites of opposition, resulting in local governments becoming allies, obstructionists, or passive actors. Next, there is an assumption that formalising urban food governance practice into government and making greater use of governance tools are desired pathways. However, some chapters raise cautions (Agyeman et al., Chapter 9; Haysom and Currie, Chapter 14; Hoey, Chapter 16; and Wegerif and Kissoly, Chapter 20). Formalising governance is only as equitable as the platform on which governance is built, which puts colonial and racist histories into question. As a result of these historical relationships, formal state governance may be in opposition to the work of other governance actors. For example, the governance of urban food markets in Africa is often, in practice, governed through contestation and everyday struggles.

Recognising the impact of historic urban food governance on current realities highlights the need for engagement in planning for uncertain and evolving futures. When developing strategies and policies there is a tendency to assume that the future will be similar to the present (Hartley et al., 2019). However, history and such recent events as the increasing negative effects of climate change, the COVID-19 pandemic, energy and food crises, disruptive politics, and wars are proving this modus operandi wrong. During the COVID-19 pandemic, many cities lacked capacity to pivot quickly to deal with supply chain issues; some FPCs were able to leverage their current governance arrangements to step in, while other cities had to turn to the private sector (Santo et al., 2021). In this context, it is imperative to explicitly embed anticipatory governance into planning exercises and actually implement tools and programmes to deal with uncertainty and increase the resilience of urban food strategies so that we can deliver sustainable food for all under different circumstances.

While futuring exercises are becoming a more familiar feature of food debates and can be a useful tool to increase the resilience of plans and strategies, there are still key gaps in current practice, as illustrated by the chapters in Part V. First, there is a need to explicitly incorporate discussions about governance into urban food futuring exercises, such as processes for access to public land for food growing and the enactment of commitments around the right to food in cities. Second, it is important to ensure fairer futuring for sustainable urban food governance by widening participation in foresight exercises to include those voices that are seldom heard and including not just procedural justice but also recognition and distributive justice elements. Finally, more inclusive communities of practice around futuring urban food governance must move debates and plans beyond the technological determinism of the private sector and elite futurists that has dominated visions of future urban food.

Principle 2: Place matters

Implementing a place-based approach to urban food governance optimises the relevance of proposed actions.

Cities and their governance dynamics are extraordinarily diverse. From Rome to Singapore, and from Belo Horizonte to Nairobi, there are thousands of mega, medium, and small cities hosting most of the world's population. This means that place-based approaches to analysis, policy, and practice are required, which involves taking into account the specific historical, socio-ecological configurations of each city and how they shape urban food governance dynamics and opportunities. It is important to unpack the three key words "urban," "food," and "governance" for each specific setting.

First, urban food scholarship and practice needs to engage more fully with the urban condition. The rapidly evolving urban scholarship shows the need to move beyond analyses that treat cities like any other place. To guide a deeper understanding of the urban dimension of food governance, we propose building on the recent approach to the urban as a trialectic, "in which the urban is viewed simultaneously as a spatial container, a conceptual terrain and a governance structure" (Moragues-Faus & Battersby, 2021, p. 4). In this framework, the urban is considered a complex socio-spatial process, which also affects non-urban environments and therefore constitutes an active agent shaping the nature and development of governance and policy processes, rather than merely being a location where these processes take place. In this regard, governance agents also actively build discourses on what the city is, who makes the city, how cities need to be governed, and what impacts cities have outside their boundaries, all of which require attention since they actively shape urban food systems and their outcomes. Not least, cities have particular governance structure characteristics that vary not only in relation to the formal competencies of each country but are also able to mobilise other forms of soft and invisible power to drive cultural, socio-ecological, and political changes.

Second, food is "the mixture of the organic and the inorganic, the material and the symbolic, and the social and the natural" (Murdoch, 2005, p. 160), and as such it constitutes a vehicle to understand and shape cultural and socio-ecological processes that transform the mineral, vegetable, and animal into edible things to maintain human life. What makes these mixtures actual "food" is contested and place-based. Different actors experience, and discursively engage with, food (and the lack of it) in various ways, from counting the calories that fuel their bodies, to using food as a medium through which relationships are formed amongst families, communities, and social groups. Therefore, food experiences and practices are very diverse and mediated by individuals and their context.

Finally, governance practices are necessarily unique to each setting due to a combination of historical, social, cultural, political, economic, and ecological configurations, as illustrated throughout this *Handbook*. As such, instead of seeking universal "best" practices, it is necessary to step back and engage with territorial or place-based approaches to conduct accurate diagnoses and design effective interventions. For example, a commonality across most cases, from Africa to the United States (aside from the Brazilian cases), is that there are few to no policy mandates for urban food governance, and the types of actors pushing for governance action necessarily vary. Food can be absent from urban agendas, requiring civil society to move agenda-setting forward. In other places, civil society may be weak, and the population may rely on the government taking the lead. In this way, suggesting a single best practice for governance arrangements based on insights from elsewhere can be detrimental to progress.

Principle 3: Relations matter

Scales, spaces, and agencies of urban food governance are co-constituted through structural and fluid interactions.

This *Handbook* shows the inherently relational character of urban food governance, which is showcased across four different dimensions: scales, space, agents, and between food systems and cities. First, the *multiscalar* perspective has been integrated into urban food governance theory and practice, with academics and practitioners acknowledging the interdependence between global, national, and local contexts and the associated drivers shaping specific urban food systems. Clear examples are the recent developments in international policy arenas linked to urban food agendas, such as the Sustainable Development Goals, the New Urban Agenda, and the Milan Urban Food Policy Pact (see chapters by Forster et al., Chapter 26, and Haysom and Currie, Chapter 14). Similarly, translocal alliances are developing at national and international scales to advance the urban food agenda in the form of city food networks, such as C40 or United Cities and Local Governments programmes (see Giordano, Chapter 27). While these translocal alliances and international agendas are rescaling the impact of urban food policies, they still have weak alignments and connections to key actors that limit their capacities to intervene effectively (Moragues-Faus, 2021). For instance, national city networks are, by and large, weakly linked to national governments, which limits their impact.

The relational character of urban food governance also has a *spatial* dimension. Indeed, translocal alliances connect cities across regions, countries, and continents but can also take the form of urban–rural (or rural–urban) linkages. This spatial relationality is often expressed through the adoption of such concepts as city region food systems or foodsheds. However, these approaches face implementation challenges in both analytical and practical ways. It is extremely difficult to map complex, multiscalar urban food system dynamics. Maps must include all the agencies involved to trace the diverse drivers of change and measure the impacts of cities beyond their administrative boundaries. Blay-Palmer et al. (Chapter 25) propose a set of tools to overcome these challenges that mainly revolve around strengthening collaboration across administrative levels and civil society; having strong civil society organisations, flexible financing, and multistakeholder engagement across sectors and scales; and promoting the importance of collective visions. However, despite their benefits, these conceptual frameworks remain elusive in practice. To date, rewiring the spatial food connections of cities constitutes an enormous challenge given the complexity, invisibility, and diversity of those relationships.

A third dimension of the relational character of urban food governance is how different *agencies* are co-constituted and operate. The practice of governance is an ever-moving target, changing over time and revealing the dynamics between civil society, the private sector, and governments. Governance requires constant tending, and there is a necessary interplay and dynamic tension between advocacy, energy, and legitimacy from civil society, and capacity and authority from local government (Haysom and Currie, Chapter 14; Rocha and Burlandy, Chapter 18; and Baker et al., Chapter 21). In this sense, it is important to acknowledge the diversity within different categories of agents. City council members are diverse and hold different skills, interests, and attitudes towards sustainable and just food transformations, from food champions to disengaged politicians or civil servants (see Vara-Sanchez et al., 2021). The same can be said for civil society organisations and the private sector, as Drimie (Chapter 22) explores in this *Handbook*. This internal diversity highlights the need to rethink the categories that we use to classify actors in governance processes and the values we attribute to them. Differentiating between more- and less-formalised governance spaces and tools and the actual governance of urban food systems becomes key to unpacking the agencies at play and their power (Moragues-Faus & Battersby, 2021). Despite wide acknowledgement of the importance of considering and engaging with multiple stakeholders in urban food governance transformation, there is an increasing critique that multistakeholderism does not clearly contend with power (see Principle 5, and McKeon, 2017; and Haysom and Currie, Chapter 14).

Finally, the relational character of urban food governance calls for a much more *fluid* understanding of the elements at play in shaping interactions between food systems and cities. For example, non-food actors and processes can be instrumental for progress in sustainable food systems and food and nutrition security in urban spaces and beyond (see Tacoli, Chapter 24). Following this line of argument, Forster et al. (Chapter 26) call for greater connections with existing institutional processes and levels of governance by explicitly adding food to existing mandates of relevant coordination committees at all levels, and in particular those related to sustainability and the Sustainable Development Goals (SDGs), or resilience and climate change, in order to enact changes effectively. It is important to look beyond the food and urban realms, but it is also important to acknowledge the usefulness of analytical tools that allow us to understand both the structural and fluid relations at work in urban food governance. For instance, Cadieux (Chapter 23) analyses land access and tenure for food cultivation in cities, where norms and bureaucratic processes, but also such conventions as the prominence of productive goals in planning procedures, are actively reproducing urban inequalities at the heart of the organising principles of cities and therefore preventing structural changes. Another example comes from the mobilisation of assemblage thinking to understanding translocal urban food governance (Santo & Moragues-Faus, 2019; Moragues-Faus & Sonnino, 2019). This approach can identify fluid and unstable interactions and allows us to understand that not only are formal processes and structures such as regulations or councils key governance tools, but also that ephemeral and informal ways of shaping and managing urban food system outcomes void of explicit rules of engagement or procedures are equally relevant to understand how food is governed in cities. For instance, alliances between cities and actors do not need to be formalised to have an effect. Being attentive to these different modes of governance will allow us to map where capacities for transformation lie.

Principle 4: Diversity matters

Dynamic and diverse critical theories, frames, and practices can help deal with complexity and co-produce new political possibilities.

Different critical theories allow us to navigate the complexity and interconnectedness of urban food governance, from lived experiences and everyday practices to structural, political, and socio-ecological configurations of the city and beyond. This *Handbook* showcases key conceptual frameworks that provide a range of entry points to understand and act upon urban food governance, such as social practices, feminist ethics of care, political economy, political ecology, and transition theory, as well as a range of concepts to guide action (e.g., foodscapes, food democracy, urban food commons, just sustainability, types of governance). There is no single concept or framework that can do it all, but there is an increasing need for transdisciplinary work and dialogue across theories that can provide multiple insights, which together have the potential to provide a more diverse, complex, and accurate account of urban food governance dynamics. The framework we are proposing here does not champion one theory or concept over another; rather, we advocate for a co-productive and transdisciplinary approach to grasp the complexity of urban food governance and design interventions accordingly. Nevertheless, we highlight the importance of adopting a critical approach, aware of how power operates across the intersection of cities, food, and governance to generate inequalities as well as opportunities for just transformations (see Principle 5 below).

Co-producing knowledge and solutions across disciplines and practices enriches our analysis and future interventions while recognising the wealth of knowledge generated beyond academic spaces. Within the expanding community attending to urban food governance, there are many examples of collaboration between academic and practitioner, examples of which include establishing a fruitful dialogue between theory and practice. In many cases, this takes the form of participatory action research or direct participation by both types of actors in shared spaces, from food policy councils to innovation projects or international policy committees. As a consequence, we can see how different theories and conceptual frameworks are slowly permeating more technical and practitioner-led mobilisations of urban food governance (as described in Halliday, Chapter 10), which focus on understanding key elements and procedures to support urban food system transformations into more equitable forms. Similarly, urban food governance practitioners have on many occasions paved the way for innovations that are later analysed and conceptualised by academics. Improved dialogue between theory and practice has resulted in some key advancements in urban food governance, such as more effective incorporation of systemic thinking into deliberations, the expansion of more participatory multi-actor engagement, and greater adoption of a territorial or place-based approach. These innovations have led cities and their inhabitants to be seen as *the* food policy pioneers of the last decade.

Finally, the co-production of knowledge and solutions by theorists and practitioners is necessary but insufficient. It must be expanded to include the knowledge that already exists in living in urban environments. Situating people's lived experiences at the centre of food system analysis and policy development is central to guaranteeing human rights, such as the right to food, and people's dignity (Freedman et al., 2022; Anderson, 2008). Evidence on lived experience is therefore critical to understanding the positive and negative impact of policies and interventions, and also integrating the agency of different actors into actively shaping their food environments and futures (Hawkes et al., 2020). A people-centred approach learns from this lived expertise and collaborates to bring forth more just solutions, as illustrated by Agyeman et al. (Chapter 9), who show how honouring this expertise can support more equitable and effective urban food governance.

Principle 5: Power matters

Engaging with normative processes and values and making a commitment to fairness requires navigating uneven patterns and relations of power.

The acts of urban food governance illustrated in this volume aim to either shift power across scales, sectors, and groups or generate greater power and influence through collective action. Much of this action is driven by a desire to increase equity and fairness, which requires attending to power and its distribution and, therefore, attending to politics, differing values, and interests. Thus, while the interface between power and governance is touched upon in each of the preceding principles, power is important enough that it is its own principle in the framework, guiding our analyses and interventions by a critical approach to the notion of governance (Moragues-Faus, 2020).

As alluded to earlier, given the historical, relational, and situated character of urban food governance, existing power relations vary. Surfacing power positions of different actors and making their interests, values, and resources explicit is a first step, but there are other forms of power that require attention. Less visible and more hidden forms of power involve inaction and nondecisions, keeping certain voices and interests out of governance processes. Less attention is paid to invisible power relations, which are often exercised through a history of colonialism and racism. Invisible power also controls the broader societal narratives and agendas, shaping thoughts and interests (Lukes, 1974; Gaventa, 2004).

It is important to question the power dynamics within all governing processes, even those that are deliberative and consensus-based, which aim to generate power through participatory processes (Lee et al., 2015). Most collaborative and multistakeholder processes and spaces are focused on consensus, which can avoid necessary conflicts that would reveal power imbalances and may obscure the desires and needs of marginalised groups. As such, there is an increasing call to embrace dissent and conflict in processes in order to enable more equitable solutions (Duncan & Claeys, 2018), including through concepts such as stretch collaboration or by fully embedding a human rights approach in defining participants and their roles (see Drimie, Chapter 22). A relational, place-based, multi-perspective approach to urban food governance needs to resituate how power is constituted and exercised and use this knowledge design process to reveal, acknowledge, and redistribute power before generating collective power. This requires humility and reflexivity from those in the powerful positions of setting up processes. Instead of a transformational governance process coming to consensus on interests and values, it could focus on revealing values, interrogating them, and reflecting on their influence on what is to be done; essentially revealing how forms of power and politics work together (Clark, 2022). Nowhere is this more important than with respect to the value of food to those who cultivate, curate, and consume it. While there are numerous political economy models in action globally, the dominance of neoliberal processes and their preoccupation with financial value and efficiency have stymied the expansion of different worlds of worth that are alluded to, for example, within the SDGs. Efforts to actualise systems that value food beyond its financial value face pushbacks from multiple and often very powerful actors, as discussed by Clark and Irish (Chapter 15).

The five principles discussed above provide a framework for urban food governance that is fit for the twenty-first century and seeks a just transition to sustainable urban food systems. In Table 1.1 below we set out a suite of questions related to these principles, which can help guide those seeking to traverse the complex landscape of urban food governance.

Table 1.1 Framework for urban food governance

Principles	*Questions*
Principle 1: Time matters	a) How have socio-ecological configurations changed over time and influenced current urban food governance arrangements in your location? Which perspectives have been considered in those **historical** accounts? b) What visions do you have for the **future** of your urban food system? What different futures might develop? What different contexts locally, nationally, and globally might impact your plans? How can considering different types of futures (plausible or not) improve the resilience of your plans? Who is involved in devising and planning for those futures?
Principle 2: Place matters	a) What do *urban*, *food*, and *governance* mean in the context of your **place** and what are the associated challenges and opportunities with these meanings? b) What elements need to be considered to translate practices from other places to your city?
Principle 3: Relations matter	a) How do dynamics unfolding at different **scales** impact the governance of your urban food system? How does your location's food governance impact other scales? b) How is your urban food system shaped by other places, from its hinterlands to far away locations, and vice versa? What types of governance tools can be mobilised to shape these **spatial relations** and accomplish desired food system outcomes? c) What and who are the **agencies and actors** shaping your urban food system? How do they relate to each other? What type of formal and informal tools do they mobilise to exercise their power and affect urban food governance? What are the values and motivations behind them? d) What are the key **intersections** between your urban food system and non-food or non-urban dynamics that affect sustainability and justice outcomes? e) What **modes of governance** – types of formal and informal arrangements, norms, regulations, processes, networks, etc. – is your city mobilising to shape its urban food system?
Principle 4: Diversity matters	a) What types of disciplines, critical theories, framings, and actors are you engaging with in your analysis and development of solutions? b) How are you ensuring a **co-productive** approach in analysing and designing interventions and actions for urban food governance? c) How are you effectively including **diverse** actors with different lived experiences to make analysis and interventions relevant for everyone, and particularly those at the margins?
Principle 5: Power matters	a) In your city, how is **power** exercised, and by whom, to shape the food system? What forms of power are visible (e.g. money, authority)? Who has hidden power, such as the power to set the agenda? What broader invisible powers (e.g. cultural norms) shape governance actors and processes? How are these powers distributed? b) Do governance processes shift power? If so, to whom? What mechanisms are put in place to recognise and act upon power inequalities, different **values**, and **interests**? c) Do governance processes aim to generate power? If so, for whom? How are the realities of historical colonial and racist histories brought into collaborative processes?

Source: Authors' compilation.

Conclusion

This *Handbook* is a collective exercise that reflects on the state of the art of urban food governance. It explores the why, who, what, where, how, and when of urban food governance. In the context of ongoing socio-ecological crises, a rapid improvement of our analyses of the challenges and opportunities for just and sustainable urban food governance is urgently required. This collection offers a valuable set of insights and tools to continue transforming our cities for good and creating sustainable food systems and just governance dynamics to build a liveable future. Rather than proposing new all-encompassing definitions, we have summarised this knowledge around a set of five principles to help guide future analysis and action. These principles support the expansion and critical capacity of the diverse urban food governance community, interpolating more actors and agencies – from housing to transport or from changes in everyday practices to global treaties – to fulfil the unquestionable potential of food, cities, and governance in shaping our lives and futures.

References

Anderson, M. D. (2008). Rights-based food systems and the goals of food systems reform. *Agriculture and Human Values*, *25*(4), 593–608.

Battersby, J., & Haysom, G. (2018). Linking urban food security, urban food systems, poverty, and urbanisation. In J. Battersby & V. Watson (Eds.), *Urban Food Systems Governance and Poverty in African Cities* (pp. 56–67) London: Routledge.

Brenner, N. (2018). Debating planetary urbanization: For an engaged pluralism. Environment and *Planning D: Society and Space*, *36*(3), 570–590.

Clark, J. K. (2022). Equitable deliberative participation design: A call to use a lens of multidimensional power. *Perspectives on Public Management and Governance*, forthcoming.

Connolly, C. (2019). Urban political ecology beyond methodological cityism. *International Journal of Urban Regional Research*, *43*(1), 63–75.

Cooksey-Stowers, K., Schwartz, M. B., & Brownell, K. D. (2017). Food swamps predict obesity rates better than food deserts in the United States. *International Journal of Environmental Research and Public Health*, *14*(11), 1366.

Demmler, K. M., & Qaim, M. (2020). Africa's changing food environments and nutritional effects on adults and children. *World Review of Nutrition and Dietetics*, *121*, 31–41. https://doi.org/10.1159/000507492

Duncan, J., & Claeys, P. (2018). Politicizing food security governance through participation: Opportunities and opposition. *Food Security*, *10*(6), 1411–1424.

Fitzgerald, L., & Davies, A. R. (2022). Creating fairer futures for sustainability transitions, *Geography Compass* (in press).

Freedman, D. A., Clark, J. K., Lounsbury, D. W., Boswell, L., Burns, M., Jackson, M. B., … & Yamoah, O. (2022). Food system dynamics structuring nutrition equity in racialized urban neighborhoods. *The American Journal of Clinical Nutrition*, *115*(4), 1027–1038.

Gaventa, J. (2004). Towards participatory governance: Assessing the transformative possibilities. In S. Hickey & G. Mohan (Eds.), *Participation: From Tyranny to Transformation* (pp. 25–41). New York: ZED Books.

Guston, D. H. (2014). Understanding 'anticipatory governance.' *Social Studies of Science*, *44*(2), 218–242. doi:10.1177/0306312713508669

Hartley, K., Kuecker, G., & Woo, J. J. (2019). Practicing public policy in an age of disruption. *Policy Design and Practice*, *2*(2), 163–181.

Hawkes, C., Fox, E., Downs, S. M., Fanzo, J., & Neve, K. (2020). Child-centred food systems: Re-orienting food systems towards healthy diets for children. *Global Food Security*, *27*, 100414.

IFPRI. (2017). *2017 Global Food Policy Report*. Washington, DC: International Food Policy Research Institute. http://ebrary.ifpri.org/utils/getfile/collection/p15738coll2/id/131085/filename/131296.pdf.

Lang, T., Barling, D., & Caraher, M. (2009). *Food Policy: Integrating Health, Environment and Society*. Oxford: Oxford University Press.

Lee, C. W., McQuarrie, M., Walker, E. T., & Calhoun, C. J. eds. (2015). *Democratizing Inequalities: Dilemmas of the New Public Participation*. New York: New York University Press.

Lukes, S. (1974). *Power: A Radical View*. 2nd ed. London: Palgrave Macmillan.

McKeon, N. (2017). Are equity and sustainability a likely outcome when foxes and chickens share the same coop? Critiquing the concept of multistakeholder governance of food security. *Globalizations, 14*(3), 379–398.

Millington, G. (2016). Urbanization and the city image in Lowry at Tate Britain: Towards a critique of cultural cityism. *International Journal of Urban Regional Research, 40*(4), 717–735.

Moragues-Faus, A. (2020). Towards a critical governance framework: Unveiling the political and justice dimensions of urban food partnerships. *The Geographical Journal, 186*(1), 73–86.

Moragues-Faus, A. (2021). The emergence of city food networks: Rescaling the impact of urban food policies. *Food Policy, 103*, 102107.

Moragues-Faus, A., & Battersby, J. (2021). Urban food policies for a sustainable and just future: Concepts and tools for a renewed agenda. *Food Policy, 103*, 102124.

Moragues-Faus, A., & Morgan, K. (2015). Reframing the foodscape: The emergent world of urban food policy. *Environment and Planning A, 47*(7). https://doi.org/10.1177/0308518X15595754

Moragues-Faus, A., & Sonnino, R. (2019). Re-assembling sustainable food cities: An exploration of translocal governance and its multiple agencies. *Urban Studies, 56*(4), 778–794.

Murdoch, J. (2005). *Post-structuralist Geography: A Guide to Relational Space*. London: Sage.

Santo, R., & Moragues-Faus, A. (2019). Towards a trans-local food governance: Exploring the transformative capacity of food policy assemblages in the US and UK. *Geoforum, 98*, 75–87.

Santo, R., Misiaszek, C., Bassarab, K., Harris, D., & Palmer, A. (2021). *Pivoting Policy, Programs, and Partnership: Food Policy Councils' Response to the Crisis of 2020*. Johns Hopkins Center for a Livable Future/Food Policy Networks. www.foodpolicynetworks.org/food-policy-resources/index.html?resource=1394

Turner, C., Aggarwal, A., Walls, H., Herforth, A., Drewnowski, A., Coates, J., … & Kadiyala, S. (2018). Concepts and critical perspectives for food environment research: A global framework with implications for action in low-and middle-income countries. *Global Food Security, 18*, 93–101.

Vara-Sánchez, I., Gallar-Hernández, D., García-García, L., Alonso, N. M., & Moragues-Faus, A. (2021). The co-production of urban food policies: Exploring the emergence of new governance spaces in three Spanish cities. *Food Policy, 103*, 102120.

PART I

Histories of Urban Food Governance

2

THE ROLE OF FOOD SYSTEMS IN SHAPING WESTERN CIVILISATION

Carolyn Steel

Introduction

Living in a modern city, it can be hard to grasp the importance of the relationship without which none could exist: that which it enjoys with its rural hinterland. As far back as 1865, George Dodd noted, 'The supply of food to a great city is among the most remarkable of social phenomena – full of instruction on on all sides' (Dodd, 1856, p. 1). Yet today, industrialisation has obscured the complex supply chains that bring food from distant lands and seas to our markets, supermarkets, kitchens and tables (Steel, 2008). Indeed, city-dwellers in the West could be forgiven for thinking that the problem of feeding cities has been solved. Yet, as ecological threats such as climate change, soil loss and mass extinction indicate, nothing could be further from the truth.

Most of our food in the Global North is produced in mega-scaled, technologically streamlined facilities, the reality of which bear little relation to the rural idylls of our imagination. From vast sheds and feedlots full of unfortunate animals and monocultural grain-fields drenched in chemicals and harvested by drone-guided combines to robotised production lines filleting fish or churning out millions of cans of baked beans, the spaces and processes that underpin our existence are as compelling as they are ruthless. In many ways, modern agri-food epitomises the fateful combination of technological prowess and ecological insouciance that now threatens us and our planet.

Our modern way of life is based on the premise of cheap food, yet when you remind yourself that food consists of living things that we kill and eat in order to live, it becomes clear that no such thing could exist. On the contrary, cheap food is an illusion of industrialisation, made possible by our cultural blindness to its multiple 'externalities', including climate change, deforestation, mass extinction, pollution, water depletion, soil degradation, declining fish stocks, obesity, diet-related disease and zoonotic pandemics. By treating food as cheap, we have brought ourselves to the brink of catastrophe; all of which makes the study of how we got here of more than passing interest. Understanding how the industrial food system gave rise to our modern way of life – and thereby questioning the assumptions upon which both are based – could prove vital to our survival.

In the pre-industrial world, things were very different. The feeding of cities was an often overwhelming task that preoccupied every city administration and shaped most aspects of urban

DOI: 10.4324/9781003055907-3

life. Above all else, what mattered to a city's fortunes was its geography. The world's first urban centres – Sumerian city-states such as Ur, Uruk and Kippur that emerged some 5,500 years ago in southern Mesopotamia – were built on a vast river delta, where the Tigris and Euphrates spilled their mineral-rich waters into the Persian Gulf. The construction of elaborate banks and ditches to control the water and use it to irrigate palm groves, orchards and grain-fields effectively represents the world's first countryside. Life in these early city-states revolved around the annual harvest, a pivotal event that was both celebrated and overseen by the temple, which acted as the city's administrative, as well as spiritual, hub. Writing, money and bookkeeping were among the artefacts and skills invented in order to help with the complex task of feeding a large, non-food-producing population. The emergence of urban food systems in ancient Sumer thus mirrors that of Western civilisation itself.

One lasting legacy of these early cities was their division of land into two distinct territories: city and country. The duality has shaped Western culture with consequences that still resound today. The identification of the city as the space of civilisation (from the Roman *civis*, citizen) in contrast to the relatively powerless and disconnected countryside is a trope that still persists, giving rise, for example, to the idea that urbanity and progress are synonymous. Another consequence of this early division was the creation of social hierarchies that would become more pronounced with time: in ancient Sumer, as in virtually every urban civilisation since, power resided in the temples, not with the farmers who toiled to fill their granaries (Standage, 2009, pp. 31–33).

Growing enough food was just one problem that early cities faced; another was the question of how to transport it so that it arrived in an edible state. Although grain – the staple food of all cities – had a reasonable shelf-life, it was heavy and bulky in relation to value, making it uneconomic to carry far overland. For this reason, most cities in the ancient world remained small, with a population of 20,000 or more considered big.

Such considerations bothered Plato and Aristotle as they considered the question of what an ideal *polis*, or city-state, should be like. Both concluded that the *polis* should remain relatively small, in order to be able to feed itself from its own territories. In their respective tracts the *Republic* and *Politics*, they described an ideal arrangement in which each citizen would have a house in the city and a farm in the countryside from which to supply it. Scaled up many times, such *oikonomia*, or household management (from Gk. *oikos*, household + *nemein*, management) would render the *polis* self-sufficient, and thus politically independent. *Oikonomia* (the root of our modern word economics) was thus the building-block of the state, in contrast to *chrematistike*, the making of money for its own sake, which Aristotle condemned on the grounds that it had no natural limits, and thus could never bring happiness (Aristotle, 1981, p. 85).

Although they never reached the perfection dreamed of by Plato and Aristotle, most pre-industrial European and Arabic cities did in fact practice some form of *oikonomia*, which is to say that they had highly productive local food economies. Towns and cities of every size were invariably surrounded by market gardens, orchards and vineyards, whose fruit and vegetables could most benefit from human and animal waste that was carefully collected to be used as manure. Households kept pigs, chickens or goats, which they fed up on kitchen scraps to be slaughtered on feast days. Food was generally grown as close to the city as possible, but since cows and sheep could walk to market, they were often reared many miles away, to be fattened up in the outskirts on spent brewers' grain before being finally brought to market and slaughtered. In general, fresh meat was a luxury that few city-dwellers could afford, and most survived on bread, and later other staples such as rice or pasta, with a little dried meat or fish, cheese and vegetables for flavour.

Rome – Consumer City

The city-state model was sufficiently successful to dominate Western urban development for the first three or so millennia. When a city eventually bucked the trend, however, it did so in such dramatic fashion as to effectively redraw the urban blueprint. That city was ancient Rome. With an estimated million citizens at its height, Rome was the first city to effectively outgrow its local hinterland. From the third century BCE, it already relied on grain imports from Sicily and Sardinia, and its conquest of Carthage and Egypt in 146 BCE and 30 BCE respectively cemented this approach, securing access to lands that expanded the capital's gastronomic as well as imperial horizons. With North Africa secured as its breadbasket, Rome was free to import other foods such as olive oil, pork, wine, honey and *liquamen* (a fermented fish sauce which most Romans considered essential) from all across the Mediterranean, Black Sea and North Atlantic coasts.

Rome thus relied on what we would now call 'food miles': a strategy of conquest and extraction enabled by its vast military might, widespread use of slave labour and mastery of the seas. The sea was vital to such a strategy since, as Neville Morley noted in *Metropolis and Hinterland*, maritime transport was around 42 times cheaper than that overland in the ancient world, and was thus the only way that bulky goods could be transported over great distances (Morley, 1996, pp. 63–65). Even so, feeding their citizens was a constant headache for Rome's leaders: during Augustus's reign, up to 320,000 received a free grain dole, the *Annona*, which Cicero reckoned cost the state one-fifth of all its revenue (Rickman, 1980, p. 170). As Tiberius noted, however, maintaining the *Annona* was essential: 'This duty, senators, devolves upon the emperor; if it is neglected, the utter ruin of the state will follow' (Rickman, 1980, p. 2).

With the bulk of the capital's food coming from overseas, farmers in the Roman *suburbium* were free to concentrate on highly lucrative *pastio villatica*, or villa farming, producing fruit and vegetables, as well as such delicacies as milk-fed snails, pond fish and nut-stuffed dormice for the luxury market – much as vertical farms and organic box schemes serve high-end markets today. While local farmers thrived, however, Rome's distant hinterlands suffered: by the third century, the soils of North Africa were exhausted, and observers wrote despairingly of the white, caked earth, a sure sign of fatal salinisation (Girardet, 2004, p. 46).

Two millennia on, it's not hard to see parallels between Rome's predicament and our own. Rome exemplified what one might call the urban paradox: the fact that city-dwellers worldwide rely on the countryside to feed them. We may call ourselves urban, but in reality we still dwell on the land. Rome was neither the first nor last civilisation to eat itself to death; the Sumerians met a similar fate, and the mass clearance of forests in ancient Greece in order to grow more wheat led to widespread soil erosion, leading Plato to describe the Attic hills as 'the skeleton of a body wasted by disease' (Plato, edited by Hamilton & Cairns, 1987, p. 1216). Today, with an estimated third of the world's arable land either lost or severely eroded, the pattern shows every sign of repeating itself.

Paris – the 'New Rome'

Politics were never far from food in pre-industrial Europe, especially when cities began to grow to unmanageable proportions once again, and supplies ran short. By 1750, Paris was one of the largest capitals on the continent, with some 650,000 citizens to feed. Dubbed the 'New Rome', the city differed from its ancient predecessor in one crucial respect: it had no direct access to the sea. The result, as Stephen Kaplan detailed in *Provisioning Paris*, was a struggle for food supplies that dominated and stifled the French rural economy. A series of 'provisioning crowns' were declared around the capital, the first of which consisted of a zone in which only grain for the city could be grown. With a good harvest, this 'first crown' could cope, but in a bad year (which came as often as one in three) the capital asserted its right, by force if necessary, to acquire its grain from a 'second crown' consisting of Picardy and Champagne, and in really bad years, a third or 'crisis' crown was invoked, consisting of much of northern France.

The Parisian authorities recognised, just as those of Rome had done, that feeding their citizens was, as one finance minister put it, 'the most essential object that must occupy the administration' (de Necker, 1778 in Kaplan, 1984, p. 24). Without access to imported grain, however, the authorities' only recourse was to attempt to control the local trade. To this end, they set up a 'grain police': an unwieldy hierarchy of thousands of officials, headed up by the king himself, known as the 'baker of last resort'. The police sent spies into the countryside to gather such information as market conditions, likely yields, local gossip and weather, reporting back at weekly meetings. Only licensed grain merchants were allowed to function within 20 miles of the city and all transactions were supposed to take place in the open so they could be monitored. The hoarding of grain was forbidden, and millers, bakers and merchants were all prevented from engaging in one another's trades, in order to prevent them from gaining too much control over the food supply.

That was the theory; in practice, a great deal of trade went on illegally, via an extensive black market that included a network of illicit 'corn exchanges' held in taverns, farms, and out on the open road. Convents and hospitals licensed to hold grain for their own consumption allowed dealers to store theirs in exchange for a cut of the profits. Millers and bakers, meanwhile, became wealthy by extending their influence up and down the food chain. Although the grain police were aware of such malfeasance, they were forced to turn a blind eye, since the black market supplied about one-third of all of the city's grain.

In an attempt to seize control, the authorities decided to concentrate all Parisian food trades in one central market at *Les Halles*. The market was split into various quarters selling different kinds of produce, each presided over by its own dynastic clan, who kept a mafia-like grip on their respective trade. *Les Halles* soon grew into a city within the city, with its own customs, rules, taverns and political opinions, the latter of which would prove pivotal. The crisis eventually came in the 1780s, when a string of poor harvests culminating in two disastrous years in 1788 and 1789 led to food shortages. As the population became restive, the market porters, or *forts*, blamed the king for the lack of food, becoming ringleaders in the subsequent revolution in which the 'baker of last resort' would lose his head.

London – Feeding the Wen

If Paris and Rome demonstrated why political leaders have generally feared being in charge of the food supply, London showed how they might avoid it altogether. Blessed with a navigable river, London was already described as a 'celebrated centre of commerce' by Tacitus just 20 years after its foundation in 43 CE, and the Roman city began as it would continue, importing all the luxuries necessary to a civilised life in the north – wine, olive oil, pine-nuts, raisins, pepper, ginger, cinnamon and of course *liquamen* – up from the Mediterranean.

London has always had plenty of options when it comes to feeding itself. The thirteenth-century capital's grain trade already dominated the economy of southeast England, and unlike their French equivalents, English market towns such as Ware, Henley-on-Thames, Faversham and Rochester flourished on the trade (Campbell et al., 1993, p. 47). When local supplies ran short, London could always import its grain from the Baltic, as it did regularly from the ninth century onwards.

London's favourable geography led its rulers to take a notably hands-off approach to feeding their capital. No English monarch ever assumed the unwelcome mantle of 'baker of last resort'; on the contrary, royal interference in London's trade was limited to continual pleas from the Palace for more ships to dock at the royal port of Queenhithe, since dues from there went to the Crown, while those from Billingsgate went to the City (Stow, 1908, p. 10).

As global navigation increased from the fourteenth century onwards, however, there was soon enough cash rolling in to keep everyone happy. While maritime cities like Venice, Amsterdam and Istanbul made great fortunes trading in grain, herring and spices, the English added sugar, after the navy's seizure of Jamaica in 1655. Sugar proved irresistible to European palates and demand grew so rapidly that by the end of the seventeenth century, plantations has been established all across the Caribbean. The dark side of this was the fact that the plantations were run on African slave labour: the shameful 'false commodity' upon which so much imperial wealth was based (Mintz, 1986, p. 43). Despite its dubious origins, the new 'white gold' soon made London a boomtown. By the early eighteenth century, one-tenth of the British population were living in the capital, a quarter of them engaged in port trades. Despite disapproving of the frivolous extravagance the boom caused, Daniel Defoe nevertheless noted that it benefitted the entire nation:

> It is not the kingdom which makes London rich, but London makes the rest of the kingdom rich...The country send up their corn, their malt, their cattle, their fowls, their coals, their fish, all to London, and London sends back spice, sugar, wine, drugs, cotton, linen, tobacco, and all foreign necessaries to the country...London consumes all, circulates all, exports all, and at last pays for all; and this is trade.
>
> *Defoe, 1726 in Dodd, 1856, pp. 110–111*

The craving for sugar, along with its bitter companions of tea, coffee and cocoa, turned Britain into the world's first consumer society. As the boundaries between need and luxury became blurred, the phenomenon that Defoe witnessed would soon create a new economic order which, as Aristotle had long ago warned, could never be sated.

The Case for Free Trade

While on a visit to Paris in 1766, the Scottish economist Adam Smith was struck by the relative torpor of the French capital compared to its booming English rival. Although the leading French economists known as the Physiocrats argued for the deregulation of trade in order to stimulate the economy, they also sought to turn France into a protectionist agrarian state. For Smith, this was a big mistake. Although he agreed with the Physiocrats that land was the ultimate source of all wealth, he also saw how such wealth could be greatly magnified though international trade, as he would later argue in *The Wealth of Nations*:

> The inhabitants of a city, it is true, must always ultimately derive their subsistence, and the whole materials and means of their industry, from the country. But those of a city, situated near either the sea-coast or the banks of a navigable river, are not necessarily confined to derive them from the country in their neighbourhood. They have a much wider range, and they may draw them from the most remote corners of the world...A city might in this manner grow to great wealth and splendour, while not only the country in its neighbourhood, but all those to which it traded were in poverty and wretchedness.
>
> *Smith, 1999 [1776], p. 502*

Although Smith didn't mention London by name, there can be little doubt as to which 'mighty city on a navigable river' he had in mind. Thanks to its favourable geography, London demonstrated what Smith called 'perfect competition': the forces of supply and demand creating a market largely unfettered by the state. The trade between city and country required no regulation, Smith argued, since the self-interest of many individuals would see to it that every economic niche was filled. The 'hidden hand' of commerce would self-regulate, to the benefit of all. Smith did acknowledge, however, that the opening up of local markets to global competition might have its casualties; an insight that has proved remarkably prescient.

'Nobody Does It'

By the mid-nineteenth century, London's position as a global centre of trade was secured. Observing all the activity around the ports, the historian George Dodd found himself wondering how such a great city was fed, and in 1856 he published the results of his research in *The Food of London*, the first comprehensive account of an urban food system. *The Food of London* is a remarkable book, describing in forensic detail all the people, spaces and systems feeding the city and logging virtually every cow, sheep, bushel and barrel entering it. Dodd was fortunate in that the port and market authorities of his day were happy to share their figures with him, as a result of which we know, for example, how many tonnes of potatoes were sold at Covent Garden in 1853 (72,000), how many head of livestock arrived in London that same year (2.2 million) and how many ships docked each day at the city's ports: 121, of which 52 came from the colonies bringing, among other things, 86 million pounds of tea from India and China. Despite amassing such data, however, Dodd admitted that explaining how this vast cornucopia reached the city was beyond him:

> It is useless to ask by what central authority, or under what controlling system, is such a city as London supplied with its daily food. 'Nobody does it'. No-one for instance, took care that a sufficient quantity of food should reach London in 1855, for the supply of two millions and a half of human beings during fifty-two weeks. And yet such a supply *did* reach London.
>
> *Dodd, 1856, p. 2*

In Dodd's day, the 'hidden hand' that fed London had barely changed for centuries: cattle were still driven down St. John Street to the livestock market at Smithfield, geese and turkeys still waddled in from Essex to be sold at Poultry, and tea clippers still sailed up the Thames. Yet things were about to change. As Dodd recognised, the railways would revolutionise the way that cities were fed. 'It is scarcely possible,' he wrote, 'to exaggerate the value of quick and easy transmission of food to so enormous a city as London; the variety of the commodities, and the prices at which they can be sold, are so intimately dependent thereon, that it becomes almost a matter of life and death to the inhabitants' (Dodd, 1856, p. 101).

The 'quick and easy transmission of food' would not only improve the quality of food available in cities, it would also emancipate cities from geography, allowing them, for the first time, to be built in any size, shape and place. The arrival of railways signalled the start of the urban age, and as cities began to expand, their rural hinterlands did likewise, as vast tracts of previously inaccessible land were opened up to farming for the first time. From now on, food would become increasingly invisible to city-dwellers, as it began travelling down specialised supply routes, often arriving at night. The nascent food industry would increasingly take control of the food supply, as political leaders heaved a collective sigh of relief, ceding responsibility for this most vital of tasks to agri-food businesses – along with the power it conferred.

Chicago – Emporium of the World

The most consequential transformation wrought by the railways was that of the American Great West. A vast swathe of open prairie roamed by tens of millions of bison and home to several Native American tribes, the area was transformed within a decade of the railroads' arrival in 1827 (through the bisons' mass slaughter and the removal of their human companions to reservations) into the largest expanse of grain production the world had ever seen.

All railroads led to Chicago, a city whose strategic position at the base of Lake Michigan and close to the head of the Mississippi watershed made it a natural trading post for the region. Before the railways, Midwestern farmers would pack their grain in sacks and either take it to the city themselves by wagon or river or pay merchants to take it for them. Once it arrived, the grain was sold in the time-honoured fashion in the open market. With the arrival of the railways, however, new methods were needed to shift the vast quantities of grain that began to flow off the Great Plains. Grain elevators were the answer: tall storage facilities that could scoop up the grain and sort it into bins according to its grade, ready for dispatch by rail to the city. As William Cronon noted in *Nature's Metropolis*, this transformation turned grain into a commodity that behaved more like a liquid than a solid (Cronon, 1991, pp. 104–132). From now on, instead of receiving direct payments for their crops, farmers would be given receipts that could be redeemed at a future date for grain of similar quality. Elevator receipts thus became tradable assets that referred, not to a particular sack of grain, but to a measurable amount of a commodified good. Since such receipts could change hands many times before delivery, soon many of those trading in them had no interest in taking delivery of the grain itself, but merely in speculating on the future price of grain: the futures market was born (Cronon, 1991, p. 126).

In 1864, the Chicago Board of Trade formalised futures contracts in an attempt to steady the extreme price fluctuations caused by variable harvests and demand surges from the Civil War. Agreeing a grain price ahead of the harvest ensured that farmers received a fair payment for their crop, while allowing buyers to speculate on the market. The move had far-reaching consequences, not just for the way in which food would be traded in future, but for global markets in general. Today, derivatives (stocks so named because they're derived from an underlying asset, such as grain) dominate global trade, effectively creating a meta-market based on pure speculation that can, ironically, fuel food price volatility in times of crisis, as happened in 2008 (see de Schutter, 2010, pp. 2–3).

Grain commodification and futures markets were Chicagoan innovations that signalled a revolution in the way cities would henceforth be fed; yet they were mere preliminaries to the invention that would really put Chicago on the map: cheap meat. With an unprecedented grain glut flowing into the city, Chicago stockmen came up with the novel idea of feeding the surplus to cattle. By 1870, Chicago's Union Stockyards (feedlots where the steers were fattened up on grain) employed 75,000 people and processed three million head of cattle a year. Slaughtered and butchered with ruthless efficiency by the city's notorious meatpackers, the cattle presented a problem in their butchered state: how to get so much fresh meat to lucrative urban markets on the East Coast in an edible condition. One of the city's biggest packers, Gustavus F. Swift, solved the problem by building a refrigerated railway – the Swift Refrigerator Line – furnished with depots of lake ice, salted blocks of which could be hung at both ends of a railway truck to keep the dressed carcasses fresh. Swift thus pioneered what is now known as the 'chill-chain': the refrigerated supply routes that are so pivotal to modern fresh food delivery. With aggressive marketing and cut-throat prices, Swift soon persuaded Bostonians and New Yorkers to abandon their traditional local butchers in favour of anonymous factory beef slaughtered hundreds of miles away: the age of cheap industrial meat had arrived.

The dependence of great cities like New York on distant markets for their food, and the potential vulnerability that this represented, was not lost on the Chief of the Port of New York Authority's Commerce Bureau, Walter P. Hedden. When a planned national railroad strike threatened to cut off the city's supplies in 1921, Hedden realised that a comprehensive reassessment of the city's food system was needed. Eight years later he published *How Great Cities Are Fed*, effectively the industrial sequel to George Dodd's *Food of London*. In it, Hedden confirmed what his Victorian predecessor had predicted, namely that railways (particularly refrigerated lines) had indeed transformed the feeding of cities. Whereas a city's rural hinterland (which Hedden dubbed its 'foodshed') was previously determined primarily by geography, the ease of rail transport meant that boundaries were now more likely to be decided by cost than by topography. 'The barriers which deflect raindrops into one river basin rather than into another are natural land elevations,' Hedden wrote, 'while the barriers which guide and control movements of foodstuffs are more often economic than physical' (Hedden, 1929, p. 17). As a result, the quality and seasonality of food now played a far greater part in deciding what cities would eat than proximity: citrus fruits from California and Florida, for example, competed in practically every important U.S. market, despite the distances travelled being considerable.

There was, however, another consequence of the industrial food system that worried Hedden: city authorities were losing control of the food supply. Unlike in Dodd's day, when 'nobody' fed London, cities now depended on a handful of powerful players such as milk conglomerates, meatpackers and railway companies, with some of the latter owned by the packers themselves. This 'vertical control' of the food chain (precisely what the *ancien régime* Parisian authorities had been so desperate to avoid) gave big food companies unprecedented power. Indeed, when the new U.S. Federal Trade Commission investigated the packing industry in 1917–18, it reported that the 'Big Five' Chicago packing firms had 'complete control of the industry from producer to consumer' (Hedden, 1929, p. 264). In response, Hedden argued for greater public control of the food industry. 'In dealing with food industries which have a high degree of concentration because of the large capital investment required for plant and equipment such as the meat packers and milk distributors,' he wrote, 'the preservation of competition itself becomes a primary objective' (Hedden, 1929, p. 279). Today we know that Hedden's words were too little, too late. Although steps were made to curtail the food industry's power, the corporate genie was already out of the bottle.

With their efficiencies of scale, logistical mastery and ruthless business practices, Chicago's meatpackers established the ground rules for an industry that would henceforth compete for ever-greater control, consolidation and profit. Today, just four packers (including JBS-Swift) control 85 per cent of U.S. beef production, and consolidation is now the name of the game across the food industry, with agri-food giants such as Nestlé, PepsiCo and Unilever enjoying annual turnovers that far exceed many national GDPs (Nestlé's sales in 2019 were worth $97 billion) (Nestlé, 2020). Such behemoths demonstrate what ancient political leaders had always known: control of food is power.

Today, the line between food and politics is blurred in the Global North, with a 'revolving door' between government and Big Food that can have grave ecological consequences. When Brazilian President Jair Bolsonaro came to power in 2018, for example, he lost no time in accelerating deforestation in the Amazon and appointing his cattle-rancher friends to key roles in government (Phillips, 2019). Similar deregulation has stripped much Indonesian rainforest to make way for palm oil plantations. A century and a half after the invention of 'cheap food', modern agribusiness represents the gravest threat to our future on the planet.

Sitopia

Whether or not we can pull back from the brink is clearly as much a political question as an ecological one. The ancient bond between city and country has long been broken in the West; here, and increasingly elsewhere, we rely on international supply chains and logistical operations wholly owned and operated by agri-food conglomerates of immense size and power. The corporate takeover of urban food systems is near complete in the industrialised world, while political appetite for more control of the food system is notable by its absence. International regulation of the food system is weak, market abuses and ecological destruction are widespread, and the food industry itself has every reason to maintain the status quo. With the increasing urgency of the need to change the food system, the question arises as to where such change will come from.

Part of the problem we face in tackling the question of how to eat better in the West is due to the fact that it is so bound up with the way we live. To alter our food system would require not just an overhaul of farming practices, but of our markets, economics, land use and lifestyles: the very foundations upon which our modern lives were built. Industrial society, as it emerged, was based on the premise of cheap food; an entity that doesn't actually exist. Unlike previous civilisations that faced a similar predicament, however, we do possess the science, experience and skill to know what to do. The question is whether or not we can summon the political will to act on it.

Another advantage we have over our forebears is the benefit of hindsight. Every civilisation in history has faced a tipping point when it has become obvious to anyone who cared to look that to continue life as normal risked catastrophe. We are at such a point now and, as ever, those bearing unwelcome news find themselves in the minority. What is remarkable, however, is how similar those voices have been.

A constant theme of utopianism – our greatest tradition of thinking holistically about the question of how to live – is the need to balance city and country. The Greek ideal of a self-sufficient *polis* was echoed by Thomas More and Ebenezer Howard in their respective tracts of 1516 and 1902, *Utopia* and *Garden Cities of To-Morrow*. While More criticised the greed and corruption of Tudor London by imagining an island nation inhabited by a network of semi-independent city-states, Howard updated the vision with the addition of railways. Recognising our human need for both society and nature, Howard dubbed his garden city a 'Town-Country Magnet', arguing that a network of dense communities of limited size could provide the benefits of city and country living, while negating the downsides of both (Howard, 1965 [1902], pp. 45–46). Crucially, all the land (both urban and rural) in the garden city would be owned by its residents in the form of a public trust, so that when values rose as a result of the city's being built, it would be local residents, not private landowners, who would benefit.

Contrary to its comfortable leafy image, the garden city was in fact a radical proposal for incremental land reform and a move towards a more regional, participatory politics. Howard recognised, as had many utopians before him, food's central role in shaping our lives. As I have argued elsewhere, this suggests that thinking through food could provide us with an alternative to utopia, which, by virtue of aiming at perfection, can never exist (Steel, 2008).[1] Since we live in a world shaped by food – a place I call 'Sitopia' (from Greek *sitos*, food + *topos*, place), food can provide us with a practical means of shaping our lives better. Since food sits at the nexus of our two most important sets of relationships – with nature and with one another – learning to value it and think through it can help us shape a more equitable, resilient world.

Effects of Good Government

The most compelling representation of what a good sitopia might look like is Ambrogio Lorenzetti's extraordinary fresco, *The Allegory of the Effects of Good Government*, painted in 1338 in Siena's great council chamber, the *Sala dei Nove*. A richly detailed evocation of daily life in the medieval city-state, it shows a prosperous city and bustling countryside coexisting in perfect harmony. As the title suggests, the image acknowledges the crucial role of government in fostering a close partnership between city and country. Had Siena's councillors glanced up at the image during one of their meetings, its message would have been clear: look after your countryside, and it will look after you.

Today, despite appearances, maintaining a balance between city and country (and thus between society and nature) remains the responsibility of our leaders. We in the industrialised world may no longer look out of our windows and see the landscapes that feed us, but our relationship with such rural territories, wherever they are in the world, remain vital to all our fortunes. The Greek *polis* and medieval Italian city-state represent two brief periods in history when this vital truth was recognised. For most of history, however, as the examples of Rome, Paris and London demonstrate, power has resided mostly in cities – which is where our historic narratives have also been written. Today, with mass urbanisation taking place at an unprecedented pace, the urban–rural imbalance is becoming a global phenomenon. One clear lesson from our past is that righting this imbalance is a matter of survival. As we enter the neo-geographical age, we must put the question of how to eat back at the heart of our thinking. We must value food again – and put the *oikonomia* back into economics.

As our current ecological crisis makes clear, food is too important to be left to the free market. While food doesn't lend itself well to political control, the absence of regulation leads to natural destruction and social injustice. Political leadership is thus needed to strike a balance between farmer and city-dweller, producer and consumer, society and nature; without it, history suggests, our civilisation will collapse.

The political instruments necessary to effect such a transformation are already available. They include taxation, environmental protections, wealth redistribution, transparent trade, regional planning and land reform – all instruments for which the Green Movement has long been calling. Such reforms are not merely essential to the prevention of ecological collapse, but to the creation of new landscapes for human and non-human flourishing. After 5,500 years of urban experimentation, rethinking how we live, work and share through the lens of food could start to heal the ancient divisions of urban civilisation.

Despite the prevailing orthodoxy (enthusiastically promoted by the agri-food industry) that 'only Big Ag can feed the world', the opposite is true. Numerous studies have shown that by adopting regenerative farming practices, wasting less and eating less meat and dairy, we could indeed feed the nine or so billion humans expected to be living on the planet by mid-century (Steel, 2020, pp. 263–265). To get there, however, will require a cultural shift towards a new idea of a good life based on living more in balance with nature and one another. One positive outcome of the COVID-19 pandemic in the Global North, indeed, has been to reveal wide public enthusiasm for such a life, at least among those able to work from home. In the UK, there has been a marked shift of interest towards living in the countryside, suggesting a shift in the future urban–rural relationship.

Crucially, food is now back on the agenda of architects and planners across the globe, and food planning is a rapidly growing field in urban and regional planning. Contemporary efforts to reconcile city and country include Dutch architects MVRDV's Almere Oosterwold masterplan, which incorporates a mix of farms, factories and housing in a deliberately fluid design, and British-based architects Viljoen and Bohn's concept of CPULs (Continuous Productive Urban Landscapes), which link underused urban spaces, such as car parks and verges, to create green corridors out into the countryside (Viljoen et al., 2005). Meanwhile, cities worldwide are joining forces to move towards more resilient and ethical food systems, with initiatives such as the C40 Cities programme, a network of 120 global cities working together to fulfil the UN's Sustainable Development Goals, the Transition Network and the UK's Sustainable Food Cities. Even the Chinese government has recently adjusted its development focus from a purely urban strategy to one that seeks a better balance between city and country, with initiatives such as its 'comprehensive rural revitalisation' programme (Wainwright, 2021).

Remarkable technologies will no doubt bring us new ways to feed ourselves in the future, but without a similarly innovative social-economic, spatial and ecological evolution, they will be worse than useless. Only by reconsidering what it means to live well, and by revaluing food and the natural world from which it comes, can we hope to build resilient lives in the future. After five and a half millennia, this could be our last chance to resolve the urban paradox.

Note

1 Utopia can either mean a good place (from Greek *eu*, good + *topos*, place, or no place, from the Greek *ou*, no + *topos*, place) (see Steel, 2008, pp. 306–9).

References

Aristotle. (1981). *The politics*. T. A. Sinclair (Trans.). Penguin.

Campbell, B. M., Galloway, J. A., Keene, D., & Murphy, M. (1993). *A medieval capital and its grain supply. Historical Geography Research Series No. 30.* Centre for Metropolitan Research.

Cronon, W. (1991). *Nature's metropolis: Chicago and the Great West.* W.W. Norton and Co.

de Schutter, O. (2010). *Food commodities speculation and food price crises: Regulation to reduce the risks of price volatility* (UN FAO Briefing Note 02). UN FAO. www2.ohchr.org/english/issues/food/docs/Briefing_Note_02_September_2010_EN.pdf.

Dodd, G. (1856). *The food of London.* Longman Brown, Green and Longmans.

Girardet, H. (2004). *Cities people planet.* Wiley.

Hamilton, E., & Cairns, H. (Eds.). (1987). *The collected dialogues of Plato.* Princeton University Press.

Hedden, W. P. (1929). *How great cities are fed.* D.C. Heath.

Howard, E. (1965 [1902]). *Garden Cities of to-morrow.* The MIT Press.

Kaplan, S. (1984). *Provisioning Paris: Merchants and millers in the grain and flour trade during the eighteenth century*, Cornell University Press.

Mintz, S. (1986). *Sweetness and power: The place of sugar in modern history.* Penguin.

Morley, N. (1996). *Metropolis and hinterland.* Cambridge University Press.

Nestlé (2020). Nestlé reports full-year results for 2019. [Press Release]. www.nestle.com/media/pressreleases/allpressreleases/full-year-results-2019.

Phillips, D. (2019). Brazil space institute director sacked in Amazon deforestation row. *The Guardian*, 2 August. www.theguardian.com/world/2019/aug/02/brazil-space-institute-director-sacked-in-amazon-deforestation-row

Rickman, R. (1980). *The corn supply of Ancient Rome.* Oxford Clarendon Press.

Smith, A. (1999 [1776]). *The wealth of nations, Books I–III* (1776). Penguin Classics.

Standage, T. (2009). *An edible history of humanity.* Atlantic.

Steel, C. (2008). *Hungry city: How food shapes our lives.* Chatto & Windus.

Steel, C. (2020). *Sitopia: How food can save the world*. Chatto & Windus.

Stow, J. (1908). *A survey of London, 1603, Vol. 2*. Ed. Charles Lethbridge Kingsford. 2 vols. Clarendon Press.

Viljoen, A., Bohn, K., & Howe, J. (Eds.). (2005). *CPULs: Continuous productive urban landscapes*. Architectural Press.

Wainwright, O. (2021) China's rural revolution: The architects rescuing its villages from oblivion. *The Guardian*, 24 March. www.theguardian.com/artanddesign/2021/mar/24/chinas-rural-revolution-architects-rescuing-villages-oblivion-tofu-rice-wine-lotus-tea

3

URBAN CHANGE AND THE MULTI-SCALAR POLITICS OF FOOD SYSTEMS IN COLONIAL AFRICA

James Duminy

Introduction

Writing an historical account of the governance of urban food systems in Africa is a challenge for several reasons. One is the enormous diversity of places and experiences within the region. Another is the fact that in many cases the actors and institutions involved in the governance of food systems have tended to frame food problems as matters of agricultural production and welfare, and therefore the responsibility of national governments rather than municipalities (de Visser, 2021). The urban has not always been an obvious scale of analysis for those interested in food. This is not to say that urban food issues have not occupied government officials in Africa. Indeed, a key argument pursued by this chapter is that, in some contexts, food problems manifesting in towns and cities were gradually rescaled into matters of wider national or imperial importance.

Scholars of African urban history have focused their studies on a diverse range of issues. Those issues include the ways that urban dynamics were drawn into national agendas, debates, and conflicts, as well as how state interests in the stabilization of urban segments of the working class were secured through practices related to planning, housing, and the built environment (Duminy & Parnell, 2020; Ferguson, 1990; Maylam, 1990; Parnell, 1993). However, less attention has been given to the role of food in the politics of African urban labour, perhaps with the exception of Frederick Cooper's (1987) study of Mombasa. Nevertheless, we do benefit from a small but sophisticated corpus of historical studies on urban food systems in various African contexts.

African food histories have predominantly addressed rural famine and transformation (de Waal, 1997; Iliffe, 1990; Moore & Vaughan, 1994; Watts, 2013). This work provides us with detailed accounts of how states intervened in times of scarcity, and how the redress and prevention of scarcity was embedded within various social, economic, and political institutions. Similarly, a rural focus on the social structures and transformations underpinning agricultural production is evident in the work addressing the 'agrarian question' in Africa, which has examined the insertion of African producers in the international economy as well as the specific forms of (post)colonial state intervention in agricultural systems (Bernstein, 1979; Mafeje,

DOI: 10.4324/9781003055907-4

2003; Watts, 1989). The relatively small body of research focusing on urban food governance has tended to address the functioning of urban food supply and marketing systems (Bryceson, 1985; Guyer, 1987; Porter et al., 2009). That work has shown how official efforts to secure urban food supply through mechanisms such as statutory marketing systems were always shaped by political forces. These efforts generated diverse effects in various contexts, in part because systems of food distribution are institutions necessarily expressed within particular kinds of social and economic structures (Guyer, 1987).

In examining the role of official actors and institutions in governing the urban food systems of colonial Africa, the focus of this chapter is on Kenya. Such a focus is warranted given the relative neglect of Kenya in existing scholarship on African food histories. It is warranted, also, in that Kenyan history reflects many of the political imperatives experienced in other colonial territories of the region – imperatives that had profound implications for how the state intervened in food systems. That diversity of political objectives arose because Kenya was caught between two sets of conflicts: the clash between settler and African producers, and that between local and metropolitan interests (Berman, 1990; Lonsdale & Berman, 1979). On the one hand, the settler community pressed for greater economic support from the Kenyan state to overcome the competition posed by less capital-intensive African producers. On the other, settlers feared and resisted what they perceived as the meddling influence of London and foreign capital on domestic affairs. Moreover, they consistently deprecated supposedly 'pro-native' British officials who considered African economic development a priority equal to or above settler demands for cheap migrant labour.

The chapter focuses on the politics of scale expressed in and through urban food systems. It will show that urban food issues and debates produced new scales through which food systems operated, were conceptualized, and governed. Such an emphasis gives us a sense of how the scalar configurations of urban food governance were reframed and contested, and of the mechanisms that mediate global crises and local conflicts (Engels, 2015). Food history is an ideal lens through which to examine the socio-political construction of scale precisely because food systems have undergone such profound transformations in terms of what people eat, where that food is produced, how it is distributed and sold, and how those processes are governed. Moreover, such an emphasis enables us to engage with recent arguments that we can and should periodize the global history of urbanization in relation to successive international 'food regimes' (Ghosh & Meer, 2020).

The focus here is on *government* policy, regulation, and intervention. That focus means that the wider array of actors and institutions involved in urban food system *governance* do not fall within our purview. While this excludes some of the broader processes of urban food governance, the emphasis here is genealogical. The key point is that we cannot understand the contemporary governance of urban food systems in Kenya and elsewhere in Africa without grasping the rationalities, practices, and legacies of colonial government in the region. In providing a 'history of the present', then, the chapter offers initial hypotheses that can be related and compared to the specific experiences of other African contexts.

The chapter follows a broad periodization of events and colonial government responses. After providing some context to Kenya as a particular case analysis, the chapter discusses the early colonial period (1890s to 1920s) that saw the rapid expansion and deepening of capitalist food markets to feed non-producing populations alongside initial attempts by the state to regulate food issues in Kenya's small but growing towns. The discussion then addresses the middle colonial period (1930s to 1945) when colonial states took on new responsibilities and commitments to support local food production in ways coloured by the demands of economic depression and war. And finally, the focus shifts to the late colonial period (1945 to 1960s) when food systems took on new political importance in the midst of rising African nationalism and international criticism of British colonial policy. These events and developments laid the framework for systems of urban food governance that continue to inform contemporary debates and practices.

The case of Kenya

Colonial authority was imposed on the area that is now modern Kenya in the late nineteenth century. Initially that authority stemmed from a charter granted to the Imperial British East Africa Company in 1888, prior to the declaration of the East Africa Protectorate in 1895. That territory was reconstituted in 1920 as the Colony and Protectorate of Kenya. Colonial status remained until the establishment of the Republic of Kenya in 1964. In the first decades of the twentieth century, the territory's towns were mainly small administrative centres, with the exception of older coastal trading ports like Mombasa and Lamu, which had previously been under Arab and Swahili control. In that period, Kenyan society and economy were overwhelmingly rural. As we will see, even after a period of rapid urban growth linked to the demands of the Second World War, the urban population constituted only around 5 per cent of the Kenyan total. While the overall urban population was limited in size, towns like Nairobi nevertheless grew rapidly to become important centres of demand for food, in the process accelerating the extension and deepening of food markets in the territory.

Food presented a pressing concern for colonial authorities, in part due to Kenya's unique spatial and environmental characteristics. The territory was and remains divided between fertile and well-watered areas suitable for intensive cultivation, concentrated in the southern inland region spanning the Rift Valley and Lake Victoria shoreline, and more arid areas with marginal environments that supported pastoral economies and societies. While Kenya enjoys a bimodal equatorial rainfall pattern comprising 'long rains' (March to May) and 'short rains' (October and November), those patterns are vulnerable to extreme meteorological events linked to the oscillations of the Indian Ocean dipole (Thielke & Mölg, 2019). As a result, Kenyans experience both extreme drought and rainfall on a periodic basis; historically, both have worked to produce or aggravate episodes of severe food scarcity.

Food also presented a problem for economic reasons. The advent and consolidation of British rule and the spread of capitalist market relations saw the development of a significant plantation econom,y producing export products such as tea, coffee, and sisal. Meanwhile, agricultural systems were increasingly dominated by the cultivation of maize, by both African and settler farmers, as a staple food crop to supply local consumers. With these farmers unable to compete with other large-scale producers in the maize export market, the question of maize production, marketing, and pricing for the domestic market became a central pivot of political contestation between African and settler producers. Those fault lines ran through the colonial history of Kenya, shaping the contours of official social and economic policy.

The specificity of Kenya's colonial history and political economy is precisely what makes it a valuable case from which to learn. Kenya hosted a relatively small but influential bloc of white settlers, concentrated in the central and fertile highland areas, who demanded that the state support their enterprise and guarantee a consistent supply of African migrant labour. Consequently, Kenya exhibited features of the settler-dominated colonial economies of Southern Africa *and* the more peasant-oriented economies of territories like Nigeria, Uganda, and Tanganyika. By examining Kenya as a case, the aim here is not to generalize Kenyan dynamics to other contexts but rather to tease out certain common features of how African colonial governments thought about and responded to problems of urban food supply and access. While that thought and practice was coloured by the specificities of Kenyan environment and political economy, there was significant inter-referencing of policies between colonial African governments. As a result, many of the ideas and practices surrounding urban food governance in Kenya had strong correlates in other contexts. That is clear in the case of concerns over urban sanitation and colonial malnutrition in the early twentieth century.

Urban food systems, sanitation, and nutrition (1890s to 1920s)

The introduction of colonial administration in Kenya facilitated the expansion and deepening of capitalist markets to feed non-producing populations. It introduced, also, official efforts to regulate food systems. However, administrators in this period seldom were animated by food problems affecting the territory's towns. In part, that was because municipal governments, where they existed in any substantial form, had few powers to intervene meaningfully in food systems (Duminy, 2019). In part, it was because government officials saw the primary problem of food as one of scarcity and famine. That problem most acutely affected rural areas with marginal environments, although undoubtedly many poorer residents of towns suffered during times of scarcity as grain farmers switched their scant supplies to more profitable channels (Herlehy, 1984). In such times, local officials and residents of coastal towns like Mombasa often relied on existing trading relations or food imports, as they did on rice imported from India during the 'Great Famine' of the late nineteenth and early twentieth centuries. That said, food systems in Kenya's growing urban centres did raise official interest through their links with problems of health and sanitation. And, in focusing on these links, urban food systems were framed, interpreted, and addressed through broader imperial anxieties and regulations surrounding public health and sanitation. In responding to problems of hygiene and disease, colonial officials sought to regulate not the producers of food so much as the urban built environment and the spaces in which food circulated.

In Kenya, urban growth in the early twentieth century amplified the risk of outbreaks of infectious diseases. Officials there, as in other British and French colonies, considered that risk an outcome of inadequate sanitation (Bigon, 2012; Swanson, 1977). Some of those anxieties directly linked to the issue of food, for diseases like typhoid fever, dysentery, and cholera could be spread through contaminated food and water supplies. To reduce the risk of contamination, colonial medical officers of health secured powers to regulate the built environment and the spaces in which food circulated. They sought also to regulate the activities of those involved in preparing, transporting, or selling foodstuffs, while ensuring that sources of food were sanitary and food items themselves free from taint.

Urban food systems linked local Kenyan debates with broader imperial discussions concerning public health, race, and segregation. Recent scholarship has been firm in asserting how Kenyan public health discourse in the first two decades of the twentieth century closely resembled those famously characterized by Swanson, in the South African setting, as the 'sanitation syndrome' (Greenwood & Topiwala, 2020; Swanson, 1977). From relatively early in the history of Nairobi, local public health officials and foreign consultants pinpointed the Indian bazaar as the principal source of the town's epidemiological risks. They used their concerns over the Asiatic community's supposed tendency to overcrowding and poor hygiene to justify the adoption of urban racial segregation as formal policy. These arguments were ultimately unsuccessful, but only after a veto from the Colonial Office finally settled the debate (Greenwood & Topiwala, 2020). Such events indicate how local colonial debates surrounding food, sanitation, and race could be inserted into, and informed by, wider imperial circulations of knowledge and practices (Njoh, 2004; Swanson, 1977; Tilley, 2011; Vaughan, 1991).

Historians of colonial public health have rightly located local urban dynamics within this broader imperial segregationist interest in sanitation. They have been less adept at examining how urban food systems, specifically, emerged as a problem through which officials secured powers to intervene directly in urban space and life. The Nairobi Township Rules, passed in 1917, offered one example of how this worked in practice. The Rules enabled officials to license and regulate the places where food was prepared, stored, and exchanged – including Indian and African eating houses, marketplaces, bakeries, abattoirs, butcheries, fishmongers, and vegetable dealers. Those operating eateries were obliged to ensure their premises were well-lit, ventilated, and constructed with hard floors. All food articles were to be kept within a dedicated store-room. People were specifically forbidden from sleeping in a room in which food was stored, prepared, or sold. Persons suffering from infectious disease were prohibited from working on the site of any food merchant. Neither could food items 'unfit for human consumption' be kept on a merchant's premises. Street vendors were to be licensed; all hawking of meat or fresh foods outside of public markets was banned – an early indication of the long-standing animosity Kenyan officials have shown towards food vendors supplying urban working-class consumers (Smart, 2017a). The Kenyan Public Health Ordinance of 1921 extended to the wider territory the kinds of powers secured by the Township Rules over the urban built environment, food standards, and trade (Duminy, 2019). Closely resembling the South African Public Health Act of 1919 in its concerns over food systems and the uses of public and private spaces, the Public Health Ordinance invested in the governor the power to regulate the establishment, control, and closure of all markets and market buildings.

Officials pursued similar practices in other settings. In Northern Rhodesia, the 1937 Market Ordinance granted local authorities powers to inspect and control market structures, the range of food articles presented for sale, trading periods, and prices (Battersby & Muwowo, 2019). Likewise, a Ugandan Markets Act secured in 1942 the exclusive rights of local officials to establish and maintain markets; those not gazetted under the Act were designated illegal (Monteith, 2019). Deborah Bryceson (1980) describes closely related legislation in Tanganyika, passed in 1928. There, part of the rationale for strict state control of marketing was the hope that, by regulating produce standards, peasant producers might compete successfully on the world market. But competitiveness in export markets was not all that was at stake. The strict regulation of marketplaces and the restriction of food vending reflected not only sanitary anxieties but also a long-standing and wider colonial disdain towards small-scale African and Indian traders or 'middlemen'. In colonial economic thought, the petty trader simultaneously was unscrupulous, unproductive, *and* a threat to the genuine productivity larger enterprises (Duminy, 2018; Harneit-Sievers, 1995; Monteith, 2019). Those ideas and motivations underpinned the development of a bifurcated food system in many colonial towns: one system operating through sanctioned places and traders, another on the fringes of the law.

The new science of public health linked together the governance of urban food systems, concerns over the local production and use of urban space, and broader racialized anxieties over 'imperial diseases' (Killingray, 2003). The latter were seen to threaten the resources of Empire, and intersected with influential discourses underscoring the risks of colonial moral and social degeneration (Stoler, 1989). Improved sanitation and medical intervention, imperial advisors and officials claimed, were critical for promoting healthier and more 'civilized' societies in colony and metropole alike (Killingray, 2003). But the interwar period also saw a second domain of scientific knowledge and technique gain official traction, in the process connecting urban food systems with wider health and economic questions. In particular, the 1920s and 1930s witnessed growing interest in the relationship between the incomes earned by working Africans on the one hand, and their cost and standard of living on the other. Such a focus on the purchasing power, health, and productivity of *urban* labour emerged within a wider colonial interest in African diets and (mal)nutrition, albeit one preoccupied initially with the diets and health of rural tribes (Brantley, 1997; Richards, 1939, 2004).

Official proposals for, and development of, dietary and ration scales for urban workers were a material outcome of the 'discovery of colonial malnutrition' in the interwar period (Worboys, 1988). In Kenya, medical officers began to show concern over the health problems of urban Africans in the 1920s, producing a schedule in 1933 of what they considered an adequate diet comprising local foods. Their recommendations were based on the minimum dietary requirements for British workers, as proposed by the British Medical Association. However, after tallying the average cost of this food and comparing it with the average going wage, officials found that a male worker in Nairobi, even without dependants, would be unable to afford an adequate diet. That realization fed concerns that low wage rates, relative to the costs of urban living, might foster labour problems related to turnover, malnutrition, and unproductivity, as well as broader social and moral evils like petty crime and prostitution (Van Zwanenberg, 1972).

The scientific knowledge of nutrition that emerged in the early twentieth century – by rendering colonial diets and bodies visible, measurable, and calculable – brought colonial labour problems into communication with wider urban anxieties over things like density, hygiene, and delinquency. Yet it also provided a means of linking local urban problems to larger networks of expertise and imperatives of governance. As we shall see, the scientific knowledge of nutrition came to play an essential role in African wartime efforts, providing a conduit through which local colonial problems became visible to metropolitan authorities, and through which imperial directives, objectives, and developments could be translated to the local level.

Depression and war (1930s to 1945)

In the face of low international prices and decreased government revenues, the 1930s saw colonial states across Africa take on new responsibilities and commitments to support and protect local food production. By the end of the Second World War, facilitated by the exigencies of global conflict and supply, state control of marketing systems had become an established means to respond to both food scarcities and wider socio-economic problems. In this period, the predominant location of food governance problems transitioned from rural areas (in the form of scarcity, famine, or rural malnutrition) to the urban domain (in a manner often closely linked to labour issues). In the process, in contexts like Kenya, local urban food problems were rescaled to become matters of regional, and indeed imperial, security.

Colonial governments initially established agricultural marketing boards with the logic that government control would boost prices, farm incomes, and export earnings – reducing marketing costs to the benefit of producers (Jones, 1987). In many colonies, settler producers saw in such boards their deserving support and protection from African competitors. The marketing of maize – as the staple food crop in many territories – assumed particular importance with respect to urban consumers. Early examples of 'maize control boards' were established in Southern Rhodesia (1931) and then Northern Rhodesia (1936), nominally to stabilize both prices and the food supply of towns and mines (McCann, 2005; Vickery, 1985). In Kenya, settler maize producers also argued for state control from the early 1930s. The Kenya Farmers Association wanted control of the internal maize market as a means to secure higher domestic prices for its members, arguing that protecting the settler maize industry was in the national interest. In the Kenyan case, however, these arguments were unsuccessful, largely due to the opposition of 'consuming interests', which included both urban consumers and rural employers like those active in the plantation industry, who feared increases in the price of food (Lonsdale, 1986). Nevertheless, when settlers did receive their desired control due to the opportunity of war, there was a precedent for thinking about maize producer and consumer prices at the scale of the *national interest.*

In this period, Kenyan officials attempted to guarantee sufficient food supplies in the territory by ensuring the production of an exportable surplus. Their interventions in the markets of African agricultural produce tied into this logic. The 1935 Marketing of Native Produce Ordinance, developed with reference to similar legislation already passed in Uganda and Tanganyika, sought to boost African production for export by stabilizing and centralizing trade – ensuring a consistent flow of goods through a limited number of officially sanctioned marketplaces, at regulated prices. It granted extensive powers to regulate the establishment and operation of marketplaces and enabled officials to restrict the outflow of produce from declared areas. Perhaps more than any other piece of legislation, the Ordinance embodied and expressed the colonial state's territorial approach to governing the food system, emphasizing the regulation of space and the operation of marketplaces. That interest in securing food supplies by stabilizing and centralizing the food system provided the context for wide-reaching changes to food system governance following the outbreak of war in 1939.

In Kenya, the Second World War consolidated a range of trends that had started in the 1930s (Anderson & Throup, 1985). One such trend was urban growth – the recovery of labour demand from the mid-1930s encouraged increasing numbers of people to seek urban employment, and the development of wartime industries accelerated that rural–urban drift. Officials initially introduced food marketing controls as a means to increase agricultural exports to supply the international war effort. However, when in 1942 heavy rains and then drought struck, decreasing the total volume of maize coming onto market, maize control staff quickly shifted their focus to supplying domestic and regional labour markets, and in particular urban consumers. The growing urban population suffered most acutely from erratic food supply through the official market, and they bore the brunt of price increases, rabid inflation on the black market, and shortages of imported goods. As wages failed to keep pace with inflated living costs, workers went on strike – initially in Mombasa but soon in other towns. Officials were forced to instigate rationing schemes, revise wage levels, and offer wartime bonuses to account for inflation. Here nutritional knowledge in the form of dietary standards was used to respond to urban labour grievances, by providing calculations of poverty and wage levels with a supposedly scientific and objective basis (Cooper, 1987).

Harvest shortfalls, and the threat of curtailing industrial production, affected the whole of East Africa, and officials recognized the problem as being regional in scope. In December 1942, they formed an East African Production and Supply Council to pool and allocate essential supplies between territories, railway and harbour authorities, and stationed military forces. Urban food systems thus emerged as a wartime priority of not only territorial but also regional inter-territorial security. Indeed, the threat of urban labour unrest was significant enough for officials to prefer to request imports using scarce imperial shipping space, rather than substitute the rations of workers with alternative foodstuffs. In contexts like Kenya, these dynamics helped to secure entitlements for urban workers in the form of preferential food access and wage subsidies from the state. Food thus became an important part of the political contract forged between state and urban labour.

Wartime scarcities and the functions of food distribution were closely tied up with an emerging politics of urban labour in Kenya and the wider region. Despite the fact that only a small minority of the total Kenyan population lived in towns by the end of the War, the problem of urban food commanded political attention at a scale far beyond the rate of urbanization would suggest. Indeed, labour agitation and official compromise established a precedent for the provision of food subsidies to urban workers, a practice that would become widespread among postcolonial African governments, providing both the context for academic and policy debates surrounding 'urban bias' and a favoured target of structural adjustment (Bryceson, 1985; Cooper, 1989; Watts, 1989). Subsidies, alongside scientific knowledge and regulation of nutrition were established as key components of an emerging system of 'welfare' directed at working urban consumers.

The late colonial period (1945 to 1960s)

Following the return of peace, food marketing controls continued to function in many African colonial territories. The governance of urban food systems also remained closely tied to the politics of labour, albeit according to slightly different objectives. Whereas, previously, urban workers were only begrudgingly accommodated in the towns of East and Southern Africa, often required to return to rural areas once their contracts had expired, colonial officials in many territories now sought the *stabilization* of a differentiated and respectable African urban working class (Cooper, 1987). In Kenya, this shift in policy arose not only due to poor living conditions and the entitlements won through social unrest and protest, but also because London's new policies of 'colonial development' made room for permanent African workers in towns (Harris, 2008). In fact, by the late 1940s, discussions around the need to confront or regulate African labour migration and to establish workers, with their families, near to their places of employment – which demanded 'good housing and diet' alongside forms of social security – extended across imperial powers (Cooper, 1989).

Kenyan officials continued to bring scientific knowledge and techniques to bear on the problem of urban labour relations and welfare, and food remained an important piece of that puzzle. In 1945, a committee appointed to enquire into labour agitation in Mombasa dwelt on the cost of living for urban workers, recommending the introduction of a comprehensive rationing scheme.[1] Reluctant to stir further discontent, officials rather focused on controlling food prices, establishing government shops and canteens, and setting out minimum dietary standard for employers to follow in their rationing.[2] Diet and nutrition were now means of progressing towards the new government objectives of detribalization and decasualization – by attracting workers, retaining labour, and boosting productivity. As the problem of African nutrition was medicalized and oriented towards the 'new' Kenyan 'labour problem', the focus of governmental attention had shifted away from the 'old' problem of rural poverty and malnutrition to the body, permanency, and productivity of the urban worker. In step, urban food systems, and what African urban residents ate, became of increasing official interest.

In Kenya, the growth in urban demand for food was an important driver of agricultural and wider development policy in the 1940s and 1950s. Growing rural landlessness, alongside increasing demand for labour in towns during and following the Second World War, underpinned the expansion of urban and non-producing populations. The national level of urbanization increased from around 5 per cent in 1948 to 8 per cent by 1962 (Ogonda, 1992). While limited in scale, this growth in domestic demand provided part of the justification for the continued existence of statutory marketing controls, including guaranteed prices for producers, over the territorial and regional food system.[3] It also justified a step change in official attitudes towards agricultural practice and development in the African reserve areas. The Swynnerton Plan of 1954, the culmination of broader shifts in Kenyan development policy towards an appreciation of the growth of cash crops by African farmers and the individualization of land tenure, was motivated in part by the desire to feed urban populations and the workforce, and to produce limited quantities for export (Thurston, 1987). The politics of urban food supply were thus central to the pursuit of the 'irreconcilable' objectives of 'intensified production and social order' in the post-war era (Cooper, 1987, p. 264).

In postcolonial Kenya, as elsewhere on the continent, securing food for urban consumers at reasonable prices would emerge as a key political imperative. That imperative has shaped state regulation of various components of urban food systems. Daniel Maxwell (1999) notes that state hostility towards urban agriculture is one consequence of agriculture-led strategies for economic growth (as pursued by numerous African countries following decolonization), as such strategies often depended on growth in domestic urban demand – an objective in principle threatened by residents growing their own food. Likewise, small-scale urban food processing, as in the form of 'hammer mills', have often found themselves at odds with government visions for the centralized large-scale processing facilities perceived as necessary to meet urban demand (Jayne & Rubey, 1993). In these ways, the politics of the urban consumer fundamentally shaped the contemporary contours of food governance.

Conclusion

Following Kenyan independence in late 1963, the postcolonial government inherited and continued a range of structures that had a fundamental bearing on urban food systems. These included a state system that directly intervened in agricultural markets in order to guarantee sufficient food supplies to urban and other non-producing populations. They encompassed a system of food subsidies geared towards urban workers. They included, too, widespread official disdain towards the presence and activities of urban informal food vendors and traders, often motivated on public health grounds (Smart, 2017b). The postcolonial inheritance was therefore a highly centralized view of, and interface with, the urban food context. It arose due to the wider issues of security that officials attached to emerging food risks in the territory's rapidly growing towns. And it was one targeted, but not completely deconstructed, by economic crisis and structural adjustment reforms in the late 1980s and early 1990s. Indeed, staple food marketing boards retain a role in national agricultural systems and food security policies. Likewise, the idea of urban food subsidies still has some influence in policy circles (Musyoka et al., 2010).[4]

The ways in which history bears on the present and future also come into focus when considering the ongoing COVID-19 pandemic. Many governments responded to the pandemic by restricting food exports (Udmale et al., 2020), echoing colonial responses to crises of scarcity. Informal workers, many involved in the food economies of African cities, faced significant barriers to their livelihoods from heavy-handed policing and strict regulation of public spaces, practices typically not faced by formal businesses (Chen et al., 2021). The pandemic has thus provided the justification for renewed exclusion and repression of critical informal food economies on public health grounds. Meanwhile, broader colonial legacies of underdevelopment and poverty, alongside dependency on international aid, have left African populations vulnerable to outbreaks of infectious disease while retarding effective local pandemic responses. Acknowledging that *history matters* in important ways, then, asks of us to avoid repeating past mistakes and debates when acting to create more equitable and resilient urban food systems.

In colonial Kenya, the growth and change of urban areas drove wide-reaching shifts in the character of the food system, in addition to the strategies and practices employed to govern that system. In particular, the emergence of an African urban working class made state intervention to guarantee and stabilize their food and nutritional security imperative. By the end of the colonial period, officials intervened in urban food systems in two main ways – increasing food production and regulating consumption. Theirs was a dualistic approach to governing food systems, working through both territorial practices of governance (regulating spaces of food production, urban built environments, marketplaces, land tenure systems, and so on) and economic mechanisms (for instance, ensuring appropriate wage levels, providing producer and consumer subsidies, and developing rationing schemes). Territorial practices were the purview of local, provincial and central governments, but the specific matter of regulating the production of the urban built environment fell to municipal officials – this was, and remains, the principal way in which African urban governments are able to intervene in and shape local food systems.

The specificity of the Kenyan case within the wider African context arises from the dilemma that officials faced in deciding whether to support either settler or African development and production. Lacking the powerful settler lobbies and mineral wealth of South Africa and the Rhodesias, yet unable to pursue the more African-centred approach of territories like Tanganyika or Uganda, Kenyan officials walked a political tightrope. Conflicting interests surrounding food production fundamentally shaped the governance of urban food systems. While the source of the specificity of the Kenyan case, the nature of these internal conflicts also enables this case to speak to wider experiences in the African region. Debates around preferential support for agriculture; the (mal)nutrition of African working bodies; the creation of statutory marketing systems; the provision of urban food subsidies; the need to regulate the built environment, food marketplaces, and vendors in the interests of public health – all featured in one way or another across the wider region. Indeed, the food systems of Kenyan towns, like those of other colonies, were inserted into wider inter-territorial and imperial circulations of knowledge and practice.

That said, a focus on the politics of scale produced through acts of food system governance warns us against deducing local events and initiatives from the influence of wider imperial, international, or global processes. In Kenya, urban food systems were not governed simply within the context of a hierarchy of objectives cascading from the imperial, to the territorial, to the local. We have seen how local and urban trends or events could raise interest and responses at the level of the central Kenyan state or, in the case of wartime developments, from imperial authorities. That recognition leads us to consider in finer detail the events that give rise to new scales of thought and action surrounding urban food systems. Moreover, a focus on scalar politics invites an examination of the ways in which different forms of scientific knowledge and calculation can provide a lens through which urban food problems become visible and amenable to actors and institutions at various scales. Scientific knowledge and practice surrounding food and eating – as with sanitary and nutritional public health, for example – may be fundamental to the emergence of new scales of thought and action.

The importance of understanding how urban events and trends shaped food systems at wider scales, and how, in turn, food systems enabled urbanization, is critical given recent debates in urban studies around the need to account for the demographic (rather than simply economic) drivers of historical urban growth and urbanization in Africa (Fox, 2017). Moreover, if we are to refine our knowledge of the historical dynamics of urbanization with reference to successive international 'food regimes', it is equally important to disaggregate our understanding of those food regimes, locating the historically and geographically specific mechanisms and operational landscapes that have enabled processes of city growth (Ghosh & Meer, 2020). This enjoins us to sharpen our understanding of the specific mechanisms through which urban food systems have been secured, and their effects, rather than relying on standard diffusionist models of history or broad systematizations of 'world-historical food regimes', models that privilege the experiences of dominant contexts over the particular scalar politics of urban food systems arising in different geographies.

Notes

1 TNA: CO 859/164/2, governor's deputy to Jones (telegram), 31 March 1947.
2 TNA: CO 859/164/2, Grant, 'Nutrition Sub-Committee Notes on Visit to East Africa', 26 June 1947; TNA: CO 859/164/2, Mitchell to Jones (telegram), 12 January 1949.
3 An East African Cereals Pool continued to operate until 1952, when it was replaced by an inter-territorial mutual supply agreement; TNA: CO 822/668, *passim*.
4 For example, the Urban Food Subsidy programme was launched with donor funding in 2012. See www.socialprotection.or.ke/national-safety-net-program/124-urban-food-subsidy-programme-ufsp, accessed 27 November 2020.

References

Anderson, D., & Throup, D. (1985). Africans and agricultural production in colonial Kenya: The myth of the war as a watershed. *Journal of African History*, *26*(4), 327–345.

Battersby, J., & Muwowo, F. (2019). Planning and governance of food systems in Kitwe, Zambia: A case study of food retail space. In J. Battersby & V. Watson (Eds.), *Urban food systems governance and poverty in African cities* (pp. 128–140). New York: Routledge. https://doi.org/10.4324/9781315191195

Berman, B. (1990). *Control and crisis in colonial Kenya: The dialectic of domination*. London: James Currey.

Bernstein, H. (1979). African peasantries: A theoretical framework. *The Journal of Peasant Studies*, *6*(4), 421–443.

Bigon, L. (2012). A history of urban planning and infectious diseases: Colonial Senegal in the early twentieth century. *Urban Studies Research*, 1–12. https://doi.org/10.1155/2012/589758

Brantley, C. (1997). Kikuyu-Maasai nutrition and colonial science: The Orr and Gilks Study in late 1920s Kenya revisited. *The International Journal of African Historical Studies*, *30*(1), 49–86.

Bryceson, D. F. (1980). Changes in peasant food production and food supply in relation to the historical development of commodity production in pre-colonial and colonial Tanganyika. *The Journal of Peasant Studies*, 7(3), 281–311. https://doi.org/10.1080/03066158008438107

Bryceson, D. F. (1985). Food and urban purchasing power: The case of Dar es Salaam, Tanzania. *African Affairs*, *84*(337), 499–522.

Chen, M., Grapsa, E., Ismail, G., Rogan, M., Valdivia, M., Alfers, L., Harvey, J., Carolina Ogando, A., Orleans Reed, S., & Roever, S. (2021). *COVID-19 and informal work: Distinct pathways of impact and recovery in 11 cities around the world*. WIEGO Working Paper No. 42. www.wiego.org/publications/covid-19-and-informal-work-distinct-pathways-impact-and-recovery-11-cities-around

Cooper, F. (1987). *On the African waterfront: Urban disorder and the transformation of work in colonial Mombasa*. New Haven, CT: Yale University Press.

Cooper, F. (1989). From free labour to family allowances: Labour and African society in colonial discourse. *American Ethnologist*, *16*(4), 745–765.

de Visser, J. (2021). Food security, urban governance and multilevel government in Africa. In R. Home (Ed.), *Land issues for urban governance in sub-Saharan Africa* (pp. 269–280). Cham: Springer.

de Waal, A. (1997). *Famine crimes: Politics and the disaster relief industry in Africa*. Bloomington and Indianapolis, IN: Indiana University Press.

Duminy, J. (2018). Ecologizing regions; securing food: Governing scarcity, population and territory in British East and Southern Africa. *Territory, Politics, Governance*, *6*(4), 429–446. https://doi.org/10.1080/21622671.2017.1306457

Duminy, J. (2019). Historical urban food governance in Africa: The case of Kenya, c. 1900 to 1950. In J. Battersby & V. Watson (Eds.), *Urban food systems governance and poverty in African cities* (pp. 83–93). Abingdon and New York: Routledge. https://doi.org/10.4324/9781315191195

Duminy, J., & Parnell, S. (2020). *Supporting city futures: The Cities Support Programme and the urban challenge in South Africa*. Cape Town: African Centre for Cities, University of Cape Town. www.africancentreforcities.net/wp-content/uploads/2020/05/8-june-csp-update.pdf

Engels, B. (2015). Contentious politics of scale: The global food price crisis and local protest in Burkina Faso. *Social Movement Studies*, *14*(2), 180–194. https://doi.org/10.1080/14742837.2014.921148

Ferguson, J. (1990). Mobile workers, modernist narratives: A critique of the historiography of transition on the Zambian copperbelt [part one]. *Journal of Southern African Studies*, *16*(3), 385–412. https://doi.org/10.1080/03057079008708243

Fox, S. (2017). Mortality, migration, and rural transformation in sub-Saharan Africa's urban transition. *Journal of Demographic Economics*, *83*, 13–30. https://doi.org/10.1017/dem.2016.29

Ghosh, S., & Meer, A. (2020). Extended urbanization and the agrarian question: Convergences, divergences and openings. *Urban Studies*, *58*(6), 1097–1119. https://doi.org/10.1177/0042098020943758

Greenwood, A., & Topiwala, H. (2020). Visions of colonial Nairobi: William Simpson, health, segregation and the problems of ordering a plural society, 1907–1921. *Social History of Medicine*, *33*(1), 57–78. https://doi.org/10.1093/shm/hky060

Guyer, J. I. (1987). *Feeding African cities: Studies in regional social history, vol. 2*. Bloomington and Indianapolis, IN: Indiana University Press.

Harneit-Sievers, A. (1995). African business, 'economic nationalism,' and British colonial policy: Southern Nigeria, 1935–1954. *African Economic History*, *23*, 79–128.

Harris, R. (2008). From trusteeship to development: How class and gender complicated Kenya's housing policy, 1939–1963. *Journal of Historical Geography*, *34*(2), 311–337. https://doi.org/10.1016/j.jhg.2007.06.001

Herlehy, T. J. (1984). *Historical dimensions of the food crisis in Africa: Surviving famines along the Kenyan coast 1880–1980*. Working Paper No. 87, African Studies Centre, Boston University.

Iliffe, J. (1990). *Famine in Zimbabwe, 1890–1960*. Gweru: Mambo Press.

Jayne, T. S., & Rubey, L. (1993). Maize milling, market reform and urban food security: The case of Zimbabwe. *World Development*, *21*(6), 975–987. https://doi.org/10.1016/0305-750X(93)90055-E

Jones, W. O. (1987). Food-crop marketing boards in tropical Africa. *The Journal of Modern African Studies*, *25*(3), 375–402. https://doi.org/10.1017/S0022278X00009903

Killingray, D. (2003). A new 'imperial disease': The influenza pandemic of 1918–9 and its impact on the British Empire. *Caribbean Quarterly*, *49*(4), 30–49.

Lonsdale, J. (1986). The Depression and the Second World War in the transformation of Kenya. In D. Killingray & R. Rathbone (Eds.), *Africa and the Second World War* (pp. 97–142). Basingstoke and London: Palgrave Macmillan.

Lonsdale, J., & Berman, B. (1979). Coping with the contradictions: The development of the colonial state in Kenya, 1895–1914. *The Journal of African History*, *20*(4), 487–505.

Mafeje, A. (2003). *The agrarian question, access to land, and peasant responses in Sub-Saharan Africa*. Civil Society and Social Movements Programme, Working Paper No. 6, United Nations Research Institute for Social Development, Geneva.

Maxwell, D. (1999). The political economy of urban food security in Sub-Saharan Africa. *World Development*, *27*(11), 1939–1953. https://doi.org/10.1016/S0305-750X(99)00101-1

Maylam, P. (1990). The rise and decline of urban apartheid in South Africa. *African Affairs*, *89*(354), 57–84.

McCann, J. (2005). *Maize and grace: Africa's encounter with a new world crop, 1500–2000*. Cambridge, MA, and London: Harvard University Press.

Monteith, W. (2019). Markets and monarchs: Indigenous urbanism in postcolonial Kampala. *Settler Colonial Studies*, *9*(2), 247–265. https://doi.org/10.1080/2201473X.2017.1409402

Moore, H. L., & Vaughan, M. (1994). *Cutting down trees: Gender, nutrition, and agricultural change in the Northern Province of Zambia, 1890–1990*. London: James Currey.

Musyoka, M. P., Lagat, J. K., Ouma, D. E., Wambua, T., & Gamba, P. (2010). Structure and properties of urban household food demand in Nairobi, Kenya: Implications for urban food security. *Food Security*, *2*(2), 179–193. https://doi.org/10.1007/s12571-010-0063-6

Njoh, A. J. (2004). The experience and legacy of French colonial urban planning in sub-Saharan Africa. *Planning Perspectives*, *19*(4), 435–454. https://doi.org/10.1080/0266543042000268813

Ogonda, R. T. (1992). Transport and communications in the colonial economy. In W. R. Ochieng' & R. M. Maxon (Eds.), *An economic history of Kenya* (pp. 131–133). Nairobi: East African Educational Publishers.

Parnell, S. (1993). Creating racial privilege: The origins of South African public health and town planning legislation. *Journal of Southern African Studies*, *19*(3), 471–488. https://doi.org/10.1080/03057079308708370

Porter, G., Lyon, F., & Potts, D. (2009). Market institutions and urban food supply in West and Southern Africa. In S. J. Shapiro, M. Tadajewski, and C. Shultz (Eds.), *Macromarketing: A global focus: marketing systems, societal development, equity & poverty. SAGE library in marketing*, 4 vols. London: SAGE Publications. http://eprints.mdx.ac.uk/4818/

Richards, A. I. (1939). *Land, labour and diet in Northern Rhodesia: An economic study of the Bemba tribe* (pp. 676–679). London and New York: Oxford University Press.

Richards, A. I. (2004). *Hunger and work in a savage tribe: A functional study of nutrition among the Southern Bantu*. London and New York: Routledge.

Smart, D. (2017a). *Consuming capitalism: Food, migration and urban life in twentieth-century Kenya*. Champaign, IL: University of Illinois Urbana-Champaign.

Smart, D. (2017b). Developing the racial city: Conflict, solidarity and urban traders in late-colonial Mombasa. *Journal of Eastern African Studies, 11*(3), 425–441. https://doi.org/10.1080/17531055.2017.1355582

Stoler, A. L. (1989). Making empire respectable: The politics of race and sexual morality in 20th-century colonial cultures. *American Ethnologist, 16*(4), 634–660.

Swanson, M. (1977). The sanitation syndrome: Bubonic plague and urban native policy in the Cape Colony, 1900–1909. *The Journal of African History, 18*(3), 387–410.

Thielke, A., & Mölg, T. (2019). Observed and simulated Indian Ocean Dipole activity since the mid-19th century and its relation to East African short rains. *International Journal of Climatology, 39*(11), 4467–4478. https://doi.org/10.1002/joc.6085

Thurston, A. (1987). *Smallholder agriculture in colonial Kenya: The official mind and the Swynnerton Plan*. Cambridge: Cambridge African Monographs.

Tilley, H. (2011). *Africa as a living laboratory: Empire, development, and the problem of scientific knowledge, 1870–1950*. Chicago, IL: University of Chicago Press.

Udmale, P., Pal, I., Szabo, S., Pramanik, M., & Large, A. (2020). Global food security in the context of COVID-19: A scenario-based exploratory analysis. *Progress in Disaster Science*, 7, 100120. https://doi.org/10.1016/j.pdisas.2020.100120

Van Zwanenberg, R. (1972). History and theory of urban poverty in Nairobi: The problem of slum development. *Journal of Eastern African Research & Development, 2*(2), 165–203.

Vaughan, M. (1991). *Curing their ills: Colonial power and African illness*. Stanford, CA: Stanford University Press.

Vickery, K. P. (1985). Saving settlers: Maize control in Northern Rhodesia. *Journal of Southern African Studies, 11*(2), 212–234.

Watts, M. J. (1989). The agrarian question in Africa: Debating the crisis. *Progress in Human Geography, 13*(1), 1–41. https://doi.org/10.1177/030913258901300101

Watts, M. J. (2013). *Silent violence: Food, famine, and peasantry in northern Nigeria*. Athens, GA: University of Georgia Press.

Worboys, M. (1988). The discovery of colonial malnutrition between the wars. In D. Arnold (Ed.), *Imperial medicine and indigenous societies*. Manchester: Manchester University Press.

4

THE HISTORICAL ROLE OF CITIES IN RECURSIVELY SHAPING GLOBAL FOOD SYSTEMS

Southeast Asia

Gisèle Yasmeen

Introduction

The purpose of this chapter is to examine the urban agglomerations in the region commonly known as Southeast Asia and their historical role in shaping, and being shaped by, global food systems. The chapter approaches the topic through the lens of foodscapes (Yasmeen, 1992), urban development and gender relations, the constellation of which is fairly unique in this socially constructed concept of a geographical region (Acharya, 2012). In all parts of the world, food has always been central to urban life and the ways in which food is governed in, and in relation to, cities has shaped wider processes at various scales of analysis, be they urban, regional or global. The chapter draws heavily on my work in Thailand, the Philippines and, to a lesser extent, Singapore, Malaysia and Indonesia, and also benefits from experience in India, East Asia and other parts of the world. The work presented here is informed both by my research experience, but also supplemented by insights sought from the historical scholars referenced in the acknowledgements.

The chapter is organized as follows. Beginning with a brief introduction to the region known as Southeast Asia and explanation of the conceptual framework employed in this chapter, I provide a cursory overview of various periods that have had an impact on, and been impacted by, urban food systems in the region. The chapter concludes with some questions as well as policy issues that have come to the fore more recently as the nexus between food systems, governance and broader social, economic, political, and environmental forces has become the topic of more concerted action by both researchers and policymakers alike.

The Southeast Asia Context

For those not familiar with the region, it is worth contextualizing the concept of Southeast Asia and how it has evolved. According to Russell Fifield (1983, p. 1):

 DOI: 10.4324/9781003055907-5

> The term Southeast Asia or a variation of it was used in scholarly literature, particularly geography and anthropology, for some time before the outbreak of World War II in 1939. The usage of the term arose from convenience – the need to name a geographical entity on the map or what could be argued as constituting a geographical entity.

The development of the term 'Southeast Asia' became increasingly popular after the Second World War. While the great empires of India and China had various terms for the lands and islands separating the two great powers, the novelty of the Southeast Asia concept points to the socially constructed nature of the region and speaks to the issue of perspective as, like the broader concept of 'Asia', it is really an outsider's term.

Nevertheless, and for the sake of convenience, the contemporary notion of Southeast Asia makes reference to 'eleven countries that reach from eastern India to China, and is generally divided into "mainland" and "island" zones' (Andaya, n.d.). Contemporary Myanmar (Burma), Thailand, Laos, Cambodia, and Vietnam are extensions of the Eurasian landmass, while Brunei, Timor-Leste, Indonesia, Malaysia, the Philippines, and Singapore are archipelagos or straddle the maritime world. The current state boundaries are colonial and contested, as the struggle for the creation of Timor-Leste in 1999 attests. 'Southeast Asia is also one of the most dynamic areas of the world economically, a factor which largely accounts for its growing international significance' (NIU, n.d.). Most students of the region comment on the impressive diversity of the region with respect to religion, culture and history. However, despite being largely a socially constructed concept, the region has some interesting commonalities when it comes to food systems in general, and urban food systems in particular.

Rice, Fish, and the Foundations of Southeast Asian Eating

Despite being, in many ways, a socially constructed concept, one of the defining characteristics of Southeast Asia as a region is the fact that its diverse societies share a few basic characteristics related to food systems and diet (Yasmeen, 2006, pp. 51–52). The primary factor is dependence on hundreds of varieties of rice as a staple. Most Southeast Asian languages equate the word for rice with food and or eating. Indeed, the region is considered home to the domestication of rice, and its wet-rice agricultural system has been looked on with fascination because of its efficiency (Bray, 1986), complex irrigation systems (Lansing, 1991), and the ability to support high population densities (Geertz, 1963).

It is often stated that Southeast Asia is a crossroads where South and East Asian influences mix with Indigenous cultural traditions (Yasmeen, 2006, p. 20). In terms of gender ideologies and practices, a 'bedrock' of typically Southeast Asian femininity persists in many rural areas today and is characterized for the most part by matrilineal descent systems, bilateral inheritance, and the importance of pre-Buddhist and pre-Islamic feminine deities/spirits (Tambiah, 1970; Potter, 1977; Reid, 1988; Sharp & Hanks, 1978). Women in this region traditionally have access to money and land – and know how to manage it well – and do not lose kinship ties after marriage. This has specific implications for how food is produced, prepared and consumed, with women playing key roles in the entire system, particularly in micro, small and medium enterprises and the informal economy in urban areas (Yasmeen et al., 2018).

Whereas on a regional scale of comparison it is true that women in Southeast Asia tend to follow the patterns described above, it is important to note the high degree of intra-regional variation. For example, Vietnam continuously stands out due to its Chinese heritage whereby patrilineal descent and patrilocal residence after marriage are the norm. Yet women there continue to dominate as food vendors in public places and are often exclusive custodians of food knowledge (Drummond, 1993; Nguyen, 1993). Similarly, Islamized societies, such as Malaysia and Indonesia, have customarily placed greater restrictions on women. An added complexity is the more patriarchal Chinese influence in the region, particularly in urban areas, which has shaped food and foodways, including what is eaten and the nature of distribution systems, as this chapter will illustrate.

Conceptual Framework

Before delving into the recursivity between urban food systems and global flows of people, knowledge, goods and services, it is important to clarify the meanings of certain terms as well as touch on general urban spatial models as a frame wherein to situate more specific issues. There is no universally agreed upon definition of what is 'urban', as opposed to 'peri-urban' or 'rural', making international comparisons difficult (Deuskar, 2015). Generally speaking, definitions of these terms in specific jurisdictions revolve around population and associated density, combined with a high percentage of non-agricultural employment. In practice, these categories of urban, peri-urban and rural can become blended, particularly in Southeast Asia.

It is important to clarify the meanings of certain terms as well as touch on general urban spatial models as a frame in which to situate more specific issues. Generally speaking, definitions of these terms in specific jurisdictions revolve around population and associated density, combined with a high percentage of non-agricultural employment. In practice, these categories of urban, peri-urban and rural can become blended, particularly in Asia in general and Southeast Asia in particular as previously mentioned, which is the home of high population densities and a number of 'mega-urban regions'. Indeed, the People's Republic of China – still home to nearly 900 million of the world's poor despite impressive economic growth over the past 20 years – has higher population densities in some of its rural areas than many of the world's cities. This is important for the urban food systems discussion, as most spatial models with respect to urban food systems include some conceptualization of the relationship between a 'city' and its 'hinterland' with food production, typically associated with concepts of 'hinterland', notwithstanding attention paid to urban and peri-urban agriculture.

The Foodscape Concept

The concept of 'foodscape' emerged in the 1990s (Yasmeen, 1992, 1995). A recent scoping review tracks the evolution of the term 'as a contraction of food and landscape [that] has been used in various research addressing social and spatial disparities in public health and food systems' (Vonthron et al., 2020).

For the purposes of this chapter, the foodscape concept will be used to look at the interface between food systems and place at the urban scale, with an added 'broad sweep' historical lens with respect to the region commonly known as Southeast Asia. My specific goal is to illustrate how regional and global patterns of trade, power relations and flows of people, goods and services have combined to form the spatial, cultural and broader socio-economic conditions we see today, including the distinctive gender relations in regards to the food system in the region.

The Early Age of Commerce – 900–1300CE

Trade in the Indian Ocean and South China Sea has been a driver of Southeast Asian urbanization and associated food systems for more than two thousand years and laid the foundations for what was to develop over those millennia both in terms of urbanization and food systems. Commerce established the region as a crossroads of cultures, which is reflected in foodways that developed in early urban settlements and their associated hinterlands.

While Eurocentric scholarship tends to pay considerable attention to the fifteenth and sixteenth centuries onward when mercantilism developed in the quest for spices, precious metals, textiles and other luxury goods from the East by the Portuguese, French, Spanish and British, according to Wade (2009, p. 222):

> the four centuries from circa 900 to 1300 CE can be seen as an Early Age of Commerce' in Southeast Asia. The thesis is that the collocation of a number of changes external to what is commonly referred to as Southeast Asia, impacted the region and provided an environment where maritime trade boomed, and that this trade boom induced political, social and economic changes throughout the region.

While much of this trade within Southeast Asia, and between the region and China in particular, revolved around ceramics and the advancements of science and technology, it was fuelled in part by high levels of agricultural productivity in China. This allowed for human time and energy to lead to ingenuity, with similar patterns emerging in Southeast Asia, which supplied precious spices to Europe, thereby influencing European foodways to this day. Recursively, influences from China, India, the Indian Ocean and Europe also profoundly influenced food systems in Southeast Asia, particularly in growing urban areas.

Even before this period, Stark (2015) argues that the period of 500BCE to 500CE – associated with Brahamization, Sanskritization and the development of small urban states – laid the foundations of what was to come at the end of the first millennium. 'Within 500 years, such settlements grew exponentially in size' (Stark, 2015, p. 77). Again, many of these settlements began as maritime polities fuelled by trade but Stark argues that religious and administrative functions were also key and that, until recently, scholars may have over emphasized the roles of India and China.

> Most early scholars working in mainland Southeast Asia wrote from an unavoidably regionalist bias that emphasized either the role of China or India in shaping early Southeast Asian cities, or the importance of Chinese documentary data. More recent approaches offer more regionally appropriate models to understand first millennium CE centers.
>
> *Stark, 2015, p. 81*

To sum up, as argued by Wade, 'Interregional maritime trade connecting the ports of West Asia to those of East Asia and through the myriad hubs along the route has been an element of the global economy for at least 2,000 years' (Wade, 2009, p. 238). This has had a distinct impact on the region's foodways, particularly in urban areas, and has also influenced food systems around the world as the next section of this chapter will argue. 'From antiquity onwards, the regional food markets of the Indian Ocean were connected for pragmatic reasons, including the redistribution of food surpluses and the sustenance of diasporic communities' (Hoogervorst, 2018, p. 528). These diasporic communities and their associated foodways, which became woven into the cultural and economic life of Southeast Asian agglomerations, included communities of Indian descent, such as Gujaratis and Tamils, as well as populations of Chinese origin, notably Hokkien and Hakka as well as Arabs and many others (Owen, 2014).

The Age of Commerce – 1450–1680

As the seminal work of Anthony Reid (1988) has demonstrated, with the European Renaissance, beginning in the fifteenth and sixteenth centuries, there was an aggressive push to trade in spices, and cash crops such as tea, resulting in the expansion of European commercial interests, supported by various 'East India' companies that made their way to and through what we now call Southeast Asia. This resulted in the growth of ever larger port or 'entrepôt' cities with associated flows of labour, goods, and services and had an influence on food and foodways both in Southeast Asia and around the world – mostly in urban agglomerations. This diverse region was therefore becoming more firmly integrated into a global trade system, with trade-based cities occupying strategic niches. The following citation sums up the relationships:

> The spice trade that animated the global boom of the sixteenth and early seventeenth centuries made possible revolutionary changes in urbanization, commercialization, state structure, and belief. Islam, Christianity, and Theravada Buddhism made rapid gains in alliance with the new states.
>
> *Reid, 1988*

Anthony Reid has argued that this 'Age of Commerce' had its roots in changes which occurred during the fifteenth century, but Wade (2009, p. 221) goes further to argue that the earlier period of commerce within the region, as well as with China and India, set the stage for this with the development of maritime trade and financial systems, giving more credit to Asian innovations. Stark also takes this position and points to a flourishing urban culture prior to the Age of Commerce with Europe, as the quote below illustrates:

> Many of the region's coasts and river valleys housed port cities and capitals with populations of 50,000–100,000 people; population density/square kilometer varied from sparsely peopled hill country to lowland agrarian areas in northern Vietnam and Bali with higher densities than those in contemporary China.
>
> *Stark, 2015, p. 74, citing Junker, 2004*

Likewise, the seminal work of K. N. Chaudhuri (1990) reframes the narrative to unpack in detail the role of food and foodways and associated trade within 'Asia', broadly defined long before extensive European contact (Bayly, 1992). By extending the approach of Braudel, Chaudhuri demonstrates how food habits and food production systems were structuring elements of cultural and economic differentiation within the region and links daily life around foodways to the rise of cities.

At the same time, Hoogervorst (2018, p. 518) points to the importance of the decline of Asia's great empires, 'including China's Qing Dynasty, the Ottomans, the Sultanate of Aceh, and the Mughals,' which left a power vacuum which Europe was ready to step into, to satisfy growing public demand in Europe for nutmeg, cloves, pepper, coffee and tea as well as other luxury products. Some of these products were sourced in Southeast Asia itself, like nutmeg, with others from China like tea, with the region serving as a convenient maritime crossroads.

The growth of urban settlements may also have had a 'supply-side' dimension related to the abundance of food in the region, thereby liberating some of the population for the development of culture and activities that typically emerge in cities as a result of food surpluses, as the following quote shows:

> Because their climate was mild and their basic diet of rice, fish, and fruits more dependably available than in most parts of the world, Southeast Asians had natural advantages in escaping from the constant struggle for subsistence. They may have had more time to devote to what would today be classified as leisure than most other peoples of that era.
>
> *Reid, 1988, p. 173*

This situation of food abundance laid the groundwork for the development of cash crops and other commodities to be produced and traded with Europe, which had a growing demand for Southeast Asian foodstuffs.

However, there were also forced displacements. It is during this period that the Dutch enslaved the Javanese and transported many to the Cape of South Africa, which was an important stop along the voyage from Europe to Asia, prior to the construction of the Suez Canal. A community persists today – with its own distinctive cuisine – and is an example of the early globalization of foodways, with urban settlements playing a key role in the shaping of, and being shaped by, long distance commerce.

Finally, Reid argues that there was a 300-year hiatus or 'Age of Crisis' beginning in the late 1700s where Southeast Asia was 'cut off' from global trade, particularly with Europe. The Dutch East India company collapsed in 1799. Nevertheless, intra-Asian trade continued between coastal cities within the region as well as inland, which had a marked impact on foodways. An example is the Peranakan community in the Straits of Melaka (Malacca), dating its origin to the intermarriage of Chinese and Malay and characterized by a distinctive culture and cuisine (Duruz, 2016; Koh, 2013).

This period set the stage for the European colonialism that followed.

European Colonialism in the Eighteenth and Nineteenth Centuries

Much of what we know about and see in Southeast Asia today has been shaped by the European colonialism of the region, which built on the mercantile relationships of the previous period that had a deep and lasting influence in the trade of food and spices, the vestiges of which are still with us to this day. The European colonial period came to a crescendo in the late nineteenth century with the Dutch, British and Spanish ascending to power in the region. The colonial period resulted in the growth of settlements and, in particular, many of the most notable cities of the region today, as well as patterns of racialized immigration, especially labourers from India and China. This significant demographic change had a drastic influence on foodways and gender patterns, as well as associated urban spatial structures.

In the case of cities like Singapore and other colonial agglomerations, the importation of laborers from China and India fuelled the demand for prepared food sold by street hawkers (Yasmeen, 2006, p. 14). The workers who migrated to these entrepôt cities were mostly men who could not cook for themselves, due to the lack of knowledge and facilities. Male hawkers ended up responding to this need and women sometimes acted as business partners in family enterprises (Lam, 1982). Bangkok, too, was the destination of many migrants, especially from China. This resulted in the institution of a similar food system, albeit one that evolved differently than in, say, colonial Malaya (now divided into Malaysia and Singapore) where ethno-cultural communities are more separated. In Thailand, the hybridization of Thai and Chinese ways fused to the point that the eating habits and cuisines transplanted by Chinese immigrants were assimilated into Thai urban culture, along with the creation of hybridized Sino-Thai identities and behavior patterns (Skinner, 1958; Keyes, 1987).

Despite the nuances, in nearly all cases the existence of the informal/worker food system can be explained 'in terms of the Dualist School and the Structuralist School in that the growth was due to the role of "re-production" of capitalism whereby goods and services were provided cheaply to workers, thus helping to reduce their cost of living' (Nirathron & Yasmeen, 2019, p. 19). As those in the Dualist and Structuralist schools of thought would explain, when workers were and are able to live on low wages, more surplus value can be retained by those who control capital.

An exciting field of historical scholarship is now trying to piece together these lost histories. An example is Daniel Bender's work on how traditional satay vendors were chased from the streets of Singapore in the name of public health (Bender, 2018), as well as Hoogervorst and Jákl's 2020 history of chefs in pre-colonial Java. There is some justifiable nostalgia for a less sanitized and Westernized past as the region forges a more decolonized sense of its past, present and future. This 'people-centered history' challenges a historiography that 'disproportionately features kings, merchants, conquerors, religious scholars, money-lenders, European colonial officials, and those with whom they interacted', in favour of (re)discovering a 'parallel world aboard ships, in harbours, tailor shops, kitchens, brothels, and prisons' (Hoogerwoorst, 2018, p. 517; Leong-Salobir, 2019).

It is within these kinds of subaltern crucibles that we can begin to unpack another dimension of the interaction of food, cities, trade and people with respect to Southeast Asia and globalization. What the emerging historical scholarship is demonstrating is that these global interactions are not new and are by no means limited to contact with Europe, which conditioned some of the previous work undertaken by Western scholars using their ethnocentric historical and geographical frames.

The Second World War and Post-War Independence Struggles

The Second World War and the independence struggles that followed represent pivotal turning points in our collective understanding of cities and their relationships to food in general and in Southeast Asia in particular. This work was also informed by more general scholarship on all things urban.

As observed by Huff and Huff (2015, p. 522), the Japanese occupation in most of Southeast Asia and the impact of either food scarcity or surpluses in urban areas were driving factors that shaped urbanization in the region in the 1940s:

> [T]wo main patterns of population movements are evident. In food-deficit areas, a search for food security typically led to large net inflows to main urban centres. By contrast, an urban exodus dominated in food surplus regions because the chief risk was to personal safety, especially from Japanese and Allied bombing. Black markets were ubiquitous, and essential to sustaining livelihoods in cities with food-deficit hinterlands. In Rangoon and Manila, wartime population fluctuations were enormous. Famines in Java and northern Indochina severely impacted Jakarta and Hanoi through inflows of people from rural areas. In most countries, the war's aftermath of refugees, revolution, and political disruption generated major rural-urban population relocations. Turmoil in the 1940s had the permanent consequences of augmenting the primacy of Southeast Asia's main cities and promoting squatter settlement.

Despite the growth in post-war literature on urban spatial models, in general, and significant upheavals in the urban food systems of Southeast Asian cities, in particular, there was little academic scholarship addressing urban food issues during this time and within this particular context until the late 1960s. Scholars and public policy experts who came of age in the post-Second World War and independence era then began developing alternative models to suit 'Third World Cities', including in Asia. Terry McGee's *The Southeast Asian City*, published in 1967, was a watershed moment, in many ways shaping scholarly debates and policymaking over the next several decades. Besides McGee, The pioneering voices on Asian urbanization and associated spatial models were those of the late David Drakakis-Smith, and Yue-Man Yeung. With the exception of Drakakis-Smith (1991), there was and is little discussion of food systems at a macro level in 'mainstream' urban geography and planning literature, though this is beginning to change as the following sections will illustrate (Cabannes & Marocchino, 2018).

Flourishing of Work in the 1970s and Resurgence in the 1990s

The 1970s represented a 'golden age' of concerted attention to the food/urban nexus, building on the groundbreaking work of McGee and his contemporaries and supported, in part, by the forward-thinking work of Canada's International Development Research Centre on the 'urban informal sector' of the cities of Asia, with much of it being relevant to food, particularly the urban food supply and distribution systems (see Box 4.1). This age represented a struggle between the forces of 'modernization' and the push for the infrastructure associated with the Global North, with voices that championed the support for the traditional 'bazaar' economy to suit the needs of the urban poor (Bucklin, 1977).

While there is no agreement on the definition of 'informal', there is widespread consensus on the work of anthropologist Keith Hart in the early 1970s being a watershed moment in the use of the term (Hart, 1973). As Ravi Kanbur explains, Hart's main objective was to show that the migrant communities he was studying in the slums of Accra were economically active – they were working (Kanbur, 2014). Hence, Hart's broad conceptualization was eventually taken up by other disciplines and divided into concepts such as informal 'sector', informal 'employment' and the broader informal 'economy' as will be explained later in this section.

In terms of the overall concept of informality, Kanbur provides one of the best descriptions:

> The informal economy comprises those economic activities, which are beyond the purview of the state because they lie outside its framework of laws, regulations and protections. A small proportion of these activities are illegal, but mostly they are activities which are simply not covered by the state's rules and regulations.
>
> *Kanbur, 2014, p. 4*

Kanbur goes on to describe how the preoccupation with informality is due to the tension between two opposing forces: first, a policy mindset assuming informality will eventually decline and disappear, and a second showing that – empirically – informality is not disappearing with economic growth and instead appears to be increasing. He goes on to describe how informality has been seen as a nuisance and symbol of underdevelopment and either 'on the other side of the wall' or 'on the way out', which does not mesh with prevailing reality and ignores the integration of various economic phenomena – including value-chains – as will be described below. The discourse has therefore evolved from one of a dichotomy between formal and informal to the notion of an integrated continuum.

Box 4.1 The History of Street Food Vending in Singapore

As early as the 1940s, when Singapore was still a British colony, efforts began to eradicate the 'scourge' of street food vendors, which was quite a typical colonial municipal response at the time with the goal of inappropriately trying to apply European frameworks (McGee, 1971). The island began to transform the spatial economy of food hawking by proposing to relocate mobile and stationary vendors in government operated hawker centres. As the previous section explained, the Second World War was a crisis time and hiatus or turning point but by the 1980s, the process was complete and the last 'real' street vendor was relocated. The only street restaurants that exist today in the city are in gentrified areas that attempt to recreate the ambience of 'Old Singapore'. They are expensive and poor imitations of the worker stalls of the past and mostly serve middle-class consumers and tourists.

Irene Tinker and her team's work on comparative street foods in the Global South in the 1980s was also a 'moment of reckoning' in the field, inspiring scholarship and policy development around the world (Tinker, 1987). Subsequently, a generation of students of the pioneers on Southeast Asian urban food systems picked up in the 1990s where the previous generation left off. The literature on urban food systems in Southeast Asia blossomed in the 1990s, resulting in a variety of ways of conceptualizing urban 'foodscapes' (Bhavivarn, 1993; Drakakis-Smith, 1990; Krowolski & Simon-Barouh, 1993; Muecke, 1992; Van Esterik, 1992; Yasmeen, 1995, 2006). This was matched by the growth of scholarly and policy work on food systems in general, and urban food systems in particular, fuelled by activism (Nirathron, 2006; Yasmeen & Nirathron, 2014; Nirathron & Yasmeen, 2019; Yasmeen, 2001).

There is a rich variety of analyses of the governance of food systems in the above-mentioned literature. Variables include differentiation of legal systems (Yasmeen, 2017) and other contextual factors. The regulation of street vending in Bangkok, for example, has often been according to the predilection of the Governor of the Bangkok Metropolitan Administration (Yasmeen & Nirathron, 2014). This is typical of Thailand's more authoritarian, top-down political system, characterized by strong military control. In the Philippines, by contrast, and since the dismantling of the Marcos régime, more grassroots activism has conditioned access to public space for livelihoods in the food sector (Yasmeen, 2017). A concrete example is the Cebu City United Vendors Association. However, the impact of the authoritarian Duterte government may have had a deleterious effect on such activism.

Asian Economic Crisis, 2008 and Now COVID-19 – Quo Vadis?

In the early to mid-1990s, as a result of the region's double-digit growth rates, Southeast Asia was seen as a miracle of rapid industrialization by mainstream economists. This growth was associated with rapid urbanization and an explosion of small home-based enterprises selling prepared food. These businesses were seen by many scholars as reducing the costs of reproducing labour, and served the interests of large-scale industry by freeing up labour, especially that of women. The widespread availability of cheap food was interpreted as facilitating and being an outcome of this labour force participation and 'subsidizing capital' by making low wages economically possible (Chua, 1994). Combined with local cultural practices, this was seen as a partial explanation for the preponderance of buying prepared food in Bangkok. Since the

Southeast Asian industrial strategy was based on high rates of female labour force participation, it challenges Mies' housewifization thesis (Mies, 1986) – or, the process by which the division of labor has attempted to relegate women to the role of housewife, including in colonial contexts – as an inevitable outcome of economic change in the region (see Bell, 1992). This was seen as one step towards explaining the resilience of the Thai 'public' sphere, as evidenced in the foodscape (Yasmeen, 2006, p. 13).

However, the Asian Economic Crisis of 1997 shook up the region and had a deep impact on the analyses of the food systems in relation to urban industrialization (Yasmeen, 2001, 2006). The economic crisis of 2008 was also a sharp turning point for scholars and policymakers alike, highlighting the centrality of spikes in food prices, and the current, global COVID-19 pandemic has brought about an even more profound shake-up that will have an impact on our thinking and planning when it comes to the recursivity of urbanization and food in the region, for decades to come. While limiting myself immediately to the work that came out of 1997 and 2008, I will attempt to address some possible implications at the end of this chapter.

As a result of the 1997 and 2008 economic crises, McGee (2001) revisited his past work in light of these crises and identified four distinctive features associated with Asian urbanization, all of which have an impact on the spatial dimensions of food systems. These four characteristics are:

1. **The domination of population giants:** specifically countries with more than 100 million inhabitants, namely China, India, Bangladesh, Pakistan and Indonesia. By 2030, Iran, the Philippines and Vietnam may join their ranks;
2. **Immense urban increments:** associated with very rapid rural to urban migration and resulting in challenges to infrastructure, livelihoods and environmental management;
3. **The prominence of megacities:** located primarily in the region's population giants, resulting in a blurring of what we think of as boundaries between urban, peri-urban and rural areas; and last but not least
4. **Uneven globalization:** Some Asian cities are highly integrated into the global economy and highly international in character, such as Seoul, Singapore, Taipei and Shanghai, whereas others, such as Phnom Penh and Vientiane, are more domestically focused, though this is changing rapidly.

All of these overall features have an impact on urban food supply and distribution and the spatial models associated with food systems with respect to cities. For example, in keeping with the theme of population density, McGee was also focused in part around the blending of what are thought of as distinct concepts of the urban and the rural, resulting in the *desakota* hypothesis of the blurring of boundaries between what we think of as urban versus rural, to explain industrialization of the countryside facilitated by high population densities (McGee, 2009). The model of the Asian city has evolved over the years and has been elaborated upon by both McGee himself and other authors. The model is important, as agriculture on the outskirts of Asia's megacities continues to merge with housing and industrial developments, resulting in specific challenges around logistics and the distribution of foodstuffs, and the presence of activities such as animal husbandry in densely populated areas. Hence, this blending of boundaries may make it difficult – on a practical level – to operationalize concepts that are contingent on a distinction between urban, peri-urban and rural, such as City Region Food Systems and other models described earlier in this chapter. Furthermore, many Asian cities exhibit other patterns associated with the globalization of the food system, concomitant with features of low and middle-income countries such as high levels of informal employment and the dominance of food microenterprises (Yasmeen et al., 2018). However, in general, the literature on patterns of Asian urbanization does not adequately interface with the literature on urban spatial food systems, so all of this requires further exploration.

In terms of pre-COVID-19 conclusions, I offer three ideas:

1. While mega-urban regions are certainly distinguishing features of Asian urbanization, recent literature has pointed to the current and future growth of small to medium-sized agglomerations. As rural populations flock to these smaller cities, many have flagged the opportunity to invest in needed infrastructure, particularly for food (ESCAP, 2017, p. 3). Urban and peri-urban areas all face similar sets of spatial challenges, some of which are itemized and expanded upon below.
2. There are several types of spatial models of urban food systems: those that focus on the relationship between the city and its 'hinterland', albeit from different perspectives; one that privileges governance issues – both in terms of horizontal multidisciplinary urban policies that consider livelihoods, public health and environmental sustainability as well as relationships between state actors at various levels (municipal, provincial/state, regional and national); and a number that are more holistic by combining internal urban challenges and the link to both domestic and international and multilateral food systems, including the Milan Urban Food Policy Pact, to which, as of February 2022, only five cities in Southeast Asia had signed up.
3. While the models of Asian urbanization have evolved over the decades, it is important to note that much literature on urbanization is based on the experience of the Global North and oftentimes may not be relevant to the Global South and the LMIC countries of Asia in particular. The fact that many Asian political and government officials, including urban planners, have been trained using these Western and Northern models may have also led to some of the challenges faced by rapidly urbanizing Asia today. Examples include the hostility of local authorities to the spatial expression of the informal economy as 'backward' rather than a distinguishing feature of cities of the Global South. Hence, viewing Asian urban, peri-urban and rural areas – however one defines them – within the political, cultural, economic context in which they have evolved is of fundamental importance, while not precluding different parts of the world from learning from each other.

However, the COVID-19 global pandemic has, in many ways, turned both scholarship and policymaking on its head. A recent report of the World Bank and FAO is one of the more recent reflections that point to this moment as a 'wake-up' call with respect to urban food systems in Asia.

> *The COVID-19 pandemic has exposed the fragility of urban food systems across emerging Asia by making it more difficult for many urban residents to access or afford staple and high-nutrient foods.* Many cities have experienced rural-to-urban supply and logistical disruptions, the temporary or prolonged shutdown of markets, schools and institutional canteens, and other venues critical to urban food supply, and exacerbated concerns about food safety and hygiene. In many cities, the livelihoods of tens of thousands of people involved in food services and delivery have also been significantly disrupted. While the pandemic's impacts are still being felt and it is too soon to reach definitive conclusions, it does seem to be the case that the prior existence of coherent food system policies, governance, and monitoring have enhanced cities' ability to respond to the food-related challenges triggered by the pandemic.
>
> *Acharya et al., 2020, p. xix; original italics*

Where do we go from here? For those who have been working for decades to move towards healthy, just and sustainable food systems around the world, with a particular pre-occupation for the urban dimension, the current context is seen as an opening for deep and lasting social and associated food systems transformation, which joins up social justice, public health and environmental preoccupations with a deep concern for sustainable livelihoods. Examples of policy and programme areas at a high level (Acharya et al., 2020) are:

- urban food system governance;
- doing more at the consumer level;
- doing more in relation to urban food logistics and marketing; and
- doing more in relation to urban and peri-urban agriculture.

However, a major policy question will be – as always – who controls this transition and who ultimately benefits in the context of a looming global food crisis, and not for lack of available food, within the context of serious environmental and climate change challenges?

Acknowledgements

The author would like to thank Terry McGee of University of British Columbia, and Jayeeta (Jo) Sharma and Daniel Bender of University of Toronto for providing valuable suggestions in the preparation of this chapter, as well as Jane Battersby and two other reviewers.

Bibliography

Acharya, A. (2012). Imagined Communities and Socially Constructed Regions. In A. Acharya (Ed.), *The Making of Southeast Asia: International Relations of a Region* (pp. 21–50). ISEAS–Yusof Ishak Institute.

Acharya, G., Cassou, E., Jaffee, S., & Ludher, E. K. (2020). *RICH Food, Smart City*. World Bank. https://openknowledge.worldbank.org/bitstream/handle/10986/35137/156620.pdf?sequence=7&isAllowed=y

Andaya, B. W. (n.d.). Introduction to Southeast Asia: History, Geography, and Livelihood. *Asia Society*. https://asiasociety.org/education/introduction-southeast-asia

Bayly, C. A. (1992). Book Review: Asia before Europe. Economy and Civilisation of the Indian Ocean from the Rise of Islam to 1750 by K. N. Chaudhuri. *The English Historical Review, 107*(424), 680–682. www.jstor.org/stable/575253.

Bell, P. (1992). Gender and Economic Development in Thailand. In P. van Esterik & J. van Esterik (Eds.), Gender and Development in Southeast Asia, *2*, 61–82. Proceedings of the 20th meeting of the Canadian Council for Southeast Asian Studies, York University, 18–21 October, Montreal.

Bender, D. (2018). *Dipping in the Common Sauce Pot: Satay Vending and Good Taste Politics in Colonial and Post-Colonial Singapore* (unpublished draft). Presented at the CityFood Workshop at New York University from November 28–30.

Bhavivarn, N. (1993). *Thai Food Culture: A Study of the Food System in Tha Prachan*. Unpublished M.A. thesis, Department of Anthropology, Thammasat University, Bangkok. In Thai.

Bray, F. (1986). *The Rice Economies: Technology and Development in Asian Societies*. Blackwell.

Bucklin, L. P. (1977). Improving Food Retailing in Developing Asian Countries. *Food Policy, 2*(2), 114–122. https://doi.org/10.1016/0306-9192(77)90057-4

Cabannes, Y., & Marocchino, C. (2018). *Integrating Food into Urban Planning*. UCL Press. https://doi.org/10.14324/111. 9781787353763

Chaudhuri, K. N. (1990). *Asia before Europe: Economy and Civilisation of the Indian Ocean from the Rise of Islam to 1750*. Cambridge University Press.

Chua, B.-H. (1994). *That Imagined Space: Nostalgia for the Kampung in Singapore*. Working Paper No. 122, National University of Singapore, Department of Sociology.

Deuskar, C. (2015). What Does 'Urban' Mean? [Blog Post]. Retrieved from http://blogs.worldbank.org/sustainablecities/what-does-urban-mean.

Drakakis-Smith, D. (1990). Food for Thought or Thought about Food: Urban Food Distribution Systems in the Third World. In R. Potter & A. Salau (Eds.), *Cities and Development in the Third World* (pp. 100–120). Mansell Publishing.

Drakakis-Smith, D. (1991). Urban Food Distribution in Asia and Africa. *The Geographical Journal,* 157(1), 51–61.

Drummond, L. (1993). *Women, the Household Economy, and the Informal Sector in Hanoi.* Unpublished M.A. thesis, Department of Geography, University of British Columbia.

Duruz, J. (2016). Love in a Hot Climate: Foodscapes of Trade, Travel, War, and Intimacy. *Gastronomica: The Journal of Critical Food Studies,* 16, 16–27. https://doi.org/10.1525/gfc.2016.16.1.16

ESCAP. (2017). *Urbanization and Sustainable Development in Asia and the Pacific: Linkages and Policy Implications: Note by the Secretariat* [E-Book]. www.unescap.org/commission/73/document/E73_16E.pdf

Fifield, R. H. (1983). Southeast Asia as a Regional Concept. *Southeast Asian Journal of Social Science, 11*(2), 1–14. www.jstor.org/stable/24490794

Geertz, C. (1963). *Agricultural Involution.* University of California Press.

Hart, K. (1973). Informal Income Opportunities and Urban Employment in Ghana. *Journal of Modern African Studies,* 11(1), 61–89.

Hoogervorst, T. (2018). Sailors, Tailors, Cooks, and Crooks: On Loanwords and Neglected Lives in Indian Ocean Ports. *Itinerario, 42*(3), 516–548. doi:10.1017/S0165115318000645

Hoogervorst, T., & Jákl, J. (2020). The Rise of the Chef in Java. *Global Food History, 6*(1), 3–21. https://doi.org/10.1080/20549547.2019.1707017

Huff, G., & Huff, G. (2015). Urban Growth and Change in 1940s Southeast Asia. *The Economic History Review, 68*(2), 522–547. https://doi.org/10.1111/ehr.12073

Kanbur, R. (2014). Mindsets, Trends, and the Informal Economy. Working Paper 2014-06, Charles H Dyson School of Applied Economics and Management, Ithaca. http://ageconsearch.umn.edu/bitstream/180155/2/Cornell-Dyson-wp1406.pdf

Keyes, C. F. (1987). *Thailand: Buddhist Kingdom as Modern Nation-State.* Westview Press.

Koh, J. (2013). Peranakan (Straits Chinese) Community. *Singapore Infopedia.* https://eresources.nlb.gov.sg/infopedia/articles/SIP_2013-08-30_181745.html

Krowolski, N., & Simon-Barouh, I. (Eds.). (1993). *Autour du Riz: Le repas chez quelques populations d'Asie du Sud-Est.* L'Harmattan.

Lam, T. T. (1982). Food for the City: The Role of the Informal Sector. *GeoJournal,* 49–59.

Lansing, J. S. (1991). *Priests and Programmers: Technologies of Power in the Engineered Landscapes of Bali.* Princeton University Press.

Leong-Salobir, C. (2019). *Routledge Handbook of Food in Asia.* Routledge.

McGee, T. (2001). Urbanization Takes on New Dimensions in Asia's Population Giants. *Population Reference Bureau,* 1 October. www.prb.org/urbanizationtakesonnewdimensionsinasiaspopulationgiants/.

McGee, T. (2009). *The Spatiality of Urbanization: The Policy Challenges of Mega-Urban and Desakota Regions of Southeast Asia.* UNU-IAS Working Paper No. 161. https://citeseerx.ist.psu.edu/viewdoc/download;jsessionid=E4D37E17F67ED55B38DC35CB9C2FCFA6?doi=10.1.1.548.2985&rep=rep1&type=pdf.

McGee, T. G. (1967). *The Southeast Asian City: A Social Geography of the Primate Cities of Southeast Asia.* Bell and Sons, Ltd.

McGee, T. G. (1971). *The Urbanization Process in the Third World: Explorations in Search of a Theory.* G. Bell & Sons.

Mies, M. (1986). *Patriarchy and Accumulation on a World Scale: Women in the International Division of Labour.* Zed Books. Doi : 10.5040/9781350221703

Muecke, M. A. (1992). Mother Sold Food, Daughter Sells Her Body: The Cultural Continuity of Prostitution. *Social Science and Medicine, 35*(7), 891–901. https://doi.org/10.1016/0277-9536(92)90103-W

Nguyen, X. L. (1993). Le Riz est Plus Parfumé: L'Alimentation des Vietnamiens en France. In N. Krowolwski & I. Simon-Barouh (Eds.), *Autour du Riz: Le repas chez quelques population d'Asie du Sud-Est* (pp. 165–196). L'Harmattan.

Nirathron, N. (2006). *Fighting Poverty from the Street: A Survey of Street Food Vendors in Bangkok. Informal Economy, Poverty and Employment: Thailand Series No. 1.* ILO. www.ilo.org/wcmsp5/groups/public/---asia/---ro-bangkok/documents/publication/wcms_bk_pb_128_en.pdf

Nirathron, N., & Yasmeen, G. (2019). Street Vending Management in Bangkok: The Need to Adapt to a Changing Environment. *Journal of Public Space, 4*(1), 15–32. https://doi.org/10.32891/jps.v4i1.562.

NIU (Northern Illinois University). (n.d.). Southeast Asian Countries. www.niu.edu/clas/cseas/resources/countries.shtml

Owen, N. G. (Ed.). (2014). *Routledge Handbook of Southeast Asian History*. Routledge. https://doi.org/10.4324/9780203763117

Potter, S. H. (1977). *Family Life in a Northern Thai Village: A Study in the Structural Significance of Women*. University of California Press.

Reid, A. (1988). *Southeast Asia in the Age of Commerce, 1450–1680: Volume One: The Lands below the Winds*. Yale University Press. www.jstor.org/stable/j.ctt1cc2k66.9.

Sharp, L., & Hanks, L. (1978). *Bang Chan: Social History of a Rural Community in Thailand*. Cornell University Press.

Skinner, G. W. (1958). *Leadership and Power in the Chinese Community of Thailand*. Cornell University Press.

Stark, M. (2015). Southeast Asian Urbanism: From Early City to Classical State. In N. Yoffee (Ed.), *The Cambridge World History* (pp. 74–93). Cambridge University Press.

Tambiah, S. (1970). *Buddhism and the Spirit Cults in North-East Thailand*. Cambridge University Press.

Tinker, I. (1987). Street Foods: Testing Assumptions About Informal Sector Activity by Women and Men. *Special Issue of Current Sociology*, 35(3), 1–110.

Van Esterik, P. (1992). From Marco Polo to McDonald's: Thai Cuisine in Transition. *Food and Foodways*, *5*(2), 177–193. https://doi.org/10.1080/07409710.1992.9961999

Vonthron, S., Perrin, C., & Soulard, C. T. (2020). Foodscape: A Scoping Review and a Research Agenda for Food Security-related Studies. *PloS One*, *15*(5), e0233218. https://doi.org/10.1371/journal.pone.0233218

Wade, G. (2009). An Early Age of Commerce in Southeast Asia, 900–1300. *Journal of Southeast Asian Studies*, *40*(2), 221–265. https://doi.org/10.1017/S0022463409000149

Yasmeen, G. (1992). Bangkok's Restaurant Sector: Gender, Employment and Consumption. *Journal of Social Research*, *15*(2), 69–81.

Yasmeen, G. (1995). Exploring a Foodscape: The Case of Bangkok. *Malaysian Journal of Tropical Geography*, *26*(1), 1–11.

Yasmeen, G. (2001). Stockbrokers Turned Sandwich Vendors: The Economic Crisis and Food-retailing in the Philippines and Thailand. *Geoforum*, *32*(1), 91–102. https://doi.org/10.1016/S0016-7185(00)00038-5

Yasmeen, G. (2006). *Bangkok's Foodscape: Public Eating, Gender Relations, and Urban Change*. White Lotus Books.

Yasmeen, G. (2017). Accessing Urban Space for a Livelihood: India, Thailand and the Philippines in Comparative Perspective. In J. A. Scutt (Ed.), *Women, Culture and the Law: Culture, Conformity and Conflict* (pp. 127–140). Palgrave Macmillan. www.palgrave.com/de/book/9783319449371

Yasmeen, G., & Nirathron, N. (2014). *Vending in Public Space: The Case of Bangkok*. WIEGO Policy Brief, Urban Policies, No. 16, Cambridge, MA. http://wiego.org/sites/wiego.org/files/publications/files/Yasmeen-Vending-Public-Space-Bangkok-WIEGO-PB16.pdf.

Yasmeen, G., Kunin, R., & Vietnam Silicon Valley. (2018). *Micro, Small, and Medium Enterprises in Agri-Food: A Study of the Philippines, Vietnam and Peru*. Asia Pacific Foundation of Canada on behalf of the Global Affairs Canada funded Asia-Pacific Economic Cooperation (APEC) Growing Business Partnership, 23 March 2018. https://apfcanada-msme.ca/research/micro-small-and-medium-enterprises-agri-food-study-philippines-vietnam-and-peru

PART II

Frames, Theories and Concepts of Urban Food Governance

5

SOCIAL PRACTICE THEORIES AND URBAN FOOD GOVERNANCE

From Problem Framing to Designing Collaborative Change Initiatives

Marlyne Sahakian and Stefan Wahlen

Introduction

How we buy and prepare food, how we eat and share meals, or how we handle food waste are tied up with an understanding of food as a social phenomenon. Food is part of complex socio-material systems, consisting of interconnected practices of production and consumption, all the more relevant in urban settings which depend on food mostly produced elsewhere. The many activities associated with food can be quite mundane, such as purchasing food in supermarkets, snacking while commuting, or preparing daily meals at home. But food can also involve more symbolic moments of consumption, such as sharing meals on celebratory occasions, harvesting an urban vegetable garden, or eating out in a fancy restaurant. Seeing food as part and parcel of everyday life habits and routines is part of a growing field of research that applies social practice theory to food studies (Warde, 2016). Practices are understood as bundles of activities that are embedded in material arrangements, social norms, and other meanings. Practices are ways of doing, oftentimes established over time as being 'normal' and thus difficult to change. Social practice theoretical approaches consider how different doings and sayings around food emerge, but also how they might be transformed in the future towards normative goals, such as healthy and sustainable food production and consumption. A focus on urban spaces offers a unique setting in which to reflect on food-related social practices, including moments of consumption but also of production. Despite the fact that food production is typically associated with rural areas, recent years have witnessed urban food initiatives for communal food preparation, urban vegetable gardens, or collective food waste reduction efforts. In urban settings, some of the boundaries between producing and consuming food become blurred.

The main aim of this chapter is to discuss the relevance of social practice approaches (SPAs) to urban food governance, not only towards a better understanding of social dynamics of food, but also as a theory that can inform social change initiatives in urban settings. In this chapter,

DOI: 10.4324/9781003055907-7

we understand the governing of food to include practices that involve collective efforts towards social change that affect systems of food provisioning. Hence, governing processes engage with different actors as carriers of a broad range of practices that aim to change how food is produced and consumed, in our case, towards more 'sustainable' ends. By considering how and in what way changes come about, we contribute to unpacking the power of urban food governance and its capacity to affect lives. We start by explaining how SPAs have emerged, in relation to more culturalist and individualistic approaches to food consumption. We discuss how SPAs can be used as a heuristic device for understanding social change, as well as towards designing interventions in practice. In parallel, we introduce our understanding of collective forms of action and social learning, and what this implies for governing processes. In the second section, we explain the relevance of such an approach to urban food governance through two case studies. We conclude by presenting an overview of how the SPA can inform change initiatives, and the policy implications of such an approach. We end with some reflections on how further developments in SPAs could be relevant to urban food governance questions.

Social practices: concepts and definitions

Food and eating have a long history in socio-anthropological theorising: over one hundred years ago, Simmel (2001 [1910]) formulated a sociology of the meal; while eating a meal is a highly individualistic act, with food ingested once and by one person, the meal as a sociological phenomenon is made up of coordinated sequences representing formal norms, as well as collective conventions. Mary Douglas (1975) described food as a socio-cultural code, which reveals social relations and follows a grammar-like structure, notably through rituals such as sharing meals with close friends and family. Norbert Elias (2016 [1969]) studied food in relation to what he termed the affective economy, focusing on the role that emotions play in regulating social norms around eating, demonstrating, for example, the ambivalent role of a knife as both weapon and cutlery. Pierre Bourdieu's (1979) seminal work on socio-cultural differentiation considers 'taste' for certain foods as socially constructed, in a dynamic relation between social class and personal dispositions. These well-established approaches have been criticised for focusing too much on social structures, or how cultural systems influence what people do.

Another body of literature on food-related consumer behaviour ranges from economic to psychological theorising. These individualist approaches often dismiss the social context in which consumption takes place and other collective dimensions (Wahlen & Dubuisson-Quellier, 2018). They tend to assume an information deficit among consumers, who only need to be informed to then change food behaviours and adopt better choices. A mechanism often discussed by individualist approaches is to set financial incentives, either by taxing or subsidising specific products in order to (re-)direct supply and demand, or getting the price right to incite purchases. More recently, individual choice editing and nudging have been considered as viable strategies – without much concern for who gets to decide what choices should be privileged over others, in what is called 'liberal paternalism'. All these individualist approaches are critiqued by scholars in practice theory, and by some in sustainability studies, as providing an oversimplified understanding of change (Shove, 2010; Cohen, 2021), often leading to policy measures that are ineffective (Davies et al., 2014). The notion of agency, or the capacity or power to be the source of action (Ortner, 1989), is one way of distinguishing these two approaches: the structuralist position would find agency in social structures that shape what people believe, say, or do, while the individualist approach gives agency to people as actors and through their consumer behaviour.

Emerging from this structure–actor tension, SPAs have gained momentum over the past decades in suggesting that agency is distributed across practices and their elements. The origins of the SPA can be found in the work of Bourdieu (1979) and Giddens (1984), with both giving primacy to neither structure nor agency. For Bourdieu, *habitus* was one way of overcoming the structure–agency dichotomy, as a disposition that could structure and be structured. For Giddens, individuals follow habits, yet also possess the critical capacity to reflect upon performances. More recent advances in practice theory are often attributed to Schatzki (2002) and Reckwitz (2002), leading to a vast literature in the sociology of consumption that engages with different social-practice inspired approaches, albeit with family resemblances. Social practices, made up of doings and sayings, are recognisable entities – like tending a garden, or preparing a meal – that imply some form of repetition. There are different ways of understanding what practices are made up of. In one approach, materials, meaning, and competences come together (Shove & Pantzar, 2005); in another and inspired by Schatzki (2002), practices are held together by understanding, engagement, and procedures (Warde, 2017).

The practice of 'preparing a meal' might involve food products and kitchen appliances, shared understandings and skills around using a knife and fork, meanings around what is a 'healthy and balanced' meal, and the embodied skills necessary for preparing it. Materiality plays an important role in practice theories, including food products, technologies, and material arrangements ranging from kitchen configurations to supermarket layouts. Practices are conducted with some common discretion, understanding, or rules on how to enact them, so that the practices are perceived as normal. Practitioners are not necessarily engaged in reflexivity when they carry out practices but make use of tacit knowledge. Practitioners may conduct the same 'normalised' practice differently to some extent, and yet even when they do not know each other, the practices might not vary greatly (Halkier, 2017). Food-related practices might differ over time and across varying geographic spaces. In terms of time, food-related practices are nowadays different from what could have been observed one hundred years ago, when industrial food production and storage, such as food canning, was only just emerging. In terms of spaces, urban food practices are nowadays shaped by food delivery services, which grew exponentially during the COVID-19 pandemic in certain cities, but which may not be prevalent in rural areas.

Practices associated with food also lead to a consideration of provisioning systems (Fine et al., 2018), which make some foods more available and accessible than others in urban settings. These systems of provision refer to how foods are produced and distributed, including power structures and cultures that underlie such systems. If we take the provisioning for food in the cities of the Global North as an example of a practice, shopping practices prevail today, whereas not too long ago, self-provisioning was more common. In some contexts, forms of self-provisioning are reviving in urban areas, through community gardens for example, whereby consumers become producers of food. Thus, 'production' and 'consumption' are not two discrete categories when it comes to studying food, and SPAs can shed processual light on different stages along the way, from producing, storing, and distributing food, to planning, shopping, storing, preparing, ingesting, and cleaning up – underlying the plurality of practices when it comes to doing food (Schatzki, 1996: 98; Warde, 2016). A social practice approach can thus serve to uncover the co-dependence of food production and consumption practices, which mutually shape each other. Practices in a system of food provision always shape the practices of consumption, and thus collective actions around food, upstream from moments of food consumption, become a relevant area of further study.

A variety of studies, inspired by practice theory approaches, scrutinise food, ranging from theoretical contributions (Warde, 2013; Domaneschi, 2012; Halkier, 2010) to studies on how to understand and support changes in food consumption (O'Neill et al., 2019; Sahakian & Wilhite, 2014; Spurling et al., 2013; Wahlen, 2011), to specific perspectives such as how prescriptions affect food practices (Plessz et al., 2016; Godin & Sahakian, 2018), including the quest for healthier (Halkier & Jensen, 2011; van der Horst et al., 2021) or more environmentally friendly forms of food consumption (Dubuisson-Quellier & Gojard, 2016; Sahakian et al., 2016; Davies, 2019). More thematic approaches include studies on food waste (Evans, 2011), or food-related appliances, such as freezers, refrigerators, or food processors (Shove & Southerton, 2000; Truninger, 2011; Sahakian, 2019). These studies emphasise that food consumption neither consists of solely individual behavioural acts, nor is it determined by social structure. They move beyond the Bourdieusian notion of 'taste' as structured by social class, the idea of eating as a solely ritual practice, or a focus on individual purchase acts, to uncover processes of preparing a meal, eating, or generating food waste. Further, they investigate how food consumption relates to doings and sayings that are embedded in historically situated socio-material arrangements, involving normative understandings of how things ought to or should be done, and the skills and competencies necessary for engaging in some practices more than others.

Food governance, social practices, and collaborative change initiatives

We understand the practice of governing food as the capacity or power to act in a way that brings about some form of social change in relation to food, and as a process that engages with different types of actors – in systems of food provisioning. The governing of food has a normative aim in this chapter, towards more sustainable forms of food production and consumption in urban settings. 'Sustainable' food involves several challenges, such as the need to safeguard consumers from under-nutrition or unsafe food, to promote healthy diets for consumers or fair wages for producers, or to reduce the negative environmental impacts of food production, distribution, and consumption. The governing of food can manifest itself in agricultural policies that guarantee stable income for farmers and affordable prices for consumers through food subsidies, yet governance can take on different forms. In complex, global, and industrial food systems, (pan-)national exertion of power is increasingly countered by local, often urban, food initiatives that are also a form of food governance. Similarly, the governing of food oftentimes leads to 'local' solutions, which are seen as a proxy for 'sustainable' food production and consumption (Godin & Sahakian, 2018), although what is meant by the 'local' merits unpacking (Born & Purcell, 2006), as the local can be the site of protectionist and non-solidarity practices.

Although many practices are rather stable, they also contain 'the seeds of constant change' (Warde, 2005): over time, some practices might become more prevalent whereas other practices might fade into meaninglessness. Rather than considering individuals as central to change, SPAs shift the gaze to how change occurs across complex socio-material arrangements that make up everyday life, involving the consuming of food but increasingly its production and provisioning. Social practice theories can help uncover how and in what way changes in urban food consumption can come about, both by understanding existing and interrelated food-related practices (production, distribution, consumption, etc.), and by imagining how social change can be acted upon through collective efforts. The SPA also reveals how food-related practices might be related to other bundles of practices, such as caring for a child or entertaining – and how such practices compete for time and require forms of coordination. In a recent study in Switzerland, tying sustainable and healthy food options into transit points and mobility offers was seen as a promising policy recommendation (Godin & Sahakian, 2018). As such, it becomes obvious that traditional governance approaches that are siloed into sectors – such as agriculture, environment, health, or urban development – do not adequately address the complexity of urban food practices. SPAs can also be applied to imagining how food might be 'governed' towards sustainable and healthy food consumption as a normative aim.

How problems are understood can have an influence on the solutions that are proposed and thus the outcomes of any intervention. Spurling et al. (2013) recognise how the process of defining the purpose and outcomes of any intervention can influence the design of such actions or interventions, and associated (urban) policies. They propose three ways of framing how social practices can change over time: (1) recrafting practices, (2) substituting practices, and (3) changing how practices interlock. First, recrafting practices is about changing 'elements of practices' (materials, meaning and competencies, in the Shove interpretation), presumably towards less resource intensity or reduced social/environmental impacts. An example would be preparing a vegetarian dish, replacing meat with alternatives such as organically produced and local vegetables. Second, substituting practices means entirely replacing one practice with another. This might entail replacing food provisioning from a supermarket with growing a vegetable garden, for example; or going from eating at home, to eating out. The third example, that of changing how practices interlock, recognises how practices can be interlinked together, either as synchronised or sequential. Examples of synchronised practices are revealed through time-use studies (Plessz & Wahlen, 2022), whereby meal preparation in a given window of time contributes to peak energy usage for cooking.

How to make social practice theory 'practicable' is a growing line of inquiry (Sahakian & Wilhite, 2014) that implies that the conceptual developments described above need to be interpreted so as to inform not only research, but also policies and actions. More recently, SPAs have been applied to design thinking towards ideating and implementing social change initiatives. A guidebook has been developed to support such approaches, which suggests that mapping the socio-material systems of any given problem is an important first step towards understanding opportunities for change (Vihalemm et al., 2015). Similarly, Hoolohan and Browne (2020) developed a 'change points toolkit', supporting practice-based interventions. They differentiate stages in designing a change process, including scoping out the unsustainable problem that needs to be addressed, identifying 'change points' in how the practices related to that problem are configured, while also accounting for diversity in how practices are performed by different groups of people, among other stages. SPAs have been applied to change initiatives that seek to reduce energy usage in homes and among everyday people (Sahakian et al., 2021; Sahakian & Bertho, 2018), or through how food habits among households might change, through a practice-based Living Lab approach (Devaney & Davies, 2017).

Underlying many of these examples is an implicit recognition of the importance of participative action and collaborative efforts towards supporting social change. This relates to literature on social learning, whereby learning is not an individual experience (common in information-deficit models) but rather a participatory and social activity, which involves situated learning in communities of practice (Lave & Wenger, 2009 [1991]). Through such a process, different groups of practitioners come together to share a common understanding of the problem that needs to be resolved, but also collaborate in devising the solution and co-designing any proposed intervention. This process recognises how forms of learning become embodied when practitioners carry out changes in practices, or when they join communities of new or emerging practices or deviate from the normal practice (van der Horst et al., 2021). These 'experiments' allow for new habits and routines to emerge, which go beyond the 'mind-centered, body-absent theoretical approaches on which public policies are mainly based' (Wallenborn & Wilhite, 2014: 61). In uncovering the process of defining the purpose and outcomes of any intervention in governing urban food, we shed light on different stages in food provisioning and consumption, as well as the process through which change initiatives take place.

Two case studies: a social practice approach for informing urban food governance

A focus on what social practice theory can bring to urban food governance places explicit attention on defining the purpose and desired outcomes of interventions, on shared understandings of social change processes, and on what aspects of practices need or can be changed, either recrafting or substituting practices, or changing how practices interlock. Such an approach is useful towards designing change initiatives in urban areas, which can range from community-supported efforts to promote local food, to city-wide or regional policy forums aimed at addressing the complexity of food in relation to everyday life. Promoting more sustainable food, whether local or vegetarian, is closely linked to how the issue is perceived as a problem and how the various practitioners involved in a change initiative frame what needs to be changed. Practice theory is particularly useful in describing the problem in its locality, because practices are time and space specific, but also in informing a co-design process towards change initiatives. The process becomes as important as the aim, as both a social practice and collaborative approach.

In this section, we detail two case studies – one Swiss and one Finnish – that consider how a social practice approach can help understand what changes can be made towards more 'sustainable' forms of food consumption in urban settings. Both examples bring forward the importance of collaborations with different actors, working together to imagine and implement change initiatives. These case studies highlight how SPAs assist in understanding what it is that needs to be governed, and how urban initiatives could be designed to achieve the goal they are aiming for. The first example illustrates a community-driven change initiative that seeks to reduce the distancing between systems of production and consumption. The second case study exemplifies a policy initiative, setting the conditions for more sustainable food consumption practices in school canteens. Both grapple with the complexity of how food-related practices play out in different urban settings.

To illustrate the centrality of shared understandings on how to address a problem, we present two different approaches to problems related to urban food governance: the individual, rational actor approach, and the social practice and collaborative approach (Table 5.1). We detail how understanding a problem might vary, but also how an understanding of practices and opportunities for social change differs. How these questions are addressed are illustrated through the two cases.

Case 1: Community-driven change initiative: Auberge des Vergers, Geneva, Switzerland

In the past few years, the city of Geneva has become the site of new developments in cooperative forms of housing, in a city that boasts among the most expensive real estate property in the world, coupled with low rates of ownership. Different cooperatives have emerged to re-appropriate the ability to decide on and use residential spaces through and for the collective. Some cooperatives are more social in their ambitions, aiming for inter-generational equity and the inclusion of low-income housing in development plans. Others are more ecological, boasting dry toilets or on-site vermicompost facilities for all waste. Les Vergers is a new neighbourhood in the Meyrin area (Geneva) where several such cooperatives have come

Table 5.1 Understanding opportunities to promote 'more sustainable' food: differences between individual and practice-based approaches

	Individual, rational actor approach	*Social practice and collaborative approach*
Understanding the problem		
How is *the problem* framed or understood?	People need to change their food (purchasing, cooking, wasting) behaviour	Practices need to change in their arrangements, including food provisioning, preparing, sharing practices, etc.
Understanding interrelated practices		
How can *the purchase* of more sustainable food be promoted?	Get the price right, where supply meets demand	Engage producers, processors and consumers in a deliberative exchange to create a common understanding
How can *the preparation* of sustainable food be promoted?	Provide information and educate on how to prepare food, or how to compost food	Demonstrate local food preparation in a community restaurant or canteen. Allow for everyday people to participate in food preparation, sharing and eating (bodily experiences)
Understanding how to engage in social change		
How can sustainable food *be trusted*?	Create a label	Ensure that consumers and producers are in relations of trust
Who should decide how problems should be addressed?	Actors providing information decide what information should be provided and what price communicated	Consumers, producers, and policymakers come together to jointly deliberate what the exact problem is and how it should be addressed
What is the role of the consumer?	An individual exhibiting bad behaviour or lacking information, both of which need to be corrected by an 'expert'	Consumers as active participants in deliberative decision-making processes
Who is responsible for change?	Individual consumers bear the responsibility	All actors across systems of food provision and interlinked practices should bear responsibility, and never the individual consumer

Source: Authors' compilation.

together, along with residential and low-income buildings. In this context, a novel food project emerged in July 2020, Auberge des Vergers: a community restaurant, a music and performance space, and guest rooms. This initiative emerged with a specific problem in mind, that of the increasing distance between the consumer and production processes, and the need to shorten the distance from farm to fork. They also recognised that food is tied up with everyday life dynamics, which involve what you buy, but also how you prepare and share meals – what can be seen as aligned with a practice-based approach. As explained in an interview with one of the founding members (December 2020), their idea was to consider 'eating' as a social practice that interconnects with systems of provision and that involves both people preparing food produce, those transforming that food into meals, and the shared experience of eating a meal.

Much of the food prepared at the Auberge des Vergers originates from *La Fève* (the Bean), a cooperative supermarket in the same eco-neighbourhood. The cooperative supermarket is made up of both producers and consumers, who work together to make choices as to what food is available and at what prices. Together they reflect on what additional labour is needed to provide pesticide-free vegetables, for example, and involving 'consumers' in that process is necessary towards rendering the value proposition visible. Thus the 'meanings' of local foods and their value are collectively deliberated and defined. This process leads to debates around prices that have to do with what people value; as such, pesticide-free production practices might have a higher price tag. Responsibility is not on individuals to make better choices, based on the limited information that might be available in a store, on a label, or on a price tag, but rather responsibility is understood as emerging from a shared understanding of related practices. Labels are no longer necessary in such a setting, as trusted relations between producers and consumers are what guarantees that food includes certain values. Producers from neighbouring farms will often come to the shop, to discuss with customers directly, which further enhances relations of trust in the material space of the community shop.

La Fève is nonetheless attractive to certain people who share a normative understanding of local foods as more desirable, and may also be 'carriers' of other practices related to collective conventions around sustainable consumption, such as privileging bicycles or public transport over car usage. The Auberge, on the other hand, attracts a wider audience, as a bistro, bar, and musical performance space. A professional cook is part of the staff, and has direct contact with local food producers. In addition to meals prepared by the chef, customers have the opportunity to propose meals and cook them together with the chef in the *Auberge* kitchen. Approximately once a week, such a meal is cooked and proposed to the community around different culinary traditions that reflect the great diversity of people living in the Les Vergers neighbourhood. In addition to demonstrating how different foods might be prepared, drawing as much as possible on local produce and towards developing new competencies, the Auberge also offers other services that are seen as complementary. Guest rooms are available, as well as a performance space; the Auberge was hosting a musical performance on a nightly basis, before confinement measures around COVID-19 were put in place. The Auberge is thus conceived of as a cultural space, where experiencing meal preparation, meal-sharing and music all come together. Different social groups are attracted by the offer, with families frequenting the Auberge mostly during the day, and younger adults arriving more in the evening – reflecting the need to understand practices in relation to the rhythms of everyday life.

While the COVID-19 pandemic and confinement measures have affected the Auberge's operations, the members feel confident that the project will be able to maintain momentum over the course of the pandemic. In a next step, members of the Auberge would like to reflect on how the chain between food production and waste could be further developed, for example through valorising food waste and collaborating with community gardens in the neighbourhood for food composting.

Case 2: A policy-driven initiative: sustainable public catering in Helsinki, Finland

The second case study refers to a change initiative that originated from a concern for unsustainable forms of producing and consuming food in Finland, leading to a policy measure that was then applied to changing systems of food provisioning in urban school canteens. A practice-inspired analysis reveals some of the intricacies and challenges associated with this initiative, for instance how the meaning of sustainable food diverged for the practitioners involved (for more information on this case see Wahlen et al., 2012). Food practices are determined by the interplay of production and consumption. The geographical position of Finland in the north-east of Europe and related climate with long winters and a short vegetation period limits the food that is produced locally, even if there is a tradition of valorising locally produced food. In 2009, the Central Finnish Government made a Council of State Decision of Principle mandating sustainable public procurement – towards not only promoting more sustainable forms of consumption by its citizens, but also serving as an example through its own practices – as the public sector is responsible for a significant share of GDP through purchases of goods and services. The Decision of Principle stipulated that sustainability measures should be set as a standard for government practices, and it included a recommendation for municipal governments to sustainably procure public catering in schools and other publicly run organisations.

Even though the policy initiative was not set up deploying SPAs, the blurring of producer–consumer boundaries assists in analysing the case: governmental bodies are involved in service provisioning practices, determining what food is prepared and eaten in public institutions. The government runs several canteens for its employees, but beyond that it is also responsible for the provision of meals in education institutions, such as schools or universities. Governmental public catering has a long tradition in Finland. Eating in an institutional setting might influence overall eating practices through embodied experiences (e.g. demonstrating deliciousness of a vegetarian dish), hence eating in canteens might impact overall everyday food consumption practices. Public catering can introduce consumers to possible alternatives and more sustainable options such as organic, seasonal, local, or vegetarian meals. Following the Decision of Principle, the City of Helsinki announced in February 2010 that it would introduce mandatory weekly vegetarian meals in local school canteens. The vegetarian day in school canteens can be interpreted as recrafting practices (Spurling et al., 2013), replacing meat with vegetarian dishes during lunch in the institutional setting. The underlying idea was, on the one hand, to stimulate sustainable consumption and production and, on the other hand, to educate children about alternative and more sustainable food – not through a campaign, but through bodily experiences of eating a vegetarian meal.

Sustainable public catering, as demonstrated by the weekly vegetarian meal in school canteens, educates pupils by recrafting lunch practices by, at least temporarily, changing the elements of a practice. Children eating at school canteens are exposed to alternative food and can get acquainted through social learning with different smells and tastes of vegetarian options to which they otherwise might not be exposed. Such embodied experiences were assumed to be taken home to their parents and families, extending towards practices in other contexts. Yet, eating more sustainable food alternatives in schools also relates to more embodied experiences in another way. Past practices also made their way into the process of governing food: the city parliament in Helsinki witnessed a very personal debate when it came to the introduction of vegetarian school food. Members of parliament referred to personal taste and preference with regard to their own practices when attending school years ago. The quality of school food back in the days was considered horrible, and it was deemed that current school kids should not experience such low-quality food in their eating practices. A collaborative effort in aligning the various perspectives of policymakers, catering professionals, and consumers (see Wahlen et al., 2012) would assist in aligning the various practices that come together in governing a change initiative and that need to be considered. Put differently, a change initiative should take practices of all practitioners into consideration, from production to preparation towards consumption practices as well as in the governing of food.

A social practice-informed analysis of the initiative reveals the simple question of 'what is a sustainable meal?' as rather contentious, with diverging meanings among government officials, catering professionals, and consumers. The initiative in Helsinki advanced 'a vegetarian meal a day' as a more sustainable option, which is aligned with scientific studies on the environmental and health impacts of meat and dairy products (Ernstoff et al., 2020). However, consumers did not necessarily care about the environmental impact of vegetarian food, but rather attributed meanings to what they saw as a 'normal' or 'healthy' meal. For example, consumers doubted whether vegetarian food would adequately nourish children in schools, leading to some resistance to the initiative. Catering professionals were also irritated by the policy: most school canteens provided different menu options, among which one vegetarian option already existed. Better understanding of existing practices and meanings, through a more collaborative and inclusive effort, could have made food governance policy measures more effective.

Conclusion

Social practice theory approaches have proven useful in informing and analysing change initiatives in the urban governing of food at a collective level. Practice-informed approaches provide a way of determining what needs to be 'governed', but also how one might go about collaboratively designing change initiatives towards the normative aims of sustainable or healthy food consumption. The two urban case studies highlight the intricacies in engaging in such change processes, such as the importance of embodied and experiential learning opportunities, demonstration sites, and public debates around what is 'sustainable and healthy' food. But SPAs also reveal some blind spots when applied to food: if the capacity to act can be seen as distributed across different elements of practices, then how can we further understand the strength of an element of practice over others, for example the abundance of commercial supermarkets as opposed to local food cooperatives in certain city centres; or the strength of certain practices over others, such as industrial food production processes over organic forms of agriculture. Behind these 'powerful practices' are certain rules and regulations (Plessz & Wahlen, 2022), but also financial incentives that make it difficult for new and alternative ways of doing to emerge and stabilise over time. Transition theories, seen by some as complementary to social practice theories (Geels et al., 2015), are one way of understanding dynamics at different levels – at what are called niche, regime and landscape levels; although, for some, practices are associated with flat social ontologies, devoid of hierarchies. Another way forward may be to consider how advances in the political economy could help inform social practice theoretical reflections (Evans, 2020), in considering the political and economic processes that underlie certain forms of food consumption and provisioning. Such consideration could expand the scale of inquiry to study not only how and in what way people or communities carry out practices at an observable scale, but also how multiple practices are interrelated, ranging from urban planning to agriculture but also packaging, production, and distribution at a global scale.

When it comes to the governing of food in urban settings, time is of the essence: practices can change over time, but they are usually quite resistant to change – and yet rapid rates of change at significant scales are needed to address compounded crises, such as climate change and biodiversity loss. Learning from experiences that seek to combine social practice theory with design interventions seems to be a promising way forward, and implies collaborations between different kinds of practitioners, from policymakers to producers, consumers, or others – humans and more than humans. Participatory methods take time, but there is increasing commitment from municipalities to support such processes, or indeed mandate them in some instances. Time also pertains to the 'sustainability' of promising initiatives over the long term: while community-driven initiatives with a focus on sustainable food governance are emerging in cities around the world, they would need to last beyond an initial or niche phase. How we can make sure that these 'sustainable solutions' are not solely carried by highly educated 'practitioners' is also a pressing issue, to ensure that sustainable food production and consumption is a default proposition for the many, rather than a privilege for a selected few. In this regard, burgeoning initiatives in urban settings to create food policy councils in the local governing of food is a promising trend (Andreola et al., 2021). Citizens and other practitioners in the food system can work together to advance healthy, local, and sustainable food in a given region, towards creating locally relevant understandings of food that take new and emerging practices seriously.

References

Andreola, M., Pianegonda, A., Favargiotti, S., & Forno, F. (2021). Urban food strategy in the making: Context, conventions and contestations. *Agriculture*, 11(2): 177. https://doi.org/10.3390/agriculture11020177

Born, B., & Purcell, M. (2006). Avoiding the local trap: Scale and food systems in planning research. *Journal of Planning Education and Research*, 26: 195–207. https://doi.org/10.1177%2F0739456X06291389

Bourdieu, P. (1979). *La distinction critique sociale du jugement*. Paris: Les Editions de Minuit.

Cohen, M. J. (2021). *Sustainability*. Medford, MA: Polity Press.

Davies, A., Fahy, F., & Rau, H. (Eds.). (2014). *Challenging Consumption: Pathways to a more Sustainable Future*. London: Routledge.

Davies, A. R. (2019). *Urban Food Sharing: Rules, Tools and Networks*. Bristol: Policy Press. doi: 10.2307/j.ctvkjb30n

Devaney, L., & Davies, A. R. (2017). Disrupting household food consumption through experimental HomeLabs: Outcomes, connections, contexts. *Journal of Consumer Culture*, 17(3): 823–844. https://doi.org/10.1177%2F1469540516631153

Domaneschi, L. (2012). Food social practices: Theory of practice and the new battlefield of food quality. *Journal of Consumer Culture*, 12: 306–322. https://doi.org/10.1177/1469540512456919

Douglas, M. (1975). Deciphering a meal. In C. Geertz (Ed.), *Myth, Symbol and Culture*. New York: W. W. Norton.

Dubuisson-Quellier, S., & Gojard, S. (2016). Why are food practices not (more) environmentally friendly in France? The role of collective standards and symbolic boundaries in food practices. *Environmental Policy and Governance*, 26: 89–100. https://doi.org/10.1002/eet.1703

Elias, N. (2016 [1969]). *La civilisation des moeurs*. Paris: Pocket.

Ernstoff, A., Stylianou. K. S., Sahakian, M. et al. (2020). Towards win-win policies for healthy and sustainable diets in Switzerland. *Nutrients*, 12(275): 1–24. https://doi.org/10.3390/nu12092745

Evans, D. (2011). Blaming the consumer – once again: The social and material contexts of everyday food waste practices in some English households. *Critical Public Health*, 21(4): 429–440. https://doi.org/10.1080/09581596.2011.608797

Evans, D. M. (2020). After practice? Material semiotic approaches to consumption and economy. *Cultural Sociology*, 14(4): 340–356. https://doi.org/10.1177/1749975520923521

Fine, B., Bayliss, K., & Robertson, M. (2018). The systems of provision approach to understanding consumption. In O. Kravets, P. Maclaran, S. Miles, & A. Venkatesh (Eds.), *The SAGE Handbook of Consumer Culture*. London, Los Angeles, Delhi, & Singapore: SAGE Publications.

Geels, F. W., McMeekin, A., Mylan, J., & Southerton, D. (2015). A critical appraisal of sustainable consumption and production research: The reformist, revolutionary and reconfiguration positions. *Global Environmental Change*, 34: 1–12. https://doi.org/10.1016/j.gloenvcha.2015.04.013

Giddens, A. (1984). *The Constitution of Society*. Cambridge: Polity.

Godin, L., & Sahakian, M. (2018). Cutting through conflicting prescriptions: How guidelines inform 'healthy and sustainable' diets in Switzerland. *Appetite*, 130: 123–133. https://doi.org/10.1016/j.appet.2018.08.004

Halkier, B. (2010). *Consumption Challenged: Food in Medialised Everyday Lives*. Ashgate.

Halkier, B. (2017). Normalising convenience food? *Food, Culture & Society*, 20(1): 133–151, https://doi.org/10.1080/15528014.2016.1243768

Halkier, B., & Jensen, I. (2011). Doing 'healthier' food in everyday life? A qualitative study of how Pakistani Danes handle nutritional communication. *Critical Public Health*, 21(4): 471–483. https://doi.org/10.1080/09581596.2011.594873

Hoolohan, C., & Browne, A. L. (2020). Design thinking for practice-based intervention: Co-producing the change points toolkit to unlock (un)sustainable practices. *Design Studies*, 67: 102–132. https://doi.org/10.1016/j.destud.2019.12.002

Lave, J., & Wenger, E. (2009 [1991]). *Situated Learning: Legitimate Peripheral Participation*. New York: Cambridge University Press.

O'Neill, K. J., Clear, A. K., Friday, A., & Hazas, M. (2019). 'Fractures' in food practices: Exploring transitions towards sustainable food. *Agriculture and Human Values*, 36: 225–239. https://doi.org/10.1007/s10460-019-09913-6

Ortner, S. B. (1989). *High Religion: A Cultural and Political History of Sherpa Buddhism*. Princeton, NJ: Princeton University Press.

Plessz, M., & Wahlen, S. (2022). All practices are shared, but some more than others: Sharedness of social practices and time-use in food consumption. *Journal of Consumer Culture*, 22(1): 143–163. https://doi.org/10.1177%2F1469540520907146

Plessz, M., Dubuisson-Quellier, S., Gojard, S., et al. (2016). How consumption prescriptions affect food practices: Assessing the roles of household resources and life-course events. *Journal of Consumer Culture*, 16(1): 101–123. https://doi.org/10.1177/1469540514521077

Reckwitz, A. (2002). Toward a theory of social practices: A development in culturalist theorizing. *European Journal of Social Theory*, 5(2): 243–263. https://doi.org/10.1177%2F13684310222225432

Sahakian, M. (2019). 'More, bigger, better' household appliances: Contesting normativity in practices through emotions. *Journal of Consumer Culture, first online*. https://doi.org/10.1177/1469540519889983

Sahakian, M., & Bertho, B. (2018). Exploring emotions and norms around Swiss household energy usage: When methods inform understandings of the social. *Energy Research and Social Sciences*, 45: 81–90. https://doi.org/10.1016/j.erss.2018.06.017

Sahakian, M., & Wilhite, H. (2014). Making practice theory practicable: Towards more sustainable forms of consumption. *Journal of Consumer Culture*, 14(1): 25–44. https://doi.org/10.1177%2F1469540513505607

Sahakian, M., Rau, H., Grealis, E., et al. (2021). Challenging social norms to recraft practices: A Living Lab approach to reducing household energy use in eight European countries. *Energy Research & Social Sciences*, 72: 101881. doi:https://doi.org/10.1016/j.erss.2020.101881

Sahakian, M., Saloma, C., & Erkman, S. (2016). *Food Consumption in the City: Practices and Patterns in Urban Asia and the Pacific. Routledge Studies in Food, Society and the Environment*. Abingdon, Oxon and New York: Routledge.

Schatzki, T. R. (1996). *Social Practices: A Wittgensteinian Approach to Human Activity and the Social*. Cambridge: Cambridge University Press.

Schatzki, T. R. (2002). *The Site of the Social: A Philosophical Account of the Constitution of Social Life and Change*. University Park, PA: Penn State University Press.

Shove, E. (2010). Beyond the ABC: Climate change policy and theories of social change. *Environment and Planning A*, 42: 1273–1285. https://doi.org/10.1068%2Fa42282

Shove, E., & Pantzar, M. (2005). Consumers, producers and practices: Understanding the invention and reinvention of Nordic walking. *Journal of Consumer Culture*, 5(1): 43–64. https://doi.org/10.1177%2F1469540505049846

Shove, E., & Southerton, D. (2000). Defrosting the freezer: From novelty to convenience, a narrative of normalization. *Journal of Material Culture*, 5(3): 301–319. https://doi.org/10.1177/135918350000500303

Simmel, G. (2001 [1910]). Sociology of the meal. In R. Kramme, A. Rammstedt, & O. Rammstedt (Eds.), *Gesamtausgabe in 24 Volumes. Vol. 12: Aufsätze und Abhandlungen 1909–1918. Vol. I.* Frankfurt: Suhrkamp.

Spurling, N., McMeekin, A., Shove, E., et al. (2013). *Interventions in Practice: Re-framing Policy Approaches to Consumer Behaviour*. Manchester: University of Manchester, Sustainable Practices Research Group. https://eprints.lancs.ac.uk/id/eprint/85608/

Truninger, M. (2011). Cooking with Bimby in a moment of recruitment: Exploring conventions and practice perspectives. *Journal of Consumer Culture*, 11(1): 37–59. https://doi.org/10.1177/1469540510391221

van der Horst, H., Wahlen, S., & Reimerink, M. (2021). Snacking practices in school: Othering and deviance in a health-normative context. *Critical Public Health*, 31(5): 595–604. https://doi.org/10.1080/09581596.2020.1713301

Vihalemm, T., Keller, M., & Kiisel, M. (2015). *From Interventions to Social Change: A Guide to Reshaping Everyday Practices*. New York: Ashgate Publishing/Routledge.

Wahlen, S. (2011). The routinely forgotten routine character of domestic practices. *International Journal of Consumer Studies*, 35: 507–513. .https://doi.org/10.1111/j.1470-6431.2011.01022.x

Wahlen, S., & Dubuisson-Quellier, S. (2018). Consumption governance toward more sustainable consumption. *Journal of Family & Consumer Sciences*, 110(1): 7–12. https://doi.org/10.14307/JFCS110.1.7

Wahlen, S., Heiskanen, E., & Aalto, K. (2012). Endorsing sustainable food consumption: Prospects from public catering. *Journal of Consumer Policy*, 35(7): 7–21. https://doi.org/10.1007/s10603-011-9183-4

Wallenborn, G., & Wilhite, H. (2014). Rethinking embodied knowledge and household consumption. *Energy Research & Social Science*, 1: 56–64.

Warde, A. (2005). Consumption and theories of practice. *Journal of Consumer Culture*, 5(2): 131–153. https://doi.org/10.1177%2F1469540505053090

Warde, A. (2013). What sort of practice is eating? In E. Shove & N Spurling (Eds.), *Sustainable Practices: Social Theory and Climate Change*. London: Routledge, pp. 17–30.

Warde, A. (2016). *The Practice of Eating*. Cambridge: Polity.

Warde, A. (2017). *Consumption: A Sociological Analysis*: New York: Palgrave Macmillan.

6

FEMINIST ETHICS OF CARE IN URBAN FOOD GOVERNANCE

Miriam J. Williams and Emma L. Sharp

Introduction

This chapter examines how a feminist ethics of care has provided, and has the potential to provide, a theoretical framework for analysing a diversity of urban food governance practices in an interdependent world. We recognise the urban as a socio-spatial process, a way of life that extends beyond the territorial confines of cities to shape non-urban environments through relationships within and beyond cities. Our approach in this chapter is expansive as we draw on a diversity of care literature from urban theory and food scholarship, documentary sources, and our research with urban food initiatives in 2019–20 (in Sydney, Australia) and 2014–18 (in Tāmaki Makaurau/Auckland, Aotearoa, New Zealand), to attend to the diverse food initiatives that take place in and beyond cities. We identify three existing domains of research on an ethics of care in urban food governance: (i) caring connections; (ii) care as a politics; and (iii) the materialities of care as brought about through relationships with and between actors. We attend to each in turn. Throughout our analysis we emphasise the potential of a feminist ethics of care, as a distinct form of care ethics, to decentre humans as the subjects of food systems (Beacham, 2018). We then highlight the possibilities and challenges of approaching urban food governance through the lens of a feminist ethics of care to support new imaginaries for care-full and just food futures.

Researchers have long been attuned to the ways in which care flows through food systems as both a guiding ethos and practice. Independent of the evidence for value-action gaps around practices such as consumption (e.g. Vermeir & Verbeke, 2006), an *ethics* of care can be seen as discrete from the *practice* of care, whilst also being intrinsically linked. Milligan and Wiles (2010, p. 737) explain that "care is the provision of practice or emotional support" and can also become an "orientation and embodied practice" (Conradson, 2011, p. 454). Tronto (2013), a pioneering scholar in care theory, conceptualises care as enacted through five phases: caring about, caring for, care-giving, care receiving and caring with. Care is not confined to the personal sphere but can be enacted through markets (Cameron & Wright, 2014; Dombroski et al., 2019; Smith, 2005) and infrastructures (Alam & Houston, 2020; Power & Mee, 2019). Care as a practice can be messy and difficult, involving acts of physical care-giving or emotional labour (Puig de la Bellacasa, 2017; Williams, 2020). Care is not innocent but can be both

 DOI: 10.4324/9781003055907-8

troubling and troubled, as power and privilege manifest through the many ways care is practised (Puig de la Bellacasa, 2017).

Multiple care ethics exist that are imbued with values and moral judgements, shaping understandings of who is responsible to/for care in urban food systems. Two discourses of care ethics are prominent in care literature: a neoliberal care ethics and feminist ethics of care (Midgley, 2016). Neoliberal care ethics dominate Western understanding of individuals as responsible for meeting their own needs either through their own labour, or through paying for care as a service (Power & Bergan, 2019). This form of care ethics can also shape understandings of how care might be practised through food systems, reinforcing the role of individuals as consumers and as enacting change through shopping (Alkon & Guthman, 2017, p. 12). For example, neoliberal care ethics might situate individuals as able to care for others through buying organic, fair trade or pesticide free products, reinforcing their subjectivity as consumer. Such products are governed by voluntary labelling and certification systems and other "market-based mechanisms" that are regulated by particular standards (Alkon & Guthman, 2017, p. 13; Moragues-Faus, 2017).

Often mobilised as a practised alternative and critique of neoliberal care ethics, a feminist ethics of care centres the political importance of questioning who is responsible to and for care, who is taking on the burden of care, and, the ways in which such responsibility is unequally borne (Midgley, 2016, p. 615). Fisher and Tronto (1990, p. 40) define a feminist ethics of care as:

> a species activity that includes everything that we do to maintain, continue, and repair our "world" so that we can live in it as well as possible. That world includes our bodies, ourselves, and our environment, all of which we seek to interweave in a complex, life-sustaining web.

A feminist ethics of care centres interconnection and relationality as its approach to responsibility and "recognises the situated, interdependent and collective relational bases of our responsibilities both to the self and to others" (Midgley, 2016, p. 615). Such a framework has been used to critique neoliberal ethics and discourses of individual responsibility, instead positing the importance of collective responsibility and activities that alter the collective infrastructures of provisioning. Grounded in a *relational social ontology* (Lawson, 2007), a feminist ethics of care draws attention to the interdependencies, responsibilities and connections that exist within and beyond food systems (Sharp, 2020) and provides a valuable lens through which to view existing practices of food governance. A feminist ethics of care is not just the act of care-giving or caring labour; it is rather more a politics and a transformative ethic that can be drawn upon to question who or what is doing the work of care and centres ways to create "as well as possible" worlds (Fisher & Tronto, 1990, p. 40).

Enacting a feminist ethics of care in the urban

We start by positioning our view, that the urban produces unique social-spatial relationships and densities that shape "care practiced across the city at an urban scale alongside the micro-spaces of care and interpersonal caring" (Power & Williams, 2019, p. 8). Massey's (2004) work encourages us to think about realms of relationships and responsibility and this includes a responsibility to near and distant others. While this might seem like a contradiction of sorts, where through relational thinking care in the 'urban' would therefore also manifest in various ways in the 'rural', Power and Williams (2019, p. 8) assist us to think more broadly about how a feminist ethics of care might be enacted in response to the specificity of relations that emerge in the urban.

Food scholars have for a long time noted the flows, connections and relationalities that shape food systems with some food networks specifically seeking to reconnect consumers and producers in order to create more caring and just food systems (Kneafsey et al., 2008). The method of following the connections between food that is on the table and its origins means tracing the intermediary forces and actors that construct it in time and place, which reveals the ethics of care for that food extending in all directions, and connecting to more-than-urban places (for example, Campbell's (2009) 'food from somewhere'). Care can, and does, emanate in response to specific urban contexts and relations, as discussed below, in various examples of community food initiatives.

Box Divvy is a fresh food box-ordering platform and a series of food hubs connecting growers on the peri-urban fringe and rural areas of Sydney directly to food hubs throughout the Sydney, Central Coast and Hunter regions of Australia (Box Divvy, 2020). OOOOBY (Out of Our Own Backyard) in Auckland, Aotearoa – and since, emergent in other locations – operates on the same principles, while encouraging smallholder (even 'backyard') growers, and promising choices for organic produce and degrees of 'localness'. Both have clear principles which are articulated in their advertising materials, detailed below:

> Pay farmers fairly by buying direct and purchasing as a group. Low food miles, no packaging, and you join a food community making a difference and good choices so helping reduce our carbon footprint.
>
> *Box Divvy, 2020, p. 1*

> We deliver fresh local and organic food to you and pay fair prices to small-scale farmers … Part of a global movement that is putting small scale food producers back at the heart of our food systems.
>
> *OOOOBY, 2020, p. 1*

Evident in the invitations for members to join is the expression of a set of values that are similar to other urban initiatives seeking to address a multiplicity of concerns evident in dominant food systems, globally. As shown in the quotes above, prospective food hub members are asked to understand their food choices in relation to other scales, places and actors, urban and more-than-urban, human and more-than-human. They are invited to take responsibility for the planet by consuming in low-carbon, no (or low) chemical ways, to care for people by considering farmer livelihoods, and to join a food community that involves negotiations of diverse priorities of care. Such ways of doing food care-fully show how actors within food systems might "…identify needs, accept responsibilities and establish caring competencies…" (Sharp, 2019, p. 764). They demonstrate care in particular spaces, with particular politics, and through particular material engagements.

However, as Puig de la Bellacasa (2017, p. 5) reminds us, care "is never neutral". Feminist care ethics ask questions of relationships of need, responsibility, privilege and politics (Lawson, 2007) and attend to the ways in which caring labour is most often carried out by the most marginalised (Puig de la Bellacasa, 2017). Such work has focused on relationships of power, particularly in the areas of domestic labour provisioning, connections between the Global North and Global South through commodity chains, and the problems of how the responsibilities for, and to, care are distributed (Cox, 2010). A feminist ethics of care serves as an evaluative framing, a set of ethical coordinates used to orient thinking and doing, that is helpful to assess practices and politics of urban governance and care inequity in particular contexts. A feminist ethics of care is a political project; a relational framework and practice that highlights what is hidden, which, in urban food governance, is often more-than-conventional food production, redistribution and consumption, and which sits in contrast to the care ethics espoused through neoliberal ideologies and which casts care as an individual responsibility rather than a collective one (Power & Bergan, 2019).

We approach governance as the diversity of formal and informal forms of "coordination, management and steering" (Painter, 2009, p. 312), enacted by diverse actors to shape food practices and systems of provisioning. Governance may involve varying levels of formality of urban 'management' by actors of the state, corporate interests, civil organisations and individuals. A feminist ethics of care has the potential to shape urban food governance – formally through mechanisms such as policy, regulation, standards, and institutional framings; and, informally through, for example, grassroots forms of governance, 'alternative' economies, peer accountability, self-regulation, and individual procuring and purchasing criteria. Attention to a feminist ethics of care prompts suggestions of how food systems might be transformed towards care-full justice (Williams, 2017a; Sharp, 2020) through connections between human and non-human others.

Caring connections: proximity and distance in urban food governance

"Come on a journey with us. Un-Supermarket"

Box Divvy, 2020, p. 1

The initiatives Box Divvy in Sydney and OOOOBY in Auckland mentioned in the previous section were established by concerned farmers (Box Divvy), food business owners, and logisticians (OOOOBY) who imagined a different food system. With their respective organisations they developed online ordering systems, supplier networks and set up the businesses as social enterprises. They wanted to support local growers and help consumers access fresher and more affordable fruit and vegetables – to enable these food actors to better govern themselves. Box Divvy sources 70 per cent of its produce from over 17 local growers (with the rest coming from other market sources), indicating that the food is "picked 24–48 hours before delivery" (Box Divvy, 2020). OOOOBY sources food locally and pays farmers at least 50 per cent of the retail value of all box deliveries. Both organisations screen farms to ensure minimal chemical inputs are used, with particular produce guaranteed organic, and have a call for backyard growers to sell into their food hubs. The goals of the organisations are to:

> Cut your food bill, without compromising on the quality, freshness and variety of food. With minimal effort, minimal packaging and food miles, and still paying farmers and suppliers a fair price for their produce.
>
> *Box Divvy, 2020, p. 1*

> Our mission is to put small-scale sustainable farming at the heart of our food system.
>
> *OOOOBY, 2020*

In these examples, Box Divvy and OOOOBY contrast the ordinary everyday practices of the 'un'caring supermarket with a different way of sourcing food, one that is based on relationships that enable people to collectively have greater control over their food procurement, sourcing and distribution. However, this care is negotiated and responsive to the food that is available, seasonal variability and extreme events such as droughts or flood. It is not always possible for food initiatives to source all the food needed locally, with Box Divvy at times providing produce from overseas, revealing how ethics are negotiated in practice:

> The few items from overseas, mostly as not available in Australia, we search for the same chemical free approach but we cannot guarantee it for anyone with sensitivities due to border inspections as they fumigate including organic produce imported – this renders it non-organic strictly speaking. The only two items we have [from overseas] are from New Zealand – kiwi when it is seasonally not available in Australia, and garlic when local is not available typically after March there is Giant Russian but this is actually a leek so we purchase … Mexican or Spanish [garlic].
>
> *Box Divvy, 2021*

All of their references to place, scale, proximity and centricity help us consider the ways in which urban food governance is assembled and negotiated through relationships of care and connection.

A feminist ethics of care approach to food systems considers the complexity of relations between actors within the industrialised, global system and more-than-profit modes of food production, distribution and consumption, and the spaces in between. The lens of an ethics of care has been applied to practices of local and global food relations between near and distant others, both human and non-human (Morgan, 2010). Engaging with a feminist ethics of care makes visible not only 'uncaring', exploitative practices involved in food systems, but also the caring potentials in both global and local food assemblages, as determined by the context of place and space (Sharp, 2018). A feminist ethics of care might flow through supply chains and involve a multiplicity of human and non-human actors caring about, for, with and giving to and receiving care from (Tronto, 2013), for example: soils, trees, packaging, carbon or producers. The wide scholarship highlights the diversity of caring community food economies (Cameron & Wright, 2014); as well as feeding publics to enable food justice and security (e.g. Dombroski et al., 2020) and sovereignty (e.g. Jarosz, 2014) whilst enabling farmer livelihood security across the Global North and South. Of emerging interest in the field has been research on care for more-than-humans in food systems more broadly (e.g. Bedore, 2018), such as for animals (e.g. Miele and Evans, 2010) and environments (Holloway et al., 2006).

Urban food experiments, or 'alternative food initiatives' (Kneafsey et al., 2008; Sharp, 2018; Sharp et al., 2015) often seek to create proximate connections between producers, consumers, growers, gardens, soil and food. Examples such as food cooperatives (Williams, 2016), verge gardens (Hsu, 2019), Community Supported Agriculture schemes (Beacham, 2018; Sharp, 2018), urban food commons (Morrow, 2019), guerilla gardening and dumpster diving (Sharp et al., 2016) reveal the diverse spaces in which care is practised in urban settings through proximate connections. Many of these self-governing, or third-sector initiatives are made possible because of their subversive nature (Goodman & Sage, 2014; Sharp et al., 2016), crossing legal, cultural, social and economic boundaries and in unlikely spaces, in order to operate. In this way, care is expressed through ethics that prioritise the flourishing of humans and non-human food relations over their exploitation and despite overly bureaucratic or ill-fitting governance frameworks that stifle flourishing.

The care ethics of urban agriculture schemes, for example, takes governance to a smaller scale, working with a term of reference that prioritises social (local and context-specific values), ecological (organic, close and low-carbon transport of produce), and local community economic benefits, often contributing to the constitution of community economies (Cameron & Wright, 2014). Such schemes emphasise the possibilities of proximate relationships that support and maintain diverse food initiatives and support a multiplicity of actors, emphasising their collective benefit. For example, Box Divvy Hubsters earn an income from running the food hubs and the food remains "roughly 30% less than online supermarkets" (Box Divvy, 2020) so that fresh, healthy food is more affordable through more proximate relationships between producer and consumer.

It is worth noting, however, that the governance of small-scale social enterprises that prioritise proximate relationships is not necessarily more care-full or ethical than that of large-scale ones (Born & Purcell, 2006). Born and Purcell observe a 'local trap', where too often 'localness' is equated with 'goodness', when in reality it is the "content of [the] agenda, not the scales themselves" that lead to sustainable or just outcomes (2006, p. 195). Feasibly, caring governance might flow through global supply chains and be mediated through global or national formal policy, regulation, advice and guidance around production and consumption (Milligan & Wiles, 2010). "The spatial extensiveness of care" (Lawson, 2007, p. 6), or ways in which care might be practised 'at-a-distance' challenges understandings of care as confined to local proximate relations (Morgan, 2010). The work that identifies how food relations engender caring about, caring for, care-giving, care receiving and caring with all food system actors, human and more-than-human, helps to make visible the (re)production of relations and social categories or the negotiation of boundaries of the public or private sphere (see Thelen, 2015). We explore this further in the next section as we engage with how a feminist ethics of care might manifest through the politics of approaches to food governance and as evaluative framing, prompting us to question who is taking responsibility to/for care in urban food systems?

Care as a politics in urban food governance: who is taking responsibility?

"We want the community to own the food system."

Box Divvy, 2020

"We're farmers and fed up with the way the food system currently operates."

Box Divvy, 2020

Above, Box Divvy makes a political statement signalling their desire for community ownership of the food system. As an enterprise they position their response and call to action as they take responsibility to care for farmers, hubsters and members. These enterprises, while formal businesses, are recognised as social enterprises that are governed by legal business practice requirements, food safety laws and human labour standards. In this domain, we identify how a feminist ethics of care might shape research attending to the politics of urban food governance in two ways: Firstly, we argue that research on a feminist ethics of care in urban food governance might reveal the ways in which particular food initiatives take responsibility to address injustices or concerns with food systems and develop particular responses. Such work might emphasise formal and informal processes that centre care, at the same time as revealing ontologies that centre values of reciprocity and interdependence. Secondly, we attend to how a feminist ethics of care might provide a lens through which to evaluate the political outcomes of systems of food governance, to reconfigure them towards care that enables human and more-than-human others to flourish. Such work draws upon existing and new place-based contextual understandings of care as it emerges.

Firstly, research on a feminist ethics of care reveals how care might be manifest in the politics that shape the goals, mission and approach of particular organisations and initiatives. For example, Beacham (2018) explores how Community Supported Agriculture schemes in north-west England aim to care for people and more-than-human others, whereas Bedore's (2018) work documents the good food box system and discusses the ways in which dignity might be facilitated through a caring organisational approach. In these analyses, a feminist ethics of care might be seen to flow through the politics of organisations, revealing how diverse actors collectively take responsibility to care for, about and with proximate and distant others. A feminist ethics of care might be expressed in the mission statements, values and approaches to food systems, and through formal practices of governance – through food policy – and informal forms of governance, the organisation of alternative markets or through voluntary labelling schemes (Moragues-Faus, 2017).

Care might flow through the politics of informal, collectively negotiated practices of food governance. Williams (2017b, p. 2226) draws on the example of Alfalfa House food cooperative, Enmore and discusses how informal buying principles have been developed to align with the objects of the cooperative, determining the food that is sold or not sold, and how it is sold. The cooperative is concerned with supplying "low-cost, ethically-produced and packaged wholefoods, cruelty-free foods, vegetarian foods, vegan foods, organic foods and genetically modified-free foods" (Williams, 2017b, p. 2225). Sometimes conflicts between personal and collective ethics arise, revealing how ethics are negotiated. These buying principles are not static but renegotiated overtime and rely upon staff and members making value judgements through their context-specific decision-making practices (Williams, 2017b). An ethics of care may shape choices by staff about whether it is more beneficial to, for example, buy Fairtrade rice from overseas or locally, where access to water may be a concern (Williams, 2017b). Another example of such an ethics is seen in their preference to support farmers by purchasing produce directly as opposed to purchasing through the organic markets where farmers receive less money for their produce (Williams, 2017b). A feminist ethics of care, which recognises the collective responsibility to care for proximate and distant others, flows through these decisions and manifests in the presence or absence of particular food stuffs or actors – care governance might enable ubiquitous availability of minimally packaged, fair trade, organic, vegetarian, local or chemical free food (Williams, 2017b).

A politics of care might be seen through ontologies that centre common being or being-in-common (Beacham, 2018). As Beacham (2018) notes in their work on a more-than-human ethics of care in the Anthropocene, a feminist ethics of care might assist us in understanding other ways food systems might be organised to create new socio-ecological relationships. In addition, these concepts might be explored through the potential of Indigenous ontologies in shaping practices of urban food governance, assisting with the reconfiguring of human and non-human relations through relational practices that emphasise connection, interdependence and reciprocity. For example, Māori *tikanga* (traditional practice) "calls for humans to be kaitiaki, caretakers of the… life-force, in each other and in nature" (Spiller et al., 2011, p. 153). Wehi and Roa (2019) discuss examples of Māori care for those in situations of food insecurity and a struggle for sovereignty to enact care on their own terms, with reciprocity as care at the heart of these interactions, for human others and non-human others. Lessons learned from these approaches are that there are other multiple ways of knowing, and that holistic and multi-dimensional approaches to value "can create multi-dimensional well-being through better personal relationships and better relationships with the natural world" (Spiller et al., 2011, p. 153).

Secondly, a feminist ethics of care might provide a lens through which to evaluate the political outcomes of systems of formal and informal food governance, to reconfigure them towards an ethics of care. Such work attends to both voluntary forms of food systems governance, and formal practices of governance by the state. Herman (2019) examines the Fairtrade wine industry in Argentina, unpacking the experiences of Fairtrade and the ability of the universal system to address injustice. Fairtrade has been critiqued by a number of authors for still reinforcing inequalities between the Global North and Global South which, according to McEwan and Goodman (2010) might exclude situated understandings of what might be considered "fair" or just trade. The systems of accountability and policymaking that inform voluntary labelling schemes as forms of food governance are shaped by power relations between stakeholders (most often between producers in the Global South, and consumers in the Global North) (Herman, 2019; McEwan & Goodman, 2010). Herman (2019) contends that Fairtrade has to be able to respond to place-based needs by providing practical support, addressing the needs of producers, fostering connections and enabling sustained representation of producers in order to enable care-full justice (Williams, 2017a) through practices of care-full governance. Herman's (2019, p. 17) work highlights the potential of a feminist ethics of care approach in reorienting Fairtrade from focussing on the ethical practice of the consumer, akin to more of a neoliberal care ethics, to instead "focus on the ethical subjectivities of all those working within the system". Such an approach would enable a diversity of stakeholder participation and governance structures that can build "global networks of solidarity and responsibility" (Herman, 2019, p. 18). For Herman (2019), an ethics of care coupled with justice as *care-full justice* (Williams, 2017a) and its ability to respond to place-based needs, provides a way to refashion the governance of Fairtrade.

A feminist ethics of care provides a lens through which to evaluate formal practices of food system governance by state actors and how they may or may not be taking responsibility for/to care. For example, in their rich work on the viscerality of food, while not explicitly framed as care, Hayes-Conroy and Hayes-Conroy (2010, 2013) expose issues surrounding the individuation of what might be seen as emotionally affected care – about, for, with, giving to and receiving from food – which makes clear a shift in responsibility of what has previously been considered the state's responsibility for food-related care. This is often narrated in terms of food security (i.e. food access, availability, stability, utilisation) (Dombroski et al., 2020), and related food policy that seeks to primarily feed the urban poor. In many jurisdictions in the Global North, charitable food banks which redistribute food surplus produced through unsustainable systems of food production have become responsible for direct food provisioning to those who are hungry (Isola & Laiho, 2020). For example, in the UK context Cloke et al. (2017) note the diversity of organisations providing food banks and how diverse their politics and the experiences of those who visit them may also be. They explain that the diversity of politics that motivate individual and organisational engagement with food banking is important to capture. Some are motivated by charity, gift-giving and understandings of the needy poor, whereas

> independent organizations bring a complicated assemblage of ethical values – including charity, equitable exchange, unconditionality, reduction of food waste, anti-war, anti-capitalism – to the table. And even the dominant, seemingly theoethically conservative faith-based models have the capacity to create compassionate affective landscapes of alternative welfare.
>
> *Cloke et al., 2017, p. 117*

Viewing the work of food relief providers through the lens of an ethics of care provides a way in which to capture the politics of how caring practice is enacted and the diverse ways in which organisations take responsibility to govern food provision for those who might be hungry. Such work has also attended to the role of the material spaces in configuring care and experiences of caring practice.

Materialities of care in urban food governance

> ...care is never a purely human phenomenon, because the very materiality of environments necessarily mediates caring relationships and comes to shape what it means to care.
>
> *Bates et al., 2017, pp. 96–97*

Emergent in research on care is the role of more-than-human others, alongside things and objects, in reciprocating, fostering, facilitating *and* inhibiting care. Although less developed, work in this area is seeking to further pay attention to the role of more-than-human agencies in enabling and inhibiting care (Power & Williams, 2019) in food governance. Care is a "socio-material practice that takes place in conjunction with *things* in the city..." (Power & Williams, 2019, p. 3). A feminist ethics of care calls us to pay attention to the configurations and material conditions that make care and caring possible. Returning to the examples of Box Divvy and OOOOBY that we have drawn upon throughout this chapter, we can see how the food itself, the bodies involved in packing boxes and ordering, the soil and farms and boxes for packing produce, alongside the absence of 'things', may play a role in enabling practices of care that constitute diverse food initiatives. In this section we focus on the ways in which an ethics of care might flow through the "objects, bodies, buildings, materials" (Power & Williams, 2019, p. 3) that constitute food systems, like OOOOBY and Box Divvy, and the ways in which they are governed.

As Box Divvy assert, one of their main motivations is to 'un-supermarket', to offer alternatives or replacements to this material storehouse for food, that for some is synonymous with exploitation of food growers, environment, other marginalised humans, and the non-human others that feed us. The two organisations manage multiple physical food hubs: Box Divvy, over 90 throughout New South Wales; OOOOBY in four regions in Australasia, including Auckland, Waikato, Christchurch, Sydney and delivering over 300,000 boxes of food to over 30,000 homes since its prototype hub was launched in 2010 (OOOOBY, 2020). These physical, material hubs are supported by virtual hubs and an online ordering system that connects the food in the soil, to the food on a plate. The trucks, boxes, fruit, soils, worms, places of packing, apps, vegetables, absence of packaging, and more, mingle together to facilitate care for bodies and worlds.

Literature on care has emphasised the ways in which "things facilitate, foster, mediate, and co-constitute caring relations and may also be enrolled in the practice of caring for human and non-human others in the city" (Power & Williams, 2019, p. 3). Materialities of care for and with urban food governance might be seen in the sensory aspects of growing and consuming food (e.g. Longhurst et al., 2009; Sharp, 2018); the practices of rescuing food (e.g. Turner, 2019); working with food waste (e.g. Spring et al., 2019); or expressed through assemblages of material food insecurity (e.g. Dombroski et al., 2020). For example, Hsu (2019) has illustrated how particular material environments, in the case of verge gardening, enable the practising of care. His work explores how care between humans and non-humans might be mediated through the presence of verge gardens, their components of biological objects, and the practice of tending plants. Flowers, herbs, and weeds themselves "enable care practices", with Hsu (2019, p. 839) reminding us how "care is a human trouble, but this does not make of care a human-only matter" (Puig de la Bellacasa, 2017, p. 2).

To take up this contradiction, we look to an example of how assembled spaces can enable or trouble caring practices in urban food governance. In their paper on food waste transitions Rut et al. (2021) discuss the 'ecologies of participation' in food waste management in Singapore, bringing the reader's attention to how care might emerge through diverse spatial configurations with sites such as dumpsters, wet markets and charities as spaces of food waste redistribution and the affective dimensions of bodies which intersect. The paper also discusses how sensorial and visceral engagements with what is material in food relations (food, bins, dirt, trucks, mobile phones) might also be enrolled in moments of 'doing' care, such as caring about food that is perishable/damaged or in surplus.

Not only do care ethics work to decentre global industrial profits in food systems, to instead re-centre them around care values that prioritise face-to-face relationships, but they also decentre the role of the human actor in food systems, giving space to the more-than-human. Beacham (2018), for example, explores the possibility of an ethics of care in reworking understandings of hierarchy between humans and non-humans, emphasising the capacity of both to be care-givers and care receivers in their exploration of Community Supported Agriculture schemes. Their work also highlights the challenges of always acting care-fully, drawing on the example of a beetle that could not be eradicated using organic pest control methods (Beacham, 2018). Limits to care and caring capacity are revealed through the ways in which actors negotiate values in response to problems such as pests. Beacham's work highlights the limits of "more than human agency" and argues that by engaging with "care for the more-than-human, we can recognise how we do not act over a world but exist within it together" (Beacham, 2018, p. 544).

Conflicts over how food is governed, and which care is enabled, are also prevalent. For example, the meanings associated with food that is past its use-by date or considered to be 'risky' has been explored in literature that studies dumpster diving. Sharp et al. (2016) examine how food activists, and food insecure individuals and groups practise care for the purposes of reducing food waste, or accessing food to eat. In any scenario the practice is illegal, socially unacceptable, and economically unadvisable for supermarkets to condone on their properties (and so issuing a trespass notice is a likely outcome). The care ethics exhibited here are demonstrated in the political projects seeking to counter food waste, environmental degradation, and to address food poverty, whilst regulations and food safety policies are ignored. Similarly, Morrow's (2019) work looks to the risk associated with food-sharing practice in community fridges in Berlin. This work attends to the ways in which the extensive rules of foodsharing.de members come into conflict with formal food safety policies seeking to mitigate risk, restricting the ability of people to care for multiple commons (Morrow, 2019). Illegal practices such as dumpster diving and informal food-sharing commons reveal the tensions that exist in how caring with food and through particular materialities is constrained by risk, government policy and negotiated by groups. Caring with food is also shaped by cultural practices, knowledge, meanings and expectations that determine when food becomes 'waste' and materialities, such as a bin that signals such a movement (Evans, 2018).

Conclusion

A feminist ethics of care is a transformative ethics that provides a lens through which to analyse and assess existing practices of urban food governance in context and points to ways in which food systems might be transformed to enable 'as well as possible worlds' Fisher & Tronto, 1990, p. 40). This chapter has addressed the dynamic, contextual and intrinsically connected relationship between care as ethics, politics and practice. The literature engaging with an ethics of care through attending to the connections, politics and materialities of food is expansive, and still emerging. We see various performances of care in the relational connections, the politics and the materialities of food systems governance, as they pertain to formal and informal governance mechanisms and institutions. We have shown that while proximity is not necessarily a precursor for an ethics of care, it enables particular types of caring relationships that are performed through embodied connections and most often self- or locally governed informal food systems. We have explored, however, how care can be exhibited at a distance, as well as locally, through examples like the global ethico-politics of Fairtrade and our case study examples of OOOOBY and Box Divvy. There is care performed across food systems at points of production, procuring, processing, retailing, consuming, as well as about, by, for and with actors, both human and more-than-human. This care can often be uneven. We have emphasised the ways in which competing ethics and politics of care may manifest and the multiple care ethics that shape understandings of who is responsible to/for care? Care is in no way neutral or value-free.

Whilst we see examples of multiple forms of care being exhibited simultaneously, sometimes care for one aspect of a food system performs neglect, or 'un'caring for another, as dependent on actors' political projects, contexts and priorities. As such, scholars who apply the framework of a feminist ethics of care need to remain mindful of the role of power and ideology in shaping the contexts in which caring practices are enacted, and understandings of who is responsible for/to care. Applying a feminist ethics of care might be troublesome due to the unequal burden of care borne by some, as Yu (2018) has explored. Such insights assist in making visible the inequalities of who is doing the work of care in our worlds and provide the opportunity for thinking through how to address injustice and neglect. As Williams (2020, p. 6) notes elsewhere, "the work of a feminist ethics of care is never done". There is need for a more conscious engagement of this ethics with urban food governance, to reveal a contextual understanding of hidden actors, materialities, policies, spaces and ways of doing food that can support bolder moves towards care-full food justice for all participants, human and more-than-human. If a feminist ethics of care truly enables us to "maintain, continue, and repair 'our world' (Tronto, 1993, p. 103) for the survival and flourishing of everything in it" (Sharp, 2019, p. 764), governance of urban food systems will require a sustained orientation of its political coordinates in this direction.

References

Alam, A., & Houston, D. (2020). Rethinking care as alternate infrastructure. *Cities, 100*, pp. 1–10. Retrieved from https://doi.org/10.1016/j.cities.2020.102662

Alkon, A. H., & Guthman, J. (2017). Introduction. In A. H. Alkon & J. Guthman (Eds.), *The New Food Activism: Opposition, Cooperation, and Collective Action* (pp. 1–27). Oakland, CA: University of California Press.

Bates, C., Imrie, R., & Kullman, K. (2017). Chapter six configuring the caring city: Ownership, healing, openness. In C. Bates, R. Imrie, & K. Kullman (Eds.), *Care and Design: Bodies, Buildings, Cities* (pp. 95–115). Chichester: Wiley Blackwell.

Beacham, J. (2018). Organising food differently: Towards a more-than-human ethics of care for the Anthropocene. *Organization, 25*(4), pp. 533–549. Retrieved from https://doi.org/10.1177/1350508418777893

Bedore, M. (2018). 'I was purchasing it; it wasn't given to me': Food project patronage and the geography of dignity work. *The Geographical Journal,* 184(3), pp. 218–228. Retrieved from https://doi.org/10.1111/geoj.12251

Born, B., & Purcell, M. (2006). Avoiding the local trap: Scale and food systems in planning research. *Journal of Planning Education and Research, 26*(2), pp. 95–207. Retrieved from https://doi.org/10.1177/0739456X06291389

Box Divvy. (2020). How it works. Retrieved from www.boxdivvy.com/how-it-works

Box Divvy. (2021). How we work with our growers. Retrieved from www.boxdivvy.com/how

Cameron, J., & Wright, S. (2014). Researching diverse food initiatives: From backyard and community gardens to international markets. *Local Environment, 19*(1), pp. 1–9. Retrieved from https://doi.org/10.1080/13549839.2013.835096

Campbell, H. (2009). Breaking new ground in food regime theory: Corporate environmentalism, ecological feedbacks and the 'food from somewhere' regime? *Agriculture and Human Values, 26*(4), pp. 309–319. Retrieved from https://doi.org/10.1007/s10460-009-9215-8

Cloke, P., May, J., & Williams, A. (2017). The geographies of food banks in the meantime. *Progress in Human Geography, 41*(6), pp. 703–726. Retrieved from https://doi.org/10.1177/0309132516655881

Conradson, D. (2011). Care and caring. In V. Del Casino Jr, M. Thomas, P. Cloke, & R. Panelli (Eds.), *A Companion to Social Geography* (pp. 454–471). Oxford: Blackwell Publishing.

Cox, R. (2010). Some problems and possibilities of caring. *Ethics, Place & Environment, 13*(2), pp. 113–130. Retrieved from https://doi.org/10.1080/13668791003778800

Dombroski, K., Diprose, G., Sharp, E., Graham, R., Lee, L., Scobie, M., … & Martin-Neuninger, R. (2020). Food for people in place: Reimagining food systems for economic recovery. *Sustainability, 12*(22), pp. 1–17 Retrieved from https://doi.org/10.3390/su12229369

Dombroski, K., Healy, S., & McKinnon, K. (2019). Care-full community economies. In C. Bauhardt & W. Harcourt (Eds.), *Feminist Political Ecology and the Economics of Care: In Search of Economic Alternatives* (pp. 99–115). Abingdon, Oxon: Routledge.

Evans, D. (2018). Rethinking material cultures of sustainability: Commodity consumption, cultural biographies and following the thing. *Transactions of the Institute of British Geographers, 43*(1), pp. 110–121. Retrieved from https://rgs-ibg.onlinelibrary.wiley.com/doi/epdf/10.1111/tran.12206

Fisher, B., & Tronto, J. C. (1990). Towards a feminist theory of caring. In E. K. Abel & M. Nelson (Eds.), *Circles of Care: Work and Identity in Women's Lives* (pp. 35–62). Albany, NY: State University Press of New York.

Goodman, M., & Sage, C. (2014). Food transgressions: Ethics, governance and geographies. In M. Goodman & C. Sage (Eds.), *Food Transgressions: Making Sense of Contemporary Food Politics* (pp. 1–14). Farnham: Ashgate.

Hayes-Conroy, A., & Hayes-Conroy, J. (2010). Visceral difference: Variations in feeling (slow) food. *Environment and Planning A, 42*(12), pp. 2956–2971. Retrieved from https://doi.org/10.1068/a4365

Hayes-Conroy, A., & Hayes-Conroy, J. (2013). Veggies and visceralities: A political ecology of food and feeling. *Emotion, Space and Society, 61*(1), pp. 81–90. Retrieved from https://doi.org/10.1016/j.emospa.2011.11.003

Herman, A. (2019). Governing fairtrade: Ethics of care and justice in the Argentinean wine industry. *Social & Cultural Geography, 22*(3), pp. 425–446. Retrieved from https://doi.org/10.1080/14649365.2019.1593493

Holloway, L., Cox, R., Venn, L., Kneafsey, M., Dowler, E., & Tuomainen, H. (2006). Managing sustainable farmed landscape through 'alternative' food networks: A case study from Italy. *Geographical Journal, 172*(3), pp. 219–229. Retrieved from www.jstor.org/stable/3873965

Hsu, J. (2019). Public pedagogies of edible verge gardens: Cultivating streetscapes of care. *Policy Futures in Education 17*(7), pp. 821–843. Retrieved from https://doi.org/10.1177/1478210318816759

Isola, A.-M., & Laiho, J. (2020). Commoning surplus food in Finland: Actors and tensions. In T. Eskelinen, T. Hirvilammi, & J. Venalainen (Eds.), *Enacting Community Economies within a Welfare State* (pp. 95–116). Christchurch, NZ: Mayfly Books.

Jarosz, L. (2014). Considering sovereignty, care ethics and policy in food politics. *Dialogues in Human Geography, 4*(2), pp. 229–232. Retrieved from https://doi.org/10.1177/2043820614537162

Kneafsey, M., Holloway, L., Venn, L., Cox, R., Dowler, E., & Tuomainen, H. (2008). *Reconnecting Producers, Consumers and Food: Exploring Alternatives* London: Berg.

Lawson, V. (2007). Geographies of care and responsibility. *Annals of the Association of American Geographers, 97*(1), pp. 1–11. Retrieved from https://doi.org/10.1111/j.1467-8306.2007.00520.x

Longhurst, R., Johnston, L., & Ho, E. (2009). A visceral approach: Cooking 'at home' with migrant women in Hamilton, New Zealand. *Transactions of the Institute of British Geographers, 34*(3), pp. 333–345. Retrieved from https://doi.org/10.1111/j.1475-5661.2009.00349.x

Massey, D. (2004). Geographies of responsibility. *Geografiska Annaler Series B: Human Geography, 86*(1), pp. 5–18. Retrieved from https://doi.org/10.1111/j.0435-3684.2004.00150.x

McEwan, C., & Goodman, M. K. (2010). Place geography and the ethics of care: Introductory remarks on the geographies of ethics, responsibility and care. *Ethics, Place & Environment, 13*(2), pp. 103–112. Retrieved from https://doi.org/10.1080/13668791003778602

Midgley, J. L. (2016). Perspectives on responsibility in practice as revealed through food provisioning offers for rough sleepers. *Critical Social Policy, 36*(4), pp. 610–629. Retrieved from https://doi.org/10.1177/0261018316640242

Miele, M., & Evans, A. (2010). When foods become animals: Ruminations on ethics and responsibility in care-*full* practices of consumption. *Ethics, Place & Environment, 13*(2), pp. 171–190. Retrieved from https://doi.org/10.1080/13668791003778842

Milligan, C., & Wiles, J. L. (2010). Landscapes of care. *Progress in Human Geography, 34*(6), pp. 736–754. Retrieved from https://doi.org/10.1177/0309132510364556

Moragues-Faus, A. (2017). Emancipatory or neoliberal food politics? Exploring the 'politics of collectivity' of buying groups in the search for egalitarian food democracies. *Antipode, 49*(2), pp. 455–476. Retrieved from https://doi.org/10.1111/anti.12274

Morgan, K. (2010). Local and green, global and fair: The ethical foodscape and the politics of care. *Environment and Planning A: Economy and Space, 42*(8), pp. 1852–1867. Retrieved from https://journals.sagepub.com/doi/abs/10.1068/a42364

Morrow, O. (2019). Sharing food and risk in Berlin's urban food commons. *Geoforum, 99*, pp. 202–212. Retrieved from https://doi.org/10.1016/j.geoforum.2018.09.003

OOOOBY. (2020). About Ooooby Auckland & Waikato. Retrieved from https://ooooby.co.nz/about-us

Painter, J. (2009). Governance. In D. Gregory, R. Johnston, G. Pratt, M. Watts, & S. Whatmore (Eds.), *The Dictionary of Human Geography*, 5th ed. (pp. 312–313). Malden, MA: John Wiley and Sons.

Power, E., & Mee, K. (2019). Housing: An infrastructure of care. *Housing Studies, 35*(3) Retrieved from https://doi.org/10.1080/02673037.2019.1612038

Power, E., & Williams, M. (2019). Cities of care: A platform for urban geographical care research. *Geography Compass, 14*(1) Retrieved from https://doi.org/10.1111/gec3.12474

Power, E. R., & Bergan, T. L. (2019). Care and resistance to neoliberal reform in social housing. *Housing, Theory and Society, 36*(4), pp. 426–447. Retrieved from https://doi.org/10.1080/14036096.2018.1515112

Puig de la Bellacasa, M. (2017). *Matters of Care: Speculative Ethics in More than Human Worlds*. Minneapolis, MN: University of Minnesota Press.

Rut, M., Davies, A., & Ng, H. (2021). Participating in food waste transitions: Exploring surplus food redistribution in Singapore through the ecologies of participation framework. *Journal of Environmental Policy & Planning, 23*(1), pp. 34–47. Retrieved from https://doi.org/10.1080/1523908X.2020.1792859

Sharp, E. L. (2018). (Re)assembling foodscapes with the Crowd Grown Feast. *Area, 50*(2), pp. 266–273. Retrieved from https://doi.org/10.1111/area.12376

Sharp, E. L. (2019). Editorial: The role of reflexivity in care-full food systems transformations. *Policy Futures in Education, 17*(7), pp. 761–769. Retrieved from https://doi.org/10.1177/1478210319874256

Sharp, E. L. (2020). Care-fully enacting diverse foodworlds in Auckland, Aotearoa New Zealand. *Gender, Place & Culture, 27*(8), pp. 1214–1218. Retrieved from https://doi.org/10.1080/0966369X.2019.1708275

Sharp, E. L., Friesen, W., & Lewis, N. (2015). Alternative framings of alternative food: A typology of practice. *New Zealand Geographer, 71*(1), pp. 6–17. Retrieved from https://doi.org/10.1111/nzg.12069

Sharp, E. L., Schindler, E., Lewis, N., & Friesen, W. (2016). Food fights: Irritating for social change among Auckland's alternative food initiatives. *Kōtuitui: New Zealand Journal of Social Sciences Online, 11*(2), pp. 133–145. Retrieved from https://doi.org/10.1080/1177083X.2016.1158197

Smith, S. J. (2005). States, markets and an ethic of care. *Political Geography, 24*(1), pp. 1–20. Retrieved from https://doi.org/10.1016/j.polgeo.2004.10.006

Spiller, C., Erakovic, L., Henare, M., & Pio, E. (2011). Relational well-being and wealth: Māori businesses and an ethic of care. *Journal of Business Ethics, 98*, pp. 153–169. Retrieved from https://journals.aom.org/doi/pdf/10.5465/ambpp.2010.54493605

Spring, C., Adams, M., & Hardman, M. (2019). Sites of learning: Exploring political ecologies and visceral pedagogies of surplus food redistribution in the UK. *Policy Futures in Education, 17*(7), pp. 844–861. Retrieved from https://doi.org/10.1177/1478210318819249

Thelen, T. (2015). Care as social organization: Creating, maintaining and dissolving significant relations. *Anthropological Theory, 15*(4), pp. 497–515. Retrieved from https://doi.org/10.1177/1463499615600893

Tronto, J. (1993). *Moral Boundaries, A Political Argument for an Ethic of Care*. New York and London: Routledge.

Tronto, J. (2013). *Caring Democracy: Markets, Equality, and Justice*. New York: NYU Press.

Turner, B. (2019). Playing with food waste: Experimenting with ethical entanglements in the Anthropocene. *Policy Futures in Education, 17*(7), pp. 770–784. Retrieved from https://doi.org/10.1177/1478210318776851

Vermeir, I., & Verbeke, W. (2006). Sustainable food consumption: Exploring the consumer 'attitude–behavioural intention' gap. *Journal of Agricultural and Environmental Ethics, 19*(2), pp. 169–194. Retrieved from https://doi.org/10.1007/s10806-005-5485-3

Wehi, P., & Roa, T. (2019). Reciprocal relationships: Identity, tradition and food in the Kīngitanga Poukai He Manaakitanga: o te tuakiri, o te tikanga me te kai ki te Poukai o te Kīngitanga. *SocArXiv Papers*, 12 December. Retrieved from https://doi.org/10.31235/osf.io/tz746

Williams, M. (2016). Justice and care in the city: Uncovering everyday practices through research volunteering. *Area, 48*(4), pp. 513–520. Retrieved from https://doi.org/10.1111/area.12278

Williams, M. (2017a). Care-full justice in the city. *Antipode, 49*(3), pp. 821–839. Retrieved from http://dx.doi.org/10.1111/anti.12279

Williams, M. (2017b). Searching for actually existing urban justice. *Urban Studies, 54*(10), pp. 2217–2231. Retrieved from https://doi.org/10.1177/0042098016647336

Williams, M. J. (2020). The possibility of care-full cities. *Cities, 98*(March), pp. 1–7. Retrieved from https://doi.org/10.1016/j.cities.2019.102591

Yu, Y. (2018). Towards a more just society? Care ethics and caregivers in urban China. *Geoforum, 96*, pp. 190–197. Retrieved from https://doi.org/10.1016/j.geoforum.2018.08.004

7
URBAN FOOD DEMOCRACY

Basil Bornemann and Sabine Weiland

Introduction

The current food system and its governance are characterised by a high concentration of power. Decisions regarding production, trade and market supply of food are largely in the hands of multinational corporations, and political and administrative elites operating in closed arenas (Lang & Heasman, 2004). Food is regarded as a commodity, and markets are in charge of regulating food supply. While some consider this organisation of the food system a prerequisite for global food security (Duncan, 2017; Fouilleux et al., 2017), an increasing number of counter-movements and alternative visions of the food system have emerged. Concepts such as food sovereignty (Patel, 2009), food justice (Alkon & Agyeman, 2011), food citizenship (Renting et al., 2012), and food democracy (Hassanein, 2003, 2008; Lang, 2005) point to critical implications and detrimental effects of the current food system and the way it is governed, including negative consequences for health, the environment and social equity. As much as the alternative visions concur in their critical diagnosis and call for food system transformation, they differ regarding the contexts in which they are articulated as well as their normative political implications (Jackson et al., 2021). 'Food sovereignty' is a concept that emerged in rural contexts in the Global South. Promoted by peasant movements, such as La Via Campesina, food sovereignty envisions a food system that provides fair access to food resources. Food is considered a human right, understood as equal access to healthy, nutritious and culturally appropriate food for everyone. Demands for 'food democracy', in contrast, are more widespread in the Global North (Carlson & Chappell, 2015). The concept attributes the problems of today's food systems to the limited opportunities for people to participate in, and to shape, food-related decisions. Food is seen as a common good, and its governance requires collaborative arrangements to meet the food needs of communities and society. Consequently, food democracy seeks to extend democratic norms, such as participation and equality, to the governance of the food system. Such democratisation is expected to lead to more equitable and sustainable food supply and consumption.

Cities, and urban areas in general, are important sites for food democracy. As urbanisation progresses, consumption, processing and, increasingly, production of food are, in large part, taking place in cities. In recent years, cities have also become important sites where calls for more democracy and democratic activism have been voiced, especially in relation to food

 DOI: 10.4324/9781003055907-9

(Haysom, 2015; Morgan & Sonnino, 2010). They are the arenas in which the "move away from a global, 'industrialised' food system to a more local (or 'alternative') one" is explored and experimented with (Harris et al., cited in Cretella, 2019, p. 4). Yet, despite the importance of cities and urban spaces for food and for democracy, a clear understanding of 'urban food democracy' does not yet exist. A recent volume entitled "Urban Food Democracy and Governance in North and South" (Thornton, 2020) provides no overall definition of the term. The book presents "examples of urban food democracy" that engage with "themes such as urban agriculture, governance, smart cities, food and social justice, and urban biodiversity issues" (ibid., p. 6). Urban food democracy is rather implicitly framed in terms of participation of food activists and social movements in urban food governance, particularly in activities that go beyond the market, emphasising the public, political and social nature of food and the need for sustainable urban development (ibid., pp. 4–5). Arguably, a systematic disambiguation of the concept is still pending.

This chapter aims to fill this gap and to develop a more nuanced understanding of 'urban food democracy'. To do so, we evoke the meaning of the concept's constituent elements. On a general semantic level, urban food democracy combines two specific articulations of democracy, each pointing to particular strands of discussion: On the one hand, democracy is thematised in relation to the specific subject area of food, bringing the concept of 'food democracy' into focus. On the other hand, democracy is addressed in relation to a specific spatial context, namely the urban space, thus activating the concept of 'urban democracy'. Together, these concepts outline the general meaning of 'urban food democracy' in terms of a realisation of democratic norms in the field of food governance in urban spaces. The resulting concept of urban food democracy can be used to critically examine the democratic quality and potential of urban food governance.

The chapter is organised as follows: Firstly, we recapitulate some existing, yet loosely developed currents of democratic thinking and analysis related to urban food governance. We then present the established notion of food democracy and highlight some recent critical extensions before we turn to the debate on urban democracy, again including critical perspectives. Finally, we bring these concepts together and define a narrow and an extended critical reading of urban food democracy. The chapter concludes with some thoughts on future perspectives for research and practice.

Democratic implications of urban food governance

A growing body of literature revolves around the democratic implications of urban food governance, broadly understood as all kinds of practices of orienting and shaping the food system (i.e., the production, distribution and consumption of food) in urban areas towards a set of common goals, such as food security and sustainability. Various authors assign democratic qualities and democratising potential to practices and initiatives as diverse as urban farming and agriculture (McIvor & Hale, 2015; Purcell & Tyman, 2015), community-supported agriculture in cities (Patel & MacRae, 2012), urban community gardening (Barron, 2017; Certomà & Tornaghi, 2015; Nettle, 2014), short food supply chains (Aubry & Kebir, 2013), urban food-sharing schemes (Davies et al., 2019), and consumer co-operatives (Knupfer, 2013). McIvor and Hale (2015), for example, highlight the potential of urban agriculture to expand and deepen democracy. Urban agriculture projects involve citizens "in conversations and actions that will shape the future course of their communities" (p. 738); they provide "space in which citizens can collaborate together on projects large and small, and these experiences of collaboration can familiarise citizens with the complexity and plurality that are inherent to democratic forms of governance" (p. 738). In a similar way, community gardeners are seen to cultivate a variety of social and political skills as well as critical perspectives that enable them to participate in promoting food democracy, and also motivate and enable democratic engagement for social justice in other areas and on other scales (Barron, 2017).

References to democratic norms can also be found in the urban food security movement. Representing a relatively recent current in the Global North, food insecurity has become a significant problem, particularly in the wake of the austerity policies that resulted from the 2008 financial crisis (Morgan & Sonnino, 2010), and again in the context of the crisis around the COVID-19 pandemic (Kinsey et al., 2020). The issue of food insecurity in otherwise 'rich' countries creates a paradox that reveals that not the lack of food supply, but rather food access and affordability, are the main problems. Further, it is now framed as a social justice concern around an empowering notion of 'community food security', which highlights the collective and structural dimension of the problem (Alkon & Agyeman, 2011; Gottlieb & Joshi, 2010). The use of a food justice framework bears linkages to wider notions of democracy and citizenship and is, in turn, part of a rights-based approach to food system transformation. Communities of colour, in particular, have made a vitally important contribution here, calling attention to their disproportionately high rates of hunger and diet-related disease, and linking these outcomes to systemic racism, colonialism, and classism in broader social structures, including the food system (Barron, 2017).

Next to the various bottom-up movements, questions of democracy have increasingly been raised in the context of more top-down forms of urban food governance over the past 20 years. This was spurred on by new currents in urban planning that are less concerned with expertise and the substantive content of planning, and more with the deliberative process, aiming to "re-integrate the 'knowing' and 'deliberative' traditions" (Morgan, 2015, p. 1382). Another case in point is that of urban food strategies, which first emerged in the early 2000s in cities like Toronto, Belo Horizonte and London, and then spread to many other places around the world. Urban food strategies contribute to the re-localisation of food production and distribution and are designed primarily around sustainability and community development goals. They are frequently assigned a positive potential to strengthen participation of, and deliberation with, the people and are widely perceived as democracy-enhancing, sustainable, and progressive governance efforts (Cretella, 2019; Sonnino & Spayde, 2014). In the same vein, food policy councils represent a form of institutionalised multi-stakeholder governance that influences urban foodscapes (Blay-Palmer, 2009; Harper et al., 2009; Sieveking, 2019). Their activity can be seen as a form of "civic engagement into shaping public opinion, culture, institutions and policies by communication, lobbying and political activism" (Renting et al., 2012, p. 300). With the aim to improve food governance, food policy councils—many of which emerge in cities—provide "a space for professionals, business, government, and community members to learn together and to galvanise collective action" (Bassarab et al., 2019, p. 32). They typically gather and share information about the structure and functioning of a food system, advise policymakers and political authorities, and develop coordinated strategies to tackle problems in the (urban) food system.

These spotlights on articulations of democratic principles and norms in urban food governance reveal, first of all, the huge practical relevance of urban food democracy. Democracy is an important point of reference for bottom-up initiatives and movements, as well as for top-down urban planning and strategy processes. To explore and consolidate the emergent diversity of meanings of 'urban food democracy' in more conceptual terms, we now turn to the debates on 'food democracy' and 'urban democracy'.

Food democracy

The notion of 'food democracy' describes a fair and transparent food system in which people are in a position to determine what and how they eat. The term was first coined by Tim Lang as a counter-concept against the colonisation of the food system through corporate control and the lack of public participation (Lang, 1999, 2005; Lang & Barling, 2012). Food democracy goes beyond adequacy of food supply and stresses the importance of the wider public good, that is, human and ecological health as well as social justice, in order to make food systems more resilient and sustainable (Booth & Coveney, 2015; Vivero-Pol, 2017). This shall be achieved by empowering the affected citizens and finding common solutions to existing food challenges. Food democracy is used to criticise existing forms of food governance and to question the democratic legitimacy of decisions made within the current institutional framework of representative government characterised by the pronounced influence of food and agricultural corporations. Beyond calling for a democratisation of the existing food system, food democracy also challenges entrenched notions and practices of (non-)democratic governance at large. The food system is seen, as it were, as a place where new ways of democratic decision-making can be developed and experimented with (Booth & Coveney, 2015).

Proponents of food democracy frequently argue for locally based and participatory forms of democratic decision-making around food and agriculture and thereby stress a distinct emancipatory potential. In a widely cited article, Neva Hassanein (2008) defines "collaborative action" and "meaningful participation…in governing and shaping [people's] relationships to food and the food system" (p. 209) as the conceptual core of food democracy. She specifies this core in terms of five key dimensions: (1) collaborating towards food system sustainability, indicating that food democracy requires not only individual participation of people in various places but also their collaboration; (2) becoming knowledgeable about food and the food system, as an act of countering corporate control of food; (3) sharing ideas about the food system with others, pointing to the deliberation of values and visions about the food systems people would like to have; (4) developing efficacy with respect to food and the food system, referring to people's capacity to be able to promote change of the food system; and (5) acquiring an orientation towards the community good, which involves people's food relations moving beyond their individual self-interest to being oriented towards the common good. These dimensions are meant as normative characteristics of food democracy and have served as criteria to empirically assess the democratic quality of various food initiatives that are presently emerging (Hassanein, 2008; Sieveking, 2019).

While food democracy has become an important reference point for scholars and activists in the field alike, the debate has seemingly come to a certain closure over the past years. Its conceptual core comprises a specific notion of empowerment and increased participation of people (Booth & Coveney, 2015; Hassanein, 2003), which is held up against a more liberal market-based and consumerist understanding of food democracy (De Tavernier, 2012; Micheletti & Boström, 2013; Lorenzini, 2019). More recently, however, new perspectives on food democracy have been raised (see Bornemann & Weiland, 2019a). Newer accounts highlight varying loci of food democracy. It can manifest itself in discourses, cognitive representations, concrete practices, or changing institutional structures. It can work through bottom-up initiatives, new networks, and various forms of participatory approaches with which people take their fate into their own hands. The boundaries between private and political, and between society, market and political system can become more fluid, for example with attempts of 'making taste public' that aim at democratising taste and food choices (Voß & Guggenheim, 2019), and forms of market-based political participation that may enlarge the action repertoire of food democracy (Lorenzini, 2019). Yet, food democracy may also be fostered through top-down policymaking processes in which state representatives act as initiators, shapers and implementers of new food policies (Baldy & Kruse, 2019; Griend et al., 2019).

To conceptualise the variety of practices and forms of food democracy in a more systematic way, we have proposed elsewhere a complex notion of food democracy (Bornemann & Weiland, 2019b; see also Behringer & Feindt, 2019). Our starting point is the progressive transformation of contemporary liberal democracies towards an increasingly complex post-liberal formation. In the face of pluralising political demands and expectations, governing arrangements are becoming more and more differentiated, involving all kinds of actors and modes of interaction—a process that has aptly been described by the emergence of 'governance'. In this constellation, however, the established forms and principles of liberal representative democracy are themselves becoming fragile (Sørensen & Torfing, 2005). When numerous organised actors participate in political problem-solving, democratic legitimacy is no longer readily available through adherence to a (liberal) representative mode of legitimacy. Rather, numerous decentred and dispersed governance practices and arrangements are involved in the generation of democratic quality. The resulting democratic quality is, in turn, to be measured against a broader set of criteria of democratic legitimacy that are based on a concept of complex democracy (Schmidt, 2013).

As a result, we argue in favour of a three-dimensional understanding of food democracy (Bornemann & Weiland, 2019b). Firstly, on the input side of the democratic process, food democracy involves increased participation of citizens and stakeholders in food-related governance. Community-supported agriculture is a case in point as it engages people in food production. Secondly, in the throughput dimension, food democracy is concerned with collaborative and deliberative interactions between involved actors. New institutionalised arenas of food governance, for example food policy councils, provide spaces in which the future of food can be debated and actors can develop capacities to collaborate (Bassarab et al., 2019; Sieveking, 2019). Thirdly, the output dimension of food democracy is about the effectiveness of collectively binding decisions that come in the form of new food policies as well as their implementation and resulting impacts. One example is the strengthening of responsibility and citizenship duties towards the food system through government education programmes.

Taken together, we propose a notion of complex food democracy that encompasses the dimensions of input, throughput, and output legitimacy. We argue that such a comprehensive notion of food democracy is necessary to capture and assess both the complexity of the democratic challenge of the contemporary food system, and the diversity of articulations and practices of food governance. In the next section, we look at the spatial dimension of food democracy by drawing on the debate on urban democracy.

Urban democracy

Historically, cities have long been the essential site of democratic practice and a reference point for democratic thought (Gabriel, 2000; Held, 1992). Cities are considered as ideal places for the emergence of democracy, as the spatial concentration of social interactions in cities creates a condensed public space that raises awareness of differences between human interests and ideas. In this way, cities foster a sense of equality and trust—both of which are prerequisites for the rise of democratic attitudes and practices, such as peaceful conflict resolution among equals (Sennett, 1998). As places where people can directly experience the working of government, cities provide a space where democratic participation is demanded and is also possible and meaningful. With the advent of modernity, however, the nation-state began to replace the city-state, and by the end of the nineteenth century, the representative nation-state democracy had become the central democratic reference (Dahl, 1967). In modern political systems organised around the integrative model of the nation-state, the democratic divide between urban and rural areas has disappeared. People living inside and outside cities enjoy the same democratic rights.

In the wake of fundamental economic and social changes, such as the transition from an agrarian to an industrial and post-industrial society, extensive socio-economic globalisation and urbanisation, and the associated shifts in political power and responsibility (e.g. supra-nationalisation and decentralisation), cities and their governance involvement have received increased political and academic attention (Kearns & Paddison, 2000). In addition to their growing economic importance, cities are regarded as important drivers of global environmental and societal change, and play a role as promoters of sustainable transformations (Bulkeley & Betsill, 2003; Castán Broto et al., 2020). Likewise, cities have returned to the centre of attention in democratic theory and practice (Purcell, 2013; Berry et al., 1993; Gabriel, 2000). Cities are spaces where social injustice and marginalisation become manifest, political demands for greater democracy are articulated, and where democratic innovations and forms of democratic experimentation are developed. In the evolving discussion about 'urban democracy', two specific interpretations of the term emerged, each highlighting a specific relationship between the urban and democracy: the urban space as an *object of democratic struggle*, and cities as *embedded sites of democratic politics* (Tawa Lama-Rewal & Zérah, 2011).

The first perspective is based on a diagnosis of democratic decay in the wake of the rampant neoliberalisation since the 1980s, the consequences of which are particularly evident in urban contexts in the form of a shrinking and increasingly fragmented public space, and a spread of isolated private economic spaces dominated by multinational corporations (Purcell, 2008). What holds for anti-democratic tendencies of neoliberalisation more broadly is especially true in urban contexts: Decisions affecting the urban space are increasingly transferred away from parliaments and citizens towards corporations and other private organisations, which follow economic imperatives and often operate detached from the contexts in which they are located (Purcell, 2006). This way, decisions about matters of common concern in the 'post-political city' (Swyngedouw, 2009) take the form of negotiations between non-elected actors, rather than being based on political dispute (Sassen, 2008).

With the aim of counteracting these post-democratic tendencies, urban democracy refers to the re-localisation of decisions affecting the urban space (Purcell, 2008). Propelled by the rise of emancipatory values, and incentivised by increasingly 'fluid' governance configurations, demands for participation and new forms of political activism have been rising. New political subjects emerging in urban contexts advance their claims by deploying a broad array of means, some of which are unconventional and radically different from the classic institutionalised forms of participation (Micheletti & McFarland, 2015). The rise of participation demands and new forms of activism is paralleled by a growing landscape of innovative, local participation formats that are supposed to deepen democracy by involving urban dwellers in policymaking and governance. A large number of these initiatives was designed and implemented with the assumption that a re-localisation of decision-making will, in turn, democratise the urban space, and result in greater social justice and sustainability (Purcell, 2006, p. 1924). They include innovations such as participatory budgeting or deliberative voting, which have been tested and institutionalised in urban contexts (Fung, 2006; Pateman, 2012; Sintomer et al., 2012). From a theoretical point of view, the new forms of urban activism and democratic innovations are based on a 'participatory' model of democracy associated with the work of authors like Carole

Pateman (1970) and Benjamin Barber (2003), who argue that people realise their full political and human potential only by participating actively and directly in political decisions. They stress the need for face-to-face interaction, argumentation and negotiation, which allows people to become (urban) citizens. Therefore, the city level is seen as the most promising context for participatory democracy.

Accordingly, urban democracy rests on the following assumption: the more localised government institutions become, the more democratic they are—which is why decentralisation of authority is said to lead automatically to more democracy. The 'local' is identified with 'the good' and therefore thought to be preferable over non-local scales (Purcell, 2006, p. 1924). Critics like Mark Purcell, however, challenge this assumption, arguing that approaches to participatory urban democracy tend to fall into the so-called 'local trap'. He finds that participation opportunities on the ground can lead to a variety of outcomes, only some of which are good (Purcell, 2006, p. 1927; see also Marvin & Guy, 1997). Accordingly, participation in urban governance can lead to a more or less democratic city. Moreover, localisation and participation may well be part of the neoliberal agenda if, for example, they promote the transfer of tasks from the state to local communities, which can lead to an overburdening of the respective municipalities (Purcell, 2006, p. 1926).

This criticism is taken up by the second perspective on urban democracy that promotes a more embedded and contextual understanding of the concept. Drawing on Henri Lefebvre's "Right to the City", Purcell stresses the possibility of generalising this concept in the direction of a right to inhabit, which is not limited to the city as such (Purcell, 2008, p. 178). This shift brings into focus how life in cities is deeply entangled with other places and levels in a multi-level governance system: the rural and regional, the national and global. Urban areas are central nodes in the global streams of goods, people and information, and in this respect powerful shapers of social relations and processes of socio-economic change, even beyond the boundaries of cities (Gabriel, 2000; Gleeson & Low, 2000). Therefore, urban affairs need to be seen as inevitably embedded in trans-local and global affairs, a fact expressed in terms such as 'glocalisation' (Roudometof, 2016). As a consequence, urban governance needs to be seen as operating in complex systems of multi-level governance (Bulkeley & Betsill, 2003). Urban governance is confronted with the task of having to tackle problems that originate from, or are shaped by, other levels of governance. This holds true for the democratic quality of urban governance as well.

The understanding of urban governance as embedded in complex multi-level structures suggests a contextual analysis and assessment of the democratic quality of urban governance. On the one hand, this includes consideration of the (non-)democratic side-effects of urban democracy upon the governance arrangements of other levels. For example, expanded opportunities for participation in urban governance may affect the legitimacy of democratic decisions at the national level if these are perceived as insufficient in the face of a developed participatory urban democracy. On the other hand, it includes acknowledging that the democratic legitimacy of urban governance arrangements is also affected by democratic practices at other levels. Haus and Heinelt (2005), for example, argue that urban democracy is always to be seen as an interplay between urban leadership and community involvement, both of which are shaped not only by governance at the city level, but also by global and national governance contexts (see also Carmichael, 2004).

Urban food democracy

The two concepts underlying a notion of urban food democracy—food democracy and urban democracy—rest on similar problem diagnoses of democratic decay and make similar propositions for democratic therapy. According to both, democratic governance is undermined by dominant economic (from a food democracy perspective) or neoliberal (from an urban democracy perspective) ideas and practices, and needs to be re-built through innovative practices that bring the people back into governance at the urban level. Moreover, both concepts have prompted critical reflections and extensions: The concept of food democracy is to include dimensions of complex democratic legitimation, while an extended concept of urban democracy calls for the embedding of democratic urban governance practices in multi-level governance arrangements.

Drawing on these strands, we see two understandings of urban food democracy—a narrow and an expanded one—taking shape (see Table 7.1). *Urban food democracy in the narrow sense* refers to the opportunities and capabilities of urban residents to participate in shaping the urban food system. This perspective emphasises the extent and quality of participation in the production, distribution, and consumption of food in bounded urban areas. Participation in urban agriculture practices, such as food-sharing networks or food councils, are current cases in point. In this understanding, improving the democratic quality of urban food governance depends directly on increasing opportunities for, and improving the quality of, participation in these practices (Hassanein, 2008).

An *expanded understanding of urban food democracy* combines a notion of complex democracy with an understanding of urban food governance as embedded in multi-level governance contexts. Firstly, an expanded understanding of urban food democracy builds on the three-dimensional concept of complex democracy. Accordingly, urban food democracy goes beyond the focus on the extent and quality of people's participation. Next to participatory practices that potentially strengthen democratic input legitimation, the expanded understanding of urban food democracy builds on other practices that are related to democratic throughput and output legitimation. In terms of throughput legitimation, the deliberative quality of urban food governance is at stake. This calls for decision-making processes that live up to democratic norms, such as transparency, accountability, inclusiveness, openness, and political deliberation. Output legitimation, in turn, refers to the problem-solving capacities of urban food governance

Table 7.1 Overview of concepts

	Food democracy	*Urban democracy*	*Urban food democracy*
Narrow perspective	Participation of people in (decisions related to) food production, distribution and consumption (at the local level)	Participation of urban dwellers in shaping the urban space	Participation of urban dwellers in the governance of urban food systems
Expanded perspective	Democratic input (participation), throughput (deliberation), and output (effectiveness) legitimation of (local) food practices	Democratic governance in urban spaces embedded in a multi-level governance context	Democratic input (participation), throughput (deliberation), and output (effectiveness) legitimation of urban food governance practices within a multi-level governance system

Source: Authors' compilation.

arrangements, for example in terms of their ability to bring about policies that are socially just and sustainable.

Secondly, an expanded understanding of urban food democracy builds on the notion that urban food systems, and likewise urban food governance, are situated in complex food chains and governance arrangements that go beyond the urban level. Consequently, any analysis of urban food democracy needs to consider the embedding of urban food (governance) practices in multi-level governance: how urban food governance affects, and is in turn affected by, regional, national, global, and transnational governance arrangements, and how these interactions can be assessed in democratic terms. This includes looking at the (un)democratic consequences of urban food governance for governance arrangements at various levels and in different geographic regions. The assessment of participatory practices that engage people in urban food governance needs to consider, for example, how these practices interrelate with and affect (un) democratic governance systems beyond the urban space. Strengthening urban participation processes and attempts to involve more people in urban food governance may stabilise or even exacerbate existing asymmetric power relations, rather than challenging and overcoming them (see Hinrichs, 2003). Thus, expanding opportunities for participation may amplify the voices of the already informed and capable, educated urban middle class, resulting in food policies that favour precisely this class and the spaces it inhabits, while marginalised groups in peripheral urban and rural areas continue to be muted and disempowered. As a result, this can lead to 'fragmented localism', a decline in cohesion between different urban areas and between urban and rural areas. Democracy-building participation must therefore be designed to account for such side-effects from the outset and incorporate them into the design of appropriate governance arrangements, for example by introducing rules of equal representation, strong incentives for participation, and expanding the space of consideration to include those potentially affected by urban food governance.

From the perspective of a broader understanding of food democracy, the potential for democratic output legitimation of a particular urban food practice must also be assessed, considering the implications of that practice beyond the urban space. Thus, the embeddedness of urban food governance in the multi-level system may constrain or enhance its democratic quality. A limiting effect on the output legitimation of urban decisions could occur if (democratic) decisions at a higher level interfere with the effectiveness of problem-solving at the urban level (Haus & Heinelt, 2005). This is the case, for example, when urban agricultural projects are constrained by agricultural or other regulations of national governments. An example of a democracy-enhancing effect emanating from the higher level is when transnational urban networks lead to the empowerment of grassroots groups in their respective urban food governance environments.

The perspective of an embedded multi-level system also makes clear that many democratic decisions affecting the food system have consequences not only for urban areas, but beyond that for rural areas as well. Hence, the democratisation of urban food systems also changes the conditions for food governance in rural areas. In an expanded understanding of urban food democracy, these consequences must be included in the evaluation of democratic practice. Taking this as a starting point for viewing the city as a strategic node for the democratisation of the food system, opens up a broader understanding of urban food democracy. It no longer refers only to democratic decision-making related to the urban food landscape, but also to all kinds of food-related decisions that are made in urban spaces but whose impacts go beyond them. This way, urban food democracy becomes a concept of democratising the food system, not only in, but also *through* urban governance.

Future perspectives

Beginning with a brief recapitulation of the democratic implications of urban food governance, we examined the two established debates about 'food democracy' and 'urban democracy' and synthesised them into both a narrow and a broad understanding of 'urban food democracy'. As a narrow concept, urban food democracy refers to practices of enabling participation in the design and governance of urban food systems. From this perspective, urban food practices, such as urban gardening and food sharing, can be interpreted as drivers of democratisation insofar as they represent loci of increased participation. In a critically expanded perspective, the concept refers to the democratic quality of all food decisions in cities considered as a part of complex multi-level systems. This perspective is based on the insight that food practices in urban areas have spillover effects on other levels of a multi-level governance system. From this perspective, the democratisation of urban food becomes a crucial lever for democratising food systems as a whole.

These understandings present challenges and opportunities for designing food governance in practice as well as for academic research on the topic. Regarding practice, the clarification of concepts opens up opportunities for positioning, critical reflection and, if necessary, expansion of the standpoints and strategies of food actors. Which understanding of urban food democracy is appropriate under which conditions, and which strategies are suitable? Which complementarities and tensions exist between different approaches? How can different urban food initiatives connect with regard to their democratisation efforts? What are effective means of inducing change in the food system?

Future research can support this by elaborating on the concepts and by empirically validating and refining them. In addition, research could identify and theoretically reflect on possible tensions between urban democracy and food democracy. For example, it is conceivable that a democratisation of the urban space undermines the conditions for urban food provision, such as in cases when the democratic process brings forth priorities other than food provision. Conversely, the adoption of food practices might close down the space for urban affairs not related to food, and thus negatively affect other democratic concerns and practices in the urban sphere. More research is also needed to show the relative contribution of democratisation of urban food governance in relation to other strategies of global democratisation—as cities are only one possible space for addressing the democratic deficits of the global food system. Finally, the question remains whether democratisation of urban food systems is also suitable for triggering sustainability-oriented transformations within cities and beyond.

References

Alkon, A. H., & Agyeman, J. (Eds.). (2011). *Cultivating Food Justice. Race, Class, and Sustainability*. The MIT Press.

Aubry, C., & Kebir, L. (2013). Shortening Food Supply Chains: A Means for Maintaining Agriculture Close to Urban Areas? The Case of the French Metropolitan Area of Paris. *Food Policy*, *41*, 85–93. https://doi.org/10.1016/j.foodpol.2013.04.006

Baldy, J., & Kruse, S. (2019). Food Democracy from the Top Down? State-Driven Participation Processes for Local Food System Transformations towards Sustainability. *Politics and Governance*, 7(4), 68–80. https://doi.org/10.17645/pag.v7i4.2089

Barber, B. (2003). *Strong Democracy: Participatory Politics for a New Age*. University of California Press.

Barron, J. (2017). Community Gardening: Cultivating Subjectivities, Space, and Justice. *Local Environment*, *22*(9), 1142–1158. https://doi.org/10.1080/13549839.2016.1169518

Bassarab, K., Clark, J. K., Santo, R., & Palmer, A. (2019). Finding Our Way to Food Democracy: Lessons from US Food Policy Council Governance. *Politics and Governance*, 7(4), 32–47. https://doi.org/10.17645/pag.v7i4.2092

Behringer, J., & Feindt, P. H. (2019). How Shall We Judge Agri-Food Governance? Legitimacy Constructions in Food Democracy and Co-Regulation Discourses. *Politics and Governance*, 7(4), 119–130. https://doi.org/10.17645/pag.v7i4.2087

Berry, J. M., Portney, K. E., & Thomson, K. (1993). *The Rebirth of Urban Democracy*. Brookings Institution.

Blay-Palmer, A. (2009). The Canadian Pioneer: The Genesis of Urban Food Policy in Toronto. *International Planning Studies, 14*(4), 401–416. https://doi.org/10.1080/13563471003642837

Booth, S., & Coveney, J. (2015). *Food Democracy*. Springer.

Bornemann, B., & Weiland, S. (2019a). Editorial: New Perspectives on Food Democracy. *Politics and Governance*, 7(4), 1–7. https://doi.org/10.17645/pag.v7i4.2570

Bornemann, B., & Weiland, S. (2019b). Empowering People—Democratising the Food System? Exploring the Democratic Potential of Food-Related Empowerment Forms. *Politics and Governance*, 7(4), 105–118. https://doi.org/10.17645/pag.v7i4.2190

Bulkeley, H., & Betsill, M. M. (2003). *Cities and Climate Change: Urban Sustainability and Global Environmental Governance*. Routledge.

Carlson, J., & Chappell, M. J. (2015). *Deepening Food Democracy. The Tools to Create a Sustainable, Food Secure and Food Sovereign Future Are Already Here—Deep Democratic Approaches Can Show Us How*. Institute for Agriculture and Trade Policy.

Carmichael, L. (2005). Cities in the Multi-level Governance of the European Union. In M. Haus, H. Heinelt, & M. Stewart (Eds.), *Urban Governance and Democracy: Leadership and Community Involvement* (pp. 129–148). Routledge.

Castán Broto, V., Robin, E., & While, A. (Eds.). (2020). *Climate Urbanism: Towards a Critical Research Agenda*. Palgrave Macmillan.

Certomà, C., & Tornaghi, C. (2015). Political Gardening. Transforming Cities and Political Agency. *Local Environment, 20*(10), 1123–1131. https://doi.org/10.1080/13549839.2015.1053724

Cretella, A. (2019). *Between Promise and Practice: Exploring the Politics of Urban Food Strategies in European Cities*. Doctoral dissertation, University of Amsterdam. https://hdl.handle.net/11245.1/d04d27a0-af62-46e2-a291-cd8468805822

Dahl, R. A. (1967). The City in the Future of Democracy. *American Political Science Review, 61*(4), 953–970. https://doi.org/10.2307/1953398

Davies, A. R., Cretella, A., & Franck, V. (2019). Food Sharing Initiatives and Food Democracy: Practice and Policy in Three European Cities. *Politics and Governance*, 7(4), 8–20. https://doi.org/10.17645/pag.v7i4.2090

De Tavernier, J. (2012). Food Citizenship: Is There a Duty for Responsible Consumption? *Journal of Agricultural and Environmental Ethics, 25*(6), 895–907. https://doi.org/10.1007/s10806-011-9366-7

Duncan, J. (2017). *Global Food Security Governance: Civil Society Engagement in the Reformed Committee on World Food Security*. Routledge.

Fouilleux, E., Bricas, N., & Alpha, A. (2017). 'Feeding 9 Billion People': Global Food Security Debates and the Productionist Trap. *Journal of European Public Policy, 24*(11), 1658–1677. https://doi.org/10.1080/13501763.2017.1334084

Fung, A. (2006). *Empowered Participation: Reinventing Urban Democracy*. Princeton University Press.

Gabriel, O. W. (2000). Introduction. In O. W. Gabriel, V. Hoffmann-Martinot, & H. V. Savitch (Eds.), *Urban Democracy* (pp. 9–27). VS Verlag für Sozialwissenschaften.

Gleeson, B., & Low, N. (2000). Cities as Consumers of the World's Environment. In N. Low, B. Gleeson, I. Elander, & R. Lidskog (Eds.), *Consuming Cities: The Urban Environment in the Global Economy after the Rio Declaration* (pp. 1–30). Taylor & Francis.

Gottlieb, R., & Joshi, A. (2010). *Food Justice*. MIT Press.

Griend, J. van de, Duncan, J., & Wiskerke, J. S. C. (2019). How Civil Servants Frame Participation: Balancing Municipal Responsibility with Citizen Initiative in Ede's Food Policy. *Politics and Governance*, 7(4), 59–67. https://doi.org/10.17645/pag.v7i4.2078

Harper, A., Shattuck, A., Holt-Giménez, E., Alkon, A., & Lambrick, F. (2009). *Food Policy Councils: Lessons Learned*. Food First/Institute for Food and Development Policy.

Hassanein, N. (2003). Practicing Food Democracy: A Pragmatic Politics of Transformation. *Journal of Rural Studies, 19*(1), 77–86. https://doi.org/10.1016/S0743-0167(02)00041-4

Hassanein, N. (2008). Locating Food Democracy: Theoretical and Practical Ingredients. *Journal of Hunger & Environmental Nutrition, 3*(2–3), 286–308. https://doi.org/10.1080/19320240802244215

Haus, M., & Heinelt, H. (2005). How to Achieve Governability at the Local Level? Theoretical and Conceptual Considerations on a Complementarity of Urban Leadership and Community Involvement. In M. Haus, H. Heinelt, & M. Stewart (Eds.), *Urban Governance and Democracy: Leadership and Community Involvement* (pp. 12–39). Routledge.

Haysom, G. (2015). Food and the City: Urban Scale Food System Governance. *Urban Forum, 26*(3), 263–281. https://doi.org/10.1007/s12132-015-9255-7

Held, D. (1992). Democracy: From City-States to a Cosmopolitan Order? *Political Studies, 40*(s1), 10–39. https://doi.org/10.1111/j.1467-9248.1992.tb01810.x

Hinrichs, C. (2003). The Practice and Politics of Food System Localization. *Journal of Rural Studies, 19*(1), 33–45. https://doi.org/10.1016/S0743-0167(02)00040-2

Jackson, P., Rivera Ferre, M. G., Candel, J., Davies, A., Derani, C., de Vries, H., Dragović-Uzelac, V., Hoel, A. H., Holm, L., Mathijs, E., Morone, P., Penker, M., Śpiewak, R., Termeer, K., & Thøgersen, J. (2021). Food as a Commodity, Human Right or Common Good. *Nature Food, 2*(3), 132–134. https://doi.org/10.1038/s43016-021-00245-5

Kearns, A., & Paddison, R. (2000). New Challenges for Urban Governance. Urban Studies, 37(5–6), 845–850. https://doi.org/10.1080/00420980050011118

Kinsey, E. W., Kinsey, D., & Rundle, A. G. (2020). COVID-19 and Food Insecurity: An Uneven Patchwork of Responses. *Journal of Urban Health: Bulletin of the New York Academy of Medicine, 97*, 332–335. https://doi.org/10.1007/s11524-020-00455-5

Knupfer, A. M. (2013). *Food Co-Ops in America. Communities, Consumption, and Economic Democracy.* Cornell University Press.

Lang, T. (1999). Food Policy for the 21st Century: Can It Be Both Radical and Reasonable? In M. Koc, R. MacRae, L. J. A. Mougeot, & J. Welsh (Eds.), *For Hunger-Proof Cities: Sustainable Urban Food Systems* (pp. 216–224). International Development Research Centre.

Lang, T. (2005). Food Control or Food Democracy? Re-engaging Nutrition with Society and the Environment. *Public Health Nutrition, 8*(6A), 730–737. https://doi.org/10.1079/PHN2005772

Lang, T., & Barling, D. (2012). Food Security and Food Sustainability: Reformulating the Debate. *The Geographical Journal, 178*(4), 313–326. https://doi.org/10.1111/j.1475-4959.2012.00480.x

Lang, T., & Heasman, M. (2004). *Food Wars. The Global Battle for Mouths, Minds, and Markets*. Earthscan.

Lorenzini, J. (2019). Food Activism and Citizens' Democratic Engagements: What Can We Learn from Market-Based Political Participation? *Politics and Governance*, 7(4), 131–141. https://doi.org/10.17645/pag.v7i4.2072

Marvin, S., & Guy, S. (1997). Creating Myths rather than Sustainability: The Transition Fallacies of the New Localism. *Local Environment, 2*(3), 311–318. https://doi.org/10.1080/13549839708725536

McIvor, D. W., & Hale, J. (2015). Urban Agriculture and the Prospects for Deep Democracy. *Agriculture and Human Values, 32*(4), 727–741. https://doi.org/10.1007/s10460-015-9588-9

Micheletti, M., & Boström, M. (2013). Political Consumerism: Consumer Choice, Information, and Labeling. In P. B. Thompson & D. M. Kaplan (Eds.), *Encyclopedia of Food and Agricultural Ethics* (pp. 1–8). Springer. https://doi.org/10.1007/978-94-007-6167-4_244-4

Micheletti, M., & McFarland, A. S. (2015). *Creative Participation: Responsibility-taking in the Political World.* Routledge.

Morgan, K. (2015). Nourishing the City: The Rise of the Urban Food Question in the Global North. *Urban Studies, 52*(8), 1379–1394. https://doi.org/10.1177/0042098014534902

Morgan, K., & Sonnino, R. (2010). The Urban Foodscape: World Cities and the New Food Equation. *Cambridge Journal of Regions, Economy and Society, 3*(2), 209–224. https://doi.org/10.1093/cjres/rsq007

Nettle, C. (2014). *Community Gardening as Social Action*. Ashgate.

Patel, R. (2009). Food Sovereignty. *The Journal of Peasant Studies, 36*(3), 663–706. https://doi.org/10.1080/03066150903143079

Patel, S., & MacRae, R. (2012). Community Supported Agriculture in the City: The Case of Toronto. *Journal of Agriculture, Food Systems, and Community Development, 2*(4), 85–100. https://doi.org/10.5304/jafscd.2012.024.003

Pateman, C. (1970). *Participation and Democratic Theory*. Cambridge University Press.

Pateman, C. (2012). APSA Presidential Address: Participatory Democracy Revisited. *Perspectives on Politics, 10*(1), 7–19.

Purcell, M. (2006). Urban Democracy and the Local Trap. *Urban Studies, 43*(11), 1921–1941. https://doi.org/10.1080/00420980600897826

Purcell, M. (2013). The Right to the City: The Struggle for Democracy in the Urban Public Realm. *Policy & Politics, 41*(3), 311–327. https://doi.org/10.1332/030557312X655639

Purcell, M., & Tyman, S. K. (2015). Cultivating Food as a Right to the City. *Local Environment, 20*(10), 1132–1147. https://doi.org/10.1080/13549839.2014.903236

Purcell, M. H. (2008). *Recapturing Democracy: Neoliberalization and the Struggle for Alternative Urban Futures*. Routledge.

Renting, H., Schermer, M., & Rossi, A. (2012). Building Food Democracy: Exploring Civic Food Networks and Newly Emerging Forms of Food Citizenship. *International Journal of Sociology of Agriculture and Food, 19*(3), 289–307.

Roudometof, V. (2016). *Glocalization: A Critical Introduction*. Routledge.

Sassen, S. (2008). The Global City. In D. Nugent & J. Vincent (Eds.), *A Companion to the Anthropology of Politics* (pp. 168–178). Wiley.

Schmidt, V. A. (2013). Democracy and Legitimacy in the European Union Revisited: Input, Output and 'Throughput'. *Political Studies, 61*(1), 2–22. https://doi.org/10.1111/j.1467-9248.2012.00962.x

Sennett, R. (1998). *The Spaces of Democracy*. The University of Michigan, College of Architecture + Urban Planning.

Sieveking, A. (2019). Food Policy Councils as Loci for Practising Food Democracy? Insights from the Case of Oldenburg, Germany. *Politics and Governance*, 7(4), 48–58. https://doi.org/10.17645/pag.v7i4.2081

Sintomer, Y., Herzberg, C., & Röcke, A. (2012). Transnational Models of Citizen Participation: The Case of Participatory Budgeting. *Sociologias, 14*(30), 70–116.

Sonnino, R., & Spayde, J. (2014). The 'New Frontier'? Urban Strategies for Food Security and Sustainability. In T. Marsden & A. Morley (Eds.), *Sustainable Food Systems: Building a New Paradigm* (pp. 186–205). Routledge. https://doi.org/10.4324/9780203083499

Sørensen, E., & Torfing, J. (2005). Network Governance and Post-Liberal Democracy. *Administrative Theory & Praxis, 27*(2), 197–237. https://doi.org/10.1080/10841806.2005.11029489

Swyngedouw, E. (2009). The Antinomies of the Postpolitical City: In Search of a Democratic Politics of Environmental Production. *International Journal of Urban and Regional Research, 33*(3), 601–620. https://doi.org/10.1111/j.1468-2427.2009.00859.x

Tawa Lama-Rewal, S., & Zérah, M.-H. (2011). Introduction. Urban Democracy: A South Asian Perspective. *South Asia Multidisciplinary Academic Journal, 5*, Article 5. https://doi.org/10.4000/samaj.3188

Thornton, A. (Ed.). (2020). *Urban Food Democracy and Governance in North and South*. Springer International Publishing. https://doi.org/10.1007/978-3-030-17187-2

Vivero-Pol, J. (2017). Food as Commons or Commodity? Exploring the Links between Normative Valuations and Agency in Food Transition. *Sustainability, 9*(3), 442. https://doi.org/10.3390/su9030442

Voß, J.-P., & Guggenheim, M. (2019). Making Taste Public: Industrialized Orders of Sensing and the Democratic Potential of Experimental Eating. *Politics and Governance*, 7(4), 224–236. https://doi.org/10.17645/pag.v7i4.2215

8

GOVERNING AND COMMONING ACTIVITIES AROUND URBAN FOOD COMMONS

Oona Morrow

Introduction

Calls for governing food and its myriad components (e.g. soil, seeds, land, water, knowledge, culinary traditions, meals, food security, nutrition and health, and organic waste) as a commons rather than primarily as a commodity have reverberated far and wide among agri-food scholars, activists, and practitioners (Vivero Pol 2017; Vivero Pol et al. 2018). Commoning food is necessary for realizing the "right to food." Recent advice by the European Union Chief Scientific advisors echoes this sentiment and makes explicit that "moving from food as a commodity to food as more of a common good" (European Commission 2020, SAPEA 2020, Jackson et al. 2021) is necessary for realizing more just and sustainable food systems. Food commons include food and all the resources needed to grow and eat it, food resources that which are jointly owned, stewarded, and/or governed by their users (Vivero Pol 2017, Rundgren 2016, Dalla Costa 2007). Urban spaces are routinely transformed into food commons through practices of commoning – in the collective reclamation of private and public property and the negotiation over shared use, care, and responsibility that this necessitates (Morrow and Martin 2019, Eizenberg 2012). However, the possibilities and challenges of governing food as a commons in cities remain underexplored. This is a significant research lacuna when we consider the diversity of food commons that are being created, cared for, and contested in cities across the world. Examples include the collection of wild edibles in urban parks and forests (Poe et al. 2013), informal gardens and fruit orchards on public and private property (Morrow and Martin 2019), community gardens and food forests, community fridges and kitchens (Chies 2017, Morrow 2018), and even whole towns like Todmorden in the UK, which has been given over to open-access food growing and harvesting (Paull 2013).

For the purpose of this chapter, I define urban food governance as governance practices (processes, decisions, policies, etc.) that shape urban foodscapes and the people and places they are interdependent with. Urban food governance is often scattered across multiple geographic scales (in national and international food policies) and multiple municipal departments and civil society organizations. Food councils and urban food strategies have emerged in an

DOI: 10.4324/9781003055907-10

effort to further consolidate and integrate urban food governance (Ilieva 2017, Candel & Pereira 2017, Gupta et al. 2018, Hoffman et al. 2019). Governance decisions may be top down, bottom up, collective, participatory, transparent, or none of the above. However they are made, decisions about land use and zoning, public space and infrastructure, public health and nutrition, education and school meals, food safety, housing and urban development, and municipal budgets all affect how equitable, inclusive, or durable food commons and their infrastructures are.

Urban food governance occurs within and around urban food commons through conflicts and negotiations over shared access, use, responsibility, and care. These negotiations can happen in informal ways, with a group of neighbors and eaters who decide to create a community garden or a community fridge, or in more formalized ways together with property owners (including the city) and public authorities who share a stake in governing these sites. Through these negotiations, commoners develop institutions and codes of conduct to help them equitably share resources, benefits, and responsibilities, and decide together what to grow, eat, or share, and who to share it with (Morrow 2018, Morrow & Martin 2019). These codes of conduct determine how inclusive or accessible a commons is and how widely the benefits are shared.

The governance of commons has long been theorized through the lens of polycentric governance, to explore how self-organized communities govern shared resources within multi-scalar governance systems (Ostrom 1999). This approach has been extended to urban governance, where legal scholars have explored how urban polycentric governance can foster commons-based urban policies though collaborative urban co-governance (Iaione 2016, Foster and Iaione 2016). Such approaches can be used to encourage the creation of urban food commons, through a variety of administrative incentives that lower barriers, reduce administrative paperwork, and encourage bottom-up citizen's initiatives. This approach has been piloted in Bologna, where the landmark "Bologna Regulation for the Care and Regeneration of Urban Commons" was passed in 2014, and a handful of municipal coalitions in Europe have embraced commoning as a mode of urban governance (Bauwens & Niaros 2017). Formalized urban food governance processes can play a critical role in the flourishing or enclosure of urban food commons.

In most cities, the governance of urban food commons takes place in a more ad hoc and informal way. Tornaghi captures this dynamic well when she writes,

> the ability of local and regional institutions to respond to these new demands [is] limited and constrained by planning traditions that have not been permeable to emerging urban cultures and their needs, failing to create flexible or more adaptable public spaces which reflect the fluidity of society. As a result, short term satisfaction of these needs is found in the possibilities left open by 'loose spaces' (Franck and Stevens, 2006) or ad-hoc negotiations (such as for the concession of land) between grassroots groups and various local institutions (councils, local businesses or organisations) but none of these go beyond the status of 'emergency' or residual practices.
>
> *2012: 350*

This leads to a number of challenges for urban food commons, which often lack a permanent or protected status, and for commoners who must dedicate considerable energy to overcoming legal and political obstacles to gaining access to urban land, and then resisting displacement (Petrescu et al. 2021, Schmelzkopf 2002, Smith & Kurtz 2003, Staeheli et al. 2002). For municipalities, the governance of urban food commons often takes the form of tolerance, turning a blind eye, or permitting temporary use, rather than a strategic plan informed by justice and equity concerns. This lack of attention to governance reproduces the reality that urban (food) commons are challenging to govern.

Commons scholars have done a great deal to demystify the governance of commons, and refute the neoclassical economics claim that resources are "ungovernable" outside of markets and the rules of private property. One starting point is the institutional analysis and development (IAD) framework (McGinnis 2011) and commons typology which Ostrom (1999) uses to categorize how different types of goods relate to their biophysical and spatial qualities; what she refers to as "subtractability of use" and "rivalry" (the difficulty of excluding beneficiaries). These terms are meant to capture the shareability of different types of resources.

Within this typology, common pool resources (e.g. grazing lands, fisheries) are characterized as both highly subtractable and difficult to exclude others from. Next to this, public goods (e.g. peace, knowledge) are described in more abundant terms, since their quality will not deteriorate from use and in fact it may even improve. Food is described as a private good that is subtractable (once consumed it can no longer be shared) and easy to exclude others from (so long as it remains a commodity that is regulated by the market and the laws of private property). The categorization of food as a private good does not acknowledge the diverse ways of provisioning and sharing food or the ethical and political implications of excluding people from the right to food by governing it as a commodified private good.

In response to the limitations of institutional approaches to theorizing commons, there has been a broad shift from commons as noun to commoning as verb (Bresnihan 2015, Bollier 2015) to examine the social practices and patterns of commoning (Bollier & Helfrich 2015) and move beyond the scarcity mindset of their presumed boundedness (Velicu & Garcia Lopez 2018). This has expanded the scholarly and political imaginary to include imperfect and impure commons, as well as emergent commons in the making. With this more expansive view of commons and commoning, scholars have removed food from the category of 'private good' and reframed it as a commons (Vivero Pol 2013). A commoning lens is useful for understanding the governance of food as a commons because of its attention to social practices that make commons – the everyday labors, conflicts, care, and negotiations. This lens is also vital if we wish to create more commons and resist the further privatization of food. Jose Vivero Pol (2017) discusses food as a tradable commodity that encompasses only one dimension of the manifold ways that people relate to, depend upon, value, and share food. As Kennedy writes, "A food commons can involve the sharing of the food itself and the property where it is cultivated, but can also extend to a 'culinary commons' of knowledge and practices that inform how food is traditionally cultivated, prepared and consumed across cultural contexts" (2020: 208). Taking a cultural and systemic perspective on food makes it impossible to sustain the claim that food is primarily encountered and governed as a commodity. Even the most commodified foods depend on a wealth of biophysical, cultural, and knowledge commons to be produced, exchanged, and consumed.

The perspective of commons as verb has informed a wealth of urban commons research, on the city as commons (Ramos 2016, Foster & Iaione 2016), housing (Huron 2015), land trusts (Krinsky & Segal 2019), and social and cultural spaces (Bresnihan & Byrne 2015) such as community gardens (Eizenberg 2012). Geographers and legal scholars have brought our attention to the unique challenges of creating and protecting commons in the often heavily financialized spaces of the city, and the related need to mobilize considerable resources and political will to claim and protect the commons. They also show that urban commons are highly unstable; their qualities are shaped by the dense and changing spatial and temporal rhythms of the city, and the needs and concerns of diverse stakeholders and communities of users (Foster 2011, Huron 2015). These shifting qualities and fuzzy boundaries can make urban commons difficult to identify, compared with more institutionalized commons studied by Ostrom which have clearly defined boundaries, material properties, and communities of users. Urban commons and commoners are perhaps most visible during moments of conflict or enclosure (Blomley 2008). I situate the concept of urban food commons at the intersection of urban commons and food commons scholarship, and use it to refer to food, as well as food resources (e.g. knowledge, seeds, soils, land, compost), that are jointly created, cared for, and enjoyed in the city. This is not to overlook the diversity of rural and peri-urban food commons (e.g. communal farm lands, forests, and fisheries) that urban residents depend on. However, in this chapter I focus on urban food commons that are located within the city, because these are the spaces that cities and citizens have the most power to govern, grow, and care for.

Urban food commons vary in their form and governance, and contain multiple property types, including semi-private club goods, community goods, and open-access public goods. However, like all commons, the governance of urban food commons cannot be fully explained by their material properties or legal status. To further complicate matters, urban food commons are nested in the multi-scalar governance of urban space, city-regional food systems, intellectual property, public health, and food safety. This can reveal considerable contradictions in how food is governed (see Morrow 2018). In many cities, food is governed as both a privately owned and traded commodity and a public good that should be healthy, safe, and accessible to everyone. This public/private or state/market binary is insufficient for governing the diverse ways in which people provision food. It can also stand in the way of achieving more just and sustainable food systems. Examining urban food governance through the lens of commons illuminates emergent and potential urban food commons as sites of governance, which are simultaneously shaped by more formalized food governance processes occurring at multiple geographic scales. These more formalized sites of urban food governance can have significant implications for commoning activities in cities.

Formal urban food governance often lags behind the everyday and informal food governance activities of residents. Furthermore, formal urban food governance spaces of decision-making, policymaking, and legislation often remain inaccessible to urban food commoners. Participating in these spaces requires considerable time (for attending meetings or court hearings), financial resources (for advocacy and legal expertise), and knowledge (about law, bureaucracy, land use, urban planning, and local politics). The challenges that commoners face in having their activities tolerated, recognized, or legalized can reveal considerable contradictions and blind spots in urban food governance strategies and policies. Such as inequalities or tensions between stakeholders, including civil society organizations, business interests, developers, public authorities, land managers, food policy councils and officers, elected officials, and civil servants. The tensions, exclusions, and power inequalities that Coulson and Sonnino (2019) observe in 'participatory' food governance arrangements suggests that much could be gained by placing commons and commoning at the heart of urban food governance, to better equip scholars, activists, and policymakers to "critically examine the exclusionary practices, power dynamics and contestations that are embedded in these new institutional configurations" (Coulson & Sonnino 2019: 171).

To date, urban food commons have been largely neglected by urban food governance scholarship and policymaking. There are, of course, exceptions, including the citizen-led Food Council Metropoolregio Amsterdam, which has adopted *Voedselcommons* (food commons) as one of their project areas. In the remainder of this chapter, I explore how urban food governance takes place in and around the urban food commons of New York City's community gardens. Through this case study I explore how urban food commons are created, cared for, and contested at the intersection of grassroots self-governance and multi-scalar urban food governance practices.

Commoning Land through Community Gardening

Scholarship on the urban commons, whether it is housing, community gardens, or cultural spaces, must grapple with the question of urban land (Huron 2015, Bresnihan & Byrne 2015). In cities, most lands are either public (e.g. parks, city-owned vacant lots, schools, libraries, sidewalks) or private (e.g. housing, businesses, vacant lots awaiting development). While both public and private lands can be sites of commoning, public lands may (in theory) be more hospitable to commoning activities, because of the responsibility that the landowner (e.g. the city, or a public authority) has to serve the public interest. The commodification, speculation, and financialization of urban land has led to a scarcity of both public and private lands and created incentives for cities to profit from the sale of public lands, along with privatization of vital public assets and infrastructure. This leads to the perception, and sometimes also the reality, that urban land is scarce, that there is simply *no room* for commoning. However, even in the most financialized cities, like New York City, there are still vacant spaces. Some of these sites have a plan or an overdue promise for their future. Others have been neglected and abandoned by their owners (public and private). Still other sites are being "warehoused" and held empty, until it is profitable enough for their owners to sell or build. And some sites are so marginal that we might not even recognize them as urban land – the margin of a sidewalk, the verge of a road, the empty space under a highway or bridge. In cities all over the world underutilized spaces have been temporarily or permanently transformed into community gardens. Community gardens are one of the most ubiquitous and widely recognized and researched forms of urban food commons (Eizenberg 2012, Follmann & Viehoff 2015, Cahn & Segal 2016, Rogge & Theesfeld 2018, Campbell & Wiesen 2009). In this case, I turn to the history and present state of the community gardening movement in New York City, in order to examine the urban food governance practices and innovations that have developed within gardens and grassroots movements in negotiation with the city and the Department of Parks and Recreation (hereafter referred to as the parks department).

In the 1970s, there were some 20,000 acres of vacant land in New York City (Gittleman et al. 2010); today there are closer to 850 acres (596 Acres). During the former period of high land vacancy, Liz Christie, the Green Guerillas, and countless other concerned residents began taking over neglected vacant lots which had attracted a number of illegal activities, including waste dumping, in Manhattan's lower east side. Gardeners began by tossing seed bombs over fences to spread flowers on neighborhood eyesores. By 1974 they had secured temporary access to these lots through Operation Greenthumb, which allowed residents to lease lots from the city for one dollar a year in exchange for removing garbage and creating safe and green community spaces (Gittleman et al. 2010, Greenthumb n.d.). The lack of care these spaces received from the city during an ongoing fiscal crisis led to what Foster (2011) identifies as "regulatory slippage" and created an opening for residents to become stewards of these neglected public spaces. The outsourcing of maintenance and care of public assets was formalized in 1978 through the city's Greenthumb program, which has gone through multiple iterations and revisions in its current administrative home with the parks department.

By the 1990s the commoning activities of gardeners had contributed to creating hundreds of community gardens across the city; these provided food for gardeners as well as a host of social, health, and ecological benefits to the wider public through education, workshops, cultural spaces, works of art, biodiversity, storm water retention, community composting, and green infrastructure (Campbell & Wiesen 2009). As community-created green spaces, the gardens offered safety, rest, and contemplation for residents who lacked access to public parks or did not feel safe in them. The success of the gardens was a mixed blessing, revitalizing but also gentrifying neighborhoods across the city. Former Mayor Giuliani sought to profit from these increased land values through the mass eviction of gardeners and the auctioning of vacant lots. This spurred a wave of grassroots, legal, and celebrity activism to save New York's community gardens and led to a number of urban food governance innovations (Brooklyn Queens Land Trust, Staeheli et al. 2002, Schmelzkopf 2002). The New York City community gardening movement emerged from, and continues to mobilize around the risks and opportunities of, vacant land (Cahn & Segal 2016).

Urban Food Governance Innovations – Tools for Commoning

Of New York's community gardens, 118 are now owned by private land trusts (Gittleman et al. 2010). Land trusts have been used as a tool for the collective long-term stewardship and conservation of (rural) nature since 1891, when the Trustees of Reservations was founded in Massachusetts. The land trust model was later introduced to cities through the community land trust (CLT) movement (Crabtree 2020). "Originating in the 1960s American civil rights movement to promote black property ownership, CLTs have since been utilised to address the pernicious effects of absentee landlordism, speculative property development and gentrification" (Thompson 2015: 1023). In 1999, when former Mayor Giuliani threatened 112 community gardens with eviction, hundreds of gardeners organized, protested, and filed lawsuits to save these spaces – giving birth to the New York City Community Gardening Coalition. As a result of years of sustained public pressure, the New York State's Attorney General Eliot Spitzer joined the gardeners lawsuit and negotiated with the city and the Trust for Public Land (a private national conservation land trust founded in 1972) to purchase and preserve 69 community gardens at a cost of 3 million USD. The remaining gardens were purchased by singer-songwriter Bette Midler on behalf of the New York Restoration Project, a private land trust which now owns 52 parks and community gardens. The Trust for Public Land has since facilitated the formation of local land trusts. These include the Brooklyn Queens Land Trust, which protects 35 community gardens in Brooklyn and Queens. The Bronx Land Trust, which protects 18 community gardens. And the Manhattan Land Trust, which protects 13 community gardens. Each land trust is a registered non-profit 501 (c) (3) organization, which owns land on behalf of communities and is governed by a board of directors who act as long-term stewards (Gittleman et al. 2010, Brooklyn Queens Land Trust). As forms of collective-private ownership, land trusts require considerable financial resources to purchase property. Once the land is held in trust it is protected from the pressures of the property market, as well as the political whims and administrative changes of the public purse. However, the necessity of private land trusts for the protection of public goods also points to the widespread failure of public authorities and elected officials to steward the commons on behalf of residents.

Land trusts are a powerful tool for creating and preserving commons of all kinds, including urban food commons (Krinsky & Segal 2019). In the 1990s, the use of land trust legislation for the preservation of urban nature in community gardens was a rarity. Since then, land trusts and community land trusts have come to play a vital role in preserving and supporting community gardens, and urban (and rural) agriculture across the United States (Yuen 2014, Crabtree 2020, DeFilippis et al. 2019). New York City is home to a number of CLTs dedicated to community development and affordable housing, and the community land trust movement is now funded in part by the municipal budget (New Economy Project 2019). To mitigate the undesired consequences of green gentrification that community gardens in New York have contributed to, it is necessary to facilitate partnerships between land trusts, community land trusts, and housing advocates in order to protect and grow affordable housing as well as gardens. These collaborations are emerging and ongoing.

The New York City parks department provides support in the form training, technical assistance, and materials to more than 550 community gardens across the city via the Greenthumb garden program. The parks department now owns the land beneath about 300 of these community created and stewarded green spaces, making it the largest landowner of community gardens in the city (Gittleman et al. 2010). In the wake of the landmark legal victories of community gardeners against the city of New York, the majority of the remaining community gardens on city-owned property were transferred to the parks department. Although the parks department had sponsored the Greenthumb program since 1978, it did not usually own the land that these gardens grew on; they were often owned by another city agency. Community gardens are not part of the mission of city agencies dedicated to housing, urban development, or transportation. And these agencies might decide that a garden does not support their mission as much as a new school, parking lot, or housing block would. The transfer of community garden ownership to the parks department is not only symbolic in that it recognizes the park-making and place-making capacities of grassroots actors, it also further consolidated formal and informal forms of urban food governance in community gardens in ways that align with their land tenure, ownership, and use.

In the State of New York, public parks are protected by the public trust doctrine. This federal legislation was developed to protect natural and cultural resources (e.g. parks, waterways, shorelines) for public use through public ownership and stewardship. The transfer of some 350 community gardens to the parks department would, in theory, place these gardens under the protection of the public trust doctrine. Under the public trust doctrine parks cannot be sold without legislative approval by the State of New York (Gresham 2001). However, the governance of community gardens differs from the governance of public parks. New York City parks are open-access, public, green spaces that are open every day to anyone. They are cared for by public employees and governed by park managers. Gardening and foraging wild food is not permitted in public parks, as this would constitute a form of encroachment or alienation of public goods for private benefit. Community gardens, on the other hand, are community created green spaces, where members can grow food for their private benefit. The gardens themselves are semi-private spaces with locked gates that are opened to the public during restricted hours. In this respect there is a risk that community gardens could become private club goods rather than inclusive commons. However, as commons, community gardens do provide the wider public with cultural, ecological, and educational services, and spaces to rest, socialize, and compost.

Community garden governance is jointly shared by the parks department and the residents who create and care for these spaces, while stewardship is in the hands of gardeners. The parks department provides training, materials, technical support, and mediation where needed. The lease agreement requires that the management body of the community garden develops a vision and governance plan, cares for the surrounding sidewalk (removing snow, etc.), and that the garden be accessible to the wider public for 20 hours a week. The gardeners decide how to design the space, what to grow, how to share responsibilities and make decisions together, and how to protect what they value in this space (Greenthumb 2019). NYC zoning allows agricultural land uses in all residential districts; food grown in community gardens can be sold, shared, and donated; chickens can be kept but roosters and fowl cannot; and honeybees are allowed but they must be registered with the department of health each year (NYC Agriculture). Structures can also be built, but they cannot be used as dwellings. However, recent changes in the parks department gardening licensing agreements have increased the financial burden and private liability of caring for a garden, while restricting the opportunities for gardens to hold events and solicit donations to fund their operations (Enman 2019, New York City Community Garden Coalition n.d.).

Community gardens are therefore ambiguous public parks. Even though some 350 community gardens are now owned by the parks department, they are still mapped as vacant land awaiting development rather than park land (Cahn & Segal 2016). Furthermore, the public trust doctrine, which offers a robust legal framework for protecting public parks, has not sufficiently protected community gardens. Legislative changes in the state Capital have permitted the sale of community gardens on a case-by-case basis, and the parks department can at any point decide that there are more desirable public uses than a garden. For example, under the parks department ownership, a community garden in Coney Island, Brooklyn was destroyed to enable a parking lot and an amphitheater to be built in its place. The parks department is also currently in the process of evicting two of the city's most productive community composting operations in Queens (to build a parking lot), and Manhattan (to renovate the east river park). These examples suggest that the food commons of community gardens are not always recognized as public goods.

Parks department ownership and governance has been a mixed bag for community gardeners. On the one hand, it has protected the gardens from the immediate threats of eviction by the city, and its more malicious Mayors, while directing public resources in the form of training, technical assistance, and education to gardeners. On the other hand, parks governance and ownership does not always align with the self-governance, autonomy, and empowerment of community gardeners. Although the parks department has proven to be a sympathetic ally to community gardens, it does not advocate on behalf of community gardeners – particularly when they are in conflict with other city agencies or development plans. In this respect, community gardeners are more tenants than constituents of the parks department. To fill this gap, a number of organizations, including 596 Acres and the New York City Community Garden Coalition, have advocated on behalf of community gardens and provided legal aid. Without this advocacy, community gardeners would be excluded from the urban food governance decisions that directly impact the urban commons they have created and stewarded.

During its existence from 2011 to 2018, the community land access advocacy organization 596 Acres provided community organizing, legal support, and land-use literacy to hundreds of community gardeners across the city of New York. During this time their efforts contributed to the creation of 40 new gardens, the protection of 55 gardens from eviction, and the transfer of 39 gardens to parks department ownership. The organization 596 Acres was founded by lawyer, Paula Segal, and mapmaker, Eric Brelsford. With their combined expertise they created the online platform and interactive map "Living Lots" to make visible the 596 acres of publicly owned vacant land that Segal had discovered in Brooklyn. Living Lots continues to function as a data commons that makes potential and emerging food commons visible; it is also complemented by sister platforms Urban Reviewer, which maps (often unrealized) urban renewal plans, and NYCommons which maps development plans and organizing efforts. Community gardeners use the Living Lots platform along with well-placed signs on fences surrounding vacant lots to organize. The signs invite passersby to organize to gain access and provide relevant contact information to get in touch with the organizers, neighbors, and the Living Lots platform (Morrow 2019).

The Living Lots platform is not only a clearing house of information, it is also an infrastructure for community organizing and participating in urban food governance. Each parcel that is mapped on the platform has extensive information about the property ownership, land-use history, organizing status, and the legal, community, and bureaucratic processes that are being navigated to secure access. Organizers for each parcel use the platform to share continuous updates, meeting minutes, photos, transcripts, court hearings, community board meetings, and correspondence with public authorities. Brelsford designed this function as an interactive "facebook" page for a parcel of property (Morrow 2019). Access to this living archive of information is essential for ensuring that organizers can share the labors of commoning, replace one another, and create inclusive organizing and governance structures for their gardens. However, access to information alone is not sufficient, it can even be overwhelming, and not all community gardeners have digital literacy or Internet access. To support these food commoners, 596 Acres employed full-time community organizers who ran a help line and supported gardeners with outreach, meetings, letter-writing, preparing testimonies, collecting signatures of support, and preparing for lengthy public meetings with local community boards, parks, city councils, and land-use boards. Community organizers sought to privilege the needs and desires of long-term residents, while using maps to make visible, reflect on, and heal from histories of structural racism in the form of red-lining and urban renewal that had created these land vacancies. Furthermore, Segal, with the support of TakeRoot Justice, has provided legal aid and representation to countless community gardens threatened by eviction in cases against absentee landlords and the city of New York. In this way, 596 Acres has helped to democratize the spaces of urban food governance, by providing food commoners with the data, tools, knowledge, and representation they need to organize, participate, and be heard.

The New York City Community Garden Coalition (NYCCGC) was founded in 1996 with the mission to promote the preservation, creation, and empowerment of community gardens through education, advocacy, and grassroots organizing. It provides a crucial platform for gardeners from across the city to practice solidarity through public rallies, direct actions, and legal advocacy, and offers a community forum where gardeners can learn from one another's successes and failures. The grassroots organizing strategies that developed through the multi-year legal battle with the city of New York continues to shape the ethos of the NYCCGC, and helps it to be a critical voice in urban food governance discussions that impact community gardens. NYCCGC continues to advocate for the 27 community gardens that are classified as "subject to development" by the department of Housing Preservation and Development, as well as recent changes in Greenthumb licensing agreements that disadvantage less wealthy community gardens. In response to some of the limitations of parks protection and the unequal relationship that community gardens hold vis-à-vis the parks department, NYCCGC and the legal aid NGO Earthjustice are currently advocating for further protection of community gardens, with a petition to extend the legal protection of Critical Environmental Areas (CEAs) to some 40 gardens. Under the New York State Environmental Quality Review Act (SEQRA), CEAs can be designated as such if they "exhibit at least one of the following characteristics: (1) a benefit to human health; (2) a natural setting; (3) agricultural, social, cultural, historic, recreational, or educational values; or (4) ecological or hydrological values that may be negatively affected by disturbances" (Earthjustice 2020: 4). Through painstaking research and social and ecological impact assessments, community gardeners and their allies have demonstrated that at least 40 gardens meet these criteria. This effort to mobilize state environmental protections for urban community gardens could be understood as a strategy for jumping scales (Cox 1998, Smith & Kurtz 2003) in the multi-level governance processes that have historically disadvantaged community-based forms of urban food governance, and to further insulate gardens from political changes in the city's administration and policy agenda.

Conclusion

Community gardeners have been engaged in practices of urban food governance since their creation. For community gardeners, urban food governance takes place through grassroots organizing, negotiating access to land, developing shared values and visions, deciding together how to use and care for their gardens, and how to share benefits and responsibilities. These governance practices are forms of commoning, or "acts of mutual support, conflict, negotiation, communication and experimentation that are needed to create systems to manage shared resources" (Bollier 2015: 2). The evolution of the parks department Greenthumb stewardship program has institutionalized many of these self-governed forms of commoning. And through funding, licensing agreements, and parks department ownership, community garden governance has been brought further into the fold of formal urban governance. This institutionalization and formalization is not without tension or conflict, and the commitments of gardeners to govern community gardens as commons do not always align with the ways in which landowners (the parks department or a private land trust) understand property, governance, or public goods. However, compared to many other cities that lack any form of land tenure for urban food commons, New York community gardens are in a privileged position.

In 2008, an additional layer of formal urban food governance was installed on top of informal food governance in various civil society organizations (including community gardens) and formal food governance in various city agencies. The Mayor's Office of Food Policy was founded to strategically align food policy activities spread across multiple city agencies with the mission to "increase food security, promote access to and consumption of healthy foods, and support economic opportunity and environmental sustainability in the food system" (NYC Food Policy). In 2015, New York signed onto the Milan Urban Food Policy Pact, and in February 2021, the Mayor's Office of Food Policy published *Food Forward*, the city's first 10-year food policy plan. The plan mentions community gardens just once as part of a shortlist of food production activities that take place in the city. Urban farming, on the other hand, is mentioned 15 times, with specific policy commitments related to increasing urban farming in order to create "modern efficient supply chains that feed the city" (City of New York 2021). In contrast, the New York City Council's 2010 *FoodWorks Vision to Improve New York Food System* mentions community gardens 12 times, and explicitly advocates for their public benefits, preservation, and growth (New York City Council 2010: 11).

The differences between the two reports, which benefited from extensive input from numerous civil society actors, state agencies, food businesses, food advocacy organizations, and scientific experts, reflect different approaches to food governance. Although *Food Forward* introduces itself as a first step toward food democracy, New York City does not have a food council or any kind of participatory public body for setting food policy. Moragues-Faus (2017: 461) describes food democracy in terms of citizens having "equal and effective opportunities to engage in shaping the food system" by "becoming knowledgeable, sharing ideas, developing efficacy in the food system, building common public goods and emphasising collective action (Hassanein 2008)." The last two points are key in recognizing the importance of common public goods (e.g. food commons), and the necessity for taking collective action to create and care for those goods. They also raise the question: just what *collectives* are taking action to shape New York City food policy? The Mayor's Office of Food Policy consists of a Director, who is appointed by the Mayor, and employs a small support staff. Members of the New York City Council, on the other hand, are immediately accountable to their local constituents, who will call them up, show up in their offices, and demand to be heard. The Mayor's Office of Food Policy could play a vital part in creating such democratic spaces, embrace commoning as a mode of urban food governance, and recognize the essential role of community gardens as food commons and spaces of food democracy and citizenship.

The pivot in food policy language from community gardening to urban farming is a concern that Kristen Reynolds and Nevin Cohen (2016) raise in *Beyond the Kale*, which chronicles how the language, funding environment, and policy processes related to urban agriculture and urban farming in New York City have marginalized and erased the contributions of people of color who work on the ground (rather than on rooftops or inside vertical farms) in food justice organizations and community gardens across the city. Many of these invisible farmers have contributed to creating, stewarding, and protecting urban food commons. At this current juncture in New York City's food governance there is a lack of alignment between the food commoning activities of thousands of community gardeners and the food policymaking activities of public agencies. This lack of alignment can result in community gardeners being pitted against other forms of urban commons, such as recreation and affordable housing, and not benefiting from funding and regulations that aim to increase food security, resilient supply chains, and sustainable food waste disposal.

The first goal of *Food Forward* is that "all New Yorkers have multiple ways to access healthy, affordable, and culturally appropriate food" (City of New York 2021: 8). Community gardens contribute to this multiplicity by providing spaces where New Yorkers can grow, eat, and share food that is healthy, affordable, and reflective of their diverse cultural backgrounds – in addition to composting food waste and growing urban soils. The omission of food commons, such as community gardens, from the current food policy plan narrows the range of possible food futures in New York City to realizing food security within the frame of food as commodity. Food commoners may have very different visions of what makes for a sustainable and equitable food system; their visions might include food sovereignty, the right to food, and food as a cultural and biophysical commons. Thankfully, urban food governance continues in many places beyond the Mayor's Office of Food Policy, in garden beds, around picnic tables, at rallies and on the steps of city hall, in court rooms and public hearings, in NYCCGC forums, in the parks department, and in dialogue with scientists, grassroots activists, businesses, and civil society organizations. To realize food democracy in New York City, it is vital to embrace commoning as a mode of urban food governance and learn from the thousands of community gardeners who are already engaged in governing food as a commons. In addition to aligning food policy with food commoning, it is also necessary to preserve community gardens as autonomous spaces of informal self-governance that strengthen the social and civic fabric of cities by providing community spaces where residents connect, organize, engage in grassroots innovation, develop their civic capacities, and demand a political voice in urban food governance processes.

Food commons could be a cornerstone of urban food governance. This would require a systemic and strategic approach to governing urban food commons, from the principles of justice and equity and within the civic infrastructures of food democracy. Although the commoning activities of community gardeners provide a glimpse of actually existing food democracy, they are also just the tip of the iceberg when it comes to urban food commons. And approaching urban food commons primarily as land, overlooks the diversity of bio-cultural commons that help people to access healthy, affordable, and culturally appropriate food, both within community gardens and in our wider food system. Governing community gardens primarily as a "land use" also leads to contradictions around commoning. Even though the land is governed as a commons, the food that is grown on this land is often a private good. This could lead to feelings of exclusion or the perception of community gardens as private club goods. Food itself is being commoned in community fridges across New York (Evans 2020), but there are missed opportunities for solidarity and cooperation between multiple forms of commons in the city. The solidarity between the community land trust movement and community gardens is instructive in this regard.

The findings from this chapter have broader implications beyond New York City and community gardening, and offer openings for rethinking the relationship between commons, commoning, and urban food governance. A commoning approach to urban food governance would nurture and protect civic spaces where city dwellers are already creating food commons and are engaged in the messy work of food democracy. Formal urban food policy and city planning can play an important role in facilitating justice and equity in the distribution of opportunities for commoning and in funding new food commons, to ensure that these resources are located in and governed by communities where they can realize the greatest public benefit and meet local needs. Finally, cities can learn from commoners who are creating social innovations for food sharing and practicing food democracy, in order to create civic infrastructures where citizens can more easily access and influence the formal food governance processes that affect their communities. Learning from and with the commons does not necessarily require formalization, institutionalization, or upscaling – in fact, depending on the context, such practices can even be detrimental to the commons and create new barriers (e.g. legal liability, etc.) (see Morrow 2019). At the same time a purely "hands off" neoliberal approach of deregulation and tolerance is insufficient – and will likely exacerbate existing social inequalities, making the food commons only accessible to those with the time, resources, and expertise to common. Making urban food commons inclusive, accessible, and durable will also require legislative changes at other geographic scales to create legal protections and supports that outlast the mayoral election cycle. By taking a systemic and strategic approach to urban food commons, cities can act in solidarity with the diversity of commons they are interdependent with in urban, peri-urban, and rural places, through public procurement, and investments in land trusts, cooperatives, and collective purchasing. In this way, cities can use municipal budgets to facilitate solidarity between the diversity of commons that make their communities livable instead of pitting them against one another in a competition over resources. This type of strategic governance does not currently take place in most cities because of an assumption that food is a commodity whose circulation should contribute to economic growth and a failure to grasp how resources could be governed outside of the binaries of public and private property. A commoning approach to urban food governance demands a paradigm shift to value, care for, and protect the many food commons that already exist in our cities, and the creativity to envision, amplify, and create new food commons that strengthen the justice, resilience, and equity of city-regional food systems.

References

596 Acres https://596acres.org/about-community-land-access-advocacy/

Bauwens, M., & Niaros, V. (2017). *Changing Societies through Urban Commons Transitions*. Berlin: Heinrich Böll and P2P Foundation.

Blomley, N. (2008). Enclosure, Common Right and the Property of the Poor. *Social & Legal Studies*, *17*(3), 311–331.

Bollier, D. (2015). Commoning as a Transformative Social Paradigm. *The Next System Project*, 1–23. Retrieved from https://thenextsystem.org/commoning-as-a-transformative-social-paradigm

Bollier, D., & Helfrich, S. (Eds.). (2015). *Patterns of Commoning*. Amherst, MA: Commons Strategy Group and Off the Common Press.

Bresnihan, P. (2015). The More-than-Human Commons: From Commons to Commoning. In S. Kirwan, L. Dawney, & J. Brigstocke (Eds.), *Space, Power, and the Commons: The Struggle for Alternative Futures*. London: Routledge. https://doi.org/10.4324/9781315731995

Bresnihan, P., & Byrne, M. (2015). Escape into the City: Everyday Practices of Commoning and the Production of Urban Space in Dublin. *Antipode*, *47*(1), 36–54.

Brooklyn Queens Land Trust. https://bqlt.org/about

Cahn, A. L., & Segal, P. Z. (2016). You Can't Common What You Can't See: Towards a Restorative Polycentrism in the Governance of Our Cities. *Fordham Urban Law Journal, 43*(2), 195–245.

Campbell, L. K., & Wiesen, A. (Eds.). (2009). *Restorative Commons: Creating Health and Well-Being through Urban Landscapes, Vol. 39*. Missoula, MT; Madison, WI; Portland, OR: USDA Forest Service.

Candel, J. J. L., & Pereira, L. (2017). Towards Integrated Food Policy: Main Challenges and Steps Ahead. *Environmental Science and Policy, 73*(C), 89–92. https://doi.org/10.1016/j.envsci.2017.04.010

Chies, B. M. (2017). Turning Food "Waste" into a Commons. *Practicing the Commons. Self-Governance, Cooperation and Institutional Change,* XVI Biennal IASC-Conference. Retrieved from www.iasc2017.org/wp-content/uploads/2017/07/chies.pdf

City of New York (2021). *Food Forward: A 10-Year Food Policy Plan*. New York: Office of Food Policy. www1.nyc.gov/assets/foodpolicy/downloads/pdf/Food-Forward-NYC.pdf

Coulson, H., & Sonnino, R. (2019). Re-scaling the Politics of Food: Place-based Urban Food Governance in the UK. *Geoforum, 98*(November), 170–179. https://doi.org/10.1016/j.geoforum.2018.11.010

Cox, K. R. (1998). Spaces of Dependence, Spaces of Engagement and the Politics of Scale, or: Looking for Local Politics. *Political Geography, 17*(1), 1–23. https://doi.org/10.1016/S0962-6298(97)00048-6

Crabtree, L. (2020). Community Land Trusts: Embracing the Relationality of Property. In J. Gibson-Graham & K. Dombroski (Eds.), *The Handbook of Diverse Economies*. Cheltenham: Edward Elgar, 292–299. https://doi.org/10.4337/9781788119962.00043

Dalla Costa, M. (2007). Food as Common and Community. *The Commoner, 12*, 129–137.

DeFilippis, J., Williams, O. R., Pierce, J., Martin, D. G., Kruger, R., & Esfahani, A. H. (2019). On the Transformative Potential of Community Land Trusts in the United States. *Antipode, 51*(3), 795–817.

Earthjustice. (2020). https://earthjustice.org/features/petition-protect-new-york-city-community-gardens

Eizenberg, E. (2012). Actually Existing Commons: Three Moments of Space of Community Gardens in New York City. *Antipode, 44*(3), 764–782. https://doi.org/10.1111/j.1467-8330.2011.00892.x

Enman, Scott (2019). City Could Lose Nearly 100 Community Gardens over Contract Dispute. *Brooklyn Daily Eagle*, October 16. https://brooklyneagle.com/articles/2019/10/16/nyc-could-lose-nearly-100-community-gardens-over-contract-dispute/

European Commission. (2020). *Towards a Sustainable Food System: Moving from Food as a Commodity to Food as more of a Common Good: Independent Expert Report*. Brussels: Directorate-General for Research and Innovation, Group of Chief Scientific Advisors, Publications Office, https://data.europa.eu/doi/10.2777/37244 (last accessed January 30, 2022)

Evans, D. (2020). Give Some, Take Some: How the Community Fridge Fights Food Insecurity. *Eater*, June 17. www.eater.com/2020/6/17/21291849/community-fridges-food-insecurity-coronavirus-covid-19-impact (last accessed January 30, 2022)

Follmann, A., & Viehoff, V. (2015). A Green Garden on Red Clay: Creating a New Urban Common as a Form of Political Gardening in Cologne, Germany. *Local Environment, 20*(10), 1148–1174.

Foster, S. R. (2011). Collective Action and the Urban Commons. *Notre Dame Law Review, 87*, 57.

Foster, S. R., & Iaione, C. (2016). The City as a Commons. *Yale Law & Policy Review, 34*(25), 65–80.

Franck, K., & Stevens, Q. (Eds.). (2006). *Loose Space: Possibility and Diversity in Urban Life*. London and New York: Routledge.

Gittleman, M., Librizzi, L., & Stone, E. (2010). *Community Garden Survey New York City Results 2009/2010*. New York: Grow NYC & Greenthumb NYC Parks Department. www.grownyc.org/files/GrowNYC_CommunityGardenReport.pdf

Greenthumb. (2019). *Gardeners Handbook*. New York: Greenthumb NYC Parks Department. https://greenthumb.nycgovparks.org/pdf/greenthumb-gardeners-handbook-2019-compressed.pdf

Greenthumb. (n.d.). *History of Community Gardens Movement*. New York: Greenthumb NYC Parks Department. www.nycgovparks.org/about/history/community-gardens/movement

Gresham, C. (2001). Improving Public Trust Protections of Municipal Parkland in New York. *Fordham Environmental Law Review, 13*(2).

Gupta, C., Campbell, D., Munden-Dixon, K., Sowerwine, J., Cappse, S., Feenstra, G., & Van Soelen Kim, J. (2018). Food Policy Councils and Local Governments: Creating Effective Collaboration for Food Systems Change. *Journal of Agriculture, Food Systems, and Community Development, 8*(B), 11–28. https://doi.org/https://doi.org/10.5304/jafscd.2018.08B.006

Hassanein, N. (2008). Locating Food Democracy: Theoretical and Practical Ingredients. *Journal of Hunger and Environmental Nutrition, 3*(2/3), 286–308.

Hoffmann, D., Morrow, O., & Pohl, C. (2019). What's Cooking in Berlin's Food Policy Kitchen? *Urban Agriculture Magazine*, *36*, 37–39.
Huron, A. (2015). Working with Strangers in Saturated Space: Reclaiming and Maintaining the Urban Commons. *Antipode*, *47*(4), 963–979.
Iaione, C. (2016). The CO-City: Sharing, Collaborating, Cooperating, and Commoning in the City. *American Journal of Economics and Sociology*, *75*(2), 415–455. https://doi.org/10.1111/ajes.12145
Ilieva, R. T. (2017). Urban Food Systems Strategies: A New Tool for Implementing the SDGs in Practice? *Sustainability*, *9*(10), 1707. https://doi.org/10.3390/su9101707
Jackson, P., Ferre, M. G. R., Candel, J., Davies, A., Derani, C., de Vries, H., ... & Thøgersen, J. (2021). Food as a Commodity, Human Right or Common Good. *Nature Food*, *2*(3), 132–134.
Kennedy, M. (2020). A Slow Food Commons: Cultivating Conviviality across a Range of Property Forms. In J. Gibson-Graham & K. Dombroski (Eds.), *The Handbook of Diverse Economies*. Cheltenham: Edward Elgar, pp. 308–315. https://doi.org/10.4337/9781788119962.00045
Krinsky, J., & Segal, P. Z. (2019). Stewarding the City as Commons: Parks Conservancies and Community Land Trusts. *CUNY Law Review*, *22*, 270.
McGinnis, M. D. (2011). An Introduction to IAD and the Language of the Ostrom Workshop: A Simple Guide to a Complex Framework. *Policy Studies Journal*, *39*(1), 169–183.
Moragues-Faus, A. (2017). Emancipatory or Neoliberal Food Politics? Exploring the "Politics of Collectivity" of Buying Groups in the Search for Egalitarian Food Democracies. *Antipode*, *49*(2), 455–476. https://doi.org/10.1111/anti.12274
Morrow, O. (2018). Sharing Food and Risk in Berlin's Urban Food Commons. *Geoforum*, *99*(August), 202–212. https://doi.org/10.1016/j.geoforum.2018.09.003
Morrow, O. (2019). Community Self-Organizing and the Urban Food Commons in Berlin and New York. *Sustainability*, 11(13), 3641.
Morrow, O., & Martin, D. G. (2019). Unbundling Property in Boston's Urban Food Commons. *Urban Geography*, *40*(10), 1485–1505. https://doi.org/10.1080/02723638.2019.1615819
New Economy Project. (2019). www.neweconomynyc.org/2019/06/nyc-takes-bold-action-to-address-the-affordable-housing-crisis-by-supporting-community-land-trusts/
New York City Community Garden Coalition. (n.d.). https://nyccgc.org/
New York City Council. (2010). *FoodWorks Vision to Improve New York Food System*. http://growingfoodconnections.org/wp-content/uploads/sites/3/1970/01/NYC-Foodworks-2010.pdf
NYC Agriculture. www1.nyc.gov/site/agriculture/faqs/frequently-asked-questions.page (last accessed January 30, 2022)
NYC Food Policy, Mayors Office of Food Policy. www1.nyc.gov/site/foodpolicy/index.page (last accessed January 30, 2022)
Ostrom, E. (1999). Revisiting the Commons: Local Lessons, Global Challenges. *Science*, *284*(5412), 278–282. https://doi.org/10.1126/science.284.5412.278
Paull, J. (2013). "Please Pick Me" – How Incredible Edible Todmorden is Repurposing the Commons for Open Source Food and Agricultural Biodiversity. In J. Franzo, D. Hunter, T. Borelli, & F. Mattei (Eds.), *Diversifying Foods and Diets: Using Agricultural Biodiversity to Improve Nutrition and Health*. Oxford: Earthscan, Routledge, pp. 336–345.
Petrescu, D., Petcou, C., Safri, M., & Gibson, K. (2021). Calculating the Value of the Commons: Generating Resilient Urban Futures. *Environmental Policy and Governance*, *31*(3), 159–174.
Poe, M. R., McLain, R. J., Emery, M., & Hurley, P. T. (2013). Urban Forest Justice and the Rights to Wild Foods, Medicines, and Materials in the City. *Human Ecology*, *41*(3), 409–422. https://doi.org/10.1007/s10745-013-9572-1
Ramos, J. M. (Ed.). (2016). *The City as Commons: A Policy Reader*. Melbourne, Australia: Commons Transition Coalition.
Reynolds, K., & Cohen, N. (2016). *Beyond the Kale: Urban Agriculture and Social Justice Activism in New York City*. Athens, GA: University of Georgia Press.
Rogge, N., & Theesfeld, I. (2018). Categorizing Urban Commons: Community Gardens in the Rhine-Ruhr Agglomeration, Germany. *International Journal of the Commons*, *12*(2), 251–274.
Rundgren, G. (2016). Food: From Commodity to Commons. *Journal of Agricultural and Environmental Ethics*, *29*(1), 103–121. https://doi.org/10.1007/s10806-015-9590-7
SAPEA (Science Advice for Policy by European Academies). (2020). *A Sustainable Food System for the European Union*. Berlin: SAPEA. https://doi.org/10.26356/sustainablefood

Schmelzkopf, K. (2002). Incommensurability, Land Use, and the Right to Space: Community Gardens in New York City 1. *Urban Geography*, *23*(4), 323–343.

Smith, C. M., & Kurtz, H. E. (2003). Community Gardens and Politics of Scale in New York City. *Geographical Review*, *93*(2), 193–212.

Staeheli, L. A., Mitchell, D., & Gibson, K. (2002). Conflicting Rights to the City in New York's Community Gardens. *GeoJournal*, *58*(2), 197–205.

Thompson, M. (2015). Between Boundaries: From Commoning and Guerrilla Gardening to Community Land Trust Development in Liverpool. *Antipode*, *47*(4), 1021–1042. https://doi.org/10.1111/anti.12154

Tornaghi, C. (2012). Public Space, Urban Agriculture and the Grassroots Creation of New Commons: Lessons and Challenges for Policy Makers. In *Sustainable Food Planning: Evolving Theory and Practice*. Wageningen: Academic Publishers, pp. 349–363.

Velicu, I., & Garcıa-Lopez, G. (2018). Thinking the Commons through Ostrom and Butler: Boundedness and Vulnerability. *Theory, Culture & Society*, *35*(6), 55–73. https://doi.org/10.1177/0263276418757315

Vivero Pol, J. L. (2013). *Food as a Commons: Reframing the Narrative of the Food System* (April 23). Available at SSRN: https://ssrn.com/abstract=2255447 or http://dx.doi.org/10.2139/ssrn.2255447

Vivero Pol, J. L. (2017). Food as Commons or Commodity? Exploring the Links between Normative Valuations and Agency in Food Transition. *Sustainability*, *9*(3), 442. https://doi.org/10.3390/su9030442

Vivero Pol, J. L., Ferrando, T., De Schutter, O., & Mattei, U. (Eds.). (2018). *Routledge Handbook of Food as a Commons*. Abingdon: Routledge.

Yuen, J. (2014). City Farms on CLTs: How Community Land Trusts Are Supporting Urban Agriculture. *Land Lines*, (April). http://staging.community-wealth.org/sites/clone.community-wealth.org/files/downloads/article-yuen.pdf

9

JUSTICE, RACE AND URBAN FOOD GOVERNANCE

Julian Agyeman, Alison Alkon and Alexandra Duprey

Introduction

Urban agriculture has enjoyed a near meteoric rise in popularity in recent years. Projects began mostly through the grassroots efforts of non-profit organizations, but now urban planners and city officials are also very interested in its interlinked economic, social, health, and environmental benefits. Many of these officials and planners see urban agriculture's greatest potential in low-income areas and communities of color where fresh food and employment opportunities can be scant, even though such desires may or may not have been articulated by community members. This presumption indicates a clear hierarchy in which those in marginalized low-income areas and communities of color are expected to quietly accept food system decisions. The detrimental nature of this paternalistic form of urban food governance is that those on the margins continue to be excluded from both the framing of urban food systems and their governance. There is the assumption by urban planners that the benefits of urban agriculture are so compelling that everyone will want it. Period.

While some communities of color have become active proponents of urban agriculture and alternative food systems (Alkon & Agyeman, 2011; Sbicca, 2018; White, 2010), critical agrarian scholars contest the presumed universal appeal of urban agriculture. They argue that urban agriculture often reflects the desires of racially and economically privileged groups that are then pushed onto communities of color (Guthman, 2008b; Slocum, 2006a, 2006b) through acts of imposed urban food governance. In this way, urban agricultural projects existing in, but not led by, communities of color remove the power of urban food self-governance, instead attributing this power to officials who apply their ideas in a top-down manner. Urban agriculture can also be viewed as fostering gentrification, as "alternative" individuals attracted by the gritty *do-it-yourselfness* of both urban farms and marginalized neighborhoods change the atmosphere into one that attracts developers and affluent consumers.

This chapter presents a case from the Dorchester neighborhood of Boston, Massachusetts, in which long-term black and brown residents initially contested a city-led urban agriculture project. The research for this chapter included interviews with Glynn Lloyd (then CEO of City Growers), Jolie Olivetti, (then Farm Manager at Victory Program's ReVision Urban Farm) and Mimi Ramos (then Executive Director of New England United for Justice). A Focus Group, comprised of five community residents and two community organizers involved in contesting

 DOI: 10.4324/9781003055907-11

the project, was held at New England United for Justice on April 24, 2012. The focus group's concerns centered on a lack of inclusion in the planning process, which they believed indicated a desire to turn control of land in their community over to non-residents, who were largely white and middle class. Of particular interest is the way in which residents initially responded to a proposed/imposed urban food governance regime by using highly racialized language to fight for spatial justice and to claim their right to the city. In this chapter, spatial (in)justice refers to an "intentional and focused emphasis on the spatial or geographical aspects of justice and injustice" (Soja, 2009, p. 2). This was widely resonant given the neighborhood's racialized environmental history (Norgaard et al., 2011), in which racial inequalities have been formed, expressed, and deepened through land-use and development processes (Agyeman, 2020). This case demonstrates what Moragues-Faus (2020, p. 73) describes as the much overlooked "conflicts of interest, winners and losers of different arrangements, and institutional deadlocks" that come with actualized food governance.

It exemplifies how a lack of participatory planning can negatively affect community responses to zoning decisions, even when the proposed land-use change has generated considerable popular attention. Participatory planning can be understood as "inquiring and learning together in the face of difference and conflict, telling compelling stories and arguing together in negotiations, coming to see issues, relationships, and options in new ways, thus arguing and acting together" (Forester, 1999, p. ix). The case also suggests that planners must develop an increased and deepened understanding of the related concepts of *recognition* (justice as recognizing the membership of all people in the moral and political community), *difference* (a more expansive, inclusive concept than "diversity") and *cultural humility*, defined by Hook et al. (2013) as the "ability to maintain an interpersonal stance that is other-oriented (or open to the other) in relation to aspects of cultural identity that are most important to the [person]" (p. 2).

Goonewardena et al. (2004, p. 12) argue that planners "retain a belief in the planner's expertise…in many instances committing the cultural injustice of non-recognition by failing to involve marginal groups directly in the planning process." This critique ultimately comes from the work of Young (1990), who notes that recognition of difference should lead not to equality of treatment but to the different treatment of groups or individuals based on the extent of their cultural and group marginalization, and lack of privilege and power. Our case suggests that cultural humility must include this recognition of difference and incorporation of cultural groups in a way that is cognizant of their relative power and privilege.

And yet, this chapter is more than just another cautionary tale emphasizing the dangers of social, racial, cultural, and community exclusion. In our case, planners responded to organized community opposition by slowing down an urban agricultural overlay zoning process to allow for community participation, and by significantly revising their land-use plan. For their part, community members participated actively in (re)negotiating the implementation plan and many, though certainly not all of them, became supportive of the project. We argue that planners initially displayed a lack of recognition of cultural humility in their approach. In response, community members deployed racialized language in order to garner recognition of social difference and yield a more just and equitable result.

Planning, Urban Agriculture, and Justice

Urban planners began to take note of the rise in grassroots urban agriculture initiatives in the early 2000s. In this era, urban agriculture projects were envisioned as "examples of citizen-initiated policy making and new forms of governance or as cases of citizen planning and grassroots democracy [because they] should be of interest to urban planners focused on various forms of citizen planning" (Wekerle, 2004, p. 379).

In 2007, the American Planning Association (APA) adopted its Policy Guide on Community and Regional Food Planning (APA, 2007), followed in 2008 by its more practical "A Planners Guide to Community and Regional Food Planning" (Raja et al., 2008). Planning scholars have argued that urban agriculture is a particularly good fit for the planning field due to compatible processes, tools, and techniques.

Campbell (2004), for example, argues that advocates' "focus on system analysis has striking parallels with comprehensive planning analysis and indicates a clear intersection between food systems work and planning" (p. 352). Beyond a systems perspective, urban agriculture and planning share a commitment to creating environmental sustainability and social justice (Agyeman, 2005; Pearsall & Pierce, 2010). Planners often celebrate urban agriculture's health benefits, namely the provision of healthy, locally sourced fruits and vegetables (Brown & Jameton, 2007; Colasanti & Hamm, 2010), environmental benefits such as reduced greenhouse gas emissions and food miles (Jansma et al., 2012; McClintock, 2010), and social benefits including increasing civic engagement (DeLind, 2002; Hale et al., 2011; Litt et al., 2011).

While the planning literature tends to regard urban agriculture, and planners' involvement in it, as a desirable outcome, critical food scholars have taken a more measured approach. Most relevant to our case are those studies that have sought to examine the relationship between race, class, and alternative food systems, an umbrella term that encompasses local, organic, slow, and other constellations of production, distribution, and consumption that comprise alternatives to the global, industrial model (Alkon & Agyeman, 2011; Sbicca, 2018).

Many scholars have noted that alternative food systems such as urban agriculture have been anchored largely in affluent and middle-class predominantly white neighborhoods and, even when located in more diverse areas, tend to appeal disproportionately to white, affluent, and middle-class individuals (Alkon & McCullen, 2010; Guthman, 2008a; Pilgeram, 2012). This is in part due to the financial pressure for urban agriculture to be profitable (Kaufman & Bailkey, 2000), which deflects practitioners' attention from the needs of low-income people (Block et al., 2011). Furthermore, critical scholars and activists have questioned whether urban agriculture projects contribute to gentrification by making marginalized neighborhoods seem attractive to more affluent individuals, business owners, and developers (Alkon et al., 2020; Zukin, 2008).

This is not to say that communities of color have not articulated a desire for, and developed, noteworthy urban agriculture projects. Often under the banner of "food justice," activists attempt to use sustainable local food systems not only to create environmental sustainability and community, but also to address racial and economic inequalities (Alkon & Agyeman, 2011; Sbicca, 2018). Detroit's D-Town Farm and the Detroit Black Community Food Security Network, for example, are significant for their emphasis on creating economic and food security in the black community (White, 2010). Immigrant communities often come from agrarian backgrounds and, for them, urban agriculture can become a way to achieve food security, maintain and celebrate cultural foodways, and create trans-local food and agricultural practices that reflect their migratory journeys (Agyeman & Giacalone, 2020; Mares & Peña, 2011; Valiente-Neighbours, 2012). Projects rooted in these communities, however, tend to be less well funded than their white counterparts and often garner less support from city agencies (Cohen & Reynolds, 2016).

This case looks to the relationship between race, class, and food system governance to argue for the importance of participatory planning, recognition of social difference, and the need for cultural humility in historically marginalized neighborhoods. This remains true even when the proposed land use seems to be generally well liked, as was the case, eventually, with urban agriculture in Dorchester.

Boston's Urban Agriculture Overlay District

In 2010, the city of Boston began the process of establishing an Urban Agriculture Overlay District (UAOD) by creating zoning to allow commercial urban agriculture. This chapter describes our research into events between the first community meeting in November 2010 and the eventual passing of Article 89 in December 2013. The Article is managed under the Mayor's Office of Food Access. Phase I of Article 89, the basis for much of this chapter, included a pilot project to attract for-profit farms to four city-owned lots in the Codman Square area at the geographic center of Boston's Dorchester neighborhood, which, as of 2010, was home to a predominantly low-income and African American community (Figure 9.1). Three of the urban farm plots were eventually developed and operated by the for-profit enterprise City Growers, while one was operated by ReVision Urban Farm. The program was administered by the Boston Redevelopment Authority (BRA) (now the Boston Planning and Development Authority), the planning authority for Boston.

Initially, community members reacted negatively to a process that seemed imposed on them and lacked participatory processes. They had not chosen commercial urban agriculture as a neighborhood land use, nor had they chosen the specific sites that would be included in the Phase 1 pilot project. Opposition was articulated in two specific ways. Firstly, the use of racialized language by then local city councilor Charles Yancey compared commercial urban agriculture to "plantations" and argued that the treatment proposed for the soil would not be sufficient to get rid of the "poison" therein (Dumcius, 2011). Local organizers and residents also decried a rushed process with minimal community input.

But, to their credit, city planners paused, listened, and reversed course. They then held a series of community meetings in which community members actively convinced planners to create a participatory process grounded in cultural humility and recognition of social difference. But perhaps, if the lessons of this case can be learned by planners interested in urban food governance more broadly, next time the ideals of cultural humility and recognition of social difference can be woven into the planning process from the beginning.

A Racialized Environmental History

After World War II, and despite its thriving commercial district in Codman Square, Dorchester was among those Boston neighborhoods classified as blighted and was "redlined." Redlining refers to the red lines mortgage lenders, insurance providers, and a federal agency, the Home Owners' Loan Corporation (HOLC), drew on maps around "hazardous," i.e. black and low-income areas. In Boston, individuals were denied loans by HOLC. The situation worsened in the 1960s and 1970s when the heads of 22 Boston savings banks designated specific neighborhoods where African Americans *could* obtain federally insured home loans (Hall, 2004). The designated areas aligned almost entirely with Boston's Jewish community, which were coincidentally unprofitable to bankers because so many of the residents had paid their mortgages off (Levine & Harmon, 1992). The program's impact on the target neighborhoods was "chaos" (Wright, 2002, p. 53). Block busting, panic selling, and racially motivated street violence and vandalism ensued, all of which contributed to a diminished demand for housing in Codman Square and other parts of Dorchester (Wright, 2002). Those who could afford to, moved away; vacancy rates soared and property values declined.

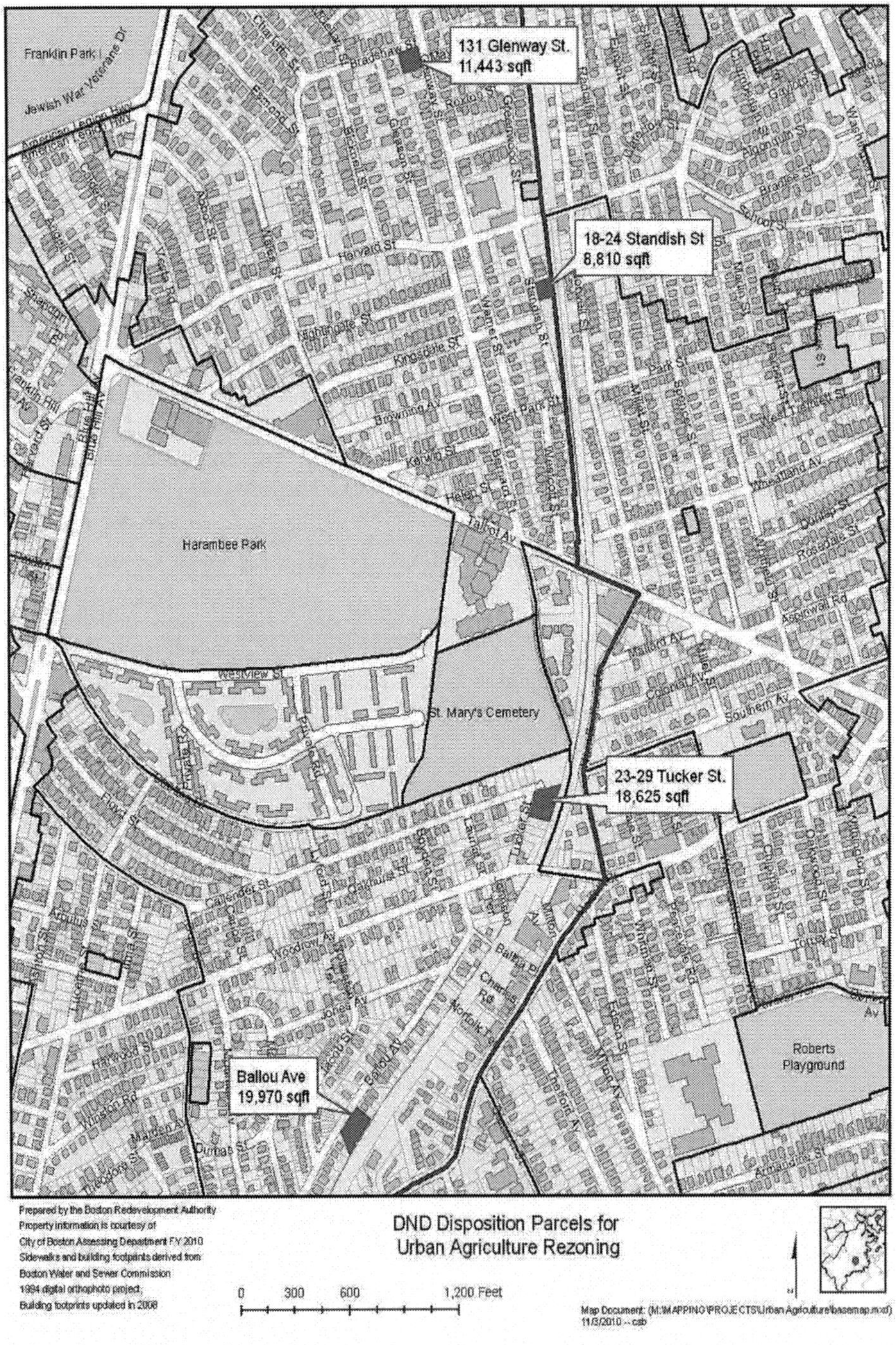

Figure 9.1 Urban agriculture rezoning – proposed parcels

Between 1950 and 1980, the city of Boston lost 30 percent of its population. This "white flight," referring to the drastic movement of white families from urban centers to the expanding suburbs, was acute in Codman Square which, during the 1970s, lost nearly 29 residents each week (Walczak, n.d.). Falling tax revenues reduced the city's ability to maintain municipal services (Warner, 1987). Historian Thomas O'Connor recounts the effects of reduced city services on the neighborhood. "Homes fell into serious disrepair, streets were no longer cleaned, garbage piled up in the alleyways, parks and playgrounds were soon neglected, and vandalism became commonplace" (O'Connor, 1993, p. 67). Rents fell, causing extensive landlord abandonment and arson.

The 2008 recession helped to shape the geography of contemporary Dorchester, increasing vacant land and thereby decreasing development pressure. These factors are likely among the reasons that the UAOD project was targeted to the area. Several scholars have observed that urban agriculture projects can serve as a "fix," helping capital to extract exchange value from underdeveloped neighborhoods (Glowa & Roman-Alcalá, 2020; McClintock, 2010; Sbicca, 2018).

These long-term processes of redlining and disinvestment create a "rent gap," in which land values are decreased sufficiently to spur investment in pursuit of future potential profits (Smith, 1987). This racialized rent gap is a primary driver of gentrification, defined as the "racial and class reconfiguration of urban, working-class and communities of color that have suffered from a history of disinvestment and abandonment" (Phillips et al., n.d.).

The UAOD was proposed at a time when the demographics of Dorchester were shifting. Today, Codman Square is home to an income-diverse group of 50,000 people from 50 countries, including immigrants from the West Indies (especially Jamaica, Barbados, and Trinidad), as well as young, predominantly white professionals relocating from the suburbs. These new residents, together with established organizations, have "revitalized" the neighborhood, initiating new businesses and raising property values (Walczak, n.d.).

Combined with the UAOD's lack of participatory processes, this demographic transition caused some residents to be suspicious of the city's newfound interest in their neighborhood. In the words of one resident:

> *If you look at the neighborhoods, it's changing a lot. Is it really for poor folks? Or is it, the neighborhood is changing and the people who are coming in will benefit from it? That's how I think. We used to have to clean the streets for ourselves. The city would never come clean the streets. Now, they're towing your car.*

This context of disinvestment and gentrification are among the reasons that participatory planning is so important in this neighborhood. As one organizer we talked to during our Focus Group put it:

> *You're coming into a neighborhood that's been through so much in the past... You have to get [residents] involved because these people have been through a lot. So you have to come and approach them.*

The lack of participatory planning processes that occurred with regard to the UAOD fits a larger pattern of disputes between the neighborhood and the city. Decades-old block groups and community organizations have long represented residents' concerns about development (Walczak n.d., p. 24). Despite this history and what former Boston city councilor Charles Yancey called a "very active" group of residents, those living in Dorchester describe it as a "forgotten" neighborhood due to its lack of investment and city services. City and charitable foundation-driven attempts have failed because, "from the perspective of its residents, the plans had been imposed from above, as thinly misguided acts of charity" (Settles, 1994, p. 12).

Area residents, for their part, were not naïve about what participating in development processes would entail. The Elmhurst Street Playground in Codman Square neighborhood, installed in 2009, took ten years of resident activism and hard work. Mimi Ramos, Executive Director of New England United for Justice (NEU4J), founded in 2010 to address racial, economic, and social injustice in Greater Boston, said that local residents "have constantly been in struggle, whether its abutting issues, vacant land concerns with the BRA...."

The debate about the UAOD needs to be understood in the contexts of this racialized environmental history, disinvestment, and gentrification. Against this backdrop, a lack of participatory planning processes can reasonably seem malicious, rather than the careless result of a rushed mayoral directive.

Dorchester Residents Resist the UAOD

Given this history, it is not surprising that many Dorchester residents had strong, negative reactions to the UAOD project. Despite the national popularity of urban agriculture, they did not automatically treat the proposed farms like a desired land use; they strongly opposed bringing in animals and had particular concerns about the quality of the soil. In addition, community members felt they were left out of the process and believed the proposed farms would benefit outsiders and newcomers rather than long-term local residents. Their anger reflected not only their experience of the planning process but their long history of marginalization through urban development.

Residents' most immediate concerns pertained to animals, rodents, and soil. At the opening community meeting, in November 2010, city staff introduced the project and potential uses of the farm sites. Concerns over animals, according to one organizer "really ticked off a lot of people... I think it's that one factor that kind of dominated the...negative views of urban farms coming into the community."

During our focus group, residents discussed their initial reactions to the city's plan to raise animals in their neighborhood. "When I first heard it," said one, "they were talking about farm animals: chickens and goats and stuff like that. That was near where I live. Oh my goodness [I thought] they can't do something like that!" Another neighbor expressed a similar reaction. "But they just said 'We're going to be bringing in pigs' and everybody said 'Oh no, you're not bringing in pigs.'"

Concern about the presence of animals was among the primary issues that motivated residents to become involved in the zoning process. A related issue was residents' fear that urban farms would drive up the neighborhood's already substantial rodent population. According to one resident who participated in our focus group: "We have a rodent problem here. And if the city isn't taking care of the rodent problem now, and yet adding all these farms, who will take care of it then?" Concerns about animals and rodents were particularly important because the city had neglected to take care of properties in the past. Residents' objections were certainly about the animals and rodents themselves, but also about their lack of faith in the city's ability to fulfill its obligations to this neighborhood. This reflects the neighborhood's historically marginalized status within the city.

Questions about soil contamination also reflected a strained history of city–community relations. Residents argued that the city had not prevented identified sites from becoming dumping grounds, and worried that these land uses had poisoned the soil. They repeatedly asked that it be tested by the city. For example, during one of the BRA meetings, a resident said the following:

> *If we are in fact going to address health issues, we don't want to end up jeopardizing them by farming on soil that is not tested prior to use and is not clearly verified as a good planting base. In addition, we would like to have whatever produce is farmed here tested before it is sold.*

A city official at the time, former councilor Charles Yancey, whose district included the Dorchester area, was particularly vocal on the issue of soils. When addressing the Zoning Commission during a meeting, he argued that one of the sites was home to a former oil company and the soil could "poison people down the line" (Gaffin, 2011).

However, Massachusetts has specific laws about cleaning up contaminated soil which the city claimed prevents them from testing the soil. With certain exceptions, these laws hold landowners liable for any hazardous materials, even if they did not cause the contamination. Senior BRA planner Tad Read said the city could not do the soil test because if contaminants were found, legally required remediation could cost millions of dollars. Instead, a city official suggested the construction of raised beds with imported soil, as had been used in nearby community gardens and was supported by soil experts.

Throughout the process described below, many community residents came to agree that this method would provide adequate protection. Others, however, remained unconvinced. Indeed, even after other concerns were resolved, fears of soil contamination remained a sticking point.

Community Input

The most commonly voiced concern by community members and organizers was that the plan had been developed without their input. Given the neighborhood's racialized history of marginalization, this concern needs to be read as a racial one in which predominantly black and brown residents felt overlooked and disrespected by a (then) predominantly white city government and planners. "People take this very personal," said one neighborhood resident. "We have no say in what's going on. It's a done deal. They had their minds made up. Evidently someone said 'Talk to the community'... And they said 'Oh. What community? You mean those folks?'" Another resident expressed similar sentiments, exclaiming, "We should not be ignored. We're taxpayers and we should be informed about what's going on. I would like to know who made the decision about turning that property over into a farm."

It is important to note the feelings of deep disrespect conveyed by the residents. From their perspective, the lack of recognition of community consultation is not accidental but stems from a belief that city officials are not concerned with their opinions, ideas, or wellbeing. This belief is supported by residents' memories of other planning processes that lacked community participation, which they recalled during the focus group, and by the neighborhood's racialized environmental history.

Perhaps the strongest words on this topic were spoken by Councilor Yancey, who, when addressing the members of the BRA, specifically referenced racial inequalities

> *I think there was a level of arrogance displayed in this process... The BRA totally ignored the community concerns when they voted to approve this project, which in reality had been already approved by assigning their staff to do it. But that's not a legitimate process... This is not a colonial regime! This is not a plantation! These are residents who deserve respect.*

Yancey's reference to a neighborhood of immigrants and African Americans as a colony and plantation were certainly not coincidental but reflect historical and present-day inequalities between the city and the community. Mimi Ramos, who would later organize city residents to participate in the UAOD process, explained this further:

> *Using [plantation] was very aggressive but [Yancey] did it because he knew that the community had this notion already... [We] connect to that race, income, equality theme and emotion that they've always had in the city.*

The city's lack of participatory planning was read in the context of past and ongoing inequalities between neighborhood residents and the city. These inequalities intersected with what, by all accounts, was a rushed process. Project leaders, under pressure from the Mayor's office, were hoping to gain official approval in just a few short months. Jolie Olivetti, who would become the farm manager when the non-profit Victory Programs eventually leased one of the sites, described community opposition in this more racially neutral way:

> *It was a matter of the City rushing into something...They talked about how they did door knocking and they tried to reach out and people weren't coming to their doors.*

But Olivetti did not believe that a rushed timeline excuses the lack of participatory processes. She continued:

> *I think that that misses the point. You can try, and if it doesn't work, that doesn't mean that you've just been given consent. Silence is not consent...If people are not responding to you, that doesn't mean go ahead and do your project.*

City representatives also scheduled community meetings, but several were canceled due to severe snowstorms. Meetings were not rescheduled until the community organized to demand additional ones. The city's decision to approach the project in this way was not inevitable. One community organizer, who participated in our focus group, offered an alternative strategy:

> *They could have taken a map and said, "Here's this area. Here are these lots. What do you think we should do with them?" I'm sure you would have heard garden. Maybe farm. But start there and let that conversation guide the discussion.*

However, the city was not prepared to undertake an open visioning process around vacant lots; they had a specific goal to find sites for urban agriculture and had no money to fund any non-farm-based suggestions. Lack of community participation was not only a question of process, but also a truly participatory process that was at odds with the city's already-chosen goal. Indeed, in city policy and planning circles, it was commonly stated that the primary motivators for the project were to increase the Mayor's prestige and reputation within the city, and to increase Boston's prestige as a green, sustainable city, in a nation that was becoming increasingly smitten with urban agriculture. In this sense, community meetings were merely a means to placate residents, to bring them on board with an already-chosen project.

Community Benefits

Most Dorchester residents, however, were generally supportive of urban agriculture but did not believe that they would benefit directly from the UAOD farms. At various community meetings and during our focus group, residents spoke favorably about school and community gardens and expressed hope that urban farms could lead to economic development. Interestingly, the previously described concerns about soil testing were never mentioned with regard to school and community gardens. Additionally, given the international demographic of Codman Square, there were sentiments expressed on the cultural connection to farming that could make such a project beneficial to community members. "I know how to dig; I know how to plant. Where I come from, that's what we do," said one resident. Another resident later noted "It's a lot of people who come from the third world and that's what they used to do: work the farm." This resident pointed out the potential for urban farming for residents "They could say to the people, 'We have these farms' and they could have put out something where they have helped them put some money for the people who know about farming."

Dorchester residents objected to the UAOD farms, however, because they did not believe this project would yield the kinds of benefits they associated with urban agriculture. During one community meeting, the BRA invited Glynn Lloyd, the founder and CEO of for-profit City Growers, to discuss the process of starting an urban farm. Lloyd estimated start-up costs to be between $5,000 and $10,000. A resident described his reaction:

> *At first when people were thinking about a farm for gardening, they were thinking about a garden that I could work in… [but] nobody in this community that I know of can afford to do the kind of farming that was talked about for this community.*

Community members quickly realized that if they were effectively prohibited from leasing these farms, that the city's goal must be to invite outside groups. In the words of one resident:

> *People in this neighborhood don't have that kind of money. So, you're talking about maybe rich white people coming into our neighborhood, taking over the community and making money off of our people.*

Another resident also couched his response in racial terms. "We've been forced to work the land all of our lives, but you're not going to give us something that we can own!" In the context of the neighborhood's racialized history, the lack of participatory planning and lack of community benefits seems particularly pernicious.

Furthermore, residents feared that they might not even have access to the produce grown on UAOD farms. As one resident put it, "We couldn't afford it at the prices they'll have to charge." "So, who are you building it for?" chimed in another. "For poor folks? Or the types of people who can buy that?" Community members recognized that the farms' high start-up costs would require the produce they sold to be more expensive than they could afford, further excluding them from not only the process, but the completed project.

While Dorchester residents were generally supportive of urban agriculture, they resisted the UAOD farms. Perhaps because residents were not able to participate in the development of the project, it was designed in such a way that they felt they would be unable to reap its benefits.

Better Late than Never: Developing Community Support

There were many reasons that community members opposed the development of urban farms in their neighborhood. Proximate concerns about animals and soil masked deeper struggles around community participation and community benefits. However, just a few short months after tensions between the city and community came to a head, many community members became active supporters of the UAOD. We argue that this dramatic transition was based on three important criteria: the existence of well-connected community-based organizations, the city's willingness to slow down the process, and the actual incorporation of community concerns into official decisions and documents. Residents' anger succeeded in garnering city planners' attention and creating space for a more participatory dialogue. This demonstrates that even in historically marginalized neighborhoods, and even when opposition is fiercely racialized, participatory planning grounded in cultural humility and recognition of social difference can lead to mutually beneficial solutions.

Silence Is not Consent: The City Listens

Once community concerns were voiced, city officials turned away from their previous tight implementation timeline to ensure that community members had ample opportunity to make themselves heard. A Zoning Commission hearing to implement the zoning change was postponed from March to November (Dumcius, 2011) and the city staff clearly modified their approach. BRA Director at the time, John Palmieri described how community concerns would affect the UAOD process as it moved forward:

> *Who is going to be selected to farm? How does the neighborhood get involved? Will children be engaged? All legitimate concerns. I think that those concerns are the concerns that will be addressed when we go through the Request for Proposals (RFP) process [to select farmers to manage the sites]. We have to prepare an RFP, vet it with the community. It won't go anywhere unless the community overwhelmingly supports the request.*

In addition, city staff scheduled two additional meetings and approached community organizations for help in revising the process. Said one community organizer:

> *If I can be very direct, they were getting their asses kicked because the community was very angry. That, at least for me, gave the neighborhood some respect when there was so much push back to give us more time... We asked the city to pause for a minute to see where people were getting confused and understanding where people need more information.*

In addition, the city redoubled its outreach efforts. City staff created educational brochures and postcards and staff–community member teams went door-to-door. Mimi Ramos praised city staff for their efforts to present the next phase of the process in easy-to-understand language:

> *I really appreciated [their] intent to come up with a menu of "What are the things that you would like to see in this RFP?" [and] to try to work that into their process. That was powerful and important.*

Residents' vocal anger prompted city planners to slow down and attempt to bring them on board. In response, residents worked through a trusted community-based organization to participate in the process.

New Process Reflects Community Concerns

In order to support effective, equitable urban food governance, urban planners need to be concerned with the existence of participatory processes from both a legal and an ethical standpoint (APA, 2009), meaning that those who are affected by planning decisions are able to share in the decision-making. But while participation is important as an end, it is more so a means to influence outcomes. With regard to the UAOD, not only did the city eventually hear from community members, but their concerns were also integrated into the process in meaningful ways.

The BRA made two decisions that quickly incorporated community concerns. First, they responded to residents' resistance to animals by permitting plant cultivation only. Secondly, the BRA eliminated one original site where residents working with a local community development corporation had long been petitioning to create a playground. Seeing their views affect outcomes encouraged community residents to continue participating in the process.

The project's next phase was to create a Request for Proposals (RFP) through which urban agriculture groups could apply to lease the remaining sites. The RFP required ongoing community participation and engagement to be a key feature of any farm's proposal. This allowed residents to be key decision makers in shaping the farm's operations. With regard to community members' concerns about soil quality, the RFP specified that farmers will be required to follow "established practices of the Boston gardening community" for separating the existing soil from contact with people and produce. Proposals were ranked based on how well they demonstrated technical farming experience and a sound business plan, as well as how they addressed community benefits, such as making produce available to residents at affordable prices or providing job training and internships for local residents.

Clearly, community input had affected both the content of the RFP and, consequently, the content and focus of the proposals that were submitted. Ultimately, two proposals were received from established farming entities, the non-profit Victory Programs' ReVision Urban Farm for the 23–29 Tucker Street lot and the for-profit City Growers for the 131 Glenway Street lot. At City Growers' September 2011 proposal meeting, only a handful of community members were actually in attendance and the sponsoring community association determined they could not hold a vote. Community members expressed that they appreciated City Growers' presentation but wanted to address the underlying issues of soil safety and farming in their neighborhood in general. It seemed that despite the City's efforts to assuage community concerns, the community members in attendance felt their concerns were as yet unresolved. After additional outreach to neighbors, City Growers was granted approval. Founder and interim CEO Glynn Lloyd described the process of getting that approval:

> *We spent many a Sunday knocking on doors. And it was like 99% in support. People were excited to talk with us and ask "Can I get a little piece? How can I help?"*

Victory Program's meeting went much more smoothly. Olivetti speculated that the organizing work that City Growers did helped to pave the way for their proposal:

> *I don't know if that's because people felt like they got their demands met, or because people who showed up to that meeting were local to that site. I do know that City Growers did tons and tons of outreach right after that experience and I know that they've got folks on board in a big way. I think that they are quite adept at community outreach.*

Since Victory Programs began farming their site, they have maintained the dedication to community concerns required by the RFP. As farm manager at the time, Olivetti had begun to attend the meetings of the various community associations representing neighborhoods that border the site. She described how one was interested in making produce available at the local corner store. "Without that type of input," Olivetti said, "I might not have thought of that, prioritised that...We'll respond to their needs and interests." Participation seems to have given community members not only influence in the permitting process, but in the operations of the farms themselves.

Lessons Learned

This chapter has mostly chronicled Phase I of the Boston UAOD Project, 2010–2013. Phase II consisted of the city-wide rezoning process, which ultimately led to the agreement to Article 89 in December 2013.

Yet in so many ways, Phase I of Boston's UAOD story is not new. Urban planners have long known, especially since Arnstein's (1969) classic "Ladder of Participation," that lack of community consultation and participatory planning, especially in communities with a history of redlining and disinvestment, can negatively affect community responses to any local change, in this case zoning decisions. They have also learned that the ethical principle of "planning for the public interest" (APA, 2009) is problematic when there is a lack of recognition of difference and that there are in fact (a) multiple publics (Sandercock, 1998), and (b) that most planners themselves neither look like nor share the values of many of those multiple publics.

Our findings therefore suggest the urgent need for an increased and deepened understanding of the concepts of recognition of social difference and cultural humility. These concepts require planners to understand the ways that urban space has been enrolled by city officials as a tool to marginalize communities of color. Without this deep cultural humility, planners imposing systems of urban food governance that are not fully negotiated will perpetuate and perhaps deepen marginalization with continued backlash from residents.

And yet, this is also a very optimistic story of democratic urban food governance through community action. The community garnered recognition from the planners and co-created space for dialogue in the planning process. Additionally, the community saw desired outcomes, such as no animals and the elimination of one site where residents wanted a playground. This was a long way for city officials to travel in a short time. But they did. And this was in no short measure due both to residents who were not afraid to voice their anger, and to the neighborhood's strong community-based organizations who offered expertise and helped residents amplify their concerns.

Community members were therefore able to disrupt the process in a way that forced city officials to address their needs. Although not every community member was eventually brought onboard—some continued to express criticism throughout the remainders of the process—many residents and neighborhood organizations seemed satisfied with the results. Several were even committed enough to join each site's Community Advisory Board. The city's rhetoric as it moved into Phase II and Article 89's city-wide rezoning was no longer about a rushed timeline but highlighted the need for community involvement in order for urban agriculture in Boston to be successful. In sum, this chapter can serve to remind planners and other city officials that there is no substitute for participatory processes in establishing a community-supported urban food governance regime.

Acknowledgments

Julian Agyeman, Alison Hope Alkon, and Alexandra Duprey extend their thanks to UEP alumnae Molly McCullagh for her interviews and running of the Focus Group and Rachel Brunner for copyediting).

References

Agyeman, J. (2005). *Sustainable Communities and the Challenge of Environmental Justice*. New York: NYU Press.

Agyeman, J. (2020). Urban Planning as a Tool of White Supremacy – The Other Lesson from Minneapolis. *The Conversation*, July 27. Retrieved from https://theconversation.com/urban-planning-as-a-tool-of-white-supremacy-the-other-lesson-from-minneapolis-142249

Agyeman, J., & Giacalone, S. (Eds.). (2020). *The Immigrant–Food Nexus: Borders, Labor, and Identity in North America*. Cambridge, MA: MIT Press. Retrieved from https://mitpress.mit.edu/books/immigrant-food-nexus

Alkon, A., & Agyeman, J. (Eds.). (2011). *Cultivating Food Justice: Race, Class and Sustainability*. Cambridge, MA: MIT Press.

Alkon, A. H., & McCullen, C. G. (2010). Whiteness in Farmers Markets: Performances, Perpetuations… Contestations? *Antipode: A Radical Journal of Geography, 43*(4), 937–955. doi:10.1111/j.1467-8330.2010.00818.x

Alkon, A. H., Kato, Y., & Sbicca, J. (2020). *A Recipe for Gentrification: Food, Power, and Resistance in the City*. New York: NYU Press.

APA (American Planning Association). (2007). *Policy Guide on Community and Regional Food Planning*. Chicago, IL: American Planning Association.

APA. (2009). *American Institute of Certified Planners' Code of Ethics and Professional Conduct*. Chicago, IL: American Planning Association.

Arnstein, S. (1969). A Ladder of Citizen Participation. *Journal of the American Planning Association, 35*(4), 216–224. doi:10.1080/01944363.2018.1559388

Block, D. R., Chávez, N., Allen, E., & Ramirez, D. (2011). Food Sovereignty, Urban Food Access, and Food Activism: Contemplating the Connections through Examples from Chicago. *Agriculture and Human Values, 29*(2), 203–215. doi:10.1177/0160597617733619

Brown, K. H., & Jameton, A. L. (2007). Public Health Implications of Urban Agriculture. *Journal of Public Health Policy, 21*(1), 20–39. doi:10.2307/3343472

Campbell, M. (2004). Building a Common Table: The Role for Planning in Community Food Systems. *Journal of Planning Education and Research, 23*, 341–355. doi:10.1177/0739456X04264916

Cohen, N., & Reynolds, K. (2016). *Beyond the Kale: Urban Agriculture and Social Justice Activism in New York City*. Athens, GA. University of Georgia Press,

Colasanti, K., & Hamm, M. (2010). Assessing the Local Food Supply Capacity of Detroit, Michigan. *Journal of Agriculture, Food Systems, and Community Development, 1*(2), 41–58. doi:10.5304/jafscd.2010.012.002

DeLind, L. B. (2002). Place, Work, and Civic Agriculture: Common Fields for Cultivation. *Agriculture and Human Values, 19*(3), 217–224.

Dumcius, G. (2011). Yancey Questions City's Urban Farming Initiative. *Dorchester Reporter*, May 26. Retrieved from www.dotnews.com/2011/yancey-questions-city-s-urban-farming-initiative

Forester, J. (1999). *The Deliberative Practitioner: Encouraging Participatory Planning Processes*. Cambridge, MA: MIT Press.

Gaffin, A. (2011). Zoning Commission Goes with Scientists over City Councilor; Approves Urban Farm Zone. *Universal Hub*. Retrieved from www.universalhub.com/2011/zoning-commission-goes-scientists-over-city-counci

Glowa, M., & Roman-Alcalá, A. (2020). Diverse Politics, Difficult Contradictions: Gentrification and the San Francisco Urban Agriculture Alliance. In A. Alkon, Y. Kato, & J. Sbicca (Eds.), *A Recipe for Gentrification* (pp. 179–201). New York: New York University Press

Goonewardena, K., Rankin, K., & Weinstock, S. (2004). Diversity and Planning Education: A Canadian Perspective. *Canadian Journal of Urban Research, 13*(1), 1–26.

Guthman, J. (2008a). If They Only Knew: Colorblindness and Universalism in Alternative Food Institutions. *The Professional Geographer, 60*(3), 387–397.

Guthman, J. (2008b). Bringing Good Food to Others: Investigating the Subjects of Alternative Food Practices. *Cultural Geographies, 15*(4), 431–447.

Hale, J., Knapp, C., Bardwell, L., Buchenau, M., Marshall, J., Sancar, F., & Litt, J. S. (2011). Connecting Food Environments and Health through the Relational Nature of Aesthetics: Gaining Insight through the Community Gardening Experience. *Social Science & Medicine, 72*(11), 1853–1863

Hall, S. (2004). *Strategies to Address Investor-owned Distressed Properties in Codman Square*. Master's thesis, Tufts University, Department of Urban and Environmental Policy and Planning, Medford, MA.

Hook, J. N., Davis, D. E., Owen, J., Worthington Jr., E. L., & Utsey, S. O. (2013). Cultural Humility: Measuring Openness to Culturally Diverse Clients. *Journal of Counseling Psychology, 60*(3), 353–366. doi:10.1037/a0032595

Jansma, J.-E., Sukkel, W., Stilma, E., Van Oost, A., & Visser, A. (2012). The Impact of Local Food Production on Food Miles, Fossil Energy Use and Greenhouse Gas Emission: The Case of the Dutch City of Almere. In A. Viljoen & J. S. C. Wiskerke (Eds.), *Sustainable Food Planning: Evolving Theory and Practice* (pp. 307–321). Netherlands: Wageningen Academic Publishers.

Kaufman, J. L., & Bailkey, M. (2000). *Farming Inside Cities: Entrepreneurial Urban Agriculture in the United States*. Madison, WI: Lincoln Institute of Land Policy.

Levine, H., & Harmon, L. (1992). *The Death of an American Jewish Community*. New York: Maxwell Macmillan International.

Litt, J. S., Soobader, M.-J., Turbin, M. S., Hale, J. W., Buchenau, M., & Marshall, J. (2011). The Influence of Social Involvement, Neighborhood Aesthetics, and Community Garden Participation on Fruit and Vegetable Consumption. *American Journal of Public Health, 101*(8), 1466–1473.

Mares, T., & Peña, D. (2011). Environmental and Food Justice: Toward Local, Slow and Deep Food Systems. In A. Alkon & J. Agyeman (Eds.), *Cultivating Food Justice: Race, Class and Sustainability* (pp. 197–219). Cambridge, MA: MIT Press.

McClintock, N. (2010). Why Farm the City? Theorizing Urban Agriculture through a Lens of Metabolic Rift. *Cambridge Journal of Regions, Economy and Society, 3*(2), 191–207.

Moragues-Faus, A. (2020). Towards a Critical Governance Framework: Unveiling the Political and Justice Dimensions of Urban Food Partnerships. *The Geographical Journal, 186*, 73– 86. Retrieved from https://doi.org/10.1111/geoj.12325

Norgaard, K., Reed, R., & Van Horn, C. (2011). A Continuing Legacy: Institutional Racism, Hunger, and Nutritional Justice on the Klamath. In A. Alkon & J. Agyeman (Eds.), *Cultivating Food Justice: Race, Class and Sustainability*. Cambridge, MA: MIT Press.

O'Connor, T. (1993). *Building a New Boston: Politics and Urban Renewal – 1950–1970*. Boston, MA: Northeastern University Press.

Pearsall, H., & Pierce, J. (2010). Urban Sustainability and Environmental Justice: Evaluating the Linkages in Public Planning/Policy Discourse. *Local Environment, 15*(6), 569–580.

Phillips, D., Flores, L., & Henderson, J. (n.d.). *Development without Displacement: Resisting Gentrification in the Bay Area*. Retrieved from https://ncg.org/sites/default/files/resources/PhilTalk_Dawn%20Phillips(1)_1.pdf

Pilgeram, R. (2012). Social Sustainability and the White, Nuclear Family: Constructions of Gender, Race, and Class at a Northwest Farmers' Market. *Race, Gender and Class, 19*(2), 37–60.

Raja, S., Born, B., & Russell, J. (2008). *A Planners Guide to Community and Regional Food Planning: Transforming Food Environments, Facilitating Healthy Eating*. Chicago, IL: American Planning Association.

Sandercock, L. (1998). *Towards Cosmopolis: Planning for Multi-Cultural Cities*. Chichester: Wiley.

Sbicca, J. (2018). *Food Justice Now! Deepening the Roots of Social Struggle*. Minneapolis, MN: University of Minnesota Press.

Settles, P. (1994). *Community Involvement in Hazardous Waste Site Cleanup in the Dudley Street Neighborhood*. Master's thesis, Tufts University, Department of Urban and Environmental Policy and Planning, Medford, MA.

Slocum, R. (2006a). *Whiteness, Space and Alternative Food Practice. Geoforum, 38*(3), 520–533.

Slocum, R. (2006b). Anti-racist Practice and the Work of Community Food Organizations. *Antipode: A Radical Journal of Geography, 38*(2), 327–349.

Smith, N. (1987). Gentrification and the Rent Gap, *Annals of the Association of American Geographers*, 77(3), 462–465.

Soja, E. W. (2009). *The City and Spatial Justice*. Justice Spatiale | Spatial Justice | No. 1, September 5. Retrieved from http://cdiwsnc.org/wp-content/uploads/2019/09/the-city-and-spatial-justice_edward-soja.pdf

Valiente-Neighbours, J. M. (2012). Mobility, Embodiment, and Scales: Filipino Immigrant Perspectives on Local Food. *Agriculture and Human Values, 29*, 531–541. doi:10.1007/s10460-012-9379-5

Walczak, W. (n.d.). *Codman Square: History (1630 to present), Turmoil (1950–1980) and Revival (1980–2000): Factors which lead to Racial and Ethnic Placement, Racial Segregation, Racial Transition, and Stable Integration*. Retrieved from www.codman.org/wp-content/uploads/2020/03/CodmanSquareHistory.pdf

Warner, S. B. (1987). *To Dwell Is to Garden: A History of Boston's Community Gardens*. Boston, MA: Northeastern University Press.

Wekerle, G. R. (2004). Food Justice Movements: Policy, Planning and Networks. *Journal of Planning, Education and Research, 23*, 378–386. doi:10.1177/0739456X04264886

White, M. M. (2010). Shouldering Responsibility for the Delivery of Human Rights: A Case Study of the D-Town Farmers of Detroit. *Race/Ethnicity: Multidisciplinary Global Perspectives, 3*(2), 189–211. doi:10.2979/rac.2010.3.2.189

Wright, D. (2002). *Saving the Square: Community Building in Codman Square (1970-1991)*. Master's thesis, Tufts University, Department of Urban and Environmental Policy and Planning, Medford, MA.

Young, I. (1990). *Justice and the Politics of Difference*. Princeton, NJ: Princeton University Press.

Zukin, S. (2008). Consuming Authenticity. *Cultural Studies, 22*, 724–748. Retrieved from http://dx.doi.org/10.1080/09502380802245985

10
CONCEPTUALISATIONS OF URBAN FOOD GOVERNANCE

Jess Halliday

Introduction

In a growing number of cities around the globe, local government officials and non-state actors are drawing up policies, plans and strategies for more just, sustainable urban food systems, and are actively implementing them. The participation of non-state actors (such as farmers, private businesses, civil society and community groups, academics, media, etc) in food policy is a hallmark of the shift from top-down government to governance in public management that has taken place in many parts of the world over the last 30 years (Stoker, 2000).

Governance of the food system is more complex than just bringing more actors into the fray, however. It is a highly contested concept, with a variety of different definitions in use across different sectors and disciplines. Urban actors who are embarking on food systems policy processes need to form an understanding of what governance is, determine what governance arrangements are best suited to their context and most likely to deliver desired outcomes, and work out how to put those arrangements in place.

Considering first what governance is, Moragues-Faus et al. (2017, p. 185) provide a definition of food security governance as: "all modes of governing encompassing activities carried out by different actors to guide, steer, control or manage the pursuance of food security – in addressing food system vulnerabilities, both conceptually and practically". This definition, which can be adapted for pursuance of other public goods related to the food system (such as public health, environment, etc), is helpful insofar as it tells us that actors can exert differing degrees of authority and influence over decision-making. 'Controlling' and 'managing' are relatively heavy-handed and interventionalist, while 'steering' and 'guiding' leave some room for autonomy on the part of non-state actors who are involved in the activity or decision-making process. It does not, however, offer urban actors any guidance in identifying suitable governance arrangements or putting them in place. To do this, it is necessary to unpack the notion of governance 'mode'.

Lange et al. (2013) regard modes of governance as falling into three dimensions: politics, polity and policy. Modes in the politics dimension concern *which actors are involved and the interactions and power relationships between them*; modes in the polity dimension concern *the rules of engagement and how, and by whom, decisions are made*; and modes in the policy dimension concern

DOI: 10.4324/9781003055907-12

the objectives of the actors' joint endeavour and instruments used to achieve them. These dimensions inform the key considerations for determining suitable governance arrangements, with the potential modes in each situated along a continuum between state intervention and societal autonomy. Modes concerning rules of engagement and decision-making (the polity dimension) are sometimes referred to as organisational arrangements or governance 'form' (Kronsell & Bäckstrand, 2010).

Urban actors often seek practical guidance on what governance form to adopt and how to do so. One source of guidance is other cities. For instance, signatory cities of the Milan Urban Food Policy Pact look to each other for inspiration on how to fulfil the recommendations on governance contained in the Pact's Framework for Action.[1] Other international networks convened by expert organisations, like the C40 Food Network and the ICLEI-RUAF CITYFOOD Network, build capacity among their members and facilitate the sharing of experience and lessons and adaptation between contexts (on city food networks, see Chapter 27 by Giordano in this volume). National networks have also emerged in some countries, such as the Sustainable Food Cities Network in the United Kingdom. Sometimes two cities exchange bilaterally, either under the auspices of a network or independently, as in the case of London (UK) and Toronto (Canada) in the 1980s and 1990s (Mah & Thang, 2013).

Another source of governance guidance for cities is the various 'how to' guides by expert consultants and civil society organisations, which have systematised lessons from pioneering food cities for the benefit of new starters (e.g. IPES-Food, 2017; Moragues et al., 2013; Burgan & Winne, 2012; Harper et al., 2009). Some of the most common lessons concern governance structures, such as the formation of an entity and its institutional home vis-à-vis local government; others are procedural and are intended to promote accountability, legitimacy, fairness and performance, as well as evidence-based and appropriate decision-making relating to food issues.

In the academic literature, cities' experiences in urban food governance are treated as case studies and analysed retrospectively through a particular conceptual or theoretical lens (e.g. Coulson & Sonnino, 2019; Doernberg et al., 2019; Halliday, 2015; Sibbing et al., 2019; Schiff, 2008). This echoes Emerson and Nabatchi's (2015, p. 9) general observation regarding collaborative governance that 'scholars are working to catch up with the advances in [...] practice [...], and new knowledge is being produced rapidly'. While it is likely that some scholar-activists draw on their conceptual knowledge in their role as members of food policy councils and partnerships in their home towns and cities, to this author's knowledge there are no accounts of city actors systematically mining the theoretical governance literature for guidance on concepts they might apply in practice. Consequently, a rich vein of expertise and inspiration remains substantially untapped.

The purpose of this chapter is to introduce six conceptualisations that are relevant to urban food governance and to provide pointers on how their key tenets might be applied – in whole or in part, individually or in concert – to enable cities to cope better with food system challenges.

The six conceptualisations were purposively selected either because they are already reflected in practice to some extent, or because they have been used as a conceptual framework in previous academic analysis of urban food governance. The conceptualisations are categorised under three types, according to whether they are a form or practice of governance, and the interactions they concern:

(1) Governance forms – between actors
  - Networked governance
  - Collaborative governance

(2) Governance forms – between governance structures, entities or levels
  - Multilevel governance
  - Polycentric governance

(3) Practices to strengthen governance
  - Reflexive governance
  - Adaptive governance

The next section discusses the conceptualisations by type. Each conceptualisation is introduced with a presentation of the theoretical origins and key tenets, followed by an exploration of their use in urban food governance and analysis to date. For each type, overlaps and/or complementarities between the conceptualisations are identified, and the case is made for urban food governance actors to gain understanding and make practical use of the conceptualisations.

The concluding section recommends that urban food governance actors be apprised of, and draw guidance from, governance conceptualisations across all three types. It identifies a key role for scholar-activists in ensuring insights from conceptual literature is available and accessible to practitioners, and in monitoring and deploying emerging conceptual thinking.

Three types and six conceptualisations

Governance form between actors

The two conceptualisations in this type – collaborative governance and networked governance – can both form the basis of interactions between actors in urban food governance and are particularly relevant to food policy councils/partnerships. There is considerable overlap between the two, but they originate from different disciplines and their processes have different ends. In networked governance the emphasis is on leveraging resources to complete a task, whereas in collaborative governance there is a broader focus on consensus-building.

Networked governance

Origins and key tenets

Networked governance refers to the mechanism of making and implementing decisions through networks of actors and organisations (Hollstein et al., 2017). It originates from Powell's (1991) observation that networks are distinct from both the hierarchy and market modes of governance, with their own operational and structural characteristics, and representing a halfway house between top-down decision-making and actors choosing their own course of action.

Huppé et al. (2012) visualise a continuum of network types. At one end are networks with active steering by the state or another organisation in which all organisations (nodes) are connected to the single steering node but not to each other (Hollstein et al., 2017). At the other end are 'self-steering' networks in which each node is connected to all others (Hollstein et al., 2017). Some networks are formed on an informal basis while others have formal rules that guide collaboration (Hollstein et al., 2017).

A key premise of networked governance is that each organisation brings resources to the table – such as, for example, knowledge and expertise, creativity and ideas, human capacity, finance or legitimacy. Resources are collectively leveraged for tasks that no one organisation could fulfil using only its own resources (Huppé et al., 2012).

Use in urban food governance and analysis

Food policy councils/partnerships are examples of networked governance, with cases spanning Huppé et al.'s (2012) continuum of network types. There is a tendency for network type to be linked to institutional home. In those that have their institutional home within local government structures, such as the Antananarivo Food Policy Council in Madagascar (Andrianarisoa et al., 2019), local government tends to both convene and steer activities. In those hosted by civil society organisations, the host may play a steering role, such as in the Durham Food Partnership in the UK, which was led by Durham Community Action (Halliday, 2015). In those that occupy a neutral space as self-standing entities there is a greater likelihood of self-steering, as occurred in the Bristol Food Policy Council (Halliday & Barling, 2018), with charismatic leaders who may emerge from certain organisations to play a steering and mobilising role.

Regarding network formality, many food policy councils/partnerships draw up terms of reference to ensure all participants know what is expected of them (IPES-Food, 2017). This is particularly helpful when membership is voluntary because motivation may wane and conflicts occur over time, as happened in Belo Horizonte (Brazil) in 1998, when the civil society food security advisory board COMASA (*Conselho Municipal de Abastecimento e Segurança Alimentar*) collapsed following internal disagreements for which no mechanisms were in place to resolve (IPES-Food, 2017).

Existing literature on food policy councils/partnerships contains reports of various actors contributing resources to fulfil collective tasks. For example, Halliday (2015) found that a civil society organisation in London, UK, has provided the resource of capacity to perform tasks that the Mayor's team could not undertake for political reasons (Halliday, 2015). Mah and Thang (2013, p. 13) claim that the Toronto Food Strategy (TFS) has been 'quietly successful in leveraging existing resources and partnerships to achieve its aims'. Likewise, Candel (2020) noted that the food strategies of both Amsterdam and The Hague explicitly state that government has limited resources to realise objectives and that other stakeholders should participate.

While Candel attributes this expectation to the Dutch policy style, it can be interpreted in two ways: (1) as a pragmatic way to overcoming an obstacle to implementation; and (2) as local government co-opting non-state actors to do their work under the guise of governance, undermining a process that is supposed to be more democratic (Moragues-Faus & Sonnino, 2018). Sibbing et al. (2019), meanwhile, signal underperformance of Dutch city authorities in leveraging their policy-based resources as they prefer 'soft' and coercive instruments over 'hard', legislative instruments. They recommend municipalities learn and draw confidence from other municipalities' successful deployment of 'hard' instruments.

Collaborative governance

Origins and key tenets

Collaborative governance emerged in the late 1980s as an alternative to top-down managerialism (in which non-state actors are consulted but not truly involved in decision-making), and to adversarial interest group pluralism. Emerson and Nabatchi (2015) identify two drivers of collaborative governance in policy decision-making. The first driver is the 'hollowing-out' of the state due to decentralisation and devolution of responsibilities to sub-national governments, combined with shrinking budgets and delegation of service provision to private enterprise and non-profit organisations. The second driver is the emergence of complex ('wicked') social problems that require the combined efforts and resources of multiple organisations and sectors.

Emerson and Nabatchi (2015, p. 10) define collaborative governance as 'the processes and structures of public policy decision-making and management that engage people across the boundaries of public agencies, levels of government, and/or the public, private and civic spheres to carry out a public purpose that could not otherwise be accomplished'. This definition is deliberately capacious and is intended to resolve differences between multiple definitions and related terms that have emerged organically, causing confusion and impairing the precision of empirical application.

Emerson and Nabatchi (2015) also revise and expand upon some aspects of Ansell and Gash's earlier (2008) explanation of collaborative.

First, they dispense with Ansell and Gash's requirement that collaborative governance be instigated by public agencies, instead proposing a typology of initiations: self-initiation by participants; independent convention by a 'boundary-spanning' organisation; and external direction by leaders in a top-down fashion.

Second, they give more detail to Ansell and Gash's (2008, p. 544) description of decision-making in collaborative governance as 'formal, consensus-oriented, and deliberative', characterised by 'small wins that deepen trust, commitment, and shared understanding'. They propose an integrative framework consisting of three mutually reinforcing cycles: principled engagement, shared motivation, and capacity for joint action. The driving force within each cycle is cross-boundary collaboration towards some degree of collective purpose, but with an emphasis on *mutual* rather than *shared* understanding – that is, comprehension and respect of others' positions without necessarily agreeing with them.

Third, they include leverage of resources within the 'capacity for joint action' cycle, alongside procedural and institutional arrangements, leadership and knowledge, contextualising actors' willingness to leverage resources to collectively achieve a task as one part of a process, rather than a stand-alone process (as in networked governance).

This attempt at a comprehensive framework notwithstanding, Asenbaum (2016) identifies a tension between the objectives of consensus-building and of diverse participation, which means that collaborative governance is not always more 'democratic, inclusive and transparent than traditional hierarchical approaches' (Emerson & Nabatchi, 2015, p. 180). Moreover, collective governance brings no guarantee of meaningful participation by disempowered and disadvantaged groups, who may be less vocal, less politically savvy and suffering from a history of oppression (Asenbaum, 2016).

Use in urban food governance and analysis

Several authors explicitly identify multistakeholder platforms such as food policy councils, food partnerships and food strategy steering groups as collaborative governance arrangements in which participants co-produce an approach to address food system issues (Hoffmann, 2019; Coulson & Sonnino, 2019; Haysom, 2020). Bassarab et al. (2019) refer to food policy councils in the United States as 'collaborative governance networks'. Others use the term 'collaboration' freely in discussion with food policy councils and similar platforms, but without putting a conceptual label on the structures themselves (e.g. McCullagh & Santo, 2012; Mah & Thang, 2013; Candel, 2020; Moragues-Faus & Sonnino, 2018).

The case study literature supports Emerson and Nabatchi's (2015) flexibility over initiation of collaborative governance. Some food policy councils/partnerships have been instigated by local government, some were formed through bottom-up processes, and others through a combination of governmental and civil society forces. No examples of initiation by 'boundary-spanning' organisations have been identified by the current author, but food policy councils/

partnerships themselves are boundary-spanning as they tackle 'wicked problems' that require a systems-oriented approach (Bassarab et al., 2019; McCullagh & Santo, 2012).

The literature also contains clues on the nature of consensus and collaboration among stakeholders. Moragues-Faus (2020) and Moragues and Sonnino (2018) provide evidence that supports the need for initial consensus in views and values, identifying sustainability as a 'consensus frame' for the UK's Sustainable Food Cities Network that enables co-production of knowledge and collaboration. Similarly, Hoffmann (2019) found a strong collaborative relationship between the Berlin civic food policy council (Ernährungsrat) and Green Party members of the coalition government as a result of political alignment.

Mah and Thang (2013, p. 104) bear out the idea that consensus found through principled engagement or shared motivation can be the foundation for joint action, as they describe the role of the Toronto Food Strategy as 'brokering of working relationships across city government divisions and directorates, and with community-based organizations, Toronto residents, advocates, academia, businesses, and the agricultural sector'. Consensus does not always lead to joint action, however. Moragues-Faus (2020) found that actors in food partnerships may agree over identification of a problem but not over how to address it, leading each to pursue their own preferred course of action individually. This signals mutual (rather than shared) understanding and means that each actor can draw only on their own resources rather than the common store.

In some contexts, such as African cities, an initial consensus frame may be extremely hard to establish due to antagonistic relations between urban actors and lived experiences of poverty and food insecurity, politics and major institutional change in response to rapid urbanisation (Smit, 2019; Haysom, 2020). While Smit (2019, p. 101) maintains that 'it is only through collaborative processes that we can begin to develop well-functioning urban food systems in Africa', he and Haysom agree on the need for preparatory work to understand existing city governance processes and to unpick the interests and power dynamics of actors involved in them.

The need for such preparatory work in all contexts is supported by a body of work that critiques food policy councils/partnerships for their lack of inclusivity and uneven power dynamics. Slocum (2006) returned a stinging verdict on unacknowledged white privilege in community food organisations in the United States, which undermines efforts to build food democracy and justice. Others have warned against creating an 'illusion of inclusion' (McCullagh & Santo, 2012) or multistakeholder platforms that 'mask' unintentional or unexamined exclusion and power asymmetries (Moragues-Faus, 2020), resulting in further alienation and missed opportunities to reconfigure structural food system failures. McCullagh and Santo (2012) find conflict to be a natural result of meaningful inclusion, but it should be seized upon as an opportunity to surface differences and forge mutually acceptable solutions.

Overlaps, complementarities and practical value

Their different disciplinary origins and end games notwithstanding, there are clearly significant overlaps between networked and collaborative governance. In particular, Emerson and Nabatchi's (2015) broad definition of collaborative governance effectively subsumes elements of networked governance, not least since both involve leveraging of resources to realise a common task. Practically speaking, Emerson and Nabatchi's integrative framework for collaborative governance may be particularly helpful as a template to be adopted (or adapted) in the deployment of urban food governance.

However, since food policy councils/partnerships have been variously identified as examples of both networked and collaborative governance, with a tendency to conflate the two in the case study literature, it is advisable for urban food governance actors to be apprised of the two conceptualisations and to draw on them in concert as they determine optimal governance arrangements. This will enable them to carry out preparatory work and to critically reflect on the appropriate role of government, power dynamics and inclusivity, including interrogation of values, privilege and politics at play. In this way, they may forge arrangements that are truly intermediary between hierarchy and market modes of governance, and that advance – rather than co-opt – democracy in urban food systems.

There is a need for actors to interrogate the extent and limits of their powers, capacities and the instruments they might deploy, including governments stepping up with hard policy instruments wherever possible.

Governance forms between governance structures, entities or levels

The two conceptualisations in this type deal with relations between local-level urban food governance arrangements and arrangements at other levels and/or in other jurisdictions. Multilevel governance concerns relations between actors and organisations at different levels through the 'vertical' dimension, while polycentric governance primarily concerns relations between organisations and governance platforms on the territorial dimension.

Multilevel governance

Origins and key tenets

Multilevel governance is the distribution of power, policymaking capacity and responsibility between supra-national, national, regional and local levels, and the sharing of decision-making between public sector and non-governmental actors at each level.

The origins of multilevel governance lie in the study of European Union administration in the 1990s, but it applies in most country contexts, each having its own framework dividing powers, responsibilities and capacities between national and sub-national levels. Broadly speaking, there has been a global tendency towards devolution over the last 40 years, at least in terms of decision-making and delivery, if not always accompanied by devolved budgets (Rodriguez-Pose & Gill, 2003).

Multilevel governance comprises two strands. The first is relatively stable legal institutional frameworks that determine which actors, at which level, can make which decisions. The second concerns decisions related to different policy issues, which is subject to continuous negotiation between actors over specific decisions. In the second strand, negotiations take place both 'horizontally' to determine policy at a given level, and 'vertically' through the framing and constraining of local-level policy by regional, national or supra-national decisions, and attempts to influence other levels (Bevir, 2009).

Use in urban food governance and analysis

The local level has been proposed as most appropriate for action over food systems because the impacts of the dysfunctional globalised food system are most evident within communities and local environments (Doernberg et al., 2019). However, developing and implementing effective local-level actions can be disrupted by a lack of conducive policies at the regional and national levels (Morgan et al., 2009).

Conducive policy frameworks are uncommon, although they do exist in a handful of countries. For example, in Kenya the 2011 Urban Areas and Cities Act requires counties to regulate urban agriculture. In Indonesia, the national, provincial and district/city levels are each required to develop a Food and Nutrition Action Plan every five years. Such frameworks undoubtedly stimulate city-level policy development, but there is a risk that cities feel obliged to address national priorities rather than different, locally relevant problems, as seen in Surabaya, Indonesia, where the national focus on food production is less relevant than urban issues of distribution and affordability (Pamungkas et al., 2020).

At the inter-national level, there are ongoing efforts to foster an enabling environment for urban food policies through national policies. The United Nations Food and Agriculture Organizations' Framework for the Urban Food Agenda includes a support area on 'effective national, urban and territorial policies and transformative institutions to enhance sustainable food systems' (FAO, 2019).

In the meantime, cities often find ways to work around multilevel governance constraints. As Coulson and Sonnino (2019, p. 171) put it: 'By opportunistically and strategically working within the cracks of multilevel governance institutions and processes, food partnerships selectively enrol policy entrepreneurs and food champions to provide place-based responses to multiscalar socioecological challenges.' An example of this comes from The Netherlands, where advertising regulation is handled at the national level. This meant the city of Amsterdam could ban unhealthy food adverts in the public transportation system, where it controls advertising space, but not across the city as a whole (Danielli et al., 2021).

Cities might also seek actively to influence regional and national food policy. One way is through sharing the positive impacts of initiatives and advocating scale-up (Doernberg et al., 2019). For example, New York City's 2008 requirement of calorie labelling on restaurant menus was adopted by federal government two years later (NYC, 2017). Another way is through translocal governance, as replication of urban food actions by multiple cities creates critical mass to leverage higher-level change. For example, Cardiff's programme to ensure school children in deprived areas have access to heathy food outside of term-time inspired similar programmes in other UK cities and contributed to a national conversation about holiday hunger (Moragues-Faus & Sonnino, 2018).

Polycentric governance

Origins and key tenets

Polycentric governance is a system in which multiple governance centres consider each other and cooperate to address a specific issue by forming a cross-jurisdictional governance unit (Carlisle & Gruby, 2019; Feldman, 2016). Governance centres can be neighbouring, autonomous municipalities whose territories overlap in some respect (such as, for example, commuter belts or water sheds and other natural resource flows). They might also be 'nested' centres at multiple levels (local, regional and national), where each has a degree of jurisdiction over the issue in question.

The concept of polycentric governance originated in the empirical observation that local governments within the same metropolitan area address cross-jurisdictional problems, such as policing, through 'inter-organizational arrangements' (Ostrom & Ostrom, 1965). Polycentric governance has been particularly useful in managing socio-ecological systems, natural resources and eco-systems, particularly through social and environmental change.

Use in urban food governance and analysis

Food governance at the city region level is an example of polycentric governance. This can be 'nested' under the auspices of a city region authority, as in the case of Greater Manchester

(United Kingdom), where the Good Food Greater Manchester food partnership is an umbrella organisation to support and enhance sustainable food activities of ten metropolitan boroughs (St Clair & Morley, 2019).

Another approach is taken by the FAO-RUAF City Region Food System programme, which identifies functional geographical areas around one or more urban centres, their surrounding peri-urban and rural hinterlands, across and between which flow people, food, goods, resources and ecosystem services (Blay-Palmer et al., 2021). As such, a city region may include all or part of several administrative areas.

Overlaps, complementarities and practical value

While multilevel and polycentric governance concerns relations between actors and organisations on the vertical and territorial dimensions respectively, there are synergies between the two.

Polycentric governance also includes vertical, 'nested' governance elements, where multiple urban food governance arrangements are framed by, or feed up to, territorial or regional arrangements. Meanwhile, there may be more actors, from both local and regional levels, involved in negotiations over a specific policy domain in places with polycentric governance arrangements.

Conducive multilevel governance has been posited as a key factor in urban food systems transformation, but the multilevel perspective should consider any polycentric governance arrangements within the territorial dimension. Conducting research on the city region food system and engaging in stakeholder mapping and dialogue can build engagement towards a common purpose both across the territorial dimension *and* at the regional level.

Polycentric urban food governance will become increasingly important, as much of the urban growth projected by 2050 will occur in small and medium towns and cities. As conurbations form and encroach on rural hinterlands, tensions will emerge over natural resources – including those essential to food production (land, nutrient-rich soil, water) – and food supplies themselves.

Practices to strengthen governance

The two conceptualisations in this type concern making changes to governance structures and mechanisms, with the aim of improving performance in dealing with food system issues. Reflexive governance is generally a deliberative process that is either retrospective or continuous, while adaptive governance is the exercise of capacity for reactive and rapid change, occurring in real time in response to a disruptive event so as to minimise the impact on the food systems.

Reflexive governance

Origins and key tenets

Reflexive governance refers to the process of continuously scrutinising and adapting the concepts, practices and institutions through which governance takes place, to enable the most effective solutions to social problems (Voss & Kemp, 2006). It emerged in the 1990s but was only applied to environmental and sustainability governance in the 2000s, as academics realised the limited efficacy of regulatory or market-based approaches in addressing these challenges (Feindt & Weiland, 2018).

Voss and Kemp (2006) identify two orders of reflexive governance. The first order concerns detecting (unintended) consequences of policies that have been introduced, and subsequent steps to handle those consequences. The second order examines the structures, systems, institutional arrangements and assumptions that underlie how problems are addressed, and how these can affect consequences. Under the second order, actors at different levels may also examine their own positionality and assumptions, which frame how problems are discussed and solutions developed, with a view to creating new discursive spaces and coming up with innovations.

Lenoble and de Schutter (2010) identify three models for conducting reflexivity over mechanisms and institutional structures: the 'relational-collaborative' model of dialogue, deliberation and participation; the 'pragmatic' model of comparing and evaluating various mechanisms in deliberative forums; and the 'generic' model of examining past experiences to inform future strategies.

Use in urban food governance and analysis

The case study literature contains examples of both first- and second-order reflexive governance during and after food policymaking, and use of all three of Lenoble and de Schutter's (2010) models.

Sonnino et al. (2014) detected reflexive governance in the multilevel governance framework of Brazil that devolves implementation of school feeding to the local level, thereby creating space for local actors to reflect on the most suitable local approach and to send post implementation feedback up to the national level. Depending on proceedings at the local level, this may include elements of the 'pragmatic' and 'generic' models.

First order reflexivity is enabled by continuous impact monitoring during implementation. In Amsterdam, The Netherlands, monitoring of interventions under the Healthy Weight Programme enabled a consequence of a policy to only provide water for children in schools to be quickly identified; parents sought to compensate for a perceived shortfall in vitamin intake by providing excessive sugary fruit juice at home (IPES-Food, 2017). The problem was remedied by educating parents that water is the healthiest drink.

Second-order reflexive governance can also take place during implementation, when governance arrangements need to respond to changing circumstances. Moragues-Faus (2020) reported on the constant need for food partnerships in the United Kingdom to reshape their structures, systems and arrangements (through the 'relational-collaborative' model) in response to, for example, changes in support from local agencies, and the need to marshal conflicting interests from participants. Moreover, organisational membership may need to be reviewed for each project to ensure all actions are appropriate and informed by knowledge and lived experience (McCullagh & Santo, 2012).

Elsewhere second-order reflexivity is a retrospective undertaking, either at the end of a specific project or as part of a programmed governance review. As Moragues-Faus (2020) points out, formal governance reviews can be hard to justify when resources are scarce. Self-assessment can be a relatively cost-effective approach, however; the Food Policy Council Self-Assessment Tool developed and tested by Calancie et al. (2017) is a 'generic' model designed to measure members' perceptions of governance structures and processes at a particular moment. Some have advocated including consideration of ensuring equity, empowerment and meaningful inclusion of diverse community residents in such reviews (McCullagh & Santo, 2012), as well as calling for all actors to exercise reflexivity over their own (racial, socio-economic or other) privilege (Slocum, 2006).

Adaptive governance

Origins and key tenets

Adaptive governance is the exercise of actors' capacity to reorganise structures, decision-making processes, and rules and norms in a bid to increase resilience of socio-ecological systems to (unforeseen) ecological and environmental change.

The origins of adaptive governance stem from the intersection of institutional theory and ecological systems theory in natural resource management. The term itself was coined by Dietz et al. (2003), who observed that stable communities have governed common resources for centuries but their ability to do so can end abruptly when sudden change occurs. They set out four prerequisites (PRQ) for adaptation taking place within governance structures:

- PRQ1: inclusive dialogue and deliberation (*analytic deliberation*);
- PRQ2: complex institutional arrangements at multiple levels (*nesting*);
- PRQ3: use of a variety of rules drawn from hierarchical top-down government systems, market incentives and community self-governance mechanisms (*institutional variety*); and
- PRQ4: facilitation of experimentation, learning and change.

Folke et al. (2005) took up this list in their exploration of the socio-ecological systems in moments of crisis and subsequent renewal and reorganisation, adding:

- PRQ5: generation and mobilisation of scientific learning from various fields (*knowledge, learning and practice*);
- PRQ6: capacity of leaders to learn from experiences and for their organisations to retain that knowledge (*organisational learning*);
- PRQ7: local community-based resource management systems working with, and receiving support from, organisations at various levels (*co-management*); and
- PRQ8: devolution of power into participatory social network structures (*social capital*).

Use in urban food governance and analysis

The concept of adaptive governance has been applied to food security governance in South Africa (Pereira & Ruysenaar, 2012) and to an analysis of how existing governance structures and processes in Queensland, Australia affected food systems actors' ability to be responsive and collaborative in endeavours to maintain food security following flooding in 2011 (Smith & Lawrence, 2018). Both these papers identified a need for more participatory arrangements involving non-state actors, corresponding to the co-management and social capital prerequisites.

Blay-Palmer et al. (2021) found that cities that had previously adopted a city region food system approach – including establishing multistakeholder governance platforms – had greater capacity to bridge supply failures and respond to emergency needs during the food crisis brought about by the COVID-19 pandemic in 2020. Even so, some cities with a long history of food governance (such as Bristol, UK) still encountered difficulties in coordinating emergency responses, signalling the need to improve performance on the eight prerequisites for adaptive capacity.

Overlaps, complementarities and practical value

There are notable overlaps between adaptive and reflexive governance. Two of the prerequisites of adaptive governance – PRQ4: facilitation of experimentation, learning and change; (Dietz et al., 2003) and PRQ6: the capacity of leaders to learn from experiences and for their organisations to retain that knowledge (Folke et al., 2005) – evoke Lenoble and de Schutter's generic model of reflexive governance, which is based on examination of past experiences to inform future strategies.

Practically speaking, adaptive capacity can be a form of second-order reflexive governance, when changes are made in real time in response to changing needs and conditions. A reflexive governance process may also be triggered in the wake of a crisis that required adaptive governance, with a view to increasing capacity and, as a result, building resilience.

Most significantly, however, the models of reflexive governance, and prerequisites (of adaptive governance), can be variously applied to the conceptualisations in the two previous 'form' types – as shown in Table 10.1 below.

An understanding of why and how to apply reflexive governance will enable urban food actors to design governance structures and processes that are optimised to each task. Moreover,

Table 10.1 Application of models of reflexive governance and prerequisites of adaptive governance to conceptualisations of governance form

	Models of reflexive governance	*PRQ of adaptive governance*
Collaborative	Relational-collaborative Pragmatic Generic	PRQ1: inclusive dialogue and deliberation PRQ4: facilitation of experimentation, learning and change PRQ5: generation and mobilisation of scientific learning from various fields PRQ8: devolution of power into participatory social network structures
Networked	Pragmatic Generic	PRQ3: use of a variety of rules drawn from hierarchical top-down government systems, market incentives and community self-governance mechanisms PRQ4: facilitation of experimentation, learning and change PRQ5: generation and mobilisation of scientific learning from various fields PRQ8: devolution of power into participatory social network structures
Multilevel		PRQ2: complex institutional arrangements at multiple levels PRQ7: local community-based resource management systems working with, and receiving support from, organisations at various levels PRQ8: devolution of power into participatory social network structures
Polycentric		PRQ2: complex institutional arrangements at multiple levels (nesting) PRQ7: local community-based resource management systems working with, and receiving support from, organisations at various levels PRQ8: devolution of power into participatory social network structures

Source: Author's compilation.

the climate crisis and potential future epidemics/pandemics mean that urban food systems will be subject to repeated, increasingly frequent disruptions in the future. The eight principles of Dietz et al. (2003) and Folke et al. (2005) may serve as a checklist for actors, either as they establish governance structures and processes or as part of reflexivity.

Conclusions and future work

This chapter has explained the origins and core tenets of six governance conceptualisations by type, and their use in urban food governance practice and analysis to date. For each type, the case has been made for urban food actors to gain an understanding of the conceptualisations and to use them – in whole or in part, individually or synergistically – to inform the design and review of food governance structures and processes.

In addition, urban food governance actors are advised to be apprised of, and to draw guidance from, all three types of governance conceptualisations, rather than focusing on just one of the form types, or the practice type in isolation. This is because, firstly, the two 'form' types relate to different arrangements – type one to arrangements between actors, and type two to arrangements between governance structures, entities or levels. Thus, the conceptualisations can inform different aspects or dimensions of urban food systems governance. Secondly, within the 'practice' type, the models (of reflexive governance) and prerequisites (of adaptive governance) can be used to strengthen governance in either (or both) of the two form types.

The limited scope of this chapter meant it was only possible to give an introduction to the key tenets of each conceptualisation. More detailed work is needed to ensure the conceptual and theoretical literature is fully exploited, and that the knowledge gained is made available and accessible to non-academic urban food practitioners. This might include production of a next generation of 'how to' guides that are informed both by the burgeoning store of practical urban food governance experiences *and* more theoretical discussions.

Within cities, scholar-activists who hold a seat on their local food policy council/partnership occupy a space at the interface between theory and practice. As such, they are in a unique position to facilitate practitioners' access to, and understanding of, conceptual literature by, for instance, drawing on their theoretical training to give tailored guidance on establishing optimal governance arrangements within a particular context. They may also keep abreast of evolving conceptual debate so that it can be rapidly deployed in the practice of urban food systems governance.

Note

1 The Milan Urban Food Policy Pact (MUFPP) is an international agreement launched in 2015 to address food issues at the city level. It has been signed by 2,011 Mayors (as of 2021). The Pact includes includes governance under its Framework for Action.

References

Andrianarisoa, O., Zuleta Ferrari, C., Currie, P., & Coetzee, I. (2019). Antananarivo Food Policy Council: Policy as Practice. *Urban Agriculture Magazine, 36*, October, RUAF.

Ansell, C., & Gash, A. (2008). Collaborative Governance in Theory and Practice. *Journal of Public Administration Research and Theory, 18*(4), 543–571. https://doi.org/10.1093/jopart/mum032

Asenbaum, H. (2016). Facilitating Inclusion: Austrian Wisdom Councils as Democratic Innovation between Consensus and Diversity. *Journal of Public Deliberation, 12*(2). https://doi.org/10.16997/jdd.259

Bassarab, K., Clark, J. K., Santo, R., & Palmer, A. (2019). Finding Our Way to Food Democracy: Lessons from US Food Policy Council Governance. *Politics and Governance*, 7(4), 32–47. https://doi.org/10.17645/pag.v7i4.2092

Bevir, M. (2009). *Key Concepts in Governance (SAGE Key Concepts series)* (1st ed.). London: SAGE Publications.

Blay-Palmer, A., Santini, G., Halliday, J., Malec, R., Carey, J., Keller, L., Ni, J., Taguchi, M., & van Veenhuizen, R. (2021). City Region Food Systems: Building Resilience to COVID-19 and Other Shocks. *Sustainability*, *13*(3), 1325. https://doi.org/10.3390/su13031325

Burgan, M., & Winne, M. (2012). *Doing Food Policy Councils Right: A Guide to Development and Action*. Santa Fe, NM: Mark Winne Associates.

Calancie, L., Allen, N. E., Weiner, B. J., Ng, S. W., Ward, D. S., & Ammerman, A. (2017). Food Policy Council Self-Assessment Tool: Development, Testing, and Results. *Preventing Chronic Disease*, *14*, 160281. https://doi.org/10.5888/pcd14.160281

Candel, J. J. L. (2020). What's on the Menu? A Global Assessment of MUFPP Signatory Cities' Food Strategies. *Agroecology and Sustainable Food Systems*, *44*(7), 919–946. https://doi.org/10.1080/21683565.2019.1648357

Carlisle, K., & Gruby, R. L. (2019). Polycentric Systems of Governance: A Theoretical Model for the Commons. *Policy Studies Journal*, *47*(4), 927–952. https://doi.org/10.1111/psj.12212

Coulson, H., & Sonnino, R. (2019). Re-scaling the Politics of Food: Place-based Urban Food Governance in the UK. *Geoforum*, *98*, 170–179. https://doi.org/10.1016/j.geoforum.2018.11.010

Danielli, S., Coffey, T., Ashrafian, H., & Darzi, A. (2021). Systematic Review into City Interventions to Address Obesity. *EClinicalMedicine*, *32*, 100710. https://doi.org/10.1016/j.eclinm.2020.100710

Dietz, T., Ostrom, E., & Stern, P. C. (2003). The Struggle to Govern the Commons. *Science*, *302*(5652), 1907–1912. https://doi.org/10.1126/science.1091015

Doernberg, A., Horn, P., Zasada, I., & Piorr, A. (2019). Urban Food Policies in German City Regions: An Overview of Key Players and Policy Instruments. *Food Policy*, *89*, 101782. https://doi.org/10.1016/j.foodpol.2019.101782

Emerson, K., & Nabatchi, T. (2015). *Collaborative Governance Regimes (Public Management and Change)*. Washington, DC: Georgetown University Press.

FAO. (2019). *FAO framework for the Urban Food Agenda*. Rome: United Nations Food and Agriculture Organization.

Feindt, P. H., & Weiland, S. (2018). Reflexive Governance: Exploring the Concept and Assessing its Critical Potential for Sustainable Development. *Journal of Environmental Policy & Planning*, *20*(6), 661–674. https://doi.org/10.1080/1523908x.2018.1532562

Feldman, D. (2016). Polycentric Governance. In Bainbridge, W. S., & Roco, M. C. (Eds.), *Handbook of Science and Technology Convergence* (pp. 877–890). New York: Springer.

Folke, C., Hahn, T., Olsson, P., & Norberg, J. (2005). Adaptive Governance of social-Ecological Systems. Annu*al* Revie*w of* Environ*ment and* Resour*ces*, 30, 441–473.

Halliday, J. (2015). *A New Institutionalist Analysis of Local Level Food Policy in England between 2012 and 2014*. Doctoral thesis, Food Policy specialization. City, University London.

Halliday, J., & Barling, D. (2018). The Role and Engagement of City Mayors in Local Food Policy Groups in England: Comparing the Cases of London and Bristol. In Barling, D., & Fanzo, J. (Eds.), *Advances in Food Security and Sustainability, Vol. 3* (1st Ed.). Cambridge: Academic Press.

Harper, A., Alkon, A., Shattuck, A., Holt-Giménez, E., & Lambrick, F. (2009). *Food Policy Councils: Lessons Learned*. Oakland, CA: Food First, Institute for Food and Development Policy.

Haysom, G. (2020). *Urban Food Governance Perspectives in Changing African and Southern Cities*, HCP Discussion Paper No. 39, Waterloo and Cape Town.

Hoffmann, D. (2019). *Collaborating towards Berlin Food Policy: Exploring Civic-State Collaboration in Current Urban Food Governance in Berlin – The Case of the Berlin Food Strategy*. MSc student Communication, Health and Life Sciences, Specialization: Health and Society. Wageningen University.

Hollstein B., Matiaske W., & Schnapp, K. U. (2017). Networked Governance: Taking Networks Seriously. In Hollstein, B., Matiaske, W., & Schnapp, K. U. (Eds.), *Networked Governance*. New York: Springer.

Huppé, G., Creech, H., & Knoblauch, D. (2012). *The Frontiers of Networked Governance*. Winnipeg: International Institute for Sustainable Development.

IPES-Food. (2017). *What Makes Urban Food Policy Happen? Insights from Five Case Studies*. Leuven: International Panel of Experts on Sustainable Food Systems.

Kronsell, A., & Bäckstrand, K. (2010). Rationality and Forms of Governance. A Framework for Analyzing the Legitimacy of New Modes of Governance. In Bäckstrand, K., Lövbrand, E., Khan, J., & Kronsell, A. (Eds.), *Environmental Politics and Deliberative Democracy: Examining the Promise of New Modes of Governance*. Cheltenham: Edward Elgar Publishing.

Lange, P., Driessen, P. P., Sauer, A., Bornemann, B., & Burger, P. (2013). Governing Towards Sustainability—Conceptualizing Modes of Governance. *Journal of Environmental Policy & Planning, 15*(3), 403–425. https://doi.org/10.1080/1523908x.2013.769414

Lenoble, J., & de Schutter, O. (2010). *Reflexive Governance: Redefining the Public Interest in a Pluralistic World*. Cumnor: Hart Publishing.

Mah, C. L., & Thang, H. (2013). Cultivating Food Connections: The Toronto Food Strategy and Municipal Deliberation on Food. *International Planning Studies, 18*(1), 96–110. https://doi.org/10.1080/13563475.2013.750941

McCullagh, M., & Santo, R. (2012). *Food Policy for All: Inclusion of Diverse Community Residents on Food Policy Councils*. Adapted from Molly McCullagh's Master's thesis research, Tufts University.

Moragues, A., Morgan, K., Moschitz, H., Neimane, I., Nilsson, H., Pinto, M., Rohracher, H., Ruiz, R., Thuswald, M., Tisenkopfs, T., & Halliday, J. (2013). *Urban Food Strategies: The Rough Guide to Sustainable Food Systems*. Document developed in the framework of the FP7 project FOODLINKS (GA No. 265287).

Moragues-Faus, A. (2020). Towards a critical governance framework: Unveiling the political and justice dimensions of urban food partnerships. *The Geographical Journal, 186*(1), 73–86. https://doi.org/10.1111/geoj.12325

Moragues-Faus, A., & Sonnino, R. (2018). Re-assembling Sustainable Food Cities: An Exploration of Translocal Governance and its Multiple Agencies. *Urban Studies, 56*(4), 778–794. https://doi.org/10.1177/0042098018763038

Moragues-Faus, A., Sonnino, R., & Marsden, T. (2017). Exploring European Food System Vulnerabilities: Towards Integrated Food Security Governance. *Environmental Science & Policy, 75*, 184–215. https://doi.org/10.1016/j.envsci.2017.05.015

Morgan, K., Marsden, T., & Murdoch, J. (2009). *Worlds of Food: Place, Power, and Provenance in the Food Chain (Oxford Geographical and Environmental Studies Series)* (Reprint ed.). Oxford: Oxford University Press.

NYC. (2017). De Blasio Administration Announces New Calories Labeling Rules. Press release. Office of the Mayor, City Hall, New York. www1.nyc.gov/office-of-the-mayor/news/318-17/de-blasio-administration-new-calorie-labeling-rules

Ostrom, V., & Ostrom, E. (1965). A Behavioral Approach to the Study of Intergovernmental Relations. *Annals of the American Academy of Political and Social Science, 359*(May), 135–146.

Pamungkas, N. P., Santoso, E. B., & Wijaya, I. (2020). Challenges Associated with Formulation of Urban-Based Food and Nutrition Policy in Surabaya City, Indonesia. *Journal of Nutritional Science and Vitaminology, 66*(Supplement), S417–S424. https://doi.org/10.3177/jnsv.66.s417

Pereira, L. M., & Ruysenaar, S. (2012). Moving from Traditional Government to New Adaptive Governance: The Changing Face of Food Security Responses in South Africa. *Food Security, 4*(1), 41–58. https://doi.org/10.1007/s12571-012-0164-5

Powell, W. (1991). Neither Market nor Hierarchy: Network Forms of Organization. In Thompson, G., Francis, J., Levacic, R., & Mitchell, J. (Eds.), *Markets, Hierarchies and Networks: The Co-ordination of Social Life*. London: SAGE Publications.

Rodríguez-Pose, A., & Gill, N. (2003). The Global Trend towards Devolution and its Implications. *Environment and Planning C: Government and Policy, 21*(3), 333–351. https://doi.org/10.1068/c0235

Schiff, R. (2008). The Role of Food Policy Councils in Developing Sustainable Food Systems. *Journal of Hunger & Environmental Nutrition, 3*(2–3), 206–228. https://doi.org/10.1080/19320240802244017

Sibbing, L., Candel, J., & Termeer, K. (2019). A Comparative Assessment of Local Municipal Food Policy Integration in the Netherlands. *International Planning Studies, 26*(1), 56–69. https://doi.org/10.1080/13563475.2019.1674642

Slocum, R. (2006). Anti-racist Practice and the Work of Community Food Organizations. *Antipode, 38*(2), 327–349. https://doi.org/10.1111/j.1467-8330.2006.00582.x

Smit, W. (2019). Current Urban Food Governance and Planning in Africa. In Battersby, J., & Watson, V. (Eds.), *Urban Food Systems Governance and Poverty in African Cities. Routledge Studies in Food, Society and the Environment* (1st ed.) (pp. 94–103). Oxon: Routledge.

Smith, K., & Lawrence, G. (2018). From Disaster Management to Adaptive Governance? Governance Challenges to Achieving Resilient Food Systems in Australia. *Journal of Environmental Policy & Planning*, *20*(3), 387–401. https://doi.org/10.1080/1523908x.2018.1432344

Sonnino, R., Lozano Torres, C., & Schneider, S. (2014). Reflexive Governance for Food Security: The Example of School Feeding in Brazil. *Journal of Rural Studies*, *36*, 1–12. https://doi.org/10.1016/j.jrurstud.2014.06.003

St Clair, R., & Morley, A. (2019). A City-Regional Strategic Food Partnership. *Urban Agriculture Magazine*, *36*, October, RUAF.

Stoker, G. (2000). Urban Political Science and the Challenge of Urban Governance. In J. Pierre (Ed.), *Debating Governance: Authority, Steering and Democracy* (pp. 91–109). Oxford: Oxford University Press. https://doi.org/10.1016/j.jrurstud.2014.06.003

Voss, J-P., & Kemp, R. (2006). Sustainability and Reflexive Governance: Introduction. In Voss, J-P., Bauknecht, D., & Kemp, R. (Eds.), *Reflexive Governance for Sustainable Development* (pp. 3–30). Cheltenham: Edward Elgar Publishing.

11

EXPLORING URBAN FOODSCAPES VIA FEMINIST POLITICAL ECOLOGY

Alice J. Hovorka

Introduction

Amidst the robust field of urban food governance, there is a timely and urgent need to generate nuanced and comprehensive insights on gendered food dynamics in cities around the world. To this end, feminist political ecology offers an important conceptual frame through which to critically assess the role of gender in shaping urban food systems and security outcomes, as well as informing urban governance trajectories.

Feminist political ecology illuminates how food 'works' through gender relations of power in the city – affecting the daily lives and livelihoods of urban residents, shaping channels of food production, distribution and consumption, and impacting food access and security. It also offers a practical frame through which to understand and transform urban food governance to facilitate more just and sustainable futures for all. Importantly, a necessarily *feminist* approach emphasises the 'political punch' that pushes gender beyond is neutral façade, reduced to a technical fix and tokenistic application (Tamale, 2006; Cornwall et al., 2004). A feminist lens exposes how power operates to establish gendered circumstances and experiences, (re)produced across scale and manifested in differential and inequitable access to food. As such, feminised scholarship exploring urban food systems and security is vital to unearth key structures and dynamics, and to facilitate appropriate urban governance interventions.

I begin this chapter with an overview of feminist political ecology (FPE), including its prevailing conceptual characteristics, seminal works, and key themes, debates, and directions over the past three decades. I then present my FPE-inspired concept of *feminist foodscapes*: specifically, a holistic, intersectional, and politicised vision of gender to serve an explanatory and emancipatory frame in the realm of urban food systems and security. My empirical research, situated in Botswana, demonstrates the pivotal role of gender in how food 'works' in and around the capital of Gaborone. Specifically, it shows that gender dynamics permeate all scales, realms, and actors associated with the urban food system, even when gender is not self-evident. It also documents the implications of gender norms for key stakeholders, structural sectors, and food security, revealing the differences and inequalities embedded within the urban foodscape. I conclude this chapter by reiterating the key conceptual contributions of FPE and offering concrete and practical steps to bring this scholarly discussion into the realm of urban governance.

DOI: 10.4324/9781003055907-13

Feminist Political Ecology

Feminist political ecology is a critical approach to understanding human–environment interactions inspired by feminist movements of the 1970s and women-centred scholarship grounded in a feminist sensibility (Sundberg, 2017). FPE emerged from spirited debate and theorising in ecofeminism, feminist science studies, and feminist critiques of development (see Elmhirst, 2015; Nightingale, 2011; Sundberg, 2017).

The seminal edited volume by Rocheleau et al. (1996) conceptualises FPE as an integrated conceptual framework with gender identified as a key variable in shaping experiences of and responses to environmental change, rooted in political and economic systems, as well as the resultant impacts on livelihoods, landscapes, and social relations. Early FPE scholarship theorises the differential, and often inequitable access to, distribution and control of resources by gender, as well as other identifiers including class, race, ethnicity, and age (e.g. Carr, 2020; Elmhirst & Resurreccion, 2008; Gururani, 2002; Harris, 2006; Hovorka, 2005; Nightingale, 2006, 2011; Rocheleau et al., 1996). Gender is conceptualised as a locally based 'meaning system' produced and reproduced through political economic relations, social and cultural institutions, and ecologically based struggles manifested across multiple scales, be they global, national, regional, or local (Rocheleau et al., 1996). Importantly, FPE engages women as political actors, agents of environmental change, and bearers/producers of environmental knowledge (Sundberg, 2017). It also legitimises local or everyday realms as important sites, spaces, and scales in their own right; individuals, households, neighbourhoods, and communities take centre stage alongside embodied practices and multifaceted social identities through which socioecological dimensions of political economic dynamics emerge and evolve.

Empirical work by FPE scholars in the 1990s and 2000s highlights themes related to gender and development, namely natural resource use and food/agrarian restructuring. It also illuminates the nuanced and complex (re)negotiation of gender roles, responsibilities, spaces, and human–environment interactions that take place at the local level in response to larger-scale transformation. Notably, these studies demonstrate how development projects or political economic restructuring disproportionately and negatively impact women's ability to fulfil their roles and secure their livelihoods while men's power and control remains intact or enhanced.

For example, work on gender relations in The Gambia demonstrates how land tenure reforms and an irrigation project specifically intended to benefit women resulted in a redefinition of traditional land rights and labour roles. The seasonal and spatial complementarity of male and female cropping systems broke down, resulting in serious conflicts at the household and community levels over both land and labour resources (Carney, 1988). The restructuring of family labour required to engage in irrigated agriculture had varying degrees of impact on men's and women's claims to resources. In particular, women's traditional floodplain fields were destroyed, and the process of wetland conversion has meant that women have reduced control over lowland resources (Carney, 1993).

Schroeder (1997) reveals that international development projects in The Gambia, on the one hand, created a pattern of gender-sensitive investments and a subsequent boom in women's market gardening. On the other hand, male landholders fought and regained what they felt were eroding land rights by working with extension agents to establish (male) orchards directly on top of women's successful garden plots. In a similar vein, Mackenzie (1998) found that the introduction and adoption of new high-yielding maize and beans caused the intensification of women's labour power during the colonial period in Murang'a District, Kenya. In turn, this reinforced and intensified men's control over women given that they controlled the resources and production associated with maize and beans. Despite their intensified workload, women resisted this intensified male control, in part by reinforcing their efforts to produce traditional millet and njahi (Kenyan Black Bean) for which they would reap the benefits of commercial sale.

Guyer's (1987) work on Cameroon presents a similar analysis of how the introduction of cocoa in the 1930s transformed Beti farming systems such that women became primary producers of household foodstuffs. Leach (1994) also found an increase in women's workloads through swamp development, promoted as an agricultural development strategy in Sierra Leone. Here husbands claimed women's labour for the increased rice transplantation involved in swamp cultivation while women lost access to intercrop-planting sites. Moore and Vaughn (1987) also found that commercialisation and technological improvements to boost agricultural productivity in Zambia meant more work for women, and thus decreased productivity in those households previously capable of sustaining their families through slash-and-burn cultivation.

New FPE debates and directions emerged in the 2010s. In terms of new debates, FPE scholars (Nightingale, 2011; Hovorka, 2015; Sultana, 2011) began to destabilise the concept of gender by emphasising intersectionality as a primary method to address social subject formation, as constituted in and through diverse and interlocking processes of differentiation, such as gender, race, ethnicity, class, and sexuality, and through material ecological relations (Sundberg, 2017). Nightingale's (2006, 2011) work is a stand-out in terms of gendered intersectionality, whereby she shifts from exploring gender roles and responsibilities in and of themselves to how gender identities and subjectivities are performed and imbued with power to shape socioecological outcomes. Her case study on community forestry in Nepal demonstrates how women of varying castes are constructed in differential and inequitable ways, as manifested in natural resource management activities. Here a group of high caste men limit women's leaf harvesting duties on supposed ecological grounds, which in turn draws out varying forms of women's protest and engagement of gendered cultural practices along caste-based inequities. Pointedly, and destabilising gender further, Mollett and Faria (2013) note that researchers privilege gender without full consideration of how it intersects with race; they engage whiteness as shaping the production of knowledge in FPE and call for a postcolonial intersectional approach to situate patriarchy and racialisation more thoroughly. Further still, recent FPE threads discuss gender as a constructed meaning system beyond-the-binary (Harcourt et al., 2015).

In terms of new directions, while FPE scholars continue to illuminate issues related to natural resources and food/agrarian restructuring (Jarosz, 2011; Kimura & Katano, 2014), they have expanded FPE work topically to include a focus on the commons and communing (Clement et al., 2019; Harcourt, 2019; Sato & Soto Alarcón, 2019), displacement (Vaz-Jones, 2018), energy (Gay-Antaki, 2016; Shrestha et al., 2019), and extractive industries (Behzadi, 2019). Other FPE scholars have engaged with the body as a site of analysis to draw in concepts of affect, emotion, and embodiment as mediating conflicts over resource access and use, environmental governance, and human–environmental relationships broadly (Carney, 2014; Doshi, 2017; Hayes-Conroy & Hayes-Conroy, 2013, 2015; Sultana, 2011; Truelove, 2011). Other FPE scholars have turned attention to nonhuman animals and human–animal relations (Hobson, 2007; Hovorka, 2015).

Notably, given the content of this volume, a necessarily *urban* body of FPE scholarship remains limited and underexplored. Early out of the gate, Freidberg (2002) focuses on the peri-urban zone in Burkina Faso to draw attention to how processes of urbanisation impact gender relations in terms of food production and labour. Freidberg argues that the redefinition of men's and women's productive roles associated with market gardening must be understood in the context of changing economic conditions, power relations, and social norms that have come about in part on account of rural–urban transformation. Drawing on the context of two market gardening villages outside Bobo-Dioulasso, her investigation reveals both the opportunities and difficulties facing men and women within the rural–urban interface. While the city offers women a means towards greater economic autonomy, it weakens their potential to engage with community-based development and conservation initiatives and their ability to maintain ties to, and control over, natural resources surrounding close settled zones.

Drawing inspiration from this early urban FPE intervention, Hovorka (2006a) engages FPE to demonstrate how agrarian restructuring and rural–urban transformation in Botswana offers women opportunities to renegotiate their marginalised position within the commercial urban agriculture sector in Greater Gaborone. While there remains some continuity of women's socio-economic disadvantages relative to men's, women are actively making claims on land and subverting their traditional roles to their advantage by dominating and succeeding in the poultry sector. Further, Shillington (2008, 2013) offers feminist perspectives on human–nature relations of home patios (gardens) in a marginalised barrio (slum) in Managua, Nicaragua. This important work draws forth the significance of domestic activities and home spaces in the (re) production of socioecological relations. Shillington details how corporeal, aesthetic, and economic relations shape human–plant–tree configurations and imaginaries in the production of habitable space in cities. Here households attempt to transform urban natures that assist in creating more liveable home and body spaces.

Moving from urban production of food and flora to water, FPE scholars offer key insights on urban water access and distribution. For example, Truelove (2011) engages FPE to reconceptualise water inequality in Delhi, India given its effectiveness at unearthing key drivers of everyday practices and micropolitics within communities. Doing so she illuminates how patterns of criminality, class, and gender are embedded in the experience of water inequalities forged on the body and within urban spaces, including households, communities, streets, open spaces, and places of work. Further, Adams et al. (2018) explore how gender dynamics influence participation in community-based urban water governance systems in Lilongwe, Malawi. They find that Water User Associations in urban informal settlements do not guarantee equitable participation given gendered politics and sociocultural practices of representation and exclusion. Ultimately women's agency is suppressed and gender-based inequalities reinforced. Buechler and Hanson's (2015) edited volume highlights both rural and urban contexts when considering issues related to women, water, and environmental change; they explicitly focus on women and gendered subjects to draw attention to those most affected or marginalised by neoliberal, colonial, and patriarchal systems in which water and climate policy are carried out.

In turn, Buechler et al. (2020) combine an FPE and water–energy–food nexus lens to gender, along with age and class in women's experiences with solar energy projects in urban and rural USA and Mexico. Their findings illuminate women's roles as important community leaders, decision makers, and labourers for livelihood-related energy use; they also shed light on how the policy and institutional context in which the small-scale projects were inserted shaped women's access to training and technologies. A particularly exciting avenue for urban FPE, and FPE more broadly, is offered by Doshi (2017), who makes the case for more rigorous treatment of the body as a material and political site in urban political ecology. Doshi grounds her argument in a feminist, anti-racist and postcolonial approach, and she proposes a conceptual focus on metabolism, social reproduction, intersectionality and articulation, emotion and affect, and political subjectivity. The urban appears as a key context through which the body is mobilised materially and politically.

In sum, FPE demonstrates how gender, in its intersectional forms, structures access to knowledge, spaces and resources, and socio-political processes; how scale, power, and nature operate in gendered human–environment relations; and how individual identities are wrapped up in and shape environmental interactions and ecological contexts. FPE provides an important foundation for attending to gendered opportunities and challenges in relation to socio-environmental change. Interestingly, with over three decades of highlighting and complexifying core concepts of gender, scale, power, and nature, FPE consistently eschews a single, narrow analytical framework. Instead, it comprises an eclectic mix of theoretical positions drawn from feminist theory, including those grounded in gender and development studies, structuralism, poststructuralism, posthumanism, postcapitalism, and postcolonial feminist theories (Elmhirst, 2015). This open-ended characteristic of FPE offers a sensitivity and malleability to the complex power relations that underlie environmental issues, rather than an emphasis on managerial, problem-solving approaches (Elmhirst, 2015).

Moreover, FPE scholarship does not limit itself to academic or theoretical realms – indeed it fully embraces the idea of praxis and an action-oriented approach to critical scholarship. FPE provides the tools for a nuanced and reflexive analysis of human–environment relations and the political actors and agencies involved. It also closes the gap and builds bridges between sectors that are conventionally kept apart – academia, policymaking institutions, and activist organisations (Elmhirst, 2015; Sundberg, 2017). In terms of practice then, recognition of gender dynamics illuminated through FPE means that planners and policymakers must evaluate how gender 'works' in a particular context so that governance interventions are necessarily just and sustainable.

Feminist Foodscapes

Inspired by the scholarly field of feminist political ecology, I applied its core tenets to explore gender relations of power in relation to food systems and security in the city. I have long engaged feminist foodscapes as an FPE-inspired conceptual frame within my research on urban food issues in Southern Africa to highlight the pervasiveness of gender relations of power, and their inequitable outcomes in the lives and livelihoods of men and women in the city. The foodscapes frame also reaffirms the importance of the social – rooted in power and knowledge and beyond biophysical and economic factors – in food dynamics, structures, and outcomes (Carr, 2006). The feminist foodscapes frame pushes us beyond simplistic ideas of gender as a women-only, local-scale variable; it alerts us to the inherent gender inequality embedded within ideological, institutional, and individual realms of society. To this end, the feminist foodscapes frame is premised upon three key tenets about the relationship between gender and food: the ubiquity of gender across scale, its complexity manifest in intersectional identities, and its inherently political nature.

First, gender is ubiquitous. It is a multi-scalar, multifaceted and not-always-obvious principle of the urban food system, shaping roles, responsibilities, expectations of men and women, shaping quantity and quality of food produced, and shaping access to, and consumption of, foodstuffs in the city. Gender operates well beyond the local scale, reaching across household, neighbourhood, municipal, regional, national, and international levels, and delimiting proper characteristics, roles and behaviours, as well as opportunities and constraints for men as much as it does for women. Further, gender manifests itself in both the material aspects of food production, distribution, consumption, as well as the symbolic construction of masculine and feminine food realms, gender identities, and relationships (Moore, 1988; Roos et al., 2001). Giving centrality to gender thus forces us to examine food from its ideological framing to production, to mealtime (Julier, 2006), and beyond. Investigating gender dynamics is not about counting all of the women present and arguing that gender is more or less important in particular parts of the urban food system, with greater or fewer women involved or obvious gender dynamics (Slocum, 2007). Rather, it is about recognising the symbolic and structural ways that gender works in the food system, which tells us things about what is valued in society and how that becomes embedded in relation to food. A multi-scaled examination of existing urban food scholarship reveals gendered topics across scales of the individual (e.g. men and women as economic actors), household (e.g. gendered livelihoods), cities (e.g. informal food systems), state (e.g. agricultural and urbanisation policies) and global (e.g. international food systems); resultant analysis facilitates integration of men's and women's daily experiences of urban food systems within broader structures and processes, shaping urban food security and governance (Riley and Hovorka, 2015). Feminist foodscapes thus conceptualise gender as operating across analytical scales and amongst all people in society, even in instances where obvious gender dynamics (e.g. women-dominated, local realms) are absent.

Second, gender is intersectional. Intersectionality is a theory and methodology of studying the relationships amongst numerous dimensions and modalities of social relationships and subject formations (McCall, 2005) and outlining interdependencies between social categories of power. Over several decades, critical race and feminist theorists (e.g. Burman, 2004; Butler, 1997; Collins, 1990; Crenshaw, 1993; Essed, 1990; hooks, 1984; Mohanty et al., 1991; Moraga & Anzaldua, 1988) have rejected essentialist categories of gender, race, ethnicity, class, orientation, age, ability, etc., advocating instead for analyses engaging how such categories intersect and emerge in relation to one another. Identities are thus emergent properties not reducible to naturally given biological essences or socially constructed role expectations. Within the urban food system, who you are in terms of identity/positionality matters in that it influences where you are located spatially and what you can do in a particular location *that in turn* produces and reproduces your identity/positionality because of the opportunities and constraints associated with a spatial location. One's identity/positionality is not only predicated on gender but also on how gender intersects with class, race, etc. such that access to land for food production, access to financial resources and social networks to pursue food-based activities, and the outcomes in terms of food quantity, quality, etc., are all directly related to one's identity/positionality.

Third, gender is political. It is an ideological system, manifested in institutional and individual realms, which reflects deeply rooted, socially constructed differences between masculine/feminine and men/women. In virtually all contexts, that which is thought of as masculine is more highly valued than that which is thought of as feminine (Harding, 1986). As a result, men benefit through relatively more favourable circumstances and opportunities than women. Feminist foodscape approaches strive to expose and explain gender difference and inequality, which ironically means re-highlighting 'women-only', given their frequent and disproportionate subordination relative to men. It does so also by recognising food as power in its own right (Arnold, 1988: 3; McMahon, 2002: 204), lying at the heart of social relations, reflecting cultural beliefs and behaviours, driving human interactions with nature, providing focus for economic activity, and shaping local, national, and global politics. Food structures and processes express, develop, and maintain social hierarchies of gender (Hastorf, 1996: 460; Counihan, 1999: 8; Slocum, 2007: 520). Food security reflects relative degrees of power in terms of access to, use of, and control over food; relations to rules and dynamics associated with the food system itself (Counihan, 1999: 8–9); and interactions with, and identity formation through, social relationships established; and performances of food-related acts and activities (Lupton, 1996; Jarosz, 2000; Probyn, 2000; Julier, 2006). Feminist foodscapes thus conceptualise gender and food as power-laden realms that produce and reproduce difference and inequality between men and women through their connections.

Illustration from Gaborone, Botswana

As an FPE-inspired conceptual frame, feminist foodscapes applied to the context of urban food systems and security offers a means through which to explore how gender 'works' given its ubiquity, intersections, and political nature. I now turn to present some of the empirical details revealed through my research in Gaborone, Botswana.

First, in terms of gender's ubiquitous nature, symbolic constructions of masculinity and femininity are evident at the national scale through policy and programming efforts that privilege cattle (in rural areas) over other agricultural sectors (that may take place in urban areas). What it means to be a 'successful man' is connected to male ownership of and responsibility for cattle, which are highly revered in Botswana society. Men reap the associated benefits of social status (whereby having more cattle is a sign of authority), resource access (whereby cattle can be sold for profit), and food security (whereby cattle are used as agricultural draught power to plough fields). National agriculture policies and programmes have long funnelled financial subsidies, land, and veterinary services towards cattle and thus towards men who hold primary control of them. The successful beef-oriented political economy and beef-focused dietary preferences are further evidence of symbolic privileging of masculinity in Botswana. The implications of such gender dynamics are that male privilege is reinforced through national policy, the political economy, food consumption patterns, and everyday access to cattle as socio-economic resources. Here, then, applying a *feminist* approach reveals that gender dynamics are ubiquitous (stretching well beyond the usual local, household level) yet not always self-evident. Explaining how and why gender operates at both specific and broader analytical scales reveals the root of difference and inequality between men and women (Hovorka, 2012).

Second, in terms of gender's intersectional nature, gender identity is often embodied and performed alongside a host of other positionality identifiers. Gendered research on food dynamics in Gaborone reveals notable intersections between gender and class. Indeed, gendered socio-economic status means that women are more limited in their access to land, and their ability to put this land to productive use. In turn, men and women operate inside different class-based hierarchies within the commercial urban food production sector, with differential and inequitable expressions of success and challenges. As excerpted from Hovorka (2005: 309):

> Low-income women operate enterprises informally and thus receive no government recognition, let alone support or services. This group of producers engages in highly intensive, efficient, and effective broiler production systems, drawing on personal social networks to sustain production at the small scale. Yet, ultimately, women are limited in their ability to expand production in residential peri-urban areas, given small plot size, or to relocate their agricultural plots, given their socioeconomic marginalization. At the middle-income level, men and women producers now have more options for their production systems since they have access to larger, more agriculturally suitable plots of land in freehold, lease, and tribal areas. Producers are formally recognised and take a more individualistic approach to agricultural production, making them reliant on relatively inadequate formal support services. Their ability to modify the environment is not stifled by lack of space per se, but rather by lack of training and assistance with intensive, commercial production. Women face particular constraints to production in this group, given that their access to land is facilitated by [government] grants, ultimately making them vulnerable to unsustainable fixed and running costs due to their relatively deflated socioeconomic status. Finally, high-income men, as women in the low-income group, operate successful enterprises on their own terms. Specifically,

> those at the top of the hierarchy come equipped with self-sufficient, business-oriented strategies and highly mechanised systems such that they do not have to rely on government support or services. They also tend to rely on their own resources, and, additionally, they have access to relatively unlimited and prime agricultural land. The success of these enterprises is reflected in their domination of the urban market.
>
> *Hovorka, 2005: 309*

Third, in terms of gender's political nature, gender differences and inequalities are fully entrenched within the commercial agriculture sector in and around Gaborone. Men access larger, more expensive plots of agricultural land located in fertile freehold areas of outright ownership; they engage in a variety of larger-scale, extensive, and diversified systems supported by many labourers and fixed asset investment; and they are employed in full-time, high-paying, steady jobs and live as part of a dual-income household. Women are concentrated on smaller, less expensive plots of land in communal tribal areas, often associated with their residence or homestead; they engage in small-scale, less-financially endowed, intensive broiler (i.e. chickens raised for meat) production enterprises, employing fewer labourers; and they farm full-time without other formal employment and live without benefit of another household wage earner. Such striking gender disparities may be explained through broader trends in education and employment structures that relegate girls and women to 'feminine' subjects, realms, and job sectors characterised as 'lesser than', and with fewer benefits than those characterised as masculine. Ultimately, men outperform women in food production (e.g. men earn 12 times the gross monthly turnover) and have access to a wide range of sub-sectors (e.g. women are overly concentrated in the broiler sector). Not only are women's individual livelihood strategies and efforts curtailed compared to men's but so too are efforts to generate locally produced foodstuffs for urban dwellers (Hovorka, 2005).

In sum, gender in its ideological, institutional, and individual manifestations, shapes which entities, products, or realms are labelled masculine or feminine, which policies and programmes result, which food-related divisions of labour and resources emerge, and what this means for individual urban dwellers. Gender shapes what food is produced for and in the city, by whom, on what conditions, and with what implications. Gender shapes people's daily interactions with food, abilities to generate income or foodstuffs for their household, and opportunities for personal empowerment. Gender, through this necessarily *feminist* conceptualisation, includes yet moves beyond women-only and local-scale foci to extensive, fluid dynamics of urban foodscapes. It also reveals substantial gender differences and inequalities that necessarily benefit men and privilege masculine realms more so than women and feminine realms.

Conclusion: Urban Food Governance Interventions

As detailed above, FPE offers the conceptual tools with which to critically assess the role of gender in shaping urban food systems and security outcomes. The FPE-inspired conceptual frame of feminist foodscapes illuminates how gender 'works' given its ubiquity, intersections, and political nature, as demonstrated through empirical research in Gaborone, Botswana. In turn, these nuanced and comprehensive insights can effectively inform urban management and policy trajectories. Here the praxis-oriented character of FPE offers a bridge between academia, policymaking institutions, and activist organisations whereby scholarly analysis can inform urban food governance interventions so that they are necessarily just and sustainable.

Importantly then, FPE presents exciting possibilities for a prospective practice-oriented agenda for urban food governance interventions through attention to numerous elements of 'gender mainstreaming' (see Riley & Hovorka, 2015; Hovorka & Lee-Smith, 2006). First, conceptual clarity is needed to recognise that gender does not refer to women's lives, livelihoods, and experiences within the household and local context alone, but rather is woven through all sorts of other scales, actors, processes, and structures within urban foodscapes. Second, practical (address the immediate situation) and strategic (transform the system) gender needs must be identified as part of urban food governance interventions. Here, assessing the type and scale of intervention – be it through programmes, planning or policies – should involve clear understanding of the local contexts and structural factors that shape opportunities and constraints for individuals. Third, political will and commitment amongst key stakeholders is required for leadership in necessarily *gendered* urban governance interventions. The awareness of gender differences and inequalities within the urban food system should guide policy responses at all levels of government and actors operating across scales.

Fourth, building capacity and allocating resources to addressing inequities must be mobilised; in turn substantive investment of funds, time, and effort reinforces the leadership and commitment of all those involved in producing and reproducing the system at large. Fifth, scholarly research on gender dynamics must be woven into urban food governance interventions. The ubiquity and complexity of gender difference and inequities mean that even rigorous gender planning may generate unintended consequences. Continued data collection and analysis through FPE framing is thus essential in shaping just and sustainable urban governance interventions. Key questions for FPE-informed interventions include: which food sectors draws the most government energy and support? To what extent, and how exactly, does this relate to ideas about masculinity and femininity? What are the implications of privileging this sector for the nation, the city, and its people? Whose privilege does it reaffirm?

In sum, this chapter articulates gender as an action-research frame, rooted in feminist political ecology, with its emphasis on scale, intersectionality, and power. For those focused on urban food governance issues, this chapter is meant to reinforce the centrality of gender as an organising principle in society and to inspire future research engaging FPE as a lens through which to understand and explain the urban realm. The paucity of research in this vein must be addressed. Moreover, the challenge for feminist, action-oriented research is how to address deeply rooted gender inequalities once realised through an FPE-inspired feminist foodscapes conceptual frame. Here the hope is to inspire researcher–practitioner collaborations to shape more just and sustainable urban food governance interventions.

Acknowledgements

Thank you to the Government of Botswana, especially the Ministry of Agriculture and Department of Women's Affairs, and the Department of Environmental Sciences at University of Botswana for their support and encouragement of my research programme over the past two decades. I am grateful for the wealth of information provided by all the farmers, entrepreneurs, and other key stakeholders who took the time to participate in my urban agriculture and food security research in Greater Gaborone. The research was funded by the Social Sciences and Humanities Research Council of Canada, the International Development Research Centre in Canada, and the National Science Foundation in the United States.[1]

Note

1 This chapter is an extension of the author's work published in *Development* (2013, Vol. 56, Issue 1, pp. 123–128) entitled 'The case for a feminist foodscapes framework: lessons from research in urban

Botswana'. Palgrave granted permission to re-use this text on 26 September 2020. It also builds on the author's work published in *Gender, Place and Culture* (2006a, Vol. 13, Issue 3, pp. 207–225) and follows reuse guidelines.

References

Adams, E., Juran, L., & Ajibade, I. (2018). 'Spaces of exclusion' in community water governance: A feminist political ecology of gender and participation in Malawi's urban water user associations. *Geoforum* 95: 133–142.

Arnold, D. (1988). *Famine*. Oxford: Basil Blackwell.

Behzadi, N. (2019). Women miners' exclusion and Muslim masculinities in Tajikistan: A feminist political ecology of honor and shame. *Geoforum* 100: 144–152.

Buechler, S., & Hanson, A. (Eds.). (2015). *A Political Ecology of Women, Water and Global Environmental Change*. New York: Routledge.

Buechler, S., Vázquez-García, V., Martínez-Molina, K. G., & Sosa-Capistrán, D. M. (2020). Patriarchy and (electric) power? A feminist political ecology of solar energy use in Mexico and the United States. *Energy Research & Social Science* 70: 101743.

Burman, E. (2004). From difference to intersectionality: Challenges and resources. *European Journal of Psychotherapy, Counselling and Health* 6(4): 293–308.

Butler, J. (1997). *The Psychic Life of Power*. Stanford, CA: Stanford University Press.

Carney, J. (1988). Struggles over crop rights and labour within contract farming households in a Gambian irrigated rice project. *Journal of Peasant Studies* 15(3): 334–349.

Carney, J. (1993). Converting the wetlands, engendering the environment: The intersection of gender with agrarian change in the Gambia. *Economic Geography*, 69(4): 329–348.

Carney, M. (2014). The biopolitics of 'food insecurity': Towards a critical political ecology of the body in studies of women's transnational migration. *Journal of Political Ecology* 21: 1–18.

Carr, E. (2006). Postmodern conceptualizations, modernist applications: Rethinking the role of society in food security. *Food Policy* 31(1): 14–29.

Carr, E. (2020). *More than (Wo)men: Why Intersectionality is Critical for Effective and Just Adaptation*. Symposium of Confronting the Climate Crisis: Feminist Pathways to Just and Sustainable Futures, organised by the Consortium on Gender, Security and Human Rights, October 7–9, 2020.

Clement, F., Harcourt, W., Joshi, D., & Sato, C. (2019). Feminist political ecologies of the commons and communing. (Editorial to the Special Feature). *International Journal of the Commons* 13(1).

Collins, P. (1990). *Black Feminist Thought: Knowledge, Consciousness and the Politics of Empowerment*. Boston, MA: Unwin Hyman.

Cornwall, A., Harrison, E., & Whitehead, A. (2004). Introduction: Repositioning feminisms in gender and development. *IDS Bulletin* 35(4): 1–10.

Counihan, C. (1999). *The Anthropology of Food and Body: Gender, Meaning and Power*. New York & London: Routledge.

Crenshaw, K. (1993). Mapping the margins: Intersectionality, identity politics and violence against women of color. In M. Albertson Fineman & R. Mykitiuk (Eds.), *The Public Nature of Private Violence*. New York: Routledge, 93–118.

Doshi, S. (2017). Embodied urban political ecology: Five propositions. *Area* 49(1): 125–128.

Elmhirst, R. (2015). Feminist political ecology. In A. Coles, L. Gray, & J. Momsen (Eds.), *The Routledge Handbook of Gender and Development*. London: Routledge, 82–90.

Elmhirst, R., & Resurreccion, B. P. (2008). Gender, environment and natural resource management: New dimensions, new debates. In B. P. Resurreccion, & R. Elmhirst (Eds.), *Gender and Natural Resource Management*. London: Routledge, 1–18.

Essed, P. (1990). *Everyday Racism: Reports from Women in Two Cultures*. Claremont, CA: Hunter House.

Freidberg, S. E. (2002). Gardening on the edge: The social conditions of unsustainability on an African urban periphery. *Annals of the Association of American Geographers* 91(2): 349–369.

Gay-Antaki, M. (2016). 'Now we have equality': A feminist political ecology analysis of carbon markets in Oaxaca, Mexico. *Journal of Latin American Geography* 15(3): 49–66.

Gururani, S. (2002). Forests of pleasure and pain: Gendered practices of labor and livelihood in the forests of the Kumaon Himalayas, India. *Gender, Place & Culture* 9(3): 229–243.

Guyer, J. (1987). Feeding Yaounde, capital of Cameroon. In J. Guyer (Ed.), *Feeding African Cities*. Bloomington and Indianapolis, IN: Indiana University Press.

Harcourt, W. (2019). Feminist political ecology practices of worlding: Art, commoning and the politics of hope in the class room. *International Journal of the Commons* 13(1).

Harcourt, W., Knox, S., & Tabassi, T. (2015). World-wise otherwise stories for our endtimes: Conversations on queer ecologies. In W. Harcourt & I. Nelson (Eds.), *Practising Political Ecology: Moving Beyond the 'Green Economy'*. London: Zed Books. 286–308.

Harding, S. (1986). *The Science Question in Feminism*. Ithaca, NY: Cornell University Press.

Harris, L. (2006). Irrigation, gender, and social geographies of the changing waterscapes of southeastern Anatolia. *Environment and Planning D: Society and Space* 24: 187–213.

Hastorf, C. A. (1996). Gender, space and food in prehistory. In R. W. Preucel & I. Hodder (Eds.), *Contemporary Archaeology in Theory*. Oxford: Blackwell Press. 460–484.

Hayes-Conroy, A., & Hayes-Conroy, J. (2013). Veggies and visceralities: A political ecology of food and feeling. *Emotion, Space and Society* 6: 81–90.

Hayes-Conroy, A., & Hayes-Conroy, J. (2015). Political ecology of the body: A visceral approach. In R. L. Bryant (Ed.), *The International Handbook of Political Ecology*. Cheltenham: Edward Elgar Publishing.

Hobson, K. (2007). Political animals? On animals as subjects in an enlarged political geography. *Political Geography* 26(3): 250–287.

hooks, b. (1984). *Feminist Theory: From Margin to Center*. Boston, MA: South End Press,

Hovorka, A. (2005). The (re)production of gendered positionality in Botswana's commercial urban agriculture sector. Annals *of the Association of American Geographers* 95(2): 294–313.

Hovorka, A. (2006a). The no. 1 ladies' poultry farm: A feminist political ecology of urban agriculture in Botswana. *Gender Place and Culture* 13(3): 207–225.

Hovorka, A. (2006b). Urban agriculture: Addressing practical and strategic gender needs. *Development in Practice* 16(1): 51–61.

Hovorka, A. (2012). Women/chickens vs. men/cattle: Insights on gender-species intersectionality. *Geoforum* 43: 875–884.

Hovorka, A. (2013). The case for a feminist foodscapes framework: Lessons from research in urban Botswana. *Development* 56(1): 123–128. (re-use permission granted)

Hovorka, A. (2015). The Gender, Place and Culture Jan Monk Distinguished Annual Lecture: Feminism and animals: exploring interspecies relations through intersectionality, performativity and standpoint. *Gender, Place & Culture* 22(1): 1–19.

Hovorka, A., & Lee-Smith. D. (2006). Gendering the urban agriculture agenda. In R. van Veenhuizen (Ed.), *Cities Farming for the Future*. Ottawa & Leusden: International Development Research Centre & Resource Centre for Urban Agriculture and Forestry, 125–136.

Jarosz, L. (2000). Understanding agri-food networks as social relations. *Agriculture and Human Values* 17: 279–283.

Jarosz, L. (2011). Nourishing women: Toward a feminist political ecology of community supported agriculture in the United States. *Gender, Place and Culture* 18(3): 307–326.

Julier, A. P. (2006). Hiding gender and race in the discourse of commercial food consumption. In A. V. Avakian & B. Haber (Eds.), *From Betty Crocker to Feminist Food Studies: Critical Perspectives on Women and Food*. Amherst & Boston, MA: University of Massachusetts Press, 163–184.

Kimura, A. H., & Katano, Y. (2014). Farming after the Fukushima accident: A feminist political ecology analysis of organic agriculture. *Journal of Rural Studies* 34: 108–116.

Lupton, D. (1996). *Food, the Body and the Self*. London: Sage.

Mackenzie, A. F. D. (1998). *Land, Ecology and Resistance in Kenya, 1880–1952*. Edinburgh: Edinburgh University Press.

McCall, L. (2005). The complexity of intersectionality. *Signs: Journal of Women in Culture and Society* 30(3): 1771–1800.

McMahon, M. (2002). Resisting globalization: Women organic farmers and local food systems. *Canadian Women Studies* 21(3): 203–206.

Mohanty, C. T., Russo, A., & Torres, L. (1991). *Third World Women and the Politics of Feminism*. Indianapolis, IN: Indiana University Press.

Mollett, S., & Faria, C. (2013). Messing with gender in feminist political ecology. *Geoforum* 45: 116–125.

Moore, H. (1988). *Feminism and Anthropology*. Minneapolis, MN: University of Minnesota Press.

Moore, H., & Vaughan, M. (1987). Cutting down trees: Women, nutrition and agricultural change in the northern province of Zambia, 1920–1986. *African Affairs* 86(345): 523–540. https://doi.org/10.1093/oxfordjournals.afraf.a097947

Moraga, C., & Anzaldua, G. (1988). *This Bridge Called My Back: Writings by Radical Women of Color.* New York: Women of Color Press.
Nightingale, A. (2006). The nature of gender: Work, gender, and environment. *Environment and Planning D: Society and Space* 24(2): 165–185.
Nightingale, A. (2011). Bounding difference: Intersectionality and the material production of gender, caste, class and environment in Nepal. *Geoforum* 42(2): 153–162.
Probyn, Elsbeth (2000). *Carnal Appetites: Food, Sex and Identities.* New York: Routledge.
Riley, L., & Hovorka, A. (2015). Gendering urban food strategies across multiple scales. In P. Dreschel & H. de Zeeuw (Eds.), *Food Systems in the City Region.* London: Earthscan, 336–357.
Rocheleau, D., Thomas-Slayter, B., & Wangari, E. (1996). *Feminist Political Ecology Global Issues and Local Experiences.* London: Routledge.
Roos, G., Prattala, R., & Koski, K. (2001). Men, masculinity and food: Interviews with Finnish carpenters and engineers. *Appetite* 37: 47–56.
Sato, C., & María Soto Alarcón, J. (2019). Toward a postcapitalist feminist political ecology approach to the commons and communing. *International Journal of the Commons* 13(1).
Schroeder, R. A. (1997). 'Re-claiming' land in the Gambia: Gendered property rights and environmental intervention. Annals of the Association of American Geographers, 87(3), 487–508. http://www.jstor.org/stable/2564065
Shillington, L. (2008). Being (s) in relation at home: Socio-natures of patio 'gardens' in Managua, Nicaragua. *Social & Cultural Geography* 9(7): 755–776.
Shillington, L. (2013). Right to food, right to the city: Household urban agriculture, and socionatural metabolism in Managua, Nicaragua. *Geoforum* 44: 103–111.
Shrestha, G., Joshi, D., & Clement, F. (2019). Masculinities and hydropower in India: A feminist political ecology perspective. *International Journal of the Commons* 13(1).
Slocum, R. (2007). Whiteness, space and alternative food practice. *Geoforum* 38: 520–533.
Sultana, F. (2011). Suffering for water, suffering from water: Emotional geographies of resource access, control and conflict. *Geoforum* 42(2): 163–172.
Sundberg, J. (2017). Feminist political ecology. In *International Encyclopedia of Geography: People, the Earth, Environment and Technology.* Hoboken, NJ: Wiley. 1–12.
Tamale, S. (2006). African feminism: How should we change? *Development* 49(1): 38–41.
Truelove, Y. (2011). (Re-)Conceptualizing water inequality in Delhi, India through a feminist political ecology framework. *Geoforum* 42(2): 143–152.
Vaz-Jones, L. (2018). Struggles over land, livelihood, and future possibilities: Reframing displacement through feminist political ecology. *Signs: Journal of Women in Culture and Society* 43(3): 711–735.

12

INNOVATION THEORY AND URBAN FOOD GOVERNANCE

Transition Thinking, Social Innovation and Transformative Change

Damian Maye, Daniel Keech and Matt Reed

Introduction

Innovation is an often-used buzzword in food policymaking. The EU's new 'Farm to Fork' strategy (European Commission, 2020), for example, calls for new 'mission-orientated' technological innovations and legislative and institutional actions, as well as behavioural changes, to transform Europe's food system to address systemic problems ('grand societal challenges'), including climate change, biodiversity loss, antimicrobial resistance and food waste (Schebesta & Candel, 2020). The emphasis is on 'system innovations' (technological, institutional or social) that enact fundamental (as opposed to incremental) change to reconfigure food systems for environmental and social well-being (Dinesh et al., 2021). The Europe 2020 strategy (European Commission, 2010) also called for innovation, orientated at that time to address 'smart, inclusive growth', including the challenges of sustainable food security. In the UK, agri-food innovation features too in policy discourse (Herbert and Lord Taylor of Holbeach, 2010), framed through the 'sustainable intensification' paradigm (Foresight, 2011) and the utilisation of existing and new technologies (genetics, robotics, nanotechnology, digitalisation, precision agriculture, big data, etc.) to enhance yields and protect environments (Ingram & Maye, 2020). This innovation paradigm was updated via the National Food Strategy (Dimbleby, 2021), which emphasises systems thinking and calls for transformative policy and market intervention to address 'destructive feedback loops'.

Behind the 'innovation' buzzword we find contested visions for sustainable food systems, particularly the competing agendas of 'technocentric' and 'ecocentric' responses, with the latter favouring 'appropriate' technologies over 'softer' innovation options (Kneafsey et al., 2021). In food policy, innovation typically refers to technology development (Ballamingie et al., 2020), such as the design of new products and services for markets. This science and technology framework may seem somewhat removed from urban food governance, but in reality urban food sustainability sits at the confluence of two innovation contexts, namely food innovation and urban innovation, the latter otherwise known as the 'smart city' agenda, which advocates ICT

DOI: 10.4324/9781003055907-14

and techno-science as solutions for urban growth (Maye, 2019). Urban agri-food innovation is a sub-set of smart city innovation.

Critics of techno-science innovation argue for greater recognition for grassroots innovation actors, placing more emphasis on people and the needs that innovations are addressing at a local level. As Bock (2012, 60) argues, innovations are born 'from collective and creative learning processes and the mutual exchange of knowledge'. In line with this thinking, this chapter argues that social innovations are critical 'acts of change' that enable sustainability transition in urban food systems. This does not discount the importance of technology or socio-technical combinations (Maye, 2019). Urban food systems represent heterogeneous assemblages of place-based innovation and action. This includes, for example, place-based food networks, such as those developing urban food strategies and partnerships, that connect actors and systems of food, agriculture, spatial planning, corporate strategy and state welfare support (Carey, 2013). Community and grassroots-based actors enable change through socio-technical innovations in organisations and through governance co-ordination.

To develop this argument, the chapter presents an overview of innovation and transition theory, using data from European and UK research projects that examine urban food systems and their governance (i.e. their ways of organising, working and doing to enact change). The innovation and transition literature is burgeoning and not always easy to navigate, so we begin by explaining the crucial relationship between innovation and transition and then introduce transition management and 'sustainability transition' (Hinrichs, 2014). This provides a useful way to understand production–consumption systems and innovations to transform them, which we then categorise at two levels: *the vertical* (i.e. strategic, system linkages) and *the horizontal* (i.e. practice, place-based linkages). Social innovation is a key process of change in both levels, particularly the horizontal. The analysis shows how transition theory is mobilised and helpful to understand processes of urban food governance. In the next section, we turn attention to an increasingly prominent and influential way to enact social and technical change on the ground, namely experimental living labs. The living lab methodology is seeping into most innovation spaces, from early testing of transformative technologies in real-world conditions to more diverse contexts, including smart cities, digital finance and sustainability transitions. This new, more transdisciplinary way of working on governance topics, particularly as a medium to engage constellations of actors in creative forms of urban (food) governance, is important to recognise. It sits alongside an emerging critique of living labs, particularly the surrender of public space to commercial interests to develop technologies (Pfotenhauer et al., 2021). This is important to recognise, but if designed in the right way, living labs, we argue, are powerful epistemological tools to transform vertical and horizontal relations, co-generating strategic and practice-orientated governance innovations for citizens, cities and regions. We use data from the ROBUST project to illustrate these points. We conclude with reflections on the COVID-19 pandemic, noting increasing calls for systemic changes to food systems and urban environments and what this means for transition theory and urban food governance.

Transition management and sustainability transition: system change through vertical and horizontal linkages

Transition has become a powerful way to think about change and the challenges involved in making systems – in this case urban food systems – more sustainable (Darnhofer, 2015). The term describes a gradual process of change (Maye, 2018), or, as Hinrichs (2014, 145) puts it, 'a gradual, pervasive shift from one state or condition to something different'. 'Transition' as a concept is also mobilised differently across sub-disciplines and epistemic communities. Food nutritionists, for example, use the term 'nutrition transition' to describe changing diets in emerging economy populations as countries grow wealthier and can afford more processed foods, fats and meat. To avoid confusion, this chapter aligns with the sustainability transition approach, which argues that innovation is essential to initiate change, disrupt the status quo and develop resources and pathways to greater sustainability. Transition studies initially examined socio-technical transitions, combining ideas from technology studies and innovation studies to examine the consequences of a new technology for social change and its potential to lead to shifts in a system. Under 'sustainability transition' studies, the focus is on examining socio-technical innovations that are aligned with sustainability agendas (Hinrichs, 2014). As Westley et al. (2011, 774) observe, the goal is to use '...innovative capacity to change the current unsustainable trajectories and support transformations toward global sustainability'. Societies, places, communities, citizens and businesses are not passive agents who experience transitions to sustainability (Maye et al., 2021); in fact, they may 'intentionally act to construct them' (Hinrichs, 2014, 145). However, transforming socio-technical regimes is not an easy task in that socio-economies have established ways of operating, with alternatives often 'locked out' or marginalised (Seyfang and Haxeltine, 2012).

The transition management approach constitutes a governance approach that focuses on pragmatic processes 'of taking action and facilitating change' (Hinrichs, 2014, 145) (policies, planning instruments, grassroots interventions) that have been applied to a number of policy fields in recent years, such as nature, the environment and 'low carbon' transitions. Sustainability transition researchers study these new socio-technical systems. Socio-technical regimes (systems of rules and principles) provide a reference for actions and behaviours and the transition approach examines processes of changing those regimes (Maye, 2018). Following Hargreaves et al. (2013) and Hinrichs (2014), the rest of this section reviews two key approaches in sustainability transition thinking: the multi-level perspective (Geels & Schot, 2007) and social practice theory (Shove & Pantzar, 2005; Shove, 2003), which, respectively, focus on different forms of system linkage (i.e. vertical or horizontal).

The multi-level perspective: vertical linkages

The multi-level perspective (MLP) is a useful approach to help understand the complexity of transitions. It conceptualises patterns of long-term change, with a focus on socio-technical regimes that are situated at three levels and labelled respectively as 'landscape factors', 'regimes' and 'niches' (Geels & Schot, 2007). In the MLP framework, the mainstream agri-food system and its governance mechanisms at different scales, including the city, represent the socio-technical regime. Niche innovations are small-scale initiatives (organic farming in its infancy in the UK, for example) which, during times of 'dynamic stability', may not be directly putting pressure on the dominant regime to change – yet may have the potential to do so. The socio-technical landscape represents pressures that are exogenous to the niches and regimes below but can significantly impact them (a zoonotic disease or health outbreak, for example, or rocketing food prices, as seen in 2007–08, or concerns about climate change). The landscape level can destabilise regimes and niches and act as a catalyst for transition (by this we mean a catalyst for change; think, for example, about ruminant livestock and meat eating which is increasingly linked to climate change and planetary boundaries). From an MLP perspective, understanding the relationship and linkages between niche and regime levels is key to understanding the nature of transitions (Darnhofer, 2015). Transition occurs because of the interactions at the different levels as well as between, thereby creating opportunities for change. In some cases, relations between niche-innovation and the existing regime are 'symbiotic' and the niche can be adopted or incorporated to improve the functioning of the regime (i.e. incremental innovation). A 'competitive relationship' is when the niche is intent on replacing the existing regime (i.e. radical innovation) (Geels & Schot, 2007).

MLP thus provides a heuristic framework that helps to position, in this case, urban food systems and governance innovations (as novelties/niches) within a wider schematic that examines their ability to interact and transform the mainstream food regime (Maye et al., 2021). MLP has been criticised, not least because of the need to examine in more detail the dynamics both between levels and between actors at the same levels (Darnhofer, 2015). The conceptual emphasis towards regimes, niches and landscapes can seem overly deterministic and 'can crowd out the importance of human agency and mute inevitable contest and politics of sustainability transitions' (Hinrichs, 2014, 149). Nevertheless, MLP is still valuable in capturing the key features of socio-technical transition and for understanding that transition is not linked to single causes but alignment of multiple processes at different levels (Geels, 2019).

Two forms of innovation also emerge from this MLP perspective (Maye, 2018): first, 'incremental innovations' (technological or social) that do not disrupt and are generated by the existing rules of the regime; and second, 'radical innovations' which respond to contradictions or negative side effects within the regime and seek to change it through the incorporation of socio-economic rules that have been generated outside the regime or by developing a new regime. In other words, sustainability transition only takes place when new socio-technical principles replace the old ones and the innovation develops coherency (Maye et al., 2021). Smith's work on the organic food sector is a good example of how a radical innovation can transform the mainstream regime, particularly in the way that organic products are now sold in supermarkets, the product of an ongoing engagement with the mainstream food regime that created new organisational arrangements and tools (Smith, 2006). The transition to a new regime is thus highly contingent on a range of different processes and constituent parts, not least due to the 'multi-level dynamics' that are likely to be involved (Wiskerke, 2003).

The social practices approach and social innovation: horizontal linkages

Attention within transition studies is focusing increasingly on further analysis of interactions between levels (Seyfang & Haxeltine, 2012; Maye, 2018), as well as combining it with complementary theoretical frameworks. Much of this work moves beyond understanding interactions between levels (i.e. vertical linkages, which is common in MLP studies) towards *social practices* as they take place at a local level within existing systems, which Hargreaves et al. (2013) characterise as 'horizontal linkages'. The social practices approach analyses 'the social organisation, continuities and possible ruptures in people's everyday practices' (Hinrichs, 2014, 149). Practices are about describing more than what people do; it is about understanding *how change takes place*; in other words, changes in practice cannot be explained and reduced to changes in status, attitude and behaviour (Maye et al., 2021).

Social practice theory examines how everyday practices (e.g. forms of cooking or commuting) become normal and routine events, which in turn reveal what might be possible and what happens when sustainable innovations are introduced. Shove's (2003) work is particularly useful, showing how practices within the home, such as showering, have evolved and become normalised as social expectations about cleanliness and comfort have emerged in parallel with new home technologies. Practices comprise three elements (Shove & Pantzar, 2005): materials (e.g. objects, tools), competence (practical knowledge to perform practices) and meaning (i.e. the social significance of the practice). Innovation is crucial to the performance of practices because it can reconfigure constituting elements, for example a new practice can emerge, practices may persist or practices may disappear. This shifts the scale of analysis from an individual to a social stance, with practices rather than individuals the centrepiece of analysis (Hinrichs, 2014, 150). A 'systems of practice' perspective is also taking shape to understand the opportunities that are available to change the practices of associated systems, for example, wider institutions and legislation governing the food system (Maye et al., 2021). This shows how a particular practice (e.g. cycling or urban gardening) can influence the meanings and discourses around it. As Langendahl et al. (2014, 5) put it, 'it is increasingly accepted that innovation does not emerge from a linear process, which proceeds from plan to implementation'.

Innovation processes are thus the co-evolution of practices, and social practice theory emphasises understanding how practices co-evolve across places. In urban food systems, there is already recognition and consensus that social innovation is a critical lever for urban food governance (Ballamingie et al., 2020). There is no consensus regarding how best to define social innovation (Neumeier, 2012). This requires understanding how social practices and associated systems change in combination with forms of collaborative action that enable social change (Marques et al., 2017). Social innovation typically delineates a fuzzy concept. Neumeier (2012, 55) provides the clearest definition, which he defines as: '[c]hanges of attitudes, behaviour or perceptions of a group of people joined in a network of aligned interests that in relation to the group's horizon of experiences lead to new and improved ways of collaborative action within the group and beyond'.

Social innovation occurs then when a network of actors changes its way of doing things and the consequence is some form of tangible improvement for those actors involved and possibly beyond. Social innovations signify 'acts of change'. Changes in attitudes, behaviour or perceptions result in a new form of collaborative action. Social innovations are non-material (Box 12.1), with complementary material outcomes (e.g. fresh food or a new community building); the focus is asset building, not needs realisation. This explains why, in contrast to technology-based and economic innovations, social innovations are difficult to identify and evaluate but 'soft changes' and 'alignment of interest', if carefully tracked, are equally transformative (Maye et al., 2021). Work on community-led 'grassroots innovations' and the development of social innovations at the community level shows, for example, how local and urban food movements are a vehicle for building collective capacity. This happens through facilitating community cohesion, healthy eating, educational enhancement and integrating disadvantaged groups into mainstream society and economy (Kirwan et al., 2013).

Box 12.1 Spaces of sanctuary and innovation – De Site

Access to land can be a limiting or enabling factor in urban agriculture. 'De Site' a community gardening project in Ghent, Belgium, overcame limits in availability by using land for a short period, planting vegetables in a brownfield site allocated for future housing development. The gardens allowed a predominantly migrant community the chance to grow food, initially for self-provisioning, although surpluses were sold to a community shop using an alternative local currency. These small gardens also provided the opportunity to meet and discuss, and to nurture a community. By liaising with the planning authority, the project representatives succeeded in securing an alternative location to which to move the gardens, once the original site was developed. In this way, the project made use of the limited period of land availability and ensured continuity of community cohesion and new food-growing opportunities. You can read more here – https://use.metropolis.org/case-studies/growth-of-small-scale-peri-urban-agriculture-in-ghent-belgium#casestudydetail.

Living labs and rural–urban food system innovation

This section considers action-orientated research that is using the experimental living labs concept as a way to co-develop governance solutions and engage constellations of actors in on-the-ground social and technical innovations. The living lab concept is prominent in urban governance settings. Living labs have potential to advance urban food governance research. We evidence this by drawing on sustainable food experiments conducted as part of a Horizon 2020-funded project, ROBUST (2016–2021), which used living labs to action governance innovations to strengthen rural–urban linkages in 11 European regions.[1]

Living lab definitions, origins and capacities to enable change

Living labs are arenas 'devised to design, test and learn from social and technical innovation in real time' (Marvin et al., 2018, 1). They have been applied in the co-creation of innovation between four main sectors – research, civil society, public institutions and the private sector. One historical origin of living labs is user-driven ICT systems design and development, such as the smart city technologies of today. Other origins focus on interdisciplinary and knowledge-sharing connections between research communities and broader society (Anderson et al., 2013), or on improving public service effectiveness in relation to citizens' expectations (Gascó, 2017). No uniform definition of the living lab exists, although several authors have highlighted distinctions between living labs and other forms of innovation. For example, Bergvall-Kareborn et al. (2009) highlight the importance of external, consumer/user input into technology innovations that have potential societal benefits, in contrast to the generally internal, firm-centric focus of open innovation prioritising market advantage. Similarly, Leminen et al. (2015) review user roles in innovation and suggest that they crucially shape innovation through real-life experiences, in contrast to more conventional R&D-based innovation, which relies on scientific or technical expertise. Thus, living labs constitute experiments that draw on real-life experience and situations, including the active involvement of prospective users to inform prototype development and refinement. Consequently, living labs have been framed as a pragmatic innovation methodology, co-produced by users to solve complex challenges (Ballon & Schuurman, 2015). When complex challenges require governance innovations, for example in tackling inequality or in community development, and are led by local authorities (Edwards-Schachter et al., 2012; Kronsell & Mukhtar-Landgren, 2018), then users are reframed as citizens. The European Network of Living Labs (ENoLL), for example, positions living labs as 'intermediaries among citizens, research organisations, companies, cities and regions'.[2]

Another important distinction of living labs, in addition to openness and user-participation, is their focus on whole systems, rather than on partial improvements, for example in services, products or business models. This has led to their application in agri-food technology where whole chain transparency is vital and requires the input of multiple actors, from farmers to consumers and beyond (Wolfert et al., 2010). Living labs are 'partnerships between sectors (often between public, private and people)' (Voytenko et al., 2016, 46), and universities often play a key role in facilitating and managing experimental iterations. Other definitions describe living labs as pilot and demonstration projects, acting as supportive tools for private actors and industry to commercialise their services, products and technologies.

Of particular interest here is the burgeoning literature on 'urban living labs' and specifically their application to address urban governance challenges. Voytenko et al. (2016, 46) define urban living labs as 'an *arena* (i.e. geographically or institutionally bounded spaces), and as an *approach* for intentional collaborative experimentation of researchers, citizens, companies and local governments'. Five urban living lab characteristics (following Voytenko et al., 2016) are:

1. *Geographical embeddedness* – which may be territorial (such as a community or district) or institutional (including contracts).
2. *Experimental learning* – using real-world conditions and time to prompt changes to governance, including testing technologies, ideas, solutions and policies.
3. *Participation and user involvement* – using the quadruple helix of government, industry, citizens and researchers to co-create solutions at all stages of design.
4. *Leadership* – clear leadership and ownership of the lab is crucial. Although participatory, labs need to be carefully coordinated.
5. *Evaluation and refinement* – it is vital that the autonomy and experimental spirit of a living lab is matched with transparency, openness to external scrutiny, and refinement of goals and outcomes as the experiment proceeds.

Urban living labs are emerging, then, as a form of collective urban governance and experimentation in response to sustainability challenges and opportunities created via urbanisation. Many social and environmental projects are now applying living lab methodologies, including innovation partnerships that support sustainable urban food and resource transition or low carbon objectives (in addition to ROBUST see, for example, REPAiR, FoodShift, FoodTrails).[3] Associated changes are needed in how systems of innovation and services are designed, organised and delivered and, as a result, different forms of urban governance are being developed and tested. These forms of the urban living lab signify a 'form of experimental governance, whereby urban stakeholders develop and test new technologies, products, services and ways of living to produce innovative solutions to the challenges of climate change, resilience and urban sustainability' (Voytenko et al., 2016, 45–46). These labs are not just technology-focused. They address also issues of consumption, civic behaviour and lifestyle (i.e. social practices and innovation, linking them with earlier forms of participative and collaborative governance, including Local Agenda 21).

In summary, living labs have origins as distinctive open innovations employed by tech-firms, researchers, public authorities and civil society networks, working together to pursue transformations beyond initial market advantage, to achieve societal improvements. In practice, urban food transformations are achieved through user behaviour, market developments and the regulation of food provisioning by city authorities whose functional food remits cover public health, waste management, spatial planning and market infrastructure. External, user-led input, combined with transparent and iterative refinement of experiments, are essential living lab characteristics that can accelerate systemic change. This has lent living labs potential, utility and popularity among governance and social innovators such as city councils, research funders and policymakers seeking multi-actor solutions to complex urban sustainability challenges, for which multiple solution pathways are possible (Marvin et al., 2018, 5). There are limitations too, of course, including their co-option and manipulation as mechanisms which, in reality, are little more than new ways to rebrand technology investment (Pfotenhauer et al., 2021). Here we emphasise their potential transformative capacity to help urban food system actors enact change when designed in the right way.

Food governance experiments: creating mechanisms to strengthen rural–urban linkages

In this sub-section, we explain how the ROBUST project applied living labs in 11 European regions to strengthen rural–urban relations, focusing on sustainable food system innovations. Living labs, by definition, are place-based and horizontally embedded, which aligns with the approaches noted in social innovation approaches, but innovations below were also in some cases more strategic (vertical, multi-level) in their governance reach.

The ROBUST project aimed to develop functional synergies between rural and urban areas. It constituted 11 living labs in different European locations, including three national capital regions (Helsinki, Lisbon and Ljubljana), two major second-tier city regions (Frankfurt and Valencia) and a range of provincial and rural settings, including Tukums (Latvia), Gloucestershire and Mid-Wales (Britain), Lucca (Italy), Ede (The Netherlands) and Styria (Austria). Each living lab was a collaboration between researchers and practice partners (a local authority or regional municipal network). Experiments to improve rural–urban linkages covered five themes: sustainable food systems, public infrastructure and social services, new business models and labour markets, cultural connections, and ecosystems services.

In each lab, a common four-stage methodology was applied. Each team made use of a participatory methods toolkit compiled by the authors. The four stages were:

- Envisioning: this included the joint development of a research and innovation agenda, following rounds of engagement with local stakeholders.
- Experimenting: here living labs tested initial ideas and scenarios through extended stakeholder engagement and refined initial objectives accordingly.
- Experiencing: more detailed experiments and ideas were implemented and tested, often at a more granular level (e.g. testing a particular approach to public procurement).
- Evaluation: the living lab partners continually reflected on the effectiveness of the process, experiments and innovation outcomes (worked as feedback loops).

Not all living labs in ROBUST worked on sustainable food innovations. We focus here only on those that did and the innovations outcomes from that work. In broad terms, five types of governance mechanism emerged from deliberations and exchanges within and between the labs (i.e. as common learning resources). Table 12.1 summarises each mechanism, including the governance objective and some examples at lab level. At face value, none of the examples are all that new, however the way the objectives were developed and deliberated is important (collective ownership). City and regional authorities developed the innovations as a range of instruments, including food strategies, supply contracts and infrastructural investments to enhance rural–urban synergies. Consumer surveys, focus groups and direct interactions with citizens and local producers (e.g. at public festivals), formed part of participatory 'user' assessments carried out by researchers and municipalities, leading to further interventions, such as investments in market and IT infrastructure by local authorities, and the revision or development of food strategies in city regional food systems. In each case, then, 'users' have been the local authorities themselves, as well as other food sector stakeholders, including where innovations were eventually

Table 12.1 Sustainable food system governance for rural–urban relations

Mechanism	*Governance objectives*	*Living lab experimentation*
Municipal food strategies	Multiple municipal actions and responsibilities covered in relation to food. Strategies link ambitions and outcomes of agriculture, urban consumption and food security.	Lucca co-developed a food strategy with the aim to unite five municipalities around a shared vision and implementation structure.
Territorial cohesion	Co-ordinated efforts to promote food-based territorial cohesion promote food system integration and market access.	Tukums LL drew on producer and gastronomic networks, branding, market infrastructure assets, and producer directories to enhance regional food identity and social inclusion.
Public procurement	Procurement contracts legally specify environmental and social food qualities that have been politically agreed.	Gloucestershire, Lucca, Ljubljana, Lisbon, Tukums, and Valencia worked with partners to improve the effectiveness of regional supply chains in school food catering.
Branding	European (PDO/PGI) and local symbols on food packaging underline the importance of food to regional identity and regulate distinctive qualities of production.	In Lucca and Tukums, local products and supply chains highlighted efforts to improve visitor awareness of local food offers, and to support value-added opportunities in local and export markets.
Sustainability indicators	Food system performance indicators help to integrate and measure food system performance across multiple dimensions.	Ede's living lab initiated a range of dashboard indicators to assess rural–urban linkages and sustainability performance in the region.

Source: Authors' compilation.

framed by national agendas. In Ede, for example, the local council directed its living lab towards national aspirations for circular farming and economy.

In forging experimental approaches to food governance to strengthen rural–urban synergies, three types of innovation from the five mechanisms listed above really stand out. They reflect the types of system linkage described earlier (vertical and horizontal), as well as technological and social interventions. Table 12.2 summarises each and a corresponding case study description below provides a more place-embedded account, bringing to life how labs worked creatively to change their urban food system. These types align, to some extent, with the urban living lab typology (Marvin et al., 2018, 8), which they label as 'strategic', 'civic' and 'organic' living labs. In Marvin et al.'s framework the urban arena for each type is a test-bed, an historically produced context, and a geographical framing by a community group or grouping. In ROBUST, urban components were part of larger territorial experimental arenas, with the governance experiments designed to foster closer functional connection between urban, peri-urban and rural places. In that sense, all are strategic and territorially embedded, with rural–urban relations strengthened through institutional, technological or social innovation. Orientations also differ in terms of where system change is targeted. Lucca, for example, is a process of food re-territorialisation via strategic multi-level policy design across five municipalities. We introduce each innovation in more detail below.

Table 12.2 Food governance innovation type and linkages

Innovation type	*Living Lab*	*Experiment*	*Innovation outcome*
Institutional (multi-level policy design – vertical)	Lucca	Extending the Intermunicipal Food Policy to enhance rural–urban synergies.	Establishment of a new intermunicipal governance model, the first of its kind in Italy.
Technological (digital platform for short food chains – vertical)	Gloucestershire	Linking the school meals service and tendering contract to new 'Dynamic Procurement System' technology.	Revision of the school meals contract wording, which enables greater market access to school meal contracts for smaller producers/SMEs.
Social practice (food study plans for schools – horizontal)	Lisbon	Enhancing sustainable food practices in the school curriculum.	Development of study plans for sustainable food linked to different classroom subjects.

Source: Authors' compilation.

In **Lucca**, five municipalities in the Plain of Lucca had been collaborating on the development of an intermunicipal food policy (IFP). The area enjoyed a well-developed network of institutional, research and grassroots organisations that were already engaged in long-standing discussions about the benefits of, and multi-functional possibilities linked to, local food (including in the lucrative tourism market), but also including spatial and environmental dimensions linked to soil sealing and urban sprawl. The Living Lab devised a new governance model, bringing together the *gestione associate* (joint municipal management structure), the food policy office, the Agora (a public forum concerned with the IFP), the Food Council and the assembly of mayors. The model represents the first exemplar of institutional, territorial strategy implementation in the Plain of Lucca, and the IFP governance model is the first case in Italy of the joint management model for sharing functions on food policies.

In **Gloucestershire**, the emergence in the food retail market of an IT innovation combined with a government-initiated trial to establish regional public procurement infrastructure crystallised the focus of the living lab. The Dynamic Procurement System (DPS) uses complex algorithms to organise supply and demand of regional food on a daily basis, allowing for seasonal supply, quality and price variations, while ensuring efficient logistics. This tech breakthrough enables smaller-scale producers to benefit from stable, consistent and lucrative public sector demand, when consolidated across institutions. The Gloucestershire living lab resulted in wording in the tender document for the catering supply which will link the contract for 18,500 daily school meals to the DPS and the regional logistics hub pilot.

In **Lisbon**, specially trained teachers are employed to consider school food nutritional standards. In one of several innovations achieved by the living lab, these specialist teachers worked together with parent groups to institutionalise five sustainable food themes in a number of classroom subjects, including science, geography and citizenship. Food topics included the productive (agricultural) cycle, ecosystems services and food, sustainable consumption, nutrition and food waste management.

ROBUST links rural and urban food spaces by creating governance innovations, designed and refined through iterative, transparent 'user-led' living labs. The project has also highlighted challenges, such as the limited capacity of local authorities for being experimental, especially when managing vital public services such as safe and healthy school meals. In addition, when extended territorial considerations are at play, for example in inter-regional food systems, it can be difficult to balance levels of stakeholder input within a living lab so that they are proportionate and inclusive, certainly for the cases reported here, which have geographically and democratically fixed administrative boundaries. In this respect, cities are useful focal points for regional innovations, because they need to secure food system resilience for their citizens, while depending substantially on agriculture outside the city limits.

Towards transformative change: 'just sustainabilities' and food justice

The previous section ended with a discussion on the sustainable food governance innovations that enhance rural–urban linkages. This highlighted the value and potential of living labs as an important socio-technical innovation to inform sustainability governance and indicated an important shift in urban research and policy priorities. Critical in this regard is the realisation that urban sustainability challenges cannot be addressed through the collection of more data or the creation of technical fixes or new institutions. As Marvin et al. (2018, 3) put it, 'transitions are required in the ways in which systems of provision and services are designed, organised and delivered in diverse urban contexts'. New technology or infrastructure fixes will not suffice; changes in markets, practice and culture are needed. This echoes earlier definitional discussions and raises a further important distinction between 'radical' and 'targeted' complementary innovations. The former seeks to significantly change the way goods or services are produced and delivered and challenges the status quo by addressing asymmetrical power relationships and inequality (Marques et al., 2017, 77). The latter describes activities that 'seek to improve the production and delivery of certain goods and services, without radically reshaping current institutional arrangements or power structures' (ibid., 8). Activities aim, then, to include end-users as citizens in the 'design and delivery of goods and services'.

The boundaries are not necessarily as clear-cut as implied here, but it draws attention to innovation, and specifically social innovation, as a concept, term and normative guide that needs to be carefully defined and problematised. The ROBUST cases, for example, arguably fall within the instrumental innovation category. This points to an important extension in socio-technical transition thinking, in the sense that we need to consider more how such innovations connect and enable the transformation of, in this case, urban food systems and associated patterns of governance. In multi-level innovation theory, one focus to address these concerns has been strategic niche management and the potential of niches to lead to regime transition (Smith & Raven, 2012; Maye, 2018). Other research calls for closer engagement with the spatial and political contexts that innovations evolve and their relationship to systemic contexts, with an emphasis on the influence of city regions in the governance of transition pathways (Marvin et al., 2018). Emphasis on the city region also provides a territorial approach to urban food systems. As Ballamingie et al. (2020, 232–233) put it, '[j]ust and sustainable food systems aimed at mitigating food insecurity among the most vulnerable (among other goals) must … be enacted where they can achieve the greatest effect: the city-region'. Crucial to this is recognition that a diversity of models may be needed rather than a one-size-fits-all approach, respecting the specificity of place and scale and the promotion of place-based approaches to urban governance (Sonnino et al., 2016), including the translation of food policy council and food partnership models. Urban sustainability and resilience are also framed in terms of climate change, but food system scholars argue that 'food serves as a portal to myriad socio-economic and environmental issues' (Ballamingie et al., 2020, 238). This means innovation must include social and ecological innovations. With municipal food systems this is best realised through a city region lens and participatory and collaborative place-based governance processes.

The COVID-19 pandemic has magnified in multiple ways the need to adopt this system perspective, as well as bringing into sharp focus the vulnerability of food systems, and interconnections with other systems, particularly social welfare. COVID-19 strengthens the case for food system planning, city region thinking and social innovation to enable just and sustainable urban food provisioning. It also requires reflection on what exactly we mean, what we need, and who is best placed to implement 'transformation'. In the final paragraphs, we review COVID-19 urban food system impacts and introduce new work which links urban food systems to 'just sustainabilities', 'food justice' and 'transformative social innovation'. These new themes offer important avenues for future urban food studies scholarship. As Carey et al. (2020) note, cities are centre stage in the COVID-19 food response, with municipal governments and city authorities critical in the promotion of equitable access to healthy food. Those already food insecure in the Global South are most at risk, including smallholder producers, but food insecurity is a serious and intensifying problem in the Global North, particularly for low-income and vulnerable populations. Soaring demand for emergency food relief has created real pressure and revealed significant weaknesses in a system that relies on the charitable sector to address food insecurity. This has also led to wider questions about the vulnerability of cities that depend on global food chains, with increasing calls for some element of food system re-localisation and the need to build diversity in sources of food. Carey et al. (2020) note that some city authorities have already taken a lead role in initiatives to address food insecurity (e.g. New York), while others are collaborating with civil society organisations (e.g. Toronto); some are creating food vouchers (e.g. Seattle) and others are building online maps so citizens can find food services and food relief (e.g. Milan). Policy tools that cities and local governments can use to strengthen their food systems are also noted, which include developing plans to respond to the immediate needs of cities in the event of future sudden shocks and the need to have well-established networks of actors from across the food system to coordinate rapid responses (Palmer et al., 2020).

What we see emerging in these responses to COVID-19 are inspiring stories of innovation, often led by citizens who 'have actively created territorialized and community food economies that champion diversity and redistribution of value to deliver wide societal and material benefits' (Moragues-Faus, 2020, 583). They are actioned through the mobilisation of physical, social and increasingly digital infrastructures, with city food networks at the heart of this. These distributive structures also lack the capacity to replace globalised food chains and concerns are raised about the wider social and economic systems and structural problems which need to be tackled, including, for example, the living wage, the price of property and rent, income support and so on. To create 'liveable and just futures for all' (ibid., 584) requires investment and support to create distributive food systems, which includes careful thought about how those innovations can best create fair redistribution of value, knowledge and power in cities and regions and across actors to deliver sustainable food security.

Transformative social innovation is a valuable guide here, if we think of social innovation as changing social relations, and transformative change as 'the process of challenging, altering, or replacing dominant institutions in a specific socio-material context' (Pel et al., 2020, 2). Increasingly, discussion about justice and equity, particularly in relation to how urban food policy councils address the dual crises of COVID-19 and structural racism, foresees these organisations modifying their principles and practices to reflect values related to racial equity, food justice and food sovereignty (Palmer et al., 2020). This emphasises the need for innovation theory to connect more directly with questions of ethics and justice. Such discourse is evident in urban sustainability transition studies, but it is important to develop a more critical governance framework for urban food studies. Particularly useful in this regard is work by Coulson and Milbourne (2020) which, informed by U.S. food justice literature, adopts a 'justice multiple' approach, conceptualising multiple ways justice intersects with food system issues. This starts by pluralising justice in terms of distributive justice, highlighting the politics of recognition (as a feature of justice and a prerequisite for fair distribution) and emphasising the importance of participatory justice in terms of the need for emancipatory strategies to empower citizens and enable participatory policymaking and democratic governance. This pluralised conceptualisation of food justice 'is not based on the top-down application of abstract norms, but enacted in situated contexts in response to multidimensional embodied injustices' (ibid., p. 4). This is a useful new way to examine social innovation transformation, particularly as it relates to urban food governance, noting too that empowerment can come through multi-scalar geographies of food justice (i.e. forging co-operative relations with networks in other localities), in line with local and trans-local linkages in social innovation networks to empower people and to gain capacity to mobilise resources for social change (Avelino et al., 2020).

This indicates also the importance of trans-localism and asserts the need for a wider interpretation of food justice that includes distribution, recognition, participation and capability-based dimensions, and that examines sustainability and justice together, as 'just' (Agyeman et al., 2003). As COVID-19 has highlighted, this requires the extension of understandings of 'alternative', 'local' and 'urban' food to address 'the structural processes that reproduce socio-environmental inequality within and beyond the food system' (Coulson & Milbourne, 2021, 13). This involves re-orientating analytical focus beyond food itself 'towards issues of (in)justice, rights and sustainable livelihoods' to create collective solutions (social and technical innovations) that tackle structural injustices through 'shared political responsibility' (Young, 2011). This new context requires urban food scholarship to combine contextualised micro-analysis of social innovation with a focus on structures of society, including social and environmental injustices and new forms of economy.

Conclusion

For governance theory and practice, this chapter reveals four key lessons for future research. First, sustainability transition is a key approach to understand urban food systems. Second, innovation – institutional, technical and especially social – is critical for sustainable urban food system transition. Governance, as collaborative collective modes of action, is central to this, allowing a shift from people being consumers to citizens who create new forms of social justice. Third, living labs are emerging as a key epistemology and methodology to enact technical and social change, including for urban food systems (as shown here using selected examples from ROBUST) and what is needed now is more understanding and appreciation of the different modalities (strategic, multi-level and policy-orientated compared with specific, internal and practice-orientated, for example). Finally, COVID-19 has highlighted systemic inequalities, including for urban food systems, and this requires new theoretical frameworks. To support social and spatial transformation, future theoretical alignments should be strengthened between urban food governance and urban sustainability, and 'food justice' and 'just sustainabilities'.

Notes

1 For details, see https://rural-urban.eu/.
2 See https://enoll.org/about-us/.
3 See http://h2020repair.eu/; https://foodshift2030.eu/; and https://foodtrails.milanurbanfoodpolicypact.org/.

References

Agyeman, J., Bullard, R. D., & Evans, B. (Eds.). (2003). *Just sustainabilities: Development in an unequal world.* Cambridge, MA: MIT Press.

Anderson, P. M. L., Brown-Luthango, M., Cartwright, A., Farouk, I., & Smit, W. (2013). Brokering communities of knowledge and practice: Reflections on the African Centre for Cities' CityLab programme. *Cities, 32*, 1–10. https://doi.org/10.1016/j.cities.2013.02.002

Avelino, F., Dumitru, A., Cipolla, C., Kunze, I., & Wittmayer, J. (2020). Translocal empowerment in transformative social innovation networks. *European Planning Studies, 28*(5), 955–977. https://doi.org/10.1080/09654313.2019.1578339

Ballamingie, P., Blay-Palmer, A., Knezevic, I., Lacerda, A., Nimmo, E., Stahlbrand, L., & Ayalon, R. (2020). Integrating a food systems lens into discussions of urban resilience: A policy analysis. *Journal of Agriculture, Food Systems, and Community Development, 9*(3), 227–243. https://doi.org/10.5304/jafscd.2020.093.021

Ballon, P., & Schuurman, D. (2015). Living labs: Concepts, tools and cases. *Info, 17*(4), 1–11. https://doi.org/10.1108/info-04-2015-0024

Bergvall-Kareborn, B., Ihlstrom Eriksson, C., Strahlbrost, A., & Svensson, J. (2009). A milieu for innovation: Defining living labs. In K. R. E. Huizingh, S. Conn, M. Torkkeli, & I. Bitran (Eds.), *2nd ISPIM innovation symposium: Stimulating Recovery – the Role of Innovation Management, 6th–9th December 2009.* New York. ISPIM.

Bock, B. B. (2012). Social innovation and sustainability: How to disentangle the buzzword and its application in the field of agriculture and rural development. *Studies in Agricultural Economics, 114*(2), 57–63. http://dx.doi.org/10.7896/j.1209

Carey, J. (2013). Urban and community food strategies: The case of Bristol. *International Planning Studies, 18*(1), 111–128. https://doi.org/10.1080/13563475.2013.750938

Carey, R., Murphy, M., & Alexandra, L. (2020). COVID-19 highlights the need to plan for healthy, equitable and resilient food systems. *Cities & Health*, S123–S126. https://doi.org/10.1080/23748834.2020.1791442

Coulson, H., & Milbourne, P. (2021). Food justice for all? Searching for the 'justice multiple' in UK food movements. *Agriculture and Human Values, 38*(1), 43–58. https://doi.org/10.1007/s10460-020-10142-5

Darnhofer, I. (2015). Socio-technical transitions in farming: Key concepts. In L.-A. Sutherland, I. Darnhofer, G. Wilson, & L. Zagata (Eds.), *Transition pathways towards sustainability in agriculture: Case studies from Europe.* Wallingford: CAB International. doi:10.1079/9781780642192.0001

Dimbleby, H. (2021). *National Food Strategy: The plan.* London. www.nationalfoodstrategy.org/the-report/

Dinesh, D., Hegger, D. L., Klerkx, L., Vervoort, J., Campbell, B. M., & Driessen, P. P. (2021). Enacting theories of change for food systems transformation under climate change. *Global Food Security, 31*, 100583. https://doi.org/10.1016/j.gfs.2021.100583

Edwards-Schachter, M. E., Matti, C. E., & Alcántara, E. (2012). Fostering quality of life through social innovation: A living lab methodology study case. *Review of Policy Research, 29*(6), 672–692. https://doi.org/10.1111/j.1541-1338.2012.00588.x

European Commission. (2010). *Communication from the Commission – Europe 2020: A strategy for smart, sustainable and inclusive growth.* Working Paper, COM (2010) 2020, European Commission, Brussels.

European Commission. (2020). *Communication from the Commission to the European Parliament, the Council, the European Economic and Social Committee and the Committee of the Regions: A Farm to Fork Strategy for a fair, healthy and environmentally friendly food system.* Brussels: European Commission.

Foresight. (2011). The future of food and farming: Final project report. London: Foresight. https://assets.publishing.service.gov.uk/government/uploads/system/uploads/attachment_data/file/288329/11-546-future-of-food-and-farming-report.pdf

Gascó, M. (2017). Living labs: Implementing open innovation in the public sector. *Government Information Quarterly, 34*, 90–98. https://doi.org/10.1016/j.giq.2016.09.003

Geels, F. W. (2019). Socio-technical transitions to sustainability: A review of criticisms and elaborations of the multi-level perspective. *Current Opinion in Environmental Sustainability, 39*, 187–201. https://doi.org/10.1016/j.cosust.2019.06.009

Geels, F. W. & Schot, J. (2007). Typology of sociotechnical transition pathways. *Research Policy, 36*, 399–417. https://doi.org/10.1016/j.respol.2007.01.003

Hargreaves, T., Longhurst, N., & Seyfang, G. (2013). Up, down, round and round: Connecting regimes and practices in innovation for sustainability. *Environment and Planning A, 45*, 402–420. https://doi.org/10.1068/a45124

Herbert, N., & Lord Taylor of Holbeach. (2010). *Science for a new age of agriculture (The Taylor Report)*. London: The Conservative Party. archive.defra.gov.uk/food-farm/farm-manage/documents/taylor-review-response-110131.pdf

Hinrichs, C. C. (2014). Transitions to sustainability: A change in thinking about food systems change? *Agriculture & Human Values, 31*, 143–155. doi:10.1007/s10460-014-9479-5

Ingram, J., & Maye, D. (2020). What are the implications of digitalisation for agricultural knowledge? *Frontiers in Sustainable Food Systems, 4*, 66. https://doi.org/10.3389/fsufs.2020.00066

Kirwan, J., Ilbery, B., Maye, D., & Carey, J. (2013). Grassroots social innovations and food localisation: An investigation of the Local Food programme in England. *Global Environmental Change, 23*, 830–837. https://doi.org/10.1016/j.gloenvcha.2012.12.004

Kneafsey, M., Maye, D., Holloway, H., & Goodman, M. (2021). *Geographies of Food*. London: Bloomsbury.

Kronsell, A., & Mukhtar-Landgren, D. (2018). Experimental governance: The role of municipalities in urban living labs. *European Planning Studies, 26*, 988–1007. https://doi.org/10.1080/09654313.2018.1435631

Langendahl, P.-A., Cook, M., & Potter, S. (2014). Sustainable innovation journeys: Exploring the dynamics of firm practices as part of transitions to more sustainable food and farming. *Local Environment, 21*, 105–123. https://doi.org/10.1080/13549839.2014.926869

Leminen, S., Nyström, A.-G., & Westerlund, M. (2015). A typology of creative consumers in living labs. *Journal of Engineering and Technology Management, 37*, 6–20. https://doi.org/10.1016/j.jengtecman.2015.08.008

Marques, P., Morgan, K., & Richardson, R. (2017). Social innovation in question: The theoretical and practical implications of a contested concept. *Environment and Planning C: Government and Policy, 36*, 496–512. https://doi.org/10.1177/2399654417717986

Marvin, S., Bulkeley, H., Mai, L., Mccormick, K., & Voytenko Palgan, Y. E. (2018). *Urban living labs: Experimenting with city futures*. London: Routledge. https://doi.org/10.4324/9781315230641

Maye, D. (2018). Examining innovation for sustainability from the bottom up: An analysis of the permaculture community in England. *Sociologia Ruralis, 58*, 331–350. https://doi.org/10.1111/soru.12141

Maye, D. (2019). 'Smart food city': Conceptual relations between smart city planning, urban food systems and innovation theory. *City, Culture and Society, 16*, 18–24. https://doi.org/10.1016/j.ccs.2017.12.001

Maye, D., Swagemakers, P., Wiskerke, J. S. C., Moschitz, H., Kirwan, J., & Jahrl, I. (2021). Transformative potential from the ground up: Sustainable innovation journeys, soft change and alignment of interests in urban food initiatives. *European Urban and Regional Studies, 29*(2), 222–237. https://doi.org/10.1177/09697764211028887

Moragues-Faus, A. (2020). Distributive food systems to build just and liveable futures. *Agriculture and Human Values*, 37, 583–584. https://doi.org/10.1007/s10460-020-10087-9

Neumeier, S. (2012). Why do social innovations in rural development matter and should they be considered more seriously in rural development research? Proposal for a stronger focus on social innovations in rural development research. *Sociologia Ruralis, 52*(1), 48–69. https://doi.org/10.1111/j.1467-9523.2011.00553.x

Palmer, A., Atoloye, A., Bassarab, K., Calancie, L., Santo, R., & Stowers, K. C. (2020). COVID-19 responses: Food policy councils are 'stepping in, stepping up, and stepping back'. *Journal of Agriculture, Food Systems, and Community Development, 10*(1), 223–226. https://doi.org/10.5304/jafscd.2020.101.013

Pel, B., Haxeltine, A., Avelino, F., Dumitru, A., Kemp, R., Bauler, T., Kuzne, I., Dorland, J., Wittmayer, J., & Jørgensen, M. S. (2020). Towards a theory of transformative social innovation: A relational framework and 12 propositions. *Research Policy, 49*(8), 104080. https://doi.org/10.1016/j.respol.2020.104080

Pfotenhauer, S., Laurent, B., Papageorgiou, K., & Stilgoe, A. J. (2021). The politics of scaling. *Social Studies of Science, 52*(1), 3–34. https://doi.org/10.1177/03063127211048945

Schebesta, H., & Candel, J. J. L. (2020). Game-changing potential of the EU's Farm to Fork Strategy. *Nature Food, 1*, 586–588. https://doi.org/10.1038/s43016-020-00166-9

Seyfang, G., & Haxeltine, A. (2012). Growing grassroots innovations: Exploring the role of community-based initiatives in governing sustainable energy transitions. *Environment and Planning C: Government and Policy, 30*(3), 381–400. https://doi.org/10.1068/c10222

Shove, E. (2003). *Comfort, cleanliness and convenience: The social organization of normality*. Oxford: Berg.

Shove, E., & Pantzar, M. (2005). Consumers, producers and practices: Understanding the invention and reinvention of Nordic walking. *Journal of Consumer Culture, 5*(1), 43–64. https://doi.org/10.1177/1469540505049846

Smith, A. (2006). Green niches in sustainable development: The case of organic food in the United Kingdom. *Environment and Planning C: Government and Policy*, *24*, 439–458. https://doi.org/10.1068/c0514j

Smith, A., & Raven, R. (2012). What is protective space? Reconsidering niches in transitions to sustainability. *Research Policy*, *41*(6), 1025–1036. https://doi.org/10.1016/j.respol.2011.12.012

Sonnino, R., Marsden, T., & Moragues-Faus, A. (2016). Relationalities and convergences in food security narratives: Towards a place-based approach. *Transactions of the Institute of British Geographers*, *41*(4), 477–489. https://doi.org/10.1111/tran.12137

Voytenko, Y., McCormick, K., Evans, J., & Schliwa, G. (2016). Urban living labs for sustainability and low carbon cities in Europe: Towards a research agenda. *Journal of Cleaner Production*, *123*(1), 45–54. https://doi.org/10.1016/j.jclepro.2015.08.053

Westley, F., Olsson, P., Folke, C., Homer-Dixon, T., Vredenburg, H., Loorbach, D., Thompson, J., Nilsson, M., Lambin, E., Sendzimir, J., Banerjee, B., Galaz, V., & Van Der Leeuw, S. (2011). Tipping toward sustainability: Emerging pathways of transformation. *AMBIO*, *40*, 762. https://doi.org/10.1007/s13280-011-0186-9

Wiskerke, J. (2003). On promising niches and constraining sociotechnical regimes: The case of Dutch wheat and bread. *Environment and Planning A*, *35*, 429–448. https://doi.org/10.1068/a3512

Wolfert, J., Verdouw, C. N., Verloop, C. M., & Beulens, A. J. M. (2010). Organizing information integration in agri-food: A method based on a service-oriented architecture and living lab approach. *Computers and Electronics in Agriculture*, *70*(2), 389–405. https://doi.org/10.1016/j.compag.2009.07.015

Young, I. M. (2011). *Responsibility for justice*. Oxford: Oxford University Press.

PART III

Practising Urban Food Governance

13

RELATIONSHIPS BETWEEN FOOD POLICY COUNCILS AND GOVERNMENT IN THE UNITED STATES

Karen Bassarab, Raychel Santo and Anne Palmer

Introduction

Food policy councils (FPCs) (also referred to as food councils, food coalitions, food and farm alliances, etc.) are groups of stakeholders from the community, governments, non-profit organizations, and businesses, which may be sanctioned by government or may exist independently of government. They address food systems issues and needs within a city, county, multicounty region, state, or tribal nation through programmes, partnerships, and policy advocacy. At the end of 2020, there were 288 active FPCs in the United States, including five FPCs in tribal nations (CLF, 2021). Of the 288, 54 per cent are in urban areas. These multi-stakeholder collaborations often arise in urban areas because current efforts only tackle singular aspects of the food system, such as hunger or urban agriculture, or because the local government only considers selective elements of the food supply chain to be within its purview. This singular approach overlooks the complexity of the food system and can perpetuate problems. FPCs bring together essential knowledge on varying aspects of the food system and build common understandings of the adaptations needed to change the system.

While FPCs exist in countries across the globe,[1] from the United Kingdom to New Zealand, this chapter examines the dynamics between FPCs and municipal governments in the United States (for a discussion of FPCs in Africa, see Chapter 14 by Haysom and Currie in this volume). Municipal authority to address food systems issues is limited and obscured by the nesting of laws, funding, and programme administration across state and federal governments. Additionally, not all local governments are granted the same authority to directly regulate elements of the food system by their state governments (Clippinger et al., 2017). Some elements of the food system, such as those related to natural resources management (agricultural production practices), social welfare programmes (food assistance benefits and school nutrition programmes), or transportation are often regulated and funded by the federal government but administered by state governments. State governments may impose additional regulations or provide funding to these programmes, within limits. There is much that local government can do to address food systems challenges, but the layering of authority constricts their power.

DOI: 10.4324/9781003055907-16

Municipal governments are in a prime position to address the complexity of their local food systems because of their access to data, financial resources, private and civil society sector stakeholders, residents, and government officials across agencies and scales, but many don't. A survey conducted in 2015 by the Michigan State University Center for Regional Food Systems and the International City/County Management Association found that, of approximately 2,000 city and county managers in the United States, the most common food activities supported by local government were keeping chickens, bees, and goats (36 per cent), establishing and managing farmers markets (33 per cent), providing land for community gardens (29 per cent), and farmland preservation (29 per cent) (Goddeeris & Newton, 2016). While within their authority, few local governments supported activities to expand access to food assistance benefits (10 per cent), connect restaurants and food retailers with emergency food providers (6 per cent), create food jobs (6 per cent), redevelop brownfields for food production (4 per cent), or establish grocery stores in underserved areas (4 per cent) (Goddeeris & Newton, 2016).

In their efforts to transform the policies and laws that shape the food system, FPCs maintain some type of relationship with government, even if it is informal or adversarial. The arrangements between FPCs and government can be considered a spectrum. FPCs can be formal arrangements mandated by government, embedded in government agencies with government staff that provides administrative support, non-profits with government staff as FPC members, or informal arrangements without direct government involvement. This spectrum, however, does not determine whether or not an FPC can influence policy. An FPC mandated by government may not be more effective at changing policy than an FPC independent of government. The shape and strength of the relationship between an FPC and government and the effectiveness of an FPC to change policy are driven by a combination of contextual factors unique to each jurisdiction.

To examine the relationship between FPCs and government, this chapter draws on data from a census of FPCs conducted by the Johns Hopkins Center for a Livable Future (CLF).[2] This survey of FPCs does not ask about the population density of the communities where FPCs work; the closest identifier is the geographic focus of an FPC. For this chapter, we define an FPC as being "urban" if it works in a municipality designated as an urbanized area, with a population of at least 50,000 people, by the United States Census Bureau (U.S. Census Bureau, 2019).[3] We also included FPCs that work at a county level in counties designated within the boundaries of Metropolitan Statistical Areas by the United States Census Bureau (U.S. Census Bureau, 2013). These Metropolitan Statistical Areas are comprised of one or more counties that encompass at least one urbanized area of 50,000 people or more plus adjacent counties that are socially and economically integrated with the nearby urbanized area through commuting. We excluded FPCs that operate at a state, tribal, or regional (multicounty or multistate) level.

We start with an overview of urban FPCs in the United States, followed by a summary of the evolution of FPCs. Next, we look at the evolution of co-governance arrangements and how power is shared between nongovernmental stakeholders and government through these collaborative models. We then review what is known about the relationships between FPCs and government using data from the CLF's annual census of FPCs, published literature on FPCs, and our experience working with FPCs. We conclude with a discussion about lingering questions for future research about the relationship between FPCs and government.

Food Policy Council Basics

Since 2013, the CLF has surveyed FPCs in the U.S. every 12–18 months about their structure and policy work, including their relationship with government. While the most recent survey was completed in 2021, we rely on data from a survey conducted in 2019 for this chapter because it included more questions relevant to the relationship between government and FPCs. At that time, only 92 urban FPCs completed our survey, with 26 per cent working at the city level, 27 per cent at the city and county level, and 47 per cent at the county level (CLF, 2019). Thirty-five per cent are embedded in government, 32 per cent are housed in a non-profit organization, 15 per cent are grassroots coalitions, 12 per cent are non-profit organizations, and 3 per cent are embedded in a university. While many FPCs are not nascent initiatives, the majority having been in existence for six years or more, they still lack substantial funding to support their work. Sixty-four per cent of urban FPCs have an annual budget of $10,000 or less, while only 11 per cent have budgets of over $100,000. Urban areas tend to attract more financial resources due to the concentration of people and problems, but most FPCs in these areas fare no better than their nonurban peers.

The creation of an FPC is a multi-year undertaking that typically starts with who is invited to sit at the table. FPCs form as a result of a recommendation in a community, an organization plan, a government mandate or executive order, or an idea of a few community members. Developing relationships is the bedrock of FPCs, which pride themselves on gathering a variety of people and sectors to work together. These partnerships are critical in addressing complex societal issues, like food systems, that involve multiple sectors. For FPCs in urban areas, this networking role is complicated. There are more stakeholders working in the food system and more resident voices to consider, but there is a less direct connection with food producers and farmworkers. FPCs spend much of their early months defining their membership and how they will work together. By connecting different sectors, FPCs work to reduce redundancy, achieve efficiencies, and build resilience.

FPCs play multiple roles in addition to influencing policy, and their existence reflects communities engaged in shaping their local food systems. Many FPCs initiate and operate food- and farming-related activities and programmes within their communities. FPCs also tend to be trusted sources for information and advice on their local food systems and policy solutions. FPCs collect data and conduct research on their food systems. They host candidate forums or public meetings, whereby political candidates are invited to discuss their platforms, summits, community dinners, and panel discussions to educate the public on food systems issues. As FPCs mature, they engage more in policy advocacy (Bassarab et al., 2019b). While much of the policy work of FPCs is aimed at government policy, FPCs also work to change institutional policy, such as hospital, university, or school district food procurement policies. Increasingly, they create opportunities for, and support, those most affected by food systems injustices to participate, influence, and lead advocacy efforts, guided by a commitment to racial and economic justice.

History of Food Policy Councils

In the late 1970s, Robert Wilson, a professor of planning at the University of Tennessee, introduced his students to the notion of food being a viable public policy topic worthy of government action and attention. Acknowledging the inequities of the food system, he recommended creating a stakeholder group to understand the complexity of food. The Knoxville Food Policy Council was formed in 1982. Growth in the formation of new FPCs remained slow until 2005, when we began witnessing an annual uptick in numbers of FPCs in the United States. FPCs and similar groups have also been emerging in other industrialized countries around the world, particularly over the past decade, and most numerously in Canada, the United Kingdom, and Germany (Santo & Moragues-Faus, 2019).

The uptick coincided with a groundswell of interest in local food systems across the nation that resulted from a convergence of factors. First, there was more awareness of the connections between the food system and societal problems, including climate change, food insecurity, diet-related health conditions, urban sprawl, immigration, and agricultural industry consolidation. Second, the federal government had made little progress in addressing complex societal problems, in part due to the New Public Management approach, which promoted disaggregation and specialization of government agencies to address public problems (Cejudo & Michel, 2017). This translated into the Department of Housing and Urban Development becoming the face of urban America, with its focus on housing issues, and the United States Department of Agriculture becoming the face of rural America, with its focus on farms and agriculture (Pothukuchi & Kaufman, 1999). Third, it was apparent that addressing complex societal problems, like food systems problems, would require the involvement of multiple sectors. The siloed government approach to public problems meant that there was no department dedicated to food systems at any level of government. Fourth, in reaction to greater awareness of the environmental and economic impact of the global food system and agribusiness, public interest in activities like urban agriculture, farmers markets, community-supported agriculture, and school food reform was growing (Feenstra, 1997; Pirog et al., 2014). The result of this growing awareness and engagement was the opportunity for people to practice food democracy by engaging with policymakers in their own backyards (Hassanein, 2003). (See Chapter 7 by Bornemann and Weiland in this volume for a broader discussion of food democracy and FPCs' role as a "through-put.")

To support the demonstration of food democracy, FPCs have benefitted from active networking, and training and technical assistance, first through the Community Food Security Coalition's food policy council activities, then later through the CLF's Food Policy Networks project. Several states have recently formed networks to convene, build capacity, align efforts, and create a collective voice for local FPCs in their states. These opportunities have likely helped fuel the growth of FPCs.

Governance and Power

The formation of the first FPC in Knoxville, Tennessee, and the subsequent increase in FPCs beginning in 2005, coincide with a national shift in civic engagement from federal to local (Cooper et al., 2006). Neighbourhood-level councils were formed in the 1980s as conduits for residents, business owners, and non-profit organizations to connect with their local governments. This shift was an acknowledgement that complex societal problems could not be solved by the government alone, and piecemeal solutions were not working. This compelled stakeholders to work together to devise solutions that would collectively be supported and acted on (Bryson et al., 2015).

Some local governments embraced these localized spaces for civic engagement as a means to share the responsibility and power of governing with citizens (Cooper et al., 2006). The degree to which governing power is shared with nongovernmental stakeholders in these arrangements depends on who is invited to collaborate, how deliberate the approach is to engaging stakeholders, and shared expectations for how the process will influence policy (Cooper et al., 2006; Fung, 2006). In other words, is the arrangement mostly invited professional experts imparting advice, is it a self-selecting group of people from a mix of backgrounds discussing and debating with government about an issue to reach a consensus on a solution, or is it a combination of these arrangements? These arrangements can instil trust and legitimize government policy decisions if the process intentionally reaches consensus through dialogue and deliberation (Cooper et al., 2006; Fung, 2006). Co-governance arrangements, and the degree to which governing power is shared, vary by local government, and by country. Variations in the authority and remits of local governments, funding landscapes, and food movement priorities, along with other political, economic, and cultural factors, influence the systems of governance in other countries. For example, based on a scan of local and regional food policy initiatives in Canada, MacRae and Donahue (2013) found that the more formal the relationship with government, the more effective the initiative. For many FPCs in the United States, co-governance is not an option, as the local government does not value food systems as a public charge (Goddeeris & Newton, 2016).

Governing power does not lie solely with government. As stated previously, the distribution of governing power between food systems stakeholders and government can be considered along a spectrum (Clark et al., 2021). The degree to which power is tilted towards more government control (multi-stakeholderism) versus food system stakeholder autonomy (self-governance) depends on the availability and mobilization of financial resources, beliefs about how change is achieved, and the socio-economic and political landscape of a place (Clark et al., 2021). FPCs fall in the middle of the spectrum as co-governance arrangements, which come in many forms, from government-led commissions to community-based coalitions that include government representatives (Emerson et al., 2012). A few councils veer towards multi-stakeholderism, whereby competition among organizations for financial and political resources to support single-issue interests can obstruct the collaborative intent of the FPC model. For these FPCs, the alignment of policy priorities among members may be more limited due to individual organization interests (Siddiki et al., 2015). Regardless of the arrangements, the FPC model is an effort to create a new, integrated system of governance for food systems.

In the following sections, we discuss how the arrangements between FPCs and government shape the distribution of power in these co-governance models.

Food Policy Council and Government Arrangements

The arrangements between FPCs and government are complex and varied, and it is challenging to categorize the shape and strength of an arrangement based on where an FPC is organizationally housed (e.g., embedded in government vs. independent of government). In this section, we discuss some of the nuances in arrangements between government and FPCs, drawing on examples of FPCs based in urban areas. We also discuss the impact of these arrangements on an FPC's relationship with community members and its policy work, two key elements to FPCs. Table 13.1 provides brief descriptions and examples of primary arrangements between FPCs in urban areas and government.

Formal Relationships with Government

An important consideration for newly forming FPCs, and particularly FPCs in urban areas, is whether to establish a formal connection to government. This formal connection can take on several forms. An FPC could be housed within the government as a board or commission, or as a project of a government agency, whereby the government provides administrative and sometimes fiscal support for the FPC. For example, the Douglas County (Kansas) Food Policy Council is a joint advisory board for the City of Lawrence and Douglas County with one staff liaison from the county who provides administrative support. The FPC could be created through legislation, like 25 per cent of urban FPCs. The FPC could be a mayor-driven initiative, like the Baltimore (Maryland) Food Policy Initiative. Lastly, an FPC could be formally

Table 13.1 Types of relationships between an FPC and local government among urban FPCs (N = 92)

	Definition	*n*
FPC is embedded in government.	FPC may be an official board or commission of the local government or an initiative of a local government agency. A local government agency may provide administrative or fiscal support for a council. A government employee may provide staff support to the FPC.	32
FPC is created or mandated by legislation.	FPC is established via a city or county resolution or ordinance. FPC does not have to be embedded in government.	23
Government employees are members of the FPC.	Staff member(s) of a government agency are official members of an FPC, potentially with the authority to vote in FPC decisions.	84
Government employees participate in FPC meetings.	Staff member(s) of a government agency may serve as a liaison or coordinator for an FPC or may provide administrative support during FPC meetings but lack the authority to vote in FPC decisions.	*
Elected officials are members of the FPC.	A city councillor, county commissioner, mayor, or other elected official is an official member of the FPC.	28
Government officials appoint members of the FPC.	An elected official or government staff member appoints FPC members, often to fill pre-designated seats for representatives of different sectors. Member appointments may be made with input from an FPC.	23
Local government supports the FPC.	Local government may provide in-kind support in the form of meeting space, research or data, or the provision of a letter of support.	51
Government seeks advice or recommendations from the FPC.	FPC may be an official advisory body to government or may be asked to provide advice on an ad hoc basis.	50

Source: Johns Hopkins Center for a Livable Future.

Note: These categories are not mutually exclusive; some councils may have many or most of these relationships with their government, while others may only have one or two.

*The survey does not distinguish government employees who participate in meetings but are not formal members from government employees who are formal members.

recognized as an advisory group to the local government, such as through a resolution. For example, the New Orleans (Louisiana) Food Policy Advisory Committee is a non-profit organization that was recognized through a city resolution as a formal advisory body to the New Orleans City Council on food and agriculture policy.

A formal relationship with government can have a mix of effects on an FPC. The most positive impact of these formal relationships is the validation that food systems matter. In urban areas, problems like lack of affordable housing, traffic, poverty, and homelessness are compounded by the population, so the investment of government resources signals the importance of an issue to the community. For instance, the Madison (Wisconsin) Food Policy Council, established in 2012 by Mayor Paul Soglin, successfully advocated for creating a Healthy Retail Access Program to provide grants to increase retail food access in select underserved neighbourhoods. The crowning achievement of the effort was the mayor allocating $150,000 annually for the grants in the 2015 Capital Budget.

A formal relationship with government may also lend credibility and legitimacy to the work of an FPC, given that an urban FPC may be one of a dozen or more food systems-related organizations or groups in a city. A social network map of the members and stakeholders engaged with the Pittsburgh (Pennsylvania) Food Policy Council contains 52 organizations.[4] Acceptance and promotion of an FPC by local elected officials or government leadership can help it garner key stakeholders' attention. For instance, the Los Angeles (California) FPC was able to recruit influential stakeholders to serve on the council because of the legitimacy the mayor gave to the nascent initiative by creating it through a directive (Gupta et al., 2018).

While a formal relationship with government may seem beneficial, that relationship can be short-lived or stymie FPC actions. FPCs that result from a mayoral directive, or are an advisory board of the local government, run the risk of becoming obsolete when administrations change. Many urban FPCs that are embedded in a local government, however, have survived the transition of elected officials, including but not limited to Austin, Texas; Baltimore, Maryland; Denver, Colorado; Madison, Wisconsin; and Minneapolis, Minnesota. As the priorities of a local government change with new leadership, an FPC may need to demonstrate its relevancy or how its work aligns with new priorities (Gupta et al., 2018). Absent a change in government leadership, an FPC may still need to consider the alignment of its priorities with those of elected officials or government agencies. FPCs created by government directives are not vested with the authority to make decisions for government; they are reliant on relationships with elected officials or government staff. For the Portland Multnomah (Oregon) FPC, differences in priorities between the FPC and elected officials, and by extension the government staff liaisons to the council, contributed to its eventual dissolution (Coplen & Cuneo, 2015). The vulnerabilities of councils that are closely intertwined with government administrations illustrate part of a broader trend in the dynamic and fluid nature of many FPCs, which often undergo deep structural changes over time to adapt to changing political, economic, or cultural environments or to dissolve altogether (Santo & Moragues-Faus, 2019).

In a few cities, two FPCs have formed, with one embedded in the local government and one separate from it. In Franklin County, Ohio, both a grassroots coalition (Franklin County Local Food Council, established in 2011) and a government-embedded group (Columbus-Franklin County Local Food Board, established in 2017) coexist. These groups work in partnership to implement the city–county Local Food Action Plan through a unique collaborative governance arrangement (Clark, 2019). More recently, the government-embedded Missoula City-County Food Policy Advisory Board formed in 2020, joining the 15-year-old non-profit FPC Community Food & Agriculture Coalition to address food systems issues in Missoula, Montana. This approach is testing the value of having councils that work from both inside and outside of government to address community concerns. While the effectiveness and efficiency of this relatively new approach remain to be seen, this model is likely to emerge mostly in urban areas with enough population to support two councils.

Food Policy Council Membership

Members are the lifeblood of an FPC, driving its priorities and diversity of work (Bassarab et al., 2019a; Siddiki et al., 2015). Government representation on an FPC can help other FPC members understand and navigate the policy process, but it can also impede an FPC's agility in working on policy and community engagement. Given this potential to inhibit policy work, most FPCs have members that represent government. The most common relationship between urban FPCs and government is when government staff participates in an FPC. Ninety-one per cent of FPCs have participating government staff, either as official members or administrative support to the council. Government staff may also serve as ex-officio representatives for their agencies. For example, the DC Food Policy Council has ex-officio members from ten government agencies, including the departments of Health Services, Transportation, and Energy and Environment. The role of an ex-officio member is to align their department's work on food systems with the priorities of the council (Council of the District of Columbia, 2014). Ex-officio members are often not permitted to vote on decisions by the FPC. Additionally, 30 per cent of urban FPCs have members who are elected officials. For example, a county commissioner serves as one of the 18 members on the Washtenaw County Food Policy Council in Michigan, whose members are appointed by the County Board of Commissioners. The members of 25 per cent of urban FPCs are appointed by government officials, and many of these FPCs were created through legislation (74 per cent), such as a city ordinance or county resolution.

Government representation on an FPC can be mutually beneficial for nongovernmental members and the local government. Through FPC meetings, government staff learn about problems facing a community food system and work with community stakeholders to identify appropriate solutions, including opportunities for the local government to be part of the solution. In the case of the San Mateo County (CA) Food System Alliance, the FPC garnered support for policies that are uncharacteristic of a health department because of the county public health officer's participation in the FPC (Gupta et al., 2018). Hearing directly from those impacted by the food system can provide an impetus for government representatives to support innovative ideas that deviate from the traditionally disaggregated approach of government. Conversely, government representatives on an FPC can educate other members about government processes and help them navigate the process or identify sympathetic staff willing to implement innovative ideas (Gupta et al., 2018).

While government representation can improve understanding of and access to the policy process, their membership can also delay and derail the policy work of an FPC. Government representatives can delay FPC decisions because they may not have the authority to act on behalf of a local government and need to seek approval before supporting a decision (Siddiki et al., 2015). They may also derail FPC decisions due to restrictions on their actions and misalignment with government priorities. Engaging in advocacy can be tricky for government employees because of restrictions on lobbying and advocacy (Chen et al., 2019; Siddiki et al., 2015). These restrictions can either result in government employees refraining from supporting FPC actions or discourage the FPC from certain policy actions. Additionally, government representatives may only be willing to act on issues that align with the priorities of a government agency or elected officials, as was the case with the Portland Multnomah (Oregon) Food Policy Council, where government staff inhibited the FPC from moving forward on its agenda by blocking communication with government officials (Coplen & Cuneo, 2015). FPCs without formal relationships with government may have more flexibility in deciding with whom they ally or partner to support their policy priorities (Gupta et al., 2018).

Community Engagement

Community engagement is essential to FPCs because it grounds their work in the needs of a community and offers a vehicle by which the community can advocate for solutions that address their needs. Ninety-eight per cent of urban FPCs have community members that serve on them. The emphasis lies most heavily on nonprofessional stakeholders, and more specifically individuals most affected by food systems problems. For FPCs, a formal association with government can bring community members to the table by raising awareness about the importance of food systems and, conversely, deter FPC engagement for certain populations. For example, farmers may be less likely to participate in an FPC that is embedded in government because of perceptions of government overreach or overregulation of farm operations (Schiff, 2008). For urban FPCs, engaging with farmers is further complicated due to the geographic location of farmers in peri-urban areas or outside of urban jurisdictions. Additionally, communities of colour may be hesitant to participate in an FPC formally associated with government because of centuries of government-sanctioned policies of discrimination that restricted access to land and financial assistance, concentrated housing for minorities, and directed transportation infrastructure through minority neighbourhoods. FPCs embedded in government can counter this distrust by intentionally taking time to build relationships with reluctant populations, which in turn can shift the priorities of local government (Gupta et al., 2018).

Policy Engagement

Policy advocacy is a key function of FPCs, and a majority of urban FPCs (73 per cent) worked on legislative or regulatory policy at some level of government (local, state, tribal, or federal) in 2018. FPCs may need to advocate for policy change beyond their local jurisdictions due to regulatory oversight of food and agriculture by federal and state governments. While most urban FPCs (86 per cent) directly engage with local policymakers, 60 per cent also engage with state policymakers, and 30 per cent with federal policymakers. For urban FPCs with no direct authority to change policy (including those embedded in government), a relationship with government staff or local elected officials, even those not directly involved with an FPC, can be a linchpin in achieving policy change. For 79 per cent of urban FPCs, a relationship with local elected officials is needed "to a great extent" or "a lot" to achieve their policy priorities. For example, in 2017, the Chicago (Illinois) Food Policy Action Council, a non-profit council with members representing government, achieved a significant policy win resulting from a relationship with the city mayor who was external to the FPC. After extensive advocacy by the council, the mayor issued a resolution calling on city departments to adopt the Good Food Purchasing Policy, an innovative idea to leverage the city's purchasing power to support the regional food system.

Urban FPCs engage with policymakers in many ways, including meeting with policymakers (78 per cent), providing policy recommendations to policymakers (77 per cent), reviewing and commenting on draft legislation (53 per cent), providing analysis or research on specific legislation (45 per cent), calling policymakers (44 per cent), and providing oral testimony (38 per cent) (Figure 13.1). A handful of FPCs survey policymakers about food systems issue(s) (22 per cent) or host candidate forums (8 per cent).

Discussion and Conclusion

While FPCs have been around for close to four decades, they are a new phenomenon for many cities, and there is still much to explore about the effectiveness of these collaborative bodies as spaces for food democracy. In general, FPCs are viewed positively as a strategy to address complex problems because they raise public awareness about the food system, build relationships across stakeholders to reduce redundancy, and advance long-term policy solutions. They embody the intent of co-governance to create space for deliberation between government and multi-sector stakeholders but, ultimately, they are reliant on government to enact policy change. The evolution of the Cass Clay (Minnesota/North Dakota) Food Partners (CCFP) exemplifies the challenges of these co-governance arrangements. The current CCFP model is

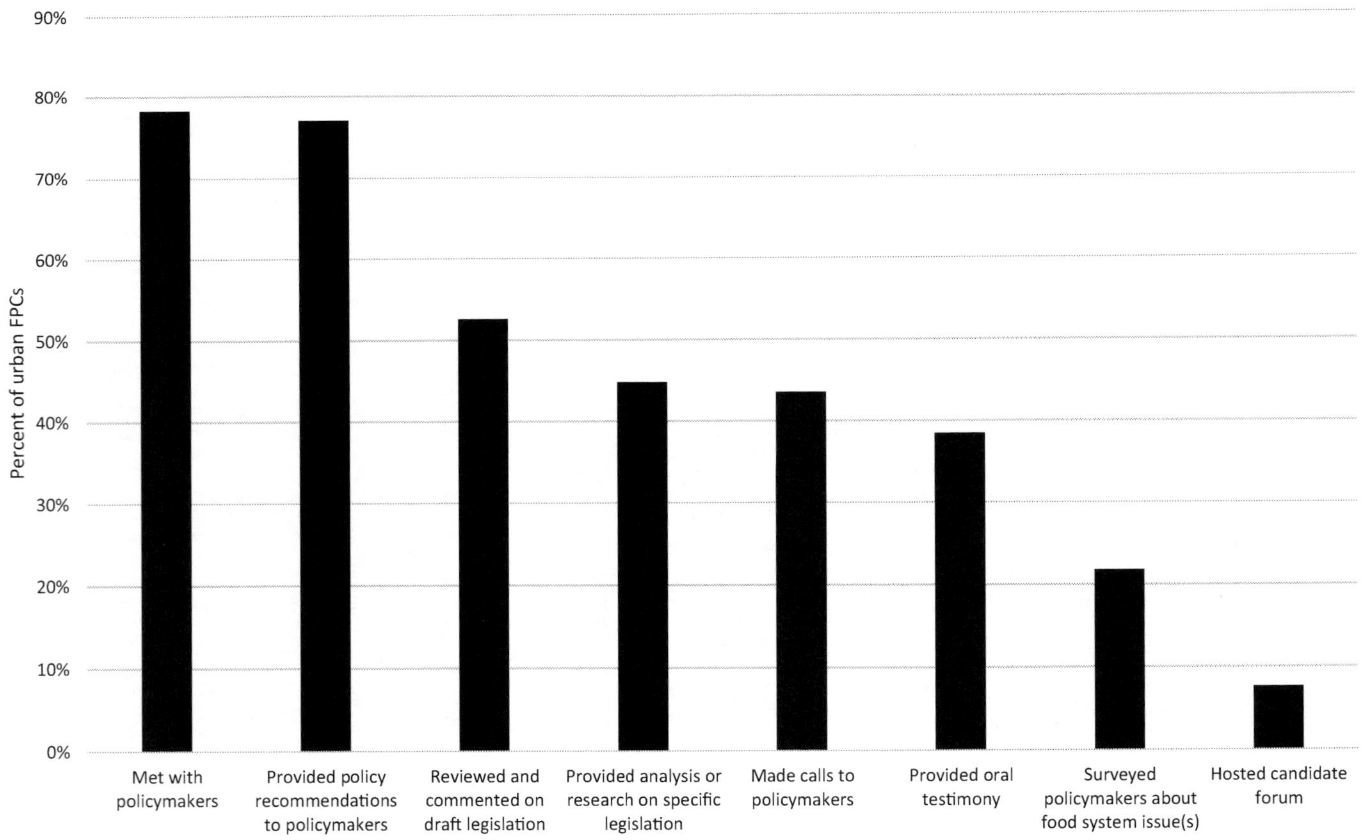

Figure 13.1 Engagement of urban FPCs with policymakers at any level of government

Note: We did not require respondents to answer all questions in the survey. The percentages above were calculated using only the respondents that answered each question (n = 78).

Source: Johns Hopkins Center for a Livable Future.

the result of oscillation between a community-driven, project-based initiative, the Cass Clay Food Systems Initiative, and a government-led commission aimed at policy change, the Cass Clay Food Commission. While the Initiative initially brought together an energetic array of stakeholders, it was unable to sustain the energy to affect policy change. The Commission arose to advance significant change through policy, but it lacked the necessary engagement of community to lend credibility to recommendations and exert pressure to act. CCFP brings together arrangements and adds an additional layer of a steering committee comprised of public, private, and civil society sector stakeholders (Gold & Harden, 2018). The evolution of CCFP highlights the complex dynamics between community and government in these co-governance arrangements.

FPCs are not a one-size-fits-all jurisdictions approach to food systems change. As the number of FPCs has increased, so have the number of cities and counties with government positions dedicated to food policy (Berglund et al., 2021). Most of these positions were formed because an FPC worked with elected officials or senior government staff to advocate for a position dedicated to food systems issues (Berglund et al., 2021). For example, the City of Baltimore (Maryland) hired a food policy director in 2010 who oversees the Baltimore Food Policy Initiative (BPFI), formed in 2010, an interagency collaboration to coordinate activities across three city agencies; the Baltimore Food Policy Action Coalition, which convenes food systems stakeholders from across the city; and the Resident Food Equity Advisors, formed in 2017 to work directly with residents on food systems solutions (Santo et al., 2014). The food policy director position has endured multiple changes in city administration, which could be attributed to the approach of the BFPI to base policy efforts on input from a network of over 60 food systems stakeholders and residents, as well as the director framing the work of BFPI to align with the priorities of each administration. The City of New Haven, Connecticut, took it a step farther in creating a city government division dedicated to food systems policy. Both the evolution of CCFP and the institutionalization of food policy in government raises the question: Are there more effective models for food systems change? Limited research evaluates the effectiveness of these models to change policy, or how the policies being advocated for are effective at achieving their desired outcomes.

In both these emerging arrangements and the existing FPCs, critical questions about the voices represented remain. Who are the voices? What is the FPC's approach to community engagement? How effective is it at including diverse voices, such as minority groups, residents of disinvested neighbourhoods and nonprofessionals? This means doing more than adjusting the location and times of FPC meetings to be more accessible to people for whom food systems are not just a job requirement; it also means changing FPCs' culture and approach to support community members in driving the agenda and advocacy efforts of FPCs. For example, the Philadelphia (Pennsylvania) Food Policy Advisory Council provides stipends to members who are not paid by their jobs to serve on the council. The San Diego Food Systems Alliance led an extensive and intentional outreach process to connect with grassroots organizations (including those not just focused on food systems issues), neighbourhood associations, and community leaders to inform a new food plan for the county. It is too soon to tell if these approaches will increase the effectiveness of FPCs in transforming policy, if elected officials will pay greater attention to the work of FPCs that they believe represent broader sets of community interests, if local governments will transform their approaches to community engagement to be more collaborative, or if more community members will engage in the policymaking process because of their participation in an FPC.

Notes

1 A list of food policy groups around the world can be found at www.foodpolicynetworks.org/councils/fpg-worldwide/.
2 Highlights from the most recent census can be found at www.foodpolicynetworks.org/councils/directory/online/.
3 Eight cities (e.g., Medford, MA; New Brunswick, NJ) were not designated individually as "urbanized areas," though they may be included as part of the "urbanized area" boundaries of a neighboring city/region (e.g., Boston, New York). For these areas, we included the FPC if the city had a population of over 50,000.
4 The Pittsburgh Food Policy Council social network map can be accessed here at https://kumu.io/pittsburghfoodpolicy/pfpc-member-directory#pfpc-member-stakeholder-directory?selection=%23health-and-nutrition-advocacy.

References

Bassarab, K., Clark, J. K., Santo, R., & Palmer, A. (2019a). Finding our way to food democracy: Lessons from U.S. food policy council governance. *Politics and Governance, 7*(4), 32–47. https://doi.org/10.17645/pag.v7i4.2092

Bassarab, K., Santo, R., & Palmer, A. (2019b). *Food Policy Council Report 2018*. Baltimore, MD: Johns Hopkins Center for a Livable Future.

Berglund, E., Hassanein, N., LaChapelle, P., & Stephens, C. (2021). Advancing food democracy: The potential and limits of food policy positions in local government. *Journal of Agriculture, Food Systems, and Community Development, 11*(1), 1–18. https://doi.org/10.5304/jafscd.2021.111.002

Bryson, J. M., Crosby, B. C., & Stone, M. M. (2015). Designing and implementing cross-sector collaborations: Needed and challenging. *Public Administration Review, 75*(5), 645–663. https://doi.org/10.1111/puar.12432

Cejudo, G. M. & Michel, C. L. (2017). Addressing fragmented government action: Coordination, coherence, and integration. *Policy Sciences, 50*, 745–767. https://doi.org/10.1007/s11077-017-9281-5

Chen, C., Santo, R., Ellison, B., & Maiolatesi, A. (2019). *Advocacy & Lobbying 101 for Food Policy Councils*. Baltimore, MD: Johns Hopkins Center for a Livable Future and Harvard Food Law and Policy Clinic.

Clark, J. K. (2019). Collaborative governance: The case of local food action planning. In P. Andrée, J. K Clark, C. Z. Levkoe, & K. Lowitt (Eds.), *Civil Society and Social Movements in Food System Governance* (pp. 164–182). New York: Routledge.

Clark, J. K., Lowitt, K., Levkoe, C. Z., & Andrée, P. (2021). The power to convene: Making sense of the power of food movement organizations in governance processes in the Global North. *Agriculture and Human Values, 38*(1), 175–191. https://doi.org/10.1007/s10460-020-10146-1

CLF (Johns Hopkins Center for a Livable Future). (2019). *Food Policy Council Census* [Data set].

CLF. (2021). *Food Policy Council Census* [Data set].

Clippinger, E., Balkus, O., Rice, C., Nielsen, A., & Broad Leib, E. (2017). *Putting Local Food Policy to Work for Our Communities* (2nd ed.). Boston, MA: Harvard Law School Food Law and Policy Clinic.

Cooper, T. L., Bryer, T. A., & Meek, J. W. (2006). Citizen-centered collaborative public management. *Public Administration Review, 66*(s1), 76–88. https://doi.org/10.1111/j.1540-6210.2006.00668.x

Coplen, A. K., & Cuneo, M. (2015). Dissolved: Lessons learned from the Portland Multnomah food policy council. *Journal of Agriculture, Food Systems, and Community Development, 5*(2), 91–107. https://doi.org/10.5304/jafscd.2015.052.002

Council of the District of Columbia. (2014). *D.C. Act, 20–483*.

Emerson, K., Nabatchi, T., & Balogh, S. (2012). An integrative framework for collaborative governance. *Journal of Public Administration Research and Theory, 22*(1), 1–29. https://doi.org/10.1093/jopart/mur011

Feenstra, G. W. (1997). Local food systems and sustainable communities. *American Journal of Alternative Agriculture, 12*(1), 28–36. www.jstor.org/stable/44502995

Fung, A. (2006). Varieties of participation in complex governance. *Public Administration Review, 66*(s1), 66–75. https://doi.org/10.1111/j.1540-6210.2006.00667.x

Goddeeris, L. & Newton, J. (2016). *The How and Why of Local Government Support for Food Systems* [presentation slides]. Michigan State University Center for Regional Food Systems. Retrieved from: www.canr.msu.edu/resources/the-how-and-why-of-local-government-support-for-food-systems

Gold, A., & Harden, N. (2018). Navigating borders: The evolution of the Cass Clay Food Partners. *Journal of Agriculture, Food Systems, and Community Development, 8*(Suppl. 2), 29–38. https://doi.org/10.5304/jafscd.2018.08B.010

Gupta, C., Campbell, D., Munden-Dixon, K., Sowerwine, J., Capps, S., Feenstra, G., & Kim, J. V. S. (2018). Food policy councils and local governments: Creating effective collaboration for food systems change. *Journal of Agriculture, Food Systems, and Community Development, 8*(Suppl. 2), 11–28. https://doi.org/10.5304/jafscd.2018.08B.006

Hassanein, N. (2003). Practicing food democracy: A pragmatic politics of transformation. *Journal of Rural Studies, 19*, 77–86. https://doi.org/10.1016/S0743-0167(02)00041-4

MacRae, R. & Donahue, K. (2013). *Municipal Food Policy Entrepreneurs: A Preliminary Analysis of How Canadian Cities and Regional Districts are Involved in Food System Change.* Retrieved from: https://foodsecurecanada.org/resources-news/resources-research/municipal-food-policy-entrepreneurs

Pirog, R., Miller, C., Way, L., Hazekamp, C., & Kim, E. (2014). *The Local Food Movement: Setting the Stage for Food Food.* Michigan State University Center for Regional Food Systems. Retrieved from: www.canr.msu.edu/resources/local-food-movement-setting-the-stage

Pothukuchi, K., & Kaufman, J. L. (1999). Placing the food system on the urban agenda: The role of municipal institutions in food systems planning. *Agriculture and Human Values, 16*, 213–224. https://doi.org/10.1023/A:1007558805953

Santo, R., & Moragues-Faus, A. (2019). Towards a trans-local food governance: Exploring the transformative capacity of food policy assemblages in the US and UK. *Geoforum, 98*, 75–87. https://doi.org/10.1016/j.geoforum.2018.10.002

Santo, R., Yong, R., & Palmer, A. (2014). Collaboration meets opportunity: The Baltimore Food Policy Initiative. *Journal of Agriculture, Food Systems, and Community Development, 4*(3), 193–208. http://dx.doi.org/10.5304/jafscd.2014.043.012

Schiff, R. (2008). The role of food policy councils in developing sustainable food systems. *Journal of Hunger & Environmental Nutrition, 3*(2/3), 206–228. https://doi.org/10.1080/19320240802244017

Siddiki, S., Carboni, J. L., Koski, C., and Sadiq, A. A. (2015). How policy rules shape the structure and performance of collaborative governance arrangements. *Public Administration Review, 75*(4), 536–547. https://doi.org/10.1111/puar.12352

United States Census Bureau. (2013). *Core Based Statistical Areas (CBSAs) and Combined Statistical Areas (CSAs), February 2013 Delineations* [Data set]. Retrieved 17 May 2021 from: www.census.gov/geographies/reference-files/time-series/demo/metro-micro/delineation-files.html

United States Census Bureau. (2019). *2010 Census Urban and Rural Classification and Urban Area Criteria. A National List of All 2010 Urbanized Areas (Including Puerto Rico and the Island Areas) Sorted by UACE Code* [Data set]. Retrieved 17 May 2021 from: www2.census.gov/geo/docs/reference/ua/ua_list_ua.xls

14

FOOD POLICY COUNCILS AND GOVERNANCE PARTNERSHIPS IN AFRICAN URBAN CONTEXTS

Gareth Haysom and Paul Currie

Introduction

There is a misconceived view that Africa is predominantly rural, a continent of smallholders (Forster & Escudero, 2014), whose production supports local food systems feeding small urban centres (Battersby & Watson, 2018; Crush & Frayne, 2014). The colonial, post-independence, and later liberalised governance approaches to urban management saw food as a rural issue, resulting in an agrarian-oriented approach to food governance (Haysom et al., 2020). Urban areas have few or no direct policy-directed mandates requiring urban food system governance (Haysom, 2015). Cities might have policies and mandates to manage components of the urban food system, such as informal food vending (Duminy, 2018), waste management, or public health (Smit, 2016), but engagement in urban food system governance is limited. In most African countries, food system policy and management are the responsibility of provincial or national governments, clearly evident in the Malabo Declaration and in details of the scale and scope of the Comprehensive Africa Agriculture Development Programme (AU, 2014). This national-scale responsibility for food security and wider food systems governance is further reinforced by donor agendas (see Smit, 2016).[1]

Africa is urbanising at a rapid rate (Pieterse & Parnell, 2014). The nature and form of this urbanisation differs across countries and regions (Pieterse et al., 2018; UNDESA, 2019). As Africa urbanises, and African cities and their food systems change as a result, governing these food systems increasingly becomes an urban challenge. How African cities are starting to engage questions of urban food governance is the focus of this chapter.

In this chapter, the term "mandate" is used to demonstrate top-down governance actions. It is understood as the governance authority to enact policy, laws, bylaws, or other government-directed instruments to achieve a particular policy outcome or goal. Globalisation has altered the relationship between cities and the nation-state, an issue that has occupied much of the urban governance discourse. This shift has been described as a move from the Fordist-oriented approaches of the 1960s to forms aligning to a more liberalised ideology of entrepreneurialism (Harvey, 1989). African cities remain embedded in traditional hierarchical governmental

 DOI: 10.4324/9781003055907-17

structures, but processes such as structural adjustment policy implementation and austerity have resulted in concentrations of power at the national scale. The challenge is how to create opportunities for other voices, such as civil society and the private sector, particularly if traditional management structures, policies, and systems remain in place (Kearns & Paddison, 2000). These other voices form part of a wider conceptualisation of governance, representing a form of bottom up, contextually specific governance that is emerging in food system change processes at different scales. When considering these different types of governance, this chapter uses the UN-Habitat framing of urban governance, which sees governance as being about both government and nongovernment actions and reflects:

> the many ways individuals and institutions, public and private, plan and manage the common affairs of the city. It is a continuing process through which conflicting or diverse interests may be accommodated and cooperative action can be taken. It includes formal institutions as well as informal arrangements and the social capital of citizens.
>
> *UN-Habitat, 2002, p. 14*

As a result of the historical governmental hierarchies and allocated mandates, most African cities have no direct mandate, or authority, to govern urban food insecurity or the urban food system. Despite absent food-specific mandates, city governing activities intersect directly with the urban food system. Many cities govern urban food markets (Battersby & Muwowo, 2018), approve development plans for new developments (Peyton et al., 2015), collect licence fees and permits from market food vendors (Sibanda & von Blottnitz, 2018), regulate informal food traders, manage market infrastructure (Battersby & Muwowo, 2018) (also see Chapter 20 by Wegerif and Kissoly in this volume), build and regulate local transportation infrastructure (Kameshwari & Kaufman, 1999), and are showing increased interest in issues of social and environmental resilience and sustainability (seen through growing membership in such urban sustainability networks as ICLEI, C40, Rockefeller's 100 Resilient Cities, the Milan Urban Food Policy Pact, etc.). They also promote urban agriculture, diversion of organic wastes, and feeding programmes in schools or communities. These governing functions generally occur in silos, with little or no food system coordination taking place (Smit, 2016). The lack of coordination and government action allows forms of rent seeking, which enable a "licence to operate," facilitated through non-state, gate-keeper, or cartel-type structures, creating different layers of governance and authorising environments[2] (Pieterse et al., 2018). These powerful alternative governance actors challenge or undermine state-enabled forms of governance (Katsaura, 2012; Simon et al., 2004), resulting in either benign or negative food system outcomes.

Internationally, there is a trend that seeks to decentralise food governance, with cities, whether through government, society, or both, taking back control of their food systems (Ilieva, 2017; MacRae & Donahue, 2013; Raja et al., 2017). Increasingly these processes are seeking ways to expand urban governance mandates, at times even seeking change beyond the urban food system (Harper et al., 2009; Moragues-Faus & Morgan, 2015; Schiff, 2008). These emerging trends are, however, largely confined to certain countries in the Global North (Sonnino, 2019; Haysom, 2015). A key trend is the emergence of pluralistic structures that bring a wide variety of urban food system actors together (Haysom, 2015; MacRae & Donahue, 2013), often referred to as "food policy councils" (FPCs). (See Chapter 13 by Bassarab et al. in this volume for a review of urban FPCs in the United States.) A review of localised FPC governance structures in North America demonstrated diverse governance positions, ranging from structures officially embedded within city governments enacting food policy processes at the urban scale, to other structures that actively sought to engage food system issues independently of city processes. The majority of these food policy structures fell between these binaries, demonstrating novel local pluralistic food governance structures (Haysom, 2015). This trend has accelerated over the past five years, with new actors supporting cities in their efforts to engage the urban food system and generate positive urban food system outcomes.

The Food and Agricultural Organisation's (FAO) Food for Cities initiative[3] and Framework for the Urban Food Agenda,[4] the Milan Urban Food Policy Pact (MUFPP)[5] and its aligned processes, ICLEI – Local Governments for Sustainability,[6] and C40 and its support for urban resilience[7] have all been active in this transition. (See Chapter 26 by Forster et al. in this volume for a discussion of the interaction of the global agenda and local practice.) The UN-Habitat New Urban Agenda (NUA) actively sought to insert food into urban governance processes (UN-Habitat, 2020). Each of the aforementioned initiatives carries a specific operational and philosophical view of where the food system challenges lie, the urban governance approaches needed, and where best to tackle these specific issues. The activities of these interventions have raised the profile of urban food policies and practices and resulted in cities adopting food policy actions.

The African urban transition demonstrates three governance-related challenges that have implications for how food policy is enacted and governed. First, cities are often seen as the strongholds of opposition parties, overly powerful or independent in trade and related processes, and as a result are often viewed with scepticism by African leaders (Pieterse & Parnell, 2014). Second, African cities face multiple infrastructural, economic, ecological, and social challenges. Finally, African cities are diverse and at different stages of urbanisation, meaning that contextually informed policies and food governance actions are paramount.

The implication of these trends is that it is unlikely that national governments will embrace city-scale governance of the food system, instead delegating power to urban managers. Also, given the multiple day-to-date challenges faced by urban managers, coupled with resourcing challenges as a result of a very thin tax base (Cirolia, 2020), urban managers and governance actors are reluctant to take on more responsibilities, despite evidence of a need. These first two points are in direct counterpoint to evidence that suggests that urban managers and urban actors are often the best placed to take action and effectively influence urban food systems. Thus, a single urban food policy or governance approach is unlikely to be applicable across the diversity of African cities.

As a result, city-scale urban food system governance actions in African cities are limited. The emergent nature of this work is most evident in the 2019 Niamey declaration, emerging under the auspices of the Milan Urban Food Policy Pact but only having 20 cities as signatories, where the preamble states that:

> Delegates recognize that, in order to adopt policies to ensure access to safe and quality food while reducing climate change's risks, there is an urgent need to strengthen local governance of food systems, in particular to facilitate collaboration between different municipal departments and agencies; to increase stakeholders' participation; to develop a disaster risk reduction strategy…
>
> *MUFPP & MUFPP Afrique, 2019, p. 1*

This chapter continues with a brief reflection on emerging urban food governance innovations, many of which are addressed in far greater detail elsewhere in this book (see, for instance, Chapter 13 by Bassarab et al. in this volume on North American FPCs). To emphasise the urgency in proactive responses to the urban food crises, the chapter then provides an overview of the state of urban food security in sub-Saharan Africa. This lays the foundation for a reflection on emerging governance interventions evident in four cities across the continent. A key trend that this chapter seeks to highlight is that there are very few African cities engaging in urban food policy or governance activities. The four cities reviewed as cases have been selected because they offer two insights: the nascent nature of these interventions and where they are housed in urban government structures. While this approach to urban food governance might align with processes in certain European countries, our review of the work of FPCs and other city-scale governance approaches outside of Africa indicates a greater trend towards pluralistic approaches, with multiple actors active in city-scale food governance. We conclude by calling for greater systematic integration of food-related governance into urban governance.

Place-based Food Governance Innovations

Emerging as part of local food movements, place-specific food governance initiatives have gained increased attention since the initiatives of the early 1980s. An FPC formed in Knoxville, Tennessee in 1982 is credited as the first FPC (Harper et al., 2009). MacRae and Donahue's (2013, p. 16) account of the increase in initiatives in Canada showed a clear escalation, from the formation of the Toronto Food Policy Council in 1990 to over 55 such councils by 2012. Innovations are not confined to North America alone, with structures also emerging across Europe (Moragues-Faus & Morgan, 2015; Sonnino, 2017) and Latin America (Dubbeling et al., 2017; Rocha & Lessa, 2009).

In certain areas, cities play a greater role in urban food system transformations, directing alternative governance approaches (see Hatfield, 2012; Rocha & Lessa, 2009). Most of the alternative urban food governance literature aligns along specific conceptual and operational lines. While fully appreciating the warning issued by Born and Purcell against the "local trap" (2006), many approaches adopt a distinctly local register. This local focus is not wrong, but it focuses on key issues experienced in a specific context.

Enacting food governance relies on a process of problem identification through discussion, debate, and the emergence of a form of agency, where those dissatisfied with food system functions, outcomes, and performance are able to debate both the problems and the pathways to agreed resolution. At times these deliberations take place within or with the support of government-aligned governance actors, but other times they are separate. Processes emerge out of deliberative spaces, and the final, agreed upon governance structure emerges from often contested but ultimately collaborative processes in which voice and agency are evident. Participation in these processes is generally voluntary, and when structures are formalised and mandated, participation by government staff is low, relying on engaged citizenry with time to participate in such structures.

It is here that this chapter seeks to reflect on the state of the food system in African cities. Understanding the nature and food system outcomes in African cities is important, as it provides the context for the remainder of the discussion on urban food governance in African cities.

The Southern Urban Food Crisis

> With few exceptions, food insecurity in the Global South has been sidelined in urban research and policy-making over the last decade.
>
> *Crush, 2016, p. 1*

The above quote highlights the challenge in understanding both the state of urban food security and the state of the urban food system in Africa. Projected to have the fastest urban growth rate in the world, Africa's cities will be home to an additional 950 million people by 2050. Much of this growth is taking place in small- and medium-sized towns (OECD/SWAC, 2020, p. 4). The United Nations Department of Economic and Social Affairs (UNDESA) figures provide greater nuance of the current state of urbanisation, demonstrating how it differs across different regions, where two of the most populous regions, Northern Africa and Western Africa, account for over 50 per cent of urban residents in Africa (UNDESA, 2018) (Table 14.1). Equally, this urban growth is taking place in the context of constrained economic growth across all regions in Africa. Urbanisation is resulting in increased informal housing and largely informal economic activities. Both housing and economic activity result in very specific urban food system realities.

National and regional policies and targets remain focused on food production as a means to address food system deficiencies and high levels of food insecurity. Examples include how food security is framed in the South African National Development Plan (NDP, 2012), and subsequent policy positions, focusing primarily on production. Food security is one of four development pillars in the Kenyan development plan (Government of Kenya, 2018).[8] At a continental scale, the Malabo Declaration directed all African government signatories to allocate at least 10 per cent of public expenditure to agriculture (AU, 2014). The dominance of a production-driven and largely availability-oriented perspective on food security presents a significant development challenge (Crush & Frayne, 2014), particularly as it overlooks the manner in which citizens access nutritious food or exercise their own choices and preferences, the nutritional quality of available food, and the wider socio-environmental impacts of processing, moving, distributing, losing, and wasting food. It also presents a significant urban governance challenge because it directs food policy and governance to scales of government beyond the urban. This has two consequences. First, local government actors, and cities more generally, have a limited mandate to engage the wider urban food system. Second, the lack of a policy mandate means that there is no fiscal mandate.

Research conducted in 2008, using USAID's Food and Nutrition Technical Assistance (FANTA) tools[9] in poor neighbourhoods in 11 cities in Southern Africa, found that 76 per cent of the sampled population were food insecure when measured according to the Household Food Security Access Prevalence Scale. When diversity of diets was measured, the mean score was five out of 12 items using the FANTA Household Dietary Diversity Score measure (Frayne et al., 2010). Importantly, a score of six or below is a proxy indicator for undernutrition.

Citywide surveys conducted in the four Southern African cities of Cape Town, Maputo, Nairobi, and Windhoek, using the same FANTA tools, found similar levels of food insecurity

Table 14.1 Percentage of urban populations across African regions

Region	*2018 Per cent urban per region*	*Net urban population*	*Per cent of urban Africa*
Africa	42.5	547,602,000	42.5
Eastern Africa	28.0	121,316,000	22.2
Middle Africa	49.5	83,484,000	15.2
Northern Africa	52.0	123,644,000	22.6
Southern Africa	63.6	41,970,000	7.7
Western Africa	46.4	177,189,000	32.4

Source: United Nations (2018) World Urbanization Prospects. The 2018 Revision. (Authors' own representation, drawn from UN, 2018 at https://population.un.org/wup/Download/.)

(Crush et al., 2018; Nickanor et al., 2018; Owuor, 2018; Raimundo et al., 2018). A multidimensional poverty index measure, the Lived Poverty Index (Mattes, 2008), was used in these same cities, where constraints in access to energy for cooking, electricity, and water were also reported (Haysom and Fuseini, 2019), demonstrating a wider systemic challenge where the nature of food access, food utilisation, and the stability of the food supply were all directly linked to the quality, nature, and reliability of infrastructure.

In Africa, given historical food supply challenges, food-related problems have been largely discussed in terms of famine or hunger (see Devereux, 2009). Recently, new challenges have emerged. The trend in South Africa of undernourished children but overweight adults, often in the same household (Shisana et al., 2013), is increasingly evident across the continent (Micha et al., 2020). The rapid rise in food-related noncommunicable diseases (e.g., diabetes) is increasingly seen as an emerging development challenge.

The rapid growth in Africa's urban areas and high levels of poverty and informality – in terms of housing types, economic activity, and food vending (Pieterse & Parnell, 2014) – coupled with infrastructure deficits, demand an integrated urban food governance approach. Some cities are beginning to engage in what may be referred to broadly as "the urban food question." All of the cities' engagements, as explored in the cases below, offer insights into the emerging practice of urban food governance in some African cities.

Case Studies

Four case studies are considered in this section. They do not reflect an exhaustive list of food governance actions, but they do offer insights into the shifts taking place. These cases were purposely selected, given the limited number of cities engaging in some form of systemic food governance, and because their plans or approaches were either publicly accessible or known to the authors. Case studies from two large and two smaller African cities are used.

Cape Town

African Food Security Urban Network research found high levels of urban food insecurity in Cape Town in 2007 (Battersby, 2011; Frayne et al., 2010). Recent surveys have found similar levels of food insecurity within poorer communities in Cape Town (Crush et al., 2018). The governance of food in Cape Town has either been assumed to be the mandate of national and provincial government spheres or, indirectly, delegated to the private sector (see Peyton et al., 2015 for a demonstration of the expansion of supermarkets across the city as one example). However, different processes have developed. In the early 2000s, city officials, after engagements with the Toronto Food Policy Council staff, and on realising a local need, began internal city-level development of an Urban Agriculture Policy, adopted in 2007 (CoCT, 2007). The impetus for the development of this strategy was threefold. The first reason was to provide a legislative framework in which various grower groups could gain a measure of policy protection. Second, the policy formed part of an economic development strategy aimed at increasing the capacity of small-scale producers. Third, it channelled social and agricultural development services through a mandated city department. This formed the foundation of a collection of processes, led by the Urban Agriculture Unit, through engagement with some growing groups and urban food system researchers, that precipitated an important change in food system engagement at the urban scale. Processes evolved, albeit slowly, and despite, at times openly hostile, views of urban food governance held by certain politicians (see Olver, 2019).

The City of Cape Town is a member of a number of international networks, including ICLEI Africa, the MUFPP, 100 Resilient Cities,[10] and the C40 network. Becoming a signatory to these processes was led by the city mayor at the time.

Over the period 2016–2019, Cape Town experienced a severe drought. In 2017, rainfall records were the lowest ever recorded since the first written records in the 1880s (Wolski, 2018). This prompted a proactive response across a number of sectors, led specifically by the city's resilience department, in alignment with the development of a Resilience Strategy, supported by the 100 Resilient Cities programme. The approaches adopted drew on research into the Cape Town food system. Combined, these culminated in a wide-reaching and novel City of Cape Town Resilience Strategy (CoCT, 2019). Food, nutrition, and the food system were prominent in this document, with improving food systems noted as a flagship action as part of Health and Wellbeing.

At the same time, the Western Cape Provincial Government[11] was developing a food and nutrition strategy. Like the Resilience Strategy, this emerging work drew on researchers across the city for input, culminating in a draft of the Household Food and Nutrition Security Strategic Framework (HF&NSSF) in 2016 (PGWC, 2016).

Through their consultative processes and content, both the City Resilience Strategy and the Provincial HF&NSSF re-energised food system actions across the city. Several working groups emerged from these processes, including a City of Cape Town-led, city-scale Food Working Group with diverse participants who were invited to participate and a Provincial Working Group comprising senior budget holders in diverse provincial government departments. Both structures focused on their specific scalar mandates. Additionally, structures such as the Western Cape Food Systems Community of Practice (CoP), convened by the Centre of Excellence in Food Security at the University of the Western Cape, was established. As the name denotes, the CoP is structured as an open space where multiple perspectives and viewpoints about the food system, often contested and passionately defended, can be shared in a neutral space. In response to the COVID-19 pandemic and associated government lockdowns, which demonstrated more clearly to many stakeholders the depth of the systemic challenges facing Cape Town's food system, a Western Cape Food Forum, mainly made up of civil society organisations, was convened by the Western Cape Economic Development Partnership.

These different processes do not yet reflect any direct form of food systems governance, despite suggestions within the CoP for some form of pluralistic governance structure, which were rejected. The reason for this was a principled one. The primary challenge that the CoP and the government-led working groups were attempting to address was high levels of food and nutrition insecurity faced by the poor. Despite efforts, the CoP has not been able to attract representatives for poor communities in the city. Planning food system change without adequate representation from these groups was deemed patronising and elitist. A second reason was that the South African government has an obligation to ensure the realisation of the right to food. Members of the CoP agreed that before setting up alternative pluralistic governance structures, greater effort was needed to hold the state accountable for ensuring the right to food and nutrition.

These food governance structures reflect an emergent process, in which urban food is being placed on the agenda and different food system actors are finding a voice. While the direct naming of food systems actions in the Resilience Strategy represents a strong political foundation for continued work on food systems, the work remains nascent, linked to and driven by passionate and dedicated public officials. It is yet to be formally adopted as a specific urban governance issue, and thus it remains vulnerable to changing political priorities and perceived needs.

Antananarivo

Madagascar is acutely affected by stunting and undernutrition. Levels of hunger are classed as "alarming," and its capital city, Antananarivo, is experiencing a progressive increase in chronic malnutrition, largely attributed to conditions of extreme poverty (Action Against Hunger, 2019).

The Antananarivo Food Policy Council evolved out of a multi-stakeholder platform originally established to enable the scaling up of the city's urban agriculture programme. The transition from an urban agriculture programme to a city-led food policy council occurred as the city drew together initiatives and actors that were working to improve food system outcomes, resulting in a widening of the platform's focus, from production to the whole food system.

The Commune Urbaine d'Antananarivo (CUA) set up the Urban Agriculture in Antananarivo programme in 2011. With the support of the French Cooperation (Ile-de-France), the CUA sought to achieve two main objectives: (i) the promotion and installation of micro-vegetable gardens in vulnerable districts of the city to improve the food and nutritional security of these communities, and (ii) the creation of income-generating activities in the form of fresh vegetable production (Andrianarisoa et al., 2019). The CUA worked to upscale the initiative by setting up a platform of actors engaged in capacity building and diffusion of urban agriculture know-how. However, the CUA did not have the requisite human or economic resources to do this, so involving external stakeholders was crucial. This promoted the establishment of a city-led platform to facilitate the expansion of urban food system plans in 2014.

In 2016, the CUA signed the MUFPP. After signing it, the CUA team started to define a strategic vision, initially identifying priorities and contributing to defining a food policy action plan for Antananarivo. To do this, a Food Policy Office (FPO) was created within the 1st Deputy Mayor's office. The food system processes evolved, resulting in the formation of the Antananarivo Food Policy Council (AFPC), driven largely by the Deputy Mayor but drawing on over 20 stakeholders involved in urban agriculture within the CUA boundaries (institutional actors, international organisations, civil society organisations, and the private sector) (Andrianarisoa et al., 2019). The Deputy Mayor articulated their food policy approach as one of policy as practice, in which relationships, rather than a core document, were the driving force of food systems action.

Until then, the focus had been on urban agriculture, but the AFPC sought to expand the work towards a systemic approach to the food chain. The AFPC action plan would include: (i) creation of an inventory of the current territorial food system using city region boundaries; (ii) construction of an open database to track the MUFPP's six working areas; (iii) the preparation of a workshop with key food system stakeholders to identify priorities; and (iv) the drafting of a working food policy guideline document to present to potential partners (Andrianarisoa et al., 2019). Governance considerations have evolved, and despite the CUA playing the lead convening role, a hybrid form of governance is emerging.

Stellenbosch

The winelands town of Stellenbosch, in the Western Cape of South Africa, represents an example of some of the potential governance pitfalls that emerging local governance bodies may encounter.

In 2010, a collection of researchers and food system activists developed a local food system strategy for the town of Stellenbosch. The funding that drove this work included a distinct local, green, sustainable, and food security-focused orientation. At face value, these are all viable and laudable aspirations, contained in many similar North American and some European city-level food strategies. After a period of research, consultation, and network development, the Stellenbosch Sustainable Food System Strategy (SSFSS) was formally adopted and received official endorsement by the town's mayoral committee, the highest decision-making body in the town, in 2011. However, as of 2020, the plan is yet to be implemented.

The Stellenbosch case demonstrates that government approval of a strategy does not equate to implementation. Given that the town had no formal food policy mandate and, as a result, no budget, Stellenbosch officials had assumed that the strategy would be implemented by civil society actors, enabled through their endorsement. On formal approval of the plan, the civil society cluster, one that had been enthusiastic about the plan, withdrew its support. This was a strategic response to a wider political skirmish taking place at the time. There was concern that the SSFSS would be used to dictate how food relief and the local social protection and feeding scheme landscape would be governed. The civic groups' withdrawal meant that claims of representation in the plan were lost. This bold response demonstrated just how political food governance processes can be. At the same time, it showed nuanced political and strategic understanding by the civic bodies.

Two factors require further consideration. First, the "local is best" vision of the SSFSS imagined the conversion of many of the vineyards to more food-type produce, often demanding higher water use, even if farmed in a sustainable manner. While laudable, and while the sustainability considerations could have mitigated some issues, this would have exposed the town to a number of stressors, undermining resilience. This became abundantly clear during the Western Cape drought, which began in earnest in 2017 and lasted until 2019. Second, while the civic groups withdrew their support, they did not reject the plan itself. Recently, due to increased food insecurity caused by COVID-19, the civic groups have again convened around the plan, adopting a more cautious approach and using the plan as a guide to convene a wider grouping of food system actors, with the ultimate goal of developing a new plan but avoiding the pitfalls of the SSFSS.

Arusha

Arusha in Tanzania is primarily dependent on food that is produced outside its administrative borders. The quality of road infrastructure, markets, transportation, and other supply chain systems present major challenges to the city's food security, especially for ensuring the safety and nutritional quality of food that is brought into the city. Agriculture and tourism are the main drivers of the regional economy (Fisher et al., 2019).

To demonstrate political commitment to improved food security for Arusha, the city signed the MUFPP in 2014. Activities to support wider urban food system outcomes were, and remain, high on the list of priorities, though implementation is slow due to high capital costs and planning processes. Nevertheless, the Arusha City Council (ACC) has focused on social interventions, improving revenue collection to support market function, and supporting the participation of vulnerable groups in food system activities. The council has built strong relationships with multiple actors that are working towards shaping a sustainable food system and has requested support in developing an urban food policy.

In framing a policy process with Arusha, facilitated through the ICLEI Africa, the concept of a food policy council remains central. In discussion about how to draw food system actors together for a shared purpose, a set of values for the Arusha food system was conceptualised. Key values propose a food system for Arusha that is:

- Safe – citizens should be confident that they are receiving food that is safe from pesticide and chemical contamination.

- Nourishing – no citizen should experience malnutrition in any form and all children should receive appropriate first 1000-day nutrition and quality food thereafter.
- Economic – food production and processing opportunities should offer improved employment, particularly for youth.
- Inclusive – the food system should ensure that all vulnerable populations, including the elderly, youth, sick, differently abled, or unemployed, are supported so that they have access to good quality food.
- Improved food system outcomes through partnering – given the nature of our food system, which crosses multiple functional and political boundaries, partnering with multiple actors across boundaries through a shared vision is essential.

With lessons from engagements with Antananarivo, which centred a policy-as-practice approach, these values were used as the basis for developing a set of policy pathways into a loose set of roadmaps that Arusha City Council, as well as private sector and civil society groups, could use to develop a food council, improve food safety and nutrition, broaden cultural and food-tourism linkages in the city, address infrastructure gaps, and begin development of a food policy. The ideas articulated in these policy pathways have not yet been broadly taken up, as the process did not result in clear articulation of responsibilities. However, an organisation that co-developed these pathways has championed the growth of a Food Safety Council, with which the ACC is a partner. This council is made up of active food-related organisations in the city and has begun to broaden its focus to the wider food system.

The four cities reviewed here demonstrate emerging engagements, with some forms of localised city-scale and city-led food governance. However, the processes discussed remain formative and are largely led by city actors. Bottom up, civic, or citizen-led actions responding to food system failures, while evident, are not driving urban-scale food system governance change. Citizen groups remain focused on issues or sectors in structures such as informal vendor networks or networks of urban growers. Such groups do not speak for wider food system actions and do not have the political support of wider city-scale food system actors. The actions of the four cities started from what could be deemed simplistic, and nonstrategic, entry points. Cape Town and Antananarivo sought initial policy and implementation processes around urban agriculture policies. Stellenbosch and Arusha, although entering the process differently, both sought to achieve more sustainable food systems. While it could be assumed that these entry points addressed food insecurity as a target, no city actively, directly sought to engage and address food system failures in a strategic manner.

Discussion and Conclusion

Given the increasingly high levels of urban food insecurity, the rise in diet-related noncommunicable diseases, and urban food system changes, there is an urgent need for African cities to adopt a proactive approach to urban food policies and urban food governance. The urgency is compounded by deeper structural issues encountered at the urban scale, specifically when food challenges intersect with other urban challenges, such as infrastructure provision.

Urban spaces in Africa remain disputed spaces, spaces where politics, histories, and the contestation over scarce resources often silence voice and agency. It is within this often volatile and contested domain that the governance question of "who wakes up and worries about urban food system outcomes?" needs to find traction. The answer is unclear, but given the diversity of urban typologies across Africa, diverse and context-appropriate urban food governance approaches are required.

In each case study, governments have either led or actively supported food policy engagement and processes, often without the clarity of a mandate. Their role in clarifying food system actions beyond a specific issue is notable. A scan of the literature indicates that there is limited civic activity aimed at challenging current urban food system actions, and where it exists, it may not be effectively connected to other stakeholder groups, with initiatives undertaken in isolation. This represents a different trend to that seen in the urban food governance approaches emerging in certain regions of the Global North, and specifically the emergence of pluralistic food policy councils.

A further trend observed in the case studies was the central role that networks or external actors, often in supporting roles, played in this process. Organisations, such as the Milan Urban Food Policy Pact, the C40 Cities Climate Leadership Group, the RUAF Global Partnership on Sustainable Urban Agriculture and Food Systems, and the ICLEI network, all played a role in either convening or supporting existing processes. Further review and critical reflection on the power of these external actors to drive on-the-ground action, beyond consultation, in the context of scarce local resources is needed.

In some European countries, city governments are playing a greater role in urban food governance, like the processes described here. This offers an interesting challenge. Given the predominance of Anglophone histories, many alliances and partnerships with the Global North are driven by language and colonial history. The role played by the MUFPP is an example of how different approaches to urban food governance can facilitate change. The MUFPP has also been influential in countries like Spain, where it has supported local food movements rather than city governments. Given the absence of local food movements in Africa, perhaps the city-led approach is the most appropriate route at this time?

All four urban food processes reviewed started from what could be deemed nonstrategic entry points, after which each city would go through a learning journey that would slowly reveal the wider interlinkages within and between food system elements. These small beginnings were essential in laying foundations for more engaged and strategically innovative food work later. Urban agriculture projects or responses to single crises can lead to far more integrated systemic processes, and any starting point is potentially productive. How these are scaled up remains a question, but external actors have played productive and generative roles in these case studies.

It is unlikely that city governments will be working in more pluralistic governance processes, similar to the FPCs of the Global North, given the levels of inequality, absence of voice, and the everyday challenges faced by most urban residents. In fact, we would go as far as calling for real caution when claims are made of inclusive, joined-up, collaborative, pluralistic urban food governance, as the likelihood that these processes are dominated by the middle and political classes is a real concern.

The cases demonstrated a sensitivity to local politics and the need for diversity and nuance in how food governance processes are managed and built out. While this may seem obvious, it does require time, network building, and reflexivity. How these emergent governance processes engage across scales and support wider food system needs will be a critical factor in their sustainability. Pluralistic structures may come with time, but a focused descaling and urbanising of food governance by the state is a critical element of Africa's urban transition.

Far more work, support, and reflection are required in the area of urban food governance in Africa. Urban food offers a lens to enliven new developmental and governance opportunities, specifically in the fields of planning, infrastructure, health, and inclusive growth, and these links are becoming more apparent to city officials. It is promising that many regional and global initiatives are creating the space for, and demonstrating the political value of, urban food system dialogue and discourse. The translation of political and theoretical interest into actions that benefit the majority of residents in these cities will require large investments and mobilisations of resources. As a first step, African cities need to embrace urban food governance. As Kami Pothukuchi (2000), speaking specifically to planning governance, noted in the early 2000s, absence is not benign, often manifesting in negative outcomes. Mitigating against negative urban food system outcomes is essential.

Notes

1 See www.rockefellerfoundation.org/initiative/alliance-for-a-green-revolution-in-africa/ and https://agra.org.
2 The term "authorising environments" is expressly used because it refers to how state and non-state structures are used or enabled to authorise a specific activity. As an example, a taxi association may or may not allow a food vendor to sell food at a taxi rank, despite the vendor holding a state-derived permit to do so. Self-authorisation may also occur in the context of government absence, in which, for example, a food vendor identifies a new niche for vending and brings nutritious food into a community through their own networks, filling a need.
3 See www.fao.org/in-action/food-for-cities-programme/en/.
4 See www.fao.org/urban-food-agenda/en/.
5 See www.milanurbanfoodpolicypact.org.
6 See https://iclei.org/en/CITYFOOD_Network.html.
7 See www.c40.org/networks/food_systems.
8 See https://big4.delivery.go.ke.
9 See Coates et al., 2007.
10 See https://www.rockefellerfoundation.org/100-resilient-cities/.
11 The City of Cape Town is a municipality in the Western Cape Province of South Africa.

References

Action Against Hunger. (2019). *Action Against Hunger Country Profiles, Madagascar*. Online. https://www.actionagainsthunger.org/countries/africa/madagascar [Accessed 8 November 2021]

African Union (AU). (2014). *Assembly of the Union Twenty-Third Ordinary Session 26–27 June 2014, Malabo Declaration on Accelerated Agricultural Growth and Transformation for Shared Prosperity and Improved Livelihoods*. Assembly/AU/2(XXIII) Malabo, Equatorial Guinea. African Union, Addis Ababa.

Andrianarisoa, O., Ferrari, C. Z., Currie, P., & Coetzee, I. (2019). Antananarivo Food Policy Council: Policy as practice *Urban Agriculture Magazine, 36*(October), 29–30. (Netherlands: RUAF).

Battersby, J. (2011). Urban food insecurity in Cape Town, South Africa: An alternative approach to food access. *Development Southern Africa, 28*(4), 545–561.

Battersby, J., & Muwowo, F. (2018). Planning and governance of food systems in Kitwe, Zambia: A case study of food retail space. In J. Battersby & V. Watson (Eds.), *Urban Food Systems Governance and Poverty in African Cities (Open Access)*. Abingdon, Oxon: Routledge, pp. 128–140.

Battersby, J., & Watson, V. (Eds.). (2018). *Urban Food Systems Governance and Poverty in African Cities*. Abingdon, Oxon: Routledge, p. 290.

Born, B., & Purcell, M. (2006). Avoiding the local trap: Scale and food systems in planning research. *Journal of Planning Education and Research, 26*(2), 195–207.

Cirolia, L. (2020). Fractured fiscal authority and fragmented infrastructures: Financing sustainable urban development in Sub-Saharan Africa. *Habitat International, 104*, 102233.

Coates, J., Swindale, A., & Bilinsky, P. (2007). Household Food Insecurity Scale (HFIAS) for measurement of food access: Indicator guide. *Food and Nutrition Technical Assistance (FANTA). Version, 3*.

CoCT (City of Cape Town). (2007). *Urban Agriculture Policy for the City of Cape Town*. City of Cape Town.

CoCT. (2019). *Cape Town Resilience Strategy*. Online: https://resource.capetown.gov.za/documentcentre/Documents/City%20strategies%2C%20plans%20and%20frameworks/Resilience_Strategy.pdf [Accessed 15 December 2020]

Crush, J. (2016). *Hungry Cities of the Global South*. Discussion Paper No. 1, Hungry Cities Partnership, Balsillie School of International Affairs, Waterloo, Canada.

Crush, J., & Frayne, B. (2014). Feeding African cities: The growing challenge of urban food insecurity. In S. Parnell & E. Pieterse (Eds.), *Africa's Urban Revolution*. London: Bloomsbury Academic, pp. 110–132.
Crush, J., Caesar, M., & Haysom, G. (2018). *The State of Household Food Security in Cape Town, South Africa (No. 12). Hungry Cities Report*. Cape Town: African Centre for Cities and Balsillie School of International Affairs.
Devereux, S. (2009). Why does famine persist in Africa? *Food Security, 1*(1), 25.
Dubbeling, M., Santini, G., Renting, H., Taguchi, M., Lançon, L., Zuluaga, J., … & Andino, V. (2017). Assessing and planning sustainable city region food systems: Insights from two Latin American cities. *Sustainability, 9*(8), 1455.
Duminy, J. (2018). Ecologizing regions; securing food: Governing scarcity, population and territory in British East and Southern Africa. *Territory, Politics, Governance, 6*(4), 429–446.
Fisher, R., Currie, P., & Mongi, R. (2019). Towards a safe, nourishing, economic and inclusive food system for Arusha, based on partnering. *Urban Agriculture Magazine, 36*, October, RUAF, Netherlands, pp. 31–32.
Forster, T., & Escudero, A. G. (2014). *City Regions as Landscapes for People Food and Nature*. Washington, DC: EcoAgriculture Partners, p. 62.
Frayne, B., Pendleton, W., Crush, J., Acquah, B., Battersby-Lennard, J., Bras, E., … & Zanamwe, L. (2010). *The State of Urban Food Insecurity in Southern Africa. Urban Food Security Series, 2*. Kingston, Canada: Queens University.
Government of Kenya. (2018). *Third Medium Term Plan 2018–2022. Transforming Lives: Advancing Socio-economic Development through the "Big Four"*. Nairobi, Kenya: The National Treasury and Planning.
Harper, A., Shattuck, A., Holt-Giménez, E., Alkon, A., & Lambrick, F. (2009). *Food Policy Councils: Lessons Learned*. Oakland, CA: Food First/Institute for Food and Development Policy.
Harvey, D. (1989). From managerialism to entrepreneurialism: The transformation in urban governance in late capitalism. *Geografiska Annaler: Series B, Human Geography, 71*(1), 3–17.
Hatfield, M. (2012). *City Policy and Programs: Lessons Harvested from an Emerging Field*. City of Portland, OR: Bureau of Planning and Sustainability.
Haysom, G. (2015). Food and the city: Urban scale food system governance. *Urban Forum, 26*(3), 263–281.
Haysom, G., & Fuseini, I. (2019). *Governing Food Systems in Secondary Cities in Africa. Consuming Urban Poverty*. Cape Town: African Centre for Cities.
Haysom, G., Battersby, J., & Park-Ross, R. (2020). *Food Sensitive Planning and Urban Design: A Blueprint for a Future South African City*. Working Paper Series, No. 7, Centre of Excellence in Food Security, University of the Western Cape, 1–101.
Ilieva, R. T. (2017). Urban food systems strategies: A promising tool for implementing the SDGs in practice. *Sustainability, 9*(10), 1707.
Kameshwari, P., & Kaufman, J. L. (1999). Placing the food system on the urban agenda: The role of municipal institutions in food systems planning. *Agriculture and Human Values, 16*(2), 213–224. https://doi.org/10.1023/A:1007558805953.
Katsaura, O. (2012). Community governance in urban South Africa: Spaces of political contestation and coalition. *Urban Forum, 23*(3), 319–342.
Kearns, A., & Paddison, R. (2000). New challenges for urban governance. *Urban Studies, 37*(5–6), 845–850.
MacRae R., & Donahue K. (2013). Municipal food policy entrepreneurs: A preliminary analysis of how Canadian cities and regional districts are involved in food system change. Online. https://foodsecurecanada.org/sites/foodsecurecanada.org/files/municipalfoodpolicyreport_may13_0.pdf [Accessed 10 December 2020]
Mattes, R. (2008). *The Material and Political Basis of Lived Poverty in Africa: Insights from the Afrobarometer*. Working Paper No. 98, IDASA, Cape Town.
Micha, R., Mannar, V., Afshin, A., Allemandi, L., Baker, P., Battersby, J., … & Dolan, C. (2020). *2020 Global Nutrition Report: Action on Equity to End Malnutrition*. Geneva: World Health Organization.
Moragues-Faus, A., & Morgan, K. (2015). Reframing the foodscape: The emergent world of urban food policy. *Environment and Planning A: Economy and Space, 47*(7), 1558–1573.
MUFPP & MUFPP Afrique. (2019). *Niamey Declaration, Third Forum of Milan Pact Cities in Africa, Niamey, Niger, 11–13 June 2019*. Online: https://www.milanurbanfoodpolicypact.org/wp-content/uploads/2020/12/Niamey-Declaration-MUFPP-_-ENG.pdf [Accessed 02 March, 2021]
NDP (National Development Plan). (2012). *National Development Plan: Vision for 2030, Our Future – Make it Work*. Pretoria, South Africa: National Planning Commission.

Nickanor, N., Kazembe, L., Crush, J., & Wagner, J. (2018). *The Urban Food System of Windhoek, Namibia.* (No. 8). Hungry Cities Report. Cape Town: African Centre for Cities and Balsillie School of International Affairs.

OECD/SWAC. (2020). *Africa's Urbanisation Dynamics 2020: Africapolis, Mapping a New Urban Geography.* Paris: West African Studies, OECD Publishing.

Olver, C. (2019). *A House Divided: The Feud that Took Cape Town to the Brink.* Cape Town: Jonathan Ball Publishers.

Owuor, S. (2018). *The State of Household Food Security in Nairobi, Kenya (No. 11). Hungry Cities Report.* Cape Town: African Centre for Cities and Balsillie School of International Affairs.

Peyton, S., Moseley, W., & Battersby, J. (2015). Implications of supermarket expansion on urban food security in Cape Town, South Africa. *African Geographical Review, 34*(1), 36–54.

PGWC (Provincial Government of the Western Cape). (2016). *Western Cape Government Household Food and Nutrition Security Strategic Framework. Draft approved by Cabinet for public comment, September 2016.* Online: https://www.westerncape.gov.za/sites/www.westerncape.gov.za/files/assets/140916_wcg_household_food_and_nutrition_security_strategic_framework.pdf [Accessed 13 February 2021]

Pieterse, E., & Parnell, S. (2014). *Africa's Urban Revolution.* London: Zed Books Ltd.

Pieterse, E., Parnell, S., & Haysom, G. (2018). African dreams: Locating urban infrastructure in the 2030 sustainable developmental agenda. *Area Development and Policy, 3*(2), 149–169.

Pothukuchi, K. (2000). *Community Food Mapping.* Address to Ontario Public Health Association workshop on community food mapping, Toronto, 11 September, 2000.

Raimundo, I., McCordic, C., & Chikanda, A. (2018). *The State of Household Food Security in Maputo, Mozambique (No. 10). HCP Report.* Cape Town: African Centre for Cities and Balsillie School of International Affairs.

Raja, S., Morgan, K., & Hall, E. (2017). Planning for equitable urban and regional food systems. *Built Environment, 43*(3), 309–314.

Rocha, C., & Lessa, I. (2009). Urban governance for food security: The alternative food system in Belo Horizonte, Brazil. *International Planning Studies, 14*(4), 389–400.

Schiff, R. (2008). The role of food policy councils in developing sustainable food systems. *Journal of Hunger & Environmental Nutrition, 3*(2–3), 206–228.

Shisana, O., Labadarios, D., Rehle, T., Simbayi, L., Zuma, K., Dhansay, A., ... & Hongoro, C. (2013). Sanhanes-1 Team. *South African National Health and Nutrition Examination Survey (SANHANES-1).* Cape Town: HSRC Press.

Sibanda, L., & von Blottnitz, H. (2018). 12 food value chains in Kisumu, Kitwe, and Epworth. In J. Battersby & V. Watson (Eds.), *Urban Food Systems Governance and Poverty in African Cities.* Abingdon, Oxon: Routledge, p. 169.

Simon, D., McGregor, D., & Nsiah-Gyabaah, K. (2004). The changing urban–rural interface of African cities: Definitional issues and an application to Kumasi, Ghana. *Environment and Urbanization, 16*(2), 235–248.

Smit, W. (2016). Urban governance and urban food systems in Africa: Examining the linkages. *Cities, 58*, 80–86.

Sonnino, R. (2017). Urban food geographies in the global North. Bollettino Della Società Geografica Italiana. *Roma, 13*(10), 39–46.

Sonnino, R. (2019). The cultural dynamics of urban food governance. *City, Culture and Society, 16*, 12–17.

UNDESA (United Nations, Department of Economic and Social Affairs), Population Division. (2018). *World Urbanization Prospects: The 2018 Revision.* Online Edition. https://population.un.org/wup/Download/ [Accessed 10 December 2010].

UNDESA, Population Division. (2019). *World Urbanization Prospects: The 2018 Revision* (ST/ESA/SER.A/420). New York: United Nations.

UN-Habitat (United Nations Human Settlements Programme). (2002). *The Global Campaign on Urban Governance, Concept Paper* (2nd Ed.). Nairobi, Kenya: The Global Campaign on Urban Governance Campaign Secretariat.

UN-Habitat. (2020). *New Urban Agenda.* UN-Habitat. Retrieved from https://unhabitat.org/the-new-urban-agenda-illustrated

Wolski, P. (2018). What Cape Town learned from its drought. *Bulletin of the Atomic Scientists*, 16 April. https://thebulletin.org/2018/04/whatcape-town-learned-from-its-drought/

15

CONCEPTUALIZING AND EXPLORING U.S. URBAN FOOD POLICY

Jill K. Clark and Aiden Irish

Introduction

In response to myriad social, environmental, and economic challenges, cities have begun exerting agency on food-related issues, becoming burgeoning laboratories of innovative "alternatives" to conventional food supply chains and addressing issues of local concern and fostering greater civic engagement and food democracy (Hamilton, 2002; Hassanein, 2003; Moragues-Faus & Morgan, 2015). Public policy tools are the language that cities are using to develop and promote these new food approaches. The mere existence of this *Handbook* is evidence of the growing importance of urban food policy.

The purpose of this chapter is to define food policy broadly and explore its application in U.S. cities. We start by taking a step back, placing food policy in the broader context of public policy. After that, we briefly outline the history of food policy and its transformation from an agricultural trade-focused national issue to its current phase of urban innovation. After this, we bring the broader policy literature and food policy literature together to propose and apply a food policy "universe" framework. This framework conceptualizes the range of potential food policies, urban or otherwise, along three dimensions that describe (a) the type of policy tool, (b) where in the food supply chain the policy intervenes, and (c) the primary goal of intervention. This universe of food policies helps us better understand which urban food policies have been applied in the U.S. Finally, we reflect on current practice and identify limitations and opportunities for growth in U.S. urban food policy.

What Is Policy?

The first step in understanding "food policy" is clarifying what is meant by policy and public policy generally. In its modern connotation, "policy" is closely tied to Enlightenment ideas of rational problem-solving, implying an understood problem and a solution (Parsons, 1995). Within the public sector (i.e., "public policy"), the most inclusive definition is "whatever governments choose to do or not to do" about a given issue (Dye, 1987, p. 1).

Other definitions offer more specificity by identifying key characteristics. For instance, Anderson (1994) defines policy as a "purposive course of action or inaction undertaken by an

DOI: 10.4324/9781003055907-18

actor or set of actors in dealing with a problem or matter of concern" (p. 5). This definition more clearly outlines a definitive set of traits: that public policy is purposeful and goal-oriented, that it is a demand-oriented response to an issue, and that it is either a positive action or an explicit inaction. For policy that is public (i.e., applied to society at large), Anderson outlines that the purposive course of action is specifically taken or not taken by a public authority (e.g., a public sector agency).

This definition highlights the use of the word "policy" to describe a decision and an objective. However, in addition to describing a decision about what to do, the word "policy" is also used to describe a policy "tool" or "instrument" that can be used to bring about the desired ends (Schneider & Ingram, 1990). Thus, rather vexingly, "policy" can refer to both the end destination and the means of getting to that destination and there may be a variety of applicable tools for any given objective. This dual use of "policy" as both objective and means reflects a long-standing debate among U.S. policy scholars about the nature and precise meaning of the word "policy" (Smith & Larimer, 2013). Throughout this chapter, we use "policy tool" to refer to this second use of policy as an instrument.

A *public* policy tool refers to an instrument that is implemented and/or backed by the authority of the public sector, as discussed above. However, the latter half of the twentieth century saw a critical shift in the practices of governing toward multi-stakeholder "governance," wherein private actors (either for- or non-profit) have greater involvement in the development and/or implementation of public policy tools (Salamon, 2000). This trend is evident in food systems policy as well (Andrée et al., 2019). In this new era of governance, the role of the public sector is increasingly to "steer" society without resorting to the exercise of authority (Stoker, 1996). For the purposes of this chapter, the most important thing to recognize about this shift toward governance is that, while public policy tools are still employed to accomplish public objectives, they do not necessarily need to be enacted by government alone (Halvey et al., 2020).

In order to better understand available types of policy tools, scholars have offered numerous approaches for assessing and/or categorizing them (Bardach, 1977; Elmore, 1987; Gormley, 1987; Lowi, 1972; McDonnell, 1988; Salamon, 2000). Salamon (2000), for example, suggests (1) assessing tools based on how they are applied (i.e., how effective, efficient, equitable, manageable, and legitimate they are) and (2) categorizing them by their characteristics (i.e., how coercive a tool is, the degree to which it is controlled by government, how easily it can be implemented, and how visible it is). This framework is particularly helpful for comparing different tools.

At their most basic, though, many categorization methods describe the different ways that policy tools structure collective action or influence individual behavior (Salamon, 2000; Schneider & Ingram, 1990, p. 513). One particularly intuitive and useful approach is to view tools as means of influencing the behavior of individuals – the "target population" – in order to achieve a desired public outcome by either promoting a new behavior or discouraging an old one (Schneider & Ingram, 1990). The target population may not yet act in the desired way because people in it (a) think they don't have clear direction or authority to act; (b) may need an incentive or capacity support to act; (c) might not agree with the values implied in either the policy means or the desired outcome; or (d) are uncertain about the nature of the problem and/or what should be done in response to it. To address these barriers, Schneider and Ingram (1990) identify five primary types of policy tools:

(1) **Authority tools** – grant or deny permission and are often accompanied by "motivating devices" that promote or deter the desired action (e.g., regulations or relaxation of regulations).

(2) **Incentive tools** – manipulate the cost–benefit calculus of action through either positive inducement (e.g., tax credits, subsidies, grants, etc.) or negative deterrence (e.g., charges, sanctions, or force).
(3) **Capacity tools** – provide information, training, education, and resources that enable action (e.g., business development support).
(4) **Symbolic tools** – influence an individual's internal, values-based decision-making process by attempting to shape subjective perceptions of an issue or the desired behavior (e.g., propaganda campaigns, such as the promotion of "victory gardens" during WWII).
(5) **Learning tools** – provide information about the need to act and/or how to act (e.g., public information campaigns).

Pursuing any given objectives may, and frequently does, employ multiple policy tools. Having outlined a way to understand the array of things that can be "policy," we now turn to a brief history of food policy.

From National Food Security to Urban Food Policy

One of the seminal definitions of food policy comes from Timmer et al. (1983), who describe it as the effort of governments to shape decision-making within production, marketing, and consumption environments. Lang et al. (2009) broaden the conceptualization by including distributional impacts and the outcomes of policy, adding "who eats what, when and how; and of whether people (and animals) eat and with what consequences" (p. 21). Clark et al. (2020) argue that the word "where" should be added to this definition to account for the spatial implications of the food system.

The character of the dominant food system and the nature of food policy has changed over time. Maxwell and Slater (2003) describe a shift to a "new food policy." Early on, food policy focused on agricultural markets and trade. Later, it came to include food security, with a focus on availability and access, before finally incorporating a variety of issues, such as health and environment. These issues emphasize a shift from social policy (linked to poverty) and rural development to a systems-based orientation that attempts to address both. Lang et al. (2009) provide a succinct history of three phases.

The first phase in the 1940s and 50s focused on agricultural production and national self-sufficiency within a "productivist" framework. Notably, the development of cities over the nineteenth and early twentieth centuries helped drive this focus on agricultural production. During this time period, the U.S. population became increasingly urban as more people moved into cities in pursuit of manufacturing jobs. This created a need to feed cities through ever more efficient agricultural production methods, even as the rural farming population decreased (Steel, 2013).

The 1970s saw oil price spikes lead to increased food prices and worldwide famines. This, coupled with the perceived failure of the productivist strategy, led to an attempt to open international markets and a focus on promoting the "green revolution" in order to increase food security while incorporating nutrition as a concern. Our current final phase has begun to highlight the ecological crisis connected to the food system and failures of markets to meet public and nutritional needs. To this third phase, we add the rise of urban food policy, which is grounded in a broader movement toward devolution, city agency in global systems, use of indirect policy tools, and collaborative governance (Moragues-Faus & Morgan, 2015; Salamon, 2000; Sonnino & Spayde, 2014). This phase emphasizes cities as sites of trial, error, change, and innovation, resulting in policies tailored to local needs while leveraging local assets and better engaging civil society.

As the level of government closest to people and their experiences on the ground, local government has become the first responder to food-related problems, such as environmental degradation, social inequity, diet-related health problems, etc. In response, cities are facilitating and supporting food systems that connect food producers and consumers through "socially just, ecologically sound, and economically viable relationships using a systems-perspective." Urban[1] food policies aim for solutions that "are civic-oriented, often place-based, focusing on community development, healthy food access, farm viability (often of small and mid-sized farms), and local and regional market and infrastructure development" (Clark et al., 2015, p. 113).

A growing number of urban governments in the U.S., and globally, have adopted and implemented plans and policies to strengthen their communities' food infrastructures (Öztekin-Günaydin et al., 2016). Globally, 210 cities have signed the Milan Food Policy Pact, a declaration of local governments' commitment to improve the sustainability of their food systems (Milan Urban Food Policy Pact, n.d.). International agencies, such as the Food and Agriculture Organization (FAO) of the United Nations, which have traditionally focused on national-scale action, have begun to recognize the opportunities afforded in subnational and urban spaces. Indeed, urban governments across the globe are emerging as the new "state" by surpassing their nations in responding to food-related challenges (Calori & Magarini, 2015), a role highlighted by the UN Food and Agriculture Organization's Urban Food Agenda.[2]

However, shifts in food policy have left cities in a complicated situation. Under U.S. federalism, states and the federal government have their own areas of responsibility and authority (Broad Leib, 2017). In the U.S., most policies shaping the broader food system originate at the federal level, covering earlier issues mentioned such as markets, trade, and national food security. Cities can also receive support and funding from the federal government. The U.S. "Farm Bill" is arguably the greatest source of support for building local food systems. Cities are subject to, and influenced by, these broader federal policies. At the same time, cities are afforded authority through their home states. This federal system gives rise to debates over which scale of government (i.e., local, state, or federal) has authority to intervene in the food system. For example, states have been pre-empting localities from instituting soda taxes to deal with diet-related disease (Crosbie et al., 2019). Even if local government has control over an issue, there are multiple sources of authority, such as municipal code or ordinance, city council resolutions, and mayoral initiatives that complicate matters (Halvey et al., 2020). Furthermore, multiple departments can adopt their own plans and programs, producing inefficient duplication or even contradiction between different plans and programs (Halvey et al., 2020). Finally, the involvement of private actors in the development and/or implementation of policy tools alluded to earlier introduces greater complexity in understanding who is accountable (Salamon, 2000).

Finally, for all the possibilities that cities represent, they are often too small to effectively tackle problems arising from a global system. Some scholars have critiqued the positioning of food governance as an urban issue because the ability of cities to create meaningful change to global problems is far from certain (Allen & Guthman, 2006; Holt Giménez & Shattuck, 2011; Ilbery & Maye, 2005). Without attention to intergovernmental approaches to implementing policy tools and support from higher levels of government, territorial limits and lack of administrative authority can hinder the ability of cities to tackle food issues that may exceed their spatial and/or administrative jurisdiction. Other critiques suggest that local policies may not have the equitable outcomes purported by advocates and may even go as far as reinforcing inequity (Allen, 2010; Allen et al., 2003; DeLind, 2011). Despite these critiques, cities are likely to remain important actors in food policy as they continue to exercise their influence in the global arena on a myriad of topics, ranging from food to climate change.

Urban Food Policy in Practice

Combining the diverse priorities and objectives of food policy with the stages of the food supply chain, and available policy tools, produces a vast array of combinations. Figure 15.1 illustrates this "universe" of potential food policies, urban or otherwise. Unlike food system frameworks (e.g., Blay-Palmer et al., 2018; Ericksen et al., 2012; Giordano et al., 2018), this universe does not conceptualize the complex relationships and feedbacks between different parts of the system, but rather offers a means of understanding the bounds of what constitutes "food policy" broadly (Calori & Magarini, 2015). Establishing these bounds provides a simple heuristic for understanding how U.S. cities have employed food policy within this universe of possibilities.

Along the left-hand side (y-axis) are the five types of policy tools outlined previously: authority, incentives, capacity, symbolic, and learning. Along the bottom (x-axis) are the basic stages in the food supply chain: production, middle infrastructure, retail/service, consumption, and waste capture. We include these stages of the supply chain as topical areas wherein food policy tools could be applied. Finally, listed front to back (z-axis) are examples

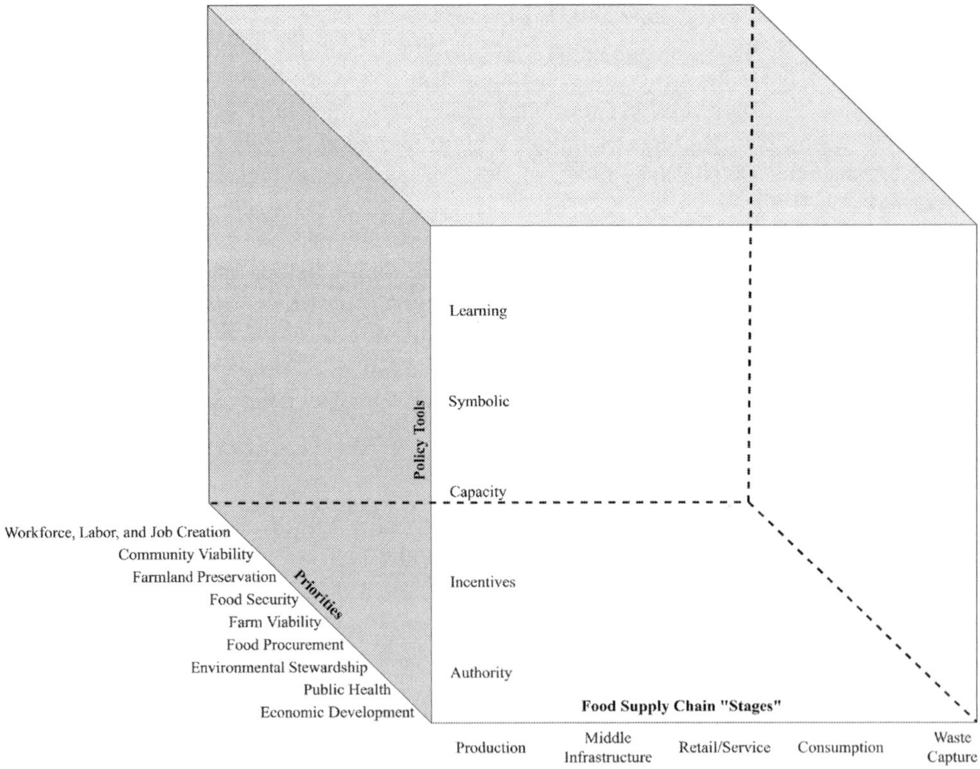

Figure 15.1 The food policy universe
Source: Created by Authors.

of the public priorities these tools are meant to address: economic development, public health, environmental stewardship, food procurement, farm viability, food security, farmland preservation, community viability, and workforce, labor, and job creation. These priorities are drawn from a U.S. nationwide survey of food policy councils conducted by the Johns Hopkins Center for a Livable Future Food Policy Network. As a result, they represent the array of policy priorities indicated by food policy councils (Bassarab et al., 2019; Öztekin-Günaydin et al., 2016).

The combination of these three dimensions produces hundreds of unique approaches. For example, a policy that provides business development assistance to beginning farmers with the goal of increasing the survival rate of new farms would be a *capacity* tool aimed at a *farm viability* priority within the *production* stage of the supply chain. Of course, not every policy fits neatly into a single quadrant of this universe. A single policy may impact multiple stages of the supply chain and/or have multiple priorities (e.g., a farmers' market promotion policy can impact both the production and retail stages of the supply chain while pursuing a variety of priorities). Nonetheless, this universe of policies can aid in understanding the food policy space and identifying sectors that might be over/underemphasized.

Table 15.1 provides a summary of example policy tools by supply chain stages, drawing on a database of implemented food policies in the U.S. assembled by Growing Food Connections (Raja et al., 2016). Blank cells in the table indicate where we could not find relevant urban examples. While we cannot say for certain the absence of any given listing in a respective cell means that it does not exist, the database represents the best available information on food policies that have been implemented in the U.S. As such, the review of this database provides the best available means of assessing what food policies have been implemented by U.S. cities.

The remainder of this section discusses what kinds of policy tools U.S. cities have used in relation to each of the food supply chain stages. This discussion elaborates on and references the policy tools noted as examples in Table 15.1.

Production. Urban food policy commonly employs zoning, land-use planning, and vacant land allocation (authority-based regulation policy tools) as methods for promoting production within or near cities (Biehler et al., 1999). For instance, Cleveland, Ohio has structured a number of local ordinances to allow urban production (Clark et al., 2020, p. 21). Frequently, authority tools used to facilitate production involve a combination of both relaxing existing regulations (e.g., zoning restrictions on agriculture) and explicit permission of authority for production. (See Chapter 21 by Baker et al. in this volume for a thorough discussion of urban agriculture governance and policy tools.)

In a survey of U.S. urban and regional planners, Clark et al. (2020) find that 71 percent of respondents reported that their city/municipality used some kind of policy tool to support agricultural production. Regulatory support (authority tool) was most common (52 percent), with incentives (34 percent) and direct administration (39 percent) being slightly less common. The most common production approaches/topics were community gardening (55 percent using any kind of policy tool), commercial agriculture (38 percent using any kind of policy tool), and small/mid-sized agriculture (29 percent using any kind of policy tool). A 2015 International City/County Management Association and Michigan State University (ICMA/MSU) survey of municipalities similarly found that residential/nontraditional livestock/beekeeping facilitation policy (29.7 percent) and farmland preservation (17.9 percent) were the most common approaches to supporting food production. Overall, regulatory/authority tools are most prevalent in promoting/facilitating agricultural production.

Although less prevalent, cities also employ a variety of educational (learning) tools, such as the promotion/facilitation of extension education, master gardeners' classes, and other agriculture and food production-related curriculum (Biehler et al., 1999). For example, Boulder, Colorado

Table 15.1 U.S. urban food policies within the universe of potential food policies

The Food Supply Chain	*Types of Policy Tools*				
	Authority	*Incentives*	*Capacity*	*Symbolic*	*Learning*
Production	Change zoning to allow production (community viability, e.g., Cleveland, OH; Detroit, MI; Baltimore, MD) Zoning permits for backyard chickens, bees, etc. (e.g., Lawrence, KS)	Reduced taxes for farming vacant land (economic development, e.g., Los Angeles, CA; San Francisco, CA) Organic conversation incentives (environmental stewardship, e.g., Woodbury County, IA)	Establishing or funding incubator farms (e.g., Cabarrus, NC)	Farmland preservation plans (e.g., Chautauqua County, NY)	
Middle Infrastructure	Zoning and regulatory definitions to facilitate commercial kitchens (community viability, e.g., Montgomery County, MD; Minneapolis, MN)	Commercial rehabilitation districts to promote food processing/distribution businesses (e.g., Marquette, MI) Contracting incentives from the city for businesses that buy local food (e.g., Cleveland, OH)	Funding or establishing incubator kitchens (e.g., Douglas County, KS) Creating or funding wholesale market infrastructure (e.g., San Francisco, CA)	Governments "pledge" to buy local (e.g., Cleveland, OH)	
Retail/Service	Zoning and code revisions to facilitate markets and food trucks (e.g., Portland, ME; Cleveland, OH; Boston, MA; Wyandotte County KS; Seattle, WA) Moratoriums on new fast food restaurants (e.g., Los Angeles, CA)	Funding for grocery stores in underserved communities (e.g., Baltimore, MD; New York, NY; Washington, DC) Incentives for food businesses (e.g., San Francisco, CA)	Healthy corner store initiatives focused on capacity support (e.g., Denver, CO) Technical support for food businesses (e.g., San Francisco, CA)	Buy local campaigns (e.g., Philadelphia, PA) – also used to support/promote local agriculture	

Consumption	School requirements for food security provision and healthy food guidelines (e.g., Washington, DC) Bans on trans-fat products (e.g., Cleveland, OH)	Funding for school-based food security and nutrition programs (e.g., Cumberland County, ME; King County, WA) Taxes on sugary drinks (e.g., Chicago, IL)	Technical support for school-based good food purchasing programs (e.g., Chicago, IL) Elder services food access programs (e.g., Cumberland County, ME)	Food plans that promote access to healthy/local food (e.g., Waterloo, ON; Cleveland, OH)	Healthy food consumption promotion programs that include educational components (e.g., El Paso, TX)
Waste	Permitting/regulation of residential composting (e.g., Chicago, IL) Mandatory recycling/compost programs (e.g., San Francisco, CA)			City resolution to reduce food waste (e.g., El Paso, TX)	
Whole Supply Chain	Zoning changes to permit farm stands on farms, and more farmers' markets (e.g., Detroit, MI; Albemarle County, VA)	Local food economy investment trust funds (e.g., Cabarrus County, NC)		Comprehensive food system plans (e.g., Columbus, OH; Multnomah County, OR)	Reporting requirements for food system metrics, aimed at informing policymakers (e.g., New York, NY)

Source: Raja et al., (2016).

Note: This table is based on policies listed in the "Local Government Food Policy Database," developed by Growing Food Connections.

parks departments, in collaboration with local nonprofits, support community garden development (Biehler et al., 1999, p. 18). This approach offers in-kind support (capacity-building tools) through the donation of water or land in addition to relaxing regulations (authority tool) to permit agriculture in parks.

Importantly, production-focused food policy is more often a federal or state-level policy domain in the U.S. While cities can promote urban agriculture and help support agriculture in the regions immediately surrounding them, they are largely dependent on production from rural agricultural regions outside of their zone of influence. This elevates the importance of intergovernmental collaboration between cities and neighboring rural counties, or cities and higher levels of government, to help shape policies that support the agricultural needs of cities.

Middle Infrastructure (Processing, Aggregation, Distribution). Promotion of middle infrastructure often employs a mix of approaches. As with production, relaxation of regulations (authority tools), such as health codes, is an important approach to facilitating small food businesses and cottage industries. Additionally, capacity-building approaches, such as providing business planning, entrepreneurial assistance, and code/permit compliance support, are also common strategies (Biehler et al., 1999, p. 7).

Another important capacity tool involves the development of virtual and relational infrastructure that helps agricultural producers, processers, distributors, retailers, and consumers connect. According to Clark et al. (2020), 14 percent of cities responding provided virtual and relational infrastructure support in supply chain networks, such as between growers and restaurants; 14 percent facilitated connections between growers and retailers; 14 percent facilitated connections between growers and local/regional wholesalers; 12 percent supported farmers' cooperatives; and 7 percent supported virtual food hubs (including online directories). One example of this relational infrastructure approach is in Franklin County, Ohio (the county that contains Columbus), where the Council of Development Finance Agencies worked with the county to create a Food Business Portal (Clark et al., 2020). Other examples include supporting virtual and in-person forums and "meet and greets," enabling farmers to connect with wholesalers and wholesalers to connect with retailers and service buyers.

However, middle infrastructure support is notably less common compared to food policies in other parts of the supply chain. According to Clark et al. (2020), only 50 percent of respondents indicated that their municipality employed any kind of policy tool to support middle infrastructure in the food system. Again, authority tools were most prevalent (33 percent), with incentives (17 percent) and direct government ownership of infrastructure (22 percent) being less common. Topically, food processing facilities, commercial kitchens, and business incubators for food processors were the most common areas supported by policy.

Retail and Service. In this particularly visible part of the food supply chain, policy support involves facilitating both the entity selling/serving the food (e.g., grocery stores, farmers' markets, restaurants, schools and other institutions, food banks, etc.) and ensuring access by consumers, particularly among low-income residents. For instance, relaxing zoning laws (authority) to permit and/or promote food retail in traditionally underserved neighborhoods is a strategy for facilitating food access on the retail side of the exchange (ChangeLab Solutions, 2012). Portland, Oregon, for example, updated its zoning bylaws to make food distribution an accessory use in most land-use categories. This allows food distribution (e.g., from an urban garden or community-supported agriculture drop-off point) in areas zoned for other purposes, such as residential (Clark et al., 2020, p. 21). Incentives for grocery store development, particularly in underserved neighborhoods, is another policy approach. On the consumer side of the spectrum, policy facilitating food access involves a variety of capacity-building tools. In addition to federal and state-run programs (e.g., federal school lunch and breakfast, SNAP

(Supplemental Nutrition Assistance Program), WIC (Special Supplemental Nutrition Program for Women, Infants, and Children), etc.), local municipalities can consider transportation planning and housing layouts in urban areas in order to help ensure access to food retail (Biehler et al., 1999). Schools partner with local pantries by providing space and access to students to increase students' access to food over the weekends through "backpack" programs (Fram & Frongillo, 2018).

As a focus for urban food policy, the retail/service sectors are frequently emphasized. In a survey of U.S. urban and regional planners, Clark et al. (2020) find that 71 percent of respondents reported that their city/municipality used some kind of policy tool to support these sectors. Of those, 53 percent indicated the use of some kind of authority tool, 25 percent indicated the use of incentive tools, and 34 percent indicated that the municipality employed direct governance. Of the particular retail/service approaches most frequently supported by policy, farmers' markets (60 percent using any tool), supermarket and grocery stores (51 percent using any tool), and restaurants (49 percent using any tool) were the most common areas of policy support. Across all surveyed areas, authority tools (either tightening or relaxing regulations) were the most common policy tool used. A 2015 ICMA/MSU survey of municipalities also found that establishing and managing farmers' markets was a common approach to supporting food retail: 9.2 percent of cities responding reported that the local government had a policy, and 6.8 percent indicated that the government alone implements the policy. However, numbers were far higher for partnerships: 21.5 percent of respondents indicated that the city was a partner on a farmers' market establishment/management policy. This illustrates the increasingly important role of nongovernmental actors in both promoting and managing municipal food policy.

Consumption. Consumption-related policy has tended to focus on promoting healthy eating habits. Given the personal choice nature of food consumption, traditional policy approaches on this front have relied more on the education of nutrition and eating education (learning tools), particularly within schools and other youth education environments (e.g., 4-H clubs, etc.) to promote healthy eating habits. When paired with school gardens and environmental curriculum, this education also provides an opportunity to inform students about agricultural production issues (Biehler et al., 1999). Learning approaches have also been aimed at the general public through newsletters, such as in New York City, or direct public outreach via farmers' market nutrition programs and community clinics (Biehler et al., 1999, p. 12).

Additional policy approaches to influence consumption have included making access to fresh food and vegetables easier for low-income residents. One such approach involves facilitating the use of Electronic Benefits Transfer (EBT) at farmers' markets so that SNAP credits can be used to purchase fresh vegetables. This is a common capacity-building tool that supports retail – including markets for small producers – and provides access to nutritious food among low-income residents (Biehler et al., 1999). Other capacity-building tools include programs such as school lunch provision and meal delivery to improve food access (Biehler et al., 1999). Furthermore, many local municipalities, such as Alamosa, Colorado, use incentive tools, like its Double-Up Bucks programs, to encourage SNAP users to shop at farmers' markets.

Waste. Waste is arguably the aspect of the food supply chain that is least represented in urban food policy. (See Chapter 19 by Warshawsky and Soma in this volume for a deeper examination of the governance of food waste.) That being said, among the most common approaches are promotion and education (learning) tools aimed at backyard composting. For instance, San Francisco provided free composting bins (capacity building) with extension resources (learning tool) to facilitate backyard composting and reduce waste (Biehler et al., 1999, p. 15).

Simultaneously, changing ordinances on how waste is paid for by consumers can be an important incentive tool for encouraging composting. San Diego, California, for example, passed an ordinance that makes payments for sewer services variable depending on the amount of waste material each ratepayer produces, which encourages restaurants to reduce the disposal of food waste down in-sink disposals (Biehler et al., 1999, p. 14). Policies like these can provide a financial motivation for reducing food waste, while capacity and learning tools help equip residents with the knowledge and/or equipment needed to realize that action.

Whole Supply Chain. Finally, we also included a category for "whole supply chain" approaches that attempt to tackle multiple parts of the food supply chain. Most notable here are comprehensive food plans, such as in Columbus, Ohio, that lay out a suite of food-related issues and associated objectives that a city aims to achieve. However, plans often do not specify the policy tools that will be used to achieve those objectives. As such, the plans themselves represent a largely symbolic commitment of a government to work on the array of food issues contained within the plan. Additionally, establishing reporting requirements in order to compile metrics for various parts of the food system so that policymakers can make more informed decisions, such as in New York City, is a kind of learning tool. Unlike other learning policy tools in this chapter, reporting requirements are aimed at changing internal government.

Where to Now?

The policy tools reviewed in the previous section represent several decades of hard-fought battles for urban food policy. Despite the merits of these efforts, this review points to a few important shortcomings of, and opportunities available to, current U.S. urban food policy. First, several key topics are largely not addressed. For instance, despite its close connection with sustainable agriculture movements, urban food policy has largely bypassed environmental issues. Yet, with 26 percent of global greenhouse gas emissions – among other environmental issues – there are important reasons for urban food policies to address the food system's environmental impacts (Poore & Nemecek, 2018). Candel (2019) offers similar findings for the Milan Pact signatory cities. There are exceptions to this, such as policies aimed at waste diversion (e.g., mandatory recycling/compost programs in San Francisco). Overall, though, there is limited attention to the topic. Similarly, labor issues (e.g., worker safety, fair pay, etc.) rarely make it into urban food policy. One exception was the 2016 increase of the minimum wage in Portland for all workers, including service workers, but despite endemic labor issues in the food industry, similar policy efforts by cities remain uncommon.

Second, U.S. urban food policy has not widely seized the opportunity to make broader social and economic impacts by strengthening middle infrastructure in food supply chains. Notably, this is not unique to the U.S., as studies of non-U.S. cities offer similar findings (Candel, 2019; Sonnino & Spayde, 2014). Access in the U.S. to publicly available and regionally oriented middle infrastructure (e.g., packing, processing, and distribution facilities) is scarce. This limits distribution options for small and mid-sized farmers and ranchers. More incentives from cities for middle infrastructure will be essential to scaling up local and regional food alternatives.

Third, current approaches to U.S. urban food policy employ a relatively narrow range of available tools. Urban food policy is still largely reliant on authority tools (e.g., zoning), which contrasts with approaches by non-U.S. cities to employ informational tools (Candel, 2019; Doernberg et al., 2019). An important future step for U.S. urban food policy will be to apply a wider array of tools, such as incentives, capacity building, and learning. Taking greater advantage of all the proverbial tools in the toolbox is an opportunity for scaling up policy impacts in order to respond to the challenges that current events continue to reveal.

Finally, ongoing demonstrations against institutional and structural racism have also brought into sharp relief how food issues are inextricably tied up with race and ethnicity. Minorities are more likely to be low-paid agricultural workers, have higher rates of diet-related chronic disease, and be food insecure (Food Chain Workers Alliance, 2012). This intersection between race and food is further highlighted by the global COVID-19 pandemic, which has disproportionately impacted minority communities that are more likely to be considered "essential" because of their agriculture and food service positions and, as a result, be at greater risk of contracting the virus. None of these are new problems. However, they raise important questions about the nature of food policy: where are the "bounds" of urban food policy? As one of the most essential needs of humanity, is the food system distinct from other problems – social, economic, environmental – with which it intersects? Or is it more akin to a connective tendril between issues? If the latter – and it seems to be – then a central challenge for the future of food policy is how to scale up its impact and comprehensiveness in order to tackle these integrated issues (Mah & Thang, 2013). These questions are essential for reflecting on the implementation of food policy at any level of government. However, as important actors in developing and implementing food policy, these questions will be particularly important to cities.

One such scale consideration for the future of food policy is geography. While progress at the city-scale in the U.S. has been made, addressing the pervasive influence and geographic distribution of sprawling food supply chains will require state and national intervention for two reasons. First, implementing a true systems approach requires greater capacity and authority than many local governments can bring to bear. Second, addressing inequality across geography (i.e., between cities) requires policymaking at the state and national levels. If U.S. food policy is to adequately respond to food system challenges, then state and national policy will need to be implemented to reinforce city-level efforts. An important next step for U.S. urban food policy is the pursuit of intergovernmental partnerships among various local jurisdictions (e.g., collaboration between cities, towns, and counties within a particular region) and across multiple levels of government (i.e., local, state, and national). Such intergovernmental arrangements will be critical governing strategies for implementing food policies that impact sufficient geographic spaces to effectively tackle food-related challenges. As noted earlier in this chapter, cities are already important laboratories for the innovative development of food policy. They can serve similar leadership roles in the creation of intergovernmental strategies for developing and implementing more geographically impactful food policies.

Conclusion

Increasingly, cities are carving out new roles for themselves in the food system by establishing sites of innovation and potential new food futures via food policy. Food policies influence who eats what, when, where, and at what cost. Cities are aiming to use these tools to create socially just, ecologically sound, economically viable food systems that are civic-oriented and place-based. Combining basic policy tools, the stages of the food supply chain, and the public goals of food policy results in a universe with hundreds of possibilities. This chapter applied this framework of possibilities to understand where and how U.S. cities have pursued food policies. While U.S. cities have adopted varied approaches, the application has been uneven. Issues such as labor, the environment, and middle infrastructure have received limited attention. Additionally, some tools are used more heavily than others. Going forward, policymakers and advocates of U.S. urban food policy should look toward changes that attend to social justice and which are backed by state and national policies.

Notes

1 In this chapter, we consider "urban" to be incorporated cities in the U.S.
2 For more information, see www.fao.org/urban-food-agenda/about/en/.

References

Allen, P. (2010). Realizing justice in local food systems. *Cambridge Journal of Regions, Economy and Society, 3*(2), 295–308. doi:10.1093/cjres/rsq015

Allen, P., & Guthman, J. (2006). From "old school" to "farm-to-school": Neoliberalization from the ground up. *Agriculture and Human Values, 23*(4), 401–415. doi:10.1007/s10460-006-9019-z

Allen, P., Fitzsimmons, M., Goodman, D., & Warner, K. (2003). Shifting plates in the agrifood landscape: The tectonics of alternative agrifood initiatives in California. *Journal of Rural Studies, 19*(1), 61–75. https://doi.org/10.1016/S0743-0167(02)00047-5

Anderson, J. E. (1994). *Public policy: An introduction* (2nd ed.). Geneva, IL: Houghton Mifflin.

Andrée, P., Clark, J. K., Levkoe, C. Z., & Lowitt, K. (2019). *Civil society and social movements in food system governance* (p. 216). New York: Routledge.

Bardach, E. (1977). *The implementation game: What happens after a bill becomes a law.* Cambridge, MA: MIT Press.

Bassarab, K., Santo, R., & Palmer, A. (2019). *Food policy council report 2018.* Baltimore, MD: Johns Hopkins Center for a Livable Future. Retrieved from https://assets.jhsph.edu/clf/mod_clfResource/doc/FPC%20Report%202018_FINAL.pdf

Biehler, D., Fisher, A., Siedeburg, K., Winne, M., & Zachary, J. (1999). *Getting food on the table: An action guide to local food policy.* Venice, CA: Community Food Security Coalition and California Sustainable Agriculture Working Group. Retrieved from http://foodsecurity.org/pubs.html

Blay-Palmer, A., Santini, G., Dubbeling, M., Renting, H., Taguchi, M., & Giordano, T. (2018). Validating the city region food system approach: Enacting inclusive, transformational city region food systems. *Sustainability, 10*(5), 1680. https://doi.org/10.3390/su10051680

Broad Leib, E. 2017. *Good laws, good food: Putting local food policy to work for our communities.* Cambridge, MA: Food Law and Policy Clinic, Harvard Law School. www.chlpi.org/flpc-releases-good-laws-good-food-putting-local-food-policy-work-communities-toolkit/

Calori, A., & Magarini, A. (2015). *Food and the cities: Food policies for sustainable cities.* Milan, Italy: Edizioni Ambiente.

Candel, J. J. (2019). What's on the menu? A global assessment of MUFPP signatory cities' food strategies. *Agroecology and Sustainable Food Systems, 44*(7), 919–946. doi: 10.1080/21683565.2019.1648357

ChangeLab Solutions. (2012). *Getting to grocery: Tools for attracting healthy food retail to underserved neighborhoods.* Oakland, CA: ChangeLab Solutions. Retrieved from www.changelabsolutions.org/sites/default/files/documents/Getting_to_Grocery_FINAL_20120514.pdf

Clark, J. K., Conley, B., & Raja, S. (2020). Essential, fragile, and invisible community food infrastructure: The role of urban governments in the United States. *Food Policy, 103*(102014). https://doi.org/10.1016/j.foodpol.2020.102014

Clark, J. K., Sharp, J. S., & Dugan, K. L. (2015). The agrifood system policy agenda and research domain. *Journal of Rural Studies, 42*, 112–122.

Crosbie, E., Schillinger, D., & Schmidt, L. A. (2019). State preemption to prevent local taxation of sugar-sweetened beverages. *Journal of the American Medical Association Internal Medicine, 179*(3), 291–292. doi:10.1001/jamainternmed.2018.7770

DeLind, L. B. (2011). Are local food and the local food movement taking us where we want to go? Or are we hitching our wagons to the wrong stars? *Agriculture and Human Values, 28*(2), 273–283. doi:10.1007/s10460-010-9263-0

Doernberg, A., Horn, P., Zasada, I., & Piorr, A. (2019). Urban food policies in German city regions: An overview of key players and policy instruments. *Food Policy, 89*(101782). https://doi.org/10.1016/j.foodpol.2019.101782

Dye, T. R. (1987). *Understanding public policy.* Upper Saddle River, NJ: Prentice Hall.

Elmore, R. F. (1987). Instruments and strategy in public policy. *Review of Policy Research,* 7(1), 174–186. https://doi.org/10.1111/j.1541-1338.1987.tb00036.x

Ericksen, P., Stewart, B., Dixon, J., Barling, D., Loring, P., Anderson, M., & Ingram, J. (2012). The value of a food system approach. In J. Ingram, P. Ericksen, & D. Liverman (Eds.), *Food security and global environmental change* (pp. 45–65). Abingdon, Oxon: Routledge.

Food Chain Workers Alliance. (2012). *The hands that feed us: Challenges and opportunities for workers along the food chain*: Los Angeles, CA: Food Chain Workers Alliance.

Fram, M. S., & Frongillo, E. A. (2018). Backpack programs and the crisis narrative of child hunger: A critical review of the rationale, targeting, and potential benefits and harms of an expanding but untested model of practice. *Advances in Nutrition, 9*(1), 1–8. https://doi.org/10.1093/advances/nmx008

Giordano, T., Ledant, C., Di Martino, D., Michel, C., & Roiatti, F. (2018). *The role of cities in the transformation of food systems: Sharing lessons from Milan Pact cities*. Rome: MUFPP. Retrieved from www.milanurbanfoodpolicypact.org.

Gormley, W. T. (1987). *Bureau-bashing: A framework for analysis*. Paper presented at the Meetings of the American Political Science Association, Chicago, IL.

Halvey, M. R., Santo, R. E., Lupolt, S. N., Dilka, T. J., Kim, B. F., Bachman, G. H., Clark, J. K., & Nachman, K. E. (2020). Beyond backyard chickens: A framework for understanding municipal urban agriculture policies in the United States. *Food Policy, 103*(2021). https://doi.org/10.1016/j.foodpol.2020.102013

Hamilton, N. D. (2002). Putting a face on our food: How state and local food policies can promote the new agriculture. *Drake Journal of Agricultural Law*, 7(2), 407–453. https://aglawjournal.wp.drake.edu/wp-content/uploads/sites/66/2016/09/agVol07No2-Hamilton.pdf

Hassanein, N. (2003). Practicing food democracy: A pragmatic politics of transformation. *Journal of Rural Studies, 19*(1), 77–86. https://doi.org/10.1016/S0743-0167(02)00041-4

Holt Giménez, E., & Shattuck, A. (2011). Food crises, food regimes and food movements: Rumblings of reform or tides of transformation? *The Journal of Peasant Studies, 38*(1), 109–144. https://doi.org/10.1080/03066150.2010.538578

Ilbery, B., & Maye, D. (2005). Alternative (shorter) food supply chains and specialist livestock products in the Scottish–English borders. *Environment & Planning A, 37*(5), 823–844. https://doi.org/10.1068/a3717

Lang, T., Barling, D., & Caraher, M. (2009). *Food policy: Integrating health, environment and society*. Oxford: Oxford University Press.

Lowi, T. J. (1972). Four systems of policy, politics, and choice. *Public Administration Review, 32*(4), 298–310. https://doi.org/10.2307/974990

Mah, C. L., & Thang, H. (2013). Cultivating food connections: The Toronto Food Strategy and municipal deliberation on food. *International Planning Studies, 18*(1), 96–110. https://doi.org/10.1080/13563475.2013.750941

Maxwell, S., & Slater, R. (2003). Food policy old and new. *Development Policy Review, 21*(5–6), 531–553. https://doi.org/10.1111/j.1467-8659.2003.00222.x

McDonnell, L. (1988). *Policy design as instrument design*. Paper presented at the Annual meeting of the American Political Science Association, Washington, DC.

Milan Urban Food Policy Pact. (n.d.). *Signatory Cities*. Rome: MUFPP. Retrieved from www.milanurbanfoodpolicypact.org/signatory-cities/

Moragues-Faus, A., & Morgan, K. (2015). Reframing the foodscape: The emergent world of urban food policy. *Environment and Planning A: Economy and Space, 47*(7), 1558–1573. https://doi.org/10.1177/0308518X15595754

Öztekin-Günaydin, B., Newton, J., Goddeeris, L., & Rybnicek, A. (2016). *2015 food systems survey*. Retrieved from www.canr.msu.edu/foodsystems/resources/brief/2015%20icma-msu%20local%20government%20food%20survey%20results%20summary.pdf

Parsons, W. (1995). *Public policy: An introduction to the theory and practice of policy analysis*. Cheltenham: Edward Elgar.

Poore, J., & Nemecek, T. (2018). Reducing food's environmental impacts through producers and consumers. *Science, 360*(6392), 987–992. doi: 10.1126/science.aaq0216

Raja, S., Hodgeson, K., Clark, J. K., & Freedgood, J. (2016). *Local government food policy database*. Retrieved from: http://growingfoodconnections.org/tools-resources/policy-database/

Salamon, L. M. (2000). The new governance and the tools of public action: An introduction. *Fordham Urban Law Journal, 28*, 1611. https://heinonline.org

Schneider, A., & Ingram, H. (1990). Behavioral assumptions of policy tools. *The Journal of Politics, 52*(2), 510–529. doi: 10.2307/2131904

Smith, K. B., & Larimer, C. W. (2013). *The public policy theory primer* (2nd ed.). Boulder, CO: Westview Press.
Sonnino, R., & Spayde, J. (2014). The "new frontier"? Urban strategies for food security and sustainability. In T. Marsden, K. Morley, & A. Sherwin (Eds.), *Sustainable food systems: Building a new paradigm* (pp. 186–205). London: Routledge.
Steel, C. (2013). *Hungry city: How food shapes our lives*. London: Random House.
Stoker, G. (1996). Governance as theory: Five propositions. *International Social Science Journal, 50*(155), 17–28. https://doi.org/10.1111/1468-2451.00106
Timmer, C. P., Falcon, W. P., & Pearson, S. R. (1983). *Food policy analysis*. Baltimore, MD: Published for the World Bank [by] The Johns Hopkins University Press.

16

STRATEGIES FOR INSTITUTIONALIZING FOOD SYSTEMS PLANNING

Lesli Hoey

Introduction

Today's global food system is increasingly blamed for fuelling the climate crisis, health epidemics, and economic inequities (IPCC, 2019). Cities – on which so many foodsheds now depend – are increasingly seen as "a pivot point" where systems-based actions could simultaneously improve food security, equitable livelihoods across rural and urban food chains, and region-wide ecological footprints (Blay-Palmer et al., 2018, 2; Haysom et al., 2020). According to the American Planning Association, food systems planning attempts to build:

> more sustainable, just, equitable, self-reliant, and resilient community and regional food systems for present and future generations... [It] emphasizes, strengthens and makes visible the interdependent and inseparable relationships between individual sectors from production to waste management... [while] leveraging connections to other health, social, economic and environmental issues.
>
> *APA, 2020*

Despite a growing number of city-led declarations that focus on food systems, peer-to-peer learning networks, and urban food policies enacted around the world (Cabannes & Marocchino, 2018), the practice of holistic food systems planning is still rare in most places. Many city governments remain entirely "food blind" (Frimpong Boamah et al., 2020, 2; Raja et al., 2014, 176). At best, urban planners inadvertently undermine food systems or do not recognize they can intervene, seeing food system failures as a market issue (Battersby, 2017; Winne, 2017). At worst, local governments are actively hostile to the human and physical infrastructure that often informally supports more equitable, health-promoting, and environmentally regenerative city food regions (Smit, 2016).

In some places, however, food systems planning is now firmly established. Rather than outline the *what* – the content of plans or actions that ideally encompass food systems planning – this chapter asks *how* cities reach a point where food systems issues become an area of focus, just as transportation, land use, housing, and other basic city functions are unquestioned as sites of ongoing urban planning visioning and intervention. Focusing on the "how" speaks to the

DOI: 10.4324/9781003055907-19

need to understand more clearly the governance dynamics and political conditions that "enable the exercise of agency" in food systems transformation (van Bers et al., 2019, 98). Armed with such knowledge, advocates could proactively, and more rapidly, expand food systems planning. Indeed, the time may be ripe to act, as many believe that the recovery process from COVID-19 could be "fertile [ground] for changing business as usual" (Juriaans, 2020), the tipping point needed to shift to a more resilient, holistic, and just food regime (Cohen & Ilieva, 2020; OECD, 2020).

Complemented by comparative research on cities across the globe, such as Belo Horizonte, Brazil, the themes outlined in this chapter are drawn primarily from cities in the United States and Canada, especially Baltimore, Buffalo, New York City, Toronto, and Vancouver, where the nascent body of policy process research on food systems planning is most robust. The remainder of this chapter offers more detail about current trends, the strategies that led some cities to focus on food systems as a regular part of government action, and the implications for practice as advocates attempt to move even more cities (more quickly) towards holistic food systems planning.

The current state of food systems planning

Particular elements of food systems – such as farmland protection, urban agriculture, food price controls, and public markets – were part of early city building (Steele, 2011), late nineteenth- and early twentieth-century utopian planning models (Ilieva, 2020), and public sector actions as late as the 1940s in the United States (Deener, 2020) and the 1970s in some parts of the Global South (Andrée et al., 2019). By the 2000s, however, most local governments played little to no intentional role in shaping food systems. Pothukuchi and Kaufman's (2000) article pointing out how food systems had become a "stranger" to the planning field in the United States sparked a series of journal articles and professional reports, including the 2007 American Planning Association (APA) *Policy Guide on Community and Regional Food Planning*. Since then, interest groups have formed in the APA, the Association of Collegiate Schools of Planning, the Association of European Schools of Planning, and the United Kingdom Sustainable Food Cities Network (Sonnino & Beynon, 2015). The same has occurred in the Global South, where the 2000 United Nations-sponsored Quito Declaration was a key turning point that inspired many city-based declarations focused on food systems (Cabannes, 2012). Later, the New Urban Agenda adopted at the UN-Habitat III Summit in 2016 identified food security and nutrition as critical parts of ensuring sustainable cities (Cabannes & Marocchino, 2018). The Food and Agriculture Organization (FAO) Food for the Cities Initiative, now encompassing a community of practice in more than 110 countries, similarly promotes the cultivation of stronger urban–rural linkages through the City Region Food Systems approach (FAO, 2020). Over 200 city signatories[1] of the Milan Urban Food Policy Pact have also pledged to develop "comprehensive, interdisciplinary and inter-institutional" food systems plans and policies (MUFPP, 2015, 1).

Despite the growing interest in food systems planning, a closer look at practice suggests that gaps still exist. In the United States, a 2014 survey of over 1,100 urban planners found that 31 per cent of the agencies they worked for had stand-alone food systems plans and 50 per cent referenced food systems in comprehensive plans, recreational plans, and land-use plans (Mui et al., 2018). Comprehensive plans commonly address food access and urban agriculture (Cabannes & Marocchino, 2018; Robert & Mullinix, 2018), while climate adaptation plans often mention green infrastructure and local food promotion (Hodgson & Moreau, 2019). On the other hand, food systems scholars have found that topics related to food waste reduction and management (Robert & Mullinix, 2018; von Massow et al., 2019), food and farm labour, local food aggregation and processing infrastructure (see Chapter 15 by Clark and Irish in this volume), and food distribution and transportation (Mui et al., 2018) are still rarely addressed. Furthermore, U.S. urban planners report that transportation and economic development plans often undermine food systems (Mui et al., 2018).

In the Global South, many city governments support urban agriculture and urban food security initiatives (Giordano et al., 2018). Cities such as Rosario (Argentina), Curitiba (Brazil), Quito (Ecuador), and Nanjing (China) have notable systems-wide strategies that integrate innovations across waste recovery, local food economies, and diverse, city-wide food retail markets, regional environmental initiatives, municipal land banks for urban and peri-urban farming, food distribution, and more (Dubbeling & Dueñas, 2016; Dubbeling & Terrile, 2016; Gianfelici et al., 2016; Haysom et al., 2020). Aside from describing the variety of initiatives in place in these cities, however, historical details about how and why their governments have so fully embraced food systems planning are not readily available.

Other research on the state of food systems planning in the Global South suggests that most city governments still see food as an "additional policy demand...rather than as a systemic entry point to develop integrated urban strategies across different sectors" (Sonnino & Coulson, 2020, 8). City governments often feel restricted in what they can do because of their inability to influence trade negotiations, national government agendas, or powerful agribusinesses (ibid.). Most data on food systems are also collected at the national level and are not sufficiently disaggregated for city-level decision-making, while local governments lack the skills to map food systems and pinpoint "leverage points" to know where to intervene (ibid., 10). Moreover, Battersby (2017) argues that "the current food system transformation in African cities is taking place *in the absence of food systems planning*" (426; emphasis added). In their attempts to "modernize" and pursue a growth agenda, many urban planners are driving supermarket expansion through infrastructure provision, zoning, regulatory reforms, tax abatements, or other means without considering – or misperceiving – its potential impact on local food systems economies or nutrition security (Battersby, 2017). At the same time, city officials often restrict or eliminate the informal food sector through laws that ban or make street food vending a criminal offence, mass removals or relocations of informal markets from public spaces to areas with less foot traffic, evictions from urban gardens and peri-urban farmland, and everyday harassment, confiscation of merchandise, or bribe-taking by state officials (Battersby & Watson, 2018; Skinner, 2018; Smit, 2016). This is all despite the fact that the informal food economy is a key source of livelihoods for the working poor and a source of the majority of the world's nutritionally biodiverse and affordable food (Steyn et al., 2013; Zimmerer & de Haan, 2020).

Moving towards institutionalization

The cities showcased in this chapter demonstrate that it is possible for governments to eventually institutionalize the practice of food systems planning, embracing the role that the public sector can and should play in proactively intervening in food systems to support equity, public health, and sustainability goals. In most examples noted here, food systems planning was integrated slowly over time through strategic incrementalism (Lindblom, 1959) as council members, bureaucrats, or legislators transformed policy over many years through small shifts and easy wins (Buchan et al., 2019). This mirrors how the Baltimore Food Policy Director operates, making decisions quickly to "gain momentum" and using available data and multiple stakeholder expertise, rather than "waiting for complete and perfect evidence" (Santo et al., 2014, 205). She also focuses on what some might see as relatively minor adjustments to policy, such as "permitting, requirements, and procedures"; as she reflects, "making changes in the small policy details has led to substantial positive impact on the city's food environment" (Santo et al., 2014, 203).

All of the cases below also demonstrate ways that more substantive changes were accomplished during what Kingdon calls "windows of opportunity," rare moments when key decision makers are aware that a problem exists, see viable solutions, and are in a political climate that supports change (Kingdon, 2003, 151). The Toronto Food Policy Council, for instance, benefited from an urban restructuring process that joined Metropolitan Toronto and its six surrounding municipalities into the City of Toronto in 1998, not long after the Council had formed. As Wayne Roberts (2014), the long-time Council Coordinator, recounted, this allowed the Council to start with a "clean slate," where "a new government with new players had no choice but to establish new foundation documents" (125).

In most cases, a combination of incrementalism and windows of opportunity pushes food systems planning forward. The common denominators are persistence and patience; the process of getting a local government to the point of fully embracing food systems planning takes decades (Cabannes & Marocchino, 2018). In other words, achieving systems-based change is "a marathon, not a sprint" (Hanleybrown, et al., 2012, 2). Policy advocates featured in *Integrating Food into Urban Planning* (Cabannes & Marocchino, 2018) set their long-term sights on entrenching food systems more firmly into urban planning practice, focusing on small-scale changes along the way, weathering setbacks, and eventually achieving milestones when opportune moments arose. In Buffalo, New York, too, food systems leaders balanced "small wins," like installing a community garden in a vacant lot, which kept food systems coalitions mobilized with a "dogged persistence" of working towards long-term efforts to transform food systems structurally through policies, such as changing land-use codes (Raja et al., 2014, 186).

This "dogged persistence" requires not only acting when windows of opportunity open on their own, but proactively *creating* the conditions that make bold action more feasible. This means that individuals or groups, either inside or outside of government, pursue varying "entry points" into food systems planning, any of which are "valid simply because they were the entry points that were *possible*" (Cabannes & Marocchino, 2018, 31; emphasis added). Examples of strategies that these policy entrepreneurs cultivated are detailed further below, along with the implications for practice.

Actively moulding policy entrepreneurs

In the cities profiled, policy entrepreneurs sometimes emerged on their own, but many eventual champions were actively moulded over time. They were encouraged by government-based advocates who saw a need for allies and cross-sector collaborators or were groomed by external coalitions who built support for their causes. Food policy councils commonly play this policy-advocacy role, educating policymakers through research and policy evaluations, running programmes as proofs of concept, coordinating across government agencies, identifying public interests, and, at times, drafting food policy and plans (Harper et al., 2009). In Buffalo, it was a food coalition made up of grassroots groups and activist-scholars who engaged urban planners on an ongoing basis, inviting city staff and public officials to food conferences and workshops to show them the connection between food and government policy (Raja et al., 2014). In Vancouver, those who initially tried to institutionalize food systems planning worked to create policy entrepreneurs at multiple levels across the public, elected officials, and "street level bureaucrats," frontline staff who implement policies and programmes (Arnold, 2015; Lipsky, 2010). They looked for people who were adept at "communicating, listening, empowering other people, enabling, and doing" and able to "read the political situation" (Buchan et al., 2019, 15).

In multiple examples, it was a symbiotic relationship between public health and urban planning staff that was key to institutionalizing food systems planning. This was apparent in a 2013 survey (Mui et al., 2018), where urban planners reported that food systems topics were most commonly incorporated into community health plans (87 per cent). In Philadelphia and a five-county collaboration in central Minnesota, managed by the Region 5 Development Commission, it was health sector partners who suggested regional food systems lenses, offered staff time to carry out food systems programmes, and tapped into sources of funding often not available to planners, such as Centers for Disease Control funding or the Affordable Care Act, which allows hospitals to purchase local foods (Mui et al., 2018). In Belo Horizonte, Brazil, too, the health department offered funding and staff time to carry out initiatives focused on food insecurity, infant mortality, and malnutrition through health posts already well established in the most vulnerable parts of the city (Chappell, 2018).

In Baltimore, the Mayor's Office, Planning Department, Health Department, City Council, universities, and non-profits had been leading a variety of food systems initiatives for nearly a decade, but never in a coordinated manner until the city's Health Commissioner suggested a meeting to identify opportunities for collaboration, especially in relation to the city's comprehensive plan (Santo et al., 2014). Similarly, in New York City, several years before the city incorporated food systems into its comprehensive plan, health staff under the Bloomberg administration launched the nation's first Food Policy Coordinator position and Office of Food Policy in 2007 and pursued a number of efforts to address the growing diabetes and other diet-related epidemics through restaurants, mobile food vendors, and farmers markets (Campbell, 2016).

In Toronto, the seeds for today's more holistic food systems focus started as early as the 1960s, with Department of Health conversations around new ways of conceiving health (Blay-Palmer, 2009). The Toronto Food Policy Council was eventually established as a subcommittee of the Toronto Board of Health and linked to the newly formed Healthy City Office in 1991. In Waterloo, Canada, as well, public health staff began doing systems-based studies on food security in the mid-1990s (Wegener et al., 2012). They then convinced urban planners to adopt a comprehensive plan in 2009 that focused on building self-reliance in the regional food economy and ensuring healthy food access through farmland protection, mixed land use, and food business and market development in urban neighbourhoods. Health staff also found ways to "transfer trust" they had built over many years with community partners to garner support for the regional planning department (Wegener et al., 2012, 4111). Urban planning staff in Waterloo later positioned themselves strategically in the health sector, recognizing that the Medical Officer of Health had more credibility than the Director of Planning to advance the food security angle of their plan (ibid.).

Establishing, tapping into, and growing a broad base of support

Regardless of whether cities relied upon a few or many policy entrepreneurs, what stands out in these cases is that none would have been effective without a widespread base of support. Diverse networks helped policy entrepreneurs develop "home-grown" interventions (Haysom, 2015, 275) and test out more comprehensive strategies when opportunities arose (Buchan et al., 2019). Policy process researchers Mintrom and Norman also explain how networks are equally important for informing policy entrepreneurs about the emerging ideas, issues, and motivations of key policy decision makers, giving them the "social acuity" to act strategically (2009, 656).

To establish collaborative relationships, the profiled policy entrepreneurs did not simply invite diverse stakeholders to the table for one-off conversations, they continuously nurtured relationships and actively engaged groups most affected by food systems issues. In Belo Horizonte, for example, the city-run Food Policy Council regularly engages church leaders, business owners, workers' organizations, and other citizen groups (Haysom, 2015). This type of relationship building requires civic engagement techniques, such as "focused outreach, trust building, power sharing," and reflexive dialogue (ibid.; Clark et al., 2017, 323). In developing the 2013 Vancouver Food Strategy, one staff member reflected, "I have been asked by other places 'Should I go straight to a comprehensive food strategy?', and I say no, unless you have a history of results and trust and relationships" (Buchan et al., 2019, 16). Staff who spearheaded the effort described how it took 20 years to build this history of results and trust through community-led mobilizing and building connections with other government staff (ibid.).

A similar story is apparent with the Toronto Food Policy Council. Despite having no authority to pass or enforce laws, scholars suggest that it was the Council's "big tent approach" that enabled it to spark a wide range of initiatives around food justice, urban agriculture, food distribution and markets, rural farm-based issues, environmental concerns, and training and education (Blay-Palmer, 2009, 403). This is apparent in its volunteer board of "community activists, physicians, gardeners, academics, UN advisors, immigrants, farmers, conservationists, planners and refugees… [which allows the Council] to provide authoritative, credible input on an extensive range of food-related issues" (ibid., 405). The Council also built the capacity of community actors to identify their own needs, write grant applications, and influence policy (ibid.). Furthermore, much of the organizing focuses not on the "act of convening" but "convening to act," ensuring that meetings are productive and action oriented (Mah & Thang, 2013, 107).

Buffalo food advocates similarly built a diverse coalition of food systems organizations that worked together for decades to transform the city's food system, with members who crossed disciplines (agriculture, environment, public health), age, governance groups (local government, farmers groups, residents), and geographic lines (urban and rural farmers). Connecting these networks strengthened the power of their demands, but as Raja et al. (2014) describe, it also provided local government officials a single place where they could engage diverse stakeholders. The coalition also offered community trainings on how to participate effectively in city-run planning forums, including an opportunity to offer input on the city's 30-year-old land-use plan and 60-year-old zoning code (ibid.).

In contrast to these cases, several examples demonstrate how failing to tap into existing networks and local knowledge can derail even the most well-financed food systems planning efforts that have high-level political support. This happened in Bolivia, for instance, where nutrition policy entrepreneurs had a rare window of opportunity to launch the Zero Malnutrition Program, an evidence-based, systems approach to reduce child malnutrition across the country. Despite being part of the election platform of the newly installed President Morales in 2007, as well as having unprecedented financial and programmatic support from international agencies, the NGO community, and many national ministries, Zero Malnutrition coordinators did not build adequate awareness, buy-in, and capacity among frontline staff and the broader public, significantly weakening the programme's implementation (Hoey & Pelletier, 2011). This mirrored a similar failure to implement systems-based nutrition policy plans in a 1970s' initiative that targeted 26 countries and was led by a team of multiple universities, international experts, and bilateral donors, but which sought little input and buy-in from local decision makers (Field, 1987; Levinson & McLachlan, 1999) The same situation occurred at the city level in Stellenbosch, South Africa, where the city council adopted a university-commissioned food systems strategy and recommendation to form a food policy council, neither of which was implemented (Haysom, 2015). Without fully engaging existing food security organizations, especially those that were distrustful of local government, and by adopting ideas that had been developed in the Global North, Haysom reflected that there was a missed opportunity to go more slowly to develop a collaborative, "home-grown" strategy based on local knowledge (ibid., 275).

Preparing ready-made solutions and codifying a focus on food

Another element that was common across cases where food systems planning took hold was the preparation of ready-made solutions that urban planners could draw upon to secure funding or to insert ideas in official planning documents or practices once windows of opportunity emerged. Ideas sometimes came from earlier government-run programmes or grassroots actions that offered precedents for particular interventions (Chappell, 2018; Reynolds & Cohen, 2016), but most often they were proposed in unofficial food strategies, food charters, and other vision statements prepared by food policy councils or networks of civil society groups. The official adoption of food systems actions in policies, plans, new departments, laws, or acts then created "intermediate points of no return at planning, policy, legal and institutional levels" (Cabannes & Marocchino, 2018, 32). As policy sustainability theorists describe it, such codification becomes a "fixed costs" for a local government, creating a "path dependency" that makes it harder to reverse course and offers advocates leverage to keep building further action (Pierson, 2000, 251).

In Belo Horizonte, for instance, after a newly elected mayor from the Workers Party launched the Municipal Food and Nutritional Security Secretariat, the directors of the Secretariat launched 27 food systems programmes in its first three years, from 1993 to 1996 (Chappell, 2018). They drew from ideas proposed by the popular, national movement, the Citizen's Action Movement for Hunger and Poverty and For Life (ibid.). They also looked at decades of experimentation and earlier innovations, reviving programmes that had been implemented for short periods, both locally in Belo Horizonte (e.g., the Popular Restaurants programme, the first of which opened in 1943) (Delgado, 2018) and at the federal level (e.g., School Meals, Popular Basket, and Straight from the Countryside farmers market programmes) (Chappell, 2018). Even programmes that had been attempted and failed 20 years prior, Chappell argues, showed some level of technical and financial feasibility, and they offered a basis on which to make improvements, "softening up" public and political support to implement modified versions (ibid., 122). Once in place, the Secretariat and most programmes have persisted, even after several generations of mayors, making Belo Horizonte the basis of the national Fome Cero Program and a global model for what food systems planning can accomplish (ibid.).[2]

In New York City, a series of unofficial visions and plans, alongside numerous city- and grassroots-led actions and efforts to fortify coalitions of diverse stakeholders, paved much of the way for action today. In the 2000s, two unofficial food visions, *FoodNYC* and *Food Works*, spearheaded by elected food policy entrepreneurs – a borough president and council member – were written with a broad base of stakeholders to demonstrate the possibility of a more systems-based approach than the health-focused nutrition interventions the city was starting to implement (Campbell, 2016). According to Campbell (2016), these visions then mobilized community gardeners to make sure that the 2011 update to the city's official comprehensive plan, *PlaNYC*, included an entire chapter on food and numerous initiatives introduced by *FoodNYC* and *Food Works*. The election of Mayor de Blasio in 2013, who made equity and social justice the basis of his administration, then led to a cascade of other initiatives, including the City Council's 2019 platform, "Growing Food Equity in New York City," along with 14 bills, two resolutions (Cohen & Ilieva, 2020) and, most recently, the first 10-year food policy plan titled "Food Forward NYC" (City of New York, 2021).

In Vancouver and Toronto, it was the initial insertion of food systems into official city plans that helped create a ripple effect. The Vancouver plan gave residents as well as policy entrepreneurs within the local government a mandate to advocate for even more change, whether to compete for funding with other departments or to apply for external grants, start conversations, generate more buy-in and cooperation from other departments, and survive administrative turnover (Buchan et al., 2019). Exactly how policy entrepreneurs succeeded in getting food systems into official planning documents is unclear in Vancouver, but the turn of events in Toronto shows what it means to be ever vigilant for opportunities to make significant, even if only symbolic, headway. Although efforts had been underway since the late 1990s, including a city food charter and food policy council, food was still not recognized by the Toronto planning department in the early 2000s. When city planners developed the first draft of a new official plan in 2002, it only mentioned food once (Wekerle, 2004). Two subsequent reports submitted by the Toronto Food Policy Council that offered detailed recommendations for ways planning could address food security produced no responses from the planning department, nor did requests to meet (Roberts, 2014). However, the Council co-chairs seized upon the opportunity when they learned that conservative and far-left groups threatened to attack the official plan only two days before printing. Knowing that the Council was well respected, the co-chairs promised that the Council would come out in support of the official plan in exchange for the chance to insert food throughout (ibid.). While these last-minute changes had to be minor – many one-word insertions of "food" – Roberts (2014, 134) recognized it as a win, a "thin edge of the wedge into the planning process" that gave the planning department a mandate to begin to pay attention to food, which helped spark more official partnerships with the Council over time.

Strategic framing to appeal to people's interests

Policy entrepreneurs in the cities profiled here also found ways to frame food systems issues and associated solutions so that they appealed to the interests of decision makers. Conversely, some learned to strategically avoid "semantic traps," in which food systems language can create opposition for proposed actions (Ilieva, 2020, 400). Coordinators of the Minnesota Good Food Charter (Berneche et al., 2017), for instance, learned that conservative elected officials often looked for key words like "equity," "justice," and "root causes" in policy proposals, which would trigger them to not adopt certain policy recommendations (4). This led the Charter coordinators to adopt a "strategic communications framing" to train food policy councils about ways to influence local planners to incorporate food systems topics into formal planning documents. Research conducted by the Frameworks Institute in Minnesota (Bales, 2006; Bales & Grady, 2005) suggested that "*Legacy*, or creating a healthy food system for future generations...and *Protection*, making sure the food supply is dependable and trustworthy" were the two "master frames" that resonated best with a wide audience of government staff in Minnesota and prompted support for food systems change, as did "fairness" or the idea of ensuring equal access to resources with rural audiences (Berneche et al., 2017, 5) A separate study conducted by the Minnesota Planning Association on enhancing health equity planning also found that planners responded well to the general frame of "health," but not when it was linked to health "disparities," "race," or "equity" (ibid., 9). Based on their experience, the

Charter coordinators concluded, "Don't change what you say – choose the strategic way to say it" (ibid., 10).

In addition to literally adding "food" to official plans when given the chance, the Toronto Food Policy Council thinks strategically about the way it frames issues so that diverse units of government see how a focus on food can achieve their goals (Roberts, 2014). Their guiding mantra, based on what Wendy Mendes (Vancouver's food planner at the time) once stated, is: "It's not what a city can do for food, but what food can do for a city" (ibid., 138). Mah and Thang describe this as seeing "food as the vehicle and not necessarily the object of policy change" (2013, 105), or what Ilieva describes as being able to "see food in all policies" in order to identify the variety of places where food planning could be inserted, even "in disguise" (2020, 401). In developing Toronto's first food charter, for instance, the Council centred food security and recommended programmes they saw as "win-win combinations that benefit the community, environment, economy, public health and also the City's budget" (Blay-Palmer, 2009, 407). After struggling for a few years to get urban planners' attention (Wekerle, 2004), Council leaders also learned how to be more strategic about their framing by intentionally learning about the urban planning process and planners' priorities. They supported other projects that planners were leading, such as pedestrian and transit issues; mentored urban planning student projects; recruited a planning scholar to the Council; spoke at planning conferences, and more (Roberts, 2014).

In Waterloo, Canada, health staff were the initial proponents of developing a comprehensive approach to addressing food insecurity. They were strategic about their use of framing to "create a climate of change" that targeted urban and regional planning staff (Wegener et al., 2012, 4107). After health staff heard that the planning department was becoming concerned with urban growth containment and protection of prime agricultural land, they started learning about the interests of planners, even hiring a public health staff member with experience in land-use planning. They also framed issues, like food deserts, in ways that would resonate with planners, talking about neighbourhood "walkability" and using community-level data that showed a preference among residents to walk to food stores (ibid., 4114).

Conversely, in New York City, according to Campbell (2016, 298), urban agriculture advocates had been adept at protecting garden sites for decades, but they were not savvy about "working with the administration's channels for making policy changes" to scale up their grassroots efforts. As one government staffer stated, activists would approach city officials as if, "well, we've already figured it out – you just need to get on board" (ibid., 298). Urban planners thought of urban agriculture as competing with affordable housing and did not see how the demands of urban agriculture activists could be "actionable" (ibid.). Urban agriculture advocates eventually learned how to capture planners' attention when they shifted their framing, proposing a local and regional food *systems* lens in plans they drafted, which Campbell says effectively brought in other allies under a "large tent," including "anti-hunger activists, rural producers, locavore consumers, and public health advocates" (ibid., 302).

Another lesson out of Belo Horizonte suggests the need to remind critical government departments of the *continuing* relevance of food systems. One reason that the newly established Belo Horizonte Secretariat for Nutrition and Food Security was able to roll out 27 new food systems programmes in the first three years was because it was able to enlist the support of many government departments, even when food security was a new concept. Secretariat directors launched a study commission and a series of seminars on malnutrition and food security with health administrators, education staff, economists, and social workers to help them uncover the food issues that existed in their city and how actions supported other department priorities (Chappell, 2018). More than 20 years later, however, other issues, like affordable housing, eventually came to dominate the city's priorities. While the most effective and established food systems programmes continue, reaching the poorest communities and least-resourced farmers was still a challenge, among other programmatic weaknesses caused by insufficient funding or attention (ibid.). Chappell argues that although the Secretariat "rests on the idea that food security is multisectoral, that does not mean that working on food security automatically addresses all other sectors," it requires actively and regularly showing how food systems continue to help other departments accomplish their priorities (ibid., 129).

Conclusion

Although food is less of a "stranger" to the planning field than it once was (Pothukuchi & Kaufman, 2000), there are still major blind spots. The cities profiled in this chapter, however, demonstrate that it is possible for policy entrepreneurs and other food systems advocates to help cities more firmly establish food systems as part of planning practice. Each case shows how the time horizon is usually long and may not always follow a linear, forward movement, but even a successive wave of small wins can eventually build systemic change. The broader lesson learned is that savvy policy entrepreneurs can create the conditions necessary for windows to open by being prepared with ready-made solutions, building and leveraging broad support to sustain momentum, including the cultivation of even more policy entrepreneurs, and strategically framing problems and solutions to capture political attention.

As cities are increasingly recognized as linchpins for reversing many of the interconnected health, environmental, and economic inequities attributed to food systems (Blay-Palmer et al., 2018; IPCC, 2019) more policy process stories about efforts to institutionalize food systems planning are needed. Policy process research is especially lacking in the Global South, where the mix of food systems actors, power dynamics, and governance models often differs, and where livelihoods, public health outcomes, and ecological challenges are more precarious than in the Global North.

In cases where the state is absent or even causing structural violence, efforts to shape food systems will likely continue to work through grassroots efforts and social movements, which currently act as the de facto food systems "planners" in many cities in the Global South (Haysom et al., 2020). In many cases, incremental, easy policy wins may have to sustain these activists in the short term, as the time horizon for achieving bigger gains may be even more protracted than the decades it took most of the North American cities profiled here. In some cases, however, if major political changes occur, radical policy change may be possible nearly overnight, as happened in Bolivia (Hoey & Pelletier, 2011) and Belo Horizonte (Chappell, 2018).

A related question that must be considered in any given context, but especially the Global South, is whether formalized planning strategies will do more harm than good. Considering the context of South Africa, Haysom et al. argue, "For many urban residents, formal planning not only excludes them, it often turns them into criminals or at best, beggars, dependent on the largess of city officials or other gatekeepers" (2020, 68). In the United States, too, historical distrust of government can lead individuals to actively avoid sharing their food systems innovations as potential strategies for institutionalizing enabling policies, out of fear that city involvement could stifle their under-the-radar initiatives (Hoey & Sponseller, 2018). In the Global South, research is particularly limited about strategies for convincing urban planners to support a human rights-based approach to engaging the corporate retail sector in a way that allows the informal sector to thrive. These types of systems-based strategies will be especially critical as part of the recovery from COVID-19, which devastated many informal food economies (Béné, 2020; ILO, 2020).

Future research might also consider the types of institutions and sectors from which food systems policy entrepreneurs tend to originate. Haysom et al. argue that "While there are a number of options open to local governments [for institutionalizing food systems planning], one of the most strategic and transversal approaches is through planning and urban design" (2020, iv). In the cities studied here, however, urban planners were rarely the first to launch food systems policies and plans, though they were the targets of policy entrepreneurs coming mainly from public health departments and coalitions of scholar-activists and grassroots groups, a pattern also found by other scholars (e.g., Hammelman et al., 2020; Mui et al., 2018). It may be worth considering whether certain government units are more amenable and enabled to engage more quickly in multidimensional food systems planning.

Notes

1 See www.milanurbanfoodpolicypact.org/.
2 See Chapter 22 by Drimie in this volume for a discussion of participatory budgeting and urban food governance in Belo Horizonte.

References

Andrée, P., Clark, J. K., Levkoe, C. Z., & Lowitt, K. (Eds.). (2019). *Civil Society and Social Movements in Food System Governance* (1st ed.). Routledge. https://doi.org/10.4324/9780429503597

APA (American Planning Association). (2020). *Food Systems Division: About*. https://apafig.wordpress.com/about/

Arnold, G. (2015). Street-level Policy Entrepreneurship. *Public Management Review*, 17(3), 307–327. https://doi.org/10.1080/14719037.2013.806577

Bales, S. N. (2006). Framing the Food System. *FrameWorks Institute*. www.frameworksinstitute.org/publication/framing-the-food-system/

Bales, S. N., & Grady, J. (2005). *Talking Rural Issues*. FrameWorks Institute. www.frameworksinstitute.org/publication/talking-rural-issues/

Battersby, J. (2017). Food System Transformation in the Absence of Food System Planning: The Case of Supermarket and Shopping Mall Retail Expansion in Cape Town, South Africa. *Built Environment*, 43(3), 417–430. https://doi.org/10.2148/benv.43.3.417

Battersby, J., & Watson, V. (Eds.). (2018). *Urban Food Systems Governance and Poverty in African Cities* (1st ed.). Routledge. https://doi.org/10.4324/9781315191195

Béné, C. (2020). Resilience of Local Food Systems and Links to Food Security – A Review of Some Important Concepts in the Context of COVID-19 and Other Shocks. *Food Security*, 12, 805–822.

Berneche, N., Adamek, M., Weiss, E., & Goebel, M. (2017). Communications Framing for Food System Change with Local Governments. *Minnesota Food Charter*. http://mnfoodcharter.com/wp-content/uploads/2018/08/Framing-Food-Access.pdf

Blay-Palmer, A. (2009). The Canadian Pioneer: The Genesis of Urban Food Policy in Toronto. *International Planning Studies*, 14(4), 401–416. https://doi.org/10.1080/13563471003642837

Blay-Palmer, A., Santini, G., Dubbeling, M., Renting, H., Taguchi, M., & Giordano, T. (2018). Validating the City Region Food System Approach: Enacting Inclusive, Transformational City Region Food Systems. *Sustainability*, 10(5), 1680. https://doi.org/10.3390/su10051680

Buchan, R., Cloutier, D. S., & Friedman, A. (2019). Transformative Incrementalism: Planning for Transformative Change in Local Food Systems. *Progress in Planning*, 134, 100424. https://doi.org/10.1016/j.progress.2018.07.002

Cabannes, Y. (2012). Pro-poor Legal and Institutional Frameworks for Urban and Peri-Urban Agriculture. *Food and Agriculture Organization of the United Nations*.

Cabannes, Y., & Marocchino, C. (Eds.). (2018). *Integrating Food into Urban Planning*. UCL Press. https://doi.org/10.2307/j.ctv513dv1

Campbell, L. K. (2016). Getting Farming on the Agenda: Planning, Policymaking, and Governance Practices of Urban Agriculture in New York City. *Urban Forestry & Urban Greening*, 19, 295–305. https://doi.org/10.1016/j.ufug.2016.03.011

Chappell, M. J. (2018). Beginning to End Hunger: Food and the Environment in Belo Horizonte, Brazil, and Beyond. University of California Press. https://doi.org/10.1525/9780520966338

City of New York. (2021). *Food Forward NYC: City Releases 10-Year Food Policy Plan*. www1.nyc.gov/office-of-the-mayor/news/123-21/food-forward-nyc-city-releases-10-year-food-policy-plan#:~:text=NEW%20YORK%E2%80%94Mayor%20Bill%20de,all%20New%20Yorkers%20that%20addresses

Clark, J., Freedgood, J., Irish, A., Hodgson, K., & Raja, S. (2017). Fail to Include, Plan to Exclude: Reflections on Local Governments' Readiness for Building Equitable Community Food Systems. *Built Environment*, 43(3), 315–327. https://doi.org/10.2148/benv.43.3.315

Cohen, N., & Ilieva, R. T. (2020). Expanding the Boundaries of Food Policy: The Turn to Equity in New York City. *Food Policy*, 102012. https://doi.org/10.1016/j.foodpol.2020.102012

Deener, A. (2020). *The Problem with Feeding Cities: The Social Transformation of Infrastructure, Abundance, and Inequality in America*. University of Chicago Press.

Delgado, C. (2018). Integrating Food Distribution and Food Accessibility into Municipal Planning: Achievements and Challenges of a Brazilian Metropolis, Belo Horizonte. In Y. Cabannes & C. Marocchino (Eds.), *Integrating Food into Urban Planning*. UCL Press.

Dubbeling, M., & Dueñas, A. (2016). A Metropolitan Agriculture Programme for the Promotion of Integrated Territorial Planning. In GIZ, FAO, & RUAF Foundation (Eds.), *City Region Food Systems and Food Waste Management: Linking Urban and Rural Areas for Sustainable and Resilient Development*. FAO.

Dubbeling, M., & Terrile, R. (2016). Operationalizing Urban–Rural Linkages through the Preservation and Improved Use of Peri-Urban Agricultural Land. In GIZ, FAO, & RUAF Foundation (Eds.), *City Region Food Systems and Food Waste Management: Linking Urban and Rural Areas for Sustainable and Resilient Development*. FAO.

FAO (Food and Agriculture Organization). (2020). *City Region Food Systems Program: Reinforcing Rural–Urban Linkages for Resilient Food Systems*. FAO. www.fao.org/in-action/food-for-cities-programme/approach-old/crfs/en/

Field, J. (1987). Multisectoral Nutrition Planning—A Postmortem. *Food Policy*, 12, 15–28.

Frimpong Boamah, E., Sumberg, J., & Raja, S. (2020). Farming within a Dual Legal Land System: An Argument for Emancipatory Food Systems Planning in Accra, Ghana. *Land Use Policy*, 92, 104391. https://doi.org/10.1016/j.landusepol.2019.104391

Gianfelici, F., Lançon, L., Bucatariu, C., Dubbeling, M., Santini, G., Ocampo, G., & Velasquez, A. (2016). Reduction and Recycling of Urban Waste in Support of Adequate Urban Diets and Prevention of On-farm Food. In GIZ, FAO, & RUAF Foundation (Eds.), *City Region Food Systems and Food Waste Management: Linking Urban and Rural Areas for Sustainable and Resilient Development*. FAO.

Giordano, T., Ledant, C., & Martino, D. (2018). *The Role of Cities in the Transformation of Food Systems: Sharing Lessons from Milan Pact Cities*. FAO.

Hammelman, C., Levkoe, C., Agyeman, J., Kharod, S., Moragues Faus, A., Munoz, E., Oliva, J., & Wilson, A. (2020). Integrated Food Systems Governance: Scaling Equitable and Transformative Food Initiatives through Scholar-Activist Engagement. *Journal of Agriculture, Food Systems, and Community Development*, 1–16. https://doi.org/10.5304/jafscd.2020.092.003

Hanleybrown, F., Kania, J., & Kramer, M. (2012). *Channeling Change: Making Collective Impact Work*. *Stanford Social Innovation Review*. Leland Stanford Jr. University.

Harper, A., Shattuck, A., Holt-Giménez, E., Alkon, A., & Lambrick, F. (2009). *Food Policy Councils: Lessons Learned*. Food First.

Haysom, G. (2015). Food and the City: Urban Scale Food System Governance. *Urban Forum*, 26(3), 263–281. https://doi.org/10.1007/s12132-015-9255-7

Haysom, G., Battersby, J., & Park-Ross, R. (2020). *Food Sensitive Planning and Urban Design – A Blueprint for a Future South African City?* Food Security SA, Working Paper Series, No. 007.

Hodgson, K., & Moreau, T. (2019). Urban and Regional Planning for Biodiversity and Food Systems. In I. W. Hawkins (Ed.), *Promoting Biodiversity in Food Systems* (pp. 211–228). Boca Raton, FL: CRC Press.

Hoey, L., & Pelletier, D. L. (2011). Bolivia's Multisectoral Zero Malnutrition Program: Insights on Commitment, Collaboration, and Capacities. *Food and Nutrition Bulletin*, 32(2_suppl2), S70–S81. https://doi.org/10.1177/15648265110322S204

Hoey, L., & Sponseller, A. (2018). "It's Hard to Be Strategic When Your Hair Is on Fire": Alternative Food Movement Leaders' Motivation and Capacity to Act. *Agriculture and Human Values*, 35(3), 595–609. https://doi.org/10.1007/s10460-018-9850-z

Ilieva, R. (2020). Urban Food Planning: A New Frontier for City and Regenerative Food System Builders. In J. Duncan, M. Carolan, & J. S. C. Wiskerke (Eds.), *Routledge Handbook of Sustainable and Regenerative Food Systems*. Routledge.

ILO (International Labor Organization). (2020). *ILO Monitor: COVID-19 and the World of Work* (3rd Ed.). ILO. www.ilo.org/wcmsp5/groups/public/@dgreports/@dcomm/documents/briefingnote/wcms_743146.pdf

IPCC (Intergovernmental Panel on Climate Change). (2019). *Climate Change and Land: An IPCC Special Report on Climate Change, Desertification, Land Degradation, Sustainable Land Management, Food Security, and Greenhouse Gas Fluxes in Terrestrial Ecosystems*. IPCC.

Juriaans, K. (2020). COVID-19 and the Chance for Fairer, more Resilient Food Systems. FAO. www.fao.org/in-action/food-for-cities-programme/news/detail/en/c/1294368/

Kingdon, J. (2003). *Agendas, Alternatives, and Public Policies*. Addison-Wesley.

Levinson, F. J., & McLachlan, M. (1999). How Did We Get Here? A History of International Nutrition. In T. J. Marchione (Ed.), *Scaling Up, Scaling Down: Overcoming Malnutrition in Developing Countries*. Gordon Breach Publishers.

Lindblom, C. (1959). The Science of Muddling Through. *Public Administration Review*, 19, 79–88.

Lipsky, M. (2010). *Street-Level Bureaucracy Dilemmas of the Individual in Public Services*. Russell Sage.

Mah, C. L., & Thang, H. (2013). Cultivating Food Connections: The Toronto Food Strategy and Municipal Deliberation on Food. *International Planning Studies*, 18(1), 96–110. https://doi.org/10.1080/13563475.2013.750941

Mintrom, M., & Norman, P. (2009). Policy Entrepreneurship and Policy Change. *The Policy Studies Journal*, 37(4), 649–667.

MUFPP (Milan Urban Food Policy Pact). (2015). *Milan Urban Food Policy Pact*. www.milanurbanfoodpolicypact.org/wp-content/uploads/2016/06/Milan-Urban-Food-Policy-Pact-EN.pdf

Mui, Y., Khojasteh, M., Hodgson, K., & Raja, S. (2018). Rejoining the Planning and Public Health Fields: Leveraging Comprehensive Plans to Strengthen Food Systems in an Urban versus Rural Jurisdiction. *Journal of Agriculture, Food Systems, and Community Development*, 8(Supp. 2), 73–93. https://doi.org/10.5304/jafscd.2018.08B.004

OECD (Organization for Economic Cooperation and Development). (2020). *COVID-19 and Global Food Systems*. OECD.

Pierson, P. (2000). Increasing Returns, Path Dependence, and the Study of Politics. *American Political Science Review*, 94(2), 251–267. http://dx.doi.org/10.2307/2586011

Pothukuchi, K., & Kaufman, J. L. (2000). The Food System: A Stranger to the Planning Field. *Journal of the American Planning Association*, 66(2), 113–124. https://doi.org/10.1080/01944360008976093

Raja, S., Picard, D., Baek, S., & Delgado, C. (2014). Rustbelt Radicalism: A Decade of Food Systems Planning Practice in Buffalo, New York (USA). *Journal of Agriculture, Food Systems, and Community Development*, 4(4), 173–189. https://doi.org/10.5304/jafscd.2014.044.015

Reynolds, K., & Cohen, N. (2016). *Beyond the Kale: Urban Agriculture and Social Justice Activism in New York City*. The University of Georgia Press.

Robert, N., & Mullinix, K. (2018). Municipal Policy Enabling Regional Food Systems in British Columbia, Canada: Assessing Focal Areas and Gaps. *Journal of Agriculture, Food Systems, and Community Development*, 8(2), 115–132. https://doi.org/10.5304/jafscd.2018.08B.003

Roberts, W. (2014). *Food for City Building: A Field Guide for Planners, Actionists and Entrepreneurs*. E-Book.

Santo, R., Yong, R., & Palmer, A. (2014). Collaboration Meets Opportunity: The Baltimore Food Policy Initiative. *Journal of Agriculture, Food Systems, and Community Development*, 4(3), 193–208. https://doi.org/10.5304/jafscd.2014.043.012

Skinner, C. (2018). Contributing yet Excluded? Informal Food Retail in African Cities. In J. Battersby & V. Watson (Eds.), *Urban Food Systems Governance and Poverty in African Cities*. Routledge.

Smit, W. (2016). Urban Governance and Urban Food Systems in Africa: Examining the Linkages. *Cities*, 58, 80–86. https://doi.org/10.1016/j.cities.2016.05.001

Sonnino, R., & Beynon, B. (2015). Rethinking Food Governance: Urban Innovations. In M. Deakin, D. Diamantini, & N. Borrelli (Eds.), *The Governance of City Food Systems* (pp. 35–48). Fondazione Giangiacomo Feltrinelli.

Sonnino, R., & Coulson, H. (2020). Unpacking the New Urban Food Agenda: The Changing Dynamics of Global Governance in the Urban Age. *Urban Studies*, 58(5), 1032–1049. https://doi.org/10.1177/0042098020942036

Steele, C. (2011). *Hungry City: How Food Shapes Our Lives*. Random House.

Steyn, N., Mchiza, Z., Hill, J., Davids, Y., Venter, I., Hinrichsen, E., Opperman, M., Rumbelow, J., & Jacobs, P. (2013). Nutritional Contribution of Street Foods to the Diet of People in Developing Countries: A Systematic Review. *Public Health Nutrition*, 17(6), 1363–1374.

van Bers, C., Delaney, A., Eakin, H., Cramer, L., Purdon, M., Oberlack, C., Evans, T., Pahl-Wostl, C., Eriksen, S., Jones, L., Korhonen-Kurki, K., & Vasileiou, I. (2019). Advancing the Research Agenda on Food Systems Governance and Transformation. *Current Opinion in Environmental Sustainability*, 39, 94–102. https://doi.org/10.1016/j.cosust.2019.08.003

von Massow, M., Parizeau, K., Gallant, M., Wickson, M., Haines, J., Ma, D. W. L., Wallace, A., Carroll, N., & Duncan, A. M. (2019). Valuing the Multiple Impacts of Household Food Waste. *Frontiers in Nutrition*, 6, 143. https://doi.org/10.3389/fnut.2019.00143

Wegener, J., Raine, K. D., & Hanning, R. M. (2012). Insights into the Government's Role in Food System Policy Making: Improving Access to Healthy, Local Food Alongside Other Priorities. *International Journal of Environmental Research and Public Health*, 9(11), 4103–4121. https://doi.org/10.3390/ijerph9114103

Wekerle, G. R. (2004). Food Justice Movements: Policy, Planning, and Networks. *Journal of Planning Education and Research*, 23(4), 378–386. https://doi.org/10.1177/0739456X04264886

Winne, M. (2017). *Stand Together or Starve Alone: Unity and Chaos in the US Food Movement*. ABC-CLIO.

Zimmerer, K. S., & de Haan, S. (2020). Informal Food Chains and Agrobiodiversity Need Strengthening—Not Weakening—To Address Food Security amidst the COVID-19 Crisis in South America. *Food Security*, 12(4), 891–894. https://doi.org/10.1007/s12571-020-01088-x

17

PUBLIC PROCUREMENT AS A TOOL IN URBAN FOOD GOVERNANCE IN BRAZIL

Luciene Burlandy, Cecilia Rocha and Patricia Camacho Dias

Introduction

The global syndemic of obesity, undernutrition, and climate change (Swinburn et al., 2019) highlights the need for a systemic approach to address these problems simultaneously. Solutions require a transformation of food systems toward healthy diets that are also environmentally sustainable and accessible to all (Willet et al., 2019). These solutions demand a paradigm shift from monoculture, industrial food production to more diverse and agroecological food systems (IPES-Food, 2016). All of this must take the present context of higher incidence of poverty among smallholder farmers, increasing urbanization throughout the world, and growing food insecurity and inequality everywhere into account.

While the needed transformation of food systems requires actions at all political levels and by all political agents, there is increasing recognition of the potential contribution of initiatives at local, municipal levels (FAO, 2019). Cities are not only where the majority of the world's population live, they also present high incidences of poverty, food insecurity, overweight, and obesity. Cities are the loci for most food commercialization and of much food waste, and they are "critical hotspots for experiencing the shocks and stresses of climate change" (FAO, 2019, p. 2). Municipal policies are thus an important entry point to address the global syndemic.

Few policy tools available to municipal governments have as much potential to contribute to the transformation of food systems as Public Food Procurement (PFP) (FAO, 2018). PFP impacts food systems beyond urban jurisdictions and helps validate a "city region food system approach" to governance (Blay-Palmer et al., 2018). PFP can create, stimulate, and support the transformative development of food supply chains and promote sustainable diets (Sonnino, 2019; Swensson, 2015). It has been implemented in different countries as an integrated tool of innovation policy to promote sustainability (Edler & Georghiou, 2007), together with socially oriented goals, such as integrating vulnerable and marginalized groups into the economy (Kanapinskas et al., 2014). Given such potential, PFP is a strategic policy tool for achieving just, sustainable, and healthier food systems.

While PFP has been practiced in many countries for many years (Stefani et al., 2017), Brazil was the first country to develop an institutional food procurement program connecting the

DOI: 10.4324/9781003055907-20

support for smallholder farmers to urban public initiatives, thus integrating production and consumption within a food and nutrition security policy (Swensson, 2015). As part of a set of instruments introduced since 2003, PFP has become an integral part of a National System for Food and Nutrition Security.

In this chapter, we look at two PFP programs in operation in Brazil: the Food Acquisition Program (*Programa de Acquisição de Alimentos – PAA*), started in 2003; and the food procurement component under the National School Food Program (*Programa Nacional de Alimentação Escolar – PNAE*), in place since 2009. Based on the literature and our personal observations of the execution of these programs in different parts of Brazil, we describe their main characteristics and identify the challenges in their implementation at the municipal level. We start, however, by describing the Brazilian context within which these programs emerged.

The Zero Hunger Strategy and the National System for Food and Nutrition Security

Launched in 2003, Brazil's Zero Hunger strategy has since attracted much attention in the world for three main reasons (Rocha, 2009, 2015). First, it was one of the key instruments helping the country reduce extreme poverty, malnutrition, child mortality rates, and general food insecurity (Silva et al., 2010). Second, it introduced bold and innovative government programs, such as the PFP programs described in this chapter, as well as many others. Third, it encouraged diverse channels for popular participation through tripartite (government, private sector, and civil society) social councils, thus exemplifying new forms of governance for food policy.

A food system approach can be detected when one looks at the list of programs composing the Zero Hunger strategy (Table 17.1). Increasing access to food was the main concern, but the strategy also aimed at supporting smallholder food producers, increasing income-generating opportunities for low-income groups, promoting healthy eating, providing food and nutrition education, and engaging civil society in the fight against hunger.

At the national level, the National Council for Food and Nutrition Security (CONSEA), an advisory body to the President on policies and general guidelines for food and nutrition security, played a decisive role in promoting and maintaining the systemic and inter-sectoral approach of the Zero Hunger strategy. With two-thirds of its members coming from civil society and the private sector and one-third from the federal government, CONSEA had representatives from labor unions, business associations, the food industry, religious groups, professional associations, academics, and nongovernmental organizations representing family farmers, Indigenous communities, and others. From 2003 until its abolition in January 2019, CONSEA was central to the institutionalization of food and nutrition security policy in the country (Burlandy, 2009; Preiss et al., 2020). In 2006, CONSEA's proposed National Law on Food and Nutrition Security (LOSAN) was adopted. Article 1 of LOSAN "establishes definitions, principles, guidelines, objectives and composition of the National System for Food and Nutrition Security – SISAN, through which the State, with the participation of organized civil society, will formulate and implement policies, plans, programs and actions towards ensuring the human right to adequate food" (Brazil, 2005). LOSAN institutionalized the right to food as both a matter of public policy and an obligation of the state. The Right to Adequate Food was then added to Brazil's constitution in 2010.

In Figure 17.1, we present a schematic illustration of the National System for Food and Nutrition Security (*Sistema Nacional para Segurança Alimentar e Nutricional – SISAN*). In construction since 2006, SISAN establishes the main components of a national system (including

Table 17.1 Zero Hunger Strategy Programs (circa 2004)

I – Food Access	
1.	Bolsa Familia – Family Grant (BF)
2.	National School Meals Programme (PNAE)
3.	Food for Specific Groups
4.	Rainwater Cisterns
5.	Popular Restaurants and Community Kitchens
6.	Food Banks
7.	Urban Agriculture
8.	Food and Nutrition Surveillance System
9.	Distribution of Vitamin A
10.	Distribution of Iron
11.	Food and Nutrition for Indigenous People
12.	FN Education for Consumption
13.	Promotion of Healthy Habits/Healthy Diets
14.	Workers Food Programme (PAT)
15.	Basic Food Basket Tax Reduction
II – Strengthening Family Agriculture	
1.	National Programme for Family Agriculture (PRONAF)
2.	Harvest Insurance
3.	Family Farming Agriculture Insurance
4.	Food Acquisition Programme (PAA)
III – Income Generation	
1.	Social and Professional Training
2.	Solidarity Economy and Productive Inclusion
3.	Food Security and Local Development Consortium
4.	Food and Nutrition Security Organisation
5.	Cooperatives of Recyclable Material Collectors
6.	Guided Productive Micro-credit
IV – Partnership and Civil Society Mobilisation	
1.	Social Assistance Reference Centre
2.	Social Mobilisation and Citizenship Education
3.	Social and Public Agents Capacity Building
4.	Volunteer Work and Donations
5.	Partnership with Private Sector and NGOs
6.	Social Development Councils

Source: Authors' compilation.

the participation of civil society) in the governance of food policy and programs, both at the federal and municipal levels.

SISAN's institutional structure aims to promote participatory governance and policy integration (CAISAN, 2009). SISAN comprises three elements, replicated at both the federal and municipal levels. First, Food and Nutrition Security Councils are composed of civil society organizations (2/3) and different government sectors (1/3). CONSEA is that body at the national level, while COMUSAN is the council at the municipal level. Second, Inter-sectoral Chambers for Food and Nutrition Security (CAISAN) are comprised of different governmental sectors implementing food and nutrition programs. At the national level, typical representatives in the CAISAN would include members from the federal ministries of health, social assistance, environment, education, and agriculture. At the municipal level, members of the secretariats

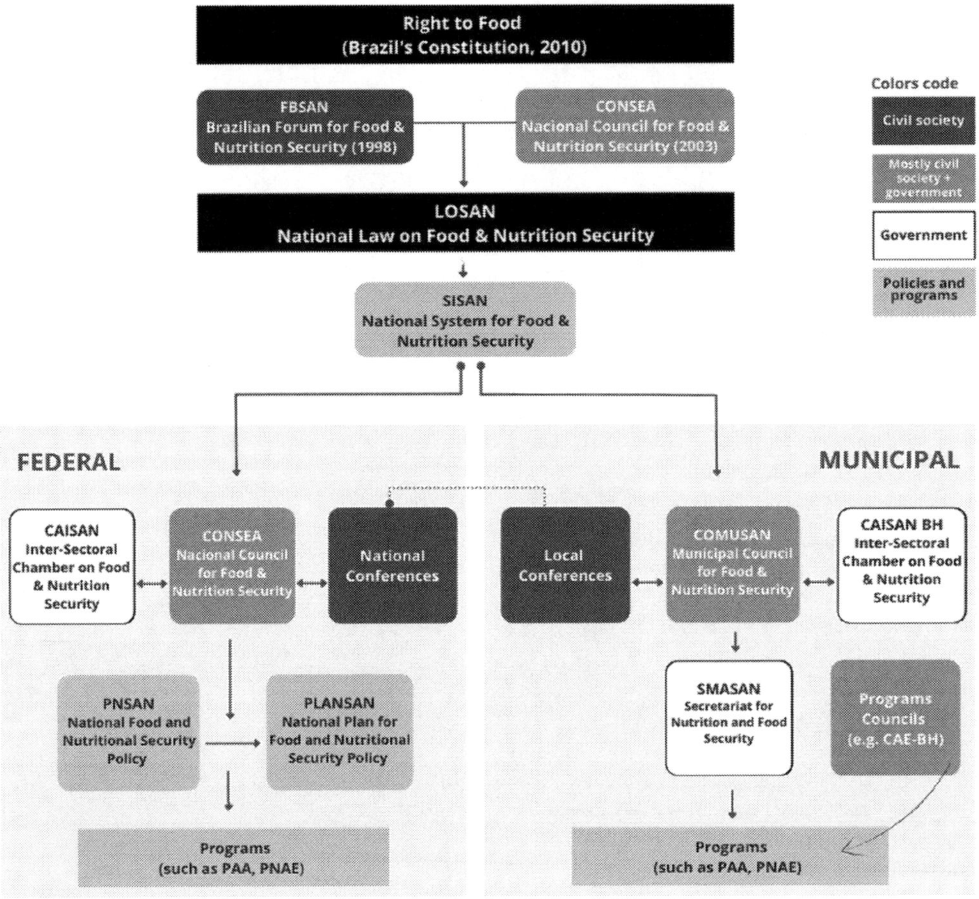

Figure 17.1 Schematic illustration of the National System for Food and Nutrition Security – SISAN
Source: Figure elaborated by C. Rocha.

in these areas would make up the municipal CAISAN. Third, there are conferences that promote participatory decision-making. At these conferences, participants from civil society organizations, academia, and government are responsible for developing policy guidelines and indicating priorities for the Food and Nutrition Security Policy at the national and municipal levels. Through its participation in conferences and councils, civil society contributes to the development, implementation, and monitoring of policies and programs, both at national and local levels.

While each of those three elements (councils, inter-sectoral chambers, and conferences) has specific attributions, they interact through joint processes and procedures. For example, both CAISANs and councils respond to priorities determined at conferences, and policy proposals originating in one of those spaces must be endorsed by the others. Furthermore, CAISAN members also participate in CONSEAs.

Thus, SISAN is a whole system for food and nutrition security, with similar, counterpart components at both the national and local levels. Municipal governments have quite high levels of autonomy in implementing their local parts of this system as long as they include the three main components (councils, inter-sectoral chambers, and conferences). The federal government, however, has a strong role in inducing municipalities to follow SISAN's guidelines through funding transfers for different programs, technical support, and monitoring of actions implemented by urban administrations. Municipal governments can also develop local policies and programs, so long as they do not violate federal legislation.

Unfortunately, the construction of this National System for Food and Nutrition Security was interrupted at the national level by the election of President Jair Bolsonaro, who abolished CONSEA on the very first day of his mandate on January 1, 2019, signaling a desire to move away from participatory democracy. However, the governance structure proposed under SISAN continues in many municipalities, which, as autonomous units in political and management terms, have their own legislation on food and nutrition security. Furthermore, many of the policies and programs introduced between 2003 and 2018 (prior to the Bolsonaro government) are well-established through national and local legislation and are not easily revoked, although some have been weakened by the lack of support from the federal government.

An example of how SISAN continues to be built at municipal levels can be found in Belo Horizonte, a Brazilian city of over 2.5 million people that is renowned for its food policies (see also Chapter 18 by Rocha and Burlandy in this volume). In the bottom part of Figure 17.1, we illustrate the key elements of SISAN at the federal level (on the left) and at the municipal level (on the right), using the case of Belo Horizonte as a municipal example. Besides its Municipal Council for Food and Nutrition Security (COMUSAN) and its Inter-sectoral Chamber for Food and Nutrition Security (CAISAN-BH), Belo Horizonte has a separate municipal department called the Municipal Secretariat for Food and Nutrition Security (SMASAN, later SUSAN) that centralizes all of the city's food programs. This separate municipal department is not a requirement of SISAN (and thus, it is not present in other cities), but it has been a part of how Belo Horizonte has organized its governance for food and nutrition security since the 1990s. A signatory to the Milan Food Pact (FAO, 2019), it is not surprising that Belo Horizonte has continued to implement a systemic food policy, despite the absence of support from the current federal government. A pioneer in developing an integrated policy for food and nutrition security (since 1993), Belo Horizonte actually inspired many of the programs in the federal Zero Hunger strategy adopted in 2003. Although not all cities in Brazil demonstrate such commitment to building SISAN, Belo Horizonte is an example of the possibility and potential of policy initiatives at the municipal level, which thrive under supportive national governments but can also be resilient under adverse political environments.

Food Procurement Programs in Brazil

It was in the inter-sectoral and participatory context of policy frameworks implemented by national governments between 2003 and 2014 that two food procurement programs, PAA and PNAE, emerged in Brazil. The PAA and the food procurement component under PNAE are examples of programs designed with the participation of civil society (through CONSEA, for example), which simultaneously address (1) issues of access to adequate and healthy food by at-risk populations and (2) issues of poverty among smallholder producers and difficulties accessing markets by family farmers (Dias & Oliveira, 2019). Despite its visible and significant presence in urban areas, poverty in Brazil is more prominent in rural areas, and it is often linked to family farming (Marconato et al., 2015). Both programs are devised by the national government and implemented at the municipal level. Municipalities are an autonomous political unity, but for federal programs, such as PAA and PNAE, they receive federal resources for local implementation (although municipalities also have to designate complementary resources for PNAE) and have to follow federal rules regarding each program. The programs are implemented by management units of municipal governments (such as SMASAN in the case of Belo Horizonte). Social control of these programs is implemented by municipal councils of food and nutrition security, which is the municipal school food council in the case of PNAE, and also by some local council of social control established by municipal governments to monitor the PAA. The composition of the local councils follows national rules. Food and nutrition security councils are composed of civil society organizations and different sectors of the government (e.g., agricultural, health, education, social assistance). The school food council is composed of representatives of the municipal government, education workers, parents, and social organizations related to education.

Part of the intent of the Zero Hunger strategy was to improve food consumption practices in institutional settings, such as schools and hospitals, and integrate them into the expansion of sustainable food production. This political process gave prominence to some actors, such as family farmers, and also to some practices, such as diversified agroecological farming, that have been historically marginalized in the context of the dominant industrialized food system (Rocha et al., 2012; Sidaner et al., 2013). Under the institutional design and political process proposed in the SISAN, civil society organizations working on issues related to family farming and agroecological production models, in partnership with organizations working on health and nutrition, became protagonists in the formulation of proposals for food and nutrition security policies (Swensson, 2015).

Brazil is one of the few countries in the world with a legal definition of "family farm". The definition became necessary in 1995 due to policies specifically designed for this group of rural producers. Four conditions must be met for a farm to be classified as a "family farm". Family farms are rural establishments (1) with no greater than four "fiscal modules" (a Brazilian measurement defined regionally and varying throughout the country from 5 to 110 hectares); (2) where work is done mostly by family members; (3) from which the household derives most of its income; and (4) that are managed by the family (Moraes & Rocha, 2016). According to the Brazilian Agricultural Census, 4.3 million rural establishments were in this category (family farms) in 2006, corresponding to 84 percent of all farms. Although family farms occupied only 24.3 percent of the total agricultural area, they produced 38 percent of the country's agricultural value. Moreover, family farms produced the majority of the staple foods consumed by Brazilians and employed 74 percent of the rural labor force (Rocha et al., 2012).

Federal legislation created the PAA in 2003 and set up how the program should be implemented at local levels. Municipalities implement the program according to national rules aiming to support family agriculture and promote smallholder farmers' economic and social inclusion (Chmielewska & Souza, 2010; Moraes & Rocha, 2016). The program fosters institutional markets through governmental purchases (federal, state, or municipal governments, depending on the modalities of the program) of food for social programs and public institutions, such as schools, popular restaurants, community kitchens, food banks, early childhood centers, nursing homes, hospitals, and shelters, most of which are administered at municipal levels. Other objectives of the program include facilitating greater and more frequent access to quality food by people at risk of food and nutrition insecurity; strengthening local and regional networks for food commercialization; promoting and enhancing biodiversity through organic and agroecological food production; encouraging healthy eating habits at local and regional levels; stimulating the development of producers' cooperatives and associations; and building up strategic stocks with family farm products (Swensson, 2015). PAA prioritizes the poorest and most vulnerable family farm producers, and it has developed special modalities to benefit women farmers and traditional community farmer organizations (Grisa et al., 2020).

Each year, the federal government establishes a total budget for the program and the maximum payment allowed for each participating family farm. Funds are transferred to municipal governments as they implement the program. Municipalities must indicate the local foods to be purchased, select producers and institutions receiving the food, define the local social control of the program (local councils), and ensure physical structures and human resources for program implementation at the local level, as well as assist family farmers in obtaining the necessary documents to sell their products to the government.

The PNAE, created in 1955, was extensively reformulated in 2009 to include the requirement that a minimum of 30 percent of the program's funding from the federal government be used for the purchase of products from family farming (Sidaner et al., 2013) for the public school system, which is administered by municipal governments in Brazil. Priority in the PFP under PNAE is given to local producers (closer to the schools where food will be delivered), but the program has also developed special conditions to favor family farmers from land reform settlements, traditional Indigenous and afro-descendant (*quilombola*) communities, and farmer cooperatives (Grisa et al., 2020). Under this legislation, 30 percent of PNAE's R$3.6 billion (approximately US$670 million) federal budget was set aside for buying products from family farms in 2016, with priority given to organic and agroecological produce (FNDE, 2017). As one of the largest social programs in the world, PNAE provides meals to over 42 million students in public schools in Brazil. In May 2020, its legislation was amended to limit the purchase of processed and ultra-processed foods to a maximum of 20 percent of expenditures, with at least 75 percent of the funds spent on the purchase of minimally processed or *in-natura* foods (NUPENS-USP, 2020). These new directives follow the 2014 Food Guide for the Brazilian Population (dietary guideline), and further benefit fruit and vegetable farmers. Also in 2020, during the COVID-19 pandemic, another amendment to the legislation allowed municipalities to deliver school food directly to the families of students while schools remained closed.

The operational design of the PAA and the PNAE is an example of an integrative policy that promotes connections between modes of production, distribution, and consumption of food (Maluf, 2007; Preiss et al., 2020; Sidaner et al., 2013). Their successful implementation, however, required some adjustment to the usual bidding processes and the traditional mechanisms of public procurement stabilized by federal guidelines for all levels of government purchases. A "special public call" for food suppliers in these programs was developed to allow bidding by family farmers only and to prevent legal challenges by larger, corporate producers. Participants in such calls must obtain an Eligibility Declaration from the National Program for Family Agriculture (PRONAF – known as the DAP, from the Brazilian acronym), which certifies that the producer can be classified as a "family farmer" (Aquino & Schneider, 2011). The "special public call" must specify the compliance of the bidding process with government guidelines linked to sustainable development; local, social, and productive inclusion; and the promotion of food and nutrition security (FNDE, 2017). As such, it minimizes the importance of lowest-price disputes among bidders and prioritizes purchases from local and more socially vulnerable producers. Indeed, one of the main factors associated with the success of public procurement for social or environmental goals in many countries is the establishment of specific legislation that guides the process (Cavalcanti et al., 2017).

Another important consideration, particularly for the successful implementation of the PAA in supporting poorer family farmers, was the recognition that these farmers would have significant difficulties in meeting the requirements of the program on their own. A large number of them live in poverty, are less educated, and have limited access to information and public resources. Applying and obtaining the DAP (Eligibility Declaration), participating in the "special public call", and being able to guarantee some minimum supply of food for public programs can be overwhelming for individual farmers. The legislation thus encourages the formation of cooperatives of family farmers to participate in the bidding process (Swensson, 2015). While the federal government is responsible for issuing the DAP, municipal governments must assist family farmers in their surrounding regions in obtaining that document.

These strategies have supported family farming as part of the Brazilian Food and Nutrition Security policy framework (Berchim et al., 2019). Both PAA and PNAE are "successful examples of intersectoral public policies that contribute to the expansion of access, the strengthening of family farming and the promotion of healthy eating" (Bocchi et al., 2019, p. 4). This kind of food procurement strategy connects the needs of both the demand (food security and public nutrition programs) and supply (family farming) sectors (Swensson & Tartanac, 2020) and supports a "socially, economically and environmentally resilient rural economy" (Wittman & Blesh, 2017, p. 100).

While PAA and PNAE are federal programs guided by federal legislation, municipal governments implement them. Federal agencies are responsible for issuing the DAP (identifying who is a family farmer eligible for participating in the programs) and for transferring the appropriate funding to local governments that will execute the procurement according to the relevant bidding process. Municipal governments are responsible for establishing the terms of the bidding process and providing support so local family farms can participate. The amount of funding transferred under PNAE is set by legislation, varying from US$0.19 to US$0.56 per student per school day in 2012 (Sidaner et al., 2013). Municipal governments complement this funding, since they must pay for the kitchen personnel and equipment (all public schools in Brazil are required to have a kitchen). By contrast, annual funding for the PAA is discretionary. As such, while funding for the PNAE is protected by legislation, the PAA is vulnerable to changes in the priorities of the federal government. Furthermore, municipal governments are not required to implement the PAA in their jurisdictions.

Challenges for Urban Governance

Although there is a growing recognition of the PFP's potential to foster a healthier and more sustainable food system, there are also many challenges in the implementation of this policy tool. The rigid "value for money" ethos and a narrow "efficiency" culture, which Soninno (2019) points out as a major barrier to embedding social goals and ethical values in public contracts, were overcome in the case of PAA and PNAE by developing a differentiated bidding process for these programs. At the same time that specific legislation and differentiated bidding processes made the transformation of food procurement into a social policy tool possible, they introduced complexities not always understood or appreciated by the local civil servants who were responsible for their implementation. Trained on, and used to following, strict minimum-cost criteria for other public procurement processes, local civil servants need clear directives to adapt their decision-making procedures to the special circumstances surrounding the PAA and PNAE. The differentiated mechanism governing these programs (procurement method, mandatory participation requirements, terms of payment, procedures for publishing tender opportunities, size of contracts) increases the "bureaucratic burden" on local governments (Swensson, 2015; Swensson & Tartanac, 2020). Instead of looking only at "lowest cost", local officials have to consider other criteria, such as the geographical location of potential suppliers (favoring those closer to schools in the case of PNAE) and if the value of each contract falls under the maximum payment allowed in the program (in the case of PAA).

In addition to this "bureaucratic burden", changes in federal legislation and federal processes initially created uncertainty and reluctance among local civil servants in some municipalities over how to implement the PNAE and the PAA. Indeed, the local PFP implementation process often faces some difficulties when local actors interpret new federal laws that allow for exceptions to long-standing rules. The local operationalization of new nationally established purchasing mechanisms and legislation requires time for institutional learning (Soninno, 2019). Local civil servants may also feel uncertain about dealing with suppliers (rural, smallholder family farmers) they do not know well and with whom they are not used to dealing. Up until very recently, smallholder family farmers belonged among "invisible" groups, without much power and without claims on urban resources (Saraiva et al., 2013). Overcoming these uncertainties demands a "strong leadership at political, administrative, cultural and commercial level and a cross-departmental commitment and cooperation" (Smith et al., 2016, p. 252).

Family farmers operating in lands within an urban jurisdiction, a very common situation in large cities, face a particular bureaucratic challenge. These urban producers are not recognized as "farmers" by the legislation, as they do not operate from rural properties. As such, urban farmers are often denied the DAP (Eligibility Declaration), which prevents them from participating in the PAA and the PNAE, even though they present all the other characteristics of the target group for these programs, including closer access to the places of delivery. In this case, local government agents need to advocate that urban farmers be exempt from the criteria of what constitutes a "farmer". The growth in the recognition of "urban agriculture", and the blurring of geographical lines between urban and rural areas in large municipalities are reducing the barriers for urban food producers.

The political will and commitment to implement new directives are stronger in some municipalities than others, leading to variance in how fast the new legislation and processes are adopted in different jurisdictions by municipal governments all over the country. For example, by 2017, eight years after the legislation, only half of all cities in the country were meeting the required minimum 30 percent of federal funding for purchases from family farmers under the PNAE (O Globo, 2019). It is interesting, but not very surprising, to note that larger cities tend to have more difficulty in meeting that quota than smaller cities. The logistics of family farmers delivering their products directly to schools is certainly more complex in larger cities (Dias et al., 2020). Indeed, researchers have found that the main reasons for noncompliance with the PNAE's 30 percent of federal funding requirement are due to difficulties faced by family farmers. These difficulties include being unable to issue invoices (thus being unable to participate in the public bid), guarantee minimum commercial standards of product hygiene and sanitary conditions, and guarantee a regular supply of particular products (Carvalhosa, 2018; Saraiva et al., 2013). Significant work needs to go into establishing the compatibility between the food products that family farmers are able to supply (quantity, quality, delivery reliability, and prices) and the menu planning process at schools, hospitals, and other public institutions (Real & Schneider, 2011). As such, municipal governments must actively engage in developing mechanisms to bring together small producers and final institutional consumers.

Overall, the Brazilian experience indicates that the implementation of federal food procurement programs at the local level is challenging. The implementation process demands new modalities of interaction between local governments and suppliers to reduce inequalities and establish a smallholder-friendly public procurement process. It requires new institutional arrangements to produce better interactions among the different sectors of the government involved with PFP, and then between these sectors and family farmers. Also, new instruments of public action and bureaucratic procedures need to be developed at the local level. The participatory councils responsible for overseeing the implementation of these programs at local levels have been important catalysts in bringing all of this together. Municipal Food Security Councils and School Food Councils are fundamental in monitoring these programs, but also in developing proposals for how to improve local implementation. In Belo Horizonte, for example, COMUSAN (the aforementioned Municipal Council for Food and Nutrition Security) is composed of 24 members, one-third of whom are representatives from the government and two-thirds of whom represent civil society, including educational or research institutions, social movements, consumer groups, agricultural workers, the food industry, and professional associations. During COMUSAN meetings, representatives of farmer organizations propose ways that agricultural extension staff in government agencies can disseminate information on public calls and help family farmers participate in the bidding process regarding both PAA and PNAE.

Another example of civil society participation in governance is the School Food Council. Under federal legislation, School Food Councils are responsible for monitoring the implementation of all aspects of the National School Food Program at the municipal level (FNDE, 2017). They make sure that the goals of PNAE are achieved, monitoring the acquisition of food and its transformation into healthy and tasty meals for students in local schools. In Belo Horizonte, the School Food Council is composed of a representative from the municipal government appointed by the mayor, a representative from workers in the education sector (for example, custodians or kitchen staff), a representative of the teachers, two representatives of parents, and two representatives of civil society organizations, such as those working with family farmers. Council members have a four-year mandate, and the Council president and vice-president are elected by the members. Difficulties following the legislation are reported at the meetings, during which members discuss possible solutions.

Civil society members in these councils bring the needs and voices of the most vulnerable groups, including family farmers and smallholders, to local decision-making. Municipal governments may be held liable if they do not comply with the regulations of the programs. As it relates to the percentage of food purchases from family farming, this is an ongoing process. Local governments are not yet "punished" for not reaching the established percentages. However, they are monitored and encouraged by the federal government to achieve the program goals. In the case of PAA, there is no federal requirement for municipalities to adopt the program. However, municipalities have a financial incentive (federal funding) to implement it. PFP programs were created in response to the national political mobilization of civil society organizations, which integrated CONSEA at the national level. At local levels, whether PFP implementation occurs in the spirit in which it was created depends on the social exercise of direct political pressure on governmental institutions by civil society groups, and often those participating in local councils.

Conclusion

PFP can be a strategic instrument of public action that simultaneously ensures that there will be an institutional market for family farmers (or agroecological and organic producers), guarantees greater access to healthy and adequate food by vulnerable groups, and promotes healthy food environments in schools, hospitals, care homes, and other social protection institutions. The experience of implementing PFP in Brazil as part of the National System for Food and Nutrition Security indicates ways to mitigate the global syndemic of obesity, malnutrition, and climate change. PFP programs in the country rely on both the creation of new institutional spaces and inter-sectoral and participatory governance processes. In Belo Horizonte, the participation of different civil society organizations in institutional government spaces gave the most vulnerable groups a voice for their demands in the decision-making process and favored the integration of institutions that dealt with food and marketing, as well as health and nutrition.

Through this dialogue, it was possible to institute public procurement as part of a synergistic, integrated solution that simultaneously affected different dimensions of food systems, including promoting healthy eating, changing the ways of producing food, and supporting family farmers through programs like the PNAE and PAA.

The role of the urban or municipal governments in these programs is to implement actions established by the federal government, strengthening local institutional structures of implementation and social participation at the municipal level, and bringing local realities to the political process. One of the main responsibilities of local governments is consolidating the institutional framework at the municipal level to implement food programs, while acknowledging the characteristics of local production processes and local farmers, including their living conditions, work conditions, and the challenges they face in establishing themselves as suppliers to government programs. Based on that knowledge, local governments can establish a political dialogue with the federal government to adjust national legislation to promote PFP based on equity principles and criteria to include family farmers. Municipal-level governments can also adjust local legislation and processes, including changing the definition of rural areas at the local level to allow family farmers to obtain the appropriate documentation, as well as the technical assistance and the political support they need.

The construction of public procurement instruments based on interactions among civil society, public managers, and government-based technical personnel that was promoted by the councils also helped in overcoming political inertia. Awareness of the reality experienced by farmers and the political mobilization promoted by civil society helped compel government managers to modify the legislation and institute processes adequate to the characteristics and needs of smallholder family farmers. In addition, this process has been fundamental in challenging criteria for valuing "efficiency" and "value for money" in public procurement processes, instead incorporating social and economic inclusion into the equation.

The action of civil society – especially of organizations committed to the interests of family farmers, the expansion of agroecological modes of production, and equitable access to adequate and healthy food – was essential in developing the policies at the federal level and in the implementation of the PFP programs at local, municipal levels. Public food procurement, particularly under the PNAE, mobilizes a large volume of financial resources. The use of this policy instrument as a tool to change the food system, support greater social and economic inclusion of smallholder family farmers, stimulate more environmentally sustainable processes, and promote healthier diets requires significant local commitment, including advocacy by urban government agents on behalf of rural and urban food producers.

The need for institutional learning and adaptation in the implementation of new but also innovative, and even revolutionary, policy instruments can be met through institutional spaces, such as food and nutrition security councils and inter-sectoral chambers, which bring together different government departments. Commitment by those occupying such spaces can overcome political inertia and reinforce political will. Many governments at the municipal level in Brazil are also loci of resistance against a federal government intent on pushing back or even destroying years of meaningful advances in food and nutrition security.

References

Aquino, J. R., & Schneider, S. (2011). 12 Anos da política de crédito do PRONAF no Brasil (1996–2008): uma reflexão crítica. *Revista de Extensão e Estudos Rurais*, 1: 309–347.

Berchim, I. I., Nunesb, N. A., de Amorima, W. S., Zimmera, G. A., da Silva, F. R., Fornasaria, V. H., Simac, M., & Guerra, J. B. S. O. A. (2019). The contributions of public policies for strengthening family farming and increasing food security: The case of Brazil. *Land Use Policy*, 82: 573–584.

Blay-Palmer, A., Santini, G., Dubbeling, M., Renting, H., Taguchi, M., & Giordano, T. (2018). Validating the city region food system approach: Enacting inclusive, transformational city region food systems. *Sustainability*, 10 (5): 1680.

Bocchi, C. P., Magalhães, E. S., Rahal, L., Gentil, P., & Gonçalves, R. S. (2019). A década da nutrição, a política de segurança alimentar e nutricional e as compras públicas da agricultura familiar no Brasil. *Rev Panam Salud Publica*, 43: e84.

Brazil (2005). *Projeto de Lei PL6047*. Brasília: Congresso Nacional.

Burlandy, L. (2009). A construção da política de segurança alimentar e nutricional no Brasil: estratégias e desafios para a promoção da intersetorialidade no âmbito federal de governo. *Ciência & Saúde Coletiva*, 14 (3): 851–860.

CAISAN (Câmara Interministerial de Segurança Alimentar). (2009). *Subsídio para Balanço das Ações Governamentais de Segurança Alimentar e Nutricional e da Implantação do Sistema Nacional*. Brasília, Brasil: Ministério do Desenvolvimento Social e Combate à Fome (MDS).

Carvalhosa, C. (2018). *Alimentação escolar como processo de mediação política: análise da trajetória histórica da compra da agricultura familiar no Brasil e nos EUA*. Doctoral thesis presented to Programa de Estudos Pós Graduados em Política Social da Universidade Federal Fluminense (UFF).

Cavalcanti, D., Oliveira, G., d'Avignon, A., Schneider, H., & Taboulchanas, K. (2017). *Compras públicas sustentáveis. Diagnóstico, análise comparada e recomendações para o aperfeiçoamento do modelo brasileiro*. Santiago, Peru: Comissão Econômica para América Latina e o Caribe (CEPAL); United Nations & Brasília: Ministério do Meio Ambiente.

Chmielewska, D., & Souza, D. (2010). *Market alternatives for smallholder farmers in food security initiatives: Lessons from the Brazilian Food Acquisition Programme*. Working Paper No. 64, International Policy Centre for Inclusive Growth, Brasília, Brazil.

Dias, T. F., & Oliveira, E. F. (2019). Agricultura familiar, políticas públicas e mercados institucionais: uma análise exploratória do programa nacional de alimentação escolar – PNAE no Rio Grande do Norte. *HOLOS*, 35 (5): e6838.

Dias, P. C., Barbosa, R. B. O., Barbosa, R. M. S., Ferreira, D. M., Soares, K. C. B., Soares, D. S. B., Henriques, P., & Burlandy, L. (2020). Purchases from family agriculture for school feeding in Brazilian capitals. *Revista de Saúde Pública*, 54, 73. https://doi.org/10.11606/s1518-8787.2020054001963

Edler, L., & Georghiou, L. (2007). Public procurement and innovation: Resurrecting the demand side. *Research Policy*, 36: 949–963.

FAO (Food and Agricultural Organization). (2018). *Strengthening sector policies for better food security and nutrition results – Public food procurement*. Policy Guidance Note 11. Rome: FAO.

FAO. (2019). *The Milan Urban Food Policy Pact: Monitoring framework*. Rome: RUAF/FAO.

FNDE (Fundo Nacional de Desenvolvimento da Educação). (2017). *Cartilha para Conselheiros do Programa Nacional de Alimentação Escolar (PNAE)*. Brasília, Brasil: FNDE/TCU.

Grisa, C., Schneider, S., & Vasconcellos, F. C. F. (2020). Compras públicas como instrumentos para a construção de sistemas alimentares sustentáveis. In P. V. Preiss, S. Schneider, & G. Coelho-de-Souza (Eds.), *A contribuição brasileira à segurança alimentar e nutricional sustentável* (pp. 69–92). Porto Alegre, Brasil: Editora da UFRGS.

IPES-Food. (2016). *From uniformity to diversity: A paradigm shift from industrial agriculture to diversified agroecological systems*. International Panel of Experts on Sustainable Food Systems.

Kanapinskas, V., Plytnikas, Z., & Tvaronavičienė, A. (2014). Sustainable public procurement: Realization of the social aspect in republic of Lithuania. *Business: Theory and Practice*, 15 (4): 302–315.

Maluf, R. S. (2007). *Segurança Alimentar e Nutricional*. Rio de Janeiro: Editora Vozes.

Marconato, M., Brambilla, M., Camara, M., Carvalho, S., & Nascimento, S. (2015). Taxa de pobreza e população rural no Brasil: análise espacial dos períodos 2000 e 2010. *Economia e Desenvolvimento*, 27 (1): 183–201.

Moraes, A., & Rocha, C. (2016). The participation of women farmers in food procurement programs in Brazil. In A. J. Fletcher & W. Kubik (Eds.), *Women in agriculture worldwide: Key issues and practical approaches*. Aldershot: Gower Press.

NUPENS-USP. (2020). *Programa Nacional de Alimentação Escolar atrela distribuição de recursos à classificação NOVA de alimentos*, May 12. São Paulo: NUPENS-USP.

O Globo. (2019). Metade das cidades não cumpre meta de uso da agricultura familiar em merendas escolares. *O Globo*, February 11.

Preiss, P. V., Schneider, S., & Coelho-de-Souza, G. (Eds.). (2020). *A contribuição brasileira à segurança alimentar e nutricional sustentável*. Porto Alegre: Editora da UFRGS.

Real, L. C. V., & Schneider, S. (2011). O uso de programas públicos de alimentação na reaproximação do pequeno produtor com o consumidor: o caso do programa de alimentação escolar. *Estudo e Debate*, 18 (2): 57–79.

Rocha, C. (2009). Developments in national policies for food and nutrition security in Brazil. *Development Policy Review*, 27 (1): 51–66.

Rocha, C. (2015). Work in progress: Addressing food insecurity in Brazil. In M. Caraher, & J. Coveney (Eds.), *Food poverty and insecurity: International food inequalities*. New York: Springer.

Rocha, C., Burlandy, L., & Maluf, R. (2012). Small farms and sustainable rural development for food security: The Brazilian experience. *Development Southern Africa*, 4 (1): 519–529.

Saraiva, E. B., Silva, A. P., Souza, A. A., Cerqueira, G. F., Chagas, C. M., & Toral, N. (2013). Panorama da compra de alimentos da agricultura familiar para o Programa Nacional de Alimentação Escolar. *Ciência & Saúde Coletiva*, 18 (4): 927–935.

Sidaner, E., Balaban, D., & Burlandy, L. (2013). The Brazilian school feeding programme: An example of an integrated programme in support of food and nutrition security. *Public Health Nutrition*, 16 (1): 989–994.

Silva, J. G., Grossi, M. E., & França, C. G. (2010). *Fome Zero: A experiência brasileira*. Brasília: Ministério do Desenvolvimento Agrário.

Smith, J., Andersson, G., Gourlay, R., Karner, S., Mikkelson, B. E., Sonnino, R., & Barling, D. (2016). Balancing competing policy demands: The case of sustainable public sector food procurement. *Journal of Cleaner Production*, 112 (1): 249–256.

Sonnino, R. (2019). Translating sustainable diets into practice: The potential of public food procurement. *Redes*, 24 (1): 14–29.

Stefani, G., Tiberti, M., Lombardi, G. V., Cei, L., & Sacchi, G. (2017). Public food procurement: A systematic literature review. *International Journal on Food System Dynamics*, 8 (4): 270–283.

Swensson, L. F. J. (2015). *Institutional procurement of food from smallholder farmers: The case of Brazil*. Rome: FAO.

Swensson, L. F. J., & Tartanac, F. (2020). Public food procurement for sustainable diets and food systems: The role of the regulatory framework. *Global Food Security*, 25 (1): 100366.

Swinburn, B., Kraak, V., Allender, S., Atkins, V., Baker, P., Bogard, J., …, et al. (2019). The global syndemic of obesity, undernutrition, and climate change: The Lancet Commission report. *The Lancet*, 393: 791–846.

Willett, W., Rockström, J., Loken, B., Springmann, M., …, et al. (2019). Food in the anthropocene: The EAT–Lancet Commission on healthy diets from sustainable food systems. *The Lancet*, 393: 447–492.

Wittman, H., & Blesh, J. (2017). Food sovereignty and Fome Zero: Connecting public food procurement programmes to sustainable rural development in Brazil. *Journal of Agrarian Change*, 17 (1): 81–105.

18

CAN PARTICIPATORY BUDGETING BE A TOOL IN URBAN FOOD GOVERNANCE?

Cecilia Rocha and Luciene Burlandy

Introduction

"Participatory democracy" refers to opportunities for citizens to directly participate in making decisions in the public policy realm. It is contrasted with "representative democracy," under which decisions are made by elected officials voted in by citizens through a democratic process. Thus, participatory democracy requires more spaces and mechanisms for greater political engagement by individual citizens beyond simply voting.

The re-democratization movement of the 1980s in Brazil, after 20 years of a dictatorial military regime (1964–1985), led to a number of innovative experiments in participatory democracy. These experiments were mostly initiated and nurtured at the local level, under elected municipal governments with close links to civil society organizations and movements (Wood & Murray, 2007). Under the country's highly decentralized political structure, progressive municipal administrations, and particularly those in large urban centres, have enjoyed significant "space" to conduct such experiments. Often, consultation processes take place in the microregions of municipalities, comprising both the urban and rural areas surrounding them.

Participatory Budgeting (PB) is probably the most iconic experiment in local participatory democracy developed in Brazil. While it can be employed in many situations, it has been popularized as an urban phenomenon in Brazil. First introduced in 1989 in the city of Porto Alegre, it has been adopted by over 200 other municipalities in the country, and it has inspired similar experiments around the world (Cabannes & Lipietz, 2018). As "a tool for shaping decisions of local communities on the use of public funds" (Filipiak & Dylewski, 2018, p. 13), PB enhances transparency and accountability in public decision-making, while strengthening civic activism by opening political spaces for groups previously denied meaningful participation in the democratic process. Its fundamental intent is to directly engage everyday citizens in becoming protagonists in the decision of allocating part of the public budget (Amaral & Carvalho, 2018) and, through this process, having citizens better understand the issues involved in the delivery of public goods and services.

DOI: 10.4324/9781003055907-21

In this chapter, we explore the possibility of using PB as a tool in advancing good urban food governance. We look at the experience with Participatory Budgeting in Belo Horizonte, a Brazilian city renowned for its innovative food policies (Chappell, 2018; Haysom, 2015; IPES-Food, 2017; Lappé & Lappé, 2002; Rocha, 2001, 2016). We describe the general rules and structures followed in the process of PB and how it has evolved through the years in Belo Horizonte. We then look at the main features of participatory food governance in the city, noting the absence of PB in its overall structure. The chapter concludes with some reflections on the potential and limitations of PB as a tool in advancing good urban food governance.

Participatory Budgeting in Belo Horizonte, Brazil

Participatory Budgeting was first introduced in Belo Horizonte in 1993, under the same municipal government (Mayor Patrus Ananias of the Workers' Party) that created a separate department for policies and programmes in food and nutrition security. Both initiatives were seen as instruments for more open, transparent, and democratic governance (Araujo, 2012; Porto et al., 2020; Wood & Murray, 2007). Overall, however, the initiatives run in parallel to each other, rarely overlapping.

As in other cities in Brazil, the PB process in Belo Horizonte was intended to deliver short-term, concrete outcomes, tending to focus on investments in municipal public works and infrastructure, such as road improvements, pedestrian bridges, sewage and water pipes, and parks. Through the years, it has also led to the construction and reform of schools, health clinics, community centres, and public housing (Walker, 2016). Between 1993 and 2016, 1,652 projects were approved through PB processes, and over 1 million people participated in them (Belo Horizonte, 2018).

PB encompasses both a "top-down" framework and a "bottom-up" process. It is "top-down" in the sense that the process is initiated and coordinated by the government, involving many departments led by the Municipal Planning Secretariat. PB is "bottom-up" in the sense that its results (the actual projects to be implemented) come from community deliberations. Some phases of the PB cycle allow for more civil society participation, while others are clearly more under the control of the government. Nevertheless, PB is a tool for increasing dialogue between the population and the government representatives it has elected.

In general, PB is a very time-consuming process, involving regional assemblies and neighbourhood meetings to decide on priorities for a given geographical area. Reaching consensus on priorities for a particular region takes significant exchange of information and lots of discussions and negotiations. The process also includes the design and estimation of costs for priority projects. Thus, while a PB process can be initiated every year, the full cycle for reaching consensus on which projects will be undertaken in a particular region can take up to two years.

PB work begins at regional assemblies (Belo Horizonte is divided into nine regions), with the presentation of the guidelines and methodology to be followed in the PB process by municipal staff. A public call for the assemblies invites all residents to attend, and at least 0.5 per cent of a region's population must be present at an assembly in order to be part of the PB process. The financial resources approved under the city's budget and made available for each region are also revealed at this initial assembly, where participants agree on the rules of the decision-making process and a tentative calendar. Subsequent rounds of the process adopt a representative model, with delegates elected by the residents present in the assemblies to form the Regional Commission for Monitoring the Execution of the Participatory Budget (COMFORÇA, in the Portuguese acronym). The Regional Commissions, along with the municipal government's PB Management Group, are then responsible for the selection of projects in each region, as well as overseeing their development and implementation. Organizing and facilitating the rounds of neighbourhood meetings to develop a list of priority projects to be costed by municipal technical staff, the Regional Commissions are the main link between the population and the municipal government in the PB process. The final project is selected after a "Caravan of Priorities," in which the delegates debate the relative merits of the various proposals put forward (Horochovski & Clemente, 2012).

In Belo Horizonte, the portion of the municipal budget dedicated to PB has varied from a maximum of 16 per cent in 2008 to less than 5 per cent in 2012, 2017, and 2020 (Porto et al., 2020). The budget is divided among the city's nine administrative regions to benefit those areas that rank lower in the Urban Life Quality Index (with indicators such as per-capita income, population density, and availability of public goods and services). Thus, PB is seen as a tool for the redistribution of municipal resources to more disadvantaged areas (Araujo, 2012).

While the above describes the more extensive Regional PB process (inaugurated in 1993), the Belo Horizonte government has created three other modalities for this tool. The Housing PB (since 1996) has a dedicated budget for the construction and renovation of public housing. The Digital PB (since 2006) allows the whole population to vote, via the Internet or phone, on projects throughout the city, such as renovation of public spaces in the city centre. The Child and Adolescent PB (since 2014) has a budget dedicated to projects geared to improving the lives of the younger residents of the city. Thus, Belo Horizonte's experiences with PB cover the more common territorially based process but have also expanded to thematic (housing) and actor-based (children and adolescents) processes.

Digital PB or ePB, described as "an innovation within an innovation" (Coleman & Sampaio, 2017, p. 756), is a pioneering experiment. It differs from the usual PB process in that the projects to be voted on, which are deemed beneficial to all residents, are predetermined by the government. It thus bypasses the participatory choice of priorities, resulting in some criticism for distorting the true intent of PB (Araujo, 2012) and being a poor representation of the potential of PB as a tool in participatory democracy. However, past city officials have defended this modality as the most effective way of increasing citizens' participation (Belo Horizonte, 2008), and particularly by young people and the middle class, both groups underrepresented in the face-to-face process in earlier years. When it was introduced in 2006, ePB only required a voter identification number for residents to cast their votes online or by phone. Coleman and Sampaio (2017, p. 759) estimated that close to 10 per cent of Belo Horizonte's registered voters participated in the Digital PB that year, compared to about 4 per cent who participated in the face-to-face process. In principle, nothing prevents a round of PB from combining the virtual and in-person processes, but it is yet to be attempted.

Since 2008, Belo Horizonte has seen a steady decline in participation in all PB modalities. In 2016 (after 22 years and 14 rounds), the newly elected mayor, Alexandre Kalil, put a halt to any new editions of the process, and the tool has not been used for approvals of new projects since then. We consider the issues that led to this situation in the next section.

Issues with Participatory Budgeting: Does the Practice Measure up to Its Promise?

The literature on Participatory Budgeting points out a few key implementation challenges (Amaral & Carvalho, 2018; Cabannes & Lipietz, 2018; Filipiak & Dylewski, 2018; Walker, 2016; Wood & Murray, 2007). These include: (1) a long-standing critique of the PB process as impractical on a large scale; (2) the process can be manipulated and controlled by the government, and thus used as political marketing; (3) it is hard to get some groups to engage and to maintain participation; (4) the process can be captured by particular groups or interests; and (5) all of the above, combined with the low or even negligible percentages of budgets available, suggest that the overall impact of PB may not be very significant.

The example of Belo Horizonte, a city with over 2.5 million inhabitants, and the diversity of situations in which PB has been tried around the world, from whole regions to small villages, suggests that the issue of geographical scale is not a significant one. The practicality of implementing a PB process depends on its careful design, which may require some adjustments before it is well established. The early years of the practice in Belo Horizonte encountered many technical difficulties, from bureaucratic and legal challenges faced by the public sector staff in adapting protocols and procedures, to the very rules of engagement for a population unfamiliar with the process. Quick recognition of, and responses to, these technical problems were fundamental so the process did not lose its credibility and to build the necessary resiliency to turn PB into more than just an ephemeral pilot project in participatory democracy. The dedication of municipal staff, the political support of the mayors from 1993 to 2008, and the support of elected members of the municipal assembly were fundamental in overcoming these early difficulties.

The question of whether PB is a legitimate tool of participatory democracy goes beyond making sure that there is space (opportunity) for meaningful participation. There are also questions about who participates (inclusion), how to maintain that participation, and who has control of the process.

There is no denying that the tool can be vulnerable to manipulation by government (as political marketing in a populist vein), or to capture by particular interest groups with power to influence or guide the votes of parts of the population. To participate in face-to-face modalities, poorer and less-educated citizens must be mobilized and organized, often through neighbourhood associations, church groups, or civil society organizations – many of which are under-resourced and not well-positioned to do this time-consuming and labour-intensive work. While concerns have been raised about particular interest groups or the government unduly influencing the decisions of participants, more studies are needed to corroborate the extent of such a capture.

The individualized, isolated voting process in Digital PB is considered less prone to the "capture problem." In Belo Horizonte, the Digital PB modality showed more participation by younger people and members of the middle class than in the face-to-face modalities. Overall participation by these groups, however, declined over the years as people became disappointed with the government-selected projects that were up for vote, which were often judged as low priority by the population (Coleman & Sampaio, 2017).

However, the main reason for declining participation in all modalities of PB in Belo Horizonte was probably the delay in the completion and delivery of the selected projects. The difference between the number of projects approved and those actually executed had been increasing steadily since 2006, until the newly elected mayor put a halt on the process in 2016, when 450 projects approved in previous years had not yet been completed (Porto et al., 2020). The intent was not to abolish the PB process, but to make sure that the projects previously approved were finalized before a new round was initiated. The delay in completing approved projects eroded the legitimacy of the PB process and led to lower participation by a disillusioned population.

Despite these setbacks, PB budgeting in Belo Horizonte is hardly dead. The preparation for municipal elections in 2020 created an opportunity for a lively discussion in the city about the role of PB in democracy, which led to a proposal to enshrine PB as part of the municipal plan legislation and to have a minimum of 5 per cent of the budget dedicated to it (Porto et al.,

2020). While this proposal continues to be debated in the municipal assembly, the re-election of Alexandre Kalil as mayor does not bode well for approvals of new projects under the PB process. The current administration will not open new rounds of PB until unfinished projects are completed, but it has dedicated less than 2 per cent of the municipal budget to this task in the past few years (Malheiro, 2021).

The Practice of Participatory Democracy in Belo Horizonte's Food Governance

Mechanisms for participatory democracy are not confined to Participatory Budgeting in Belo Horizonte. In fact, we find no connection between PB processes and the system of food governance for which the city is famous.

In 1994, the same year as the first PB exercise in the city, the municipal government created a new department (the Municipal Food Supply Secretariat, which is today the Sub-Secretariat for Food and Nutrition Security-SUSAN) to plan and coordinate all policies and programmes for food and nutrition security (FNS) in Belo Horizonte (IPES-Food, 2017; Rocha, 2016). SUSAN has divided its programmes into seven "lines of work": (1) subsidized food sales, (2) food and nutrition assistance, (3) food supply and market regulation support for urban agriculture, (4) support for urban agriculture, (5) education for food consumption, (6) job and income generation, and (7) management of public policies in FNS. The department coordinates 17 programmes that reach more than one million people daily (Belo Horizonte, 2020). Principles guiding the programmes include the right to adequate food, social justice (favouring marginalized and low-income groups), universality (most of its programmes, such as the Popular Restaurant, are open to all people, residents and non-residents alike), and food quality and safety.

Following the national Zero Hunger strategy announced in 2003, congressional approval of the National Law on Food and Nutrition Security in 2006, and the amendment to add the Right to Adequate Food to the country's constitution in 2010, Brazil embarked on developing a National System for Food and Nutrition Security (SISAN). One of the guiding principles of SISAN (see Chapter 17 by Burlandy et al. in this volume for more on SISAN) is social participation in the development, implementation, and monitoring of policies and programmes. Participatory Budgeting, however, is not contemplated in the system. Instead, SISAN requires the formation of councils with the participation of civil society and government representatives at the municipal level. Thus, popular participation in the governance of food under SISAN is through the required councils.

In Belo Horizonte, two councils deserve special notice. The Municipal Council for Food and Nutrition Security (COMUSAN) is responsible for assuring people's constitutional right to adequate food through the municipal government's policies and programmes. COMUSAN is composed of 24 members, with one-third representing the government and two-thirds representing civil society, including educational or research institutions, social movements, consumer groups, agricultural workers, the food industry, and professional associations. Another example of civil society participation in governance is the School Food Council. Under federal legislation, School Food Councils are responsible for monitoring the implementation of the National School Food Program (*Programa Nacional de Alimentação Escolar – PNAE*) at the municipal level (FNDE, 2017). One of the largest school food programmes in the world, PNAE offers healthy meals as well as food and nutrition education in all public schools in the country (see Chapter 17 by Burlandy et al. in this volume). In Belo Horizonte, the School Food Council is composed of one representative from the municipal government who is appointed by the mayor, one representative from education workers, one representative of the teachers, two representatives of parents, and two representatives of civil society organizations (Belo Horizonte, 2011). Councils' staff members are municipal civil servants working for SUSAN. Thus, while representatives from civil society are volunteers (appointed or elected to serve by their organizations), the work of the councils is supported by a secretariat paid by the municipal government. Councils have a four-year mandate, their presidents are elected from the civil society members, they have regular meetings, and decisions are reached by consensus.

In sum, "participatory democracy" in urban food governance in Belo Horizonte is mostly represented in the work of the councils. Despite the city's significant experience with Participatory Budgeting, the tool has not yet been used in its very successful food governance model.

Discussion

Participatory Budgeting is proposed as a way to deepen everyday citizens' participation in politics and policymaking, and it can certainly do that. For many years, a great part of the population (close to 14 per cent at a certain point) in Belo Horizonte showed willingness to be part of the process, and over 1,650 projects had been approved by 2016. Among the final results and impacts of PB, it is worth highlighting the political learning provided to those who engaged in it, not only for everyday citizens but also for public managers, professionals, and public sector staff. This is especially important in countries with a history of authoritarian governments, such as Brazil. PB has an impact on the local government bureaucracy and on public agents, making them more aware of the demands of the population.

However, many problems have emerged, including questions about how to institutionalize the process and maintain a significant level of legitimate participation. Even after 26 years, Participatory Budgeting has not yet been consolidated as an institution in the general governance of the city.

The challenges regarding the implementation process of Participatory Budgeting cannot be wholly attributed to the tool itself, or at least they are not exclusive to PB. These challenges (e.g., manipulation by the government, difficulties with engagement of the population, capture by interest groups) have also been identified in other democratic instruments and institutional arenas of social participation. PB is an instrument of public action that is part of the whole scenario of public policy implementation at the municipal level. Its potential impacts depend on how much the process as a whole is guided by democratic values and how it can mobilize different types of resources (political, financial, and institutional). The decision-making process in PB is complex, involving different groups and interests. The political and economic contexts that influence managers' decisions at local levels can change rapidly, considering the balance and asymmetry of power in settings characterized by inequalities. These contextual changes can occur within the municipal realm, but also at the state and national levels, with significant implications for local governance. The principles of accountability and transparency embedded in the PB process are essential to promote the engagement of the population and confidence in local government. However, these principles must go beyond the PB instrument of public action and drive the whole process of municipal planning.

While PB has the potential to be part of a more comprehensive and systemic approach in public policy to advance good urban food governance, this has not happened in Belo Horizonte, which is somewhat surprising. The city is renowned for both its PB processes and its innovative food governance, but these two realms have rarely intersected. In the list of over 1,650 projects approved through the PB process in Belo Horizonte, few are directly related to food, although construction and reform of schools would include the kitchens and cafeterias in the School Food Program.

Nevertheless, given the inter-sectoral nature of food security, infrastructure projects that benefit lower-income populations (voted for under the PB process) also enhance conditions for greater food security. It is important to establish, as part of urban food governance, connections among actors and institutional structures responsible for food and nutrition security policies and the respective policy sectors responsible for other thematic issues (such as housing and urban infrastructure) covered by PB. This demands an integrated municipal planning process and strong political will to face conflicts of interest in the disputes around the public budget and other public resources (such as institutional spaces) that are mobilized by food and nutrition policies.

A more direct way for PB to advance good urban food governance in Belo Horizonte would be to develop a specific modality dedicated to food projects, such as the one dedicated to housing. Projects for selection or popular voting could include urban gardens, community kitchens, and farmers markets, for example. This particular modality would follow the same rules as those specified for the general PB process that are intended to benefit lower-income areas and more marginalized groups.

However, to avoid some of the main problems plaguing the PB process in the past few years, and particularly the lack of consolidation as an institution in the general governance of the city, this food modality could be implemented under the already well-established Municipal Council for Food and Nutrition Security (COMUSAN). This would have the advantage of a stable institutional setting under the National System for Food and Nutrition Security.

Conclusions

Participatory Budgeting practices reflect the constant tension that exists whenever tools of participatory democracy are introduced in a representative democracy model. How much decision-making power are legitimately elected governments willing to give up for greater popular participation? When do everyday citizens expect to participate, and when do they expect their elected government representatives to make decisions on their behalf? How can one prevent democratic institutions and practices from being captured by powerful interest groups? These concerns suggest, once again, the importance of careful design to guarantee spaces for the legitimate and meaningful participation of civil society.

Under the National System for Food and Nutrition Security in Brazil, food councils are an established, reliable mechanism for democratic participation. We suggest that a dedicated PB food modality could be embedded in such spaces, further improving Belo Horizonte's food governance. Combined with the proposal to guarantee a minimum budget percentage by law, this could revive the PB process in the city.

More generally, Belo Horizonte's experience with Participatory Budgeting confirms its potential as a mechanism to deepen democracy, but it also points out some general principles for its effective implementation. A constant preoccupation with the design of PB projects to make sure they include marginalized sectors and prevent capture by particular interest groups is essential and requires continuous innovation. Completion of projects selected under this process in a transparent and timely manner would be needed to maintain people's trust in the tool. However, this would require government commitment to the tool, in particular, and to participatory democracy, in general. Greater institutionalization through legislation and established participatory spaces (such as food councils) can protect the credibility of processes like PB from the vagaries of government changes in a democracy.

References

Amaral, C. T. G., & Carvalho, F. T. (2018). Democracia e deliberação: A escolha popular das políticas públicas locais – o caso do Orçamento Participativo de Porto Alegre (OPPOA). *Revista de Direito da Cidade, 10*(1), 463–486.

Belo Horizonte. (2008). *Orçamento Participativo de Belo Horizonte – 15 anos*. Prefeitura de Belo Horizonte.

Belo Horizonte. (2011). Decreto no. 14.264, de 27 de janeiro de 2011, *Diário Oficial do Município (DOM)*, Ano XVII.

Belo Horizonte. (2018). *Empreendimentos do orçamento participativo*. Prefeitura de Belo Horizonte, Mapas, Estatísticas e Indicadores. https://prefeitura.pbh.gov.br/estatisticas-e-indicadores/orcamento-participativo/empreendimentos (accessed 8 November 2020)

Belo Horizonte. (2020). *Segurança alimentar e nutricional: Política de abastecimento e segurança alimentar e nutricional da capital*. Prefeitura de Belo Horizonte, Secretaria Municipal de Assistência Social, Segurança Alimentar e Cidadania, Subsecretaria de Segurança Alimentar e Nutricional. https://prefeitura.pbh.gov.br/smasac/susan (accessed 20 February 2020)

Cabannes, Y., & Lipietz, B. (2018). Revisiting the democratic promise of participatory budgeting in light of competing political, good governance and technocratic logics. *Environment & Urbanization, 30*(1), 67–84.

Chappell, M. J. (2018). *Beginning to end hunger: Food and the environment in Belo Horizonte, Brazil and beyond*. Oakland, CA: University of California Press.

Coleman, S., & Sampaio, R. C. (2017). Sustaining a democratic innovation: A study of three e-participatory budgets in Belo Horizonte. *Information, Communication & Society, 20*(5), 754–769.

de Araujo, R. M. (2012). *Orçamento participativo: Uma experiência de gestão e planejamento urbano em Belo Horizonte*. Master's thesis, Administration Program, FUMEC University, Belo Horizonte, Brazil.

Filipiak, B. Z., & Dylewski, M. (2018). A real or a marginal trend in participatory budgets in local governments. *Financial Internet Quarterly, 14*(4), 12–21.

FNDE – Fundo Nacional de Desenvolvimento da Educação. (2017). *Cartilha para conselheiros do Programa Nacional de Alimentação Escolar (PNAE)*. Brasília: FNDE/TCU.

Haysom, G. (2015). Food and the city: Urban scale food system governance. *Urban Forum, 26*, 263–281.

Horochovski, R. R., & Clemente, A. J. (2012). Democracia deliberative e orçamento público: Experiências de participação em Porto Alegre, Belo Horizonte, Recife e Curitiba. *Revista de sociologia e política, 20*(43), 127–157.

IPES-Food. (2017). *What makes urban food policy happen? Insights from five cases*. International Panel of Experts on Sustainable Food Systems.

Lappé, F. M., & Lappé, A. (2002). *Hope's edge: The next diet for a small planet*. New York: Tarcher/Putnam.

Malheiro, F. (2021). Orçamento participativo em BH perde espaço em gastos da prefeitura. *O Tempo*, 16 August.

Porto, H., Oliveira, M. R., & Silva, P. (2020). Participação social da constituição à cidade: O orçamento participativo em Belo Horizonte. *Cartografia do Orçamento Participativo*, UFMG. https://opbh.cartografia.org/2020/11/05/participacao-social-da-constituicao-a-cidade-o-orcamento-participativo-em-belo-horizonte/ (accessed 13 November 2020)

Rocha, C. (2001). Urban food security policy: The case of Belo Horizonte, Brazil. *Journal for the Study of Food and Society, 5*(1), 36–47.

Rocha, C. (2016). Opportunities and challenges in urban food security policy: The case of Belo Horizonte, Brazil. In M. Deakin, N. Borrelli, & D. Diamantini (Eds.), *The governance of city food systems: Case studies from around the world*. Milan: Fondazione Feltrinelli.

Walker, A. P. P. (2016). Self-help or public housing? Lessons from co-managed slum upgrading via participatory budget. *Habitat International, 55*, 58–66.

Wood, T., & Murray, W. E. (2007). Participatory democracy in Brazil and local geographies: Porto Alegre and Belo Horizonte compared. *Revista Europea de Estudios Latinoamericanos y del Caribe, 83*, 19–41.

19

THE FORMAL AND INFORMAL GOVERNANCE OF URBAN FOOD WASTE IN CITIES

Case Studies in the United States and Indonesia

Daniel N. Warshawsky and Tammara Soma

Introduction

More than one-third of the global food supply is lost upstream by growers and suppliers and wasted downstream by retailers and consumers (FAO, 2019). These large volumes of food waste contribute to negative social, environmental, and economic outcomes. This includes less access to edible food, environmental degradation from poor land management, increased methane emissions associated with climate change, and loss of ecological and economic resources. The United Nations' Sustainable Development Goal 12: Responsible Production and Consumption sub-component on Food Loss and Waste (SDG 12.3) highlights the enormity of the food waste crisis (United Nations, 2020). In addition, as noted by many recent efforts to proactively reduce food waste, SDG 12.3 has contributed to increased attention to the global food waste crisis across sectors, scales, and global contexts (Flanagan et al., 2019; ReFed, 2016).

Food is wasted at each stage in the system from production to consumption. Within the last two decades, North American and European companies, governments, and civil society organizations have incorporated the food recovery hierarchy to prioritize various food waste prevention methods. This food waste hierarchy promotes food waste reduction in this order: source reduction, feed hungry people, feed animals, industrial uses, composting, and landfill or incineration (Environmental Protection Agency, 2006; European Union, 2008). Although the food waste hierarchy originated in North America and Europe, it has become increasingly utilized as a best practice framework in many corporate and government institutions across the globe.

In cities, the challenges associated with food insecurity and food waste are increasingly connected to the issue of food system governance, as the structure and roles of different institutional players define what is possible for food system management strategies and practices at the local and household levels. Food loss and spoilage are often used to describe food lost in the production and distribution phases of the food system, while food waste is used to denote food lost in the retail and consumption phases of the food system (FAO, 2021). To this point, while Gille (2013) highlights the difference between surplus food in the system versus wasted food at

 DOI: 10.4324/9781003055907-22

the end of the system, food waste is employed in this chapter to denote any edible food that is lost within any part of food systems (Gustavsson et al., 2011).

In this chapter, the urban governance of food waste is defined as the institutional organization and delivery of food system processes and services and the set of governance mechanisms which determine how food systems are controlled (Warshawsky, 2021). The food system is governed through a range of governments, businesses, non-profits, and households in cities. Although many formalized institutions have developed highly efficient structures and processes to manage food systems, other components of the food system are more ad hoc and disorganized. In addition to the more formalized structures in food systems, such as food manufacturers and food retailers, street vendors, households, and other local players engage in a breadth of informal strategies to handle food waste. These processes include composting, feeding scraps to pets, sewer disposal, giving to charity or neighbours, dumpster diving, and dumping or incineration (Reynolds et al., 2014).

This chapter therefore pays attention to both formal and informal systems of food waste governance, as well as food waste generation and mitigation within both formal and informal sectors of the food system. For the purpose of this chapter, informal food waste governance is defined as food waste management that occurs outside officially sanctioned institutional activity, often within ad hoc networks, markets, vendors, and traders in the shadows or invisible to the state or corporations (Helmke & Levitsky, 2004; Wegerif, 2020). Although these informal methods may be beyond quantitative measurement, they are key daily practices in many communities and households across the world. With the emergence of the COVID-19 pandemic, severe disruptions in the production, distribution, and availability of food have created new challenges in food waste management as institutions at all scales have had to rethink their relationship to food (FAO, 2020). In many contexts, this has produced new formal and informal strategies to cope with food waste, food insecurity, and the inequalities in the global food system.

To analyse the challenges associated with food waste governance in greater detail in an urban context, this chapter examines two case studies. Both case studies are reflective of the challenges associated with food waste governance in their respective food system contexts. The first case study examines Dayton, a moderately sized metropolitan region of 800,000 people in the post-industrial U.S. Midwestern state of Ohio. Even though there is some interest shown amongst leaders in government and industry in reducing food waste in the Dayton region, the lack of political support, infrastructure to process food waste, and economic incentives have delayed the development of a more comprehensive food waste strategy. In this way, Dayton is reflective of the challenges of urban food waste governance in many contexts.

The second case study analyses the City of Bogor, Indonesia, a dense population centre of one million people in the province of West Java. Rapid urbanization, population growth, and urban sprawl, combined with the increased prevalence of plastic food packaging, have contributed to issues which complicated the onsite management of food waste as residents have become increasingly dependent on municipal waste collectors rather than decentralized household food waste management strategies. This has become quite problematic as food waste volumes are amongst the highest per capita in the world and have contributed to environmental hazards for those living near open dump sites. In West Java, municipal waste is not thrown in sanitary landfills as none currently exists, but rather in open and unmanaged dump sites resembling mountains of waste. In Bogor, formalized mechanisms to share unwanted food from businesses have emerged to complement the range of informal food waste practices; however, the city's approach is arguably quite disorganized and uneven in impact.

This chapter starts with a discussion on the conceptualization of formal and informal food waste governance in cities. Then, through the case studies of Dayton and Bogor, the chapter critically analyses the range of formal and informal food waste strategies employed in each city and the challenges associated with food waste governance in each context. The chapter ends by exploring the implications of these case studies and the future of food waste governance in the world's cities.

Conceptualizing Food Waste Governance

The urban governance of food waste is conceptualized as the organization and implementation of food system processes and services and the set of governance mechanisms controlling how food systems are managed (Warshawsky, 2021). Food system governance is managed through a wide range of institutions, including intranational, national, provincial, and local governments; global corporations and local businesses; international non-governmental organizations, community non-profits, and households; and other ad hoc organizations operating in different contexts. Informal food waste governance is conceptualized as the food system processes operating within networks, markets, or other spaces outside state or corporation control (Helmke & Levitsky, 2004; Wegerif, 2020).

As the responsibility of programmes shifts towards the local or non-governmental organizations, urban governance has facilitated the reduction in governmental services, increased roles for non-governmental organizations and for-profit enterprises, and reshaped the definitions of citizenship, territoriality, and governmental control (Pieterse et al., 2008). This shift in governance structure has produced new management strategies which often emphasize entrepreneurship and self-sustaining enterprise models of service delivery. These dynamics contribute to new practices at the level of state governance for individuals, as people and institutions learn how to negotiate new governance regimes of service delivery (Brenner & Theodore, 2002). In addition, as noted below, although food systems are comprised of formal and informal food institutions, organizations often exist as hybridized or where the formal and informal meet. Formal food corporations do not always operate within bounded spaces, and seemingly informalized charities, co-ops, and social enterprises often have clear logics and systems of operation.

Formal Food Waste Governance in Cities

In the wake of growing awareness of the volumes of food wasted, a range of actors in the private, government, and non-profit sectors have moved towards governing food waste management in cities (Hoover, 2017). While some of these food waste systems may be more formalized in design in parts of Europe, North America, or Australia, most food waste governance in the world's cities remains ad hoc, disorganized, and not systematically managed. Very often, governance vacuums have been created because of weak food waste policies and the atomization of food waste management to individual consumers (Busa & Garder, 2015). Although food waste in higher-income countries is often created in the supply chain through practices related to food consumption, households and consumers have been delegated significant responsibility to reduce food waste, even though they might not have the capacity, interest, or time to properly manage food waste (Evans, 2011; Warshawsky, 2019).

To mitigate these extremes, the food recovery hierarchy has been widely adopted to shift food waste management practices. This hierarchy provides a framework for food waste prevention, reduction, and recovery in the form of an upside-down pyramid; outside of addressing reduction at the source (the most desirable), the framework encourages the distribution of edible food to 'feeding people in need' (Environmental Protection Agency, 2006, European Union, 2008). The framework also suggests that the next step to address the food waste that is not suitable for human consumption is to feed it to animals, to use it for industrial purposes (e.g. rendering), to compost, and to only use landfilling as a last resort when there are no other options (Environmental Protection Agency, 2006; European Union, 2008). However, for the reasons noted above, without adequate incentive or regulation, food is thrown away in the garbage, the last stage in the food waste hierarchy.

To more thoroughly understand the aforementioned challenges in food waste governance, scholars have examined the range of institutions which engage in the governance of food access and food waste (Galli et al., 2019). Researchers have articulated how the central state and food companies have actively recast the origins and solutions to food insecurity and food waste through the neoliberal devolution, decentralization, and privatization of food system governance to local non-profit organization, households, and consumers (see Busa & Garder, 2015; Guthman, 2008). Although a plethora of alternative food movements have developed to empower local communities and transform the priorities and operations of regional food systems, deeply entrenched inequalities in the global food system have limited achievements in food justice and the right to food in many contexts (Goodman et al., 2012; Sonnino, 2016). Also, race, class, and gender have played a significant role in shaping the potential and limitations of measurable impacts in city spaces, as state food programs, corporate philanthropies, and anti-hunger organizations operate with their own hierarchies, contradictions, and limitations (Heynen et al., 2012; Reynolds, 2015).

Importantly, the neoliberal shift to local governance has created a political and economic space for food waste governance to be delegated to consumers (Evans, 2011). As noted by Riches (2018), many governments have taken advantage of this opportunity to reduce their role in food waste management. In addition, food corporations, arguably the key players in the creation of food waste (Cloke, 2020), often cast blame on consumers as the cause of food waste, even though they are the institutions that typically create the retail environment in which consumers buy food. Although consumers clearly have a significant role to play in food waste management, the state and food corporations have leveraged the neoliberal devolution, decentralization, and privatization of food systems to elide their responsibilities in food waste governance (Warshawsky, 2015, 2019).

The social construction of the consumer as the source of the problem and the solution to food waste governance is arguably the result of a mass consumption culture within contemporary capitalism (Hebrok & Boks, 2017). Food retailers and restaurants actively shape how food is produced, transported, presented, and sold to the consumer. Profitability, appearance, and quality are prioritized over food waste reduction (Gunders, 2017). Moreover, food corporations have utilized philanthropy and food waste charity as a way to recast their companies as sustainable and socially just, so there is significant incentive for them to enhance their brand and deflect attention away from food waste generation, high food prices, or any aspect of the food system that makes them look like bad actors (Ionescu-Somers, 2004; Lohnes, 2021; Warshawsky, 2016). In this way, it is arguably a false binary to distinguish between food waste from food retailers and that of consumers (Parfitt et al., 2010).

Most recently, the COVID-19 pandemic has created significant problems for the governance of food waste in cities. Challenges have included the transportation of food, extreme fluctuations in food demand from food retailers, restaurants, and households, as well as large volumes of food left on farm fields or ploughed over (Yaffe-Bellany & Corkery, 2020). The disconnect between those who need food and the large volumes of wasted food have highlighted the contradictions, excesses, and warped incentives that determine how food is produced, sold, transported, and consumed by various institutions in the food system (Clapp, 2020). Although the Coronavirus Food Assistance Program was passed in the U.S. context to mitigate some food waste through increased delivery of edible food to the food relief network, much of the work to rescue food across the world was completed through a somewhat disorganized ad hoc process whereby groups of people or individuals rescued food, cooked food, or developed other creative methods to reduce food waste (Corkery & Yaffe-Bellany, 2020). Building on these challenges in the formalized context, the following section will examine food waste governance in the informal setting.

Informal Food Waste Governance in Cities

Informal approaches to food waste governance occur in both cities of the Global North and South. In this chapter, informal food waste governance is defined as food waste disposal and management, as well as the sharing of unwanted or unmarketable edible food, outside of the formal system of waste management (state-led), retail markets and businesses, and those governed through informal institutional arrangements. In many cities, particularly in the Global South, informal food networks, markets, vendors, and traders, play an important role in the food supply chain (Wegerif, 2020). Informal governance and informal institutions, as defined by Helmke and Levitsky (2004), are socially shared rules that are usually unwritten, including rules that are enforced out of officially sanctioned channels. According to Christiansen and Neuhold (2012) understanding informal governance is quite challenging as it is an attempt to study the shadow, the invisible, and below-the-surface opaque practices.

In a study conducted by Reynolds et al. (2014), it was found that there are five dominant informal food waste disposal practices. These include composting in the household, repurposing food scraps to pets, donating food to community members, chucking food into the dumpster or incinerator, and throwing food into the neighbourhood sewer system. Unlike formal waste management systems that enable the measurement of food waste (e.g. through solid waste departments or municipalities), informal food waste management and governance at the household level includes many of the five food waste practices identified by Reynolds et al. (2014). Although the informal waste stream may appear to represent only a small proportion of the total food waste management system, Reynolds et al. (2014) found that 20 per cent of household food waste diverted from the landfill was channelled through informal food waste routes. As such, simply targeting the formal route of food disposal practices (e.g. municipal compost pickup) or understanding the issues of food waste from a formal governance lens would be incomplete.

The sharing of unwanted food is a common informal food waste management strategy at the household level in the Global South and the Global North, where practices include giving unwanted food to neighbours, domestic helpers, and waste collectors (Soma, 2017a). It is important to note that this 'sharing' may be rooted in patron-based relationships where the poor have no other choice but to accept unwanted foods from their employers. In addition, as Davies (2019) noted in the European context, the act of sharing can also be a way to improve status within hierarchical social settings, and even as a response to avoid punishment from others in the group. Evans (2014) also found that depending on the culture, food sharing between neighbours, particularly surplus food, is not always accepted as there are potential concerns around food safety, allergies, tastes, and preferences.

As noted in the Global North context, informal sharing may be facilitated with anonymity through communal refrigerators, also known as 'solidarity fridges,' which potentially reduce these hierarchies in power through enabling anonymous donation and receipt. The communal refrigerators allow individuals, and in some cases (depending on the scale) businesses and restaurants, to share extra food. This approach to sharing is based on trust. However, due to the unregulated nature of the communal refrigerators, many have been shut down due to potential health risks as well as due to the need to place the fridge in a public space which may be against local government by-laws (Parikh & Fagan, 2015).

Another form of food waste diversion is the provision of food scraps to domestic livestock (e.g. chickens, catfish) (Soma, 2019; Katongole et al., 2012), and community or neighbourhood composting (Cofie et al., 2009). In most developing countries, community-based composting initiatives have arisen due to the inability of local governments to provide sufficient services in waste collection and management (Colon & Fawcett, 2006; Parizeau et al., 2006). As noted by Ali and Snel (1999), waste management is one of the most expensive services within the budgets of most municipalities and the inability to carry out this service gives rise to local and informal initiatives such as community-based waste management. For countries in the Global South, informal food waste governance is an important part of an integrated sustainable food waste management system as 50 to 80 per cent of the waste generated in most developing countries is organic (Yedla, 2012; Oberlin & Szántó, 2011; Parizeau et al., 2006).

While the literature on neighbourhood or community-based composting is quite established, informal networks of food sharing between friends and neighbours have only recently received more attention in academic literature (Davies et al., 2019). With regards to food acquisition, other informal food waste reduction practices include dumpster diving and freeganism, whereby individuals obtain their food from food discarded by businesses or retailers (Barnard, 2016). The practice of dumpster diving is key to understanding the complexities, tensions, and conflict that may occur in informal urban food waste governance. Of course, informal food acquisition practices by consumption of 'wasted foods,' such as dumpster diving, may come with a steep price. The case of Steven De Geynst, a.k.a 'The Muffin Man,' in March of 2010 highlights how a simple act of taking two bags of muffins from a waste bin in Rupelmonde, Belgium, resulted in him being charged for robbery and tried in court (O'Brien, 2012). While he was eventually released, his act of rescuing food was not one that was celebrated by the state.

In sum, informal food waste governance broadly encompasses the wide range of practices that exist within and across networks of people, ideas, and places. While informal strategies are often most visible within households or across communities, they are also present in markets and places which can best be described as hybridized spaces. Thus, informal food waste governance is not simply a catch all for practices outside formalized food system governance in the Global South. Rather, the presence of formalized, informal, and hybridized mechanisms of food waste governance are found across the globe in various contexts. In what follows, we highlight two case studies exemplifying these complex processes of food waste governance in two very different urban contexts, one in Dayton, Ohio (United States) and the other in Bogor, West Java (Indonesia).

Case Studies

Dayton, Ohio, United States

This case study examines the urban governance of food waste in the U.S. Midwestern city of Dayton, Ohio (see Figure 19.1).[1] Recent studies have estimated that 15 per cent of waste in Dayton area landfills is food. This amounts to 75,000 tonnes of food (Warshawsky, 2021). As in other cities across the U.S. (Shannon, 2014; Slocum, 2007), race and class shape the food

Figure 19.1 Case study location: Dayton, Ohio, United States
Source: Created by Author.

system in the Dayton region, as West Dayton, East Dayton, and parts of the semi-urban fringe, are food deserts (Dayton and Montgomery County Public Health, 2015). Food insecurity has remained high in Dayton since deindustrialization accelerated in the 1970s, producing large-scale manufacturing layoffs and disinvestment (Friedhoff et al., 2016). By 2014, Dayton was ranked as the ninth most food insecure city in the U.S., with 23 per cent of its population being food insecure (Food Research and Action Center, 2014). Although Dayton's food insecurity rate decreased between 2014 and 2019 as the U.S. economy started to rebound from the Great Recession of 2008 and 2009 (Dayton and Montgomery County Public Health, 2015; Food Research and Action Center, 2018), these gains were quickly lost in 2020, as the COVID-19 pandemic decimated the local economy and contributed to increased unemployment and lost wages for many households. As a result, food insecurity rates rose dramatically during 2020, with some estimates pointing to a doubling of hunger in the state of Ohio due to the pandemic (Meibers, 2020).

To address food system inequalities in the Dayton region, key county, city, private, and non-profit organizations have developed programmes to address both food insecurity and food waste over the past decade, as discussed in the following paragraphs (Cuy Castellanos et al., 2017). Although these programmes have arguably had limited impact in the community, given the scale of the challenges associated with food system inequality, they have resulted in increased regional discussions about food insecurity, food waste, and food justice in the Dayton area, as new stakeholders across sectors have committed to addressing food insecurity.

Like many of their U.S. Midwestern counterparts, the primary county and city governments in the Dayton region do not maintain any significant governmental programmes to divert food waste from landfills, except for a small composting programme that is limited in its impact given its focus on wasted food rather than surplus food earlier in the supply chain (see Mourad, 2016). This is due to the lack of mandates in existing legislation, low cost of landfills, and dearth of facilities to process food waste in the region. Although many local governmental administrators have explored the idea of developing new anaerobic digestion facilities, private food waste hauling services, and new composting areas to provide regional commercial and residential customers increased opportunities to participate in food waste mitigation, support is growing but remains limited (see Montgomery County Solid Waste Management District, 2019). Also, the development of new food waste management infrastructure may take years to fund and build. More broadly, most residents support food waste management at the household or consumer level through food waste composting and food surplus source reduction associated with individual personal responsibility, as there is concern amongst many residents that increased regulation will increase service costs and taxes (see Warshawsky, 2021) even though 'strong sustainability' methods may cost less in the long run (Mourad, 2016).

In addition to government, large corporations play a role in food waste reduction in the Dayton region. Kroger, one of the world's largest food retailers, operates the Zero Hunger Zero Waste program to increase food donations of healthy food, reduce waste within its food system, and develop a new fund to develop innovative food waste solutions (Kroger Company, 2017). Rumpke, one of the largest waste operators in the U.S. Midwest, manages a large recycling programme in the region (Rumpke, 2019). Although both companies have expressed interest in a partnership with Dayton's Montgomery County to promote food waste reduction, the infrastructure to process food waste does not exist. Moreover, even though it is admirable that they want to partner with regional governmental entities to reduce food waste, it is also important to recognize the public relations and financial benefits these companies receive through food waste reduction efforts as they position themselves as sustainable and socially just companies (Ionescu-Somers, 2004; Lindenbaum, 2016).

Many non-profit organizations are also engaged in food waste reduction in the Dayton region. Advocacy organizations, such as the Hall Hunger Initiative and Partners for the Environment, publicize the challenges pertaining to food waste and develop local partnerships in the community to address these needs. Compost Dayton actively works to develop sustainable and economically viable approaches to composting.

The Dayton food bank, known as The Foodbank, is the largest and most impactful player in the region. It functions by taking food donations from corporations, governments, and individuals and warehousing them in its headquarters before distributing them to community food pantries and other beneficiary organizations. In addition to the millions of pounds of food it delivers to its member agencies within its region (The Foodbank, 2018), it has also built an anaerobic digester to reduce food waste next to its warehouse, a type of technology which is still under critical review for its environmental impact (De Meester et al., 2012) Although this machine may be scaled out in terms of its impact, it remains at the food bank's headquarters location for now. The Foodbank has been criticized for its partnership with Feeding America and its expansive network of 200 food banks and 60,000 beneficiary organizations across the U.S. and its perceived micromanagement of member agencies and oversized voice on food system issues in the region, as it strongly influences the conceptualization, causes, and solutions of food insecurity, management of poverty and food insecure people, and the types of services and anti-hunger solutions that are developed (Poppendieck, 2014; Riches, 2018). This influence on the food system occurs even though The Foodbank is non-profit and not democratically elected or accountable to the population it serves. At the same time, The Foodbank has also played a key role during COVID-19 to address dramatic increases in food insecurity, as the institution worked on the frontlines to mitigate food insecurity during the height of the pandemic's economic crisis (The Foodbank, 2020).

In the North American context, scholars have long been concerned with the development of food banks as they can enable governments to offload their welfare state responsibilities, facilitate corporate capture of food systems, and have limited capacity to reduce food insecurity or food waste on the large scale (Poppendieck, 2014; Riches, 2018). While the charity-based patchwork of food relief helped many during the pandemic, the crisis also revealed the structural weaknesses of a network which is based on excess food redistribution from corporations (Kulish, 2020). Repurposing corporate food waste to the food insecure is not a sufficient way to overcome extreme poverty, unemployment, or low wages tied to inequality in the global food system or distribution of wealth. Moreover, the generation of food waste is often internalized as an accepted cost of business practices, even though it has significant economic and social costs to society (Lohnes, 2021).

According to a recent survey of Dayton households (Warshawsky, 2021),[2] most residents wasted food regularly because of inadequate consumer knowledge, concern, time, or ability to reduce food waste. While residents recognized some roles for food companies in the production of food waste, Dayton area residents blamed consumers as the primary source of food waste creation, a point noted in other studies (Evans et al., 2017). On a more hopeful note, the survey reveals that Dayton residents might be more open to progressive food waste policies, increased regulations, and household changes in food waste management if more infrastructure, such as kerbside pickup of food waste or presence of food waste bins, was available to dispose or process food waste.

Bulkeley and Gregson (2009) argue that it is important to note that consumer preferences and behaviours are shaped by the actions of a range of global, national, and regional food system actors, such as states, corporations, and restaurants, which shape the broader mass consumption culture. Although consumer psychology is clearly important to understand (Schmidt & Matthies, 2018), household decisions are shaped by class, culture, and infrastructure availability (Soma, 2017a, 2017b; Spring et al., 2020). Moreover, powerful food system actors, such as the state and food corporations, need to remain at the centre of the discussion about causes and solutions pertaining to food waste governance, given that the social construction of food waste as a local consumer issue only helps deflect attention to the structural causes of food waste generation, such as the dominance of global food corporate profitability motives, inefficiencies in food systems, and the lack of systematic mechanisms for consumers to repurpose or reduce their food waste. However, as noted in the following case study, food system dynamics are organized quite differently in the Global South.

Case Study: Bogor, Indonesia

The following case study features the City of Bogor, Indonesia and highlights similarities to, as well as differences from, the food waste governance case study in Dayton. This case study in Bogor highlights the diverse informal food waste management approaches and the food waste governance regime (or lack thereof) in Indonesia. The waste governance regime that currently exists does not enforce policies that stress the importance of waste reduction and the need to disincentivize waste generation, and it is one that makes it very easy and cheap to waste. The lack of enforcement of policies and regulations means that those responsible for creating an environment where waste management becomes complex and burdensome (e.g. corporations), are externalizing the negative impact of their business model on to citizens. Moreover, while this governance regime relies on informal waste collectors and pickers to address the gaps in service, these groups also bear the highest burden on their health, safety, and precarity.

The City of Bogor, in the province of West Java, Indonesia, is a densely populated city with over one million people (Statistics Bogor City, 2014) in an area of only 11,850 hectares. The urban core is extremely dense with several hundred thousand people living in an area of

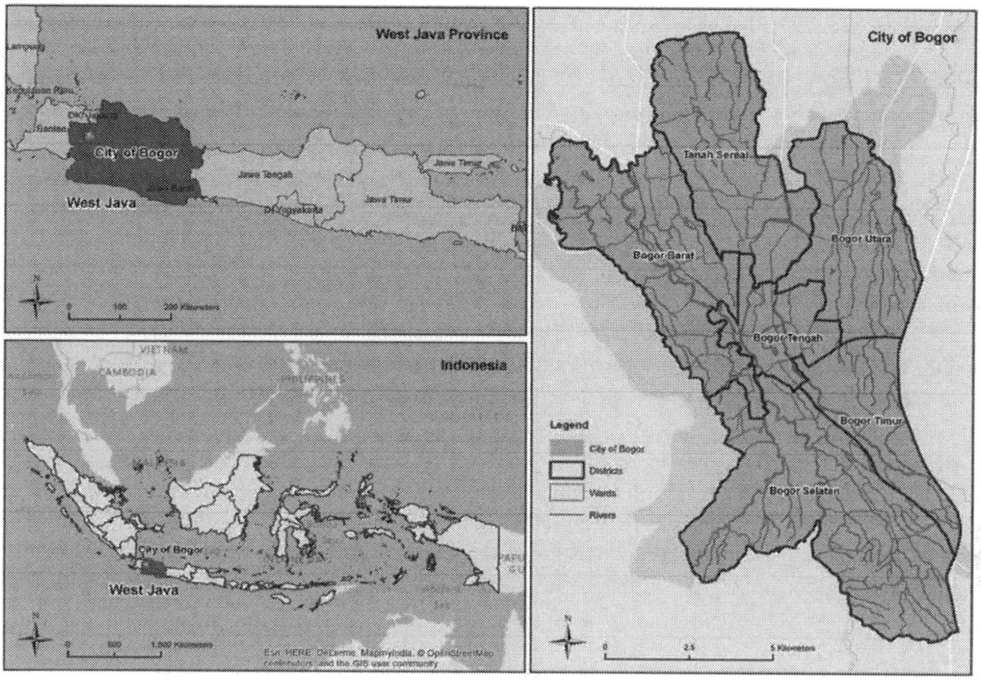

Figure 19.2 Location map of the City of Bogor, West Java

Source: Maps created by Asya Bidordinova, based on GfK GeoMarketing GIS data from the University of Toronto Map and Data Library; and for the Indonesia map, Asia GIS File; and for the City of Bogor map, Somma Radite GIS files.

approximately 20 square kilometres. Strategically located only 60 kilometres south of Indonesia's capital city Jakarta, Bogor is part of the Greater Jakarta region. Due to Bogor's strategic location near the capital city (see Figure 19.2), it has experienced rapid urbanization, population growth, and sprawl.

Urban sprawl and a growing population have resulted in the city rapidly losing its farmland to urban development. According to the 2013 agricultural census, the agriculture sector in Bogor decreased by almost 20 per cent from 2003 to 2013 (Andriamasari, 2015) with 47,953 hectares of land converted into urban development (Fajarini, 2014). More recent estimates identified only 131 hectares of arable land left in the city for farming (Haryudi, 2020). It was only in 2010 that the planning department for the municipality started to take the issue of sprawl seriously and embarked on vertical growth instead of single-family households. Within the context of scarce land, growing population, and rapid urbanization, Bogor is also faced with a growing waste crisis and a landfill crisis. Rapid urbanization has resulted in the paving over of farmlands and has made it more difficult to foster a circular food system and the recycling of nutrients. Urban development has also made land so scarce that what are typically known as 'landfills' in Indonesia, are actually open dumps that are still being used despite being severely overcapacity.

Prior to the rise of plastic packaging, it was possible for Bogor residents to manage their food waste onsite and therefore return nutrients back to the soil. The most common approach was to bury the food waste by digging a hole, or to feed the food waste to animals, mostly the chickens that often roam around the neighbourhoods, and in some cases catfish (see Soma, 2017b). Even when the poor used to throw food scraps or organic waste in the river, there were few issues since all the waste was biodegradable and plastics were not prevalent. Food-related packaging was usually made of banana leaves, or other plants such as palm fronds, and old newspapers. However, the rise of plastics and other non-biodegradable packaging, as well as rapid urbanization has made on-site treatment, such as composting or burying food waste, difficult due to the growth of different types of associated packaging waste resulting in more contamination, as well as the lack of space. This has resulted in the residents of Bogor having to be increasingly reliant upon an unevenly distributed and deficient waste collection service from the municipality whereby those with privilege have access to waste collection as they can afford to pay the waste fees, while others may have to walk quite a distance to reach a temporary dumpsite or would resort to burning and dumping waste in rivers and ravines.

In Bogor and most of Indonesia, it is the households' responsibility to throw their waste in a temporary dumpsite, and the municipality will then send a truck to collect the waste. However, temporary open dumpsites are not always easy to find, and if they are near a neighbourhood, there are issues around smell, leaching, pests, and litter. The inconvenience of going to the temporary dumpsite also may result in littering. According to the municipal solid waste estimates, food waste comprises 69 per cent of the total household solid waste collected, and only 67 per cent of the Bogor residents are serviced by the municipality (Municipality of Bogor, 2011). Addressing the issue of food waste in Indonesia has become one of great urgency as food waste in urban areas of Indonesia is projected to grow by 49 per cent between 2005 and 2025 (Adhikari et al., 2006). A new study recently conducted by the Indonesian Ministry of National Development and Planning (2021) estimated food loss and waste generation of 115–184kg/capita/year over the period from 2000 to 2019. It is projected that if Indonesia maintains the status quo (business as usual), it will generate 344 kg/capita/year by 2045 (Ministry of National Development and Planning, 2021). It is important to note that currently, almost all the household solid waste is mixed and there is a lack of composting programmes or formal diversion programmes that are designed for dealing with food waste and recycling waste.

In the context of Indonesia, the dumping of food waste in dumpsites can result in fatal consequences due to landfill fires, methane explosions, and garbage avalanches. In the city of Bogor, there have been several fatal garbage avalanches at the Galuga open dumpsite that have killed waste pickers, including youth waste pickers (Humaeni & Widjaya, 2010). Galuga is Bogor's only landfill and has reached its maximum capacity since 2005 but was still used at the time of the case study (2014–2015). Similar to many developing countries, the 'landfill' (i.e. open dump) is improperly managed by the government. The site is not environmentally managed to deal with leachate or methane gas emission. While composting food waste would be one approach to reducing the amount of organic waste sent to the landfill, currently there is no official composting programme nor is there a mandate by the city to source separate organic waste from inorganic waste. The city did start a pilot programme to test recycling and composting in 13 neighbourhoods in 2011. However, it is not clear that the programme has been scaled up to other areas of the city. A household survey study in Indonesia (n = 323) found that 26.6 per cent of low-income respondents, 43.0 per cent of middle-income respondents and 59.7 per cent of high-income respondents know how to compost food waste. However, 92.6 per cent of the respondents stated that they 'never' compost their food waste. The issue of space was raised as a barrier as only those of the upper-income and middle-income households have some space for composting (Soma, 2019). For low-income people in the case study, space is non-existent as they often live in highly crowded urban slums/villages.

There are many examples of practices on the ground that highlight the different steps that households take when managing unwanted food and food scraps. In Bogor, 56.7 per cent of respondents give their leftover or surplus food to someone else. In Indonesia it is quite common for upper- and middle-income households to employ domestic helpers and often give extra food to them and to waste collectors, labourers, security guards etc. (Soma, 2019). Income shapes household food-sharing practices, with 77.4 per cent of higher-income respondents stating that they give leftover foods to others in comparison to 42.9 per cent of low-income respondents. However, the process of giving unwanted or surplus food is based on the dynamic of unequal power and class relations, and sometimes an upper-income household may take on a 'ridding' approach rather than a 'gifting' approach to food sharing, with low-income households taking on the role of, what can possibly be seen as, human waste management infrastructure (Soma, 2017a). In a Global North context, Giles (2013) also noted that as caloric intake has risen in the U.S., the body itself has become the site of accumulation. There are similar issues around the unequal power dynamics between the donor and recipient organizations (e.g. food banks) in the Global North context, where food recovery organizations may feel pressured to take whatever surplus is provided (Riches, 2018).

While activities around food recovery, sharing, and composting have been based on informal and individual approaches (Soma, 2019), a growing recognition by the Government of Indonesia of the issue of food waste has resulted in the publication of a new national strategy to reduce food loss and waste and a more strategic approach to address this issue. The amount of energy and nutrients lost was calculated, resulting in an estimation that if such waste had not occurred it could have fed 61–125 million Indonesians (Ministry of National Development and Planning, 2021).

In line with the Indonesian government's plans to formally address food waste, a growing formalized network of non-governmental food banks and food recovery organizations has developed with a plan to distribute food to the poor that would otherwise be wasted (see foodbankindonesia.org; gardapangan.org). While these organizations play an important role, it is necessary to explore how this model of 'food waste governance' may impact the need for integrated efforts to prevent food waste, and systematically address food insecurity. This model of food recovery may help prevent edible food from being landfilled and it can be helpful to recover good quality and nutritious food for those who are food insecure; however, the danger in conflating the issue of food waste with food insecurity is well documented (Arcuri, 2019; Fisher, 2017; Riches, 2018; Spring & Biddulph, 2020; Tarasuk & Eakin, 2005). Some of these concerns include, but are not limited to, governments reneging on their roles in ensuring the citizen's right to food by relying on charitable efforts; issues around a secondary market of lower-tiered, lower-quality foods; the stigmatization of food recipients; the normalization of poverty, and the failure to address the causes of food waste (Caplan, 2017).

Conclusion

In this chapter, the complexities of urban food waste governance have been analysed through the two cities of Dayton and Bogor. In particular, these two case studies have highlighted how formal, informal, and hybridized food waste management strategies operate in vastly different urban contexts in the Global North and South. It is highly illuminating to consider that, in the context of the Global South, food waste governance (or the lack thereof) may lead to fatalities, such as the example of the methane induced landslide which killed waste collectors and waste pickers who work in the vicinity of Bogor's open dump sites (Humaeni & Widjaya, 2010). As such, there is much at stake in this field, particularly as urban food waste governance is relatively understudied. In dealing with the governance of food recovery or food sharing, both the case of Dayton and Bogor clearly demonstrate the growing dependency of various communities around the world on charitable models such as food banks. In fact, food banks and charities have become the go-to infrastructure for corporations to reduce their food waste.

We found that inadvertently (or perhaps advertently), the dominant model of governance treats the poor as a 'food waste management infrastructure' and herein lies the issue when food waste reduction is governed through a charity and a neoliberal market-based approach. While the public sector may take on some role in addressing the issue of food waste around organic waste management downstream (e.g. through municipal government), these efforts in Bogor have been limited to the piloting of a few composting programmes in neighbourhoods, or a few composting programmes in Dayton. Although there is a diversity of governance structures across various contexts in the Global North and South, the two case studies analysed in this chapter highlight the challenges associated with formal and informal food waste governance. In particular, the chapter has highlighted the limits of exporting formalized governance structures into the Global South as they may disrupt already existing food waste reduction strategies at the local level. In addition, this dynamic has underscored the value that informal food waste strategies can provide to offset weaknesses in formalized food waste governance models in the Global North and South. For these reasons, formal and informal food governance approaches should be understood and deployed in complement not in opposition, as they already exist in hybridized forms in many contexts.

This chapter has identified a research gap on the food waste governance mechanism that may support upstream solutions and food waste prevention, therefore calling on future governance and food waste scholars to explore alternative solutions and governance approaches that promote circular and equitable solutions in urban centres of the Global North and South. While uneven consumer interest in food waste reduction and the lack of infrastructure for households to repurpose or reduce their food waste collectively contribute to food waste downstream, much larger volumes of food loss are produced upstream by food system processes which emphasize corporate profitability and reinscribe system inefficiencies. For this reason, it is important that the governance of food surplus earlier in the food system and food wasted towards the end of the food system are both prioritized, as food waste management is not a replacement for source reduction in the global food system.

Importantly, the neoliberalization of the global food system has reinforced corporate strategies for profit maximization through the trope of sustainability and corporate social responsibility. This has resulted in the continuation of food waste production and a refocus on consumers as the cause of food waste. While mitigation measures based on the food recovery hierarchy provide some avenues for food waste reduction, they operate within a context of food system inequalities, and yet do not speak to the causes of food waste, food insecurity, or food system inequality. Formal and informal food waste strategies are forced to operate within this context at the local level in cities and communities. Although the potential for food waste reduction may be limited for this reason, local food waste reduction initiatives continue to emerge in many places, as individuals, households, and communities mobilize their efforts towards systemic change to reduce waste and propose ways to diminish contributions to global warming. Although initially small, these seemingly disparate local movements have the potential to increase the political support required to pass meaningful food waste policies, regulate food companies, and build infrastructure to process waste sustainably.

Notes

1 This research included 31 interviews with city and county government administrators; food retailers, food vendors, and restaurants; local food non-profits, and households and food consumers between 2016 and 2020. For more information on these methods, see Warshawsky (2021).

2 This phone survey was conducted with 386 residents in the Dayton metropolitan area. It was designed to be geographically and demographically representative of the study region. For more information on these methods, see Warshawsky (2021).

References

Adhikari, B. K., Barrington, S., & Martinez, J. (2006). Predicted growth of world urban food waste and methane production. *Waste Management & Research, 24*(5), 421–433. https://doi.org/10.1177/0734242X06067767

Ali, M. & Snel, M. (1999). *Lessons from community-based initiatives in solid waste: task no: 99.* Water and Environmental Health at London and Loughborough, London School of Hygiene & Tropical Medicine.

Andriamasari, H. (2015). *Potensi dan Strategi Pengembangan Pertanian Periurban di Kabupaten Bogor.* Dissertation, Bogor Agricultural University. http://repository.ipb.ac.id/handle/123456789/79264

Arcuri, S. (2019). Food poverty, food waste and the consensus frame on charitable food redistribution in Italy. *Agriculture and Human Values, 36*(2), 263–275. https://doi.org/10.1007/s10460-019-09918-1

Barnard, A. V. (2016). Making the city 'second nature': freegan 'dumpster divers' and the materiality of morality. *American Journal of Sociology, 121*(4), 1017–1050. https://doi.org/10.1086/683819

Brenner, N., & Theodore, N. (2002). Cities and the geographies of 'actually existing' neoliberalism. *Antipode, 34*(3), 349–379. https://doi.org/10.1111/1467-8330.00246

Bulkeley, H., & Gregson, N. (2009). Crossing the threshold: municipal waste policy household waste generation. *Environment and Planning A, 41*(4), 929–945. https://doi.org/10.1068/a40261

Busa, J. H., & Garder, R. (2015). Champions of the movement or fair-weather heroes? Individualization and the (a)politics of local food. *Antipode, 47*(2), 323–341. https://doi.org/10.1111/anti.12108

Caplan, P. (2017). Win-win? Food poverty, food aid and food surplus in the UK today. *Anthropology Today, 33*(3), 17–22. https://doi.org/10.1111/1467-8322.12350

Christiansen, T., & Neuhold, C. (Eds.). (2012). *International handbook on informal governance.* Edward Elgar Publishing.

Clapp, J. (2020). Spoiled milk, rotten vegetables and a very broken food system. *The New York Times*, 8 May. www.nytimes.com/2020/05/08/opinion/coronavirus-global-food-supply.html

Cloke, J. (2020). Vastogenic regimes in the 21st century. In C. Reynolds, T. Soma, C. Spring, & J. Lazell (Eds.), *Routledge handbook of food waste* (pp. 65–77). Routledge. https://doi.org/10.4324/9780429462795

Cofie, O. O., Drechsel, P., Agbottah, S., & van Veenhuizen, R. (2009). Resource recovery from urban waste: options and challenges for community-based composting in Sub-Saharan Africa. *Desalination, 248*(1–3), 256–261. https://doi.org/10.1016/j.desal.2008.05.063

Colon, M., & Fawcett, B. (2006). Community-based household waste management: lessons learnt from EXNORA's 'zero waste management' scheme in two South Indian cities. *Habitat International, 30*, 916–931. https://doi.org/10.1016/j.habitatint.2005.04.006

Corkery, M., & Yaffe-Bellany, D. (2020). 'We had to do something': trying to prevent massive food waste. *The New York Times*, 2 May. www.nytimes.com/2020/05/02/business/coronavirus-food-waste-destroyed.html

Cuy Castellanos, D., Jones, J. C., Christaldi, J., & Liutkus, K. A. (2017). Perspectives on the development of a local food system: the case of Dayton, Ohio. *Agroecology and Sustainable Food Systems, 41*(2), 186–203. https://doi.org/10.1080/21683565.2016.1263893

Davies, A. R. (2019). *Urban food sharing.* Policy Press. www.jstor.org/stable/j.ctvkjb30n

Davies, A. R., Cretella, A., & Franck, V. (2019). Food sharing initiatives and food democracy: practice and policy in three European cities. *Politics and Governance,* 7(4), 8–20. https://doi.org/10.17645/pag.v7i4.2090

Dayton and Montgomery County Public Health. (2015). *The geography of opportunity: Montgomery County, Ohio.* www.mcohio.org/departments/human_services_planning_and_development/MC_Opportunity_Map.pdf

De Meester, S., Demeyer, J., Velghe, F., Peene, A., Van Langenhove, H., & Dewulf, J. (2012). The environmental sustainability of anaerobic digestion as a biomass valorization technology. *Bioresource Technology, 121*, 396–403. https://doi.org/10.1016/j.biortech.2012.06.109

Environmental Protection Agency (United States). (2006). *Putting food to good use*. https://archive.epa.gov/wastes/conserve/tools/rogo/web/pdf/food-guide.pdf

European Union. (2008). *Directive 2008/1/EC of the European Parliament and of the Council of 15 January 2008 concerning integrated pollution prevention and control*. https://eur-lex.europa.eu/legal-content/EN/TXT/PDF/?uri=CELEX:32008L0001&from=en

Evans, D. (2011). Blaming the consumer – once again: the social and material contexts of everyday food waste practices in some English households. *Critical Public Health, 21*(4), 429–440. https://doi.org/10.1080/09581596.2011.608797

Evans, D. (2014). *Food waste: home consumption, material culture and everyday life*. Bloomsbury Publishing.

Evans, D., Welch, D., & Swaffield, J. (2017). Constructing and mobilizing 'the consumer': responsibility, consumption and the politics of sustainability. *Environment and Planning A, 49*(6), 1396–1412. https://doi.org/10.1177/0308518X17694030

FAO (Food and Agriculture Organization). (2019). *The state of food security and nutrition in the world*. www.fao.org/3/ca6030en/ca6030en.pdf

FAO. (2020). *Impacts of COVID-19 on food security and nutrition: developing effective policy responses to address the hunger and malnutrition pandemic*. September. High Level Panel of Experts, United Nations. www.fao.org/3/cb1000en/cb1000en.pdf

FAO. (2021). *Food loss and waste*. www.fao.org/food-loss-and-food-waste/flw-data

Fajarini, R. (2014). *Dinamika perubahan lahan dan perencanaan Tata Ruang di Kabupaten Bogor*. Thesis, Bogor Agricultural University. http://repository.ipb.ac.id/handle/123456789/73120

Fisher, A. (2017). *Big hunger: the unholy alliance between corporate America and anti-hunger groups*. MIT Press. https://doi.org/10.7551/mitpress/10987.001.0001

Flanagan, K., Robertson, K., & Hanson, C. (2019). *Reducing food loss and waste: setting a global action agenda*. World Resources Institute. https://files.wri.org/s3fs-public/reducing-food-loss-waste-global-action-agenda_1.pdf

Food Research and Action Center. (2014). *How hungry is America? FRAC's national, state, and local index of food hardship*. www.frac.org/research/resource-library/hungry-america-fracs-national-state-local-index-food-hardship-april-2015

Food Research and Action Center. (2018). *How hungry is America? food hardship in America: a look at national, regional, state, and metropolitan statistical area data on household struggles with hunger*. http://frac.org/research/resource-library/hungry-america-fracs-national-state-local-index-food-hardship-july-2018

Friedhoff, A., Wial, H., & Wolman, H. (2016). *The consequences of metropolitan manufacturing decline: testing conventional wisdom*. www.brookings.edu/wp-content/uploads/2016/06/1216_manufacturing_wial_friedhoff.pdf

Galli, F., Cavicchi, A., & Brunori, G. (2019). Food waste reduction and food poverty alleviation: a system dynamics conceptual model. *Agriculture and Human Values, 36*(2), 289–300. https://doi.org/10.1007/s10460-019-09919-0

Giles, D. B. (2013). *'A mass conspiracy to feed people': globalizing cities, world-class waste, and the biopolitics of food not bombs*. Unpublished doctoral dissertation, University of Washington.

Gille, Z. (2013). From risk to waste: global food waste regimes. In D. Evans, H. Campbell, & A. Murcott (Eds.), *Waste matters: new perspectives on food and society* (pp. 27–46). Wiley-Blackwell.

Goodman, D., DuPuis, E. M., & Goodman, M. K. (2012). *Alternative food networks: knowledge, practice, and politics*. Routledge. https://doi.org/10.4324/9780203804520

Gunders, D. (2017). *Wasted: how America is losing up to 40 percent of its food from farm to fork to landfill*. 2nd ed. Natural Resources Defense Council. www.nrdc.org/sites/default/files/wasted-2017-report.pdf

Gustavsson, J., Cederberg, C., Sonesson, U., van Otterdijk, R., & Meybeck, A. (2011). *Global food losses and food waste*. Food and Agriculture Organization of the United Nations. www.fao.org/docrep/014/mb060e/mb060e00.pdf

Guthman, J. (2008). Thinking inside the neoliberal box: the micro-politics of agro-food philanthropy. Geoforum, 39(3), 1241–1253.

Haryudi. (2020). Lahan Pertanian Kota Bogor Tersisa 131 Hektare: Bima Arya Jaga 'Surga' Yang Tersisa. *SindoNews*. https://metro.sindonews.com/read/118086/171/lahan-pertanian-kota-bogor-tersisa-131-hektare-bima-arya-jaga-surga-yang-tersisa-1596089259?showpage=all

Hebrok, M., & Boks, C. (2017). Household food waste: drivers and potential intervention points for design: an extensive review. *Journal of Cleaner Production, 151*, 380–392. https://doi.org/10.1016/j.jclepro.2017.03.069

Helmke, G., & Levitsky, S. (2004). Informal institutions and comparative politics: a research agenda. *Perspectives on Politics, 2*(4), 725–740. https://doi.org/10.1017/S1537592704040472

Heynen, N., Kurtz, H. E., & Trauger, A. (2012). Food justice, hunger and the city. *Geography Compass, 6*(5), 304–311. https://doi.org/10.1111/j.1749-8198.2012.00486.x

Hoover, D. (2017). *Estimating quantities and types of food waste at the city level.* Natural Resources Defense Council. www.nrdc.org/sites/default/files/food-waste-city-level-report.pdf

Humaeni, A., & Widjaya, I. (2010). Longsor Sampah di Bogor, 4 Remaja Tewas. *Viva*, 12 March. http://nasional.news.viva.co.id/news/read/136750-longsor-sampah-di-bogor-4-remaja-tewas

Ionescu-Somers, A. (2004). The food and beverage industry. In U. Steger (Ed.), *The Business of Sustainability* (pp. 178–198). Palgrave Macmillan.

Katongole, C. B., Nambi-Kasozi, J., Lumu, R., Bareeba, F., Presto, M., Ivarsson, E., & Lindberg, J. A. (2012). Strategies for coping with feed scarcity among urban and peri-urban livestock farmers in Kampala, Uganda. *Journal of Agriculture and Rural Development in the Tropics and Subtropics, 113*(2), 165–174.

Kroger Company. (2017). Zero hunger zero waste: Kroger's plan. www.thekrogerco.com/wp-content/uploads/2017/08/Kroger-ZeroHungerZeroWaste-Plan.pdf

Kulish, N. (2020). Food banks are overrun, as surging hunger meets dwindling supplies. *The New York Times*, 8 April. www.nytimes.com/2020/04/08/business/economy/coronavirus-food-banks.html

Lindenbaum, J. (2016). Countermovement, neoliberal platoon, or re-gifting depot? Understanding decommodification in US food banks. *Antipode, 48*(2), 375–392. https://doi.org/10.1111/anti.12192

Lohnes, J. D. (2021). Regulating surplus: charity and the legal geographies of food waste enclosure. *Agriculture and Human Values, 38*, 351–363. https://doi.org/10.1007/s10460-020-10150-5

Meibers, B. (2020). Coronavirus: food insecurity has doubled locally, across Ohio. *Dayton Daily News*, 29 June. www.daytondailynews.com/news/local/coronavirus-food-insecurity-has-doubled-locally-across-ohio/cIXo5K5pzcIGbhKhF4lgmO/

Ministry of National Development and Planning. (2021). *Executive summary for policy makers food loss and waste in Indonesia: supporting the implementation of circular economy and low carbon development.* https://lcdi-indonesia.id/wp-content/uploads/2021/07/Executive-Summary-FLW-ENG.pdf

Montgomery County Solid Waste Management District. (2019). *Solid waste management plan.* www.mcohio.org/Montgomery%20County%202019%20SWMP_%20RATIFIED.pdf

Mourad, M. (2016). Recycling, recovering and preventing 'food waste': competing solutions for food systems sustainability in the United States and France. *Journal of Cleaner Production, 126*, 461–477. https://doi.org/10.1016/j.jclepro.2016.03.084

Municipality of Bogor. (2011). *Layanan Kebersihan.* https://kotabogor.go.id/index.php/page/detail/96/informasi-laporan-penyelenggaraan-pemerintahan-daerah-kota-bogor-tahun-2011

Oberlin, S., & Szántó, G. (2011). Community level composting in a developing country: case study of KIWODET, Tanzania. *Waste Management & Research, 29*(10), 1071–1077. https://doi.org/10.1177/0734242X11402871

O'Brien, M. (2012). A 'lasting transformation' of capitalist surplus: from food stocks to feedstocks. *The Sociological Review, 60*, 192–211. https://doi.org/10.1111/1467-954X.12045

Parfitt, J., Barthel, M., & Macnaughton, S. (2010). Food waste within food supply chains: quantification and potential for change to 2050. *Philosophical Transactions of the Royal Society B: Biological Sciences, 365*(1554), 3065–3081. https://doi.org/10.1098/rstb.2010.0126

Parikh, A., & Fagan, J. M. (2015). Proposal for a community 'Solidarity' refrigerator that would both feed the hungry and lessen food waste. *Colloquium: ethics in science and society.* https://rucore.libraries.rutgers.edu/rutgers-lib/49382

Parizeau, K., Maclaren, V. W., & Chanthy, L. (2006). Waste characterization as an element of waste management planning: lessons learned from a study in Siem Reap, Cambodia. *Resources Conservation and Recycling, 49*(2), 110–128. https://doi.org/10.1016/j.resconrec.2006.03.006

Pieterse, E., Parnell, S., Swilling, M., & van Donk, M. (2008). Consolidating developmental local government. In M. van Donk, M. Swilling, E. Pieterse, & S. Parnell (Eds.), *Consolidating Developmental Local Government* (pp. 1–23). University of Cape Town Press.

Poppendieck, J. (2014). Food assistance, hunger, and the end of welfare in the USA. In G. Riches & T. Silvasti (Eds.), *First World Hunger Revisited*, 2nd. ed. (pp. 176–190). Palgrave Macmillan.

ReFed. (2016). *A roadmap to reduce U.S. food waste by 20 percent*. www.refed.com/downloads/ReFED_Report_2016.pdf

Reynolds, C. J., Mavrakis, V., Davison, S., Høj, S. B., Vlaholias, E., Sharp, A., Thompson, K., Ward, P., Coveney, J., Piantadosi, J., & Boland, J. (2014). Estimating informal household food waste in developed countries: the case of Australia. *Waste Management & Research, 32*(12), 1254–1258. https://doi.org/10.1177/0734242X14549797

Reynolds, K. (2015). Disparity despite diversity: social *in* justice. *Antipode, 47*(1), 240–259. https://doi.org/10.1111/anti.12098

Riches, G. (2018). *Food bank nations: poverty, corporate charity and the right to food*. Routledge.

Roever, S. (2016). Informal trade meets informal governance: street vendors and legal reform in India, South Africa, and Peru. *Cityscape, 18*(1), 27–46.

Rumpke. (2019). *Awards and honors*. www.rumpke.com/docs/default-source/default-document-library/waste-recycling-industry-awards-for-rumpke.pdf?sfvrsn=2

Schmidt, K., & Matthies, E. (2018). Where to start fighting the food waste problem? identifying most promising entry points for intervention programs to reduce household food waste and overconsumption of food. *Resources Conservation and Recycling, 139*, 1–14. https://doi.org/10.1016/j.resconrec.2018.07.023

Shannon, J. (2014). Food deserts: governing obesity in the neoliberal city. *Progress in Human Geography, 38*(2), 248–266. https://doi.org/10.1177/0309132513484378

Slocum, R. (2007). Whiteness, space and alternative food practice. *Geoforum, 38*(3), 520–533. https://doi.org/10.1016/j.geoforum.2006.10.006

Soma, T. (2017a). Gifting, ridding and the 'everyday mundane': the role of class and privilege in food waste generation in Indonesia. *Local Environment, 22*(12), 1444–1460. https://doi.org/10.1080/13549839.2017.1357689

Soma, T. (2017b). Wasted infrastructures: urbanization, distancing and food waste in Bogor, Indonesia. *Built Environment, 43*(3), 431–446. https://doi.org/10.2148/benv.43.3.431

Soma, T. (2019). Space to waste: the influence of income and retail choice on household food consumption and food waste in Indonesia. *International Planning Studies*, 1–21. https://doi.org/10.1080/13563475.2019.1626222

Sonnino, R. (2016). The new geography of food security: exploring the potential of urban food strategies. *The Geographical Journal, 182*(2), 190–200. https://doi.org/10.1111/geoj.12129

Spring, C., & Biddulph, R. (2020). Capturing waste or capturing innovation? Comparing self-organising potentials of surplus food redistribution initiatives to prevent food waste. *Sustainability, 12*(10), 1–19. https://doi.org/10.3390/su12104252

Spring, C., Soma, T., Lazell, J., & Reynolds, C. (2020). Food waste. In C. Reynolds, T. Soma, C. Spring, & J. Lazell (Eds.), *Routledge handbook of food waste* (pp. 1–20). Routledge.

Statistics Bogor City. (2014). Area and total population by sub-districts in Bogor City in 2014. https://bogorkota.bps.go.id/statictable/2016/01/05/16/penduduk-kota-bogor-menurut-kecamatan-dan-jenis-kelamin-2014.html

Tarasuk, V. & Eakin, J. (2005). Food assistance through 'surplus food': insights from an ethnographic study of food bank work. *Agriculture and Human Values, 22*, 177–186. doi:10.1007/s10460-004-8277-x

The Foodbank. (2018). Backgrounder. https://thefoodbankdayton.org/learn/the-backgrounder/

The Foodbank. (2020). COVID-19 update: continuing our relief efforts in a still-uncertain economy, May. https://thefoodbankdayton.org/2020/05/

United Nations. (2020). *Sustainable development goal 13: responsible consumption and production*. www.un.org/sustainabledevelopment/sustainable-consumption-production/

Warshawsky, D. N. (2015). The devolution of urban food waste governance: case study of food rescue in Los Angeles. *Cities, 49*, 26–34. https://doi.org/10.1016/j.cities.2015.06.006

Warshawsky, D. N. (2016). Food waste, sustainability, and the corporate sector: case study of the Kroger company. *The Geographical Journal, 182*(4), 384–394. https://doi.org/10.1111/geoj.12156

Warshawsky, D. N. (2019). The challenge of food waste governance in cities: case study of consumer perspectives in Los Angeles. *Sustainability, 11*(3), 847–868. https://doi.org/10.3390/su11030847

Warshawsky, D. N. (2021). The limits of food waste governance in cities: case study of Dayton, Ohio. *Geographical Review, 111*(3), 352–372. https://doi.org/10.1080/00167428.2020.1776124

Wegerif, M. C. (2020). 'Informal' food traders and food security: experiences from the Covid-19 response in South Africa. *Food Security, 12*(4), 797–800. https://doi.org/10.1007/s12571-020-01078-z

Yaffe-Bellany, D., & Corkery, M. (2020). Dumped milk, smashed eggs, plowed vegetables: food waste of the pandemic. *The New York Times*, 11 April. www.nytimes.com/2020/04/11/business/coronavirus-destroying-food.html

Yedla, S. (2012). Replication of urban innovations-prioritization of strategies for the replication of Dhaka's community-based decentralized composting model. *Waste Management & Research, 30*(1), 20–31. https://doi.org/10.1177/0734242X10380116

20

PERSPECTIVE FROM AN AFRICAN CITY

Food Market Governance in Dar es Salaam

Marc C. A. Wegerif and Luitfred Kissoly

Introduction

This chapter discusses the nature of urban food market governance as found in many African cities. This is important given that, as many authors have pointed out, there is a lack of research and work on urban food system governance, policy and planning in Africa (Battersby & Watson, 2018; Smit, 2016), and theories of how cities function 'remain rooted in the developed world' (Roy, 2005: 147). Just as Fred Block (1990) has argued that new analysis and institutions are needed to deal with a post-industrial economy in the United States of America, so we argue that new ideas are even more needed for urban food governance in African cities that are not part of highly industrialized economies today and moreover they never were.

This chapter's goal, therefore, is to bring a perspective of urban food market governance from a large and fast-growing city in Africa, the type of city where much of the world population growth is going. Governance for us is not limited to the role of government; urban food market governance in this context is the outcome of ongoing contestation between the range of actors involved.

The food markets we are referring to include what we call public markets, often also referred to as wet markets or open markets. These are public spaces within and around which many traders sell their produce. In Dar es Salaam and similar cities, most of these market spaces appear in government plans and some of the traders in them are registered, their names appearing on lists of members held by market leadership and the responsible municipalities. Around each government-designated public market area there is almost always a wider trading area that does not appear in the government plan, an area filled with traders who are not on the official lists of members, but who run the same kinds of enterprises as those who are. There are also public markets and traders in them that do not appear on any government plans or lists, that have occupied land and do business without any official permission.

As well as including all these forms of public markets, we also look at the governance of other forms and spaces of food trading of importance for cities like Dar es Salaam. These include the small local grocery shops, fruit and vegetable stalls, street traders and street food vendors. Thus, we are looking at the wider concept of food markets as the places of food

DOI: 10.4324/9781003055907-23

wholesaling and retailing, covering a range of forms with differing legal status, although across them we find some common characteristics of their governance.

We do not write about supermarkets, because there are very few of them[1] in Dar es Salaam and they serve the expatriate and certain Tanzanian elites, not the vast majority of residents. Further, the supermarket operations, including their supply chains, follow a logic drawn from the Global North that is well written about elsewhere. We are interested here in the governance realities and logic of the dominant food markets in cities like Dar es Salaam.

Dar es Salaam is used as an example to illustrate the arguments made; to show details of food market governance realities in such a context. Dar es Salaam is one of the fastest growing cities in the world and, like other such cities in poorer countries, is seeing increasing poverty and food and nutrition insecurity among these growing urban populations as urban job opportunities and services fail to meet expectations (Balineau et al., 2021; Dodman et al., 2017). As with other primary cities in African countries, Dar es Salaam also has the largest concentration of population and economic activities in the country, making it a key market for food and other agricultural produce from across the country. The governance of food markets in such cities, therefore, has profound implications for the food security of urban residents and the livelihoods of farmers and others involved in food production, processing and distribution.

This chapter is informed by extensive qualitative field research carried out in Dar es Salaam, ongoing research and participation in food system governance discussions in other countries in Africa, as well as a review of literature on the topic. We shall start, in the next section, with an overview of the nature of food market governance in such contexts, before explaining details of the Dar es Salaam case.

The nature of urban food market governance in Africa

Urban food governance is understood to involve the full range of actors and their interactions that shape the nature and operations of urban food systems and markets. This includes the government and its various roles. It also includes organizations and actions of the full range of civil society and private sector actors in as far as these impact on the operations of food markets. It involves the ways that different individuals and groups express and exercise their interests and how disputes manifest and are mediated. Ultimately, it is about how markets operate as they do. As Lindell (2008: 1883) put it, based on her work in Mozambique, governance should not just be about policymaking, but rather 'encompass a wider range of activities or practices through which the state and other actors steer the economy and society'.

We agree with Warren Smit (2016) that studies of urban food governance in Africa have tended to 'focus too much on what should be rather than helping understand what is' (Smit, 2016: 80). We have, therefore, sought to understand how urban food markets are actually governed, without limiting our scope to already visible and recognized forms of governance. As others studying African markets have argued, governance of markets is in practice polycentric with no single hegemonic vision, but with multiple discourses and actions (Chikulo et al., 2020), where relations between civil society groups, not just state and civil society, need to be looked at (Lindell, 2008).

The literature on informal markets confirms that the nature of markets we are focused on are widespread and the main source of food, especially for poorer urban residents, as they are accessible and affordable (Battersby & Watson, 2018; Roesel & Grace, 2015; Skinner, 2018). In this chapter, we focus on the under-documented and little theorized elements of urban food market governance that we believe are applicable in many African cities. We are aware of the significant differences between African cities, but are confident from what we have seen, heard, and read about in a range of countries (Battersby & Watson, 2018; Kiaka et al., 2021; Rudolph et al., 2021), that much of what we describe here can be found, albeit with variations, in most cities in Africa. Our approach may also be applicable in cities elsewhere, especially where what are often referred to as traditional and/or informal food markets form a core part of food distribution. Indeed, we see many parallels in writing on the subaltern and urbanization in cities of South Asia (Bayat, 2000; Benjamin, 2008; Roy, 2005).

Food systems and the African urban food governance context

It is now widely accepted that food systems, and the urban food markets within them, need to address poverty and deliver jobs and income-earning opportunities – in rural and urban areas – as well as making food accessible (FAO, 2018; HLPE, 2020; Tefft et al., 2017). This is much more important in most African countries where, firstly, large proportions of the population live in rural areas and depend on agriculture and related activities for their livelihoods. Secondly, there are far too few economic opportunities outside agriculture, even in urban areas (Jayne et al., 2018). Thirdly, rapid urbanization is posing new risks and creating new challenges to ensuring access to affordable and healthy diets, with 'traditional produce markets' playing a key role in this regard. More than half of Africa's urban population lives in informal settlements; there is very high urban and youth unemployment, and even though moving to an urban area is often done to seek new opportunities, there is increasing urban poverty and food and nutrition insecurity (Balineau et al., 2021; Dodman et al., 2017; FAO et al., 2020). Urban food governance approaches in Africa have to address this diversity of considerations.

We can only properly understand market governance and socio-spatial arrangements within particular contexts, including history, culture, and geography (Chikulo et al., 2020; Jessop et al., 2008; see also Chapter 3 by Duminy in this volume). In African cities, that context includes how colonialism and imperialism shaped, and still shapes, food markets, what food is eaten and produced and how. Colonial food governance focused on the interests of the colonial powers and white settlers, while acting punitively against African food traders who were seen as a hazard rather than as running important businesses (see Chapter 3 by Duminy in this volume for further elaboration on historical governance of food in African cities). We continue to see the effect of this history on government efforts at urban food market governance and wider urban planning approaches that are not a good fit for local realities. As with the wider arena of sustainable development in Africa, food governance will have to consciously challenge imperialist power structures, including their dominant discourses, economic structures, and political and governance influences that are not working in the best interests of the majority (Tandon, 2015).

One of the consequences of Africa's history and position in the world economy, is that it sits on the wrong side of global terms of trade and an accelerating concentration of ownership in food systems that is driving greater inequalities of power and accumulation. International corporations – such as finance institutions, agri-businesses, food processors and supermarkets – are aggressively seeking investment opportunities and markets in Africa (Nolte et al., 2016; Wegerif & Anseeuw, 2020). Given this situation, some regulation to protect national agriculture production and food markets becomes important.

There was a colonial obsession in many African countries with the health hazards assumed to exist in African food markets and this colonial framing has contributed to a situation where the most powerful departments dealing with food within local governments are still often those dealing with environmental and public health issues. It is important to note that, in reality, the translation of potential food hazards in African markets into actual risks causing harm, has been found to be low and no greater than in 'formal' markets, even for higher risk meat products (Roesel & Grace, 2015). Traditional handling and preparation practices, as well as the speed with which produce goes from processing to consumption, tend to mitigate against negative health impacts, even in far from ideal food handling environments.

Low government capacity is a given in many African countries (Battersby & Watson, 2018). Programs, such as market upgrading, often just do not materialize or are driven by foreign donors or investors that don't understand or have an interest in the local conditions. When states do have some capacity there is greater risk, exacerbated during the COVID-19 pandemic, of them destroying urban markets through rigorous enforcement of inappropriate regulations or overt attacks, often still justified by claims of health concerns, against those enterprises they see as informal (Chikulo et al., 2020; Kiaka et al., 2021; Lindell, 2008; Smit, 2016; Wegerif, 2020b).

Urban plans and regulations, such as the Dar es Salaam Master Plan, that include space for a diversity of many public markets, small shops and hawkers are of great value. Lessons can also be learned from policies like the 'crawling peg', which is applied in some cities in China to ensure space is set aside for public markets, small-scale traders and fresh produce sales (Zhong et al., 2019). It is not that these are expected to be fully and exactly implemented as planned, but they contribute by setting aside space for markets in some cases and, as importantly, through creating the justification – it is in the plans – for economic actors to take space to trade.

Food markets (including the shops, processors and others in the food system) are an important source of revenue, especially for local government, even though this is often not well acknowledged by the state. Further, a government depending on particular revenue streams will tend to look more favorably on, and give some protection to, those who generate that revenue. A taxation system that works well in such contexts is structured in a way that (1) is administratively as easy as possible for the smallest enterprises to adhere to, and (2) applies progressive tax rates, giving exemptions to the smallest economic actors and then taxing on a sliding scale with lower rates for smaller enterprises and higher rates for larger ones. Any overly complex tax requirements applied across the board favor the larger businesses that have more resources to meet stringent requirements.

Recognized civil society and private sector

Various associations, such as market committees and religious groups, as well as non-government organizations and corporate private sector companies and their business associations, exist and play a role in urban food market governance. These recognized actors are often focused on engagements with the state and are visible to the state and to other institutional actors, such as international development organizations (Benjamin, 2008). Like the state, the recognized parts of civil society and the private sector have limited capacity to consistently and effectively organize food markets that serve the subaltern, and they have particular interests that are often contradictory to the interests of the majority of poorer rural and urban residents (Benjamin, 2008; Shivji, 2007).

The 'private sector' mentioned in most literature and by government and NGOs, and that we have seen in our personal capacities over years get invited into multi-stakeholder processes, is invariably corporate and of a larger scale, 'for example big supermarket chains and chambers of commerce' and 'multinational food production companies' (Smit, 2016: 82). Of greatest concern is how this recognized private sector and their allies push corporate and investor interests, such as promoting supermarkets, capital intensive large-scale agriculture, mall developments and other elements of 'modern' food supply chains and urban planning (Benjamin, 2008; Wegerif &

Guereña, 2020). As these models are not accessible on beneficial terms for most local smaller-scale farmers, processors and traders, their successes are a threat to the more inclusive urban food markets that currently exist and sustain hundreds of millions of enterprises across Africa (for further discussion on issues of power within multi-stakeholder processes, see Chapter 14 by Haysom and Currie in this volume).

The traders and farmers associations, as well as market committees, are important and the closest part of the recognized civil society to the actors that make up the markets. Yet, these structures often have entrenched challenges of low levels of participation, power struggles, and poor levels of representivity, in particular around issues of gender, class and ethnicity (Lindell, 2008). Leadership is too often self-appointed and even when elected, as we have seen in a number of markets in Dar es Salaam, largely made up of men who serve for indefinite periods and derive their influence from being able to talk the language that government and NGOs want to hear. Such leadership can, however, be useful in some instances in advancing the interests of actors within food markets, but their role as representatives of the people should not be over-romanticized.

NGOs, especially international NGOs and donors, often play a contradictory role, at times siding with elites in modernization initiatives that don't work for the subaltern and attempting to demobilize and discipline unruly civil society (Bayat, 2000; Benjamin, 2008; Shivji, 2007). NGOs can, however, also play a positive role at times if they are self-aware about their compromised position in relation to power and money, and stand in solidarity with people in poverty, including through facilitating international solidarity, and supporting people's mobilization (Roy, 2005; Shivji, 2007).

The subaltern and symbiotic food systems

The food systems that serve the majority, in particular the urban poor, in African cities are what we call symbiotic food systems. They are made up of multitudes of socially embedded economic actors who operate largely in symbiotic relations (Wegerif, 2020a). As Bayat (2000: 548) has observed 'the poor tend to function as much as possible outside the boundaries of the state and modern bureaucratic institutions, basing their relationships on reciprocity, trust and negotiation'. These relations do not involve 'organizations and deliberate networking' (Bayat, 2000: 552), they are rarely structured in the ways of recognized civil society with elected leaders and prearranged meetings or bank accounts. These economic relations are also not structured by a high level of 'marketness' – responding almost exclusively to price – but are instead 'embedded in a more complex web of social relations' (Block, 1990: 53). The economic actors involved are private market actors, but very different from the recognized private sector, and so socially embedded that they are also very much a part of the community (civil society) where they live and work.

The mode of ordering and governance in such systems is based on an interdependence among people who know each other, or are at least familiar with each other, are relatively equal in the scale of their economic enterprises, and are operating out of the same cultural repertoires and norms. Central to these relations is the management of the age-old tension between autonomy and group membership; being an individual and part of the collective. Such relations are often linked to ethnic identity or people coming from particular regions, but they are not confined to such groupings. In cosmopolitan cities, these relations are constantly contested and recreated and reach beyond ethnic or other narrow group identities (Wegerif, 2020a; Wegerif, 2018).

It is through these symbiotic relations that shop owners link to each other, and their customers and suppliers, and the food markets expand through replication, as actors already in the market assist others they know to start enterprises, rather than scaling up their individual operations. Traders engage in many collaborations with each other, just as they also compete with each other and contest market space and organization. Those who step outside the accepted norms are chastised or ostracized (Wegerif, 2018). This is not governance according to set regulations, it is 'rules and regulations that are continuously shaped and reshaped by people's practices and relationships' (Chikulo et al., 2020: 26).

The extent to which food markets governed through symbiotic relations are egalitarian and effective in meeting the food and economic needs of the majority, depends on the social embeddedness of the economic actors involved. The more that relatively equal actors are embedded within the society of the people they serve, in particular the impoverished majority, the better the chance that markets will be responsive to their common needs. Higher levels of inequality and significant market actors, living divorced from the social dynamics of those who depend on the market, increase the risk that markets will not serve the needs of the majority. Greater inequality and social dislocation also undermine the interdependent relations the symbiotic system relies on, as actors can turn to other means to meet their needs and reduce their mutual commitments within the system.

Food markets primarily relying on symbiotic relations for their governance are showing great resilience and reshaping urban space and market governance. These markets are created and defended as the economic actors unite, often with no fixed or clear leadership, in everyday forms of struggle and resistance. They employ 'quiet encroachment' (Bayat, 2000) and the 'weapons of the weak', more often associated with the peasantry; the mundane, but determined contestation with the authorities and elites over land, a place to trade, to pay less taxes, to resist exploitation (Scott, 1986; Scott, 1985; Van der Ploeg, 2008). Beyond this, these actors in markets are, together with small-scale farmers, constituting modes and circuits of production and distribution that work for them and increase their autonomy from the corporate food systems (Van der Ploeg, 2008).

New markets are created as people set up stalls at a promising spot, or as women put out mats and their pots in the street and sell to nearby residents and passers-by. Existing public markets are reshaped as groups of market traders create structures for themselves within or outside designated public markets when municipalities fail to provide the basic shelter they need. A group of traders may decide that a particular corner would be a good place to sell milk in the morning. If authorities ask them to vacate today they will be back tomorrow. As Bayat (2000: 550) pointed out, referring to Cairo and Istanbul, such street traders 'simply retreat into the back streets once the municipality police arrive, but immediately resume their work as soon as they are gone again'. Some see the outcomes as chaotic, and at times they may be, but there is a logic, a form of ordering that works for those involved and has resilience.

The interface across these spheres of food system governance

The recognized mode of joint governance – and one commonly used in the development of urban food policies and strategies in the Global North – is multi-stakeholder forums where different parts of government sit together with parts of the recognized civil society and private sector (see Chapter 10 by Halliday in this volume for elaboration on the types of multi-stakeholder processes that have developed). Such forums may discuss strategies and policies, but in the African context there has been little success in reaching agreements that get implemented. Importantly, the economic actors among the subaltern and their real interests are rarely present or well represented in such forums, normally convened in hotel or office boardrooms, where multi-stakeholder discussions happen and where most grassroots leaders are at a disadvantage and risk becoming distant from their base. One of the core challenges of multi-stakeholder processes, that is too often overlooked, is that the outcomes are shaped by power, and in African cities the power inequalities are great and the stakes are high.

Jessop et al. (2008) have argued that we should reject 'premature harmonization of contradictions' and instead emphasize 'the importance of contradictions, conflicts, dilemmas, marginalization, exclusion, and volatility, at once within and among each of these sociospatial forms' (Jessop et al., 2008: 394). Governance of urban food markets in Africa is, in practice, often governed through contestation and everyday struggles, just as the nature of urbanization in other cities of the Global South is one of ongoing contestation and struggle (Bayat, 2000; Roy, 2005). A struggle that often exploits the gray areas of unclear regulations and limited state capacity, through which space is used and expanded in a relentless process of take and give and take again, 'quiet encroachment', that the socially embedded economic actors are particularly adept at using to advance their interests. The fresh produce trader doesn't start or expand their operation by negotiating for trading space in a multi-stakeholder forum, they simply set up stall, likely on a road alongside a recognized market, thus slowly expanding the real marketplace.

While elites, from government, academia and international donors, want to see clear plans being implemented, 'cities as political entities are necessarily "unruly" and constituted by multiple and fluid spaces. This is problematic for the metro elite and large international donors pursuing neoliberal "urban reforms"' (Benjamin, 2008: 725). What results out of the contestations between actors in the city was never planned for and will look very different from any strategy coming out of a boardroom, even if many stakeholders were involved. As Chikulo et al. point out for the largest food market in Harare, 'Mbare Musika's logic does not follow a predetermined track but rather is the negotiated outcome among the sociopolitical and material elements that together constitute the market' (Chikulo et al., 2020: 2). The contestation is not a failure of governance, it is the nature of actual governance in such a context.

The case of Dar es Salaam

Dar es Salaam is a coastal city that covers a total land area of 1,590 square kilometers, has a population above 5 million (in 2020) and is subdivided into five municipal areas: Ilala, Kigamboni, Kinondoni, Temeke and Ubungo. From being a small fishing village, Dar es Salaam was established as a trading port with strong Arab influence in the 1800s and then became the seat of the German colonial rulers, before the British took over in 1919 and kept the city as their administrative center. After independence for Tanganyika in 1961 and the formation of Tanzania in 1964, the official capital of the country became the inland city of Dodoma in 1974, but Dar es Salaam remains the commercial and cultural hub of the country.

The dominant food system in Dar es Salaam involves multitudes of small-scale economic actors that are deeply socially embedded with the subaltern and operating in symbiotic relations with other actors of a similar scale, embedded in similar social relations. There is no agreed or decreed explicit food policy or strategy for Dar es Salaam, but there is a de-facto form of food market governance that is described in more detail below.

Planning of market spaces

From the government's perspective, the Dar es Salaam Master Plan 2016–2036 (DMP), which is prepared and approved by the Ministry of Lands, Housing and Settlements Development, is the key planning instrument that impacts on market spaces in the city. It was developed with some consultative processes that included the municipal councils and local residents who were involved during field surveys. The DMP includes markets and commercial facilities as part of basic services that are to be provided in every neighborhood unit of approximately 24,000 people and 48 hectares. The DMP calls for a total of 1.5 hectares for three different commercial areas and 0.2 hectares for a market within each neighborhood unit in the city. The plan also provides for: home-based enterprises; vendors at busy transportation routes/nodes; and commercial space for a range of emerging sectors, which includes food processing.

Despite the guidelines in the plan, the DMP acknowledges that there is a proliferation of small-scale trading, especially of food, in almost all available spaces. The set standards are largely unenforced in what many see as the uncontrolled expansion of the city. Nevertheless, these planning guidelines, especially the commitment to make space available for markets, are used by the economic actors involved to justify their occupation of space, with no formal approval, to set up local shops, market spaces and roadside trading. In new informal settlements there is an acute demand for market spaces as there was no prior planning. In response, all five Dar es Salaam municipalities have opted to allow roadside spaces for *Gulio* markets (open markets) that operate on specific days of the week.

Public markets and their governance

There are dozens of public markets on municipal land across Dar es Salaam, that constitute key nodes for food supply to city residents. These are officially recognized, in that they are registered and listed as markets with the municipalities and identified in the DMP. Most have fairly rudimentary structures of wooden poles supporting zinc roofs, with mud floors and traders constructing their own stalls. Only the famous Kariakoo market building, near the center of town, and a few more recently built markets, have cement floors and more solid roofs and structures. There are also public markets that are not officially registered, they have resulted from direct occupation of land by traders and do not appear on the lists of markets or in the government's urban plans. Mabibo is an example of such an unregistered market, yet it is also one of the largest wholesale markets for bananas and potatoes in the city.

Mabibo was formed by traders occupying land in 2001 and refusing to move to another area, where the government wanted them to go, which they deemed less suitable, in part due to its distance from major transport routes. To date, the market still occupies this contested land, which was originally set aside for industrial development (that did not materialize) and is still officially owned by a company. Late in 2020, just before national elections, the President of Tanzania (the late John Magufuli) intervened directly to say that this market should continue to be run by the traders. The traders run the market through their associations, who collect from each trader a daily levy (very similar to the registered markets) to cover costs of operating the market, such as to pay for security, administration, utilities and waste management.

As well as there being markets that are not registered at all, every registered public market is surrounded by traders who operate outside the area designated by the municipality for the market. The market is in practice made up of the officially recognized core and the trading activities that fill the streets surrounding that core. Those traders that overflow and extend the market into the surrounding streets either operate with no physical market structures, or put up temporary shelters to get some limited protection from the sun and rain. In many cases the number of registered traders occupying the designated market areas are fewer than those operating in and around the market. Some, not all, of the traders who operate outside the officially designated market areas and are not registered (listed) with the municipality, pay levies (in some cases at lower rates than those in the designated market area) to the market committees to contribute to services, such as cleaning and security that they benefit from, and to be able to claim some rights and legitimacy as traders. This is, of course, useful revenue for the market, and most is not recorded or paid to the municipality. The amounts and level of enforcement of payment depend on factors such as the size and permanence of the stalls and the distance from the core designated market area. Theoretically the traders not listed with the municipality have less secure rights to the trading places they occupy, but in practice in Dar es Salaam these traders rarely face harassment or removal and tend to be protected by market committees and leaders.

The municipalities are the level of government responsible for the organization of public markets. Their main roles involve the establishment and development of markets in line with the DMP; maintenance and improvement of market infrastructure; waste collection and sanitation services; safety and security; and the collection of levies and charges. Each market has a municipal appointed market manager who is responsible for overseeing day-to-day operations. Officially, this responsibility is for the designated market area and registered traders, but in practice there is no clear distinction between these and the wider real market that overflows out of that. Once market spaces are designated, it is the responsibility of municipalities to enact and enforce regulations regarding the use of the market space, as well as instituting regulations on the day-to-day operations of the markets. Again, in practice, there is a lot of shaping and reshaping the actual practices among the actors within the markets themselves.

Market traders often invest individually and collectively to build structures, especially in the early days of markets or for particular sections of the markets. In some cases, the first market structures were built by groups of traders who had started operating in an area before it was designated as a market. In another example, chicken sellers in some markets have pooled resources to build their own improved structures – for keeping live birds and for slaughtering – within the wider markets. Some wholesale marketplaces are primarily open grounds or streets where trucks park and agents sell the produce directly from the back of trucks.

A number of committees are, according to municipal by-laws, supposed to exist in the public markets. These include the market committee, which is responsible for the general running of the market and improving the welfare of traders, ensuring discipline and observance of regulations, and fostering development of their markets. These committees, in particular the main market committee, are supposed to be elected at annual general meetings by market members (who are all the traders operating at the market), in a democratic process presided over by officials from the municipality. In smaller markets this is normally a direct election by all members, while in some larger markets the main committee is comprised of members elected by each commodity group operating in the market (e.g. vegetables, fruits, grains, meat, etc.). These annual general meetings, however, are often delayed, sometimes for years. Sub-committees that are identified in by-laws, but are often not operating, include those dealing with infrastructure and environment, finance, administration, and safety and security.

Revenue at the markets is collected as per municipal by-laws that specify the amounts per stall or kiosk, and also per volume – normally per sack or crate – for certain produce delivered at the market. The larger kiosks and shops that fall within the markets normally pay monthly, while the stall holders pay daily.

There is a range of associations not specified in by-laws but organized more informally by the various actors dealing with particular functions in public markets, such as vegetable sellers, fruit sellers, butchers, the porters, and transporters. Members of the markets support each other in numerous ways through these associations and through social networks outside of them. It is the norm that market members contribute to assist each other with life events like funerals and weddings. Information sharing among market members, which happens through friend networks and general chat in and around the market, is essential to success, as are joint activities, such as traders sharing common transport when buying stock. Market members are also customers and suppliers to each other, for example women who cook food in the market buy stock from market traders and in turn sell their cooked food back to them.

Local shops and street stalls

Dar es Salaam is home to thousands of small local grocery stores (*dukas*), one or more on almost every street, which form the backbone of food retailing in the city. Every *duka* needs to have an operating license, obtained annually from the municipality, and a taxpayer identification number from the Tanzania Revenue Authority (TRA). Located in converted parts of residential houses most *dukas* are rented by the owners from the homeowner. They occupy and, with home extensions, push the boundaries of a gray area between little-enforced regulations of commercial and residential properties and the provision in the DMP for home-based enterprises.

The typical *duka* falls under the category of small businesses whose annual turnover does not exceed TSHS 100 million (USD 43,500). These businesses pay tax in terms of the 'presumptive tax system', at a rate of 3–3.5 percent of annual turnover. This system is supportive of small businesses in that it does not require any financial record keeping and exempts businesses with an annual turnover of less than TSHS 4 million (USD 1,740) from paying any tax (TRA, 2020). The approach also allows a level of negotiation as the turnover to be taxed is estimated based on assessments based on observation by TRA officials. *Duka* owners attempt to reduce these estimations through understating their expenses and income, among other strategies. The TRA officials are aware of such practices and try to factor this into their estimations. The room for negotiation, including corrupt practices, is clear.

Larger shops, including supermarkets, fall into the category of mid-sized to big businesses if they have an annual turnover above TSHS 100 million. These are required to pay Value Added Tax (VAT) and are assessed for a corporate tax that is 30 percent of net income, based on financial records that must be kept.

From 2015, the TRA attempted to introduce tax receipt machines to be used in all shops to accurately calculate turnover and due taxes. *Duka* owners resisted this, arguing that the receipt machine was too expensive; but they were also opposing a system that would have removed the room for maneuver and negotiation available under the presumptive system. They resorted to closing their shops when tax officials came around – word of mouth and cellphones were used to pass the message between *duka* owners – and opening again after the officials left. Eventually the government relented and the smaller businesses remain exempt from using the tax receipt machines.

The regulations for small street stalls (*genge*) are somewhat silent, particularly for those of a temporary nature (i.e. made with temporary materials) and situated in open spaces, such as on roadsides. A recent arrangement, championed by President Magufuli, requires that these traders pay 20,000 TSHS (USD 8.70) for which they get an annual identity card, which will enable them to trade without harassment or eviction (Msikula, 2018). While this has provided an accessible form of a right to trade, it has not involved an allocation of any specific space to trade, thus there is still a contestation that includes evictions from particular areas by city authorities who claim these sites are not for petty traders.

Although the *duka* and *genge* owners work more autonomously in their own spaces, compared to those with stalls or kiosks in the public markets, they use many of the same modes of organizing. They collaborate with each other when it is mutually beneficial. They buy from and sell to people closer to them in terms of location or networks. They tend to be part of the community where they do business, joining in with life events like weddings and funerals, contributing when there is a need in the neighborhood.

Food vendors and street hawkers

Numerous hawkers and vendors sell all manner of items, including foods, in the streets, especially at main transport routes and nodes, such as bus stops and road junctions. If the authorities move them away because they are deemed to be operating outside designated areas or do not have the officially required permits, they regroup nearby, or return again as soon as they can. In some places, as they get established, they start to build structures and a more permanent market emerges. There are also door-to-door food sellers who go on foot or by bicycle on regular routes along which they build up a customer base that they deliver to. These hawkers are almost entirely beyond any state regulation and formal associations.

There are many street food vendors (people selling cooked foods) in and around public markets and in the streets across the city. These include the renowned *Mama Ntilie* or *Mama Lishe* who typically sell tea and local donuts (*mandazi*) or chapatti in the morning, and then dishes such as Rice and Beans for lunch and dinner. These women often have no more than a mat to sit on next to their pots. Some construct rudimentary wooden benches, tables and rough shelters when they feel more established. The other ubiquitous street food vendor is the potato chip seller found on the sides of many roads or congregated near shops and bars. These are normally young men with rough wooden tables, who cook chips in large wok-like pans full of oil on charcoal fires. Some also have a grill for meat on sticks (*mishikaki*) and for preparing a popular omelet-like chip and egg dish (*chips mayai*). These operators follow the same mode as others in encroaching on space, and gradually getting more established, which then sometimes involves them getting trading licenses as they become more visible and want the security of being able to stay in one place.

Mills and abattoirs

Mills and abattoirs, as well as being key nodes for food processing that supply other markets, are markets in themselves from where maize flour (*sembe*) and meat are bought and distributed.

There are thousands of small-scale mills operating in Dar es Salaam and a larger number of different *sembe* traders, many sharing mills. The maize is trucked from all corners of the country and ground into *sembe* for the majority of city residents, most of whom cook it into the staple food of maize porridge (*ugali*) (Wegerif & Wiskerke, 2017). The mills can be found in and around public markets and business centers as well as in residential areas, making affordable *sembe* accessible. They get annually renewable business licenses from the municipalities that accept their operations. In addition, there are a few large milling companies that focus more on wheat (which is imported) and on some maize products for the middle- and upper-class consumers. These large mills are located in industrial zones.

Dar es Salaam has only a few large public abattoirs processing cattle, goats and sheep. Despite upgrades, the facilities and infrastructure in these abattoirs is basic. Like the public markets, the abattoirs are approved by the municipality (although some began as the initiatives of groups of butchers) and are run by market committees. The market committees in the abattoirs are elected, from among themselves, by all the butchers who are members of the market and slaughter there. These butchers buy the live cattle and, along with their employees, arrange the slaughtering, skinning, meat carving and selling. Many other actors in and around the abattoirs deal with different but related operations from the selling of animal skins to the processing and sale of dried blood. After slaughtering, the meat is distributed to thousands of butchers across the city. Poultry slaughtering takes place at public markets where live birds and chicken meat are sold.

All businesses dealing with food processing are required to register with the Tanzania Bureau of Standards (TBS) and to adhere to good hygienic practices in production, storage and distribution. The TBS can inspect and revoke registration if there are contraventions of the regulations. There is routine inspection by health officials at abattoirs and during the slaughtering. What one can observe, however, is that these regulations are applied flexibly and in a way that enables operations to start and run with limited capital. Overly stringent requirements would be hard to maintain in Dar es Salaam with its poor infrastructure, including non-existent mains sewerage, and unreliable water and electricity supplies.

Food sources

Important for the functioning of the markets in Dar es Salaam is that foods, whether from urban agriculture or from across and outside the country, are largely made available in the same small and flexible quantities through networks that fit these markets. This is due to the distribution, even with staple foods from distant production locations, being through the same symbiotic food system comprised of many small-scale and socially embedded economic actors, including the many transporters, traders, wholesalers and public markets. Even the typical wholesaler and maize miller in Dar es Salaam is a small family-owned business (Wegerif & Wiskerke, 2017). Thanks to the dominant retail position of the public markets and *dukas*, the few large food companies and most importers also arrange some of their distribution to supply these small-scale market outlets.

There is also an important level of protection from the vagaries of international food markets, which is perhaps the most important government intervention in food market governance in Dar es Salaam. Tanzania cooperates with the rest of the East African Community[2] (EAC) in applying common external tariffs. These provide protection across most food items, from fresh vegetables to live goats, that are covered by a 25 percent import tariff (EAC, 2017). There are also foods identified as 'sensitive items' for which special tariffs are applied. Notably, all rice imports are subject to a 75 percent or a $345 (whichever is higher) per metric ton duty. All sugar cane, beet sugar and sucrose are subject to a 100 percent or $460 (whichever is higher) per metric ton duty (EAC, 2017). There are also complete bans on the imports of some items, like chickens. These protections contribute to sustaining domestic production and distribution patterns that fit with the nature and scale of food market governance in Dar es Salaam.

Discussion and conclusion

The actual day-to-day governance of food markets is an outcome of contestation between different actors and driven in large part by the everyday forms of resistance (Scott, 1985), or quiet encroachment (Bayat, 2000) of the multitudes of economic actors socially embedded with the subaltern. And this is not a bad thing, even if it may not look like the grand plans of government or the modern city ideals of the elite and recognized private sector and civil society actors. For as long as the majority of the economic actors involved are socially embedded with the subaltern and the core ordering principle is symbiotic, the outcomes will be reasonably equitable and responsive to the food and nutrition needs of the majority of residents in African cities.

This does not mean that the state is irrelevant, far from it. The state at all levels plays a key role in shaping the nature of urban food governance: providing infrastructure that supports particular forms of food system; protecting certain modes of production and retailing; preventing or assisting in the accumulation by a few, or by many, within food markets; choosing to turn a blind eye to certain activities or intervening harshly to try and stop them; and sending out a message as to what is acceptable through policy and political announcements. In their quiet encroachment the subaltern rarely openly defy, they rather take advantage of the spaces created and push the boundaries in the gray areas on the periphery of the plans and the regulations.

Regulation of international food trade, as is done to some extent in Tanzania, is essential to urban food market governance in most African contexts. Each country needs to analyze their situation to determine the right mix of tariff and non-tariff barriers, but integration into global food and agricultural markets, with no protection, will undermine the sustainability and equitability of local production and food markets.

Most urban food governance interventions, and much of the literature, focuses on governments collaborating with recognized civil society, often through multi-stakeholder forums, in the development of urban food policies and strategies. Such processes can be useful but are far removed from the realities of most residents in cities in Africa and are potentially problematic due to the interests represented and those excluded.

More research is needed to understand urban food market governance as it exists in Africa, in particular on two areas that this chapter has underscored. First, the sphere of the symbiotic food systems through which the subaltern organize markets. We need to know more about how these operate, including the power dynamics as well as the modes of collaboration within them. Second, the role and nature of the contestation that happens at the interface of state plans and people's actions, which needs to be understood as central to the nature of governance in such a contact, not the exception to it.

Elinor Ostrom (2010: 25) stated that 'a core goal of public policy should be to facilitate the development of institutions that bring out the best in humans'. The challenge to researchers and policymakers interested in urban food markets, is to recognize and enable the positive norms, values and practices around which socially embedded economic actors govern markets.

Acknowledgments

Some of the research conducted for this chapter was carried out with the aid of a grant (No. 109580-001) from the International Development Research Centre, Ottawa, Canada. The views expressed herein do not necessarily represent those of IDRC or its Board of Governors.

Notes

1 Large supermarket groups – Shoprite from South Africa and Nakumat and Uchumi from Kenya – all closed their stores in Tanzania between 2013 and 2017.

2 The EAC is a regional economic community made up of Burundi, Kenya, Rwanda, South Sudan, Tanzania, and Uganda.

References

Balineau, G., Bauer, A., Kessler, M., & Madariaga, N. (2021). *Food Systems in Africa: Rethinking the Role of Markets*. World Bank Publications. https://openknowledge.worldbank.org/handle/10986/34919

Battersby, J., & Watson, V. (2018). *Urban Food Systems Governance and Poverty in African Cities*. Routledge. https://doi.org/10.4324/9781315191195

Bayat, A. (2000). From 'dangerous classes' to 'quiet rebels': Politics of the urban subaltern in the Global South. *International Sociology*, *15*(3), 533–557. https://doi.org/10.1177/0268580900015003005

Benjamin, S. (2008). Occupancy urbanism: Radicalizing politics and economy beyond policy and programs. *International Journal of Urban and Regional Research*, *32*(3), 719–729. https://doi.org/10.1111/j.1468-2427.2008.00809.x

Block, F. L. (1990). *Postindustrial Possibilities: A Critique of Economic Discourse*. University of California Press. https://doi.org/10.1525/9780520910133

Chikulo, S., Hebinck, P., & Kinsey, B. (2020). 'Mbare Musika is ours': An analysis of a fresh produce market in Zimbabwe. *African Affairs*, 119(476), 311–337. https://doi.org/10.1093/afraf/adaa003

Dodman, D., Leck, H., Rusca, M., & Colenbrander, S. (2017). African urbanisation and urbanism: Implications for risk accumulation and reduction. *International Journal of Disaster Risk Reduction*, *26*, 7–15. https://doi.org/10.1016/j.ijdrr.2017.06.029

EAC. (2017). *Common External Tariff: 2017 Version*. www.eac.int/documents/category/eac-common-external-tariff

FAO. (2018). *Sustainable Food Systems: Concept and Framework*. www.fao.org/3/ca2079en/CA2079EN.pdf

FAO, IFAD, UNICEF, WFP, & WHO. (2020). *The State of Food Security and Nutrition in the World 2020: Transforming Food Systems for Affordable Healthy Diets*. Food and Agriculture Organisation of the United Nations. www.fao.org/documents/card/en/c/ca9692en/

HLPE. (2020). *Food Security and Nutrition: Building a Global Narrative towards 2030*. CFS – Committee on World Food Security. www.fao.org/3/ca9731en/ca9731en.pdf

Jayne, T., Chamberlin, J., & Benfica, R. (2018). Africa's unfolding economic transformation. *The Journal of Development Studies*, *54*(5), 777–787. https://doi.org/10.1080/00220388.2018.1430774

Jessop, B., Brenner, N., & Jones, M. (2008). Theorizing sociospatial relations. *Environment and Planning D: Society and Space*, *26*(3), 389–401. https://doi.org/10.1068/d9107

Kiaka, R., Chikulo, S., Slootheer, S., & Hebinck, P. (2021). 'The street is ours': A comparative analysis of street trading, Covid-19 and new street geographies in Harare, Zimbabwe and Kisumu, Kenya. *Food Security*, *13*, 1263–1281. https://doi.org/10.1007/s12571-021-01162-y

Lindell, I. (2008). The multiple sites of urban governance: Insights from an African city. *Urban Studies*, *45*(9), 1879–1901. https://doi.org/10.1177/0042098008093382

Msikula, A. (2018). IDS For 'Machinga' Launched. *Daily News*, December 11. https://dailynews.co.tz/news/2018-12-115c0f4aad6c071.aspx

Nolte, K., Chamberlain, W., & Giger, M. (2016). *International Land Deals for Agriculture. Fresh insights from the Land Matrix: Analytical Report II*. Centre for Development and Environment, University of Bern; Centre de Coopération Internationale en Recherche Agronomique pour le Développement; German Institute of Global and Area Studies; University of Pretoria; Bern Open Publishing. https://landmatrix.org/publications/

Ostrom, E. (2010). Beyond markets and states: Polycentric governance of complex economic systems. *American Economic Review*, *100*, 408–444. https://doi.org/10.1080/19186444.2010.11658229

Roesel, K., & Grace, D. (2015). *Food Safety and Informal Markets: Animal Products in Sub-Saharan Africa*. Routledge. https://doi.org/10.4324/9781315745046

Roy, A. (2005). Urban informality: Toward an epistemology of planning. *Journal of the American Planning Association*, *71*(2), 147–158. https://doi.org/10.1080/01944360508976689

Rudolph, M., Kroll, F., Muchesa, E., Paiker, M., & Fatti, P. (2021). Food security in urban cities: A case study conducted in Johannesburg, South Africa. *Journal of Food Security*, *9*(2), 46–55. https://doi.org/10.12691/jfs-9-2-2

Scott, J. C. (1985). *Weapons of the Weak: Everyday Forms of Peasant Resistance*. Yale University Press. https://yalebooks.yale.edu/book/9780300036411/weapons-weak

Scott, J. C. (1986). Everyday forms of peasant resistance. *The Journal of Peasant Studies*, *13*(2), 5–35.

Shivji, I. G. (2007). *Silences in NGO Discourse: The Role and Future of NGOs in Africa*. Fahamu/Pambazuku. http://fahamubooks.org/book/?GCOI=90638100112660

Skinner, C. (2018). Contributing yet excluded? Informal food retail in African cities. In J. Battersby & V. Watson (Eds.), *Urban Food Systems Governance and Poverty in African Cities* (pp. 104–115). Routledge. https://doi.org/10.4324/9781315191195

Smit, W. (2016). Urban governance and urban food systems in Africa: Examining the linkages. *Cities*, *58*, 80–86. https://doi.org/10.1016/j.cities.2016.05.001

Tandon, Y. (2015). Development is resistance. *Africa Development*, *40*(3), 139–159. www.ajol.info/index.php/ad/article/view/124758

Tefft, J., Jonasova, M., Adjao, R., & Morgan, A. (2017). *Food Systems for an Urbanizing World*. World Bank. https://openknowledge.worldbank.org/handle/10986/32502

TRA. (2020). *Presumptive Tax System*. Tanzania Revenue Authority. www.tra.go.tz/index.php/income-tax-for-individual

Van der Ploeg, J. D. (2008). *The New Peasantries: Struggles for Autonomy and Sustainability in an Era of Empire and Globalization*. Earthscan. https://doi.org/10.4324/9781849773164

Wegerif, M. (2020a). The symbiotic food system. In J. Duncan, J. S. Wiskerke, & M. S. Carolan (Eds.), *Routledge Handbook of Sustainable and Regenerative Food Systems* (pp. 188–203). Routledge. https://doi.org/10.4324/9780429466823

Wegerif, M., & Anseeuw, W. (2020). *Unearthing Less Visible Trends in Land Inequality*. https://d3o3cb4w253x5q.cloudfront.net/media/documents/land_inequality_conceptual_paper_2020_11_unearthing_less_visible_trends_en_spr_lavhFDK.pdf

Wegerif, M. C., & Wiskerke, J. S. (2017). Exploring the staple foodscape of Dar es Salaam. *Sustainability*, *9*(6), 1081. https://doi.org/10.3390/su9061081

Wegerif, M. C. A. (2018). An ethnographic exploration of food and the city. *Anthropology Today*, *34*(5), 16–19. https://doi.org/https://doi.org/10.1111/1467-8322.12460

Wegerif, M. C. A. (2020b). 'Informal' food traders and food security: Experiences from the Covid-19 response in South Africa. *Food Security*, *12*(4), 797–800. https://doi.org/https://doi.org/10.1007/s12571-020-01078-z

Wegerif, M. C. A., & Guereña, A. (2020). Land inequality trends and drivers. *Land*, *9*(4), 101. https://doi.org/https://doi.org/10.3390/land9040101

Zhong, T., Si, Z., Crush, J., Scott, S., & Huang, X. (2019). Achieving urban food security through a hybrid public–private food provisioning system: The case of Nanjing, China. *Food Security*, *11*(5), 1071–1086. https://doi.org/10.1007/s12571-019-00961-8

21

URBAN AGRICULTURE PRACTICE, POLICY AND GOVERNANCE

Lauren Baker, James Kuhns and Joe Nasr

Introduction

It is unclear how many urban farmers or people are involved in food production in cities, from input supply to processing and marketing. It is also difficult to determine where urban agriculture (UA) is more or less prevalent, and the scale and scope of these activities across urban settlements, larger and smaller worldwide, is hard to grasp. However, UA's global scale is far beyond common perceptions. In the mid-1990s, UA pioneer Jac Smit estimated that 15–20 percent of the world's food was produced in urban areas, and that this percentage was increasing (Smit et al., 1996). While no accurate overall figures exist on the true global scale of UA, some partial indications do exist. For example, a team at Arizona State University and Google estimated the annual value of UA production to be between \$80 and \$160 billion and documented a host of associated ecosystem services (Clinton et al., 2018). This study has a narrower definition of "urban" that does not include peri-urban space, and so it challenges the Smit et al. (1996) estimate of 15–20 percent of food produced in urban areas. However, Clinton et al. (2018) outline significant potential for urban agriculture when incentivized as part of a city's green infrastructure.

Multiple definitions of UA speak to differences in geography, context, scale, and scope. UA includes food systems activities in and around cities and involves input supply, production, processing, and distribution from farm to fork, as well as waste management. One recent definition of urban and peri-urban agriculture, which builds on several commonly cited definitions, describes it as "the growing of food and other outputs through agricultural production and related processes, taking place on land and other spaces within cities and surrounding regions" (FAO et al., 2021).

UA spans all actors, communities, activities, places, and economies that focus on biological production in a spatial context, which – according to local standards – is categorized as "urban." It takes place in intra- and peri-urban areas, and it is structurally embedded in the urban fabric. It is integrated into the social and cultural life, the economies, and the metabolism of a city. Urban agriculture is at once specific to the "agriculture" aspect of growing food in cities, and broad in relation to the connections between growing food and other value chain and food systems activities.

DOI: 10.4324/9781003055907-24

Cohen and Wijsman (2016, p. 216) define practices as "simply the routine things people do to achieve various goals. They consist of three elements: (1) competencies, or the knowledge of how to do things; (2) material items, including technologies and infrastructure; and (3) meanings, or the ideologies, goals, and cultural understandings that make certain practices acceptable and normal." A wide spectrum of UA practices exists, which cuts across scales (from a retiree growing herbs on a balcony to investors pouring millions of dollars into controlled-environment rooftop greenhouses); across geographies (from a community greenhouse in a village above the Arctic circle to an enterprising farmer raising small livestock in an equatorial megacity); and across contexts (covering intra-urban and peri-UA as part of city region food systems, both in the Global North and the Global South). The who, what, where, how, why, and when of UA vary dramatically, thus transcending any attempts at generalization (FAO et al., 2021; Gorgolewski et al., 2011; Smit et al., 1996).

Given the unique contextual, spatial, social, cultural, and economic aspects of UA, it is an important example of the complexities of "practicing urban food governance." This chapter explores the intersections between UA practice, policy, and governance. We explore these issues in the context of global, regional, and local food systems, food security, food sovereignty, food justice, resilience, urban–rural linkages, and broader global policy priorities, all of which are explored throughout this *Handbook*. From a governance perspective, we are interested in UA's relationship with governance processes, from the local or territorial level to the global, and how these activities shape landscapes and city regions (see Chapter 25 by Blay-Palmer et al. in this volume), bolster food security and sovereignty, and enhance environmental sustainability in and around cities (RUAF, n.d.). Urban agriculture practice, policy, and governance are intricately connected to and nested across scales and within broader urban issues and governance. UA governance is multidimensional, can be both formal and informal, and is often connected to different governance platforms that shape programs, rules, and regulations. In cities, these platforms are usually new political and multi-stakeholder places for deliberation and discussion. UA governance mirrors broader food systems governance and involves coalitions of actors (state, market, individuals, civil society, collective networks) who shape and reshape both landscapes and the governance mechanisms themselves (laws, policies, regulations, norms, power).

This chapter reveals key governance tensions and challenges in UA, such as access to land, space, and resources. It reviews opportunities to support UA through various programs, activities, policy tools, and approaches. The forms of multi-stakeholder dialogue and governance that emphasize the involvement of civil society and other actors are highlighted vis-à-vis their relationship with UA, and the linkages between UA and a number of pressing global priorities, including climate change, urbanization, poverty reduction, health, and equity, are made. Case studies from Toronto, Paris, Nairobi, and Quito explore how different actors and municipalities are working to enable the effective practice of UA and overcome its challenges.

Urban agriculture challenges and implications for governance

Given the wide spectrum of practices and settings, a number of challenges confront UA practitioners on a daily basis. Consequently, governance responses to these challenges have to be as diverse as the wide spectrum of UA itself. At the heart of the challenges facing UA lie preconceived attitudes about the activity, including that it is temporary, marginal, uneconomical, unproductive, archaic, dirty, dangerous, and unsightly (Smit et al., 1996, pp. 6–8), which influence the state's engagement with UA. A number of the structural challenges that occur across many settings are outlined briefly below, along with some critical governance issues related to these challenges.

Key challenges facing urban agriculture

Land and space are probably the factors most frequently cited as a major limitation to UA. (For a discussion of land tenure, structural inequity, and governance, see Chapter 23 by Cadieux in this volume.) Land is a fixed resource, where multiple actors compete for multiple uses, pushing many to creatively utilize other spaces (e.g., roofs, walls, building interiors). At least as challenging as the *availability* of land and space is their *accessibility*. While access can be limited through physical means, it is more commonly constrained through legal, regulatory, and procedural means: from ownership and leasing mechanisms, to zoning, bylaws and building codes, and rules defining eligibility.

Competing demands for scarce land resources are frequently governed by the planning maxim of the "highest and best use" of land, which often relegates UA to an interim activity, such as installing a community garden in raised beds for a few years until the land is properly "developed" (McClintock, 2014). Land use is governed by comprehensive plans and zoning, which often either leave out any agricultural activities or present many problems when they are mentioned. UA is a fluid and ever-changing activity, and such new practices as vertical farming and rooftop greenhouses can present challenges to planning departments and the people trying to begin projects. Municipal and other governments are generally not adept at making changes or accepting new land uses in a timely manner.

Financial resources can represent critical obstacles in different sectors of UA, impacting both for-profit businesses and non-profit ventures. A survey of commercial urban farms in the United States (Rangarajan & Riordan, 2019) highlighted a range of financial issues that growers, whether for-profit or non-profit, face. Even though federal funding and grants are available in the U.S. (United States Department of Agriculture, 2016), there is little awareness of them among urban farms, and their time and complexity level are issues. In a 2014 North American survey, community garden managers across North America cited funding as the most challenging issue gardens face (Drake & Lawson, 2015). Support from cities is variable, leaving garden groups and the nongovernmental organizations that frequently manage them to chase competitive grants for programming.

In the Global South, UA can represent a significant part of the economy (Cabannes, 2012), while it is fast growing as an investment area in the Global North. However, many governments and funders in richer countries tend to view it as a leisure activity (Corcoran & Calvin, 2015), while municipalities in poorer countries have long viewed UA with suspicion and repressed it (Prain et al., 2010).

Financial pressures often combine with other challenges for many types of practitioners, given the common belief that UA can serve multiple functions and provide multiple benefits simultaneously. Daftary-Steel et al. point out that urban producers are often expected to generate income and create jobs, provide food to low-income individuals, and provide leadership, job training, and work experience for people. They conclude by terming this "the unattainable trifecta of UA," describing it as a "myth that UA can and should, alone and without long-term funding investments, simultaneously achieve these three goals" (Daftary-Steel et al., 2015, p. 21).

Equity is another structural challenge, with unequal access to financial and spatial resources being two among several major issues inevitably impacting UA practices. Lack of financial or spatial capital is intimately tied to lack of power and privilege and, consequently, lack of ability to access resources and influence governance. A lack of connections with funders or resources to secure land tenure skews where and how UA is practiced, and ultimately who practices it. Flashy new expressions of UA, such as rooftop farms with remote sensing, attract funding, while more conventional projects in underserved areas are often passed over.

Consideration of gender and race is increasingly recognized as essential to examining how resources related to UA are distributed and accessed. Gendered differences in food production, processing, and marketing practices vary significantly between countries, with an uneven burden on women common across them (Hovorka, 2006). Racialized communities often do not have the economic, social, and political capital to succeed when it comes to fundraising or accessing land (Reynolds & Cohen, 2016). Multi-stakeholder platforms also may not be of use, as inclusion remains a challenging issue for many governance bodies and platforms. (See Chapter 9 by Agyeman in this volume for a discussion of structural inequity and urban agriculture planning processes.) Equity issues have been highlighted more clearly during the COVID-19 pandemic, as cities struggle to grapple with rising food insecurity. Many smaller civic organizations responded to the crisis by pivoting their work and adapting the purposes and operations of their gardens, farms, and community food distribution models to sources supplying food to the most vulnerable members of society, often with uneven governmental support (Global Alliance for the Future of Food, 2021).

Urban agriculture governance tensions

Various legal instruments (from zoning codes specifying how many of which livestock can be raised where, to municipal rule books that community garden coordinators must follow to use City-owned land) control and regulate UA practices. Legal and regulatory instruments interact with all forms of governance, from formal and informal networks and cooperatives to other forms of collaborative entities. These hybrid governance approaches are common across UA, and they enable the formation of spaces where different stakeholders interact. However, hybrid governance is rife with tensions that impact the ability to practice UA and the forms of the practice in multiple ways, creating tensions that are connected to the abovementioned challenges.

Manganelli (2022) suggests that the hybrid governance that is characteristic of urban food movements, including UA, triggers different forms of negotiation and bargaining but can also "usher alliances, coalitions, advocacy-networks at different scales, strategizing for more enabling political spaces and more supportive multi-level policies." She suggests that tensions are common around three aspects of the hybrid governance of urban food movements: *resources, organizations, and institutions*. The tensions are interrelated, trigger mobilization across actors, and often require mediation across institutions.

Governance tensions can be found in relation to all the ways that UA is characterized: who, what, where, how, why, and when. This is reflected in the many forms of regulations and policies that define the modalities of UA. Restrictions on *who* can practice UA range from refugees who do not have the right to access land for cultivation, to women who do not hold title to a farm property. *What* cannot be produced in urban areas or parts of them, particularly many types of livestock, is often spelled out in zoning codes. Constraints on *where* urban gardening or farming can take place, and where processing and marketing of the products can occur, may be the most pervasive restrictions, enforced through zoning codes, bylaws, land-use plans, and code enforcement officers. *How* UA occurs is also impacted through the same means, whether by defining the way hens are housed or the manner in which fertilizers are applied. *Why* UA is practiced may also be controlled, with any commercial food production in residential zones or in community gardens often prohibited. Even *when* or *how long* UA can be practiced is often constrained due to the very common limited duration of leases, leading to precarious farms and lack of investment by growers.

In addition to consequences from the *presence* of problematic UA governance emanating from many institutions and organizations, a *lack* of governance can also have negative impacts on practices. Gaps in regulations and policies create voids that lead to practitioners taking risks by acting without guidance, and enforcement officers interpreting regulatory frameworks that do not explicitly state what is and is not allowed. This impacts innovations, and the emerging practices in terms of locations, products, and processes, in everything from rooftop greenhouses to the interiors of industrial buildings, cricket farms, and aquaponics systems, have encountered challenges in recent years.

Governance challenges facing urban agriculture practices – Toronto

Toronto, Canada, is known globally for its pioneering work on UA and food policy through such municipal bodies as the Toronto Food Policy Council, civil networks like Toronto Urban Growers, and official policy documents like the GrowTO: UA Action Plan (City of Toronto, 2012). Despite several decades of various kinds of policy support in this area, Toronto illustrates a range of governance-related challenges.

For example, while some scattered actions identified in the GrowTO Plan have been realized through formal City support since the Plan was approved in 2013, most actions have remained either unimplemented or have been led by UA practitioners, networks, and advocates. A Toronto Agriculture Program was established soon after the approval of the Plan to serve as an interdepartmental platform (with some representation from civil society groups) and address the range of challenges that GrowTO identified. After early promises, the interdepartmental platform's single accomplishment has been the establishment of a new program, the Community Engagement and Entrepreneurial Development (CEED) Gardens, combining community economic development, sustainable food production practices, and skills development for disadvantaged populations on newly created, publicly accessible green spaces. The process of creating these new spaces has highlighted the difficulty of collaborating across multiple silos in City departments and other public authorities, as evidenced by the more than six years, and the large human and financial resources, it took to establish the first two CEED Gardens in 2020–2021 (Hammelman, 2019). Now that the CEED Gardens have been enabled by the City and public authorities, residents, community organizations, funders, and others are collaborating to oversee the garden programs.

In support of UA, Toronto has clarified the rules for growing and selling food and provided public health guidance on assessing soil contamination when gardening in urban areas. However, the integration of enabling UA policies and programs within the City's governance remains far from fulfilled. Overall, the Planning Department has barely engaged in food system planning in the ways that some other cities around the world have done in recent years. The addition of UA into the City's new zoning code was limited to adding the single, limited category of "market garden." Individual projects of many types have been impacted by the patchwork of regulations and their interpretation by various municipal staff, combined with a lack of funding for UA. The City of Toronto's experiences exemplify the challenges related to a lack of systematic support for food system actors in general, and UA in particular.

From challenges to supports for urban agriculture

The constraints and challenges faced by urban agriculture practitioners can be addressed with a number of supportive legislative, economic, educational, communications, and planning and design instruments (Halvey et al., 2020). Supportive mechanisms include creating a conducive and enabling policy environment for UA and its formal acceptance as an urban land use, expanding access to land and land tenure security, providing support services to enhance the productivity and economic viability of UA, encouraging investments from various levels of government and the private sector, promoting gender equity and social inclusion, and practices that reduce the health and environmental risks associated with UA. Enabling policies, planning, and governance mechanisms should take into account the variation in types of urban farming and related activities, each with their own characteristics and specific opportunities and limitations. If favorable policies to practicing food production in urban areas were enacted, regulatory frameworks and institutional structures were altered to remove obstacles to such practices, and municipal staff were trained to accommodate such practices, how would all these shifts be put in place, given the highly diverse and ever-changing nature of UA and the multitude of stakeholders involved? Addressing this overall challenge lies at the center of determining how to address structural limitations tied to governance. The next section will address governance-related responses to challenges facing UA practices and show ways to capture UA's synergies with other systems, as well as opportunities for multifunctionality.

City government roles and responsibilities

Higher levels of governance (national/federal, regional, provincial/state) play some roles in the governance of UA in various parts of the world. However, it has largely fallen to cities to set the operating framework for UA. This makes sense, as the world continues to urbanize at a rapid rate, and UA activities are local activities. In addition, the municipal level is frequently viewed as being closest to the people, with the greatest ability to respond quickly and "get things done" (Moragues-Faus & Morgan, 2015). With cities increasingly becoming major actors in food policy governance, it follows that UA governance is emerging as an important sector that needs to be addressed. However, many practitioners feel that cities both overregulate UA and under-support it (Thibert, 2012), while many officials do not take it seriously (Corcoran & Calvin, 2015).

A basic and daunting question for cities is deciding where UA fits in a municipal authority or where its institutional home should be. There is no one-size-fits-all answer, as every city has different economic and social challenges that affect how it views UA. Unlike many activities that occur in cities, UA touches on a range of city departments, from economic development to public health, and many in between. Competition between departments, the "silo" effect, adds to the complexity of making coherent policy and building relationships with practitioners (Sonnino et al., 2019).

Effective municipal governance of UA requires a clearly defined institutional home that communicates effectively with stakeholders and, equally importantly, promotes UA within municipal departments and agencies (IPES-Food, 2017). If buy-ins from multiple city departments occur, UA may be taken seriously and incorporated into the work plans of multiple departments (Cohen & Wijsman, 2016).

Emerging tools, approaches, promising practices

Cities that wish to further UA can take many routes. As cities' roles related to the food system become more prominent with the adoption of strategies and charters (Sonnino, 2019), UA may come to be viewed as an area that fits into the food narrative while also making contributions to other agendas at the municipal level.

Two of the tools that are available for cities to demonstrate support of productive UA are food strategies and action plans, which are often the result of sustained advocacy by UA supporters. The tools sometimes address broader social or environmental policy priorities, while at other times they are focused specifically on a food system or UA. In all cases, once adopted and then fully implemented, they can provide guidance on how to advance UA. In the northwest, the cities of Seattle, Portland, and Vancouver have each created plans with the intent of promoting UA. For instance, action steps in the case of Vancouver included updating existing land-use policies and zoning to assist in the establishment of community gardens (City of Vancouver, 2013). Vancouver also required the provision of a range of "food assets," such as markets, gardens, farms, grocery stores, and other urban food infrastructure, in any new large development.

These documents are created for many reasons, including bringing together the many stakeholders of UA, both inside and outside of government, to examine what enabling actions are needed to raise the profile and effectiveness of a city's UA initiatives. London, Ontario, is a city of 380,000 people located in southwest Ontario, and is known as a center for health care and education. In 2017, the City's planning department released a UA strategy to guide its development in the city, building on the work of the Middlesex-London Community Food Assessment, and using community-based consultation to engage long-standing UA and food advocates. The strategy's goal is to "help the municipality and the diverse communities of London work together, and support each other, in developing a positive, enabling environment for UA in the city" (Evergreen, 2017, p. 4). London developed a series of guiding principles to support the implementation of the UA strategy and reflect a shared vision while respecting and honoring diverse perspectives. These principles are broad, but of particular interest is the desire to complement the adjoining region's rural agricultural sector and create an enabling policy environment for UA by encouraging the development of supportive municipal policies, regulations, and bylaws and removing policy barriers (Evergreen, 2017). In a nod to multi-stakeholder engagement, community-based decision-making and leadership is cited as a means to promote partnerships and collaboration. Linkages with the regional Agricultural Committee and Food Policy Council are emphasized. The effectiveness of these plans is determined by whether they are used by the various stakeholders involved, including multiple city departments, to address barriers and create more enabling conditions for UA.

Creating space for urban agriculture – Paris

Paris, France, has a rich history of UA, and its position has been elevated in recent years due to some policy moves made mostly by the City of Paris and championed by its recent Mayors. As early as 2003, Paris instituted a program intended to support the creation of community gardens, which were assigned to local associations so Parisians could come together to practice their gardening skills. A management code, the *Charte Main Verte* (The Main Green Charter) governs the behavior of gardeners, while the City provides the participating gardens with a variety of support (advisory services, topsoil, water, a utility shed) (Ville de Paris, 2020; Carrot City, n.d.a). This is one example of the priority given to the use of municipal and other properties as new spaces for UA by the City.

Food and UA are addressed indirectly through the City's Climate Plan (Ville de Paris, 2018), which has set ambitious targets in many areas. Preservation of farmland in the Île-de-France area is a focal point of intervention. Within the city, strong financial support was given to community gardens, along with a pledge to identify spaces to create more in underserved areas.

The most effective UA innovation is the municipal Parisculteurs project. Designed to set up notable UA projects around Paris, the project identified suitable sites and organized competitions to choose teams of partners to implement the vision. Competitions include many forms of agriculture, thereby involving many different groups and organizations, and workshops are held to orient competitors to the world of UA. Many of these projects are located on rooftops, as part of an ambitious goal of creating 30 hectares of new green roofs within the dense city (Les Parisculteurs, n.d.). Paris shows that a variety of approaches can be adopted by local governments to support UA, particularly in relation to the climate agenda and even in dense megacities.

Where UA is formally allowed to take place, it is governed by municipal land-use regulations and bylaws that spell out permitted uses for a piece of land or space and can either hinder or support UA. Sometimes UA stakeholders request clarification of these rules to enable urban agriculture. Other times, clear rules and regulations make it more difficult for UA practitioners (Witt, 2013). The ever-changing nature of UA puts cities at a disadvantage, as they need to catch up with what is happening on the ground. This situation may also be impacted by city planners, who may not appreciate the benefits that UA can deliver to a city (Meenar et al., 2017). Still, this is an important area where positive changes can occur. Multi-stakeholder dialogue is essential to reach solutions that work for practitioners while advancing a city's interest.

Municipalities have access to other instruments to enable UA. Economic instruments, such as tax abatement or microcredit for small entrepreneurial urban growers, can be employed to enable UA. Regulations around preparing and selling food can be beneficial to urban farmers, and many cities provide meals to their citizens in a variety of settings. Having rules in place for local procurement is a nonfinancial tool that serves multiple purposes. Notably, demand for local produce can be stimulated while simultaneously addressing other city goals, such as the provision of safe and healthy food (Dillemuth & Hodgson, 2015). Moreover, in places where one can only sell food that has been prepared in a commercial kitchen, home cottage laws make it easier to sell value-added products, allowing farmers to diversify their income sources. While having laws and regulations can be stifling for adding value to urban food production in some places, it can be enabling for UA in others.

For some municipalities, and especially those facing adverse economic conditions, creative zoning that permits certain agriculture practices can have positive impacts on food security, economic development, and social cohesion. UA advocates (including some from the local government) were instrumental in creating and implementing a new Urban Garden District zoning category in Cleveland in 2007 through the Cuyahoga Food Policy Coalition, opening the door for other changes, such as allowing the keeping of animals and bees, a few years later (Meenar et al., 2017; Growing Food Connections, 2016).

Cities can also help producers by providing compost to growers. In addition, funds can be allocated to agricultural extension and training programs that can make urban farming more productive. A ground-breaking report from Baltimore (Baltimore Office of Sustainability, 2013) shows what a city can do to enable UA. Actions in the plan include increasing land security relevant to a range of growers, from community gardeners to commercial farmers, innovative measures to ensure maximum water for growers, and a pledge to educate citizens about UA and engage with growers.

Land inventories are tools that can inform growers where vacant land may be available. Unusually sized parcels of land or land in areas where other uses are not possible, such as power corridors, can be used to grow and green a city. Further, inventories can help cities plan for UA and other sustainability goals (Mendes et al., 2008).

Promoting multi-stakeholder engagement

In most jurisdictions, the rules, regulations, and resources provided are examples of contested spaces that require dialogue and deliberation in order to arrive at a place where governance functions smoothly. This equilibrium state can be encouraged by engaging the multiple stakeholders of UA. Multi-stakeholder engagement occurs in places of deliberation, such as food policy councils or committees (Moragues-Faus & Morgan, 2015).

Multi-stakeholder processes encourage the participation of various food system actors in transparent and open planning and policymaking processes (de Zeeuw & Dubbeling, 2015). UA stakeholders are individuals, groups, or organizations (including governments) that are involved and have an interest (*stake*) in UA activities within or near urban areas. There are many reasons for creating and supporting multi-stakeholder forums to help govern UA. These processes allow for higher quality decision-making through a better understanding of priority issues and the needs of the different stakeholders involved. They improve the likelihood of UA implementation through enhanced ownership, improved mechanisms and processes for coordination, and more effective use of available human, technical, and financial resources. They give both the process and results higher credibility, contribute to more participatory governance, and can lead to interesting partnerships. Finally, they can improve the problem-solving and innovation capacity of the participating actors. The result is a more holistic and multifunctional approach to UA planning and policymaking that recognizes the complexities of cities, where countless priorities must be considered and balanced.

One of the biggest challenges remaining for local governments is engaging with food system networks and community groups, and in particular a city's most excluded groups. Unless urban producer groups and other key food system stakeholders are able to build their collective capacity and form legitimate organizations, it will remain challenging for them to participate in policy decisions that impact them (Mougeot, 2005).

Food policy councils (FPCs) have emerged in North America, and to a lesser extent in Europe, as bodies that impact how UA is governed. North American councils tend to focus more on issues of food justice, while European councils tend to be more focused on developing policy (Prové et al., 2019). If constituted inclusively, FPCs can address many issues that concern UA, from social justice to land access and funding issues. However, while some FPCs are embedded in municipal governments, most are advisory bodies (Prové et al., 2019). How much power and agency they wield differs from city to city. Still, some sort of formal and informal channels between government and civil society are needed for effective governance in the sector.

UA multi-stakeholder forums can function smoothly and produce results if participants are committed, institutional links exist, and the body is representative of its stakeholders. Equity and accessibility should be top concerns when constituting multi-stakeholder bodies. However, alternate solutions are needed when current governance and communications with stakeholders are failing. Termed by Hajer (2003) as "new political spaces" (cited in Cohen & Reynolds, 2014), these alternative solutions are sought when current mechanisms are unable to resolve problems. However, building these "new political spaces" is easier said than done.

Engaging government – Nairobi

Nairobi, Kenya, offers a compelling case study of how civil society engaged the government, resulting in the passing of the 2015 Nairobi City Council UA and Regulation Act. Prior to 2010, UA was widely perceived as an illegal activity. Measures against farmers were inconsistently enforced, and a lack of clarity about the rules made it difficult for this important part of the economy to function. Constitutional change in 2010 devolved the power of the central government to newly created Counties. Equally important was moving the administration of sectors such as agriculture to the County level of government (Gore, 2018).

The lengthy process required to fully legitimize UA shows the importance of building relationships with and knowledge for all stakeholders involved. In Nairobi, the Mazingira Institute (a civil society organization) was the lynchpin needed for success. It initiated the Nairobi and Environs Food Security, Agriculture and Livestock Forum (NEFSALF) in 2004. This bottom-up initiative brought together farmers and stakeholders from the private and public sector, which was an important step towards the institutionalization of UA (Gore, 2018). Engaging multiple partners at the government level was accomplished through NEFSALF forums and a 2016 capacity-building workshop for senior county officials (Lee-Smith, 2019).

The Nairobi County Integrated Development Plan (2018) sets out a broad range of objectives for UA, including zoning urban and peri-urban land for agriculture (Nairobi City Council, 2018). The plan pledges to create an enabling environment for UA practitioners and invest in different agriculture industries, as well as value addition and value chain development.

The process used in Nairobi reflects some of the enabling factors found in the IPES-Food (2017) report on what makes urban food happen. The policy was supportive at the national level, especially because of the multi-actor and multi-sector policy process that occurred in Nairobi. Lobbying and relationship building by the Mazingira Institute was critical in creating buy-in and commitment to the evolving urban agriculture policy, which came to fruition. Momentum generated by this work in Nairobi led the City Council to endorse and sign the Milan Urban Food Policy Pact.

From local to global: Urban agriculture policy linkages

UA governance and policy are usually focused at the local or territorial level. Over the past decades, with increasing global attention on "sustainable development" and urbanization, UA has been placed in the context of global policy priorities via the Sustainable Development Goals (SDGs). Interest in local food systems and concerns about ecological footprints and

Linking UA to the Sustainable Development Goals

Goal 1. No poverty
UA's main support for the no poverty goal are its contributions to household, community, and urban food security, along with job and income-generation.

Goal 2. Zero hunger
UA often supplements food and enhances household income, supporting access to healthy affordable food and reducing food insecurity.

Goal 3. Good health and well-being
UA can enhance nutrition and reduce susceptibility to and the effects of disease and illness.

Goal 5. Gender equality
A large percentage of urban farmers are women, and UA provides special opportunities for poor urban women (especially female-headed households).

Goal 6. Clean water and sanitation
UA may recycle and use such resources as urban organic waste and wastewater.

Goal 8. Decent work and economic growth
UA offers an opportunity for employment creation in production. For urban youth, market-oriented UA, or linked enterprises, such as waste management or processing, provides a relatively accessible entry into the urban job market.

Goal 11. Sustainable cities and communities
UA improves rural–urban partnerships, enhancing green infrastructure by creating jobs and strengthening social and cultural connections through food.

Figure 21.1 Linking urban agriculture to the Sustainable Development Goals

climate change, food security, and sustainable cities has meant that UA is increasingly relevant to national-level governments seeking to fulfill their global sustainable development commitments. Linkages to the global policy agenda are now formalized and clear, demonstrating how policy and planning for UA supports cities and countries in addressing urgent issues, including climate change, urbanization, equity, and poverty reduction.

The SDGs set out targets for reducing poverty and improving livelihoods by the year 2030. One could argue that all 17 SDGs are relevant to UA, but the goals on zero poverty, gender equality, good health and well-being, clean water and sanitation, decent work and economic growth, and sustainable cities and communities are particularly relevant (Figure 21.1).

The SDGs, and specifically Goal 11 (known as the urban goal), complement the *New Urban Agenda*, which focuses specifically on urban areas and territorial development, and emphasizes the need for urban–rural food systems linkages. Although food systems and land use have only just begun to be addressed via the Climate Convention, it is possible that nationally determined contributions will include targets related to diets, food production, shortened food supply chains, sustainable production and consumption, and sustainable land use. UA is relevant for both climate change mitigation and adaptation.

UA practitioners and advocates emphasize how it can play a role in creating more green and social cities, while at the same time reducing their ecological footprints. Cities have rallied around these global goals and targets, creating networks that strengthen their roles in contributing to the global agenda. Networks include the C40, ICLEI, and the Milan Urban Food Policy Pact, which were created to support cities in mobilizing their food systems, with an emphasis on local production and consumption. Here we see strong linkages between UA (inputs, processing, production, marketing, food waste) and integrated landscape approaches, city region food systems, and global policy priorities.

Resilience strategy – Quito

In 2017, Quito, Ecuador launched its resilience strategy by partnering with the 100 Resilient Cities Initiative and with long-term support from the UN's Food and Agriculture Organization and international NGO RUAF. Quito's strategy supports the city in facing future challenges by strengthening urban systems, including the food system. The program builds on Quito's Participatory Urban Agriculture Program (AGRUPAR), which promotes the production, processing, marketing, and distribution of organic food from urban and peri-urban gardens. In its over 19 years of existence, AGRUPAR has advanced food security, job creation, income generation, environmental management, gender equity, social inclusion of vulnerable groups, and entrepreneurship (ConQuito, n.d.; Carrot City, n.d.b).

In 2017, a group of participants were invited to build the platform for the city's food policy. Initially, a multi-stakeholder body was formed, including different levels of government, food companies, farmers, consumers associations, universities, NGOs and international organizations, and civil society organizations. This platform was later transformed into the Agrifood Pact of Quito (PAQ), informing the creation of an Agrifood Charter and the Agrifood Strategy of Quito.

The vision for Quito's Resilience Strategy is as follows: "Quito in 2040, will be a city with a high quality of life, capable of successfully facing all the challenges that arise in the social, cultural, economic and environmental fields and in the territory. It will thus become a resilient city and will have ensured the sustainable development of its population" (Government of Quito, 2017, p. 14).

Food and UA are mentioned throughout, with goals to strengthen:

1. The Quito food system
2. The UA program in Quito
3. The sustainable agricultural production program

Quito illustrates how cities can plan to address pressing issues, such as urban land use, climate change, and poverty. Within each of the plans or strategies, the food system is identified as a priority, and UA is mentioned as an action area. The municipality of Quito has provided one of the most interesting and comprehensive responses to the urban food system and UA by a city region in Latin America.

Conclusion

This chapter reveals key governance tensions and challenges in UA, such as access to land, space, and resources, as well as opportunities to support UA through various policy tools and approaches. The forms of multi-stakeholder dialogue and governance that emphasize the involvement of civil society and other actors are highlighted vis-à-vis their relationship with UA. The linkages between UA and a number of pressing city, territorial, and global priorities, including climate change, urbanization, poverty reduction, health, and equity, are made. Given the extensive and pervasive nature of UA globally, it remains marginalized and underappreciated in key planning and policy domains. A sustainable future for global city regions will require more dedicated attention to food systems broadly and UA specifically. How can city and regional governments support complex and diverse UA practices? How can the rigid legislative and policy and planning frameworks in cities be expanded to provide an enabling environment for UA? How can UA's diverse constituents be engaged in policymaking processes to shape their communities and cities? These questions should be taken up by anyone interested in urban futures.

References

Baltimore Office of Sustainability. (2013). *Homegrown Baltimore: Grow Local. Baltimore City's Urban Agriculture Plan*. Baltimore, MD: Baltimore Office of Sustainability.

Cabannes, Y. (2012). Financing urban agriculture. *Environment and Urbanization, 24*(2), 665–683.

Carrot City. (n.d.a). Programme Main Verte. Retrieved from www.ryerson.ca/carrotcity/board_pages/city/main_verte.html

Carrot City. (n.d.b). AGRUPAR. Retrieved from www.ryerson.ca/carrotcity/board_pages/city/agrupar.html

City of Toronto. (2012). GrowTO: Urban Agriculture Action for Toronto. Retrieved from www.toronto.ca/legdocs/mmis/2012/pe/bgrd/backgroundfile-51558.pdf

City of Vancouver. (2013). What feeds us: Vancouver Food Strategy. Retrieved from https://vancouver.ca/files/cov/vancouver-food-strategy-brochure-what-feeds-us.pdf

Clinton, N., Stuhlmacher, M., Miles, A., Uludere Aragon, N., Wagner, M., Georgescu, M., & Gong, P. (2018). A global geospatial ecosystem services estimate of urban agriculture. *Earth's Future, 6*(1), 40–60.

Cohen, N., & Reynolds, K. (2014). Urban agriculture policy making in New York's "new political spaces": Strategizing for a participatory and representative system. *Journal of Planning and Education Research, 24*(2), 221–234. doi:10.1177/0739456X14526453

Cohen, N., & Wijsman, K. (2016). The coevolution of urban-agriculture practice, planning and policy. In J. Dawson & A. Morales (Eds.), *Cities of Farmers: Urban Agricultural Practices and Processes* (pp. 215–229). Iowa City, IA: University of Iowa Press.

ConQuito. (n.d.). AGRUPAR. Retrieved from www.conquito.org.ec/tag/agrupar/

Corcoran, M. P., & Calvin, J. S. (2015). Introduction. In F. Lohrberg, L. Lička, L. Scazzosi, & A. Timpe (Eds.), *Urban Agriculture Europe*. Jovis.

Daftary-Steel, S., Herrera, H., & Porter, C. M. (2015). The unattainable trifecta of urban agriculture. *Journal of Agriculture, Food Systems, and Community Development, 6*(1), 19–32. http://dx.doi.org/10.5304/jafscd.2015.061.014

de Zeeuw, H., & Dubbeling, M. (2015). Process and tools for multi-stakeholder planning of the urban agro-food system. In H. de Zeeuw & P. Drechsel (Eds.), *Cities and Agriculture – Developing Resilient Food Systems*. London: Earthscan.

Dillemuth, A., & Hodgson, K. (2015). Local, healthy food procurement policies. In K. Hodgson & S. Raja (Eds.), *Planning & Policy Briefs*. Buffalo, NY: Growing Food Connections.

Drake, L., & Lawson, L. (2015). Results of a US and Canada community garden survey: Shared challenges in garden management amid diverse geographical and organizational contexts. *Agriculture and Human Values, 32*(2), 241–254. doi:10.1007/s10460-014-9558-7

Evergreen. (2017). *London Urban Agriculture Strategy*. Retrieved from https://unitedwayem.ca/wp-content/uploads/2019/02/Urban-Agriculture-Strategy-London.pdf

FAO, RUAF, & Rikolto. (2021). *Urban and Peri-urban Agriculture Sourcebook – from Production to Food Systems*. Rome: Food and Agriculture Organization of the United Nations.

Global Alliance for the Future of Food. (2021). *Beacons of Hope: Stories of Food Systems Transformation during COVID-19*. Toronto: Global Alliance for the Future of Food.

Gore, C. D. (2018). How African cities lead: Urban policy innovation and agriculture in Kampala and Nairobi. *World Development, 108*, 169–180.

Gorgolewski, M., Komisar, J., & Nasr, J. (2011). *Carrot City: Creating Places for Urban Agriculture* (1st ed.). New York: Monacelli Press.

Government of Quito. (2017). Quito Resilience Strategy. Retrieved from http://gobiernoabierto.quito.gob.ec/wp-content/uploads/documentos/resiliente/resilencia.pdf

Growing Food Connections. (2016). Cleveland, Ohio: A Local Government's Transition from an Urban Agriculture Focus to a Comprehensive Food Systems Policy Approach. Retrieved from https://growingfoodconnections.org/comminnovat/city-of-cleveland-ohio/

Hajer, M. (2003). Policy without polity? Policy analysis and the institutional void. *Policy Sciences, 36*(2), 175–195.

Halvey, M. R., Santo, R. E., Lupolt, S. N., Dilka, T. J., Kim, B. F., Bachman, G. H., Clark, J. K., & Nachman, K. E. (2020). Beyond backyard chickens: A framework for understanding municipal urban agriculture policies in the United States. *Food Policy, 103*(2), 102013.

Hammelman, C. (2019). Challenges to supporting social justice through food system governance: Examples from two urban agriculture initiatives in Toronto. *Environment and Urbanization, 31*(2), 481–496.

Hovorka, A. J. (2006). Urban agriculture: Addressing practical and strategic gender needs. *Development in Practice, 16*(1), 51–61.

IPES-Food (International Panel of Experts on Sustainable Food Systems). (2017). What makes urban food policy happen? Insights from five case studies. Brussels: International Panel of Experts on Sustainable Food Systems.

Lee-Smith, D. (2019). Nairobi and environs food security, agriculture and livestock forum. *Urban Agriculture Magazine, 36*, 35–36.

Les Parisculteurs. (n.d.). Les Parisculteurs (official website). Retrieved from www.parisculteurs.paris/

Manganelli, A. (2022). *The Hybrid Governance of Urban Food Movements: International Perspectives and Cases from Toronto and Brussels*. Cham, Switzerland: Springer.

McClintock, N. (2014). Radical, reformist, and garden-variety neoliberal: Coming to terms with urban agriculture's contradictions. *Local Environment, 19*(2), 147–171.

Meenar, M., Morales, A., & Bonarek, L. (2017). Regulatory practices of urban agriculture: A connection to planning and policy. *Journal of the American Planning Association, 83*(4), 389–403.

Mendes, W., Balmer, K., Kaethler, T., & Rhoads, A. (2008). Using land inventories to plan for urban agriculture: Experiences from Portland and Vancouver. *Journal of the American Planning Association, 74*(4), 435–449.

Moragues-Faus, A., & Morgan, K. (2015). Reframing the foodscape: The emergent world of urban food policy. *Environment and Planning A, 47*(7), 1558–1573.

Mougeot, L. J. A. (2005). *Agropolis: The Social, Political, and Environmental Dimensions of Urban Agriculture*. London: Earthscan.

Nairobi City Council. (2018). County Integrated Development Plan (CIDP) 2018–2022. Working draft. Retrieved from www.kpda.or.ke/documents/CIDP/Nairobi%20County%20Intergrated%20Development%20Plan%20(CIDP)%202018-2022.pdf

Prain, G., Karanja, N., & Lee-Smith, D. (2010). *African Urban Harvest: Agriculture in the Cities of Cameroon, Kenya and Uganda*. Springer: New York.

Prové, C., de Krom, M., & Dessein, J. (2019). Politics of scale in urban agriculture governance: A transatlantic comparison of food policy councils. *Journal of Rural Studies, 68*, 171–181.

Rangarajan, A., & Riordan, M. (2019). The promise of urban agriculture: National study of commercial farming in urban areas. Retrieved from https://smallfarms.cornell.edu/wp-content/uploads/2019/12/Promise-of-Urban-Ag_Full_102919-1.pdf

Reynolds, K., & Cohen, N. (2016). *Beyond the Kale: Urban Agriculture and Social Justice Activism in New York City*. Athens, GA: University of Georgia Press.

RUAF. (n.d.). Urban agriculture and city region food systems: What and why. Retrieved from https://ruaf.org/urban-agriculture-and-city-region-food-systems/#urban-and-peri-urban-agriculture

Smit, J., Ratta, A., & Nasr, J. (1996). *Urban Agriculture: Food, Jobs and Sustainable Cities*. New York: United Nations Development Programme.

Sonnino, R. (2019). The cultural dynamics of urban food governance. *City, Culture and Society, 16*, 12–17.

Sonnino, R., Tegoni, C. L. S., & De Cunto, A. (2019). The challenge of systemic food change: Insights from cities. *Cities, 85*, 110–116.

Thibert, J. (2012). Making local planning work for urban agriculture in the North American context: A view from the ground. *Journal of Planning Education and Research, 32*(3), 349–357.

United States Department of Agriculture. (2016). Urban agriculture toolkit. Retrieved from www.usda.gov/sites/default/files/documents/urban-agriculture-toolkit.pdf

Ville de Paris. (2018). Paris Climate Action Plan. Retrieved from https://cdn.locomotive.works/sites/5ab410c8a2f42204838f797e/content_entry5ae2f905a2f4220ae645f026/5af7316614ad660b652531de/files/Paris_-_Paris_Climate_Action_Plan.pdf?1526890697

Ville de Paris. (2020). Les jardins partagés. Retrieved from www.paris.fr/pages/les-jardins-partages-203

Witt, B. (2013). Urban agriculture and local government law: Promises, realities, and solutions. *University of Pennsylvania Journal of Law and Social Change, 16*(3), 221–235.

PART IV

Scales and Agencies in Urban Food Governance

22

THE ROLE OF THE PRIVATE SECTOR IN URBAN FOOD GOVERNANCE

Scott Drimie

Introduction

This chapter provides an analysis of the private sector in urban food governance. As literature reflecting directly on this question is limited, the chapter draws on a broad range of perspectives and experiences to offer a critical reflection around this key food systems actor. The complexity of the urban food challenge calls for holistic approaches that transcend sectoral responses that fail to address underlying barriers to food availability, access and utilisation. Comprehensive and cross-cutting urban food strategies are required that transform the whole urban food system (Battersby & Haysom, 2016). Urban governance actors can impact on food systems in a variety of ways; for example, through the governance of the production of food in and around cities; the functioning of urban and peri-urban transport systems that impact on food distribution; formal and informal food retail; and food safety (Smit, 2018).

The Global Panel on Agriculture and Food Systems for Nutrition (2018) argues that the private sector could be a positive force in the urban context for food systems change, especially through increasing the availability, affordability and aspiration of sustainable and healthy foods. The Panel argues that decision makers within the public sector need to be realistic about their own limits and pragmatic in seeking to persuade industry partners to play a more active role in improving diets. A related argument is that "civil society and private sector actors bring their own arsenals of resources and instruments to complement those of the public sector" (Halliday, 2019, p.63) and that involving non-governmental actors, including private-sector actors, is useful for ensuring additional perspectives, capacity and to leverage additional resources (Halliday et al., 2019).

Yet, the inclusion of the private sector in the governance of food systems remains deeply contentious considering the immense power that some actors have in dominating and shaping these systems. The food industry has long been criticised for its part in making food environments 'unhealthy' (Nestle, 2002, 2018). The World Health Organisation found in 1990 that the food industry could do much to develop healthy and nutritious foods, but instead chooses to produce and advertise sugary, fatty and salty foods due to increased profitability (Popkin, 1993). Arguably this situation has persisted 30 years on. Significantly for urbanising populations, the food industry has been a major driver of the nutrition transition through the

DOI: 10.4324/9781003055907-26

increased availability, affordability and aspiration of foods that are highly processed, high in protein, and/or energy dense (Popkin, 1993; Haysom, 2015; Battersby, 2017).

The cynicism of some large food corporations has accentuated the distrust that many proponents of transforming food systems have in engaging the private sector. A case in point is a report documenting over 300 examples of manufacturers of ultra-processed food and drink products leveraging the COVID-19 pandemic for commercial gain (Collin et al., 2020). This raises concerns about corporate behaviour during the pandemic of industries that are fuelling the burden of non-communicable diseases (NCDs) and placing people at greater risk of severe COVID-19 outcomes. For example, the global marketing of a sugary beverage strongly associated with poor diets, obesity, type-2 diabetes, and heart disease, all well-established risk factors for poor outcomes of COVID-19, drove a campaign celebrating the 'everyday heroes' of doctors, caregivers and educators in combatting the pandemic.

Considering a terrain characterised by deep mistrust, conflicting perspectives and possibly irreconcilable agendas, how should new forms of urban food governance include and engage the private sector? To address this question, the chapter draws together conceptual work and academic approaches with advances in international political debates and experiences pertaining to private-sector engagement in urban food governance.

In the next section, urban food governance is framed as a process of making and implementing decisions by a community of actors in order to shape food systems. They do this by defining appropriate actions and policies that deliver better food systems outcomes for people living in these places. It is argued that adopting a systems approach elevates the need for more holistic forms of governance. Types of governance should enable coordination and coherence as well as mediate or moderate power dynamics entwined within competing priorities. In the following section, it is argued that a nuanced understanding of the private sector is needed to allow for a diversified strategy in engaging actors. Recognising and acting on this diversity, recognising different agendas, becomes a key strategic governance opportunity.

Building on this notion, the chapter explores the inclusion and exclusion of different private-sector actors so as to influence the structures and mechanisms of food systems governance. A key question is then posed: how should power dynamics that emerge through competing priorities of different actors be mediated? The chapter goes on to discuss co-governance arrangements that address institutional constraints, foster synergies, and strengthen capacity. Adaptive governance arrangements are considered an important option as they rely on more open, inclusive processes for decision-making than traditional, centralised approaches. The idea of stretch collaboration is surfaced to propose governance processes that incorporate dissent and conflict as a way of raising tensions and enabling solutions. These arguments and perspectives are finally drawn together into a section that suggests some components of a strategy to engage different kinds of private-sector actors in urban food governance.

Governing urban food systems

A food system can be defined as

> the chains of market and non-market activities and actors connecting food production, aggregation, transportation and storage, processing and catering, distribution, preparation and consumption, waste and resources management, as well as agro-input suppliers and the associated regulatory institutions and activities. While these activities and actors are inter-connected by the circulation of food, each of them can be

> considered as sub-systems with specific interactions with other activities and actors that are not part of agriculture or food.
>
> *Bricas, 2019, p.16*

This includes complex relationships and interactions between the environment, people, inputs, processes, infrastructure and institutions – across different scales and levels – including the way in which food supply chains and local food environments influence the behaviour of consumers (Swart et al., 2020). Thus, food systems encompass vast networks of actors connected in a variety of intricate ways, all with different aims and approaches towards realising their own interests. These interests may be survival, well-being, pursuing a food-related livelihood, providing food for the household, community, or, more broadly, citizens, or capturing profits, subsidies, land or other resources (Walls et al., 2020).

In the wake of rapid urbanisation, questions of governing urban food systems have come to the fore. The New Urban Agenda, adopted by the United Nations (UN) in 2016, recognises the need for strengthening food systems governance, including planning and "improving food security and nutrition" in urban areas (UN, 2016, p.11). Hawkes and Halliday (2017) argue that urban food policies have the potential to address a wide spectrum of challenges within cities, including access to food, nutrition-related diseases, climate change and waste, and unemployment. This argument was echoed by the EAT–Lancet Commission on healthy diets from sustainable food systems, which claimed that by shifting diets, local governments can leverage biodiversity protection, climate change mitigation, citizens' health and food security (Willett et al., 2019). Cities have great potential to shape dietary patterns by enabling access to healthy and sustainable food and, by extension, are in a strategic position to intervene with the nutrition transition (Cabannes & Marrochino, 2018).

This brings to the fore the importance of governance. Urban food governance is a process of making and implementing decisions that shape food systems to deliver better outcomes for people living in those places. In other words, it is a process that ensures that urban food systems are influenced by a community of actors dealing with common challenges by defining and implementing appropriate actions and policies (TP4D, 2018). An analytical concept of governance reflects the "range of political, organisational, and administrative processes through which stakeholders (including citizens and interest groups) articulate their interests, exercise their legal rights, take decisions, meet their obligations, and mediate their differences" (Bakker et al., 2008, p.1894). This process-orientated approach is reflected in the Milan Urban Food Policy Pact (MUFPP), which supports municipalities to adopt comprehensive and interdisciplinary approaches, connecting food policies with other urban challenges. It calls for multi-stakeholder collaboration to develop food-related policies and initiatives, and policy coherence between all government spheres (MUFPP, 2015).

Approaching food from a systems perspective reveals important challenges and opportunities, as it highlights the need for more holistic forms of governance (Termeer et al., 2018). A systems approach clarifies that food cannot be dealt with appropriately when approached in the fragmented way that the institutional architecture of prevailing food governance encourages. The food system itself involves many interacting subsystems and is at the confluence of these other systems. This means it cannot be reduced to narrow problem frames that do not address system intricacies. As such, Candel (2014) argues that the governance system should be made more coherent and harmonised, better integrated and coordinated, and more inclusive. Beyond coordination and coherence, making and implementing decisions that shape food systems to deliver better outcomes for people raises questions about mediating or moderating the power dynamics that will emerge through the competing priorities between different actors.

This implies that governance processes should give voice to those most affected by food systems and hold those making and implementing decisions to account for their actions. McKeon (2017) argues that governance arrangements require clear parameters to ensure effective participation by the marginalised and to avoid the "capture" by more powerful actors, in particular corporate actors. McKeon describes "an abyss" between "multi-actor" processes and what has come to be known as "multistakeholderism" in which everyone enters the room on the same footing, ignoring differences in interests, roles, and responsibilities among the parties, and negating power imbalances (2017, p.380).

Termeer et al. (2018) pertinently ask what forms of governance are most appropriate to govern food systems in a more holistic and inclusive way and that moderate power differentials. They propose a framework to diagnose food governance arrangements based on five principles crucial for a food systems approach: (1) system-based problem framing, (2) boundary-spanning structures, (3) adaptability, (4) inclusiveness, and (5) transformative capacity. Highlighting a key issue, these imply that institutional frameworks to govern the food system must "address legitimacy, accountability, justice, fairness, and equity" (Termeer et al., 2018, p.87). As argued by McKeon (2017) and Moragues-Faus (2020), ensuring social differentiation and the 'voice' of marginalised people is core to this. Involving existing local networks and communities can contribute to more holistic and systems-based approaches, since civil society actors often transcend silos in practice and link "issues related to food, for example, food access, obesity, food supply, and nutrition" (Siddiki et al., 2015, p.537). Although these arguments extend to the inclusion of different private-sector organisations, emphasis is on inclusion of the marginal under principles of equity, justice and fairness.

Responding to the food system will require innovations in governance that appreciate complexity and that reflect a systems approach to problem-solving, informed by greater participation of and engagement with multiple actors with a recognition of the different power dynamics at play. The role of the private sector in governance arrangements requires careful consideration, the dimensions of which will be explored below.

Differentiating private-sector actors in urban food governance

The private sector encompasses a vast range of actors from small-scale farmers and informal vendors to large-scale corporations and 'Big Food', all of which have a role within food systems. Indeed, the role of the private sector is pervasive in food systems, including in their intersection with health and environmental systems (McKee & Stuckler, 2018; Moodie et al., 2013). There is immense diversity within the private sector, beyond the differences in simply large and small, formal and informal. Within each of these are significant variation and similarity.

There are also complicated relationships between them, including competition and contestation and overlap and interdependency (GAIN, 2020). For example, the construction of modern food retail, such as malls anchored by supermarkets, is often favoured by (local) governments over informal food retail, which is seen as a threat to public health due to issues of food safety and disrupting modern city planning. Informal food retailers often source stock and ingredients from the formal food sector, such as wholesalers, formal markets and supermarkets (Crush & Frayne, 2011). Formal and informal food retail also target different consumers: people primarily visit informal food retail points for fresh produce, whereas formal food retail is commonly used for staple products (Berger & van Helvoirt, 2018). These relationships reflect the complexity of making and implementing decisions that consider the multiple interests of a range of private-sector actors that shape food systems.

Wegerif (2020) argues that the categories used to differentiate between private-sector actors reveals how different actors are treated by officialdom. He argues that there needs to be a change of language, including moving away from the concept of "informal", as describing people and their enterprises by what they are *not* has a built-in assumption of their insignificance and that the other – the formal – is superior. This leads to simplistic interventions that aim to formalise them in the image of large corporations rather than building on how they operate and the benefits they provide. For example, supporting informal trade might involve removing regulatory barriers while improving existing trade through the provision of storage space, easier registration mechanisms and developing trading plans. Such approaches could emerge in effective urban food governance that 'listen' to the realities of the informal sector. Indeed, the Milan Pact has recommended that cities should acknowledge the importance of the informal food sector, drawing them into the governance structures of the food system (MUFPP, 2015).

Recognising the variety in the private sector and their complex interrelations allows for a more nuanced and diversified strategy in engaging the private sector. This implies that acknowledging and engaging this diversity and the connotations of the categories of language– including small-scale and informal – are a key strategic governance imperative.

Including the private sector in governance arrangements

The inclusion and exclusion of different actors influences the structures and mechanisms of food system governance as well as the substance of decisions made. Candel (2014) argues that although private corporations and related associations are increasingly involved in food security governance, in comparison to civil society organisations, they have received relatively limited attention. This is partly because most of their activities and impacts remain relatively hidden, although the presence of private-sector organisations is more visible in global forums and organisations like the *Food System Dialogues* and the *Scaling Up Nutrition* (SUN) Initiative.

There are increasingly strident arguments that private-sector actors, including large corporations, should be further embedded in food security governance. David Nabarro, Senior Advisor to the Food Systems Summit Dialogues, strives for effort to enable greater alignment and collaboration amongst multiple food systems actors at global, national and local levels, including corporates, to enable different paths for food systems transformation responding to local and national expectations (Caron et al., 2018). The Global Panel on Agriculture and Food Systems for Nutrition (2018), as another example, emphasises that solutions cannot be found in public-sector actions alone, as national policies are only one part of the puzzle, and that food systems provide the nexus where policies, investment plans, regulations, free markets and consumer behaviour interface with each other.

In calling for a 'new global research agenda for food', several high profile academics argue that the failing global food system demands urgent and collaborative effort, including analysing business incentives, understanding supply and demand, and identifying economic levers for change to transform diets and transition to a sustainable system (Haddad et al., 2016). Very recently, the World Business Council for Sustainable Development began convening a series of Science-to-Policy Dialogues, bringing together business, science and civil society to co-construct transformative food systems-related policy asks (WBCSD, 2020). Multi-stakeholder collaboration and public–private dialogue are becoming more mainstream at the global level.

In several countries, private-sector entities have acknowledged that they can do more to support public health agendas (Allen & Bloomfield, 2016). Taking this perspective to the urban level, the Global Alliance for Improved Nutrition (GAIN) has argued; "developing effective policies and programmes to address malnutrition" requires coordinated action across sectors within city governments and the involvement and participation of urban stakeholders, such as the private sector, civil society, and academia (Platenkamp et al., 2020, p.1). This builds on an approach offered by Haddad that a failure to incentivise businesses to do more to improve nutrition results in a missed opportunity: "businesses – small, medium, and large – are the key investors in the system and, within the imperative to maximize profit, can do things that are more or less positive for nutrition outcomes" (2019, p.1). Incentivising corporates to be part of the solution provides an opportunity to do more to improve nutrition results, in addition to policies that punish corporates for promoting unhealthy food (Haddad, 2018).

Nonetheless, Haddad (2018) acknowledges that corporate mistrust means that opportunities to encourage corporates to do good for nutrition are being missed. Hoddinott et al. (2016) maintain that there may be a place for public–private partnerships in improving nutrition but caution is required as there is an inherent competitive nature that may retard collaborative efforts. Taking this much further, Gillespie (2020) argues that there are commercial determinants of malnutrition, which implies that for progress to happen with corporates, the underlying drivers that incentivise market and consumption growth need to be acknowledged and addressed. Unless such companies take responsibility for their cross-cutting effects on food systems and demonstrate both intention and action to do no harm, their participation in policy processes should be limited to adhering to regulation.

The implication for urban governance is that the involvement of such companies in governance arrangements introduces conflicts of interest and may legitimise corporate irresponsibility. As McKeon argues,

> Transnational corporations' rights are protected by hard laws with strong enforcement tools, while their obligations – such as they are – are backed only by soft laws and voluntary guidelines. How to correct this imbalance is one of the greatest challenges that need to be addressed in order to defend common goods and peoples' rights, and the task becomes more arduous the more corporations assume regulatory responsibility and enter into governance spaces.
>
> *2017, p.393*

Thus, a challenge emerges of finding ways to harness the potential of private-sector engagement in food governance without compromising the need for transformation. In other words, a key challenge for urban governance is to adopt the processes, form or shape that primarily support its intended purpose: governing the urban food system for the benefit of its denizens. As Moragues-Faus (2020) has argued, governance mechanisms should fully incorporate the political dimension inherent in the production of and access to food. The governance of urban food systems is complex and challenging because of "the interdependencies of actors and their activities, as well as their different framings of the problem of food insecurity" (Pereira & Drimie, 2016, pp.25–26). The actors involved in urban governance have very different interests and agendas, requiring processes for resolving competing interests and reaching consensus (Smit, 2018). A key dimension here is the analysis, acknowledgement and mediation of power.

Analysing, understanding and mediating power

Despite some of the concerns raised earlier, the Global Panel on Agriculture and Food Systems for Nutrition argues that the private sector has "considerable potential to make food environments healthier" (2018, p.8). This centres on the sector's shaping of the production of wholesale and retail food, influencing people's attitudes, perceptions and desires, and underpinning the affordability of key food items in local and global markets. Gillespie and Nisbett (2019), in highlighting the power of large transnational corporations, acknowledge that the products and practices of private-sector organisations may help address problems encountered in food systems – or they may drive, exacerbate, or deliberately confound it. Surely, they surmise, public agencies, need to ask themselves questions about whether to engage with certain private-sector organisations, for what purpose, when and how. They avoid a general binary – between extremes of engaging with the private sector or not – indicating that there is important space where negotiations can take place and collaborations can be developed.

Gillespie and Nisbett (2019) do, however, make it clear that non-engagement with certain companies is necessary, as it is in other arenas such as public health, climate change, and green investment, where there are clear cases of 'no-go companies' – tobacco, climate disinvestment, child labour, alcohol, gambling. Moodie et al. (2013) argue that unhealthy commodity industries should have no role in the formation of national or international policy relating to NCDs, for example. This challenges the pervasive practice of accepting industry self-regulation and public–private partnerships, as public regulation and market intervention are the only evidence-based mechanisms to prevent harm caused by the unhealthy commodity industries (Moodie et al., 2013).

These 'no-go companies' aside, questions about whether to engage remain complicated. Some companies, particularly larger organisations, have corporate social responsibility units and foundations which may be "supporting pro-nutrition activities that in themselves are positive for nutrition" whilst their core business practices "encompass products and practices that continue to damage nutrition – at a much larger scale" (Gillespie & Nisbett, 2019). How to judge whether and when a company's net impacts are sufficiently positive for the food system to become eligible for potential collaboration becomes a key question. By implication, engagement principles are needed to provide clear, practical guidelines. Gillespie and Nisbett (2019) argue that these issues need to be surfaced and debated openly, as part of a consensus-building process led by those convening the governance arrangement, including where and how to draw red lines. In considering this, they argue that companies need to show pro-nutrition *actions*, and not rhetoric, over a reasonable length of time before discussions on engagement or partnerships begin.

Towards a human rights approach

A key question for urban food governance is thus how to mediate or moderate power dynamics that emerge through competing priorities between different actors – and which perpetuate systems that favour the powerful.

Walls et al. (2020) use the word *power* to describe "what allows or prevents people from realising these interests; why and how systems including food systems tend to favour particular groups over others over time; why resources accrue to some and not others; who gets to set societal norms and beliefs and how this affects individuals or groups; and how people may struggle against and resist this" (p.2). The authors make the point that power imbalances permeate all relationships concerning nutrition and not just regarding food companies (Walls et al., 2020). The use of financial, epistemic and normative power permeates the entire food system, influencing the relationships between various actors, and has a direct bearing on its outcomes. In particular, the issue of a lack of representation of the poor and marginalised in systems of local and national government and health governance is raised (Harris & Nisbett, 2018 cited in Walls et al., 2020).

Walls et al. (2020) argue that people and institutions exert their power openly but also behind 'closed' doors, or in privileged spaces, such as within global food and nutrition forums, and are challenged only when these spaces are contested. This same power can be exerted at any level, including within an urban locality. The hidden nature of private-sector organisations, partly as a result of the profit motive within a competitive system, reiterates the need for democratic control of private-sector interests (Moodie et al., 2013). Indeed, Walls et al. (2020) emphasise the power of large companies who market unhealthy foods and beverages, or lobby in backrooms against public health measures, as corporate entities are heavily incentivised by profit maximisation and related efforts to reduce (public health) regulation.

Another use of the notion of power is to understand and act on the 'centres' of power and their interconnections, offsetting the dominant by building accountability through a social compact. Walls et al. (2020), drawing on studies from a range of countries, suggest that civil society activism and other participatory approaches can create bottom-up demand for better nutrition and challenge power structures in various contexts (p.4). If this is commensurate with accountability mechanisms to support governance processes, the influence of corporate and other actors can be constrained, and civil society engagement reinforced (Swinburn et al., 2015). Following Haddad's (2019) analysis of the role of the state in setting the rules of the game in a food system and positively incentivising the private sector, the importance of the state lies in regulation, oversight, and ensuring human rights are protected (Headey et al., 2017).

Walls et al. (2020) argue that the "one existing framework with clear potential to redress power imbalances within and among states" is "the global human rights system" (p.5). In their analysis, the authors reflect that successive United Nations Rapporteurs on food and nutrition have called for placing power as a central consideration of food systems using human rights as a mechanism, providing a focus on better outcomes and on more equitable processes in the drive for better population nutrition (De Schutter, 2019 cited in Walls et al., 2020, p.5). Practically speaking, this implies that urban governance should pivot on rights-based guidance on food systems and diets, utilising "international human rights law, institutions and mechanisms" for norm setting, advocacy and accountability. Such a framework has been described conceptually by Fanzo et al. (2018) and considered in more practical terms for a non-academic audience by Hossain and te Lintelo (2018). Apart from the conceptual and practical elegance of such an approach, adopting a human rights framework has considerable traction globally (Walls et al., 2020, p.5).

Equitable processes that embrace human rights should be used to counter and balance the neoliberal economic paradigm in which food systems exist – "an economic and political ideology with an inherent focus on reshaping the regulatory environment in favour of the market" (Bell & Green, 2016). As the neoliberal perspective considers the responsibility for food choice and nutritional outcomes to lie with the individual, a counter narrative within a rights-based framework can offset its hegemony. Thus, instead of simply blaming unhealthy dietary choices on citizens and offering nutrition education, resolving underlying causes of food insecurity is imperative (Pereira et al., 2015). The transition towards healthy and sustainable diets calls for a holistic and integrative approach, touching on all areas of the urban food challenge and one that embeds a human rights approach at its centre.

Inclusive participatory governance and stretch collaboration

There is growing consensus on the need to involve relevant municipal departments and stakeholders in food governance arrangements to effectively address the existing systemic, multi-dimensional challenges (Willet et al., 2019; MUFPP, 2015; Global Panel on Agriculture and

Food Systems for Nutrition, 2018; Battersby & Haysom, 2016). This perspective holds that city governments and other actors from civil society, business and research should develop co-governance systems to identify barriers and opportunities, overcome institutional constraints, foster synergies, and build capacity (Halliday, 2019; Matacena, 2016; MUFPP, 2015). Thus, governance actors should recognise the systemic nature of the food challenge, aim for innovative solutions at a local level, and involve learning and reflection to improve action over time. The United Nations System Standing Committee on Nutrition (UNSCN, 2020) proposed that inclusive economic, social and environmental sustainability could be achieved by taking a holistic, integrative approach, working to develop a common vision, valuing the meaningful participation of and partnership among stakeholders, and developing clear roles and actions for them.

The UNSCN suggests that adaptive governance provides a solution to addressing food systems challenges as it relies on open, inclusive processes for decision-making compared to traditional, centralised approaches. Food policy councils have been suggested as positive examples of formal collaborative governance structures that include private-sector actors (Matacena, 2016). Proponents of such councils and food charters argue that they have generated regional and municipal food plans informed by declarations of values, principles and priorities, which are useful for bringing actors together to develop a common vision (Cabannes & Marrochino, 2018). Halliday et al. (2019) provide examples of actions that have been put in place in cities around the world, including governance mechanisms to improve nutrition. A key lesson is that city governments should find opportunities to collaborate early, so that key partners are involved in all phases, from planning to implementation and review. Another lesson is that when engaging the private sector, the business case for involvement must be clear, particularly when mandatory regulations or restrictions are involved, to avoid exploitation of loopholes or legal challenges.

However, in a critique of food policy councils, Moragues-Faus (2020) argues that such analyses have been imbued in an optimistic philosophy depicting such experiences as pragmatic "depolitized processes of collaboration" that in many instances overlooks conflicts of interest, winners and losers of different arrangements, and institutional deadlocks. Existing power imbalances and potential lack of inclusivity create challenges for structures such as food policy councils. Doernberg et al. (2019) reveal in a study of urban food policy and planning in German cities that activities remain fragmented and often based on individual initiatives within the administration. As such, integrated urban food policies and their implementation are an exception in major cities in Germany. In analysing food partnerships in the United Kingdom, Moragues-Faus (2020) elaborates how those with 'no-voice' at the margins of the food system, such as groups experiencing food poverty, or different ethnicities, continue to be excluded in the new reframing of urban food systems. Finding ways to enable inclusive participation of a wide range of actors, especially grassroots voices, are crucial for a formal platform to be effective.

Rather than embracing food policy councils as democracy-enhancing processes, without a deeper examination of the values and politics at play, Moragues-Faus (2020) raises questions about how these initiatives incorporate discontent, and calls for egalitarian spaces where people have the capacity to act politically. Arguably, many of the approaches around collaboration within food policy councils are based on the premise that common ground can be found by identifying a problem, finding potential solutions, developing a plan of execution, defining clear roles and responsibilities, and establishing a common purpose. Yet the high levels of mistrust, particularly of many private-sector organisations, and substantial differences in understanding what the problem is, let alone how to solve it, can rapidly polarise efforts. In these situations, unconventional *stretch collaboration* may be necessary.

Stretch collaboration abandons the assumption of control, giving up unrealistic notions of harmony, certainty, and compliance, and embraces the messy realities of discord, trial and error, and co-creation. Adam Kahane (2017) has argued that stretch collaboration can enable people to get things done even in complex situations where people do not agree or trust each other. The higher potential of collaboration with diverse others is that a greater understanding of the situation will emerge and new options created that are better than the ones imagined or implemented separately (Drimie et al., 2018). Stretch collaboration reflects a way of working *with* the system, rather than trying to control or force changes. It requires an approach of accepting that the future cannot be controlled but rather influenced. The definition of success in this kind of collaboration is not to come up with a solution, but to be working towards it.

To give this practical resonance, a case study from South Africa is illustrative (Cockburn et al., 2019). This investigates how collaboration can be fostered in contested landscapes. The challenges included water catchment management, soil management, invasive alien species management, fire management, unsustainable farming practices, and biodiversity conservation. Collaborative arrangements were established amongst government officials, large-scale commercial farmers, small-scale farmers and other interest groups. Yet deep divisions existed between people of different race groups, accentuated by a long history of colonialism and apartheid. Interaction was characterised by a lack of communication and high levels of distrust. High social diversity, inequity, and contestation, including power disparities based on historical dispossession and exploitation, were prevalent. Collaborative approaches were found that embraced these divisions. Identifying and building on existing initiatives where forms of collaboration existed was key. These included identifying shared interests based on the livelihoods or business needs of the actors in the landscape. The authors suggest an approach that focuses on enhancing individual and social-relational enablers, based on a bottom-up engagement premised on the notion of pluralism (Cockburn et al., 2019).

Drawing this into the realm of urban food systems governance, spaces should be created to allow conflict to emerge and be recognised as a productive process of contestation that unmasks interests and helps new perceptions to emerge (Pereira et al., 2020). These spaces should be underpinned by the engagement principles suggested by Gillespie and Nisbett that provide clear, practical guidelines (2019) and support the mediation or moderation of power dynamics (Walls et al., 2020). Some of the principles for a relational, pluralistic approach to collaboration can be discerned from both the South African case study and other work (Cockburn et al., 2019) including:

(1) Support the development of individual and collective agency and new interpersonal relationships among diverse actors, including private-sector actors.
(2) Recognise pluralism as a fundamental feature of the food system and embrace diversity, including within the private sector, rather than trying to control it.
(3) Build collaboration from the bottom up by meshing existing patches of collaboration and strengthening informal networks to develop the trust needed to make higher level, more formal, platforms work.
(4) Support local practitioners to reflexively learn-by-doing in their efforts to foster collaborative experiences, rather than recommending the naïve implementation of externally developed design principles or guidelines for collaboration.
(5) Appreciate that collaboration is situated in a context shaped by history, culture, politics, and existing power dynamics, and
(6) Understand that building relationships with and amongst actors takes time and requires leadership skills.

Conclusion

Engaging the private sector within urban food governance is a complex undertaking that embraces the fault lines in food systems, especially those characterised by social and ecological injustice and inequity. The actors involved in urban food systems have starkly different interests and agendas, and there are few processes for reaching consensus or resolving competing interests. These issues have to be recognised when considering the question of governing the urban food system.

Urban food governance includes a range of processes of making and implementing decisions that shape food systems in order to deliver better outcomes for people living in those places. These processes should create the space for different actors to articulate their interests, exercise their legal rights, take decisions, meet their obligations, and mediate their differences. They should also allow for conflict to be a productive process of contestation, of unmasking interests and rethinking perceptions. This is imperative considering the low levels of trust between actors in this system.

A key question for urban food governance is how to mediate or moderate power, particularly that of large food companies and corporations. The power dynamics that emerge through competing priorities between different actors perpetuate systems – including food systems, as well as wider social and economic systems. As they are currently construed, these systems favour the powerful. Understanding and mitigating power should be an issue at the core of processes within urban food governance that include different private-sector actors.

It is becoming received wisdom that governance systems should be made more coherent and harmonised, better integrated and coordinated, and made more inclusive. Yet principles of engagement are required to provide clear, practical guidelines for multi-actor processes. Human rights frameworks, in particular, provide much to guide food systems governance that seeks to "address legitimacy, accountability, justice, fairness, and equity" (Termeer et al., 2018, p.87) and thus enable ways for the participation of a wide range of actors, especially grassroots voices. This is crucial for a formal platform to be effective.

In directly engaging the private sector in governance processes, collaborative efforts are required, including analysing business incentives, understanding supply and demand, and identifying economic levers for change to transform diets and transition to a sustainable system. Taking a systems approach facilitates for the recognition of the variety of actors in the private sector and their complex interrelations, which allows for a diversified strategy for engaging them.

The essentials of food systems governance are that efforts should recognise the systemic nature of the food challenge, aim for innovative solutions at a local-level, and involve learning and reflection to improve action over time. In terms of 'modes of engagement', particularly with the private sector, stretch collaboration reflects an innovative way of working *with* the system, rather than trying to control or force changes. It requires an approach of accepting that the future cannot be controlled but, rather, influenced.

References

Allen, L., & Bloomfield, A. (2016). Engaging the private sector to strengthen NCD prevention and control. *The Lancet, Global Health*, 4(12): e897–e898.

Bakker, K., Kooy, M., Shofiani, N.E., & Martijn, E.-J. (2008). Governance failure: Rethinking the institutional dimensions of urban water supply to poor households. *World Development*, 36(10): 1891–1915. doi:10.1016/j.worlddev.2007.09.015

Battersby, J. (2017). Food system transformation in the absence of food system planning: The case of supermarket and shopping mall retail expansion in Cape Town, South Africa. *Built Environment*, 43(3): 417–430.

Battersby, J., & Haysom, G. (2016). *Africa's Urban Food and Nutrition Transition: A Call to Action*. Consuming Urban Poverty Project, Working Paper No. 1, African Centre for Cities, University of Cape Town.

Bell, K., & Green, J. (2016). On the perils of invoking neoliberalism in public health critique. *Critical Public Health*, 26(3): 239–243. doi:10.1080/0958159 6.2016.1144872

Berger, M., & van Helvoirt, B. (2018). Ensuring food secure cities: Retail modernization and policy implications in Nairobi, Kenya. *Food Policy*, 79: 12–22.

Bricas, N. (2019). The scope of the analysis: Food systems. In S. Dury, P. Bendjebbar, E. Hainzelin, T. Giordano, & N. Bricas (Eds.), *Food Systems at Risk: New Trends and Challenges*. Rome, Montpellier, Brussels: FAO, CIRAD and European Commission, pp. 15–18.

Cabannes, Y., & Marrochino, C. (2018). *Integrating Food into Urban Planning*. London: UCL Press; Rome: FAO. www.fao.org/3/CA2260EN/ca2260en.pdf.

Candel, J.J.L. (2014). Food security governance: A systematic literature review. *Food Security*, 6(4), 585–601.

Caron, P., Ferrero y de Loma-Osorio, G., Nabarro, D., Hainzelin, E., Guillou, M., Andersen, I., Arnold, T., Astralaga, M., Beukeboom, M., Bickersteth, S., Bwalya, M., Caballero, P., Campbell, B.M., Divine, N., Fan, S., Frick, M., Friis, A., Gallagher, M., Halkin, J.P., Hanson, C., Lasbennes, F., Ribera, T., Rockstrom, J., Schuepbach, M., Steer, A., Tutwiler, A., & Verburg, G. (2018). Food systems for sustainable development: Proposals for a profound four-part transformation. *Agronomy for Sustainable Development*, 38(41), 1774–0746.

Cockburn, J., Cundill, G., Shackleton, S., Rouget, M., Zwinkels, M., Cornelius, S., Metcalfe, L., & van den Broeck, D. (2019). Collaborative stewardship in multifunctional landscapes: Toward relational, pluralistic approaches. *Ecology and Society*, 24(4): 32. https://doi.org/10.5751/ES-11085-240432

Collin, J., Ralston, R., Hill, S.E., & Westerman, L. (2020). *Signalling Virtue, Promoting Harm: Unhealthy Commodity Industries and COVID-19*. Geneva, London, New York: NCD Alliance, SPECTRUM.

Crush, J., & Frayne, B. (2011). Supermarket expansion and the informal food economy in Southern African Cities: Implications for urban food security. *Journal of South African Studies*, 37(4): 781–807.

De Schutter, O. (2019). The political economy approach to food systems reform. *IDS Bulletin*, 50(2): 13–26. doi:10.19088/1968-2019.115

Doernberg, A., Horn, P., Zasada, I., & Piorr, A. (2019). Urban food policies in German city regions: An overview of key players and policy instruments, *Food Policy*, 89. https://doi.org/10.1016/j.foodpol.2019.101782

Drimie, S., Hamann, R., Manderson, A.P., & Mlondobozi, N. (2018). Creating transformative spaces for dialogue and action: Reflecting on the experience of the Southern Africa Food Lab. *Ecology and Society*, 23(3): 2. https://doi.org/10.5751/ES-10177-230302

Fanzo, J., Cordes, Y.K., Fox, E.F., & Bulman, A. (2018). Tying the knot: An interdisciplinary approach to understanding the human right to adequate nutrition. *Columbia Journal of Transnational Law*, 57: 62–114.

GAIN. (2020). *Informal Food Retail in Urban Areas*. Urban Governance for Nutrition Programme Fact Sheet. www.gainhealth.org/sites/default/files/publications/documents/informal-food-retail-in-urban-areas.pdf

Gillespie, S. (2020). Focus on the political and commercial drivers behind the double burden of malnutrition. *IFPRI blog*, 7 January. www.ifpri.org/blog/focus-political-and-commercial-drivers-behind-double-burden-malnutrition

Gillespie, S., & Nisbett, N. (2019). Principles, practice and the private sector's role in malnutrition: Time to review red lines?, *Research Programme on Agriculture for Nutrition and Health*, unpublished blog, 29 May. https://a4nh.cgiar.org/2019/05/29/principles-practice-and-the-private-sectors-role-in-malnutrition-time-to-review-red-lines/

Global Panel on Agriculture and Food Systems for Nutrition. (2018). Improving diets in an era of food market transformation: Challenges and opportunities for engagement between the public and private sectors. Policy Brief No. 11. London: Global Panel on Agriculture and Food Systems for Nutrition.

Haddad, L. (2018). Reward food companies for improving nutrition. *Nature*, 556(7699): 19–22. doi:10.1038/d41586-018-03918-7. PMID: 29620753.

Haddad, L. (2019). How can businesses operating in the food system accelerate improvements in nutrition? In S. Fan, S. Yosef, & R. Pandya-Lorch (Eds.), *Agriculture for Improved Nutrition: Seizing the Momentum*. London: International Food Policy Research Institute, pp. 113–120.

Haddad, L., Hawkes, C., Webb, P., Thomas, S., Beddington, J., Waage, J., & Flynn, D. (2016). A new global research agenda for food. *Nature*, 540(7631): 30–32. doi:10.1038/540030a. PMID: 27905456.

Halliday, J. (2019). Cities' strategies for sustainable food and the levers they mobilize. In C. Brand, N. Bricas, D. Conaré, B. Daviron, J. Debru, L. Michel, & C.-T. Soulard (Eds.), *Designing Urban Food Policies*. Cham., Switzerland: Springer, pp. 53–74.

Halliday, J., Platenkamp, L., & Nicolarea, Y. (2019). A menu of actions to shape urban food environments for improved nutrition. Switzerland, Italy, The Netherlands: GAIN, MUFPP, and RUAF.

Harris J., & Nisbett, N. (2018). Equity in social and development-studies research: insights for nutrition. In *UNSCN News 43: Advancing Equity, Equality and Non-Discrimination in Food Systems: Pathways to Reform*. UK: UNSCN, pp. 57–63.

Hawkes, C., & Halliday, J. (2017). *What Makes Urban Food Policy Happen? Insights from Five Case Studies*. Brussels: IPES-Food.

Haysom, G. (2015). Food and the city: Urban scale food system governance. Urban Forum, 26(3, September): 263–281.

Headey, D., Hoddinott, J., & Park, S. (2017). Accounting for nutritional changes in six success stories: A regression-decomposition approach. *Global Food Security*, 13: 12–20. doi:10.1016/j.gfs.2017.02.003

Hoddinott, J., Gillespie, S., & Yosef, S. (2016). Public–private partnerships and undernutrition: Examples and future prospects. *World Review of Nutrition and Dietetics*, 115: 233–238. doi: 10.1159/000442110. Epub 2016 May 19. PMID: 27198661.

Hossain, N., & te Lintelo, D. (2018). A common sense approach to the right to food. *Journal of Human Rights Practice*, 10(3): 367–387.

Kahane, A. (2017). *Collaborating with the Enemy: How to Work with People You Don't Agree with or Like or Trust*. Oakland, CA: Berrett-Koehler Publishers.

Matacena, R. (2016). Linking alternative food networks and urban food policy: A step forward in the transition towards a sustainable and equitable food system? *International Review of Social Research*, 6(1): 49–58.

McKee, M., & Stuckler, D. (2018). Revisiting the corporate and commercial determinants of health. *American Journal of Public Health*, 108(9): 1167–1170. doi:10.2105/ajph.2018.304510

McKeon, N. (2017). Are equity and sustainability a likely outcome when foxes and chickens share the same coop? Critiquing the concept of multistakeholder governance of food security. *Globalizations*, 14(3): 379–398. doi:10.1080/14747731.2017.1286168

Moodie, R., Stuckler, D., Monteiro, C., Sheron, N., Neal, B., Thamarangsi, T., Lincoln, P., Casswell, S., & Lancet NCD Action Group. (2013). Profits and pandemics: Prevention of harmful effects of tobacco, alcohol, and ultra-processed food and drink industries. *Lancet*, 381(9867): 670–679. doi:10.1016/s0140-6736(12)62089-3

Moragues-Faus, A. (2020). Towards a critical governance framework: Unveiling the political and justice dimensions of urban food partnerships. *The Geographical Journal*, 186(1): 73–86.

MUFPP (Milan Urban Food Policy Pact). (2015). *Milan Urban Food Policy Pact*. www.milanurbanfoodpolicypact.org/text

Nestle, M. (2002). *Food Politics: How the Food Industry Influences Nutrition and Health*. Los Angeles, CA: University of California Press.

Nestle, M. (2018). *Unsavory Truth: How Food Companies Skew the Science of What We Eat*. Berkeley, CA: University of California Press.

Pereira, C., McLachlan, M., & Battersby, J. (2015). Understanding fruit and vegetable consumption: A qualitative investigation in the Mitchells Plain sub-district of Cape Town. *European Journal of Nutrition & Food Safety*, 5(5): 745–746.

Pereira, L., & Drimie, S. (2016). Governance arrangements for the future food system: Addressing complexity in South Africa. *Environment: Science and Policy for Sustainable Development*, 58(4): 18–31.

Pereira, L., Frantzeskaki, N., Hebinck, A., Charli-Joseph, L., Drimie, S., Dyer, M., Eakin, H., Galafassi, D., Karpouzoglou, T., Marshall, F., Moore, M.L., Olsson, P., Siqueiros-García, J., Van Zwanenberg, P., & Vervoort, J. (2020). Transformative spaces in the making: Key lessons from nine cases in the Global South. *Sustainability Science*, 15: 161–178. 10.1007/s11625-019-00749-x

Platenkamp, L., Polack, S., Mbuya, M.N.N., Demmler, K.M., Kushitor, S.B., Moragues-Faus, A., Battersby, J., & Drimie, S. (2020). *Urban Governance for Nutrition: Implications for Enabling Better Nutrition for Cities*. Global Alliance for Improved Nutrition (GAIN). Discussion Paper Series No. 3, Geneva, Switzerland. www.gainhealth.org/sites/default/files/publications/documents/gain-discussion-paper-series-4-defining-urban-governance-for-nutrition-implications-for-enabling-better-nutrition-for-cities.pdf

Popkin, B.M. (1993). Nutritional patterns and transitions. *Population and Development Review*, 19(1): 138–157. doi:10.2307/2938388.

Siddiki, S.N., Carboni, J.L., Koski, C., & Abdul-Akeem, S. (2015). How policy rules shape the structure and performance of collaborative governance arrangements. *Public Administration Review*, 75(4): 536–547.

Smit, W. (2018). Current urban food governance and planning in Africa. In J. Battersby & V. Watson (Eds.), *Urban Food Systems Governance and Poverty in African Cities*. Abingdon, Oxon: Routledge, pp. 94–103.

Swart, R., van der Merwe, M., & Drimie, S. (2020). Child-centred food systems: Ensuring healthy diets for children. In J. May, C. Witten, & L. Lake (Eds.), *South African Child Gauge 2020*. Cape Town: Children's Institute, University of Cape Town.

Swinburn, B., Kraak, V., Rutter, H., Vandevijvere, S., Lobstein, T., Sacks, G., Gomes, F., Marsh, T., & Magnusson, R. (2015). Strengthening of accountability systems to create healthy food environments and reduce global obesity. *Lancet*, 385(9986): 2534–2545. doi:10.1016/s0140-6736(14)61747-5

Termeer, C.J.A.M., Drimie, S., Ingram, J.S., Pereira, L., & Whittingham, M.J. (2018). A diagnostic framework for food system governance arrangements: The case of South Africa. *NJAS–Wageningen Journal of Life Sciences*, 84(March): 85–93. www.sciencedirect.com/science/article/pii/S157352141730012X

TP4D. (2018). *Fostering Territorial Perspective for Development. Towards a Wider Alliance*. White paper. AFD, BMZ, Cirad, European Commission, FAO, GIZ, Nepad, OECD, UNCDF.

UN. (2016). For further information see: www.un.org/en/development/desa/population/migration/generalassembly/docs/globalcompact/A_RES_71_256.pdf.

UNSCN. (2020). *Urban–Rural Linkages for Nutrition: Territorial approaches for sustainable development*. Discussion Paper, January. www.unscn.org/uploads/web/news/document/Urban-rural-linkages-for-nutrition-EN-WEB-OK-Feb.pdf

Walls, H., Nisbett, N., Laar, A., Drimie, S., Zaidi, S., & Harris, J. (2020). Addressing malnutrition: The importance of political economy analysis of power. *International Journal of and Health Policy Management*, 10(12): 809–816. doi:10.34172/ijhpm.2020.250

WBCSD. (2020). *Science to Policy Dialogue for a Food and Agriculture Policy Roadmap*. Summary outcome paper for discussion, 6 October, WBCSD, Geneva. www.wbcsd.org/Programs/Food-and-Nature/Resources/Science-to-policy-dialogue-for-a-food-and-agriculture-policy-roadmap-Summary-outcome-paper-for-discussion

Wegerif, M.C.A. (2020). "Informal" food traders and food security: Experiences from the Covid-19 response in South Africa. *Food Security*, 12: 797–800. https://doi.org/10.1007/s12571-020-01078-z

Willett, W., Rockstrom, J., Loken, B., Springmann, M., Lang, T., Vermeulen, S., Garnett, T., Tilman, D., De Clerck, F., Wood, A., Jonell, M., Clark, M., Gordon, L.J., Fanzo, J., Hawkes, C., Zurayk, R., Rivera, J.A., De Vries, W., Sibanda, L.M., Afshin, A., Chaudhary, A., Herrero, M., Agustina, R., Branca, F., Lartey, A., Fan, S., Crona, B., Fox, E., Bignet, V., Troell, M., Lindahl, T., Singh, S., Cornell, S.E., Reddy, K.S., Narain, S., Nishtar, S., & Murray, C.J.L. (2019). Food in the Anthropocene: The EAT-Lancet Commission on healthy diets from sustainable food systems. *The Lancet*, 393(10170): 447–492.

23

GOVERNING URBAN LAND FOR COMMUNITY FOOD CULTIVATION

Kirsten Valentine Cadieux

Introduction: Supporting food land uses as normal and desirable in cities

Urban food cultivation sites are rich in relationships. From an ecosystemic view, urban agroecosystems are diverse sites for practicing local and traditional ecological knowledge, particularly in urban landscapes. At a broader scale, efforts to address the climate crisis identify food and agriculture as the largest sector likely to be able to reduce greenhouse gas contributions, and perhaps draw down atmospheric CO_2 concentrations by resequestering carbon in soils via agroecological farming methods (Campbell et al., 2017) and breaking historical patterns of ecological apartheid (Grant, 2017). In the Twin Cities metropolitan region of Minnesota, as in many regions, considerable analysis of local demand for land for producing food shows that many farmers and aspiring farmers are interested in agroecological methods, and in farming near population centers—but that their aspirations are unlikely to be successful under current regulatory and market conditions (HEAL Alliance and the Union of Concerned Scientists, 2020). Their largest barrier is maintaining land tenure (Rippon-Butler, 2020).

Further, social inequalities manifest in an exaggerated way in food production due to intersectional racism, along with differential opportunities and barriers associated with socio-economic status and gender identity. The gap between aspirations to support BIPOC (Black, Indigenous, and People of Color)-led food system and climate justice reform has prompted efforts to rethink farm land access, tenure, and supports for operation (LaShae, 2021). The chapter explores this rethinking in the U.S. state of Minnesota, with attention to governance mechanisms for providing community food land tenure to farmers in ways that address the challenges of land markets. I review key arguments supporting and opposing governance mechanisms for urban community food land tenure via a case study in the capital county of Minnesota, in the geographical context of the Twin Cities metropolitan region. I also briefly review how parallel cases have addressed the barriers they faced, reminding us that community food land tenure aspirations are not unrealistically utopian, but reflect long-standing, diverse mechanisms that communities use to meet basic needs.

I begin by summarizing the argument promoting community land for urban food production. I then consider central barriers and opponents to providing land tenure for community

DOI: 10.4324/9781003055907-27

food production. I then contextualize this land tenure struggle by discussing how urban food cultivators and their networks of support have met challenges. This work is based on public statements and activities to secure long-term access to food land in the Twin Cities over the past decade. These examples suggest strategies and tactics for shifting the lens of urban food land governance from a land-use model that sees food production as a transitional, interim, or marginal land use to viewing food land as a more integrated part of contemporary and future urban form (Soil Nexus, 2021; cf. WinklerPrins, 2017, concluding chapter).

Governance issues involved in providing land for urban food cultivation

Land-use governance is a foundational part of urban food governance. Land is the basis of most food produced for urban consumption, and land tenure regimes for growing food within cities face challenging political and governance issues. Despite offering multiple layers of positive public benefits, both urban and agroecological food farming tend to produce monetary returns that are both variable and low, relative to land values in Minnesota (Nopar, 2011; Belz, 2019). Further, despite the introduction of mechanisms to support modes of urban agriculture that encourage ecological integrity and economic justice (such as the recent Minnesota Department of Agriculture granting program for urban farming, MDA, 2020; see also Egerer & Cohen, 2020, especially Bowness, 2020 in that collection, for more on social and ecological intersections in urban agroecology), most positive effects beyond food are *externalities*, not currently rewarded by markets or by other governance mechanisms (Camps-Calvet et al., 2016). Structural disincentives are built into contemporary food, land-care, and social structures, particularly by the expectation that food production should be profitable, and the often implicit expectation that positive contributions of food production, such as education and cultural transmission, ecological integrity, and economic justice, do not need dedicated resource streams, but should be subsidized by the returns from selling food (Daftary-Steel et al., 2015; Penniman, 2018; Shoemaker, 2020; Calo et al., 2021). More substantive attention to the value of urban agroecologies could help communities—especially those in the position to translate between community land-use practices and regional economic development frameworks and evaluation—build a land base to support community food sovereignty.

Arguments supporting relational governance of urban food land

Displaced agrarian communities are disproportionately represented in U.S. urban and community agriculture; hence, addressing the obstacles to urban community food land tenure is an issue of both racial equity and food sovereignty, as recently well outlined in the HEAL Alliance's policy brief *Leveling the Fields* (HEAL Alliance & UCS, 2020—an important intervention in part for the shift it represents toward centering alliances of those who work across the food chain in implementing food systems governance). Broader engagement with the goals of racial equity and food sovereignty has significantly shifted the conceptual frameworks relevant to governing community food land tenure. This shift may be usefully understood as moving away from community development ideals that have often been used to frame urban agriculture as a means to remediate "urban blight."[1]

This framing has often been embedded in narratives of a "war on poverty" that stops short of grappling honestly with the structural racism of urban planning and land investment (Chumbler et al., 2015a; Rosenthal, 2018). In contrast, what Monica White (2018) describes in *Freedom Farmers* as "collective agency and community resilience" can be better supported by frameworks that acknowledge centuries of discrimination and aim to repair the resulting injuries, traumas, and community wealth and health impacts via building community health and wealth, capacity for economic and social self-determination, and joyful thriving.

Historically, advocacy for urban food cultivation has centered arguments on the tax benefits to cities, rather than the well-being or economic health of their residents, attempting to gain legibility for community food cultivation in cities by projecting property tax increases (Bremer et al., 2003, p. 20; Voicu & Been, 2008). However, the very real cost of such a justification is that food cultivation land uses can become the means of displacing the very residents they were meant to serve. Beyond problematic charity models, this view also reinforces mechanisms of support from governments that instrumentalize urban food cultivation sites as low-cost ways to address "blight." These often rely on extensive volunteer labor by society's most overworked, underemployed, and undernourished sectors, because cities tend to grudgingly allow, but not encourage or supportively enable, community agriculture. This allowing often occurs in the name of providing basic access to food and land, that should be basic human rights (Patel, 2012), to marginalized people about to be displaced, often away from the food land infrastructure and soils they have struggled to build.

Instead, contemporary food systems advocates argue against the transitional or gentrifying views of urban food cultivation, in favor of explicit understandings of urban food land uses having a legitimized place in current and future cities, as a base for non-displacing modes of economic development and community wealth generation, and as stable sites of community activity and mutual support (WinklerPrins, 2017; White, 2018). They articulate the right to the city as including equitable access to community greenspaces, with interactive management regimes determined and carried out by community members (Santo et al., 2016; Ventura & Bailkey, 2017). Community members organize to govern food land in various ways, including via community land trusts that incorporate food land in their purview (for example, in Chicago, Providence Rhode Island, Madison Wisconsin, Athens Georgia, and Oakland California, in addition to the Twin Cities efforts described here) and via related community land networks like the Detroit Black Food Security Network, the Food Project in Boston, and parallel efforts in New Jersey, Vermont, Maine, Oregon, Washington, Baltimore, Washington, DC, Virginia, and many other metro regions in the U.S. and beyond (including the MST's urban-allied projects in Brazil, agroecological industrial parks in Argentina [Soil Nexus, 2021], networked efforts across Canada, and advocacy for urban and peri-urban food cultivation worldwide [RUAF, 2021]).

These efforts to advocate for food cultivation as a multifunctional part of healthy neighborhoods help to articulate multiple ways that community farming contributes to healthy cities beyond food—and in contrast to gentrification. Milwaukee, like many similar cities, and consistent with contemporary understanding of the important relationship between broader planning processes and thriving food systems (APA, 2007), has contextualized its Urban Agriculture Plan within the broader goals of its comprehensive planning. Several cities participating in Spain's Network of Agroecological Cities have developed instruments centering food as an essential service, like water, energy, and transportation, with details ranging from the preservation of food land and examination of public space to enhance food systems in Barcelona, to the conversion of 80 hectares of parkland to food land in Madrid, to the development of instruments easing farming access after failed or stalled redevelopment plans in Valencia (Soil Nexus, 2021). Baltimore, in developing its Urban Agriculture Plan, identified the following goals "to be achieved at least partially through urban agriculture:

1. Increasing availability of fresh produce in close proximity to consumers;
2. Promoting economic development and job creation;
3. Improving the natural environment and contributing to sustainability;

4. Making productive use of vacant lots;
5. Increasing green space;
6. Increasing community resilience to natural disasters;
7. Promoting a sense of community; and
8. Providing educational opportunities."

(Chumbler, 2015a; cf. www.baltimoresustainability.org/homegrown-baltimore-plan/)

Arguments against—or limiting—urban food land governance relationships

Although this chapter focuses largely on the way that community-food land regimes help address the inequalities built into the dominant organizing principles of twentieth-century urban form, it is important to understand the challenges embedded within the status quo, and the reasons used to reject arguments for multifunctional community agriculture in urban areas. Many bureaucratic processes interweave to support and maintain the status quo. Challenges to the structural inequalities built into the current system, such as those presented by attempts to remove land from property relations (Case, 2018), face active resistance, passive opposition, and lack of comprehension or ability to collaborate. Consequently, strategies to build public literacy and political will to address the need for community food land should consider arguments designed to reach across the spectrum of allies and also opponents. These include, most obviously, community and regional economic development and planning professionals who will need to update codes and procedures, as well as evaluation strategies and vocabulary, to address emerging challenges like climate change and food security. Similarly, investors, developers, and financial services sector representatives (like land speculators) are likely to find paradigm changes threatening, and, along with urban businesses and residents, may need coaching to understand (or at least be able to co-exist with) multifunctional possibilities of urban land as interactive greenspace, including for food production. These also include rural agriculturalists who may see urban infrastructural provision as unfair subsidy or competition—or who may be defensive about challenges to the structural racism that has been reinforced by fee simple ownership of agricultural land. Although this specific argument falls largely beyond the scope of this chapter, it is addressed here by focusing primarily on food cultivation with community-centered rather than extractive goals, goals that may include livelihood payments beyond the paradigm of "not-for-profit" community, but that do not yield investment profit (see Shoemaker, 2020, for a comprehensive review of possibilities for transforming food land ownership regimes via a view of all food lands as public goods).

One of the central understandings used to argue against extended land tenure for food cultivation is that food cultivation is often considered a non-compliant use of urban land. As WinklerPrins reviews in the overview of her 2017 *Global Urban Agriculture*, this perspective sees urban food cultivation as outdated, too rural, or too lower class and "unsightly," by class-aspiring "city beautiful" standards—or as outright illegal, especially in locations where colonial labor regimes have relied on alienating potential workers from food supplies. More commonly, such land uses are deprioritized as not "highest and best" uses, that would bring in optimal tax revenues, or transitional, on the way to more lucrative uses (Minnesota Revisor of Statutes, 2008). Status quo, "modern" food systems have been optimized for cost reduction, uniformity, and adequate safety at the expense of labor and land relationships. Privileging highly capitalized and extractive agri-food industry, this model encourages high capital inputs and hazard controls on large land blocks tended by underpaid labor and reduces the diversity of models of food production. This is particularly disadvantageous to the smallest-scale producers growing food in urban areas, who are perceived as not meeting the safety or scale requirements expected of "real" farmers, growing marketable commodities "at scale," which usually means at a scale of enterprise considered worthy of financial investment.

Further exacerbating the divides in access and socio-ecological impact between the commodity farming perceived as "successful" and smallholder and community farming more likely to be practiced in urban areas, the spatial arrangement of settlement patterns and community land access in the United States also reveals American hierarchies of race, class, and gender. Spatially concentrated areas of wealth and poverty show ongoing segregation by race and also by socioeconomic status (Henderson, 2018). These patterns have shaped distinct ecologies reflecting structural racism that, in turn, require additional ecological repair work to sustain healthy communities or agroecologies (Cadieux et al., 2019; Schell et al., 2020). The dominant forms of single-family housing neighborhoods separated from commercial and manufacturing districts[2] reinforce ideals of male breadwinners supporting nuclear families. These spatial arrangements of contemporary cities demonstrate the intersectional effects of sexism, classism, and attachment to imagined White ideals of normalcy that together can disincline possible supporters from considering urban food cultivation to be a desirable or feasible land use. Investment patterns in both urban and rural areas have contributed to community land access regimes that have further separated where people live and where community food land access is located—as well as where necessary infrastructure is sited.

Enmeshed with systemic racism, such investment patterns and prejudices against small-scale and urban food producers, who are likely to be growing food for home and community consumption more than for profit, are multiply problematic. Systemic racism already significantly influences the operation of agriculture, for example in credit systems necessary for seasonal industries such as food production (Carpenter, 2012). Racism is also mobilized against agrarian migrants whose imported farming habits (often from places where they have been forcibly displaced from land through war, racist violence, or land appropriation [McMichael, 2010]) may visibly contrast lauded modern agricultural practices and exacerbate anti-immigrant sentiments (Stokes, 2013).

As discussed in the case study below, these dynamics intersect with agricultural support programs to marginalize urban and near-urban food producers who run afoul of policies meant to reduce tax evasion. Urban food lands are considered a plausible vehicle of tax evasion when developers hold land speculatively and attempt to reduce their tax burden by allowing land to be used by food producers in the interim. This further contributes to uncertain land tenure and the perception of urban food cultivation as an easily displaced land use. This perception also prevents access to support programs that could be helpful, because such short-term urban agriculture (that has likely not had the time and resources to build regenerative practices) is so often seen as a marginal version of extractive agriculture meant to be a source of tax revenue and a land use to be kept away from conservation land, rather than as a source of community food security, economic development, and ecological resilience.

Urban food cultivation can be difficult to define, given diversity in methods, cultures, and goals. Urban smallholder agriculture *may* be about building economic wealth, or may be mostly about fresh food provision, or about cultural transmission and stewardship of, and interaction with, the more-than-human world. Consequently, to representatives of relevant bureaucracies, supportive infrastructure often seems dauntingly complicated to develop and administer. Even to those who have supported urban community farms and gardens and related businesses when it was relatively straightforward to do so (OLA, 1913, highlights how vacant lot garden facilitation is practical only when community organizing is not required, for example), the social complexity of diverse urban food cultivation communities often exceeds the capacity local governance organizations are willing to devote. Discussing the development of labor- and time-intensive mediation techniques in the civil rights context of the 1960s, which remains particularly relevant to urban food governance, McCorkle and Reese (2019, p. 11) note that "as neighborhoods and businesses become more diverse in ethnicity, gender, nationality, age, and lifestyle, it is imperative to develop channels of communication to manage the predictable clashes of values, style, and goals that will accompany this diversity."

Community and public land conservation efforts that may have the resources to mediate competing land relationships tend to be concentrated away from population centers, differentially contributing to property value increases for the wealthy who own the land or adjacent land (Raymond & Fairfax, 2002). At the same time, well-intentioned densification and redevelopment of urban areas continues to displace lower-income urban communities—a process often aided by community investments in community food-producing spaces. And existing programs supporting farmland preservation often disqualify urban farmland, privileging the larger acreages and row crop agriculture that have more data to support their value. Even when this is justified in terms of food security, commodity or investment yields tend to be used as rubrics of success rather than more holistic measures of community wealth, health, and culture—starkly contrasting what many communities seek from urban food cultivation (Daftary-Steel et al., 2015; Santo et al., 2016; WinklerPrins, 2017). This is particularly notable in the context of Indigenous and agrarian dispossession, as discussed below in the context of the Twin Cities case study.

Community food land access and urban food governance in the Twin Cities

The Minnesota, U.S., "Twin Cities" of Minneapolis and Saint Paul, is a metro city region of seven counties and over one hundred and fifty cities and townships. It is a significant site of urban food cultivation, both historically, with early twentieth-century Canadian legislative reports using an international perspective to describe the importance of their innovative governance of agricultural uses of vacant lots during boom periods of house building (OLA, 1913), and recently, particularly with the in-migration of several agrarian communities (Cadieux et al., 2019; Nicklay et al., 2020). Many dispossessions have contributed to the contemporary urbanization of agrarian communities and households.

This includes the settler colonial history of Minnesota, which has been a thriving Indigenous agricultural site for thousands of years (Case, 2018). It also includes the history of racist enslavement, particularly of people of African descent, whose relationship with farmland is complicated by this history, and who have participated in twentieth-century Great Migration and earlier northward relocation to metropolitan regions like the Twin Cities (White, 2011; Williams & Holt-Giménez, 2017). Additional dispossession has occurred in the often-violent displacement of many agrarian refugee communities, such as Hmong communities relocated to Minnesota from Southeast Asia following the American war in Vietnam (the Twin Cities metro area hosts the largest Hmong community in the U.S., with a significant concentration of agrarian knowledge; see the Minnesota Historical Society for more details at www.mnhs.org/hmong), or Latinx labor and structural-adjustment migrants.

In the light of this history, and considering the question of how communities imagine their rights to access food land, the conventional history and understanding of farmland acquisition and conservation is notably linked to exclusive imaginations of how people secure access to land to produce food. Conservation is understood as rural. It tends to privilege taking land out of food production, and although small-scale agroecological farming methods are technically allowed on many conservation easements, smallholder farming has not been broadly respected as legitimately contributing to either agricultural economies or ecological integrity. Instead, many gatekeepers of programs designed to support farming see smallholder agriculture largely through a lens of concern that expanding the definitions of farming will create tax evasion loopholes for wealthy exurbanite "hobby farmers," and that resulting land uses, especially if diverse, will be difficult to evaluate and manage for program compliance.

Popular imaginations of nature and farmland conservation—which undergird the political will supporting existing farm and conservation programs—have also been bound up in representational and political struggles over who is a good steward of land and water, and hence a legitimate agricultural land user. Settler colonial imagination of land relationships is firmly embedded in state infrastructure. The state seal of Minnesota contentiously shows a male pioneer farmer plowing the land while an Indigenous man rides a horse into the sunset. Both Indigenous peoples and environmental stewardship interests contest this settler agrarian dominance, often alongside immigrant advocacy positions, noting the agroecological prowess of the Central American and Asian agricultural labor force (Main Street Project [now Sharing Our Roots], 2020; Case, 2018).

Such contests contribute to ongoing definitional struggles around what "counts" as agriculture and worthy of public support, for example in relation to stewardship incentive programs for farmers to reduce sediment and nutrient loss from land into water (Russell, 2019), or privileging conservation funds for expansion of hunting and wildland habitat. Such imaginations of the settler agrarian ideal intensify the degree to which urban agrarians are excluded from programs designed to support food production. They also exacerbate hostile, exclusionary social dynamics that continue to associate urban areas as the "appropriate" locale for BIPOC communities, a dynamic made even more visible during the Trump era by the prevalence of flags signaling a lack of welcome and safety for BIPOC farmers and further intensifying challenges to secure land tenure.

The Twin Cities metropolitan area is often described as one of the nation's most racially segregated urban areas, with accompanying racial disparities in income, wealth, and health outcomes—unequal at the same time it is touted as having some of the highest quality of life (for White residents) (Minnesota Housing Partnership, 2021). It is also located in the heart of the Midwestern agricultural "breadbasket," with a strong cultural association with agriculture and food production, which still accounts for a significant proportion of the state's economy. Extractive property regimes are heavily associated with agrarian settler societies such as those of the United States', meaning that forms of agriculture supported by policy and infrastructural investments tend to be export-oriented, heavily subsidized by environmental and racialized labor externalities (Patel, 2012; Cadieux et al., 2019), and disproportionally organized around commodity production, rather than food provision (Cassidy et al., 2013). And, in addition to being the current home of the nation's largest urban Indigenous community, it is a significant destination for agrarian immigration. However, despite this wealth of experience and history, contemporary land allocation has significantly disadvantaged agrarian communities' access to food land.

My methods of participation in the discourses and politics reported here have largely been centered around roles teaching community food systems in public and higher educational contexts and organizing land access advocacy with a large community network connected via the Twin Cities Community Agricultural Land Trust (cf. Cadieux et al., 2019; Nicklay et al., 2020; Bowness et al., 2020). Building on analyses gathered for these purposes, I proceed to consider how the governance of urban food land is called by community to better facilitate the project of supporting relationship to land and place in ways that address current crises of climate disaster and food apartheid (Brones & Washington, 2018). This entails considering the conditions that support or challenge the existing benefits, possibilities, and transformations imagined for food land relationships in Minnesota and more broadly.

Social dynamics in the governance of urban food land

Within a state context conducive to agriculture, boasting the nation's fifth largest agricultural economy (MDA, 2021), multiple programs exist to help support agricultural land access and preservation. These include programs similar to those in many other places: a metropolitan agricultural land preserve (Metropolitan Council, 2019), which is a "current use" tax program that taxes urban land on its current agricultural use rather than development values; another statewide agricultural land tax subsidy, the Minnesota Agricultural Property Tax Law (commonly known as the Green Acres program, Hinze, 2012), that disincentivizes transfer of agricultural land into development with reduced tax rates (clawed back in the case of development); and a beginning farmers' tax credit (MDA, 2019), subsidizing land access for new farmers. Despite these programs' intentions and Minnesota's strong history of land conservation and agricultural land preservation, however, attempts to use these programs to meet the growing need for long-term access to land for urban (or near-urban) food uses have been remarkably unsuccessful (West, 2008; Murray, 2012). Instead, these policy mechanisms would need to be updated to support successful governance of contemporary urban food cultivation.

The agricultural preserve and Green Acres programs require a minimum of 40 and 10 contiguous acres, respectively, for example, far more than the median amount available to be used by urban food producers. The tax incentive program has also been challenged to meet the needs of small producers (despite efforts of many farmer aid organizations to build more financial outreach capacity), many of whom often do not have capacity to engage tax advisors or the tax-support infrastructure needed to make sense of such programs. And instead of responding accommodatingly to the migration of people with agrarian expertise to cities (in part because of the land dispossessions and racist patterns in farm lending noted above), metro municipalities have not substantively allocated urban land for food production (Metropolitan Council, 2014), notably following class and racial exclusion programs in zoning and planning regimes (Ramer, 2019).

In recent decades, a series of specific incidents has raised the visibility of urban food producers' struggle to retain land access in this region, and highlighted additional ways that opponents to such access operationalize their objections. Hmong farmers produce a disproportionately high amount of the food sold in local markets in the Twin Cities. In 2009, a group of Hmong farmers, working at the eastern edge of the metro area, were threatened by an exurbanite waving a rifle at them for farming at the end of the day, and hence interrupting his attempts to attract deer to his property for viewing. This incident brought attention to the tenuous land access shared by most immigrant farmers—often year-to-year handshake agreements with landowners, under ongoing pressure from exclusionary zoning (Stokes, 2013). Further incidents of racial profiling were reported around enforcement of building, zoning, and other, permitting for small-scale and backyard production and sales. For example, Latinx and Hmong farmers report being required to remove chicken houses and season extension infrastructure such as hoop houses, and get tickets for parking delivery trucks in residential neighborhoods. Literacy and advocacy campaigns have helped with these struggles to some degree. Successful tactics have involved designing around the challenges, with the Sharing Our Roots (formerly the Main Street Project) modular sheds for regenerative chicken farming as a prime example of building coops adequately within the zoning requirements as to reduce the friction of encounters with enforcement bureaucracy.

In the metro core during this time, long-term community gardeners have been facing increasing development pressure on land, accentuated by privatization of public land by municipal entities. This tendency toward public land disposal illustrates additional significant problems with reliance on the market disposal of property, even beyond excessive focus on maximizing tax base (West, 2008; Raymond & Fairfax, 2002), and beyond governance reinforcement of settler colonial ideas of land as property (Case, 2018). The market model approach to "re/development" tends not to consider whether proposed land uses will be able to provide more public benefits in lieu of taxes than their market tax potential. This lens on land use tends to emphasize the tax revenue generation potential of land for urban food cultivation, without accounting for the actual mechanism of that potential, which usually is achieved by gentrification—displacing the community advocating for, and attempting to benefit from, community farming or gardening.

The many dispersed offices with land governance responsibilities have tended to downplay the importance and persistence of demand for community farming or gardening space, or the relevance to their offices. The number of recognized gardens has grown by an order of magnitude in the last decade (Prather, 2016). Public listening sessions, for example of the Saint Paul Ramsey County Food and Nutrition Commission (in 2018) and the Ramsey County COVID-19 food security response team (2020), highlight public concern that two of the food security issues on which the city and county have made least progress are supporting urban food land access and coordinating permissions for using public lands for growing food.

Emergence, challenges, and current directions of urban food land governance

As community farming and gardening continue to gain relevance as mechanisms of community food security and food sovereignty, as well as of justice and mutual capacity building (White, 2018; Bowness et al., 2020), urban food cultivation sites continue to foster community governance strategies. Responses to the COVID-19 food security crisis have highlighted the persistent challenges of eliciting coordinated support from the multiple layers of official government entities who control zoning, taxation, and other land-use policies, especially around risk management on public land. COVID-19 food security responses have also showcased the remarkable and ongoing history of community organizing that has attempted to meet the demand for urban food land.

Some civil society organizations are stepping up to provide land and food (particularly grown by BIPOC farmers and prepared by underemployed food workers, such as in the Minnesota Central Kitchen project), supplementing public provision of some land. They are also helping to remind food providers, preparers, and contracting agencies that the production of the food itself could be creating more local, culturally appropriate employment, along with jobs built via other charitably and publicly supported food programs. This holistic advocacy makes more visible the extensive relational infrastructure required to turn land access into long-standing, regenerative agroecosystems and community food systems—and to maintain these. Networking and coordinating roles have been played by a variety of organizations. These include:

- peer-to-peer farm and garden organizing groups in many neighborhoods, such as the Urban Farm and Garden Alliance in Saint Paul's Rondo neighborhood and Project Sweetie Pie on Minneapolis's North side,

- garden projects connecting neighborhoods with non-profits in coalitions, such as Minneapolis's Northside Fresh or the 24th Street Urban Farm Coalition,
- and geographically more extensive networking efforts, such as those during the early 2000s of refugee assistance and faith groups, especially with Hmong and Karen agrarian communities, and continuing with partnerships with many individual farmers, gardeners, neighborhoods, and private and public organizations such as the State Horticultural Society, the public schools, Extension agents, public housing offices, churches, and the urban participants in a regional "Farmland Access Hub" that includes dozens of farm support organizations and commons efforts (Farmland Access Hub, 2021).

Convergence between all these organizations confirms the importance of a few central themes in urban food land governance. Expectations of what urban food cultivation can deliver, especially in terms of community benefits, vastly outstrip support streams. Urban plans continue to imagine urban food production occurring largely in the context of single-family housing, while renters comprise the majority of residents in the urban core of the Twin Cities, and where BIPOC homeownership is currently 35 percent lower than White, with the Twin Cities' high rates of racial disparities in housing (Minnesota Housing Partnership, 2021). Approaches to urban food cultivation centering racial equity and leadership, along with cross-cultural competency, are crucial, especially given a strong tendency of state, civic, and civil society actors in community food spaces to act through a lens of charity. Urban agriculture communities in the Twin Cities have cultivated a strong ethos of community agency rather than doing for others, with an accompanying *commons* ethic (Grant, 2017; Williams & Holt-Giménez, 2017). Although food knowledge may be shared in the course of growing, harvesting, and preparing food together, perhaps the most powerful community organizing efforts center around collaborative land tenure governance in the context of a richly varied heritage of community agriculture traditions.

Efforts to strengthen and change governance mechanisms are often highlighted in the context of organizing aspirational community food producers and those threatened with displacement. For example, around a large, thriving community garden on regional water authority land in Ramsey County, land slated for redevelopment had been granted temporarily to gardeners on the condition that they not protest future land-use changes—but many immigrant elders and other gardeners are now organizing to seek appropriate replacement for garden access that has been conveniently accessible by metro bus routes—or to advocate inclusion of food cultivation space in the proposed redevelopment designs. Slow shifts toward enriching the agricultural bureaucracy to better serve all farmers—especially BIPOC farmers, who are more likely to live in urban areas and more likely to focus on food crops in Minnesota—also are supporting more attention to urban food land governance. The Minnesota Land Trust's new strategic plan (2019) features a shift toward conservation directly supporting diverse communities, for example, including food land. Policy reviews in Minneapolis and Saint Paul have attempted to ease barriers to food cultivation, including possibilities for agriculture in all zoning districts, for example, although barriers remain to implementation of suggested collaborations between departments, such as conservation, energy, housing, redevelopment, and especially risk management. The Minnesota Department of Agriculture has recently launched an "Emerging Farmers" working group, serving and representing BIPOC farmers, and has included urban agriculture in its competitive grants program for the past few years, building a framework for officially recognizing urban food cultivation as part of the state's agricultural economy, served by its official governance bureaucracy.

Governance frameworks helping legitimize urban food cultivation

Governance frameworks, such as those discussed in the prior section, name urban food cultivation as a legitimate urban land use for several specific reasons, and also provide specific avenues for the supports needed to make such land uses successful and sustainable. Naming specific goals prevents the abuses of supports such as agricultural tax abatement programs—since anxious protection of these programs against exurban abuses appears to still be a significant hurdle for expanding these programs to urban regions in many places—and also makes legible the many strands of work that go into urban food cultivation. The recent Minnesota Department of Agriculture grant program for urban agriculture, for example, helpfully names several plausible specific outputs of urban food cultivation: urban youth agricultural education; urban agriculture community development; positive environmental impact such as promotion of clean water, healthy soils, carbon sequestration, and pollinator habitat, reduction of waste or more efficient use of energy, water, nutrients, or other inputs, promotion of organic and sustainable agriculture; commitment to economic justice such as through the creation of living-wage jobs, provision of entrepreneurial education and skills training, protection of land tenure, expansion of urban lands for agricultural use, reducing or eliminating health disparities related to food access; and service to communities of color or Native American tribal communities as specific benefits of urban agriculture worthy of tax-funded community supports (MDA, 2020).

These named benefits help people, including supporters, neighbors, and potentially those not yet convinced of the value of including and supporting food cultivation in cities, to see how much goes into—and comes out of—urban food cultivation. Detailing specifics raises literacy beyond superficial understandings of community agriculture as charity or as healthy-eating training for the disadvantaged, and provides evaluative lenses more likely to pick up easily overlooked relational benefits of urban food cultivation (Nicklay et al., 2020; Bowness et al., 2020). It can also help reduce excessive emphasis on expectations of commercial success as "real farming"—a barrier that contributes to the frequent bypassing of BIPOC farming efforts, more likely to be embedded in the many community dynamics named in the paragraph above, in favor of supports to White college-graduate market farmers whose efforts may be more legible as compatible with the goals of developers, landlords, and financial industries (Beckett & Galt, 2014; Valliant & Freedgood, 2020). This more detailed understanding may also help address barriers such as ignorance, for example on the part of mortgage lenders or land sellers, of existing programs that can help support the financial viability of urban food production, including tax reduction programs, tax credits and other tax incentives—both for producers and supporters (e.g. land providers, as in California's urban agriculture enterprise zones or Florida's community contribution tax credit), green credits (e.g. for stormwater management facing climate threats), and valuation programs such as the current use tax valuation strategies used to reduce tax burdens on agricultural land in urbanizing regions in many states (Chumbler et al., 2015b).

Maryland's recent urban agricultural support law defines "agricultural purposes" "to include not only crop production but also stormwater abatement, groundwater protection, recreational activities, food donations and preparation, canning classes, job training, sales to restaurants and institutions, and on-site sales of produce grown on-site" (Chumbler et al., 2015b), and Missouri, New Jersey, California, Utah, and Washington DC also have similar specific new laws. The development and evaluation of these laws, as they are implemented, are helping to identify and address further barriers, such as the challenge of finding both agricultural land and housing (the Maryland law subsequently struck down prohibitions to living on-site), or the weight of excessive permitting processes.

Conclusion: Valuing urban community food land

In states like Minnesota—which already use governance mechanisms to limit investment purchase of agricultural land (National Agricultural Law Center, 2019), as well as to limit property tax limitations conferred by conservation easements (MN statute 273.117)—arguments in favor of community food lands as important parts of thriving urban regions should be straightforward to support. Beyond the provision of fresh food in places that need it, urban community food lands support a model of economic development that includes a focus on basic needs and livelihoods as more than extractive, and feature community engagement and racial equity (since, for example, these two themes are explicitly the central policy organizing frameworks of urban counties such as Ramsey, Minnesota's capital county), along with the ability to build wealth and learning, and to invest elsewhere when basic needs are met.

Official COVID-19 food security responses in Ramsey County have highlighted the degree to which urban food land is the most underdeveloped plank in the platform, demonstrating plausible space to move toward supporting community food land, especially with the arguments above helping to establish possible domains for governance negotiation and improvement. Affordable food land faces many of the same biases as affordable housing (advocates suggest relabeling the category "accessible," also noting that initial "access" is only helpful if supported by infrastructure to maintain access and community food sovereignty (LaShae, 2021)). Addressing opposition may be assisted by positive sentiment toward agriculture, widespread recognition of the public health crisis of inequitable access to fresh and adequate food (demonstrably exacerbated during COVID-19), and increasing public literacy about histories of dispossession and trauma in relation to forced labor and migration (Chang et al., 2020; Raja, 2020; Anindya & Sekhar, 2021).

These perspectives all help people to recognize that some land and some exchanges are not best arranged by markets, that land relationships are more than resources, and that the status quo of "highest and best use" to maximize tax returns and redevelopment income leaves many more valuable and multifunctional community benefits unrealized. This perspective also helps us to recognize emerging community food land governance mechanisms that may be particularly well suited to urban areas. These include community land trust approaches to agriculture (Beckett & Galt, 2014), parallel models removing food land from speculative lane economies and debt such as Agrarian Commons (Agrarian Trust, 2020), land access extensions to farm incubator programs (Calo & De Master, 2016), and other policy and financial incentives (Valliant & Freedgood, 2020). These have recently been described as some of a multiplicity of governance strategies contributing alternatives to our current crises of climate, racial equity, and healthy food and basic needs sovereignty.

Urban food cultivation in this context can be seen as an important knowledge ecosystem for racial justice, social and ecosystemic healing, and rebuilding of moral integrity (Grant, 2017; Williams & Holt-Giménez, 2017; Schell et al., 2020). It is valuable to identify and share themes, cases, strategies, and specific mechanisms by which districts are supporting urban food cultivation, particularly as we proceed to support, refine, and respond to these movements—especially since those who think about urban food governance are often asked to help support the praxis of orientation, collaboration, and critical, reparative, developmental evaluation of local, regional, state, and federal development frameworks (Bowness et al., 2020). For example, the U.S. Farm Service Agency is currently creating more urban county committees and the USDA is establishing a national advisory committee for urban agriculture (FSA, 2021).

Although it may seem like urban food land governance requires considerable coordination work from existing bureaucracies—and that it may call accepted premises of city planning into question, creating additional work—it is also true that this investment has the demonstrated potential to leverage considerable community effort to meet basic needs well for remarkably modest government investments (Daftary-Steele et al., 2015; Ventura & Bailkey, 2017). However, rather than accept the existing tradeoffs—encouraging labor, then displacing the laborers—a forward-looking approach to urban food land would expand existing programs that endorse community agriculture as amenities that developers currently may have the option to use as part of their landscaping (see, for example, the Minneapolis Code of Ordinances around planned unit developments), into a more basic requirement, like parking, so that it can become more recognized as an engine of community economic development, wealth, and accessibility/affordability. Further work should be done to share suites of policies (with a specific focus on zoning, tax, tenure, and operational mechanics) that have been facilitative or obstructive, to better support community urban agriculture and particularly to support the mentor farmers and gardeners who make it happen. Finally, especially where tax revenue has been carefully preserved by avoiding tax evasion through conservation easements, as in Minnesota, funding for land conservation should more regularly be used to secure land for urban food cultivation.

Notes

1 Brentin Mock's 2017 review of the use of the "urban blight" metaphor provides valuable context, relying on three main sources that are excerpted here from his review:

> (1) From the Virginia Tech Metropolitan Institute's Vacant Properties Research Network report: "Urban reformers in the first quarter of the 20th century started to use the language of blight as a metaphor in their descriptions of vast numbers of problems they noticed in cities. They borrowed the term from ecological studies of plant blight with the intent to make their studies of cities seem as rigorous as those of traditional sciences. … 'Blight' does not shed light, as it should, on the actions and processes that contribute to the blighting of particular places or the underlying socioeconomic drivers of conditions that cause or generate different types of blight. Governmental and nongovernmental (i.e., philanthropic) funders continue to direct resources to projects that target something called 'blight' and all 50 states and the District of Columbia have adopted anti-blight legislation. What these groups are really talking about, however, is spatial change and how to manage it."
>
> (2) University of Pennsylvania property law scholar Wendell Pritchett's 2003 paper "Public Menace of Blight" in the *Yale Law & Policy Review, Vol. 21*: "Blight was a facially neutral term infused with racial and ethnic prejudice. While it purportedly assessed the state of urban infrastructure, blight was often used to describe the negative impact of certain residents on city neighborhoods. This 'scientific' method of understanding urban decline was used to justify the removal of blacks and other minorities from certain parts of the city. By selecting racially changing neighborhoods as blighted areas and designating them for redevelopment, the urban renewal program enabled institutional and political elites to relocate minority populations and entrench racial segregation."
>
> (3) And a 2015 essay by New York City urban planner Justin Garrett Moore: "Why do I consider 'blight' a problematic word when it comes to describing our cities and communities?… The violence of urban renewal (versions 1.0, 2.0 and now 3.0 beta) used this terminology of disease to describe a place and its people to justify the use of constitutional police power 'the betterment of the health, safety, morals' to take property and wealth, remove people, and to literally destroy places. Think about cities and communities where there is geographic decline and disinvestment. What exactly is the disease? Vacant buildings? Untended naturalizing lots? Poor people? Brown people? How is the disease treated? Historically the response has been at various scales of action and impact to wipe it out and start again with something new."

2 Note in contrast, however, failures of zoning in cities like Houston, that have led to environmental justice crises of refineries amidst housing (see Texas Environmental Justice Advocacy Services, T.e.j.a.s.).

References

Agrarian Trust. (2020). *Agrarian Commons FAQ—Agrarian Commons*. Retrieved February 3, 2021, from https://agrariantrust.org/agrariancommons/faq/

Anindya, B., & Sekhar, K. N. (2021). Reassessment of urban sustainability and food security in the light of COVID-19. In C. Chakraborty, S. Roy, S. Sharma, & T. A. Tran (Eds.), *The Impact of the COVID-19 Pandemic on Green Societies: Environmental Sustainability* (pp. 31–55). Springer. https://doi.org/10.1007/978-3-030-66490-9_2

APA (American Planning Association). (2007). *APA Policy Guide on Community and Regional Food Planning*. Retrieved February 4, 2021, from www.planning.org/policy/guides/adopted/food.htm

Beckett, J., & Galt, R. E. (2014). Land trusts and beginning farmers' access to land: Exploring the relationships in coastal California. *Journal of Agriculture, Food Systems, and Community Development*, *4*(2), 19–35.

Belz, A. (2019). A tough row to hoe as farmers age: Young ones can't buy land. Young farmers find little land to buy, acres of obstacles to get loans. *Star Tribune*, November 4. www.startribune.com/a-tough-row-to-hoe-as-farmers-age-young-ones-can-t-buy-land/564328302/

Bowness, E., Nicklay, J. A., Liebman, A., Cadieux, K. V., & Blumberg, R. (2020). Navigating urban agroecology with the social sciences. In M. Egerer & H. Cohen (Eds.), *Interdisciplinary Research in Urban Agroecology* (pp. 275–298). CRC Press.

Bremer, A., Jenkins, K., & Kanter, D. (2003). *Community Gardens in Milwaukee: Procedures for Their Long-term Stability & Their Import to the City*. University of Wisconsin-Milwaukee, Department of Urban Planning.

Brones, A., & Washington, K. (2018). Karen Washington: It's Not a Food Desert, It's Food Apartheid. *Guernica*, May 7. www.guernicamag.com/karen-washington-its-not-a-food-desert-its-food-apartheid/

Cadieux, K. V., Carpenter, S., Liebman, A., Blumberg, R., & Upadhyay, B. (2019). Reparation ecologies: Regimes of repair in populist agroecology. *Annals of the American Association of Geographers*, *109*(2), 644–660.

Calo, A., & De Master, K. T. (2016). After the incubator: Factors impeding land access along the path from farmworker to proprietor. *Journal of Agriculture, Food Systems, and Community Development*, *6*(2), 111–127.

Calo, A., Mckee, A., Perrin, C., Gasselin, P., Mcgreevy, S., Sippel, S. R., Desmarais, A., Shields, K., Baysse-Lainé, A., Magnan, A., Beingessner, N., & Kobayashi, M. (2021). Achieving food system resilience requires challenging dominant land property regimes. *Frontiers in Sustainable Food Systems*, *319*.

Campbell, B. M., Beare, D. J., Bennett, E. M., Hall-Spencer, J. M., Ingram, J. S., Jaramillo, F., Rodomiro Ortiz, R., Ramankutty, N., Sayer, J. A., & Shindell, D. (2017). Agriculture production as a major driver of the Earth system exceeding planetary boundaries. *Ecology and Society*, *22*(4).

Camps-Calvet, M., Langemeyer, J., Calvet-Mir, L., & Gómez-Baggethun, E. (2016). Ecosystem services provided by urban gardens in Barcelona, Spain: Insights for policy and planning. *Environmental Science & Policy*, *62*, 14–23.

Carpenter, S. (2012). The USDA discrimination cases: Pigford. In re Black Farmers, Keepseagle, Garcia, and Love. *Drake Journal of Agricultural Law*, *17*(1).

Case, M. (2018). *Relentless Business of Treaties: How Indigenous Land Became US Property*. Minnesota Historical Society Press.

Cassidy, E. S., West, P. C., Gerber, J. S., & Foley, J. A. (2013). Redefining agricultural yields: From tonnes to people nourished per hectare. *Environmental Research Letters*, *8*(3), 034015.

Chang, M., Green, L., & Cummins, S. (2020). All change. Has COVID-19 transformed the way we need to plan for a healthier and more equitable food environment? *URBAN DESIGN International*. https://doi.org/10.1057/s41289-020-00143-5

Chumbler, M., Negro, S. E., & Bechler, L. E. (2015a). The Tax Implications of Urban Agriculture: Liabilities and Incentives. In M. Chumbler, S. E. Negro and L. E. Bechler (Eds.), *Urban Agriculture: Policy, Law, Strategy, and Implementation*. American Bar Association, Section of State and Local Government Law.

Chumbler, M., Negro, S. E., & Bechler, L. E. (2015b). Land Use and Zoning Tools: Integrating Agriculture into the Urban Landscape. In M. Chumbler, S. E. Negro and L. E. Bechler (Eds.), *Urban Agriculture: Policy, Law, Strategy, and Implementation*. American Bar Association, Section of State and Local Government Law.

Daftary-Steel, S., Herrera, H., & Porter, C. M. (2015). The unattainable trifecta of urban agriculture. *Journal of Agriculture, Food Systems, and Community Development*, *6*(1), 19–32.

Egerer, M., & Cohen, H. (Eds.). (2020). *Urban Agroecology: Interdisciplinary Research and Future Directions, Vol. 23*. CRC Press.

Farmland Access Hub. (2021). *Farmland Access Hub Partners.* www.renewingthecountryside.org/farmlandaccesshubpartners

FSA. (2021). *County Committees for Urban Agriculture.* www.fsa.usda.gov/news-room/county-committee-elections/index

Grant, S. (2017). Organizing alternative food futures in the peripheries of the industrial food system. *Journal of Sustainability Education, 14.*

HEAL Alliance and the Union of Concerned Scientists. (2020). *Leveling the Fields: Creating Farming Opportunities for Black People, Indigenous People, and Other People of Color.* www.ucsusa.org/sites/default/files/2020-06/leveling-the-fields.pdf

Henderson, J. (2018). National Equity Atlas: Data to support community change processes. APHA's 2018 Annual Meeting & Expo, November 10–14.

Hinze, S. (2012). Minnesota's Green Acres program and other property tax programs for rural lands. House Research Short Subjects Report, Research Department of the Minnesota House of Representatives. www.house.leg.state.mn.us/hrd/pubs/ss/ssgrnacres.pdf

LaShae, T. (2021). *Emerging Farmers Conference Keynote*, January 31. https://youtu.be/eY53McTwvVU?list=PL3dw6bg9IAwNdMv2iRR-sJyWI93MOx-Ct

Main Street Project. (2020). About Us. *Main Street Project.* https://mainstreetproject.org/about (now called Sharing Our Roots: https://sharing-our-roots.org/about/)

McCorkle, S., & Reese, M. J. (2019). *Mediation Theory and Practice*, 3rd edition. Sage Publications.

McMichael, P. (2010). Food sovereignty, social reproduction and the agrarian question. In A. H. Akram-Lodhi & C. Kay (Eds.), *Peasants and Globalization: Political Economy, Rural Transformation and the Agrarian Question.* (pp. 300–324). Routledge.

MDA (Minnesota Department of Agriculture). (2019). *Beginning Farmer Tax Credit.* www.mda.state.mn.us/bftc

MDA. (2020). *AGRI Urban Agriculture Grant | Minnesota Department of Agriculture.* www.mda.state.mn.us/grants/grants/urbanaggrant

MDA. (2021). *Economic Analysis and Market Research.* www.mda.state.mn.us/business-dev-loans-grants/economic-analysis-market-research

Metropolitan Council. (2014). *Thrive MSP 2040 Plan.* https://metrocouncil.org/Planning/Projects/Thrive-2040.aspx

Metropolitan Council. (2019). *Decades-old Program Helps Preserve Metro Area Ag Land.* https://metrocouncil.org/News-Events/Communities/Newsletters/Preserving-metro-area-agricultural-land.aspx (See also: www.leg.mn.gov/docs/2018/mandated/180302.pdf).

Minnesota Housing Partnership. (2021). *State of the State's Housing: Twin Cities Region Key Findings.* www.mhponline.org/publications/2021-state-of-the-state-s-housing

Minnesota Land Trust. (2019). *Twin Cities Metro Conservation Program Area Plan 2017–2027.* https://mnland.org/2019/11/20/twin-cities-metro-conservation-program-area-plan/

Minnesota Revisor of Statutes. (2008). 6122.0200 DEFINITIONS: §Subp. 6. www.revisor.mn.gov/rules/6122.0200/

Mock, B. (2017). The Meaning of Blight: A word that was originally about plant diseases became "infused with racial and ethnic prejudice" when it moved to the city. *Bloomberg CityLab*, February 16. www.bloomberg.com/news/articles/2017-02-16/why-we-talk-about-urban-blight

Murray, K. (2012). *CURA-Supported Local Food Systems Research, 2007–2012.* Center for Urban and Regional Affairs.

National Agricultural Law Center. (2019). *Corporate Farming Laws—An Overview.* https://nationalaglawcenter.org/overview/corporatefarminglaws/

Nicklay, J. A., Cadieux, K. V., Rogers, M. A., Jelinski, N. A., LaBine, K., & Small, G. E. (2020). Facilitating spaces of urban agroecology: A learning framework for community–university partnerships. *Frontiers in Sustainable Food Systems, 4*, 1–26. doi: 10.3389/fsufs.2020.00143.

Nopar, D. (2011). *Look Who's Knockin'.* Land Stewardship Project. https://landstewardshipproject.org/morefarmers/lookwhosknockin

OLA (Ontario Legislative Assembly). (1913). *Vacant Lot Gardening in Minneapolis.* Sessional Papers—Legislature of the Province of Ontario, pp. 33–39. www.google.com/books/edition/Sessional_Papers_Legislature_of_the_Prov/FHVOAAAAMAAJ

Patel, R. C. (2012). Food sovereignty: Power, gender, and the right to food. *PLoS Med, 9*(6), e1001223.

Penniman, L. (2018). *Farming While Black: Soul Fire Farm's Practical Guide to Liberation on the Land*. Chelsea Green Publishing.

Prather, S. (2016). Community gardens more than triple in Twin Cities. *Star Tribune*. www.startribune.com/community-gardens-more-than-triple-in-twin- cities/392254821/

Raja, S. (2020). Planning and pandemics COVID-19 illuminates why urban planners should have listened to food advocates all along. *Agriculture and Human Values*, 1–2. https://doi.org/10.1007/s10460-020-10090-0

Ramer, H. (2019). *Urban Agriculture, Race, and Real Estate: The Minneapolis Garden Club 1910–1925*. Agriculture, Food, and Human Values Society meeting, Anchorage.

Raymond, L., & Fairfax, S. K. (2002). The "shift to privatization" in land conservation: A cautionary essay. *Natural Resources Journal*, *42*, 599–639.

Rippon-Butler, H. (2020). *Land Policy: Towards a More Equitable Farming Future*. National Young Farmers Coalition. www.youngfarmers.org/land/wp-content/uploads/2020/11/LandPolicyReport.pdf

Rosenthal, C. N. (2018). *Democratizing Finance: Origins of the Community Development Financial Institutions Movement*. FriesenPress.

RUAF. (2021). *Resource Center for Urban Agriculture and Forestry Homepage*. RUAF Urban Agriculture and Food Systems. Retrieved February 4, 2021, from https://ruaf.org/

Russell, T. (2019). Legislation could protect public wells with clean-water crops. *Friends of the Mississippi River*, February 20. www.fmr.org/legislative-updates/working-lands-drinking-water-program-legislation-introduced

Santo, R., Palmer, A., & Kim, B. (2016). Vacant lots to vibrant plots: A review of the benefits and limitations of urban agriculture. John Hopkins Center for a Livable Future, May.

Schell, C. J., Dyson, K., Fuentes, T. L., Des Roches, S., Harris, N. C., Miller, D. S., Woelfle-Erskine, C. A., & Lambert, M. R. (2020). The ecological and evolutionary consequences of systemic racism in urban environments. *Science*, *369*(6510).

Shoemaker, J. A. (2020). Fee simple failures: Rural landscapes and race. *Michigan Law Review*, *119*, 1695.

Soil Nexus. (2021). *Policy Learning for Urban and Peri-Urban Soil Regeneration*, May 27 and 28. www.eventbrite.com/e/workshop-policy-learning-day-1taller-aprendizaje-politicas-publicas-dia-1-tickets-155715373875#

Stokes, S. (2013). Justice for Hmong farmers in Minnesota. *Clearinghouse Community*. www.povertylaw.org/clearinghouse/stories/stokes

T.e.j.a.s. (n.d.). *Toxic Tours*. www.tejasbarrios.org/toxic-tours

Valliant, J., & Freedgood, J. (2020). Land access policy incentives. *Journal of Agriculture, Food Systems, and Community Development*, *9*(3), 1–8.

Ventura, S., & Bailkey, M. (2017). *Good Food, Strong Communities: Promoting Social Justice through Local and Regional Food Systems*. University of Iowa Press.

Voicu, I., & Been, V. (2008). The effect of community gardens on neighboring property values. *Real Estate Economics*, *36*(2), 241–283.

West, E. F. (2008). Minneapolis community gardens: A study of public policies in Minneapolis and Hennepin County. CURA NPCR 1274 Report in collaboration with GardenWorks. https://conservancy.umn.edu/handle/11299/203829

White, M. M. (2011). Sisters of the soil: Urban gardening as resistance in Detroit. *Race/Ethnicity: Multidisciplinary Global Contexts*, *5*(1), 13–28.

White, M. M. (2018). *Freedom Farmers: Agricultural Resistance and the Black Freedom Movement*. UNC Press Books.

Williams, J. M., & Holt-Giménez, E. (2017). *Land Justice: Re-imagining Land, Food, and the Commons*. Food First Books.

WinklerPrins, A. M. (2017). *Global Urban Agriculture*. CABI.

24

WHY SMALL TOWNS MATTER

Rural–Urban Linkages and Food Systems in the Global South

Cecilia Tacoli

Introduction

At around the turn of the century, the majority of the world's population became predominantly urban-based (Ritchie & Roser, 2018). Greater attention has since turned to the implications for food and farming of this unprecedented transition, and to whether the growing and changing demands for food from urban consumers can be met by the agricultural sector while addressing rural and urban poverty, reducing greenhouse gas emissions and increasing resilience to the impacts of climate change (Satterthwaite et al., 2010). More recently, the coronavirus pandemic crisis has highlighted the extent of food insecurity and inequalities, intensifying calls for greater attention and investment in improving the sustainability of food systems, also in view of the anticipated climate-related disruptions (FSIN and Global Network Against Food Crises, 2021; World Bank, 2021).

The links between rural and urban areas, people and enterprises are central to food systems and to policies aiming to strengthen them. There is often, however, an implicit assumption that there is a relatively simple and unilinear connection between the 'rural' as the site of food production and the 'urban' as the site of food consumption. As a result of what is essentially a focus on production, policy debates are largely framed around the main question of whether the future of food should be local or global. This reductionist view overlooks how rural–urban linkages reflect the diversity of urban systems and urbanisation processes, as well as the complex and context-specific dynamics of rural transformation (Battersby & Watson, 2019a; Crush et al., 2020; Tefft & Jonasova, 2020). It also neglects the critical role of small towns and large, 'urbanising' villages in the transition from largely agrarian economies to economies where most of the population is employed in industry and service sectors. These emerging urban centres are also often, but not always, key nodes in food systems, linking networks of producers, traders and consumers (Agergaard et al., 2019). A better understanding and recognition of the role of small towns is integral to more sustainable food systems. Achieving this, however, requires developing effective and accountable governance systems that build on context-specific opportunities and challenges.

This chapter examines how food systems are shaped by and shape the closely interrelated and dynamic processes of urbanisation and rural transformation, with specific attention to small towns

DOI: 10.4324/9781003055907-28

in low and middle-income countries and regions. Following a definition of rural–urban linkages that focuses on functional interactions between areas, people and enterprises, it summarises the main dimensions of processes of rural transformation. It then examines the demographic and socio-economic factors underpinning the emergence of small urban centres, and their role in local economic development and specifically in food systems. Finally, it assesses emerging territorial approaches to governance and the key issues they need to address in order to succeed.

What do we mean by rural–urban linkages? Some basic definitions

The linkages and interactions between rural and urban areas, people and enterprises have become increasingly intensive and an important element of livelihoods and economies in most regions of the world. They are also, however, extremely diverse and context-specific, reflecting local and national socio-cultural and economic transformations, including the systems and institutions that manage natural resources, the nature of agricultural production systems, the nature and location of manufacturing and of extractive industries, as well as the overall shape of national and regional urban systems. Rural–urban linkages have substantial impacts on livelihoods and, depending on individuals' and households' access to opportunities and assets, they can contribute to poverty reduction but also to social polarisation and marginalisation. Indeed, complexity is the one characteristic shared by all rural–urban linkages regardless of their location, and they are better defined as a complex web of connections between rural and urban areas, people and enterprises, rather than a linear relationship.

While there is a general, intuitive understanding of what is meant by rural–urban linkages, effective policies need to be based on clear definitions. Rural–urban linkages have both spatial and sectoral dimensions. Spatially, they include the tangible and intangible exchanges between rural and urban areas, people and enterprises. These links are spatial in that they involve the physical movement of goods, people, money, information and waste (see, for example, UN-Habitat, 2019); and the social networks and relations that span rural and urban locations. This definition is useful to describe the density and directions of linkages; however, it does little to capture the dynamics that underpin these exchanges.

A sectoral definition focuses more narrowly on the interactions between different economic sectors: agriculture, industry and services. These can include agricultural production backward linkages (the manufacturing of inputs) and forward linkages (processing, transport and distribution) (see, for example, Winters et al., 2002). While this broader definition goes some way towards capturing the functional links between people, activities and enterprises in different locations, it too, however, has limitations. To fully understand and support rural–urban linkages what is needed is a combination of sectoral (or functional) and spatial dimensions, and how these are framed by social relations and political and institutional contexts. As described in the next sections, examples of positive rural–urban linkages – that is, interactions that contribute to social, environmental and economic sustainability – typically share one key factor: the added value produced through functional linkages is retained and reinvested locally, where, with appropriate institutional support, it can serve as the engine of local sustainable development and poverty reduction. How this happens in practice is closely related to the context-specific nature of rural transformation, and to local processes of urbanisation.

Rural transformation

Rural–urban linkages are central to the concept of 'structural transformation' intended as the shift from largely agrarian economies, with large parts of the labour force engaged in farming, to service economies, where labour markets are dominated by industry and services (Losch et al., 2012; McMillan & Headey, 2014). Globally, since about 1980 the economically active population employed in manufacturing and services has exceeded that employed in agriculture (Satterthwaite, 2007). Currently around one-third of the world's labour force is engaged in agriculture, and the sector generates 2–3 per cent of global value added, although this does not take into account subsistence production and the added value produced by the manufacturing and distribution of food and other agricultural raw materials (Satterthwaite et al., 2010). With the major shifts in the global, regional and national structures of the economy, the non-farm share of rural households' incomes has become increasingly important. Figures vary and should be interpreted with caution since part-time and seasonal employment are typically under-counted, especially if in the informal sector, which is estimated to account for 61 per cent of global non-agricultural employment, and 90 per cent in low-income countries (ILO, 2018).

Even then, the proportion of rural incomes derived from non-agricultural sources is high and growing. Estimates put it between 30 and 50 per cent in sub-Saharan Africa, about 60 per cent in South Asia and roughly 40 per cent in Latin America (Reardon et al., 2001). Even in countries where agriculture remains the main economic base, such as Tanzania, the share of rural non-farm income went from 11 per cent in 1991 to 46 per cent in 2000 (Haggblade et al., 2007) and Bhutan, where in 2012 non-farm activities accounted for over 60 per cent of rural households' incomes (Rahut et al., 2016). An important question here concerns the nature of rural non-farm employment, and whether and how it affects food systems.

Closely related to these shifts in rural employment is the sharp rise in rural land acquisitions by urban-based investors, especially but not only in sub-Saharan Africa (Steel et al., 2019; Zoomers et al., 2017). Demographic and Health Survey data from Ghana, Kenya, Rwanda, Tanzania and Zambia show that urban-based 'emergent investor farmers' own 10 to 35 per cent of total agricultural land, and a disproportionate share of national farm holdings over 20 hectares (Jayne et al., 2014). This trend, coupled with increasing land subdivision, soil degradation and the impacts of the climate and environmental crisis, exacerbates constraints on smallholders' access to land and contributes towards explaining the move out of agriculture.

One important consequence of rural transformation is that a growing proportion of rural households produce less food than what they consume and rely on market purchases. In Vietnam, the second largest exporter of rice in the world, more than half the rural population are net rice buyers (Hoang et al., 2015), while in West Africa own agricultural production accounts for less than half the economic value of food consumed by rural households (Bricas & Tchamda, 2015). In Guatemala, the rural poor were the group most adversely affected by the food price hikes of 2008–2009 (de Janvry & Sadoulet, 2010).

Since non-farm income-generating activities are usually located in urban settlements, the general trend towards the diversification of rural households' income sources is closely linked to increased mobility. This includes migration in its many forms, especially internal migration on a permanent and temporary/seasonal basis, and daily mobility, often to local towns. Small urban centres are a central feature of rural transformation and its links with urbanisation.

Small urban centres: a diverse category

The academic and policy interest in small urban centres and rural–urban linkages has increased in recent years, although it has been central to regional planning since the 1970s (Satterthwaite & Tacoli, 2003). Demographic considerations are a key reason for the renewed interest in small towns, while economic growth and structural transformation, decentralisation and reducing migration to larger urban centres are increasingly important. The growth of small towns is explicitly promoted by local, national and international policies such as the New Urban Agenda, and there is increased recognition of the critical role small towns can play in adaptation to the impacts of climate change.

Globally, a significant and growing proportion of the urban population live in urban centres other than the larger cities. Currently, close to half the world's urban residents are estimated to live in centres with less than 500,000 inhabitants and in many cases just a few thousand inhabitants, with large variations across regions: in Africa, more than half the urban population live in this settlement category, compared to close to two-thirds in Europe but just one-third in North America (UNDESA, 2015). But such a broad category is unlikely to provide much detailed information.

A recent United Cities and Local Governments' report (UCLG, 2016) divides the world's urban settlements into three categories: metropolitan areas, intermediate cities and small towns of up to 50,000 inhabitants. While overall one-fifth of the world's population live in small towns, the average figure for Africa – 26.4 per cent – hides substantial regional differences between West and East Africa, both with 30 per cent of their urban residents living in small towns, and Central Africa, where this proportion is only 12.7 per cent. Among high-income regions, Europe has a higher-than-average proportion of its urban residents living in this category of settlements, while in North America this is only 10.9 per cent. This high level of diversity reflects wider socio-economic contexts, including the shape and nature of national urban systems, of which small towns are an important part.

Alternatively, recognising that even the 50,000 threshold may exclude smaller centres that do not have administrative urban status but may fulfil important urban functions, the Africapolis database defines an agglomeration as urban if its population exceeds 10,000 people and its built environment contains no unbuilt spaces wider than 200 metres. This results in a striking number of 'unofficial' urban centres throughout Africa. These new urban agglomerations, many rooted in rural transformations, play a vital part in reducing distances between urban and rural populations, in structuring urban networks, and in connecting the local and regional to the continental and global. The heightened proximity between rural and urban environments gives rise to new and unique urban forms, increasingly blurring the lines between the 'rural' and the 'urban' (OECD SWAC, 2020).

Both the UCLG and the Africapolis definitions attempt to address the key difficulty in international comparisons of small towns, namely the widely different definitions used by national governments, which in some cases also change over time. Most national definitions have a population threshold for settlements to be considered as urban; however, this varies from a few hundred inhabitants to 20,000. Additional criteria may include the nature of the economic base, such as the proportion of residents employed in non-farm activities; infrastructure, including roads and public services such as schools and hospitals; and administrative status. For analytical and policy purposes, however, it is more useful to consider small towns based on their functions, including the provision of services, facilities and infrastructure to their population and that of the surrounding region. These functions are largely shaped by the national and regional economic base and urban systems rather than by population size, and by administrative arrangements, including decentralisation or indeed the lack of it.

Small-town urbanisation and food systems

What drives the emergence of small urban centres? While large cities play an important role in national and regional economies, smaller urban centres have the potential to play a more direct role in the development of their rural region. They are in many ways the crucial connection between rural and urban areas, people and enterprises, the drivers of more diversified local economic bases and the links to wider markets; in so doing, they can contribute to poverty reduction and to more sustainable food systems.

The interdependence between urban-based enterprises, rural producers and urban markets, and the reliance of many households on both urban and rural resources and assets are often stronger around and within small towns. These can provide access to markets for small-scale producers, especially those who cannot fulfil the consistent quality and large quantities demanded by large supply chains. Nationally, as incomes grow, domestic demand for locally produced perishable goods such as fresh fruit and vegetables increases, supporting related processing activities in small towns. In Vietnam, demand for speciality fruit has stimulated the growth of several small towns in the south of the country, with local traders connecting small-scale producers to a network of markets. Unlike large supply chains and supermarkets, the towns' traders are able to buy all grades of produce which they then sell on different markets – high quality for urban consumers in the large cities, medium quality to consumers in secondary towns and low grade to rural markets. In addition, activities directly related to the production, processing and transport of food have created new jobs and stimulated local demand for a variety of services, from restaurants to hairdressing (Hoang et al., 2015). Along similar lines, a review of the links between agriculture, urbanisation and income growth in sub-Saharan Africa over a period of 40 years (1960s to 2000s) shows that there is very limited evidence that export crop production is the key to economic growth. In contrast, access to local urban markets and increased demand from urban consumers are the key drivers of farmers' multiple small investments in technologies and products, often financed by remittances and earnings from non-farm activities (Tiffen, 2003).

But there are great variations in the extent to which small urban centres can fulfil their role as engines of regional development. A good indicator is whether towns grow or instead stagnate and even decline. And this is closely related to agricultural production systems and markets. A good example is that of Ghana's Central Region where, between 1970 and 1984, the proportion of the urban population declined from 28.5 per cent to 26.5 per cent, in counter-tendency with national urbanisation levels which continued to grow. This was due to the collapse of international prices of cocoa, a commodity central to the economy of the Central Region. Small towns were depending on the cocoa trade, and as this dried up their residents moved out. As populations shrank, small towns were reclassified as rural settlements (Songsore, 2000).

Small towns have varied economic bases, including small-scale mining (Bryceson & Yankson, 2010). In some regions they are the primary destination for rural populations displaced by conflict and insecurity (Büscher & Mathys, 2019). But in most cases, it is the link to a prosperous agriculture providing adequate incomes to a large number of farmers that underpins more sustainable urbanisation. This implies a relatively equitable access to assets, especially land; adequate natural resources such as good soil quality and access to water; and whether crops are sold primarily on more stable domestic and regional markets, or on more volatile export markets.

In agricultural regions where production is dominated by large commercial farms, local small towns may not play a significant role as market nodes. As large volumes of cash crops bypass local centres, the low wages of agricultural workers fail to stimulate demand for goods and services. Even where production is by small-scale farmers but integrated in global export value chains, rapid changes in requirements can negatively affect local economies. In southern Ghana, pineapple production for export markets drove local agricultural growth from the 1990s until 2005, when buyers switched to smaller, sweeter varieties better grown in Central

America, resulting in the stagnation and often the economic and demographic decline of small towns in the region (Gough & Fold, 2010).

In Zimbabwe, land reform initiated in 2000 has radically transformed the agricultural economy and generated new opportunities in local small towns. In the last 20 years, their populations have more than tripled, and continue to attract commuters from rural areas. Land reform has created a large number of small and medium-sized producers out of what were previously large commercial enterprises. Higher incomes are reinvested and spent locally, generating demand for services such as street vendors, sellers of phone credit, mobile repair operations, transporters and so on (Scoones & Murimbarimba, 2021). Women and young people are especially important players in the new and largely informal economy of Zimbabwe's small towns, and the ones more likely to engage in non-farm activities. This reflects findings from an earlier study of a small town in northwest Tanzania, showing a striking difference in the number of women-headed households (30 per cent) compared with the surrounding rural areas (7 per cent), suggesting that urban labour markets offer far more opportunities for women, who may often have less rights to farmland than men and who also often head smaller households with less labour capacity (Baker, 1995). In all the case studies cited in this chapter, women and young people are a large proportion of those employed in food processing, marketing and transport.

Access to adequate natural resources is also an important factor in small-town development: a study of such settlements in Malawi found that poor soil quality can limit the development of cash crops and hamper the 'virtuous cycle' of rural–urban connections whereby higher incomes from farming trigger the urban functions provided by the small town (Nchito, 2010). The negative impacts of climate-induced changes in rainfall and temperatures can affect not only farming and food production, but entire local economies and small-town development.

Small urban centres' trajectories are in many cases determined by the specific value chain dynamics of the crops that dominate local agricultural production. In Tanzania, smallholder-produced perishable cash crops, such as tomatoes and maize destined mainly to domestic and cross-border urban markets, have spurred a myriad of related small enterprises providing packaging, storage, processing and transport and located in the local small towns. Other small urban centres have grown around the agro-processing of crops, such as tea and sugarcane grown through contract farming schemes where farmers only cultivate the crop and receive seeds, fertilisers and other inputs from the local large commercial farm and all post-harvest activities – cutting, loading, transport to the processing factory – are carried out by private contractors. The dominance of large estates also has financial implications, as their taxes are paid to regional, rather than local governments (Lazaro et al., 2019).

Perhaps the most important role of small towns in food systems is the provision of market nodes, with produce moving first to the local small town to then move on to other towns and further to large urban markets and in some cases to regional and international markets. Effectively, goods travel through, rather than just to, small urban centres (Karg et al., 2019). This highlights the significance of accessibility, in transport infrastructure as well as communications, and especially the role of mobile phones, in linking producers, traders and consumers. However, improved infrastructure such as roads and transport networks may not benefit small towns that can be bypassed by links to larger cities (Douglass, 1998). But lessons from empirical studies are often set aside when national governments opt to invest in more visible infrastructure projects based on generalisations instead of a careful understanding of the local context, rather than supporting long-term processes such as expanding the capacity of local governments and civil society organisations through shared learning.

Territorial approaches and the governance of small towns: implications for food systems

Governance arrangements in small towns have important implications for food systems within and beyond their administrative boundaries. However, they remain largely understudied and the capacity of local governments in this category of settlements is, in many instances, severely limited, as discussed below (Satterthwaite, 2017; Tacoli, 2010).

Urbanisation has a powerful influence on rural locations where food demand spurred by higher urban incomes and changing dietary patterns drives rural transformation. At the same time, however, growing competition over resources, especially land, contributes to increasing social polarisation and the gradual dispossession of low-income groups. The need for inclusive urbanisation is as important in small towns as it is in large urban centres, as the most vulnerable groups often cannot obtain a secure urban home or job but find their rural opportunities declining. Yet, while, historically, urbanisation has been recognised as central to economic growth, for a very long time urban growth policies have accepted rising inequalities and declining environmental conditions within and around urban centres as inevitable and best addressed once the necessary economic resources are available.

One example is the 2009 World Bank's World Development Report, sub-titled 'Reshaping Economic Geography', which explicitly excluded the social and environmental impacts of a changing economic geography from the report (World Bank, 2008). This effectively rejected responsibility for the social and environmental consequences of their recommended approach to the rural–urban transition, based largely on spatially blind, 'one-size-fits-all' policies that include strengthening formal institutions to enforce the rule of law and protect private assets, investing in transport infrastructure and creating larger internal markets. By focusing on dynamic areas around larger urban centres, these policies run the very concrete risk of exacerbating economic underdevelopment in remote rural areas, leading to greater regional and territorial inequalities and poverty (Rigg et al., 2009).

In contrast, place-based or territorial approaches acknowledge the centrality of local contexts. Increasingly recognised as an efficient way to integrate the rural–urban transition in global agendas, such as the SDGs and the New Urban Agenda, they advocate stronger rural–urban linkages fostering spatial inclusion and, as a result, achieving economic growth and reducing regional inequalities (UN-Habitat, 2019). Small towns, and especially networks of urban centres of different sizes, are clearly an important element of territories that encompass rural and urban locations, although they are not always explicitly mentioned.

Territorial approaches to governance put at their centre both formal and informal institutions and integrated, multi-sectoral and comprehensive strategies. The explicit geographic focus builds on local conditions and advantages and, in so doing, aims to increase resilience and reduce regional inequalities. As a bottom-up approach, it involves local stakeholders in planning and implementing development strategies, stimulating dialogue and co-production of solutions between local government and civil society, and providing greater transparency and accountability. In addition, territorial approaches call for regional-level development strategies that mobilise assets and harness complementarities (Barca, 2009; OECD, 2013; UCLG, 2016).

Here too, however, there is insufficient attention to socio-economic and, in many cases, cultural polarisation and growing inequalities (Andersson Djurfeldt, 2021). Where competition over resources increases, tensions between different and often new interest groups affect governance. In sub-Saharan Africa, inconsistencies between customary and modern institutions can lead to conflict between elected representatives and unelected (and unaccountable) traditional chiefs around control over land, affecting food production, and urban planning, affecting market and transport infrastructure (Brown, 2021). Mobility and migration can also influence and sometimes radically change the dynamics of governance at the local level. In countries such as Senegal where international remittances are vital to local economies and livelihoods, decentralisation has opened up opportunities for migrants to participate in local politics in small towns and, in so doing, becoming a powerful new interest group extending control over land and planning (Sall, 2010).

In the context of food system policies, rural–urban linkages are framed primarily as the links between producers and consumers, with a focus on local supply or short chains. The city region food system (CRFS) is defined as "all the actors, processes and relationships that are involved in food production, processing, distribution and consumption in a given city region that includes a more or less concentrated urban centre and its surrounding peri-urban and rural hinterland" (FAO, 2019). While the links to national and global food systems are recognised as necessary, the approach advocates local food production to reduce dependence on imports and market price volatility (Battersby & Watson, 2019a; on the city region approach, see also Chapter 25 by Blay-Palmer et al. in this volume). Closely aligned to both territorial and CRFS approaches, the Urban–Rural Linkages: Guiding Principles and Framework for Action promoted by UN-Habitat (UN-Habitat, 2019) aim to strengthen urban–rural linkages and implement integrated territorial development. In the process, the terminology has changed from rural–urban to urban–rural linkages, reflecting the perceived role of urban centres as the drivers of economic development within their region.

This view is not new and has been central to the highly influential 'urban functions in rural development' approach developed in the 1990s, which sees urban centres, including small towns, as promoters of rural development by supplying services, agricultural inputs and consumer goods to rural populations (Belsky & Karaska, 1990; Rondinelli, 1985). While this approach still influences regional planning models, including territorial approaches, it has been widely criticised for missing the crucial point that low rural consumption is the result of social inequality and low incomes rather than difficult access to supply and markets (Hardoy & Satterthwaite, 1986; Pedersen, 1997; Simon, 1992).

Current approaches to food systems such as the CRFS and the Urban–Rural Linkages framework for action similarly underestimate the ample evidence showing that food poverty in urban centres is the outcome of multidimensional urban poverty, including income and non-income aspects, rather than of insufficient supply (Battersby & Watson, 2019b; Boonyabancha et al., 2019; Crush et al., 2020; Haysom, 2020; Tacoli, 2017). They also underestimate the fact that rural poverty, including food poverty, is not so much the result of inadequate access to markets – including local urban food markets – but rather that of inequality in access to land, capital and labour. A more explicit focus on consumption rather than the current one on production and supply would go a long way in identifying the priorities for food systems that serve the urban and the rural poor.

From a governance perspective, territorial approaches build on decentralisation reforms widely promoted since the late 1990s with mixed results, whereby powers, resources and responsibilities are devolved to increasingly autonomous and legitimate sub-national authorities. While this is a model that can work well in the Global North, implementing it in low-income nations proves to be much more problematic. The factors behind the relatively high rate of failure of decentralisation have been analysed at length (for a review, see Satterthwaite & Tacoli, 2003). For territorial approaches to succeed it is important that they address the key issues that hampered decentralisation. The first and perhaps most important is the underestimation of macroeconomic policies, pricing policies and sectoral priorities, including policies related to agrifood systems that do not make explicit reference to spatial dimensions (such as, for example, supporting export-oriented food production). Equal access to land and secure tenure are also critical, as the examples of successful small towns in this chapter clearly show. Neglecting the powerful influence of such policies is a major reason for the failure of local and territorial development, as local governance is deeply influenced by policies and strategic choices made at the macro level. As the world faces a global post-pandemic recession and a climate and ecological crisis, these will be ever more important.

The second reason that hampers territorial approaches is the lack of adequate information and reliable data that reflect the huge diversity of small towns and of the nature and scope of the rural–urban linkages underpinning them. Data about local needs, priorities and resources, and of the impacts of sectoral policies, are needed to support the design and implementation of effective local initiatives. In most low and middle-income nations, the lack of sub-national data on economic activities – especially the large proportion of informal enterprises; demographic changes due to migration and mobility – especially seasonal and temporary movement; and poverty and vulnerability – including access to housing and basic infrastructure and services, is a severe constraint for local government action. Small towns and their surrounding regions that depend on agricultural production are extremely vulnerable to the impacts of climate change. Access to and understanding of accurate and fine-grained data is a key element of local governance and is essential to ensure the sustainable management of natural resources and to face what can well be an existential crisis for these territories.

The third reason is that while the centrality of local governance systems, including institutions and governments, is increasingly recognised, this has not been accompanied by an appropriate fiscal and financial architecture that enables them to perform their role (UCLG, 2016). This is especially the case for low- and middle-income countries: while in Europe the proportion of local government revenue is above 35 per cent of total government revenue, in African countries on average it is only 7 per cent (OECD, 2015). In India, government funding for services is often better in rural panchayats (village councils) than in small towns, which are often underfunded under several national large schemes despite their increasing demographic and socio-economic significance (Zerah & Denis, 2017). This makes local governments heavily dependent on central government transfers and limits their ability to invest according to local priorities and needs. Virtually all the case studies of small towns cited in this chapter report of the difficulties encountered of local governments in raising local taxes from businesses. On the one hand, large commercial farms tend to pay taxes to central government; small local businesses, on the other hand, often justify their unwillingness to pay local taxes with the perception that these are not used to provide needed services. This shows that to achieve legitimacy, local governments need to be accountable to their citizens, often in a difficult context of competing institutions such as national sectoral institutions, traditional authorities and powerful private-sector actors. Transparency on expenditure and collaboration with civil society, starting from collecting locally relevant information, are crucial ways to increase legitimacy.

Conclusions

A better understanding of the role of small towns as market nodes and centres for rural non-farm employment and income-generating activities is central to the understanding of the governance of food systems. By contextualising food systems within wider socio-economic transformations that affect both rural and urban areas, it highlights the importance of context and the need to pay special attention to processes of social polarisation. In turn, this requires a switch from a linear and essentialist conceptualisation of the 'rural' as the location of food production and the 'urban' as that of food consumption. Policies that assume that rural producers and urban consumers are effectively homogenous groups are likely to neglect the specific drivers of both rural and urban food (and non-food) poverty. While a clear improvement from earlier regional planning, both the CRFS and, to a lesser extent, the Urban–Rural Linkages framework for action run the risk of adopting a sectoral approach which misses the importance of non-food factors in determining the sustainability of food systems and in reducing food and nutrition insecurity.

References

Agergaard, J., Tacoli, C., Steel, G., & Ørtenblad, S.B. (2019). Revisiting rural-urban transformations and small town development in sub-Saharan Africa. *European Journal of Development Research*, 31: 2–11. https://doi.org/10.1057/s41287-018-0182-z

Andersson Djurfeldt, A. (2021). Theorising small-town urbanisation in sub-Saharan Africa: A multi-scalar approach. *Town Planning Review*, 92(6): 667–676. https://doi.org/10.3828/tpr.2021.16

Baker, J. (1995). Survival and accumulation strategies at the rural–urban interface in north-west Tanzania. *Environment and Urbanization*, 7(1).

Barca, F. (2009). *An Agenda for a Reformed Cohesion Policy: A Place-based Approach to Meeting European Union Challenges and Expectations*. Brussels: European Commission.

Battersby, J., & Watson, V. (2019a). The planned 'city region' in the New Urban Agenda: An appropriate framing for urban food security? *Town Planning Review*, 90(5). http://dx.doi.org/10.3828/tpr.2019.32

Battersby, J., & Watson, V. (Eds.). (2019b). *Urban Food Systems Governance and Poverty in African Cities*. London: Routledge.

Belsky, E.S., & Karaska, G.J. (1990). Approaches to locating urban functions in developing rural areas. *International Regional Science Review*, 13(3): 225–240.

Boonyabancha, S., Kerr, T., Joshi, L., & Tacoli, C. (2019). How the urban poor define and measure food security in Cambodia and Nepal. *Environment and Urbanization*, 31(2): 517–532. https://doi.org/10.1177/0956247819863246

Bricas, N., & Tchamda, C. (2015). Sub-Saharan Africa's significant changes in food consumption patterns. *A Question of Development – Syntheses of AFD Studies and Research*, n° 26.

Brown, D. (2021). Towards a comparative research agenda on in situ urbanisation and rural governance transformation, *International Development Planning Review*, 43(3): 289–320. https://doi.org/10.3828/idpr.2020.15

Bryceson, D., & Yankson, P. (2010). Frontier mining settlements: Livelihood promises and predicaments. In J. Agergaard, N. Fold, & K. Gough (Eds.), *Rural-Urban Dynamics: Livelihoods, Mobility and Markets in African and Asian Frontiers*. London and New York: Routledge.

Büscher, K., & Mathys, G. (2019). War, displacement and rural–urban transformation: Kivu's boomtowns, Eastern D.R. Congo. *European Journal of Development Research*, 31: 53–71. https://doi.org/10.1057/s41287-018-0181-0

Crush, J., Frayne, B., & Haysom, G. (Eds.). (2020). *Handbook on Urban Food Security in the Global South*. Cheltenham: Edward Elgar.

De Janvry, A., & Sadoulet, E. (2010). The global food crisis in Guatemala: What crisis and for whom? *World Development*, 38: 132–139.

Douglass, M. (1998). A regional network strategy for reciprocal rural–urban linkages. *Third World Planning Review*, 20(1).

FAO. (2019). *City Region Food Systems Programme*. Rome: FAO.

FSIN and Global Network Against Food Crises. (2021). *Global Report on Food Crises 2021, Rome*.

Gough, K., & Fold, N. (2010). Rise and fall of smallholder pineapple production in Ghana: changing global markets, livelihoods and settlement growth. In J. Agergaard, N. Fold, & K. Gough (Eds.), *Rural–Urban Dynamics: Livelihoods, Mobility and Markets in African and Asian Frontiers*. London and New York: Routledge.

Haggblade, S., Hazell, P., & Reardon, T. (2007). *Transforming the Rural Non-farm Economy*. Baltimore, MD: Johns Hopkins University Press.

Hardoy, J., & Satterthwaite, D. (1986). *Small and Intermediate Urban Centres: Their Role in National and Regional Development in the Third World*. London: Hodder and Stoughton.

Haysom, G. (2020). Perspectives on urban food-system governance in the Global South. In J. Crush, B. Frayne, & G. Haysom (Eds.), *Handbook on Urban Food Security in the Global South*. Cheltenham: Edward Elgar.

ILO (International Labour Organization). (2018). *Women and Men in the Informal Economy: A Statistical Picture* (3rd ed.). Geneva: ILO

Jayne, T.S., Chamberlin, J., & Headey, D. (2014). Land pressures, the evolution of farming systems, and development strategies in Africa: A synthesis. *Food Policy*, 48: 1–17. https://doi.org/10.1016/j.foodpol.2014.05.014

Karg, H., Bellwood-Howard, I., Akoto-Danso, E.K., et al. (2019). Small-town agricultural markets in Northern Ghana and their connection to rural and urban transformation. *European Journal of Development Research*, 31: 95–117. https://doi.org/10.1057/s41287-018-0171-2

Lazaro, E., Agergaard, J., Larsen, M.N., Makindara, J., & Birch-Thomsen, T. (2019). Urbanisation in rural regions: The emergence of urban centres in Tanzania. *The European Journal of Development Research*, 31(1): 72–94. https://doi.org/10.1057/s41287-018-0185-9

Losch, B., Fréguin-Gresh, S., & Thomas White, E. (2012). *Structural Transformation and Rural Change Revisited*. Washington, DC and Paris: World Bank and AFD.

McMillan, M., & Headey, D. (2014). Introduction: Understanding structural transformation in Africa. *World Development*, 63: 1–10. https://doi.org/10.1016/j.worlddev.2014.02.007

Nchito, W.S. (2010). Migratory patterns in small towns: The cases of Mazabuka and Kalomo in Zambia. *Environment and Urbanization*, 22(1): 91–106. https://doi.org/10.1177/0956247810362846

OECD. (2013). *Rural–Urban Partnerships: An Integrated Approach to Economic Development*. Paris: OECD Publishing.

OECD. (2015). *African Economic Outlook 2015: Regional Development and Spatial Inclusion*. Paris: OECD Publishing.

OECD/SWAC. (2020). *Africa's Urbanisation Dynamics 2020: Africapolis, Mapping a New Urban Geography. West African Studies*. Paris: OECD Publishing. https://doi.org/10.1787/b6bccb81-en.

Pedersen, P.O. (1997). *Small African Towns: Between Rural Networks and Urban Hierarchies*. Aldershot: Avebury.

Rahut, D.B., Ranjan Jena, P., Ali, A., Behera, B., & Bahadur Chhetri, N. (2016). Rural nonfarm employment, income, and inequality: Evidence from Bhutan. *Asian Development Review*, 32(2): 65–94. https://doi.org/10.1162/ADEV_a_0005

Reardon, T., Berdegué, J., & Escobar, G. (2001). Rural nonfarm employment and incomes in Latin America: Overview and policy implications. *World Development*, 29(3): 395–409.

Rigg, J., Bebbington, A., Gough, K.V., Bryceson, D.F., Agergaard, J., Fold, N., & Tacoli, C. (2009). The World Development Report 2009 'reshapes economic geography': Geographical reflections. *Transactions of the Institute of British Geographers*, 34(2): 128–136.

Ritchie, H., & Roser, M. (2018). Urbanization. Published online at https://ourworldindata.org/urbanization.

Rondinelli, D. (1985). *Applied Methods of Regional Analysis: The Spatial Dimensions of Development Policy*. Boulder, CO: Westview Press.

Sall, M. (2010). Straightforward critics or would-be candidates? International migrants and the management of local affairs and development: The case of the Senegal River Valley. *Environment and Urbanization*, 22(1): 81–90.

Satterthwaite, D. (2007). *The Transition to a Predominantly Urban World and its Underpinnings*. Human Settlements Discussion Papers Series – Urban Change 4, IIED, London.

Satterthwaite, D. (2017). The impact of urban development on risk in sub-Saharan Africa's cities with a focus on small and intermediate urban centres. *International Journal of Disaster Risk Reduction*, 26: 16–23. https://doi.org/10.1016/j.ijdrr.2017.09.025

Satterthwaite, D., & Tacoli, C. (2003). *The Urban Part of Rural Development: The Role of Small and Intermediate Urban Centres in Rural and Regional Development and Poverty Reduction*. London: IIED.

Satterthwaite, D., McGranahan, G., & Tacoli, C. (2010). Urbanization and its implications for food and farming. *Philosophical Transactions of the Royal Society B*, 365: 2809–820. https://doi.org/10.1098/rstb.2010.0136

Scoones, I., & Murimbarimba, F. (2021). Small towns and land reform in Zimbabwe. *European Journal of Development Research*, 33: 2040–2062. https://doi.org/10.1057/s41287-020-00343-3

Simon, D. (1992). Conceptualizing small towns in African development. In J. Baker & P.O. Pedersen (Eds.), *The Rural–Urban Interface in Africa: Expansion and Adaptation*. Uppsala: The Scandinavian Institute of African Studies

Songsore, J. (2000). *Towards a Better Understanding of Urban Change: The Ghana Case Study.* Urban Change Working Paper 2, IIED, London.

Steel, G., Birch-Thomsen, T., Cottyn, I., et al. (2019). Multi-activity, multi-locality and small-town development in Cameroon, Ghana, Rwanda and Tanzania. *European Journal of Development Research*, 31: 12–33. https://doi.org/10.1057/s41287-018-0183-y

Tacoli, C. (2010). Editorial: Governance, migration and local development. *Environment and Urbanization*, 22(1): 5–11. https://doi.org/10.1177/0956247810364111

Tacoli, C. (2017). Food (in)security in rapidly urbanizing, low-income contexts. *International Journal of Environmental Research and Public Health*, 14(2): 1554. www.mdpi.com/1660-4601/14/12/1554

Tefft, J., & Jonasova, M. (2020). Food systems transformation in an urbanizing world. In J. Crush, B. Frayne, & G. Haysom (Eds.), *Handbook on Urban Food Security in the Global South.* Cheltenham: Edward Elgar.

Tiffen, M. (2003). Transitions in sub-Saharan Africa: Agriculture, urbanisation and income growth. *World Development*, 31(8): 1343–1366.

UCLG. (2016). *GOLD IV: Fourth Global Report on Decentralization and Local Democracy: Co-creating the Urban Future.* Barcelona: UCLG.

UNDESA (United Nations, Department of Economic and Social Affairs), Population Division. (2015). *World Urbanization Prospects: The 2014 Revision, (ST/ESA/SER.A/366).* New York: UNDESA.

UN-Habitat. (2019). *Urban–Rural Linkages: Guiding Principles Framework for Action to Advance Integrated Territorial Development.* Nairobi: UN-Habitat.

Winters, P., Davis, B., Reardon, T., & Stamoulis, K. (2002). *Promoting Farm/Non-Farm Linkages for Rural Development: Case Studies from Africa and Latin America.* Rome: Food and Agriculture Organization of the United Nations.

World Bank. (2008). *World Development Report 2009: Reshaping Economic Geography.* Washington, DC: The World Bank.

World Bank. (2021). For further information, see www.worldbank.org/en/topic/agriculture/brief/food-security-and-covid-19.

Xuan Thanh, H., Thu Phuong, D.T., Thanh Hoa, D.T., & Dinh Lap, L. (2015). *Urbanisation and Rural Development in Vietnam's Mekong Delta: Revisiting Livelihood Transformations in Three Fruit-growing Settlements, 2006–2015.* IIED Working Paper, IIED, London.

Zerah, M.H., & Denis, E. (2017). Introduction: Reclaiming small towns. In E. Denis & M.H. Zerah (Eds.), *Subaltern Urbanisation in India.* Berlin: Springer.

Zoomers, A., van Noorloos, F., Otsuki, K., Steel, G., & van Westen, G. (2017). The rush for land in an urbanizing world: From land grabbing toward developing safe, resilient, and sustainable cities and landscapes. *World Development*, 92: 242–252. https://doi.org/10.1016/j.worlddev.2016.11.016

25

THE CITY REGION FOOD SYSTEM

Broadening Space for Urban Governance

Alison Blay-Palmer, Jess Halliday, Guido Santini, Joy Carey, Roman Malec, Makiko Taguchi, René van Veenhuizen and Laine Young

Introduction

This chapter builds from ongoing explorations and critiques of the City Region Food System (CRFS) approach (Blay-Palmer et al. 2018, 2021; Jennings et al. 2015; Battersby & Watson 2020). A CRFS 'aims to foster the development of resilient and sustainable food systems within urban centres, peri-urban and rural areas surrounding cities by strengthening rural-urban linkages' (RUAF n.d.). The CRFS approach helps to understand and harness the potential of existing local food systems. As Clancy and Ruhf explain, 'the region is more than the sum of its "locals"' (2010: 4). The CRFS approach is explicitly place-based, offering a territorial approach that can focus on cities of all sizes and their surrounding regions and work within existing regional strengths and weaknesses (Battersby & Watson 2020; Berdegué et al. 2014; UNDESA, 2019; Clancy & Ruhf, 2010).

This chapter is based on research conducted by the authors since 2015 around city region food systems. There have been two phases of research. During each phase, local actors were supported by RUAF-FAO expert teams as they determined their visions, built multi-actor teams, established priorities for their work based on their existing capacities, and then worked toward achieving changes for their city regions. In the first phase from 2015–2018, pilot city projects (Colombo, Sri Lanka; Kitwe and Lusaka, Zambia; Medellin, Colombia; Quito, Ecuador; Toronto, Canada; Utrecht, Netherlands) were guided as they developed and tested how CRFS could move them in more sustainable directions. The outcome of that work is a toolkit and indicator framework that cities and their regions can use to move in greener, healthier, more accessible and fairer territorial food systems. The second step of the project is ongoing. This phase aims to understand how CRFS can be more resilient in the context of climate change, pandemics and other shocks and hazards. This work is taking place in Colombo, Sri Lanka; Kigali, Rwanda; Melbourne, Australia; and Tamale, Ghana (FAO 2021a; RUAF 2021). An online training manual for this work has been launched and will be available in 2022.

DOI: 10.4324/9781003055907-29

While findings from the pilot projects are preliminary and case-study based, insights linked to urban governance from this ongoing exploration will be highlighted in our chapter to describe the emerging CRFS approach in more detail. The CRFS approach is grounded in, and builds on, decades of research and practice into multi-stakeholder engagement, asset-gap/SWOT analysis and related insights about place-based development and policy development (e.g. FAO 2021a; Dubbeling & de Zeeuw 2011; Raja et al. 2017; Moragues-Faus & Sonnino 2019). As we get a better understanding of CRFS pilot projects in the context of these long-standing research pillars, three key insights are emerging about CRFS. Given that the particulars of every CRFS are unique to each city region, the resulting food system and its related governance will also be one-off. Starting from this recognition, the CRFS approach is:

1. Intended to guide the understanding around and development of increasingly sustainable and shock resistant CRFS, providing a flexible and dynamic approach with examples that may be taken up as is, but more often are springboards for place-based action. In this regard, the CRFS approach and the related tools are not prescriptive;
2. The process builds more effectively through the leadership of inclusive multi-stakeholder platforms, which cross sectoral and policy silos and reach across scales; and
3. As part of understanding the particulars of each place, it is beneficial to have guiding priorities that help to steer participants. This can take the form of a collective vision developed by a multi-stakeholder engagement team but can also be a simpler list of priorities developed on a more ad hoc basis. This knowledge guides each city region towards understanding more about its existing resources and challenges in the context of the CRFS goals.

Given these considerations, the CRFS approach can help make rural–urban linkages more coherent and identify how to close material resource flows by understanding and weighing opportunities and challenges in a CRFS (Dreschel 2020; Blay-Palmer et al. 2018; on rural–urban linkages, see also Chapter 24 by Tacoli in this volume). Through diverse food chains of different lengths, it can support small-scale producers and businesses along the food system. It can also provide economic opportunities in rural settings, helping to stem the flow of migration from rural to urban. Getting more fresh local produce to consumers, especially marginalized communities, helps build food and nutrition security. This, in turn, offers localized opportunities to protect and conserve biocultural diversity (Egal & Forster 2020; Pimbert 2016). By offering economic and biocultural diversity solutions it can help address climate change, poverty and food security, and biodiversity loss.

This chapter uses as its starting point the ideas articulated in Chapter 10 (by Halliday in this volume) that urban food governance is evolving, ongoing and fluid. This leads to the central question for this chapter: what types of iterative and exploratory governance could be well aligned, in support of not only cities but also their surrounding regions, with the goal of building more resilient sustainable, shock resistant food systems? In particular we note the challenges raised by Battersby and Watson (2020), along with other urban initiatives, that CRFS often operate within resource poor, and as a result, conflictual government realities; that boundaries are difficult to determine as they are context dependent and can include political, foodshed, biogeographical, and ecological considerations, among others, making the projects difficult to realize; and that there are frequent data challenges, in particular across hard to define boundaries. In addition, Jennings et al. (2015) refer to the 'governance gap' and point to a lack of multi-dimensional policy and planning for food systems. Drawing on Salet et al. (2015), they remind us that within a CRFS, governance 'depends on the existence of strong, well-resourced local governments willing to collaborate, as well as well-developed civil society and advocacy groups – characteristics which do not hold in many parts of the world and are especially lacking in parts of the global South' (Battersby & Watson 2020: 509). There is also the reality that city regions must increasingly compete for the slim available financial and other resources, pitting various regional and city governments against each other (Battersby & Watson 2020: 509). On the other hand, decentralization (e.g. Kenya), rapid growth of smaller cities and towns, the creation of new local municipalities (Nepal, Uganda), and young educated staff with local authorities, offer opportunities to improve or create new forms of governance.

Collaborative measures to overcome these limitations include: (1) implementing governance frameworks that are more coherent and inclusive; (2) using spatial planning and building suitable infrastructure to ensure long-term value; (3) using public procurement to create a more stable demand and involve local suppliers; (4) promoting business, innovation and entrepreneurship to create and capture CRFS benefits; and, (5) making information more accessible and transparent (Jennings et al. 2015).

While some of these CRFS concerns and possibilities are explored elsewhere (Blay-Palmer et al. 2018, 2021), we use this chapter to continue to reflect on the opportunities and challenges that have emerged in the second phase of the project and are focused on addressing climate change and other shocks and hazards. The main aim of the chapter is to look at the CRFS approach through the lens of urban governance. The chapter provides insights into the global context for the CRFS approach, the CRFS as a place-based process, and the role of multi-functional engagement across various spatial considerations. With this overview, we then turn our attention to Quito to provide concrete examples of how the CRFS can broaden the space for urban governance. We end the chapter with a discussion about CRFS as it intersects with governance. The conclusions point to the need for flexible resources to support the process; the engagement of multiple actors to build robust networks; and a strong vision to help steer the process.

CRFS and governance context and insights

While the CRFS approach is unique to each city region, each CRFS is influenced by, and influences, governance at multiple scales. It is also place-based and grounded in the unique assets and challenges of each city region. The CRFS is improved through multi-stakeholder engagement offering opportunities to build network linkages across government departments and sectors. Food is inherently multi-functional and enables action and policy linked to health, economic development, social inclusion and ecosystem well-being levers, among others, that can improve the CRFS through more coherent governance within cities and across scales.

The global context

There are a number of global initiatives that address the need for more sustainable food systems. Together, three recent initiatives provide the conceptual context for the CRFS to both respond to, and be supported as, a pathway to more sustainable food systems. First, at the national scale, there are several Sustainable Development Goals (SDGs) that link food to specific actions. SDGs 1 and 8 point to economic activities and the opportunity to reduce migration. Food can enable more robust economic opportunities in rural areas, curbing the need for migration (Smith & Wesselbaum 2020). SDGs 4, 5 and 10 link learning and improved gender equality to food. SDG 3 connects to health through improved food and nutrition security. Goals 7 and 13 can use more sustainable food systems to mitigate climate change through climate cooling production approaches (Blay-Palmer et al. 2018; FAO 2019). Secondly, the Milan Urban Food

Policy Pact (MUFPP) provides an entry point for municipalities and surrounding regions to engage in coherent regional food policy and programme initiatives that focus on governance; sustainable diets and nutrition; social and economic equity; and food production, distribution, waste reduction, and recovery. The MUFPP supports these six themes through an indicator framework to monitor progress and case studies to provide workable examples for change. Finally, the New Urban Agenda paragraph 123 suggests food as an entry point for urban and regional planning to address food and nutrition security, coordinate more equitable and less wasteful food systems, and address environmental resilience and biodiversity. By acting as a connector point, CRFS can deploy these resources to build increasing resilience.

More specifically, there has also been a significant global effort to provide guiding frameworks that link rural and urban food regions – a hallmark of the CRFS approach. These include the FAO World Committee on Food Security (CFS) 2018 document 'Addressing Food Security and Nutrition in the Context of Changing Rural–Urban Dynamics', the work on urban–rural linkages by UN-Habitat including 'Urban–Rural Linkages: Guiding Principles Framework for Action to Advance Integrated Territorial Development' (Egal & Forster 2020; Tefft et al. 2017) and the Territorial Perspective for Development (TP4D) (Caron et al. 2017). These global initiatives have the potential to provide guidance about governance in cities and their regions as they point to gaps and opportunities across the rural/urban continuum. They can set the stage for place-based approaches, connections across urban and rural spaces through multi-stakeholder engagement and provide opportunities for multi-spatial multi-functional engagement.

CRFS as a place-based approach

Every city region food system is different. Each one has its own governance system nested within regional and/or national and/or supranational governments/governance. These systems all have unique production, distribution, market and consumer flows that impact ecologies, cultures and economic factors. These systems are relatively more or less resilient, sustainable and circular. Key goals of the CRFS approach are to understand existing city region strengths and challenges, set a course, measure and monitor, and work in the direction of meeting the established goals, and aim to constantly improve as a way to build sustainability. This is necessarily an ongoing and iterative process, typically fraught with challenges and some successes.

As a result, the tools needed to move the sustainability needle are not the same across the board and are not prescriptive. That said, there are common needs that are emerging as part of CRFS research. The initial online toolkit (first launched in 2017; FAO 2021b), developed based on pilot project research in Colombo, Kitwe, Lusaka, Medellin, Quito, Toronto, and Utrecht, includes tools that support establishing a multi-stakeholder task force, defining a shared vision, determining the boundaries for the CRFS, conducting a scan of initial resources, engaging in an in-depth assessment, exploring governance considerations as well as developing policy supports, and engaging in planning. Given that every CRFS is different, there is no one entry point and we have had cities and their regions begin from any number of spaces. What we find is that these eventually are the steps that CRFS engage in and that together they provide a good sense of where cities regions are and where they want to go and determine how to get there. For example, in the second iteration of the project with the focus on creating training modules – on topics such as building multi-stakeholder engagement and indicators, climate risk rapid scan of the CRFS, and food systems and climate – guidance, examples and tools are provided to CRFS actors to enable them to move forward with a process that works for them. This flexibility is important as, according to the High Level Panel on Food Security and Nutrition (FSN) (cited in Battersby & Watson 2020), the FSN system 'gathers all the elements (environment, people, inputs, processes, infrastructures, institutions, etc.) and activities that relate to the production, processing, distribution, preparation and consumption of food, and the outputs of these activities, including socioeconomic and environmental outcomes' (HLPE 2014: 12).

In the same way 'collaborative governance' has always existed in one form or another, naming it in the 1980s helped to clarify and realize benefits by having a deeper understanding of the principles (see Chapter 10 by Halliday in this volume). The same is true of CRFSs. The elements for the CRFS approach have existed since we have had food moving from rural to urban areas but are now being understood using a more explicit, interconnected, coherent lens to capture the benefits of a more clearly defined approach. This includes food system governance.

Broadening the conversation: Multi-spatial multi-functional engagement

Multi-stakeholder engagement across various government departments can make the CRFS process increasingly inclusive and robust and is one of the dimensions of building a CRFS. As described in CRFS material including the toolkit (FAO 2021b; RUAF 2021), recommended stakeholders include government officials from city, rural, regional and national governments with representatives of the environment, food, health (including food and nutrition security), social inclusion and diversity, and economic development (recognizing the importance of informal markets). Actors across the food chain are also key and should include representatives for producers, processors, distribution, wholesale, markets, retail, consumers and waste management. The more individuals sitting around the table, the more problems will be identified and addressed. Effective engagement and facilitation are important so that stakeholders are included and able to participate. It is also important to realize the capacity-building potential for vulnerable groups and the informal sector if they continue to participate in the governance project. Other challenges include: the need for stable funding; linking food and planning so that food is included in urban planning efforts; and, the need to seek continuity in sustainable forms (RUAF 2019). As well, addressing the informal sector and the inclusion of vulnerable groups is a pressing challenge, post-agenda setting, as projects are operationalized (see Bellwood-Howard et al. 2015 on Tamale in Cabannes & Marocchino 2018).

One of the benefits of food is its multi-functionality. In agriculture, multi-functionality is defined as the capacity to go beyond producing food, fibre, and fuel to include related and interconnected benefits. These include employment, economic development, ecosystem and soil revitalization, biodiversity, the preservation of agricultural plants and animals as well as those in the wild, recreation and tourism, aesthetic amenities, and education and skill-building, all with a view towards becoming more prosperous and more resilient. This can help build more sustainable and resilient communities with more robust social, natural, financial and cultural capitals (Knezevic et al. 2017). There is a challenge that exists in the valuation of these opportunities, and that is weighing these against current globalized food systems, and subsequently defining investment needs of local and national authorities. The CRFS process brings these issues to the table and invites parties to address these by connecting biodiversity and environmental health policy across urban–rural spaces, which can also open up sustainability benefits from food. As Egal and Forster point out:

> The consolidation and concentration of post-harvest processing activities and the adoption of new legal and regulatory measures have also presented barriers to micro,

small and medium-size enterprises. Smallholder producers and food enterprises which traditionally fed the local population have been relegated to an informal economy that receives little support from government authorities, when not actively discouraged or even barred from the market.

from Berdegué & Proctor 2017 in Egal & Forster 2020

Ideally, the CRFS approach enables trust building between typically disjointed stakeholders such as the local government and those working in the informal economy (e.g. Zuluaga Orrego and Santini 2020).

The Case of Quito – CRFS governance in action: Context and complementary initiatives

With more than 1.9 million people spread over 4,200 square kilometres, the metro area of Quito is an extensive urban, peri-urban and rural agglomeration. From 2011 to 2016, the urban sprawl of the Municipality of the Metropolitan District of Quito (MDQ) increased by 11.17 per cent despite municipal planning and regulations. The agricultural production sector is a significant presence on the landscape, taking up 35.5 per cent of the area with production occupying 28.2 per cent (Young 2019: 154). The MDQ includes 32 urban parishes and 33 rural and sub-urban parishes, along with regional powers assigned by the national government in 2008. As such, it represents a coherent administrative city region system.

Over the past two decades, Quito's food system has been increasingly recognized and used as a lever for change. This growing recognition began in 2002 when AGRUPAR, a Participatory Urban Agriculture project, was launched by the MDQ (RUAF 2020) as a response to increasing poverty and food insecurity prompted by an economic crisis that had resulted in a 48 per cent poverty rate. While AGRUPAR was originally part of the social development structure mandated to support vulnerable groups, including women, young people, vulnerable children, the disabled, and Indigenous and African Ecuadorians (Young 2019: 155; Rodriguez 2020; Halliday et al. 2020), in 2004 it was moved into CONQUITO, the economic development office for the MDQ. The division of the economic and social development occurred to support more people (Young 2019). AGRUPAR operates with the 2008 Ecuadorian constitution (updated 2011) as a reference point. Ecuador was one of the first nations to include food sovereignty in their constitution. In terms of rights and food, the constitution states:

Article 13. Persons and community groups have the right to safe and permanent access to healthy, sufficient and nutritional food, preferably produced locally and in keeping with their various identities and cultural traditions.

The Ecuadorian State shall promote food sovereignty.

Republic of Ecuador 2008, updated 2011

Based on interviews with CONQUITO, Young reported that, as of 2018:

... participants in Quito's AGRUPAR project grow in over 3,600 gardens implemented across the city. They estimate that there are 4,500 beneficiaries of the program per year. Over 21,000 farmers have been trained by AGRUPAR to date on organic farming practices and market sales. There are 17 bioferia [organic] markets in Quito where AGRUPAR participants can sell their excess products to consumers. This provides approximately US$175 of extra income per month to the growers, which is 3.5 times the government human development funding available to those living in poverty. Approximately 84% of the participants in this program are women.

Young 2019: 155

When Quito joined the Milan Urban Food Policy Pact in 2016, as well as the FAO-RUAF City Region Food Systems Programme, it further acted on its commitment to developing an integrated city food policy (van Veenhuizen 2020; Dubbeling & Santini 2018). As part of the CRFS programme, Quito undertook an assessment of where food was being produced in the region and who had access to it. This analysis divided the capacity of the food system to supply food to Quito into three rings. The first ring included the urban and rural areas for the city district of Quito which supplied about 5 per cent of the food to the city region. The second level draws in food from the province representing 16 per cent of CRFS food. The third, outer ring, includes food from 12 more distant provinces and can supply 262 per cent of Quito's food needs.

In 2017, as part of this CRFS project led by AGRUPAR and supported by RUAF, a multi-stakeholder process began to identify relevant actors in the city region food system who could anchor food policy. The final group was broadly inclusive, with 24 institutions and organizations, and included the Municipality of Quito, government ministries, officials from Pichincha province, food companies, farmer and consumer organizations, universities, cooperative organizations and civil society organizations (Santandreu et al. 2019; Young 2019). Ultimately this group became the Quito Agri-Food Pact (PAQ), which was recognized and formed its own council, not one within city government. This reinforces the cross-cutting nature of the PAQ within the city region (Santandreu et al. 2019). The PAQ identified five areas of focus: managing food resources for the future; food and nutrition security, including food sovereignty; building a more inclusive food economy and urban–rural linkages; managing waste; and governance. These pillars were addressed through 16 participatory workshops that worked to address the themes in a cross-cutting way. By October 2018, the Agri-food Charter of Quito was signed with the PAQ publishing Quito's first Agrifood Strategy in April 2019 (Young 2019; Santandreu et al. 2019). There was broad commitment to the Agri-Food Charter and its dissemination. It:

> ...was signed by the members of the PAQ, including the national and provincial government, food industries, farmer and consumer organisations, universities and various civil society organisations. Through social networks, almost 2,000 people and organisations have supported the actions contained in the charter. In parallel, the PAQ designed and implemented a communication strategy to help disseminate the charter and the different achievements of the policy, transforming food into a municipal political agenda issue.
>
> *Santandreu et al. 2019*

An Action Plan was developed as part of the strategy through a broad consultative process that included 57 meetings, 16 workshops and 14 interviews with government partners and other actors in the agri-food system (Santandreu et al. 2019; Informa 2018).

The results of the CRFS Quito-region findings generated enough evidence as to the relevance of food for it to be included in the City's Resilience Strategy and Vision 2040 (the strategic and participatory planning of the city by 2040). It promoted a high level of awareness and activism among actors within the agri-food system and helped to define a common objective and vision. Quito also collaborated with the MUFPP and RUAF, supported by FAO and the Water Land and Ecosystem Programme (WLE), in a pilot project to start working with the MUFPP monitoring framework locally, and shared what they learned with other cities (RUAF 2020). This resulted in the identification of specific indicators from the MDQ that were compatible with the MUFPP themes and its guiding indicators. Quito was also part of the Rockefeller 100 Resilient Cities initiative which named food as a pillar for the development of a resourceful and solid economy (100 Resilient Cities 2017) (see Table 25.1).

Young's (2019) research into AGRUPAR initiatives points to future options and confirmed the need to build more disaster resilience for Quito's food system. Respondents suggested that AGRUPAR seek additional funding for the organization through increased resources from the City of Quito and other municipal government secretariats, or to work towards project self-sustainability by building partnerships with other municipal governments, through more sales based on increased promotion to the public, or by increasing ties to community partners. As well, those interviewed indicated the knowledge created in the Quito CRFS could be shared through urban agriculture networks (Young 2019: 156).

Food initiatives in Quito and the MDQ have been recognized as leading the world towards increased food system resilience and sustainability. In 2018, it received the Future Policy Silver Award 2018 from the World Future Council, in partnership with FAO and IFOAM – Organics

Table 25.1 Timeline of initiatives that underpin and/or reinforce the CRFS process

	MDQ, City Region	*National*	*Global*
2002	AGRUPAR funded for social development	Economic crisis	
2004	AGRUPAR moved to CONQUITO, economic development		
2008		Ecuador passes new constitution that recognizes food sovereignty and confirms the right to food	Economic meltdown, global food price spikes through 2009
2015	New Urban Agenda meeting in Quito		New Urban Agenda; MUFPP initiated UN Sustainable Development Goals established
2016	Signs on to MUFPP; initiates CRFS project		
2017	Initiates MUFPP indicator project; Resilience Strategy launched with support of Mayor; Food included in 2040 Vision		
2018	AgriFood Pact established		
2019	AgriFood Strategy and Action Plan published		COVID-19 Pandemic begins
2021	Food key facet of COVID-19 response		

Source: Authors' compilation.

International. This award recognized AGRUPAR's '...impressive socioeconomic and environmental impact, its participatory and holistic approach involving the most vulnerable groups, and its full respect for the Future Justice Principles and Elements of Agroecology' (Future Policy 2021). In addition to being selected as a pilot city for the MUFPP indicator pilot project, Quito was a recipient in 2020 of a Milan Urban Food Policy Pact award in the Food Production category for its use of urban agriculture as a response to COVID-19 (Milan Urban Food Policy Pact 2021). Funding has been secured to implement the Food Pact in neighbourhoods, as a further step in CRFS assisting in this process, going beyond the city boundaries, but also challenging to go deeper within.

Discussion and conclusion

Here we return to the questions posed at the start of the chapter where we asked how/whether iterative and exploratory governance could be well aligned in support of not only cities but also their surrounding regions with the goal of building more resilient, sustainable, shock resistant food systems. In particular, the focus is on the need for a flexible process and tools; the importance of multi-stakeholder engagement that bridges sectors, policy silos and scales; and the value of having a collective vision or set of priorities to guide the CRFS work.

As seen through the example of Quito, in addition to the engagement of multi-state and non-state stakeholders in the CRFS process, the approach can provide the benefit of silo busting within governments and across sectors, as people from the public sector, private business and civil society from health (food access for consumers), economic development (rural and urban access to livelihood opportunities), ecosystem well-being (sustainable food production) among other political and sectoral spaces, all work together to improve food system sustainability and resilience. Additionally, a CRFS approach offers the benefit of networks and multi-level governance interactions between state and non-state actors that enable knowledge co-creation, sharing and dissemination. Ideally, as seen in Quito, these networks are a hybrid of active and self-steering initiatives so civil society organization stakeholders are well-connected and resourced but at the same time have enough agency to be empowered as the CRFS process unfolds. Multi-level governance is also well served for CRFS if the principle of subsidiarity is taken up and respected so that decisions are made as close to the ground as possible. The devolution of power to the Quito city region, MDQ, provides an excellent example of how empowerment at the relevant community scales can catalyse positive action through organizations, such as AGRUPAR, which use food to find solutions to intertwined social, ecological and economic challenges.

While it is clear that the inclusion of multiple actors has value for food systems governance, there have been concerns raised about the politics of global multi-stakeholder processes in the wake of the UN Food Systems Summit and the role of multi-national corporations within it (Clapp 2021). Given the space that opened up to corporate domination during the FSS, there is an active call for caution in this regard. Civil society and some national governments are calling for a move away from multi-stakeholderism in favour of multilateralism (Canfield et al. 2021; Prato and Adams 2021). This is relevant for urban governance as the power dynamics at play can undermine cities as national governments align with corporate interests over other priorities.

The vision needed to map out and realize change is also found in the Quito example as captured in the City's Resilience Strategy and Vision 2040. To make this vision a reality, city and regional governments need both financial capital and political power to determine and enact the policies and regulations needed for their CRFS. Initiatives are also needed to support decentralized funding of national governments, coupled with donor funding to support territorial initiatives. The right national policies are required as a frame for local policies, by-laws, regulations, and ultimately action. Food can also be included in strategic planning accompanied by incentives and appropriate policy frameworks. Connections to other cities at the national and international levels, through, for example the MUFPP and Resilient Cities Network initiatives, provide pipelines to outside knowledge that can help to stimulate new forms of governance, such as the PAQ and the Agri-Food Strategy in Quito. As Battersby and Watson (2020) explain, 'It also supports their [i.e. Born and Purcell, 2006; Jennings et al. 2015] call for recognition of contextual specificity and the need to understand and support the entire food system, which is likely to be more resilient where it draws on a combination of local, wider regional and international food networks.' The CRFS approach can accomplish these goals, whereas defensive localism is only about protectionism through provisioning, with inherently closed governance of supply chains. Looking to the future, through better engagement with national policymakers, there are opportunities to bring more inclusivity to City Region Food Systems, especially women, youth, and the environment, making these initiatives at once more responsive and relevant to the socio-economic needs of communities

Acknowledgements

We are grateful for the financial support this publication and underlying work received from the German Federal Ministry of Food and Agriculture Project Identity Number GCP-FAO2018-1, CGIAR Research Programme Water Land and Ecosystems led by IWMI, the Social Sciences Humanities Research Council of Canada (award number 895-2015-1016), and Wilfrid Laurier University/Laurier Centre for Sustainable Food Systems for the financial support to the CRFS programme. We would also like to thank the anonymous reviewers for their constructive comments.

References

100 Resilient Cities. (2017). *Resilient Quito: Resilience Strategy, Metropolitan District of Quito*. https://resilientcitiesnetwork.org/downloadable_resources/Network/Quito-Resilience-Strategy-English.pdf (accessed 20 April 2021).

Battersby, J., & Watson, V. (2020). The planned 'city region' in the New Urban Agenda: An appropriate framing for urban food security? In J. Crush, B. Frayne, & G. Haysom (Eds.), *Handbook on Urban Food Security in the Global South*. Edward Elgar Publishing.

Bellwood-Howard, I., Häring, V., Karg, H., Roessler, R., Schlesinger, J., & Shakya, M. (2015). *Characteristics of urban and peri-urban agriculture in West Africa: results of an exploratory survey conducted in Tamale (Ghana) and Ouagadougou (Burkina Faso), Vol. 163*. International Water Management Institute (IWMI).

Berdegué, J. A., Proctor, F. J., & Cazzuffi, C. (2014). Cities in the rural transformation. *Journal Environment and Urbanization, 22*(2).

Blay-Palmer, A., Santini, G., Dubbeling, M., Renting, H., Taguchi, M., & Giordano, T. (2018). Validating the city region food system approach: Enacting inclusive, transformational city region food systems. *Sustainability*, 10(5), 1680.

Blay-Palmer, A., Santini, G., Halliday, J., Malec, R., Carey, J., Keller, L., Ni, J., Taguchi, M., & van Veenhuizen, R. (2021). City region food systems: Building resilience to COVID-19 and other shocks. *Sustainability, 13*(3), 1325.

Born, B., & Purcell, M. (2006). Avoiding the local trap: Scale and food systems in planning research. *Journal of Planning Education and Research, 26*(2), 195–207.

Cabannes, Y., & Marocchino, C. (Eds.). (2018). *Integrating Food into Urban Planning*. UCL Press.

Canfield, M., Anderson, M. D., & McMichael, P. (2021). UN Food Systems Summit 2021: Dismantling democracy and resetting corporate control of food systems. *Frontiers in Sustainable Food Systems*, *5*, 103.

Caron, P., Valette, É., Wassenaar, T., Coppens, D. E., & Papazian, V. (2017). *Living Territories to Transform the World* (p. 274). éditions Quae.

Clancy, K., & Ruhf, K. (2010). Is local enough? Some arguments for regional food systems. *Choices*, *25*(1).

Clapp, J. (2021). The problem with growing corporate concentration and power in the global food system. *Nature Food*, *2*(6), 404–408.

Dreschel, P. (2020). *Strengthening City Region Food Systems during and beyond COVID-19*. CGIAR, Water Land Ecosystem Programme. https://wle.cgiar.org/thrive/2020/04/08/strengthening-city-region-food-systems-during-and-beyond-covid-19

Dubbeling, M., & de Zeeuw, H. (2011). Urban agriculture: Advances, opportunities and application. In H. S. Geyer (Ed.) *International Handbook of Urban Policy: Issues in the Developing* World, Vol. 3 (pp. 190–224). Edward Elgar.

Dubbeling, M. & Santini, G. (2018). City region food system assessment and planning. *Urban Agriculture Magazine*, *34*(May), 6–9.

Egal, F., & Forster, T. (2020). Biodiversity, food systems and urban-rural linkages. In D. Hunter, T. Borelli, & E. Gee (Eds.), *Biodiversity, Food and Nutrition: A New Agenda for Sustainable Food Systems* (pp. 189–205). Routledge.

FAO. (2019). The state of the world's biodiversity for food and agriculture. In J. Bélanger & D. Pilling (Eds.), *FAO Commission on Genetic Resources for Food and Agriculture Assessments*. FAO, 572 pp. (www.fao.org/3/CA3129EN/CA3129EN.pdf)Licence: CC BY-NC-SA 3.0 IGO.

FAO. (2021a). *City Region Food Systems Programme – Pilot Cities*. www.fao.org/in-action/food-for-cities-programme/pilotcities/wherewework/en/

FAO. (2021b). *City Region Food System Toolkit*. www.fao.org/in-action/food-for-cities-programme/toolkit-old/getting-prepared/stakeholder-engagement/en/.

Future Policy. (2021). *Quito's Participatory Urban Agriculture Programme* www.futurepolicy.org/global/quito-agrupar/

Halliday, J., Joshi, D., Young, L., & van Veenhuizen, R. (2020). Gender in urban food systems. *RUAF Urban Agriculture Magazine*, July. https://cgspace.cgiar.org/bitstream/handle/10568/109186/UA-Magazine-37_web.pdf?sequence=1

HLPE. (2014). *Food Losses and Waste in the Context of Sustainable Food Systems*. A Report by the High Level Panel of Experts on Food Security and Nutrition of the Committee on World Food Security, Rome.

Informa. (2018). *Pacto Agroalimentario una apuesta al presente y futuro de Quito*. www.quitoinforma.gob.ec/2018/10/02/quito-suscribe-pacto-agroalimentario/

Jennings, S., Cottee, J., Curtis, T., & Miller, S. (2015). *Food in an Urbanised World: The Role of City Region Food Systems in Resilience and Sustainable Development*. Research Report, Food and Agricultural Organization of the United Nations. www.alnap.org/help-library/food-in-an-urbanised-world-the-role-of-city-region-food-systems-in-resilience-and

Knezevic, I., Blay-Palmer, A., Levkoe, C. Z., Mount, P., & Nelson, E. (Eds.). (2017). *Nourishing Communities: From Fractured Food Systems to Transformative Pathways*. Springer.

Milan Urban Food Policy Pact. (2021). *Milan Pact Winners, 2020*. www.milanurbanfoodpolicypact.org/milan-pact-awards/milan-pact-awards-2020/

Moragues-Faus, A., & Sonnino, R. (2019). Re-assembling sustainable food cities: An exploration of translocal governance and its multiple agencies. *Urban Studies*, *56*(4), 778–794.

Pimbert, M. (2016). *Food Sovereignty, Agroecology and Biocultural Diversity*. Routledge.

Prato, S., & Adams, B. (2021). Reimagining multilateralism: A long but urgently necessary journey. *Development*, *64*(1), 1–3. https://doi.org/10.1057/s41301-021-00320-1

Raja, S., Morgan, K., & Hall, E. (2017). Planning for equitable urban and regional food systems. *Built Environment*, *43*(3), 309–314.

Republic of Ecuador. (2008). *Republic of Ecuador Constitution*. Political Database of the Americas (Updated 2011). https://pdba.georgetown.edu/Constitutions/Ecuador/english08.html

Rodriguez, A. (2020). *How Quito's Urban and Peri-urban Agriculture Contributes to the COVID-19 Response*. www.fao.org/in-action/food-for-cities-programme/news/detail/en/c/1274823/

RUAF. (2019). *RUAF Magazine*, October, Issue No. 36. Food Policy Councils. https://ruaf.org/assets/2019/11/Urban-Agriculture-Magazine-no.-36-Food-Policy-Councils.pdf

RUAF. (2020). *City Region Food System Toolkit*. https://ruaf.org/news/quitos-journey-to-better-food-security/ RUAF https://ruaf.org/news/city-region-food-system-toolkit/

RUAF. (2021). *City Region Food System Toolkit.* https://ruaf.org/news/city-region-food-system-toolkit/
RUAF. (n.d.). *City Region Food Systems.* https://ruaf.org/focus-area/city-region-food-systems/#:~:text=A%20City%20Region%20Food%20Systems,by%20strengthening%20rural%2Durban%20linkages.&text=With%20FAO%20and%20the%20Milan,developed%20a%20set%20of%20indicators.
Salet, W., Vermeulen, R., Savini, F., & Dembski, S. (2015). Planning for the new European metropolis: functions, politics, and symbols. *Planning Theory and Practice, Interface, 16*, 251–275.
Santandreu, A., Rodriguez, A., Jácome, D., Cruz, C., & Pinto, N. (2019). *RUAF Urban Agriculture Magazine, 36*(October).
Smith, M. D., & Wesselbaum, D. (2020). COVID-19, food insecurity, and migration. *The Journal of Nutrition, 150*(11), 2855–2858.
Tefft, J., Jonasova, M., Adjao, R., & Morgan, A. (2017). Food Systems for an Urbanizing World. World Bank Group.
UNDESA. (2019). *World Urbanization Prospects: The 2018 Revision* (ST/ESA/SER.A/420). United Nations, Department of Economic and Social Affairs, Population Division, New York.
van Veenhuizen, R. (2020). *Resilient and Participatory: How Quito is Setting the Standard on Urban Food Systems.* https://wle.cgiar.org/news/resilient-and-participatory-how-quito%E2%80%99s-setting-standard-urban-food-systems
Young, L. (2019). Growing food in the city: Urban agriculture in Quito, Ecuador, through a feminist lens. *Journal of Agriculture, Food Systems, and Community Development, 9*(Suppl. 1), 151–158. https://doi.org/10.5304/jafscd.2019.091.040
Zuluaga Orrego, J., & Santini, G. (2020). *City Region Food Systems in Medellin, Colombia: A Pathway of Governmental and Territorial Integration to Face the COVID-19 Crisis.* City Region Food Systems Programme. www.fao.org/in-action/food-for-cities-programme/news/detail/en/c/1273338/

26

INTERNATIONAL AGENDAS AND URBAN FOOD SYSTEMS GOVERNANCE

Informing, Integrating and Operationalizing the SDGs

Thomas Forster, Florence Egal and Ana Puhac

Introduction: From food security to food systems

Global recognition of urban food governance builds upon the convergence of parallel processes starting in the 1970s and stretching over four decades. First, the global narrative on food and agriculture expanded into a food system narrative and from a rural- to a national-level focus on agriculture, food security and nutrition. Second, the food systems narrative enabled a larger variety of actors to engage with food and agriculture, including consumer and environmental movements, and local, subnational governments. Third, local and regional food systems evolved into self-recognized urban and territorial food systems with and without the support of national governments. Interaction between parallel processes quickened and intensified after 2015. This chapter will summarize the progressive interactions between global and local food systems governance narratives over nearly a half-century.[1]

Global agendas in food and agriculture evolved over the decades from a mostly rural focus on agricultural production to include sustainable development, global urbanization and sustainable diets.[2] Important benchmarks in global food governance between the 1970s and 2015 can be traced back to the 1974 World Food Conference, convened in the wake of the Bangladesh famine. The Universal Declaration on the Eradication of Hunger and Malnutrition, signed on this occasion, affirmed that it is a fundamental human right to be free from hunger and malnutrition, so that one can develop both mental and physical faculties fully (OHCHR, 1974). At this time the Committee on World Food Security (CFS) was set up as a United Nations intergovernmental body, hosted in the Food and Agriculture Organization (FAO), to serve as a forum for review and follow-up of national food security policies in a global context increasingly dominated by policy priorities of industrial food production and trade liberalization.

Mobilization of small and peasant farm movements together with other nongovernmental and civil society organizations created a "counter narrative" to global food governance. In 1993,

DOI: 10.4324/9781003055907-30

the concept of food sovereignty was introduced by La Via Campesina (LVC) – an organization of farmers, peasants and landless workers organizations in every region of the world. The motivation for many of the organizations that make up the social movements (of which LVC is the largest) is that the impacts of global food governance are more negative than positive, as it did not respond adequately to the real needs and challenges of practitioners, including smallholder farmers and landless peoples.[3] "Food sovereignty" places emphasis on the right of individuals and communities to define the processes that regulate their own food systems, from production to consumption. Contrary to a concept of food security that started from a global macro-economic entry point to then focus on household food security, food sovereignty seeks to build alternatives to homogenized global food systems, challenging the commodification of food and instead positioning food as a universal human right, secured through bottom-up, grass-roots approaches.[4]

Engagement of civil society in the debates around critical issues that stemmed from a food sovereignty perspective helped to shape several key benchmarks in global food governance, which later influenced urban food governance. One example is the Voluntary Guidelines to Support the Progressive Realization of the Right to Adequate Food in the Context of National Food Security (FAO Council, 2005), endorsed by the Committee on World Food Security (CFS) in October 2004. The universal human right to food anchors global food policy in practice at the local level, although it is seldom incorporated into operational legal tools at municipal or subnational levels. Another recent example is the United Nations Declaration on the Rights of Peasants and Other People Working in Rural Areas (Human Rights Council, 2018).

Almost all of the global food debates before 2008 centered around "food and nutrition security" and were marked by a narrow view that rural small farmers need to be integrated into globalized and urban markets and value chains, overlooking the multifunctionality of agriculture and the potential of multiple linkages that exist within, and among, more diversified markets embedded in territorial food systems. Until then, food and agriculture were very much considered to be "rural" issues. After the world population turned more urban than rural in 2007, and the food price surge in 2007–8 triggered a wave of political protests in more than 60 countries, even in high income countries, global development discourse deepened to consider more complex, relational interactions between rural–urban and global–local scales, as well as potential trade-offs and synergies between nutritional (diet quality), environmental (sustainability and resilience), and social (distribution, culture, equity) outcomes.

Coinciding with the "food price crisis" and the reform of the Committee on Food Security, global narratives and debate began to account for increasing concerns with social, economic, and health impacts of intensive agro-industrial food systems. As defined by FAO, food systems "encompass the entire range of actors and their interlinked value-adding activities involved in the production, aggregation, processing, distribution, consumption and disposal of food products that originate from agriculture, forestry or fisheries, and parts of the broader economic, societal and natural environments in which they are embedded" (FAO, 2018a). Since food systems include the web of production, distribution, marketing, consumption and food waste in urban and peri-urban areas, the mainstreaming of the food systems narrative prepared the ground for engaging with local and subnational regional governments (cities and territories), who also began to adopt their own food systems frameworks.[5]

While global food governance debates and policy outcomes clearly had a major impact at the local level, cities and local governments were not represented in most of these global governance mechanisms. Malnutrition was mainly seen as a rural problem until recently. Even as global policy agendas began to move toward a food systems perspective, the contribution of urban food systems governance for advancing the food systems framework only started being acknowledged as important after 2015. By 2020, cities and local governments were increasingly demanding that their implementing role be acknowledged and that they be represented in the policy spaces convened by UN agencies, such as FAO and the CFS, or by international finance and agriculture research institutions such as the World Bank. The rise of food systems thinking before 2015 influenced emerging frameworks for urban and territorial food governance, which evolved between 2015 and 2020 through processes to be described in the next sections.

Normative policy negotiated at different levels (local, national and international) have been accompanied by principles and frameworks for action curated by the institutions with mandates to help governments, nonstate actors and networks implement food policy. As we will see, there are significant implications for more inclusive and resilient food systems and sustainable development as a multi-level food policy governance narrative becomes more widely adopted. The COVID-19 pandemic, which started in 2020, showed both the vulnerability and weaknesses of present food systems and the key role of local institutions and local actors in addressing not only the health impacts, but also the social and economic impacts of emergencies. The urgency of managing a resilient and inclusive food system for growing urban and territorial populations, in the midst of rural transformation and crisis management from multiple stresses, conflict and shocks, presents new opportunities for multi-level and multi-sector governance.[6] Efforts to reposition agriculture in the context of resilience to climate change, biodiversity conservation, and ecosystem restoration benefited from the articulation of "food systems". This also brought to the debate on the future of food a wider range of actors pursuing sustainable development goals in international agendas.[7]

Sustainable cities and early stages of urban food system governance

Over the same four-decade period of evolving global food governance, the governance framework for sustainable urbanization also evolved and became increasingly complex, with benchmarks including the successive United Nations Conferences on Human Settlements between 1976 and 2016. At Habitat I (1976) in Vancouver, governments recommended regional planning as a means to reconcile and coordinate the objectives of urban and rural development. In 1996 in Istanbul, Habitat II added to the goal of adequate shelter for all, goals of making human settlements safer, healthier and more livable, equitable, sustainable and productive in harmony with nature (see Habitat II, 1996). As forums for global deliberation on priorities for human settlements, Habitats I and II, however, did not specifically address the growing engagement of cities in food security and nutrition.

In the mid-1980s, urban community-driven initiatives for improved housing, urban and peri-urban land tenure and governance of urban resources and public services (such as participatory budgeting, community architecture, urban community land trusts, etc.) had brought attention to the need for a shift in governance around urbanization issues.[8] In the late 1980s, technicians and researchers in agri-food systems had started to engage in a variety of topics such as urban/peri-urban agriculture, markets, urban forestry, street foods, urban nutrition and urban–rural linkages, sharing scholarly and field experiences through different academic and civil society networks. However, food and agriculture were not explicitly included in the "sustainable urbanization" debate for another decade.

From 2001, civil society, academia and UN organizations started to systematically bring up food security, urban forestry and nutrition, and set up related side events and exhibitions in successive biennial World Urban Forums for awareness-raising and networking purposes. But it was not until the preparation for Habitat III in 2015 that urban food and governance issues became explicit in formal intergovernmental policy. Indeed, practitioners and actors

Figure 26.1 Long arc of convergence between global and local/regional food governance 1970s–2015

from both urban development and food arenas were aware of parallel governance gaps between the reality and needs of people in their everyday lives and the policy narratives promoted at global and national levels. Increasing interaction between communities of practice across governance levels helped to create a paradigm shift in the model of development governance from a macro-oriented global outlook to more place-based, human-centered and participatory approaches, which contributed to the adoption of "the right to the city" theme during negotiations of Habitat III. These two narrative streams, one from the global mainstreaming of food systems framing, and one from engagement in food policy by cities and local governments, are represented as an "arc of convergence" in Figure 26.1 below.

Still, until 2015, food systems remained largely absent from sustainable urbanization debates, apart from urban and peri-urban agriculture research projects and occasional food security workshops at conferences and side events.[9] Legal frameworks and initiatives addressing food safety, market regulation, public food procurement and land-use zoning were present in many local and regional governments, but there were only a few local efforts to integrate all the different food system issues into a comprehensive urban food policy framework. This "puzzling omission" of food in urban policy and planning was detected by urban planning scholars who started asking why, unlike the other areas essential for human development (air, land, water, housing), food was never a stand-alone topic of interest for urban policy and planning (Pothukuchi & Kaufman, 1999). Beginning in the early 2000s, the urban planning profession began to incorporate food, for example in the American Planning Association, but it would take several more years for food systems policy to emerge in formal governance mechanisms for local and regional governments.

Engagement of local and regional governments in the global development agenda

International city networks, dating as far back as the early twentieth century, advocated for new political spaces that allowed cities to emerge to the global level[10]. None of these networks engaged with food until recently (on city food networks, see Chapter 27 by Giordano in this volume). But their engagement with different themes (in particular climate and biodiversity) did contribute to the emergence of a "systems" perspective that has been applied to food and agriculture. Through their representative networks and associations, cities started to engage with the global sustainable development agenda in three Rio Conventions: the UN Framework Convention for Climate Change (UNFCCC), the Convention on Biodiversity (CBD), and the UN Convention to Combat Desertification (UNCCD).

The sea change in the global profile for cities in a general sense occurred after the 2007 State of World Population report, *Unleashing the Potential of Urban Growth*, which brought to the world's attention that in 2008, for the first time, more than half of the world's population would be living in urban areas, and that by 2030, towns and cities would be home to almost 5 billion people (Montgomery, 2007). International organizations such as FAO, UN-Habitat, the World Bank, the European Commission, OECD and others began to shift mandates and programs to give greater emphasis to the relation of cities to the development agenda. In 2011–2012, during the negotiation of the Rio+20 outcome *The Future We Want* (UN General Assembly, 2012), city networks fought hard for a first global goal for sustainable cities "Make cities and human settlements inclusive, safe, resilient and sustainable" as one of the 17 Sustainable Development Goals (SDGs) set up by the UN General Assembly in 2015. There was a reference to the importance of "Strengthening urban–rural linkages" in relation to food systems in the Future We Want (paragraph 110). The role of local and regional governments was not included in SDG 2 targets, but a reference to the integration of urban, peri-urban and rural planning for sustainable development did become a target for SDG 11. Target (11.a) calls for integrating urban, peri-urban and rural communities in sustainable development planning.

The United Cities and Local Governments (UCLG) was the first global network of cities, which celebrated its 100-year anniversary in 1919, but food policy has only become a UCLG priority in recent years. The network for Local Governments for Sustainability or ICLEI, founded in 1980, did make food a priority in 2013 and partnered with the global urban and peri-urban agriculture NGO, RUAF (the Global Partnership on Sustainable Urban Agriculture and Food Systems). The Global Taskforce of Local and Regional Governments was set up, also in 2013, to bring the perspectives of local and regional governments to the preparation of the SDGs, the Paris agreement, the Sendai Framework for Disaster Risk Reduction and the New Urban Agenda (NUA). It convenes elected local and regional leaders from around the world in the World Assembly of Local and Regional Governments to undertake joint advocacy work relating to global policy processes. Together with the United Nations Development Programme and UN-Habitat the Global Taskforce has drawn up a roadmap for localizing the SDGs to support cities and regions in delivering the 2030 Agenda.

In addition to the Global Taskforce, UCLG, ICLEI and the network for subnational regional governments, Regions4, are the designated organizing partners for the United Nations Local Authorities Major Group (LAMG).[11] The LAMG is recognized in the 2030 Agenda to help bring the voices of urban and subnational governments to follow up and review SDG implementation. ORU-FOGAR (United Regions Organization), created in 2007 to be the voice of the intermediate governments in parliaments, was the first network to take up food sovereignty as a core theme, before the national governments and international bodies, and to organize from 2010 a series of Summits of the World Regions on Food Security. Despite the fact that these networks for local and regional governments (LRGs) worked hard on SDG 11, the gap between SDG 2 and SDG 11 was not addressed by either cities or by countries engaged in negotiation of the SDGs.

The SDG 2–11 gap was however addressed during preparation and negotiations for Habitat III in 2016, a year after the launch of the SDGs. Food and urban governance issues would be explicitly linked by Member States in negotiations during the Habitat III process. This would also be the first time that cities and their networks and allies would make an effort to shape global food policy. The Rome-based UN food agencies (FAO, International Fund for Agricultural Development, and the World Food Programme) were also engaged in the Habitat III process. But as we will see, it was the concerted efforts of city networks and allied groups that delivered food governance alongside the territorial dimension of sustainable urbanization. Before telling that story, it is necessary to describe the autonomous, parallel international effort to bring food systems into the policy and planning of municipal governments.

Urban and multi-level food governance reaches the international stage

The launch of the 2030 Agenda for Sustainable Development with a goal for cities was one of three parallel and simultaneous processes in 2015 and 2016, including the launch of the Milan Urban Food Policy Pact (MUFPP) and the negotiation of the New Urban Agenda, the outcome of Habitat III. These three global agendas, negotiated separately by national governments (SDGs and NUA) and local governments (MUFPP), came to be regarded as mutually supportive frameworks for integrating urban and territorial food system governance. The follow-up and implementation of these agendas at different governance levels has seen food system governance emerge as a thread connecting local and national governance and integrating different dimensions of sustainable development. These three global agendas from 2015 and 2016, and the implementation frameworks developed after their launch, are summarized in Figure 26.2 below.

Cities themselves led the articulation of urban food governance internationally by linking with other cities to find consensus on priorities for urban food systems. Two years before the launch of the New Urban Agenda at Habitat III, on the occasion of the fifth biennial C40 Cities Mayors Summit in February 2014 in Johannesburg, the Mayor of Milan made a proposal for a pact on urban food policies to be signed during Expo 2015: Feeding the Planet, Energy for Life. A participatory six-month drafting process was assisted by a technical team and an advisory group including the UN and research and nongovernmental agencies. The Milan Urban Food Policy Pact (MUFPP, 2015), was signed on World Food Day by 108 cities in October 2015 and handed to the UN Secretary General. Since the launch of the Milan Pact, signatory cities have exchanged food practices and policies in annual global and regional summits, spreading the urban food governance principles and actions to new cities and networks of local and regional

Figure 26.2 Normative guidance for local, regional, and national multi-level food governance

governments. Signatory cities of the Pact then began to participate in follow-ups to the SDGs, the NUA and global agendas, including climate change, biodiversity, nutrition, among others.

The Milan Urban Food Policy Pact[12] includes a voluntary Framework for Action, built upon actual experiences and practices of 48 original city partners. Mayors of signatory cities identify governance as a priority challenge, recommending

- a comprehensive, inter-disciplinary and multi-actor approach for the formulation and implementation of all food-related policies, programs and initiatives;
- coherence between municipal food-related policies and programs and national, regional and international policies and processes; and
- the involvement of cities and neighboring territories in negotiating, operationalizing and/or contributing to international processes.

While no single city has instituted all the dimensions of urban food governance recommended in the Milan Pact, the Framework for Action has provided guidance to cities willing to improve their urban food governance. In the first few years after the promulgation of the Milan Pact, many cities were more interested in learning from other cities than directly engaging the SDGs and global policy agendas. However, since 2018, the interplay between urban food governance and global agendas has become more active with the involvement of city networks (see Chapter 27 by Giordano in this volume) and local and regional governments in the follow-up and implementation of the SDGs and the NUA.

The Milan Pact was a global agreement between mayors of cities and, as of December 2021, there are 210 signatory cities. The NUA is an agreement of all countries in the United Nations. In October 2016, national governments confirmed in the New Urban Agenda that they would promote a new model of urban development, able to integrate all facets of sustainable development (as represented in the 2030 Agenda for Sustainable Development). The NUA calls for coherence between goals and measures of sectoral policies, "at different levels and scales of political administration, across administrative borders and considering appropriate functional areas, in order to strengthen integrated approaches to urbanization and implement integrated urban and territorial planning strategies that factor them in".[13]

National governments committed to "support the implementation of integrated, polycentric and balanced territorial development policies and plans, encouraging cooperation and mutual support among different scales of cities and human settlements, strengthening the role of small and intermediate cities and towns in enhancing food security and nutrition systems" (United Nations, 2016). The concept of functional territories emerged to strengthen integrated approaches to urbanization and implement integrated urban and rural planning strategies.[14] The model of urban development in the NUA also calls for new approaches to urban governance, and urban food governance would turn out to be one of the fields of innovation for sustainable urban development generally.

The inclusion of food systems in connection with sustainable urbanization in the first global agenda for sustainable urbanization was not accidental and there were multiple channels of advocacy. These channels included engagement by cities, experts and organizations pushing for inclusion of food in the NUA, inside and outside the negotiation process. Parallel to the drafting of the Milan Pact in spring and summer of 2015, negotiations by Member States were underway for the United Nations Conference on Housing and Sustainable Urban Development, or Habitat III. Organizations, including city networks and those drafting the Milan Pact on urban food systems governance issues, engaged in negotiations on related provisions in the New Urban Agenda adopted the following year in Quito, Ecuador (United Nations, 2016). Habitat

III aimed to systematize the alignment between cities and towns and national planning objectives in their role as drivers of national economic and social development. Extensive urban and peri-urban food systems development in the Habitat III host City of Quito and the Province of Pichincha were showcased during the conference with support from the international NGO network RUAF and FAO.

Debate on sustainable urbanization recognized the importance of urban–rural linkages that came into issue papers and multiple expert group meetings. Members of the MUFPP technical team and advisory group participated in the preparations for negotiation. The result is that urban planning and policy is linked to territorial planning and policy throughout the NUA. The definition of urban–rural linkages (URLs) as the flows of goods, services, people, money and information made inclusion of food systems an easy addition. For the first time, text negotiated by UN Member States explicitly mainstreamed food security, nutrition and food systems at the urban and territorial level throughout the document.[15] In the NUA there are many paragraphs calling for integrated urban and territorial planning and development.

After the successive launches of the 2030 Agenda in 2015 and the New Urban Agenda in 2016, the two UN agencies responsible for monitoring and follow-up to these agendas started to initiate new programs that raised awareness of the need to link global food governance and urban food governance. The agencies whose mandates intersect the most in the city–food nexus are the Human Settlements Program (UN-Habitat) and the Food and Agriculture Organization (FAO). In years immediately following the launch of the SDGs and the NUA, both agencies launched new initiatives to support implementation of the new global agendas and are respectively custodians of targets for SDGs 2 and 11. Figure 26.3 below shows the interactions of global agendas, frameworks, and governance supporting urban and territorial food systems.

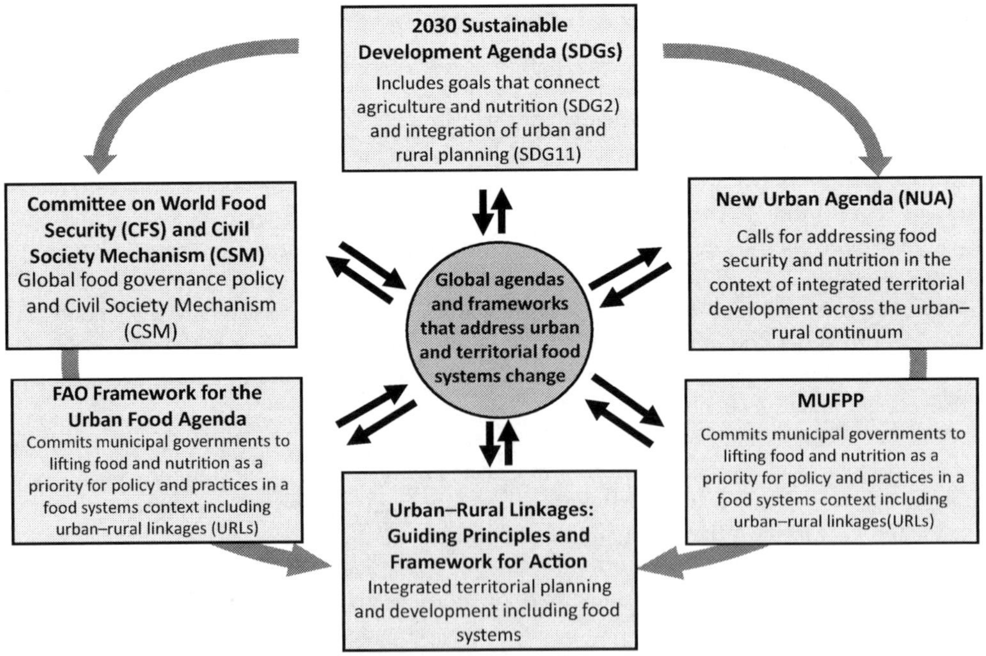

Figure 26.3 Global agendas and frameworks that address urban and territorial food systems change

UN-Habitat began to work with countries to develop national urban policies (NUPs), a major proposed action in the New Urban Agenda. Responding to the call to integrate urban and rural planning and development (SDG 11.a), UN-Habitat published in 2019 Urban–Rural Linkages: Guiding Principles (URL-GP) and the Framework for Action to Advance Integrated Territorial Development (United Nations Human Settlements Programme, 2019). The URL-GP text has a similar structure to that of the MUFPP, with a short high-level commitment (the principles) and suggested voluntary operational actions (the Framework for Action). The URL-GP was developed with a view to supporting national, regional and local governments, planners and development agencies committed to improving urban–rural relations in the context of sustainable urbanization. UN-Habitat, and over 130 actors who contributed to the elaboration of the URL-GPs, held the position that integration of urban and rural development would contribute to the operationalization of both the SDGs and the New Urban Agenda, alongside other global policy goals (United Nations Human Settlements Programme, 2021).

FAO has had technical teams working with urban-related issues for decades, in areas such as urban and peri-urban agriculture, urban markets, urban nutrition, urban forestry or street foods. These work streams were initially coordinated through informal internal and external networks until Food for Cities was recognized in 2005 as a FAO Priority Area for Interdisciplinary Action. Ensuing processes included the launch and management of a global open-access listserv "Food for Cities" and the development of a series of projects, initiatives and knowledge products, such as the city region food system (CRFS) assessment tools (FAO, 2018b) and actively contributing to the elaboration of the Inter-Agency Standing Committee (IASC) strategy on Meeting Humanitarian Challenges in Urban Areas (IASC, 2010). FAO supported the drafting and launching of the Milan Pact and hosted the first Mayors Summit in October 2016. A collaborative assessment of *The Role of Cities in the Transformation of Food Systems: Sharing Lessons from Milan Pact Cities* was published in 2018 (FAO, 2018c). In an effort to bring together the range of FAO work with cities, a Framework for an Urban Food Agenda was launched (FAO, 2019), followed by a Greening Cities Initiative (GCI) in 2020 that puts urban food systems into a broader framework for promoting nature in cities. These events and processes, among others, signaled a formal commitment to work with cities on urban food governance and related urban food systems issues.

Other UN agencies, such as the World Health Organization (WHO) and the UN Environment Program (UNEP), developed their own engagements with urban health and environmental issues that relate to food systems. Together with partner UN agencies and other organizations and actors, local and regional governments have organized forums at the annual High Level Political Forum (HLPF) to review progress on the 2030 Agenda and then more recently with the UN Food Systems Summit (UNFSS) in 2021. Coalitions to support urban and territorial food systems emerged from the UNFSS, supported by national governments, as well as many of the agencies and actors mentioned in this chapter. The G20 meeting hosted by Italy parallel to the UNFSS produced a "Rome Declaration" that for the first time addressed the role of cities and the circular economy as key to the localization of SDGs.[16]

Advancing toward multi-level food governance: Challenges and opportunities

The processes described in the section above demonstrate an increasing convergence of urban food policy with the sustainable development agenda. While the framework for sustainable urbanization firmly integrates food systems and their governance by Member States in the NUA, the modalities to operationalize urban food governance were left to be established.

A shared goal for both cities and international organizations going forward is therefore to operationalize urban food governance principles and actions in the following five challenge areas. The good news is that all five of the challenges suggested below to operationalize urban and territorial governance are found in recommendations of the key UN agencies, including FAO and UN-Habitat, and in the recommendations of the MUFPP, the Organization for Economic Cooperation and Development (OECD, 2015, 2020a), the World Bank Group, and other organizations and networks working to support the role of local and regional food systems in the transformation of food systems at national and international levels.

- **Intersectoral collaboration:** Operationalizing food systems approaches is increasingly acknowledged as a "whole of government" agenda. Cities and local governments should therefore bring together departments and sectors that usually have different jurisdictions, regulations and procedures.
- **Inter-institutional collaboration:** Joining forces to reorient food systems requires the involvement of all actors (government, civil society, academia, private sector, etc.), any of which are generally not used to working together, have different priorities, ethics, culture and funding mechanisms, and do not really know each other.
- **Multilevel governance** (from local to national, global and back) is difficult in many contexts where decentralization often remains theoretical and trust is lacking or tensions exist between levels of governance. Such tensions were on display in the wake of COVID-19, but so were positive examples of highly responsive multilevel governance.
- **Territorial integration:** Partnerships between cities and neighboring rural communities to agree on win–win institutional arrangements is essential but made difficult by the persistence of separate policy and planning between rural and urban areas. Too often cities do not collaborate within metropolitan or regional governments.
- **City-to-city collaboration** continues to be one of the easier ways that cities and regions learn about each other's practices and cities play an important diplomatic role. The city-to-city exchange fits in many cities' programs, and international organizations are supporting cities in related knowledge management and lessons learned.

Urban food governance practices have been shown to strengthen food system resilience to current and future crises. The COVID-19 pandemic struck major cities first and then spread to towns and cities of all scales and rural areas. Subnational governments –regions and municipalities – have been, and continue to be, at the frontlines of crisis management and recovery, and are confronted by COVID-19's asymmetric health, economic, social and fiscal impacts. No country or government was prepared for the scale, length or impacts of the pandemic and measures had to be taken rapidly on an unprecedented scale. From one day to the next, municipalities had to deal with the health dimensions of the pandemic but also apply instructions to prevent further spread of the virus, with major socioeconomic consequences and significant food systems disruption.

The global crisis generated by the COVID-19 outbreak pushed local and regional governments to give immediate answers to an emergency that seriously threatened (and continues to threaten) not only citizens' health, but the social cohesion, the economy and the functioning of territories (OECD, 2020b). Municipal governments and local institutions (and in particular civil society and the private sector) have demonstrated enormous potential in collaborating, coordinating, exploring and supporting community-based solutions. Cities engaged in urban food governance prior to COVID-19 have proved better prepared to manage the situation, confirming the key role of urban food governance to manage crises and support inclusive and resilient food systems.[17] Food governance impacts and efforts to address food system vulnerability, build back from the pandemic, and prepare for future crises has become a crucial arena for innovation. COVID-19 has been an eye-opener to all forms of inequalities across people and places, in particular in large cities, and of the need for better urban–rural linkages and more resilient territorial food systems. The crisis has contributed toward unblocking previous institutional obstacles, limiting collaboration between municipalities and civil society, or small-scale producers and municipalities. Examples include new working relations between health, planning, social protection, economic development and other municipal departments. Responses to the pandemic also focused attention on the need for better alignment and collaboration between local, territorial and national governance levels. And it has often confirmed people's perception that local governments, rather than national governments, are the first port of call to concretely handle complex emergencies (United Cities and Local Governments, 2020).

Urban food governance and territorial development can help to unblock the 2030 Agenda. With less than ten years left to 2030, the Sustainable Development Goals remain as valid and as urgent as ever. And they need to be dealt with together and not in isolation. The 2021 UN Food Systems Summit has confirmed the importance of context-specific approaches to transform food systems. Urban food governance may well be one of the keys to accelerating the 2030 Agenda and to mitigating future health, climate, and other crises. Cities and local governments should therefore be acknowledged as key actors and sit in national, regional and global governance mechanisms. Existing legislation, regulations and procedures should be reviewed and revised in order to ensure an enabling environment for food systems transformation, training and financial support provided to local authorities and partner institutions to plan, implement and coordinate territorial development strategies and programs, and experiences shared, reviewed and disseminated. But this will also require institutional and behavior change within all development partners (including academia and donors who are still organized along separate rural and urban lines).

Alignment of local, subnational and national policies and programs in the food system context is receiving more attention as a result of the interplay of urban, territorial and global governance described in this chapter.[18] This is an area where UN agencies that have turned toward the localization of the global agenda in general, and specifically to urban food governance, can be of assistance and must join forces. Although localization of SDGs and alignment of policy across governance levels has mainstreamed, there is still a long way to go to integrate urban and rural policy and planning. The historical relations between UN and international organizations with national government ministries, often through country offices, can be brought to bear to support local and regional governments in reorienting their food systems as part of localizing the SDGs; however, subnational experiences and priorities also need to inform national policies. Cities have much to contribute to and benefit from national efforts to implement the SDGs, but the interaction of local, regional and national governments needs to be transversal, not just top-down, where possible (United Nations Human Settlements Programme, 2021). Networks of local and regional governments have been engaging in various ways with UN agencies, at both country and headquarter levels, to help in the multilevel alignment of policies and programs. These actors need to be present in the decision-making spaces of intergovernmental policy debate and follow-up of global agendas, such as the HLPF and CFS, among others.

The priority is to build upon existing resources and experience. It is important to acknowledge that any process seeking interdisciplinarity, multi-actor participation and human rights is central to good food governance but also that a food system approach can bring added value and help operationalize such processes. It would therefore be counter-productive to multiply time-consuming committees at only local levels, and priority should be given to connecting with existing institutional processes and levels of governance. Food should be explicitly added to the existing mandates of relevant coordination committees at all levels (in particular those related to sustainability and SDGs or resilience and climate change). But food can also constitute an operational entry point for bringing together and discussing trade-offs between different dimensions of development, related to health and other social issues, the economy and environment.

As reports have emerged from cities, networks, governments and international organizations across the horizon, the interactions of urban, national and global food governance in the context of COVID-19 reinforce the necessity for new governance approaches. It is therefore important for cities and local governments to convene all actors to discuss the way forward and embark on action-learning processes, in partnership with counterpart institutions at local, central and global levels but also with other cities and local governments facing similar challenges.

Notes

1 The three co-authors of this chapter participated directly in many of the phases of policy convergence between urban food governance and global policy agendas described in this chapter as well as assisting implementation of urban and territorial food policy through technical and knowledge exchange to support practice to policy alignment from urban to national levels.

2 Policy reports of the High Level Panel of Experts (HLPE) of the Committee on World Food Security collectively provides a detailed overview of the evolution of global food system narratives in the last decade. Retrieved from www.fao.org/cfs/cfs-hlpe/hlpe-reports/en/.

3 Managing complex food systems in different parts of the world has required coordination and alignment between local and national governance for years, but the food system impacts of COVID-19 and recovery efforts in all countries have coincided with a first United Nations food systems summit (UNFSS). One outcome of the food systems summit is global attention to the role of local and regional governments in food policy and governance. This chapter addresses a few of the lessons and findings from the 2021 confluence of local and global dimensions of food systems that link policy and practice across levels of food governance.

4 There is a growing literature on the scope of the food sovereignty narrative and a foundation for this narrative includes the Declaration of Nyeleni (Mali) at the 2007 World Forum on Food Sovereignty (https://nyeleni.org/spip.php?article290). While the food sovereignty movement was originated by smallholder and peasant/campesino movements in Latin America and spread to all regions, there are also governments at local, subnational and national levels that incorporate food sovereignty as a food policy framework.

5 At the global level, the debate over what a food systems approach means for governance is a contentious field of debate, as seen in the fraught process of both the negotiation of the Voluntary Guidelines on Food Systems and Nutrition in the Committee on Food Security (CFS 47) and the UN Food System Summit, both in 2021.

6 Managing complex food systems in different parts of the world has required coordination and alignment between local and national governance for years, but the food system impacts of COVID-19, and parallel to the recovery efforts in all countries, there has been a first United Nations Food Systems Summit (UNFSS). These two parallel experiences have generated significant new global attention to the role of local and regional governments in food policy and governance. This chapter addresses only some of the lessons and findings from this, still unfolding, set of experiences that link policy and practice at all levels of food governance.

7 The wider range of actors engaging in food systems debates at the global level includes the civil society and private sector mechanisms of the CFS in Rome, Major Groups and other Stakeholders (MGoS) in the context of the global sustainable development debates (New York), and other global stakeholder mechanisms such as those engaging with the United Nations Environment Program (UNEP) and the United Nations Human Settlements Program (UN-Habitat).

8 Of particular relevance was the IDRC, Canada 1993–2002 Cities Feeding People (CFP) research program, in collaboration with the CGIAR Urban Harvest program, FAO and UN-Habitat, which gave birth in 1997 to the international Support Group for Urban Agriculture (SGUA) that eventually evolved into the Global Partnership on Sustainable Urban Agriculture and Food Systems (RUAF). CFP influenced the programs of its main international partners – in particular FAO's Interdepartmental Working Group and subsequent Priority Area for Inter-disciplinary Action (2002–2007) on Food for the Cities – along with many regional and national institutions, through building regional networks, linking researchers with policy advisors and urban planners at city and regional levels and developing joint policy briefs.

9 A good example of the richness of the urban food movements, before the policy linkages of urban food governance to territorial development and urban–rural linkages became more of a priority after 2015, can be seen in the collection of excellent essays in Cities and Agriculture: Developing resilient urban food systems (De Zeeuw & Dreschel, 2015).

10 Since the first global gathering in 1913, networks of municipalities have been multiplying at national, regional and international levels to foster city-to-city exchange and to influence policy at national and international levels. In 1984, Metropolis was set up as a hub and platform for major cities and metropolitan areas. In 1980, ICLEI was founded as the "International Council for Local Environmental Initiatives". In 2002, Regions4 was established in Johannesburg as the Network of Regional Governments for Sustainable Development. In 2004, mayors and political leaders from all over the world founded the World Organization of United Cities and Local Governments (UCLG) with the view to unite many of the major local and regional government associations. In 2005, the Mega-Cities Climate Leadership Group (now C40) was convened in London to forge an agreement on cooperatively reducing climate pollution.

11 The Local Authorities Major Group (LAMG) was one of the nine original Major Groups authorized by Member States in Agenda 21, the outcome document of the United Nations (section III. 28.1–7): https://sustainabledevelopment.un.org/content/documents/Agenda21.pdf.

12 While the MUFPP is not a network and has a small secretariat, the Pact has been taken into multiple national, regional and international city networks, mayors associations and intergovernmental bodies such as the European Commission.

13 The incorporation of territoriality in the New Urban Agenda was the product of strategic advocacy efforts linking civil society, city networks, UN agency and country actors. A dedicated coalition-building effort to this effect was funded by the Ford Foundation. "Communitas Coalition" was a well-organized coalition which used multiple channels that culminated in supporting negotiation by specific countries in the NUA negotiations. While not only about food systems, this advocacy prepared the ground for inclusion of urban food systems in the NUA. For more information, see www.fordfoundation.org/work/learning/learning-reflections/strong-partnerships-for-a-sustainable-future-the-legacy-of-the-communitas-coalition/.

14 Two seminal studies emerged on territorial approaches for food security and nutrition. The first was published in 2014 by the Latin American Rural Development Center (Rimisp): www.rimisp.org/wp-content/files_mf/1422296516InclusiveRural_UrbanLinkages_edited.pdf, and the second by OECD in 2015: www.oecd.org/cfe/regionaldevelopment/territorial-fsn-launch.htm.

15 One example of NUA final text, paragraph 123, was inspired by actors and cities engaged in the Milan Pact process:

> 123. We will promote the integration of food security and the nutritional needs of urban residents, particularly the urban poor, in urban and territorial planning, in order to end hunger and malnutrition. We will promote coordination of sustainable food security and agriculture policies across urban, peri-urban and rural areas (…). We will further promote the coordination of food policies with energy, water, health, transport and waste policies, maintain the genetic diversity of seeds, reduce the use of hazardous chemicals and implement other policies in urban areas to maximize efficiencies and minimize waste.

16 The Rome Declaration endorsed a G20 Platform on SDG Localization and Intermediary Cities, with the support of the OECD and UN-Habitat, both strong supporters of multi-level governance and territorial approaches: www.g20.org/wp-content/uploads/2021/10/G20-ROME-LEADERS-DECLARATION.pdf.

17 There have been a number of reports that share the key messages on urban and territorial responses to the pandemic and demonstrate the value of integrated multi-level governance in mitigating the

impacts of health and other crises, including environmental and political crises. Among these are two from FAO and one from UN-Habitat: www.fao.org/documents/card/en/c/cb0407en/ and https://unhabitat.org/issue-brief-covid-19-through-the-lens-of-urban-rural-linkages-guiding-principles-and-framework-for).

18 Approaches to territorial governance have become a way to embrace the inclusive and balanced interaction of local, regional and national governance with a major White Paper, "Fostering Territorial Approaches to Development (TP4D): Towards a wider alliance" published in 2019. This led to the 2021 "Territorial Approaches to Sustainable Development: Stocktaking and Synthesis Report" published by GIZ. Both reports influenced policy debates and key messages in the UN Food Systems Summit organized through an Ad Hoc Working Group for Territorial Governance.

References

Committee on World Food Security. (2021). *Voluntary Guidelines on Food Systems and Nutrition*. Retrieved from www.fao.org/cfs/vgfsn/en/

De Zeeuw, H., & Dreschel, P. (2015). *Cities and Agriculture: Developing Resilient Urban Food Systems*. London: Routledge.

FAO (Food and Agriculture Organization of the United Nations). (2018a). *Sustainable Food Systems: Concept and Framework*. Rome: FAO. Retrieved from www.fao.org/3/ca2079en/CA2079EN.pdf

FAO. (2018b). *City Region Food System Toolkit*. Rome: FAO . Retrieved from: www.fao.org/urban-food-actions/resources/resources-detail/en/c/1133524/

FAO. (2018c). *The Role of Cities in the Transformation of Food Systems: Sharing Lessons from Milan Pact Cities*. Rome: FAO. Retrieved from www.milanurbanfoodpolicypact.org/wp-content/uploads/2018/10/CA0912EN.pdf

FAO. (2019). *FAO Framework for the Urban Food Agenda: Leveraging Sub-national and Local Government Action to Ensure Sustainable Food Systems and Improved Nutrition*. Rome: FAO. Retrieved from www.fao.org/3/ca3151en/CA3151EN.pdf

FAO. (2020). *Cities and Governments at the Forefront in Building Inclusive and Resilient Food Systems*. Rome: FAO. Retrieved from www.fao.org/documents/card/en/c/cb0407en/

FAO. (2021). *Transforming Agri-food Systems: Legislative Interventions for Improved Nutrition and Sustainability*. Rome: FAO. Retrieved from www.fao.org/3/cb6016en/cb6016en.pdf

FAO. (2019). *Sustainable Healthy Diets: Guiding Principles*. Rome: FAO. Retrieved from www.fao.org/3/ca6640en/ca6640en.pdf

FAO Council. (2005). *Voluntary Guidelines to Support the Progressive Realization of the Right to Adequate Food in the Context of National Food Security*. Adopted by the 127th Session of the FAO Council November 2004, Food and Agriculture Organization of the United Nations. Retrieved from https://www.fao.org/3/y7937e/Y7937E.pdf

Habitat I. (1976). The Vancouver Declaration on Human Settlements. *United Nations Conference on Human Settlements, Vancouver, Canada, 31 May to June 1976*. Retrieved from https://mirror.unhabitat.org/downloads/docs/The_Vancouver_Declaration.pdf

Habitat II. (1996). The Istanbul Declaration on Human Settlements. *United Nations Conference on Human Settlements, Istanbul, Turkey, 3 to 14 June 1996*. Retrieved from https://mirror.unhabitat.org/downloads/docs/2072_61331_ist-dec.pdf

Human Rights Council. (2018). *United Nations Declaration on the Rights of Peasants and Other People Working in Rural Areas*. Resolution adopted by the Human Rights Council on 28 September 2018, United Nations. Retrieved from https://digitallibrary.un.org/record/1650694#record-files-collapse-header

IASC. (2010). *IASC Strategy Meeting Humanitarian Challenges in Urban Areas*. New York: IASC. Retrieved from https://reliefweb.int/sites/reliefweb.int/files/resources/Full_Report_501.pdf

Milan Urban Food Policy Pact. (2015). *Milan Urban Food Policy Pact*. Milan: MUFPP. Retrieved from www.milanurbanfoodpolicypact.org/

Montgomery, M. (2007). United Nations Population Fund: State of world population 2007: Unleashing the potential of urban growth. *Population and Development Review*, 33(3), 639–641. Retrieved from www.unfpa.org/publications/state-world-population-2007

OECD. (2015). *Adopting a Territorial Approach to Food Security and Nutrition Policy*. Paris: OECD. Retrieved from www.oecd.org/cfe/regionaldevelopment/territorial-fsn-launch.htm

OECD. (2020a). *A Territorial Approach to Sustainable Development Goals*. Synthesis Report, OECD Urban Policy Reviews. Paris: OECD. Retrieved from www.oecd.org/cfe/a-territorial-approach-to-the-sustainable-development-goals-e86fa715-en.htm

OECD. (2020b). *The Territorial Impact of COVID-19: Managing the crisis across levels of government*. Paris: OECD. Retrieved from https://read.oecd-ilibrary.org/view/?ref=128_128287-5agkkojaaa&title=The-territorial-impact-of-covid-19-managing-the-crisis-across-levels-of-government

OHCHR (Office of the United Nations High Commissioner for Human Rights). (1974). *Universal Declaration on the Eradication of Hunger and Malnutrition*. Retrieved from www.ohchr.org/en/professionalinterest/pages/eradicationofhungerandmalnutrition.aspx

Pothukuchi, K., & Kaufman, J. L. (1999). Placing the food system on the urban agenda: The role of municipal institutions in food systems planning. *Agriculture and Human Values*, 16(2), 213–224.

UCLG (United Cities and Local Governments). (2020). *Dialogue for the Post COVID-19 Era: An Opportunity to Take Responsibility Towards Future Generations*. Barcelona: UCLG. Retrieved from www.uclg.org/sites/default/files/decalogue_for_the_post_covid-19_era.pdf

UN (United Nations). (2016). *New Urban Agenda*. New York: United Nations, Retrieved from https://unhabitat.org/sites/default/files/2019/05/nua-english.pdf

UNGA (United Nations General Assembly). (2012). *The Future We Want*. New York: United Nations. Retrieved from www.un.org/ga/search/view_doc.asp?symbol=A/RES/66/288&Lang=E

UNGA. (2015). *Transforming Our World: the 2030 Agenda for Sustainable Development*. New York: United Nations. Retrieved from www.un.org/ga/search/view_doc.asp?symbol=A/RES/70/1&Lang=E

UN-Habitat. (2019). *Urban-Rural Linkages: Guiding Principles Framework for Action to Advance Integrated Territorial Development*. Nairobi: UN-Habitat. Retrieved from https://unhabitat.org/sites/default/files/2020/03/url-gp-1.pdf

United Nations Human Settlements Programme. (2019). *Urban-Rural Linkages: Guiding Principles. Framework for Action to Advance Integrated Territorial Development*. Nairobi: UNHSP. Retrieved from https://unhabitat.org/sites/default/files/2020/03/url-gp-1.pdf

United Nations Human Settlements Programme. (2021). *Global State of National Urban Policy: Achieving Sustainable Development Goals and Delivering Climate Action*. Nairobi: UNHSP. Retrieved from https://unhabitat.org/global-state-of-national-urban-policy-2021

27

THE ROLE OF TRANSNATIONAL CITY FOOD NETWORKS IN SUPPORTING URBAN FOOD TRANSFORMATION

Thierry Giordano

Introduction

City food networks have been emerging at national, regional and international levels over the past decade in the wake of the growing awareness of the unsustainability of food systems (Webb et al., 2020). Most of these networks are being set up in Europe and North America. They are highly diversified—pursuing different objectives, conducting different activities, integrating different members (big, intermediary and/or small cities, sometimes even other actors like local civil society organizations), with different degrees of political commitment and activities in policy arenas (Moragues-Faus, 2021). Yet they pursue the same overarching goal: to transform urban food systems to ensure their sustainability.

This chapter focuses on transnational city networks (as opposed to national or regional networks). It explores the role of these networks as agents of change in the governance of food security and nutrition by unpacking the functions they are currently fulfilling. The chapter draws on a literature review and builds on the author's experience and interactions with such networks over the 2016–2019 period in his role as a decentralized cooperation advisor to the Director of the Partnerships Division at FAO. The chapter specifically analyses the four transnational networks that have emerged over the past decade: the Milan Urban Food Policy Pact (MUFPP), C40 Cities Climate Leadership Group (C40), ICLEI Local Governments for Sustainability (ICLEI) and United Cities and Local Governments (UCLG). The chapter is organized as follows. The subsequent section depicts the history of these networks, which sometimes have close relations with national or regional networks—these are mentioned when they shed light on the way transnational networks operate. This is followed by a section that unravels the main functions and the means these networks use to fulfil them. Three key functions are identified: (1) building a community for exchanges of knowledge and good practices; (2) providing political support to help cities in their quest for legitimacy on food; and (3) seeking financial resources for their functioning and for their members. This section focuses on the

DOI: 10.4324/9781003055907-31

resources that networks have at their disposal, the activities they develop, and their motivations. However, it does not aim to determine the relationships between outputs (network activities), outcomes (how network members grasp, use, adapt or transform these outputs) and impacts (on members and beyond), as this would require additional data and analysis. The final section explores a fourth potential function of transnational networks regarding their global advocacy role. The final section provides concluding remarks and recommendations.

Emergence of transnational city food networks

Transnational city food networks are recent, yet they are built on a long history of transnational city networks tracing back to 1913 and the creation of the Union Internationale des Villes (Gaspari, 2002). Since then, networks have traditionally focused on cities and their built environment, with growing concern regarding the unsustainability of urban development models. In recent years, there has been a clear shift from framing cities as sustainability problems to sustainability solutions. This has led to the widespread idea that "cities can save the planet" (Angelo & Wachsmuth, 2020). City networks have embraced this idea, leading to a tremendous increase in network numbers. Acuto and Leffel (2020) estimate that there are 300 city networks worldwide.

The growing need for food system transformation to allow all urban dwellers to access and consume healthy food has prompted cities to take action. This transformative dimension stresses the fact that "for urban sustainability to be achieved and progressed, deep transformations are required in systems, relations, policies and governance approaches" (Frantzeskaki et al., 2021). Faced with limited, ready-to-use transformative solutions or evidence, cities have turned to networking as a means to speed up transformation in their territorial space (Moragues-Faus & Morgan, 2015). Many city food networks have emerged over the past decade at different scales, including two types of transnational networks, that is, networks created specifically to prioritize urban food, and already existing transnational networks that are setting up thematic sub-networks on food.

Milan Urban Food Policy Pact (2015): a game changer in the city network scene

In February 2014, at the C40 Summit in Johannesburg, Giuliano Pisapia (the then Mayor of Milan) put forward the idea of an international initiative on urban food policies. The Milan Urban Food Policy Pact emerged after an intense one-year effort. The Pact was presented to the Secretary General of the United Nations (SGUN) on World Food Day following the 2015 Milan Universal Expo. Over 100 cities then signed the Pact, which represented the first international agreement on sustainable urban food systems. The number of signatories had grown to 217 in January 2022. When signing the Pact, cities commit to sustainable food systems that are inclusive, resilient, safe and diverse. They also pledge to engage in some or all of the 37 actions in the six working areas of the MUFPP Framework of Action: (a) governance, (b) sustainable diets and nutrition, (c) social and economic equity, (d) food production, (e) food supply and distribution, and (f) food waste.[1]

The MUFPP network has no legal status. The City of Milan hosts the Secretariat of the Pact and organizes the main network activities, including the annual gathering of members, the best practice awards process supported by the Cariplo Foundation, and some regional gatherings or capacity-building events. MUFPP members also elect a board responsible for overseeing the activities of the Secretariat. As outlined in the next section, the Pact gave a new dimension to the role of cities in food system transformation, due to its heightened visibility after being showcased to the Secretary General of the United Nations, its capacity to last, remain active and inclusive, while providing a benchmark for other transnational city networks.

Food as a novel area for existing transnational networks: ICLEI (2013), UCLG (2016) and C40 (2016)

MUFPP may have prompted some transnational city networks to realize that food systems were becoming critical in ensuring urban sustainability. We briefly review here how and when ICLEI, UCLG and C40 created their food system networks.

ICLEI was founded in 1990 as the International Council for Local Environmental Initiatives. In June 2013, ICLEI and the RUAF Foundation, that is, an NGO focused on urban agriculture and food systems, launched the "CITYFOOD network on resilient city-region food systems and urban agriculture" at the ICLEI Resilient Cities Conference in Bonn (ICLEI & RUAF, 2013). Twenty city leaders signed the Bonn Declaration of Mayors, which focused mainly on adaptation to climate change, while including a paragraph on the importance for cities of developing resilient city region food systems (ICLEI, 2013). Despite this announcement, the network remained discreet before being re-launched as the ICLEI-RUAF City Food Network at the ICLEI Resilient Cities Conference in Bonn in May 2017. Its main goals are to provide training, technical assistance, policy advice and facilitate exchanges and learning between cities facing similar challenges (ICLEI, 2018).

UCLG is one of the major transnational, cross-sectoral local government networks, which was founded in 2004 following the merger of some of the oldest networks in the world: the International Union of Local Authorities,[2] the Fédération Mondiale des Cités Unies,[3] and Metropolis.[4] UCLG has the unique feature of pooling all types of local governments, including provinces, and many national local government networks. In 2015, a UCLG member, Régions de France, the French association of provincial governments, proposed the creation of a community of practice (CoP) on "Territorial governance, food security and nutrition transition". This was quite a remarkable move in this flourishing city network setting, since it advocated a broader territorial approach including urban and rural areas, thereby addressing rural–urban linkages. The CoP was then launched at the UCLG World Assembly in Bogota in October 2016.[5]

C40—a network initially devoted to climate actions—also turned its sights on food system sustainability. C40 was created in 2005 and gathers 97 large cities or metropoles from around the world. It revolutionized the functioning of transnational city networks. Firstly, Bloomberg Philanthropies has been backstopping C40 since its inception by providing financial support for network functioning, thus providing substantial leeway for experimentation. Secondly, the network is very inward-looking, working with and for their purposely limited number of members, while sharing little information with the outside world. Finally, C40 uses climate change experts positioned at the highest possible municipal levels to help cities design and implement a climate strategy. The same model was applied to the C40 food system sub-network created in 2016 in partnership with the philanthropic EAT Initiative. In October 2019, the C40 Food Systems Network took a new turn when 14 cities signed the C40 Good Food Cities Declaration—progressing from experience exchange and learning to becoming truly transformative. By signing the Declaration, mayors and city leaders commit to aligning their food procurement policies to the Planetary Health Diet,[6] fostering increased healthy plant-based food consumption, while reducing food waste and loss (C40, 2019a).

There has been a tight bond between C40 and MUFPP from the outset. The City of Milan is a C40 member, and Mayor Pisapia tested the idea of the MUFPP at the C40 Summit in 2014. The appointed head of the C40 Food Systems Network in 2016 was a former advisor to Mayor Pisapia, and one of the architects of the MUFPP. Not surprisingly, the focus areas of the C40 Food Systems Network share similarities with the MUFPP framework of action—it focuses on food procurement, food environment, food waste, regenerative agriculture and governance.

The main functions of transnational city food networks

While transnational city food networks have different origins, their objectives revolve around a core set of functions upon which they build their legitimacy. These functions can be divided into three areas that closely resemble those of other global public policy networks (Streck, 2002): (a) to create a community of cities sharing practices to inspire others, and spark new local food initiatives; (b) to support food as a fully fledged remit of cities; and (c) to mobilize resources for networks and their members to engage in transformational activities. These areas are described in the three subsections below.

To build a community for the exchange of knowledge and good practices

Capacity building by fostering the exchange of knowledge and cooperation between cities is a core function of most city networks. This is certainly the most dominant function when it comes to city food networks. While cities had developed different tools to secure food, especially cereals, for their urban populations since antiquity, they lost their urban food system management capabilities with the rise of the nation-state in the sixteenth century (Daviron et al., 2017). Pothukuchi and Kaufman (1999) explain why food issues long remained beyond cities' scope in the twentieth century. Firstly, cities took their food system for granted, without raising questions about food access or availability. Secondly, cities developed around specific urban-centric issues, while food and agriculture were deemed rural. Thirdly, technologies of the industrial revolution facilitated urban food supply even when agricultural land traditionally used to feed cities was disappearing due to urban sprawl. Finally, rural and urban development in many countries has been the responsibility of different departments with little or no coordination. Hence, when cities initiated actions around food, this process was more reactive than proactive and was based on a piecemeal rather than a comprehensive approach, without due consideration of the food system as a vital urban system (Pothukuchi & Kaufman, 2000).

The most committed and capacitated cities started to innovate, mostly through trial and error in the 1980s and 1990s, with the support of local food experts and researchers. When transnational networks were set up, the most advanced cities became role models, as many cities were unable to engage in food initiatives without external support. This was particularly the case in developing countries where the decentralization process was faltering, financial resources were scarce and local capacities limited. The exchange of practices between cities became critical in this setting. City food networks acted as knowledge brokers and facilitators through the exchange and promotion of good practices and peer-to-peer learning activities. All networks put a great emphasis on supporting cities in developing countries. Through networks, cities could then learn from one another, showcase their actions, get inspired and spark new food initiatives. Transnational city food networks thus use and combine different tools and mechanisms to engage cities, as explained below.

Workshops and meetings

Networks convene city officials and their technical teams through online or in-person meetings to activate city communities and present how they politically and technically address the challenges they face.

The C40 Food Systems Network regularly organizes online thematic workshops with members, to present initiatives, raise concerns, get feedback, etc. Similarly, ICLEI CITYFOOD runs online workshops, that is, a so-called city hub. It allows cities to showcase their food policies, projects and programmes. The MUFPP Secretariat does not have the means of C40 to organize regular workshops for its entire network, but together with the City of Milan it leads the "Eurocities Working Group Food", a European network of large cities created in 1986, including 140 members in 39 countries (Moragues-Faus, 2021).

The "Eurocities Working Group Food" is a transversal "creative hub" for sharing information, ideas and solutions regarding local food governance, education to achieve sustainable food, reducing food waste, providing access to food to all social groups, fostering wellness, the environmental and agricultural dimensions of food systems, trade, etc. (EUROCITIES, 2021). Its aim is to strengthen cooperation and synergies between Eurocities' members and EU institutions regarding food, to share knowledge and agree on advocacy messages and actions, and thus to promote interactions of cities with diverse stakeholders (private and public sectors, EU institutions, NGOs, etc.). The City of Milan has been very active, and to some extent it acted as a *de facto* secretariat for this working group until 2020, so it could be viewed as the main European arm of the MUFPP. In 2020, the network secured a €12 million European project, that is, the Food Trails project. Its main goal is to support 11 European cities (including nine MUFPP members) in developing and launching their food policies. It also includes knowledge sharing and advocacy on the role of cities in the transformation of urban food systems (see https://foodtrails.milanurbanfoodpolicypact.org/).

Awards and monetary prizes

Awards and prizes also facilitate knowledge sharing and are quite prevalent amongst city networks. These awards identify, label and promote good practices and thus boost recognition and enhance the reputation of winning cities. For instance, with Cariplo Foundation support, MUFPP launched the Milan Pact Awards in 2016, with an award for each of the six categories of the MUFPP Framework for Action. In addition, two monetary prizes (€15,000 each) are geared towards peer-to-peer assistance as an incentive to further city-to-city cooperation. Four hundred practices have been documented over the last six years through the awards process, constituting a rich collection of transferable practices to speed up learning and foster collaboration between cities. Participating in these awards is a great way for cities to showcase their own food policies and programmes, to gain visibility and legitimacy and even tap into new financial resources. In 2020, the Secretariat innovated by asking for video submission of cities' practices.

C40 grants the "C40 Cities Bloomberg Philanthropies Awards", which recognize outstanding and innovative actions implemented by cities to adapt to and mitigate climate change and support city resilience. Awards cover seven categories on The Future We Want theme, that is, the future we want "is resilient", "relies on green mobility", "runs on renewable energy", "engages all citizens", "breathes clean air", "requires transformative change" and "uses green technologies". These awards are directly linked to the annual Cities100 publication (C40, 2019b). It features innovative programmes, policies and projects developed by cities to tackle climate change effects while serving as a policy guide and an inspirational tool for members. When submitting an entry for this publication, cities can ask for their application to be considered for the C40 awards, thereby illustrating the core thrust of these prizes: collecting knowledge and stimulating exchanges of good practices through competition between cities. However, following the creation of the C40 Food Systems Network, no food-related awards were granted at the last two editions of the Awards (2017 and 2019).

Develop shared technical capacities

Beyond exchanges, networks can also help build members' capacities through technical assistance. City food networks centralize information and foster the capitalization and promotion of skills and knowledge. For instance, collective workshops on methodology and assessment processes contribute to enhancing the capacity building of local stakeholders and the network.

The MUFPP monitoring framework is part of this capacity-building function of networks. FAO funded the development of the Monitoring Framework and provided an internal technical team to oversee the technical work of the RUAF Foundation, a lead ICLEI-RUAF City Food Network partner. The monitoring framework includes a set of indicators covering the six areas of the Framework of Action and its 37 actions. It includes the structure of each indicator, the data needed to build it, and the way data could be collected (FAO, MUFPP, & RUAF, 2019). It aims at facilitating information collection on the state of city food systems. This information could be used to trigger policy initiatives, projects and programmes, while the indicators could then be used for monitoring as a first step towards an evidence-based policy. The indicators have thus been built and selected over a two-year period and were finalized in 2019 in close collaboration with a few voluntary MUFPP cities from both developed and developing countries. The latter agreed to participate in the process and provide inputs and feasibility assessment according to their local context, and their own financial and technical capacities. This is a critical step towards the potential adoption of the indicators by the largest number of cities. A handbook was then drawn up to help cities implement the Monitoring Framework (Carey & Cook, 2021).

Contrary to the WHO Healthy Cities Network and its specific set of indicators (Webster & Sanderson, 2013), the MUFPP Monitoring Framework does not seek to cross-evaluate cities and ensure comparability. This option was discarded from the start to prevent despondency by cities leading initiatives and/or those with limited resources.

Political support to cities' quest for legitimacy on food

A second key function of transnational city food networks is to support their members in positioning food higher on the city political agenda and legitimize urban food initiatives. The COVID-19 pandemic has underpinned this trend.

Three levels of legitimacy

Transnational networks foster this legitimacy at three levels. The first one stems from the inner structure and functioning of cities. Officials in charge of food policy have to convince other officials and elected representatives to mainstream food in other sectoral policies—many sectoral initiatives and decisions, apparently remote from food, actually shape local food systems. They also need to develop initiatives and policies specifically targeting the many unsustainable dimensions of food systems, so they must be transformative. Competition is fierce between urban sectors with regard to credits, positions or political support, and the addition of another remit is a further challenge. It is therefore critical to legitimize the actions of food teams within municipalities, build their reputations and develop local branding.

The second level relates to the complexity of food systems, the diversity and multiplicity of actors within and around them: large private companies, small businesses, civil society organizations, communities, associations of producers and consumers, retailers, transporters, informal workers, etc. They are part and parcel of the food systems, and many initiatives are doomed to fail without their support. However, cities are new players in the field. Long-standing traditional urban food stakeholders must accept local governments as new legitimate actors and partners.

A third level concerns the need to gain support from their constituencies. Networks can ensure public acknowledgement of urban food policies through marketing campaigns and contribute to anchoring food issues at the local level. Beyond the democratic stakes, ensuring a close connection with citizens is critical to bolster the effectiveness of cities' local policy or food initiatives. These campaigns help raise public awareness on the unsustainability of food systems and encourage new behaviour and practices. For networks, it ensures visibility with regard to their work and the solutions they put forward.

Publications and members' meetings as key legitimization instruments

Transnational city food networks play a critical role in assisting cities in two different ways. Firstly, networks use publications as tools to collect, frame and spread knowledge, thereby legitimizing cities' role. These outreach publications are a means for city officials to show colleagues what it is possible to do, to provide elected officials with evidence of the engagement of other cities and create constructive competition, and to establish cities as new partners of well-established stakeholders.

Some publications are geared towards mapping members' initiatives and providing an overview of cities' engagement and concrete initiatives. Through the Milan Pact Awards of 2016, 2017 and 2018, the MUFPP documented and published a series of practices, as well as an analysis of what MUFPP signatories have been focusing on (MUFPP et al., 2018). UCLG, under the leadership of Régions de France and via its collaboration with the French NGO Résolis, also published a series of practices, but by region or country: in France (Résolis, 2015), Quebec (Résolis, 2016c), Costa Rica (Résolis, 2016b), the Mediterranean region (Résolis, 2016a), and Santa Fe province in Argentina (Divay, 2017).

As cities have become increasingly aware, active and able to broaden the scope of their activities to tackle food challenges, network publications have tended to become less generic and to focus on more in-depth specific themes. Examples include the MUFPP and Barilla Center for Nutrition report on the role of urban food policies in achieving the Sustainable Development Goals (SDGs) (BCFN & MUFPP, 2018), the MUFPP report on nutrition (Halliday et al., 2019), and the C40 consumption report to meet the 1.5°C target to combat climate change, which includes food as one of its six key consumption categories (C40, 2019a).

In 2016, to support the dissemination of good practices and strengthen the legitimacy of local governments, transnational food networks collaborated with FAO to develop the Urban Food Actions Platform, an online knowledge hub aimed at gathering extensive relevant information on urban food solutions to achieve sustainability.[7]

Secondly, most networks organize annual or bi-annual gatherings. These high-level events welcome mayors, vice-mayors, ministers, international organizations and other special guests and partners. They seek to anchor food as a fully fledged remit of cities. Networks bring cities together and provide a framework in which a community of cities committed to developing sustainable food systems can collaborate and build a common vision. The audience is a critical element here.

When sharing good practices, cities also showcase their local efforts to build more sustainable and resilient food systems to other food systems actors. They strive to demonstrate their legitimacy and ability to act on food issues. At each gathering, the audience is much broader ranging than cities themselves. Host cities develop campaigns targeting their citizens and other stakeholders, while inviting ministers, actual or potential funding partners. Examples are the annual MUFPP summit and the C40 Food Systems Network bi-annual summit meeting. Since 2013, ICLEI has put food on the agenda in most of its annual Resilient Cities Conferences. Moreover, the MUFPP Secretariat has also overseen regional gatherings in Africa, Latin America, North America and Asia, often in partnership with other organizations—12 such gatherings took place between 2015 and 2020. The aim is to incite cities with similar socio-economic dynamics to tackle urban food challenges.

Unexpected consequences of the COVID-19 pandemic

The COVID-19 crisis has dramatically challenged local food systems, pushing cities to the frontline, thereby boosting their legitimacy. Local food systems have been under pressure but have also emerged as a critical element of food system resilience (Kolodinsky et al., 2020; O'Connell et al., 2021; Thilmany et al., 2021; Thulasiraman et al., 2021). The crisis has triggered new initiatives to facilitate access to food in response to the rising level of food insecurity in urban areas, due mainly to lockdown-related measures (Campbell, 2021; FAO, 2020).

Transnational food networks have been pivotal in displaying and legitimizing the role of cities through different means, for example, ICLEI and its African branch (Rikolto, 2020; Daring Cities, 2022), Eurocities and MUFPP organized webinars on cities' responses to the COVID-19 pandemic (see EUROCITIES, 2022; MUFPP, 2020a). The 5th Anniversary of the MUFPP was mainly devoted to coping with the COVID-19 pandemic, and the MUFPP awards 2020 released in December showcased videos of many urban food solutions tailored to COVID-19-induced food challenges (MUFPP, 2020b; MUFPP, 2020c), C40 published blog pieces (C40, 2020), while UCLG produced briefing and learning notes co-published with Metropolis and UN-Habitat, entitled "Food systems: Lessons learnt from the Pandemic" in July 2020, following a webinar organized a few weeks earlier (UCLG et al., 2020).

Attracting financial resources for their members

The third core function of transnational city networks deals with finance, a factor that is critical for at least two reasons: (1) as a vehicle to enable networks to pursue their activities and fulfil their objectives; and (2) as an incentive for cities to join and be an active member of a network when it is able to raise money for their members and activities. This latter dimension may be crucial in encouraging the long-term involvement of cities in a network (Betsill & Bulkeley, 2004).

The first reason questions the continued sustainability of transnational networks, some of which charge members annual fees in order to benefit from the network services (e.g. UCLG and ICLEI). However, these are multi-sectoral networks, where food is just one issue amongst many others. Food is often not high on their agendas because they have to prioritize due to their limited resources. Sub-network managers hence must raise their own funds to underpin their activities—the sub-network dynamics are thus heavily dependent on the sub-network manager's mettle.

Bloomberg Philanthropies has supported C40, guaranteeing an initial multi-year budget for C40 to hire a highly qualified team to plan and implement its strategy. C40 has therefore been able to rapidly build partnerships and diversify its funding sources by enlisting other philanthropic foundations, bilateral governmental donors and some private companies. Hence, the C40 Food Systems Network was created in partnership with the EAT Initiative.

The MUFPP Secretariat is funded by the City of Milan, thereby enabling it to conduct a minimum set of activities, including liaising with members, organizing online seminars, annual gatherings and the award process. Cariplo Foundation supports MUFPP by funding the awards prizes. The Italian and French Foreign Offices have directly or indirectly funded some regional gatherings. A Letter of Intent with FAO was critical to enable FAO staff to provide technical and financial support to the Secretariat and some cities.

These networks have minimum resources, yet they also have to raise money to develop activities and support some of their members in launching new initiatives. A small share of these supplementary funds comes from grants negotiated directly with partners: Régions de France used to apply for a small grant offered by the Decentralized Cooperation Office of the French Ministry for Europe and Foreign Affairs, which allowed the association to carry out some studies used by the UCLG CoP. Both ICLEI and MUFPP benefited from FAO grants for backstopping studies and publications, and for organizing regional workshops. Meanwhile C40 benefited from an FAO grant for seconding a city food system advisor to the Nairobi County (based on its model of seconding climate change experts to municipalities to speed policy development and programme implementation). The expert enhanced the technical capacities of the municipality and participated in the development of the Nairobi urban food strategy (Nairobi County et al., 2020).

However, the bulk of the funding often comes from competitive project financing, which is a relatively uncertain funding source that may lead to the ebb and flow of network activities. Activities of the ICLEI-RUAF City Food Network are highly reliant on competitive project financing. The facilitator and aggregator roles of the network, in drawing up project call submissions together with its members, are thus crucial, especially in Europe where financing opportunities arise from different European Commission grant programmes. European networks have developed technical expertise to underpin European funding calls and manage European projects, while their monitoring and strategic understanding of EU decisions, project grants and programmes are facilitated by their linkages. This enables networks to identify a consistent consortium of cities, draft comprehensive proposals based on shared views, and even foresee or lobby for future topics of interest for its stakeholders. These capacities were critical in enabling the Eurocities Working Group Food—led by Milan and Warsaw—to win a few tenders and thereby strengthen European urban food dynamics. Through the Food Trail project mentioned earlier, for instance, cities will thus receive from €200,000 to €900,000 for its implementation.

Note here that the originality of the URBACT Programme is primarily funded by the European Regional Development Fund of the European Commission. Created in 2002, it aims at fostering sustainable integrated urban development in cities across Europe through capacity building, transnational exchange, policy design and implementation, knowledge sharing and dissemination. Food is one of the many urban topics URBACT seeks to address by financing temporary networks of cities working together on specific food-related issues, for example the Biocanteens network, Food Corridors network and the Rurban networks, just to mention the ones that are currently operational (URBACT, 2022). While transnational urban food networks do not benefit from URBACT, many of their European members are leaders of these temporary food networks.

C40 has probably gone the furthest of all transnational networks in facilitating members' access to project finance in emerging and developing countries. The Cities Financial Facility (CFF), founded in 2017, is a joint initiative implemented by C40 and the German International Cooperation Agency (GIZ), and funded by USAID, BMZ and the UK Government. It facilitates funding access by providing technical assistance to develop cities' sustainability priorities into bankable investment proposals—a major project finance barrier that mayors and city leaders have to overcome (C40, 2022). However, so far none of the 14 already-funded projects target urban food systems.

The CFF experience confirms a wider conclusion that food systems do not seem to leverage the same kind of funding as other urban sectors (transport, sanitation, energy, waste, etc.). Networks will continue to struggle in meeting their fundraising goals. This might explain why they do not promote good practices in accessing specific funding sources through the dissemination of success stories or the development of funding guides that include potential funding sources, support services or innovative financing schemes. However, national networks like Sustainable Food Places in the UK (Davies & Messer, 2018) and research groups are more active in this respect (Santo & Horrigan, 2019).

While such activities do not directly benefit networks, funding access is critical in strengthening network seriousness and attractiveness. This is exactly what CFF does in sharing its experiences, or what the Global Covenant of Mayors for Climate and Energy—a network of EU cities that was launched in 2008—does by regularly showcasing how some of their members managed to access grants and loans allocated by national governments, the European Commission or the European Investment Bank to fund energy-related projects.[8] Unfortunately such financing mechanisms do not currently exist for food system projects, but might in the near future under the new EU Farm to Fork Strategy (European Commission, 2021).

Next step: towards a global advocacy role?

The core functions of the previously described transnational city food networks do not differ from those of other thematic or broader transnational city networks. Exploring their effectiveness in supporting food system transformation is beyond the scope of this chapter. However, one critical dimension for achieving this goal must be questioned, and that is their capacity to advocate the role of cities in global food governance and weigh in on the global food agenda.

The capacity of cities to transform the urban environment goes beyond their territories, and depends on other levels of governance—provincial, national, regional or international. Transnational city networks have gradually invested in advocating their role as strategic players and critical implementers of innovative solutions. They have thereby engaged in other governance arenas to influence the way questions and solutions are framed and achieve recognition for their actions. Indeed, over the last decade, nation-states have struggled to respond to rising global challenges, which has boosted the influence of many non-state actors and their transnational networks in international governance (Betsill & Bulkeley, 2006). City networks are no exception. They have been increasingly involved in global policy processes, initially around climate change, then regarding the SDGs (Acuto et al., 2017; Curtis, 2016), and more recently the COVID-19 pandemic (Pipa & Bouchet, 2020).

City Networks aim at emboldening other levels of governance to push for more ambitious goals and more comprehensive policies via which local initiatives could thrive. This role has been particularly clear in climate change negotiations, where ICLEI, the Covenant of Mayors and C40 have been particularly vocal and influential by collectively committing to more ambitious targets as compared to nation-states. However, transnational city networks, and even more so their members, lack capacities in so-called city diplomacy to ensure that they play a greater role (Kosovac et al., 2020).

Why would it be different for transnational city food networks? Local food systems do not operate in isolation, and they have many provincial, national, regional or global connections. Collective thinking and actions are hence required when other levels of governance inhibit cities' capacities to deal with local challenges. They aim at overcoming hurdles that are beyond the city's remit. Being active in global policy arenas is a new function for transnational city food networks. Global involvement of city networks in efforts to meet the SDGs translates into mainstreaming food challenges into different fora, as reviewed below in chronological order (for more on international agendas and urban food governance, see Chapter 26 by Forster et al. in this volume).

UN-Habitat and the New Urban Agenda (2015)

Following the endorsement of the SDGs in 2015, a Global Taskforce of Local and Regional Governments was created as a consultation and coordination mechanism to weigh in on global policy processes.[9] ICLEI and UCLG are members of this taskforce, yet food issues are low on the agenda. One of the first shifts occurred when UCLG, C40 and ICLEI, together with partners, successfully pushed for the inclusion of food on the New Urban Agenda, adopted at the United Nations Conference on Housing and Sustainable Urban Development (Habitat III) in October 2016 (UN, 2016). This was a learning process for city food networks on how to participate in global policy discussions. It enticed them to follow up on the New Urban Agenda process and participate in biennial World Urban Forum sessions. They regularly organize side events on the role of cities in food system transformation.

Urban 20 and G20 (2020)

C40 and UCLG launched Urban 20 (U20) in 2017, during the One Planet Summit in Paris. U20 gathers mayors from G20 countries with the aim of influencing G20 discussions and actions and putting cities higher on heads of state agendas. In 2020, under the Saudi Arabian presidency, U20 organized three task forces, including one on "Nature-based urban solutions" chaired by Durban. It led representatives from Rio de Janeiro to produce a white paper on "Empowering cities for the development of sustainable food system policies" (U20, 2020b).

The communiqué of the Urban 20 Meeting (October 2020) subsequently included a resolution on food. Cities committed to

> [guaranteeing] food security for all by strengthening urban-rural linkages and investing in physical and social infrastructure that fosters resilient and sustainable food consumption and production systems, along with revising the G20 Principles on Habitat and Regional Planning to balance agriculture development with natural habitat protection, by reinforcing capacity building in rural environments and protecting the rights of food workers, and by generating city-level data in order to monitor world supply and price developments reliably during food and health crises.
>
> *U20, 2020a*

The Italian Government hosted the G20 Meetings in 2021. The City of Milan was involved in the U20 work, but the food agenda was not as high as could have been expected, given that Milan was overseeing MUFPP. However, the June 2021 communiqué still called for governments to acknowledge the critical role of cities in the recovery from the COVID-19 pandemic and this included transforming food systems (U20, 2021).

UN Convention on Climate Change and COP26 (2020)

Transnational networks have a long history of involvement in climate change negotiations (Kona et al., 2018), but food was not on their agenda until December 2020. ICLEI and MUFPP then signed the Glasgow Declaration (2021), initiated by IPES-Food with the technical support of FAO, "a commitment by subnational governments to tackle the climate emergency through integrated food policies and a call on national governments to act". This Declaration was officially presented at the Conference of Parties 26 of the Climate Change Convention (COP26) in November 2021. According to ICLEI (2021), "the Glasgow Food and Climate Declaration leaves a lasting legacy by setting the groundwork for bridging the gap between food and climate through the voices of the local and regional governments".

UN Food Systems Summit (2021)

In 2019, the Secretary General of the United Nations announced that a Food Systems Summit would take place in 2021. A secretariat was set up, with a special envoy, and a highly complex organizational process. An Urban Food Systems Working Group was created in 2020, comprising city networks (C40, Global Resilient Cities Network, ICLEI, UCLG), academic institutions and other organizations (Cardiff University, Consumers International, EAT Foundation, Food Foundation, GAIN, IPES-Food, Nourish Scotland, Rikolto, RUAF and The Prince's Foundation), as well as UN agencies (FAO, UN-Habitat, UNCDF, UNEP, UNICEF, UNSCN, WHO). This multi-stakeholder group is probably the biggest achievement of the Summit as far as local governments are concerned. In parallel, to support the involvement of cities in the preparation process and make cities' voices heard, FAO worked with ICLEI to organize a series of independent dialogues in different cities.[10]

In July 2021, the Italian Government hosted a pre-summit where most of the discussions took place. The Urban Food Systems Working Group was very active. It organized a plenary session on "Cities and local food systems". In addition, an official dialogue on "Empowering cities and local governments to improve food systems globally" was convened by FAO, GAIN, the Global Taskforce of Local and Regional Governments and the Summit Secretariat (UNFSS, 2021).

The Summit took place in New York in September 2021.[11] One of its outcomes might become important with respect to the advocacy role of local governments in food system transformation, that is, the creation of Coalitions to follow up on concrete actions. FAO and GAIN are actively working on using the Urban Food System Working Group as the basis for the creation of this "Coalition on sustainable and inclusive urban food systems".[12]

Committee on World Food Security

The Committee on World Food Security (CFS) of the United Nations is the most important international forum on food. It is an intergovernmental platform created in 1974 to ensure food security and nutrition for all. It was reformed after the food crisis of 2008 to include two mechanisms to facilitate the participation of civil society and the private sector in the debate. Such mechanisms do not exist in any other international fora.

There is no formal room for transnational networks in CFS, while their growing legitimacy on food could warrant this. Yet in October 2016, Régions de France, on behalf of UCLG, participated in a plenary session of the Committee to advocate the role of local government in supporting the food system transformation.[13] This was the first and only time a transnational city network was granted a speaking slot since the creation of CFS. Several reasons could be put forward to explain this situation. Firstly, networks do not have the resources needed to participate in and follow the CFS discussions, which are time consuming and demanding. Secondly, while there is a CFS mechanism to ensure private sector and civil society participation, there is not one for local governments. This does not mean that it would not be possible to offer one, but CFS member states would have to agree on it.

Conclusion

Transnational city food networks are still new actors in food systems, as shown by their recent emergence, while being founded on a long tradition of city-to-city exchanges and collaborations. They are gradually building their legitimacy in providing services to their members. This chapter presents a broad range of examples to illustrate how they fulfil their core functions: creating communities of cities sharing good practices to inspire others and spark food-related initiatives; promoting food as a fully fledged remit of cities; and tapping resources for their members and functioning.

They have clearly managed to put food higher on the agenda of mayors and elected representatives. They have progressively been playing a greater role in some international arenas, using different fora and channels to mainstream food into the urban, climate change and G20 agendas, and the UN Food Systems Summit. They are, however, still not involved in the Committee on World Food Security, which is the most important international food governance arena. Whether they will manage to enter this arena is still unclear. Transnational city food networks will certainly have to pursue their advocacy efforts. Hurdles lie ahead due to the lack of both human and financial capacities, and national governments must acknowledge the right of local governments to participate in global food governance.

Outputs related to their core function are very clear and focused on knowledge sharing and exchange, yet it is hard to identify the extent of traction gained by knowledge exchange or the long-term effects of networks on elected representatives and practitioners. Outcomes and impacts have to be quantified, while paving the way for a new research agenda, which would be critical to ensure the sustainability of these networks. To be more active, they will have to mobilize resources while supporting their members so that they can be more transformative in their actions and sustainable in their activities.

Notes

1 www.milanurbanfoodpolicypact.org/wp-content/uploads/2020/12/Milan-Urban-Food-Policy-Pact-EN.pdf
2 IIULA was founded in 1913 in the Netherlands to promote local governance with a specific focus on European cities.
3 FMCU was launched in 1957 in France to support city-to-city twinning as a way of promoting peace around the world, with members on all continents.
4 Metropolis was set up in 1980 and pools cities and metropolitan regions of 1 million inhabitants and over.
5 The UCLG food network was founded the work of the Organisation des Régions Unies (ORU-Fogar), a transnational network of provincial governments created in 2008. The same year, ORU-Fogar launched a Core Group on Food Sovereignty following a Memorandum of Understanding with FAO. Its goal was to promote provinces as a relevant governance level to deal with food security, through the development of regional food policy and the promotion of cooperation between regions.

ORU-FOGAR briefly joined UCLG in 2015, participated in the launch of the UCLG food network in 2016, but rapidly seceded from UCLG—regretting the weak weight of provinces over cities in the discussions.

6 The idea of a planetary Health Diet derives from the EAT-Lancet Commission (Willett et al., 2019) and is supported by the EAT Initiative: https://eatforum.org/learn-and-discover/the-planetary-health-diet/#targetText=The%20planetary%20health%20diet%20is,of%20fruits%2C%20vegetables%20and%20nuts

7 www.fao.org/urban-food-actions/en/

8 For instance: www.eib.org/en/events/covenant-of-mayors-webinar-elena-european-local-energy-assistance-inspiration-from-successful-projects

9 See more information www.global-taskforce.org/

10 See, for instance, the Dialogues for African cities: https://africa.iclei.org/2021-african-city-food-exchange/

11 See www.un.org/en/food-systems-summit

12 See https://foodsystems.community/commitment-registry/coalition-on-sustainable-and-inclusive-urban-food-systems/

13 See www.fao.org/cfs/home/plenary/cfs43/en/

Acknowledgement

The author would like to thank Nicolas Bricas, Soisic Ollion, and Alice Jan for early discussions on this chapter.

References

Acuto, M., & Leffel, B. (2020). Understanding the global ecosystem of city networks. *Urban Studies, 58*(9), 1758–1774. doi:10.1177/0042098020929261

Acuto, M., Morissette, M., & Tsouros, A. (2017). City diplomacy: Towards more strategic networking? Learning with WHO healthy cities. *Global Policy, 8*(1), 14–22. doi:10.1111/1758-5899.12382

Angelo, H., & Wachsmuth, D. (2020). Why does everyone think cities can save the planet? *Urban Studies, 57*(11), 2201–2221. doi:10.1177/0042098020919081

BCFN & MUFPP. (2018). *Food and Cities: The Role of Cities for Achieving the Sustainable Development Goals*. Retrieved from: www.barillacfn.com/media/material/food_cities.pdf

Betsill, M. M., & Bulkeley, H. (2004). Transnational networks and global environmental governance: The Cities for Climate Protection program. *International Studies Quarterly, 48*(2), 471–493. doi:10.1111/j.0020-8833.2004.00310.x

Betsill, M. M., & Bulkeley, H. (2006). Cities and the multilevel governance of global climate change. *Global Governance, 12*(2), 141–159. doi:10.2307/27800607

C40. (2019a). *Good Food Cities: Achieving a Planetary Health Diet for All*. Retrieved from: https://c40-production-images.s3.amazonaws.com/other_uploads/images/2405_C40_Good_Food_Cities_Declaration_EN_Final_-_CLEAN.original.pdf?1570711845

C40. (2019b) World's seven best climate projects announced as 2019 C40 Cities Bloomberg Philanthropies Awards winners. Press release. Retrieved from: www.c40.org/news/c40-awards-2019/

C40. (2020). Can the COVID-19 crisis help reboot urban food in Africa? Press release. Retrieved from: www.c40.org/news/opinion-can-the-covid-19-crisis-help-reboot-urban-food-in-africa/

C40. (2022). Developing projects to address climate change in cities. C40 Cities Finance Facility. Retrieved from: www.c40cff.org/

Campbell, C. G. (2021). The impact of COVID-19 on local government stakeholders' perspectives on local food production. *Journal of Agriculture Food Systems and Community Development, 10*(2), 71–88. doi:10.5304/jafscd.2021.102.035

Carey, J., & Cook, B. (2021). *The Milan Urban Food Policy Pact Monitoring Framework: A Practical Handbook for Implementation*. Rome: FAO. Retrieved from: www.fao.org/3/cb4181en/cb4181en.pdf

Curtis, S. (2016). Cities and global governance: State failure or a new global order? *Millennium, 44*(3), 455–477. doi:10.1177/0305829816637233

Daring Cities. (2022). For more information, see https://daringcities.org/about/

Davies, S., & Messer, B. (2018). *Financial Sustainability Guide: Experiences from the SFP Network and Beyond.* Retrieved from: www.sustainablefoodplaces.org/resources/files/SFP_Toolkit/Financial_Sustainability_Guide.pdf

Daviron, B., Perrin, C., & Soulard, C. T. (2017). Histoire des politiques alimentaires urbaines en Europe, de la ville antique à la ville industrielle. In C. Brand, N. Bricas, D. Conaré, B. Daviron, J. Debru, L. Michel, & C.-T, Soulard (Eds.), *Construire des politiques alimentaires urbaines.* Versailles, France: Éditions Quæ, 43–66.

Divay, V. (2017). *Iniciativas de alimentación responsable y sustentableen la provincia de Santa Fe: Identificación de buenas prácticas.* Retrieved from: www.uclg.org/sites/default/files/iniciativas_de_alimentacion_responsable_y_sustentable_en_la_provincia_de_santa_fe.pdf

EUROCITIES. (2021). *Food Systems.* Retrieved from: https://eurocities.eu/goals/food-systems/

EUROCITIES. (2022). Live updates COVID-19. European cities respond to the coronavirus crisis. *Blog.* Retrieved from: https://covidnews.eurocities.eu/category/covidnews/food-supply/

European Commission. (2021). Farm to fork strategy. Retrieved from: https://ec.europa.eu/food/horizontal-topics/farm-fork-strategy_en

FAO. (2020). *Cities and Local Governments at the Forefront in Building Inclusive and Resilient Food Systems: Key Results from the FAO Survey "Urban Food Systems and COVID-19".* Retrieved from: www.fao.org/documents/card/en/c/cb0407en

FAO, MUFPP, & RUAF. (2019). *The Milan Urban Food Policy Pact: Monitoring Framework.* Rome: FAO. Retrieved from: www.fao.org/3/ca6144en/ca6144en.pdf

Frantzeskaki, N., McPhearson, T., & Kabisch, N. (2021). Urban sustainability science: Prospects for innovations through a system's perspective, relational and transformations' approaches. *AMBIO.* doi:10.1007/s13280-021-01521-1

Gaspari, O. (2002). Cities against states? Hopes, dreams and shortcomings of the European Municipal Movement, 1900–1960. *Contemporary European History, 11*(4), 597–621. doi:10.1017/S0960777302004058

Glasgow Declaration. (2021). *The Glasgow Food and Climate Declaration.* Retrieved from: www.glasgowdeclaration.org/the-glasgow-declaration

Halliday, J., Platenkamp, L., & Nicolarea, Y. (2019). *A Menu of Actions to Shape Urban Food Environments for Improved Nutrition.* Italy/Netherlands/Geneva: MUFPP/RUAF/GAIN. Retrieved from: www.gainhealth.org/sites/default/files/publications/documents/gain-mufpp-ruaf-a-menu-of-actions-to-shape-urban-food-environments-for-improved-nutrition-2019.pdf

ICLEI. (2013). *Bonn Declaration of Mayors. Mayors Adaptation Forum 2013.* Bonn: ICLEI. Retrieved from: www.google.com/url?sa=t&rct=j&q=&esrc=s&source=web&cd=&cad=rja&uact=8&ved=2ahUKEwilhK-s9JbuAhVBxoUKHa8TBC8QFjAAegQIBRAC&url=https%3A%2F%2Fsustainabledevelopment.un.org%2FgetWSDoc.php%3Fid%3D792&usg=AOvVaw04ospgM0lZVUUO8z0vLiNj

ICLEI. (2018). *Invitation to the ICLEI-RUAF CITYFOOD Network.* Bonn: ICLEI. Retrieved from: https://ruaf.org/assets/2019/12/CITYFOOD_Network_brochure.pdf

ICLEI. (2021). Glasgow Food and Climate Declaration: Putting local and regional food systems on the table of the UN climate negotiations. *City Talk,* a blog by ICLEI. Retrieved from: https://talkofthecities.iclei.org/glasgow-food-and-climate-declaration-putting-local-and-regional-food-systems-on-the-table-of-the-un-climate-negotiations/

ICLEI, & RUAF. (2013). *CITYFOOD: Linking Cities on Urban Agriculture and Urban Food Systems.* Bonn/Netherlands: ICLEI/RUAF. Retrieved from: https://ruaf.org/assets/2019/12/CITYFOOD-Linking-Cities-on-Urban-Agriculture-and-Urban-Food-Systems.pdf

Kolodinsky, J., Sitaker, M., Chase, L., Smith, D., & Wang, W. (2020). Food systems disruptions: Turning a threat into an opportunity for local food systems. *Journal of Agriculture, Food Systems, and Community Development, 9*(3), 5–8. doi:10.5304/jafscd.2020.093.013

Kona, A., Bertoldi, P., Monforti-Ferrario, F., Rivas, S., & Dallemand, J. F. (2018). Covenant of mayors' signatories leading the way towards 1.5 degree global warming pathway. *Sustainable Cities and Society, 41,* 568–575. doi:10.1016/j.scs.2018.05.017

Kosovac, A., Hartley, K., Acuto, M., & Gunning, D. (2020). *Conducting City Diplomacy: A Survey of International Engagement in 47 Cities.* Chicago, IL: Chicago Council on International Affairs and University of Melbourne.

Moragues-Faus, A. (2021). The emergence of city food networks: Rescaling the impact of urban food policies. *Food Policy, 103,* 102107. doi:10.1016/j.foodpol.2021.102107

Moragues-Faus, A., & Morgan, K. (2015). Reframing the foodscape: The emergent world of urban food policy. *Environment and Planning A, 47*(7), 1558–1573. doi:10.1177/0308518x15595754

MUFPP. (2020a). *Milan Pact Talks on Food Aid*. Retrieved from: www.milanurbanfoodpolicypact.org/milan-pact-talks-on-food-aid/

MUFPP. (2020b). *MUFPP 6° Online Global Forum & Milan Pact Talks 2020*. Video retrieved from: www.youtube.com/watch?v=siHHdRVX2YE&ab_channel=MilanUrbanFoodPolicyPact

MUFPP. (2020c). *Milan Pact Awards 2020*. Retrieved from: www.milanurbanfoodpolicypact.org/milan-pact-awards/milan-pact-awards-2020/

MUFPP, FAO, & ESTA. (2018). *Role of Cities in the Transformation of Food Systems: Sharing Lessons from Milan Pact Cities*. Retrieved from: www.fao.org/3/CA0912EN/ca0912en.pdf

Nairobi County, FAO, & C40. (2020). *Nairobi City County Food System Strategy*. Retrieved from: www.devolutionhub.or.ke/file/90185692-nairobi-city-county-food-system-stra.pdf

O'Connell, C., Gay, R., McDonald, N., & Tayal, S. (2021). COVID connections: Lessons from adaptations to COVID-19 as strategies for building food system resilience. *Culture, Agriculture, Food and Environment, 43*(2), 123–136. doi:10.1111/cuag.12276

Pipa, A. F., & Bouchet, M. (2020). Multilateralism restored? City diplomacy in the COVID-19 era. *The Hague Journal of Diplomacy, 15*(4), 599–610. doi:10.1163/1871191X-BJA10043

Pothukuchi, K., & Kaufman, J. L. (1999). Placing the food system on the urban agenda: The role of municipal institutions in food systems planning. *Agriculture and Human Values, 16*(2), 213–224. doi:10.1023/a:1007558805953

Pothukuchi, K., & Kaufman, J. L. (2000). The food system. *Journal of the American Planning Association, 66*(2), 113–124. doi:10.1080/01944360008976093

Résolis, J. (2015). *Systèmes alimentaires Territorialisés en France: 100 initiatives locales pour une alimentation responsable*. Retrieved from: https://resolis.org/journal/systemes-alimentaires-territorialises-en-france-100-initiatives-locales-pour-une-alimentation-responsable-et-durable/4586e8c6-bb4d-41ab-8ddb-ee3275137ec9

Résolis, J. (2016a). *Les systèmes alimentaires territorialisés en Méditerranée: Initiatives pour une alimentation responsable et durable*. Retrieved from: www.alimenterre.org/system/files/ressources/pdf/996-resolis-sat-mediterranee.pdf

Résolis, J. (2016b). *Sistemas alimentarios territorializados en Costa Rica: 100 iniciativas locales para la alimentación responsabley sostenible*. Retrieved from: www.alimenterre.org/system/files/ressources/pdf/995-resolis-sat-costa-rica.pdf

Résolis, J. (2016c). *Systèmes Alimentaires Territorialisés au Québec: 100 initiatives locales pour une alimentation responsable et durable*. Retrieved from: www.chaireunesco-adm.com/IMG/pdf/resolis_sat_quebec-2.pdf

Rikolto. (2020). *Covid-19 and Cities: Lessons on Maintaining Access to Good Food*. Retrieved from: www.rikolto.org/en/news/covid-19-and-cities-lessons-maintaining-access-good-food

Santo, R., & Horrigan, L. (2019). *Changing the Food System Takes More than Change: Stories of Funding Food Policy Councils*. Baltimore, MD: Food Policy Networks/Johns Hopkins Center for a Livable Future. Retrieved from: https://assets.jhsph.edu/clf/mod_clfResource/doc/Funding_guide_formatted_2021_01-05.pdf

Streck, C. (2002). Global public policy networks as coalitions for change. In D. Esty & M. Ivanova (Eds.), *Global Environmental Governance: Options and Opportunities*. New Haven, CT: Yale Center for Environmental Law and Policy.

Thilmany, D., Brislen, L., Edmondson, H., Gill, M., Jablonski, B. B. R., Rossi, J., ... & Schaffstall, S. (2021). Novel methods for an interesting time: Exploring U.S. local food systems' impacts and initiatives to respond to COVID. *Australian Journal of Agricultural and Resource Economics, 65*(4), 848–877. doi:10.1111/1467-8489.12456

Thulasiraman, V., Nandagopal, M. S. G., & Kothakota, A. (2021). Need for a balance between short food supply chains and integrated food processing sectors: COVID-19 takeaways from India. *Journal of Food Science and Technology, 58*(10), 3667–3675. doi:10.1007/s13197-020-04942-0

U20. (2020a). *Communiqué from the Urban 20 (U20)*. Retrieved from: www.urban20.org/wp-content/uploads/2020/10/U20-2020-Communique.pdf

U20. (2020b). *Empowering Cities for the Development of Sustainable Food System Policies*. Retrieved from: www.urban20.org/wp-content/uploads/2020/11/Empowering-Cities-for-the-Development-of-Sustainable-Food-System-Policies.pdf

U20. (2021). *Urban 20 Calls on G20 to Empower Cities to Ensure a Green and Just Recovery*. Retrieved from: www.urban20.org/wp-content/uploads/2021/06/U20-2021-Communique-Final.pdf

UCLG, UN-Habitat, & Metropolis. (2020). *Food Systems: Lessons from the Pandemic*. Retrieved from: www.uclg.org/sites/default/files/briefing_lle_food_systems-_pdf.pdf

UN. (2016). *The New Urban Agenda*. Retrieved from: https://uploads.habitat3.org/hb3/NUA-English.pdf

UNFSS. (2021). *Food Systems Summit Dialogues Official Feedback Form: Empowering Cities and Local Governments to Improve Food Systems Globally*. Retrieved from: https://summitdialogues.org/dialogue/24573/official-feedback-24573-en.pdf?t=1627637625

URBACT. (2022). *URBACT Networks*. Retrieved from: https://urbact.eu/all-networks?topic=82

Webb, P., Benton, T. G., Beddington, J., Flynn, D., Kelly, N. M., & Thomas, S. M. (2020). The urgency of food system transformation is now irrefutable. *Nature Food, 1*(10), 584–585. doi:10.1038/s43016-020-00161-0

Webster, P., & Sanderson, D. (2013). Healthy Cities indicators: A suitable instrument to measure health? *Journal of Urban Health, 90*(Suppl. 1), 52–61. doi:10.1007/s11524-011-9643-9

Willett, W., Rockström, J., Loken, B., Springmann, M., Lang, T., Vermeulen, S., … & Murray, C. J. L. (2019). Food in the Anthropocene: The EAT–Lancet Commission on healthy diets from sustainable food systems. *The Lancet*. doi:10.1016/S0140-6736(18)31788-4

PART V

Urban Food Governance Futures

28

TOWARDS GOVERNANCE FOR OPEN URBAN FOOD FUTURES

Jaz Hee-jeong Choi, Sara Heitlinger, Alex Taylor and Viktor Bedö

Introduction

We begin this chapter by acknowledging the immense challenges many people continue to face, further aggravated by the COVID-19 pandemic—a pandemic which we are still grappling with at the time of writing. To think about urban food governance now is not possible without acknowledging the deep structural fractures and failures as evidenced in the stark socio-economic and racial inequities amplified by COVID-19. Profound uncertainties and fear have led to panic-buying and hoarding for those able to afford it. At the same time, a sharp and sustained increase in food insecurity has been observed, leading to a myriad of consequences ranging from reduced physical activity of children to hunger and worsening mental well-being (Power et al., 2020).

The World Food Programme predicts that the continued impact of the pandemic will "exacerbate existing vulnerabilities, with the number of people suffering acute food insecurity likely to almost double from 135 million to 270 million" (World Food Programme, 2020, p. 7). These conditions raise the question of who had, and continues to have, secure access to resources, including appropriate food, shelter, and now "social-distance."

During the pandemic, the movement to and of food has come to be an especially significant concern, in particular for those who are already socio-economically marginalised across the world. For example, the impact of persistent and widespread mobility injustice became acutely evident in India when, in late 2020, a hard lockdown was rapidly enforced in response to the country's "first wave." Required to isolate within four hours, much of the population battled to return home or at least find places of refuge. Such a drastic restriction of mobility at street level posed an immediate challenge to local access to food (commonly acquired through local markets and street stalls), and significant threats to the livelihoods of people whose income is generated through local and informal supply chains.

These levels of deprivation and marginalisation stand in stark contrast with the opposite extreme: the obscene profits accrued within the oligopolistic global industrial food system, in which the planet's natural resources are enclosed and value is extracted and concentrated in the hands of a few individuals and multinational corporations (Woodall & Shannon, 2018). This presents a threat not just to personal livelihoods or individual life, but to the abundance of life

DOI: 10.4324/9781003055907-33

on the planet and whether it can be sustained. Today, one million species are threatened with extinction and over 75 per cent of all cultivated crop diversity has been lost (IPBES, 2019). These losses are rooted in anthropocentric activities driven by capitalist agendas, with industrial agriculture being a major driver, as demonstrated by the 1 per cent of farms that operate 70 per cent of the world's farmland (Watts, 2020), and four corporations controlling more than 50 per cent of the world's seeds (Shield, 2021).

While our chapter is not focused specifically on COVID-19, it is our ethical impetus as scholars at this point in history to acknowledge the manifold conditions of injustice that exacerbated the pandemic's impact, and that continue to shape the places we cohabit with other-than-human beings. We believe that action towards more liveable futures is only possible with an explicit acknowledgement of what we did not do, or what we did not know but should have. For urban food futures and its governance, such a need for critical inspection now feels more pressing than ever.

In the following, we will first examine the current uneven structural conditions of food governance. In particular, we will draw attention to the increasing reliance on cyber-physical systems to improve food production and supply at scale, yet they often exacerbate the unevenness, because they operate in the same structures of governance driven by capitalist agendas. Acknowledging the need for a radically different kind of governance, we will then introduce the notion of the commons as an alternative model centred on equity and evenness. Following this, we draw from emerging calls to seek new ways of questioning and relating, to move towards open, commons-based urban food futures, highlighting the need for scaling-out rather than scaling-up. We will put forward a case for transdisciplinary and creative practices as an inherent part of radical reimagining of food futures, as a means of raising questions rather than solving predefined or assumed problems, thereby creating spaces for new forms of governance to emerge, based on equity, justice, and pluralism.

Uneven Terrains of Urban Food Governance

Governance is concerned with sustaining structures and processes in accordance with certain sets of values and principles specific to the system in question. For food governance in cities, we might imagine the unrestricted and even flow of food to all should drive such structures and processes. However, the spatial configurations of cities and the imperative of growth act as immediate constraints in conforming to these values. As cities expand and megacities form, the food landscape fragments. Food production, supply, and consumption splinter and spread unevenly across urban, peri-urban, and rural terrains. This kind of fragmentation is often intensified by zoning policies and the limits of delivery services, as well as supply chain issues such as food hygiene and packaging. In effect, the city and megacity multiply the forms of distancing, to include not just the geographic but also the economic, cognitive, and political (Bricas, 2019). What results is an amalgam of variedly accessible, bounded food systems with different levels of possible mobilities within and between them.

Consider food production through farming as an example. This form of food production is challenged by an intensification of mobilities, in this case mobilities that concentrate flows and growth towards urban areas and towards capital-intensive food production. A growing number of studies (Daghagh Yazd et al., 2019; Hagen et al., 2019; Lunner Kolstrup et al., 2013) point to how the direction of travel from rural to urban, and the distances involved, render farming a particularly precarious form of livelihood. With small, local farms on the decline—as large, industry-scale food production intensifies—we see either the movement of a rural, agricultural labour force into urban or peri-urban areas, or reskilling amongst workers (particularly women) to find employment in the non-manual or service-oriented jobs of the city (Sanghi et al., 2015). Again, the structures of governance—both private and public—are the source of an unevenness dictating who travels to the sites of food production and also how those in rural areas are forced to respond (Marsden, 1995).

Unsurprisingly, technological systems promise to alleviate some of the pressures on the production, supply, and consumption of food, in effect optimising the structures and processes of food governance. The shrinking workforce in farming, for example, has been met with two major mitigation measures operating within a "smart farming" paradigm: precision agriculture and distributed ledger technologies. Central to precision agriculture is optimising efficiency and minimising the variability of food production through integrated data-driven technologies. Through a combination of networked sensors, cloud computing, and Artificial Intelligence, food production is constantly monitored, and adjustments can be made in response to any variance caused by environmental factors such as changes in temperature and water availability. Doing this at scale aims to compensate for a declining workforce while also reducing human harms such as the exposure to health hazards.

Aligning with this *productivist* model of food supply (Halfacree, 2007; Mather et al., 2006), distributed ledgers have been fast emerging as a dominant technological solution to the transparency and efficiency issues of the current global food systems. Offering a form of automated governance (though arguably free from governing), distributed ledger technologies use shared, synchronised, and replicated databases to authenticate and process transactions. This distributed approach to consensus can increase transparency, efficiency, and security of data processing, reducing the need for centralised or intermediary authorities. Considering some of the limitations of the legacy and current systems, if adopted, the approach has the potential for radical transformations in the political, economic, environmental and social foundations of society.

Yet such technological systems cannot fully address the unevenness of food production and supply. Even with optimised production logics and the possibilities of bypassing cumbersome governance procedures, challenges persist around who has the rights, and means of access, to innovations and "progress." For example, automation measures often assume and demand the baseline conditions of already digitally connected and large-scale systems to achieve their potential. The costs, however, of establishing and maintaining adequate digital access (including 5G and beyond, as well as new hardware and software requirements) can be unfeasible for smallholder farms, many of which are already facing emerging "climatic, health, price, and financial risks and challenges" (Fan & Rue, 2020, p. 14), further distancing them from the current and future opportunities to participate in food systems. Disparities are evident further "down" the food supply chain. The new technological infrastructures, heralding greater yields and efficiencies, serve only the upper-middle classes and elites of society who can capitalise on these technologies or pay the prices of food that is technologically validated as "quality" and "trustworthy."

The longer-term impact of technological infrastructures on food system ecologies is also uncertain. While optimising technologies have the potential to reduce the overall carbon emission in farming, the scale of reductions depends on the farm's size: bigger is better (Soto Embodas et al., 2019). Likewise, blockchain technologies evolve on the promise of more carbon efficient consensus mechanisms. However, they continue to accelerate extraction and rely on the exploitation of natural resources, as well as people at the socio-economic margins (Wang, 2020). The result, again, is an intensification of socio-economic inequalities.

A similar unevenness relating to how benefits are distributed by technological systems is evident in cities where most of human food consumption occurs. An illustrative case is the rapidly growing food delivery service sector. According to a report on the future of the last-mile delivery ecosystem by the World Economic Forum (2020), the food delivery sector is expected to grow by 10 per cent globally, contributing to the already increasing emissions from delivery traffic to reach 32 per cent over the next decade. The resulting rise in traffic congestion is expected to be 21 per cent, which equates to 11 additional minutes of daily commute time for each passenger. A decade of research has shown a direct correlation between longer commuting time and the decline in subjective well-being of the commuter (Nie & Sousa-Poza, 2018; Office for National Statistics, 2014; Olsson et al., 2013), and that those engaged in informal labour, such as women, are more negatively affected by long commuting time (Clark et al., 2020; Roberts et al., 2011).

Broadly speaking, we must recognise that the production and maintenance of technological systems—that govern the processes of production, supply, and consumption, ranging from blockchains to tracking sensors on chickens (Wang, 2020)—have intersecting and significant impacts on the environment and people. The consequences, though hard to disentangle, are stark:

> [E]nvironmental injustices and economic injustices are two faces of the same problem, each contributing to the other ... in the form of uneven distribution of access to transport, energy, and the fundamental life requirements of clean air, water, food, and shelter. These human [and nonhuman] rights are now ... riskily financialized as tradeable "ecosystem services."
>
> *Sheller, 2018, p. 16*

What we see here is that a greater dependence on such technology-led forms of food governance risks reinforcing rather than challenging the problematic systems and values of technocapitalism (Suarez-Villa, 2009, 2012) and further marginalising those already at the margins. Urban food governance must take a radically different form to be able to address these fundamental systemic concerns. Doing this, we argue, requires moving away from rendering foods as commodities and bolstering a paradigm shift to valuing and governing food as *commons*, fundamentally a social and cultural transformation towards justice and equity.

Commoning Food

Collectively and individually, the work we have been conducting as researchers has sought to respond to the inequities and injustices made visible through a prism of food governance. We take as a starting point the idea that the governing structures and processes that are being designed to optimise food supplies and meet demand, especially in densely populated spaces such as cities, are unsustainable. As we have discussed above, these self-same structures and processes are built on a scaling-up of production, supply, and consumption. This is a scaling-up built around consumption driving expansion and profit, and the corresponding wealth creation for the few. What the structures and processes of governance do little, if anything, to address is what alternatives there might be and how such alternatives might afford sustainable food futures for the many not just human but also other-than-human inhabitants of the spaces we inhabit.

What brings much of our work together is an interest in commoning, and in large part whether the commons might interject new structures and processes for governance. Here, we see the commons involve the inclusive practices of negotiating, managing, and maintaining accessible resources for the common good. This notion of the commons has been re-emerging as a radical governance paradigm for the past few decades, in response to the growing inequalities, contradictions, and threats of contemporary neoliberal and capitalistic societies (Savic et al., 2020). Shiva (2019, p. 233) presents a helpful frame for the commons when she declares, "a life support base can be shared; it cannot be owned as private property or exploited for private profit." This, she continues, provides an impetus for all to "have access to and responsibility for" the means of sustaining lives. We believe that this presents a compelling frame to apply to food governance and across food's production, supply, and consumption.

Commoning presents a useful expansion of the commons, drawing attention to the essential and ongoing work of putting the commons into practice. Linebaugh (2008, p. 279) argues, "the commons is an activity and, if anything, it expresses relationships in society that are inseparable from relations to nature. It might be better to keep the word as a verb, rather than as a noun, a substantive." Bollier and Helfrich in *Patterns of Commoning* (2015) map out the diverse and relational nature of the commons, stating that commoning is neither a punctual historical curiosity, nor confined to small face-to-face networks as a matter of course, "but a robust contemporary reality."

Food Commoning and Cyber-physical Systems

It is this ongoing and active process of constituting the commons—commoning—that we believe offers a different way to cut through the relationship between food governance and technology. To put it succinctly, our thinking is led by a shift away from the monolithic logic of *scaling-up* production and supply, intrinsic in profit-driven governance, and towards a *scaling-out*: a proliferation of diverse, commons-based food futures that prioritise equality and multi-species abundance, and often require imaginative experimentation and creative processes in restructuring social and ecological relations. From this perspective, we understand technology not merely as a solution to maximising yields or optimising supply chains in the interests of corporate expansion, but rather, we aim to see technology as a resource for scaling-out food commons, a resource that can not only provide pragmatic support but also create the conditions for diverse urban networks of producers, suppliers, and consumers, being responsive to the uneven terrains enacted through the *status quo* in food governance. We explain below.

Recurring patterns of food commoning paint a picture of "idiosyncratic creativity, improvisation, situational choices, and dynamic evolution" (Bollier & Helfrich, 2015). Taking into account different commons with different principles, interests, and scales operating in parallel with one another at all times is a new and significant challenge for urban food governance. Computing's growing capacity for automated learning, and transparent decision-making and implementation, even in complex, changing environments, may be able to provide some pragmatic support, as shown in projects such as Platform Cooperative Consortium[1] and P2P Models,[2] the blockchain-based platform for supporting commons-driven communities.

Many forms of urban food communing, such as community and allotment gardening, are hyperlocal, typically involving the most immediate neighbourhood. Technology might be used to compose cyber-physical systems that scale differently, not seeking only extraction but the ingredients for creative and experimental ways to form new conditions for food commons. Cyber-physical systems are "composed of interacting arrangements of digital information-processing systems, objects, humans, and environments" (Lawless et al., 2020, p. 342). As such, they can flexibly adapt to multiple aspects of food (ranging from practices to material) and scalar possibilities of food governance (ranging from hyperlocal to planetary), creating new conditions for food commoning. For example, the life of food as perishable material can fall into the operational governance of urban logistical platforms, which may favour and enforce standardisation and reduced diversity. When rescued edible food is ejected from the shops by logistics and health and safety regulations, it can still potentially enter a next stage of its life as commons, governed by different sets of rules, protocols, and processes. These may include culturally specific ways to prepare and consume food, and stewardship and long-term maintenance (Cardullo, 2018) of related place-specific infrastructures.

These "[n]on-cartographic concepts of scale are not a smooth zooming in and out but involve jumps and discontinuities" (Clark, 2012, p. 149). Here, differences in scale constitute differences of kind rather than degree. It raises questions about how they can be approached from the perspective of design and governance (Woods, 2014) of constellations of cyber-physical networks, and possible instruments and methods that can be used in the process. The scalar possibilities of such a perspective on food governance are not in one direction, "up" but, as we say, "out." Governance for food commons would thus benefit from moving away from the technocratic vision of progress measured by growth and scaling-up in production and profit. To genuinely realise the promises of commoning for sustainable and equitable futures, the focus of governance must be on enabling diverse commons that can support multiple, many new, relation buildings within and across themselves.

What we need is a fundamental shift in how the new conditions for urban food futures and governance can be imagined, built, and maintained, with and by whom. This under-explored epistemological and methodological intersection is where we see the key opportunities and challenges for future urban food governance. There is urgency to building capacity for radical speculations and imaginings. Speculation and alternative imaginaries about food as commons instead of commodity can identify a wide range of sites where food is ejected from its social life as commodity (Appadurai, 1986), and explore how these sites can be reclaimed, rebuilt, and repaired with and through the social practice of commoning. Doing this will help sustain an *open system* for new forms and trajectories of urban food governance to emerge.

Towards Open, Commons-based Food Futures

According to Sennett (Sennett, 2018, p. 5), an open system allows "for fitting together the odd, the curious, the possible," and are necessarily complex, experiential, adversarial, and importantly, learning and (therefore) evolving. The current surveil-and-control model, driven by algorithmic forecasting, flattens the richness of such complexities into patterns and sequences; it is fundamentally a closed system. Learning in the context of open systems involves building capacity in two inter-related domains: critical understanding of the current closed systems; and accepting that some things, especially those that are critical to sustainable futures, simply cannot be flattened or measured. For instance, endeavouring to flatten or measure "pleasure" in relation to producing, creating, and consuming food, and the socialising that accompanies these experiences, would likely be an impossible and futile exercise.

Central to this dual-capacity building in the context of food futures is radical (re-)imagining of urban food governance as described in the previous section. Creative arts offer rich and powerful potential for enabling this. Creative arts have proven their ability to reveal different ways for relating with, rather than othering, the unfamiliar, and for imagining multiple different futures, thereby helping people build capacities to cope with uncertainties and entanglements. In other words, they can empower people to become more aware of and move across geographic, economic, cognitive, and political distances (Bricas, 2019) to relate with one another, and to create open food systems based on equity, justice, pluralism, and care. This points to what we believe to be two critical objectives for future urban food governance:

1. Repairing and repurposing current closed systems to become more open; and
2. Building capacity in learning to cope with complex relational conditions, bringing with them uncertainties, differences, and emergence of the new.

Below we discuss these objectives in more detail. We will present examples that illustrate how the objectives can be addressed through and with creative practices, weaving them with Sennett's practical suggestions for assembling "synchronous, punctuated, porous, incomplete and multiple forms" (Sennett, 2018, p. 205) as an open system.

Repairing and Repurposing Closed Systems

Repairing and repurposing closed systems to make them more open must start with rich, nuanced insights into, and respect for, their existing operating conditions. This requires engaging with research methodologies that can help understand the complex relations that form socio-material interactions and infrastructures. This understanding helps us design things that we can, with some confidence, call both reparative and regenerative. Across disciplines, qualitative and creative methods of research and engagement are increasingly recognised for their potential to be deeply regenerative in various social conditions. Yet, continued concerns exist about how such methods and resulting data are designed to be used for "governing at a distance" (Rose & Miller, 2010, p. 271). This means that the process loosely but unmistakably fits into the prefigured "sequence of linked activity ... a seamlessly connected chain of problem-research-data-analysis-policy-solution." Following the sequence, by the time the policy informed by the research outcomes is being applied, the initial conditions have already changed, diminishing the potential impact and relevance of the solutions (Torrance, 2018, p. 734).

This critique is a useful caution for us to take seriously the need to reframe research and data as emergent and relational. The *process* of doing research—often through multiple forms of engagement with multiple stakeholders—is equally valuable, if not moreso, to its outcomes such as data and insights. This also indicates that there is real danger in simply applying established methods or cookie-cutter tools of scientific and creative inquiry, expecting richer insights that can lead to regenerative transformation towards openness; this is unfortunately an all-too-familiar image of the so-called design thinking or design innovation, a discourse widely adopted by the public and private sectors alike but increasingly being criticised for this precise reason. Instead, the process should morph dynamically and dialogically with changing conditions that shape, and are shaped by, the research. The reciprocal and process-centred nature of participatory and co-creative engagements can strengthen and establish feedback loops to question "what might work," instead of "what works," and help avoid reinforcing "the policy status quo, the already-assumed-to-be-perfect solution which is built into the evaluation and feedback procedure of a closed system" (Torrance, 2018, p. 739).

This also highlights that honouring indigenous knowledges and practices in epistemological reimagining is not only beneficial but also crucial. For example, Kimmerer's *Braiding Sweetgrass* (2013) brings together her ways of knowing as a botanist and a member of the Citizen Potawatomi Nation, demonstrating the power of pluralist and reciprocal knowledge making. Kimmerer (2013, p. 368) writes:

> We do indeed stand at the crossroads. Scientific evidence tells us we are close to the tipping point of climate change, the end of fossil fuels, the beginning of resource depletion ... In the valleys below the hill, I see the people of the Seventh Fire walking towards the crossroads with all they have gathered. They carry in their bundles the previous seeds for a change of worldview. Not so they can return to some atavistic utopia, but to find the tools that allow us to walk into the future. So much has been forgotten, but it is not lost as long as the land endures and we cultivate people who have the humility to and ability to listen and learn. And the people are not alone. All

along the path, nonhuman people help. What knowledge the people have forgotten is remembered by the land. The others want to live, too.

A notable characteristic of indigenous cultures is the embeddedness of arts and creative practices as regenerative means for knowledge sharing and making through generations, often through storytelling. For example, Fujikane's *Mapping Abundance for a Planetary Future: Kanaka Maoli and Critical Settler Cartographies in Hawai'i* (2021), challenging the settler capitalism centred on the notion of scarcity, was a culmination of the author's deep engagement with Kanaka Maoli scholars, activists, artists, and cultural practitioners through a wide range of activities and events.

Building Capacity for Learning and (therefore) Evolving

Reparative and regenerative agendas, as outlined above, call for co-creative approaches to making interventions that do not replace or remove the existing, or formalise informal, relations, but enable new ones in ways that are respectful of the existing conditions. Fundamentally, this could mean actively endeavouring to decolonise systems of knowledge, particularly as colonialism has been at the root of ongoing socio-ecological crises (Liboiron, 2021; Mahony & Endfield, 2018). Practically, this could mean conducting smaller but multiple interventions that encourage experimenting with different relationships, dialogues, and agreements within the particular community, prompting new forms of governance, providing much-needed learning opportunities for all stakeholders, thereby strengthening resilience for uncertainty (Sennett, 2018; Torrance, 2018).

An illustrative case is the Connected Seeds Library (Heitlinger et al., 2018), an ongoing community resource resulting from participatory design research which took place in east London over 18 months. The project involved local and community-level engagements with different stakeholders such as urban growers, organisers, activists, and technologists. It drew on their different knowledges and experiences to experiment with the potential for the Internet of Things (IoTs) to play a role in sustainable cities through seed-sovereignty, increasing biodiversity, knowledge sharing, and community building. Through this long-term engagement, participants developed knowledge and skills in using digital technologies and urban farming and cultivated social connection and community-building. A co-created outcome of the process was a free mobile seed library with a digital audio function and photographs for each seed (Figure 28.1). It is still in operation, allowing people to physically interact with the library to learn more about the seeds and growing them; take seeds home or bring some back to maintain the living stock; and keep the library and community growing through ongoing engagements.

Co-creative methods are increasingly used to decentre the human in urban contexts (Clarke, 2020; Forlano, 2016) and to provide inclusive means for engaging people who have the different levels of technical knowledge required for imagining and designing fairer food futures (Dolejšová et al., 2020). These kinds of co-creative speculative projects take into account the complex socio-technical networks that evolve with the changing values and contexts of specific communities, including those who may not otherwise have access to, or understanding of, emerging technologies or food systems (for a detailed example, see Chapter 30 by Heitlinger et al. in this volume). They create spaces for collaborative exploration of many different possible futures, while at the same time interrogating issues of ethics, values, and social interactions, and the consequences of technologies on these.

Figure 28.1 The Connected Seeds Library

Along with diverse locally specific matters, urban food governance must also address the need to build capacity to grasp and respond to broader concerns—for example, those emanating from societal and planetary crises that are already taking place and will increase with deteriorating ecological and social conditions. Doing so requires more expansively speculative, and at times spectacular, engagements, to bring about larger ontological change. The engagements must be able to raise deeper questions about the more-than-human worlds, and shift different values and paradigms with a common aim of de-centring humans, ultimately creating spaces for *pluriversal* (Escobar, 2018, 2020) thinking, feeling, and action. Within the specific context of urban food governance, this may include taking seriously the possibility of other-than-humans having a voice and a stake in urban food systems, as a way of addressing the inequalities and power imbalances within the global industrial food systems.

An example of creative work that engages people to question and shift familiar values and paradigms is *Feral Atlas: The More-than-Human Anthropocene*.[3] It is an online platform, which resulted from a multi-year curatorial project by Tsing and colleagues (2020), involving over 100 scientists, humanists, and artists to explore "un-designed effects of human infrastructures." It presents rich detail on what has become "feral," which refers to something that was once recognised as part of human infrastructures but has since evolved out of human control. An example is camels imported to Australia in the nineteenth century, to be used as transport across desert. With the introduction of locomotives, over time they were abandoned, grew in large numbers in areas less visible to human infrastructures, and are now violently killed en masse through "feral culling." Instead of mapping and providing standardised definitions for each "feral entity," Feral Atlas encourages the viewer to reflect on the more-than-human relations that render it feral by playfully and, in their own ways, exploring cross-disciplinary, field-based, and historically grounded texts, artworks, and media.

Other examples include *Mitigation of Shock* (2017–2019) and *Refuge for Resurgence* (2021) by the design studio Superflux. These life-sized installations recreating, respectively, a London apartment set in the future transformed by food insecurity and climate extremities; and a large table designed for multi-species (humans, snake, a beaver, a raven, a wasp, a mushroom, a fox, a wolf, a wild boar, an old cow, a rat, and a pigeon) commensality in a speculative post-Anthropocene world (Figure 28.2).

By immersing themselves in these para-natural multisensory environments, audiences are invited to question their "sense of stability in and mastery over the world, and to reveal the 'true' nature of our subjectivity as fragmented and decentred [and, as a result, become more] equipped to negotiate our actions in the world and with other people" (Bishop, 2005, p. 133) as a result.

Figure 28.2 Refuge for Resurgence (2021) by Superflux

Conclusions

This chapter came to existence during the COVID-19 pandemic, when socio-ecological fractures and fragilities became rapidly amplified. The pandemic exacerbated the already existing conditions that enabled the growing socio-economic divide. Now more people face food insecurity and poverty as a result. Witnessing this provided us, the authors of this chapter, with an impetus to carefully assess opportunities and perils of socio-technical networks supposedly equipped to provide more certainty, which would in turn move the world towards more sustainable and liveable futures. Doing so revealed the unevenness in food systems offering different levels of possible mobilities, within and between them, to different people. Cyber-physical systems rapidly grow in their data-processing power, promising greater transparency and solutions to complex problems across varied urban contexts. Yet, dependence on technology-led forms of food governance risks reinforcing the unevenness in the access to, and mobilities within, the current food systems built on the values of techno-capitalism, further marginalising those already at the margins. We argued for a need to cut through the relationship between food governance and techno-capitalism and suggested a shift of focus from scaling-up to scaling-out, and from reliance on computing to building capacity in imagining and creating a radically new commons-based paradigm for urban food governance.

Building on Sennett's (2018) account of the ethics of designing open systems, we then identified the need to ensure more openness in food infrastructures, which necessarily evolve through experimentation. Creative practices provide a strategic and urgently needed space to expand speculative and imaginative possibilities for such experimentations. Consequently, we made two directional suggestions for urban food governance: first, it must form reparative and regenerative agendas by engaging with research methodologies to achieve a rich, nuanced understanding of existing conditions, focusing on the diverse relations that form socio-material interactions and infrastructures; and second, it must build capacities for learning to make, through co-creative and participatory engagements, interventions that enable new relations in ways that are respectful of the existing conditions, thereby increasing infrastructural resilience. In addition, we argued that the capacity building must extend to coping with large-scale uncertainties and potential crises, which requires expansively speculative and potentially spectacular engagements to bring about ontological change, ultimately creating spaces for pluriversal (Escobar, 2018, 2020) thinking, feeling, and action.

Imagining food futures is at the centre of life of all intelligent species. It is a matter of livelihood and vitality to ensure sustainable food futures for oneself and one's social groups in different scales through times of varying needs—for example, climatic seasons, times of war, natural disasters, and health crises. The need and desire to imagine futures to secure appropriate amounts and kinds of food have been expressed in art and rituals from prehistory right up to the present day. Transdisciplinary and creative practices provide spaces for new forms of governance to emerge through radical, diverse questioning rather than solving problems predefined or assumed by a few. They can lead to ontological and collective transformation towards open urban food futures, and therefore must be considered an inherent part of food governance.

Notes

1 https://platform.coop/
2 https://p2pmodels.eu
3 https://feralatlas.org

References

Appadurai, A. (1986). *The Social Life of Things: Commodities in Cultural Perspective*. Cambridge: Cambridge University Press.

Bishop, C. (2005). *Installation Art: A Critical History*. London: Tate Publishing.

Bollier, D., & Helfrich, S. (2015). *Patterns of Commoning*. Amherst, MA: Levellers Press. Retrieved from https://patternsofcommoning.org/overture-2/

Bricas, N. (2019). Urbanization Issues Affecting Food System Sustainability. In C. Brand, N. Bricas, D. Conaré, B. Daviron, J. Debru, L. Michel, & C.-T. Soulard (Eds.), *Designing Urban Food Policies: Concepts and Approaches* (pp. 1–25). Cham: Springer International Publishing.

Cardullo, P. (2018). *Commoning the Smart City: A Case for a Public Internet Provision*.

Clark, B., Chatterjee, K., Martin, A., & Davis, A. (2020). How Commuting Affects Subjective Wellbeing. *Transportation, 47*(6), 2777–2805. doi:10.1007/s11116-019-09983-9

Clark, T. (2012). Derangements of Scale. *Telemorphosis: Theory in the Era of Climate Change, 1*, 148–166.

Clarke, R. E. (2020). Ministry of Multispecies Communications. *Paper presented at the Companion Publication of the 2020 ACM Designing Interactive Systems Conference, Eindhoven, Netherlands.* https://doi.org/10.1145/3393914.3395845

Daghagh Yazd, S., Wheeler, S. A., & Zuo, A. (2019). Key Risk Factors Affecting Farmers' Mental Health: A Systematic Review. *International Journal of Environmental Research and Public Health, 16*(23), 4849. doi:10.3390/ijerph16234849

Dolejšová, M., v. Gaalen, S., Wilde, D., Raven, P. G., Heitlinger, S., & Light, A. (2020). Designing with More-than-Human Food Practices for Climate-Resilience. *Paper presented at the Companion Publication of the 2020 ACM Designing Interactive Systems Conference, Eindhoven, Netherlands.* https://doi.org/10.1145/3393914.3395909

Escobar, A. (2018). *Designs for the Pluriverse: Radical Interdependence, Autonomy, and the Making of Worlds*. Durham, NC: Duke University Press.

Escobar, A. (2020). *Pluriversal Politics: The Real and the Possible: Latin America in Translation/En Traducción/Em Tradução* (pp. 1 online resource (xl, 192 pages)). Retrieved from www.degruyter.com/isbn/9781478012108

Fan, S., & Rue, C. (2020). The Role of Smallholder Farms in a Changing World. In S. G. y. Paloma, L. Riesgo, & K. Louhichi (Eds.), *The Role of Smallholder Farms in Food and Nutrition* Security. Cham: Springer.

Forlano, L. (2016). Decentering the Human in the Design of Collaborative Cities. *Design Issues, 32*(3), 42–54. doi:10.1162/DESI_a_00398

Fujikane, C. (2021). *Mapping Abundance for a Planetary Future: Kanaka Maoli and Critical Settler Cartographies in Hawai'I* (pp. 1 online resource (321 pages)). Retrieved from https://ebookcentral.proquest.com/lib/mit/detail.action?docID=6452820

Hagen, B. N. M., Albright, A., Sargeant, J., Winder, C. B., Harper, S. L., O'Sullivan, T. L., & Jones-Bitton, A. (2019). Research Trends in Farmers' Mental Health: A Scoping Review of Mental Health Outcomes and Interventions among Farming Populations Worldwide. *PLoS One, 14*(12), e0225661. doi:10.1371/journal.pone.0225661

Halfacree, K. (2007). Trial by Space for a 'Radical Rural': Introducing Alternative Localities, Representations and Lives. *Journal of Rural Studies, 23*(2), 125–141. https://doi.org/10.1016/j.jrurstud.2006.10.002

Heitlinger, S., Bryan-Kinns, N., & Comber, R. (2018). Connected Seeds and Sensors: Co-designing Internet of Things for Sustainable Smart Cities with Urban Food-Growing Communities. In *Proceedings of the 15th Participatory Design Conference: Short Papers, Situated Actions, Workshops and Tutorial—Volume 2, Hasselt and Genk, Belgium*. https://doi.org/10.1145/3210604.3210620

IPBES. (2019). *Global Assessment Report on Biodiversity and Ecosystem Services*. Bonn, Germany: IPBES secretariat.

Kimmerer, R. W. (2013). *Braiding Sweetgrass: Indigenous Wisdom, Scientific Knowledge and the Teachings of Plants* (1st ed.). Minneapolis, MN: Milkweed Editions.

Lawless, W., Mittu, R., & Sofge, D. (2020). *Human-Machine Shared Contexts*. San Diego, CA: Elsevier Science & Technology.

Liboiron, M. (2021). *Pollution Is Colonialism* (pp. 1 online resource (217 pages)). Retrieved from https://ebookcentral.proquest.com/lib/mit/detail.action?docID=6527589

Linebaugh, P. (2008). *The Magna Carta Manifesto: Liberties and Commons for All*. Berkeley, CA: University of California Press.

Lunner Kolstrup, C., Kallioniemi, M., Lundqvist, P., Kymäläinen, H. R., Stallones, L., & Brumby, S. (2013). International Perspectives on Psychosocial Working Conditions, Mental Health, and Stress of Dairy Farm Operators. *Journal of Agromedicine, 18*(3), 244–255. doi:10.1080/1059924x.2013.796903

Mahony, M., & Endfield, G. (2018). Climate and Colonialism. *WIREs Climate Change, 9*(2), e510. https://doi.org/10.1002/wcc.510

Marsden, T. (1995). Beyond Agriculture? Regulating the New Rural Spaces. *Journal of Rural Studies, 11*(3), 285–296. https://doi.org/10.1016/0743-0167(95)00027-K

Mather, A. S., Hill, G., & Nijnik, M. (2006). Post-productivism and Rural Land Use: Cul de Sac or Challenge for Theorization? *Journal of Rural Studies, 22*(4), 441–455. https://doi.org/10.1016/j.jrurstud.2006.01.004

Nie, P., & Sousa-Poza, A. (2018). Commute Time and Subjective Well-being in Urban China. *China Economic Review, 48*, 188–204. https://doi.org/10.1016/j.chieco.2016.03.002

Office for National Statistics. (2014). *Commuting and Personal Well-being, 2014*. Retrieved from www.ons.gov.uk/ons/dcp171766_351954.pdf

Olsson, L. E., Gärling, T., Ettema, D., Friman, M., & Fujii, S. (2013). Happiness and Satisfaction with Work Commute. *Social Indicators Research, 111*(1), 255–263. doi:10.1007/s11205-012-0003-2

Power, M., Doherty, B., Pybus, K., & Pickett, K. (2020). How COVID-19 has Exposed Inequalities in the UK Food System: The Case of UK Food and Poverty. *Emerald Open Research, 2*, 11. doi:10.35241/emeraldopenres.13539.2

Roberts, J., Hodgson, R., & Dolan, P. (2011). "It's Driving Her Mad": Gender Differences in the Effects of Commuting on Psychological Health. *Journal of Health Economics, 30*(5), 1064–1076. https://doi.org/10.1016/j.jhealeco.2011.07.006

Rose, N., & Miller, P. (2010). Political Power beyond the State: Problematics of Government. *The British Journal of Sociology, 61*(s1), 271–303. https://doi.org/10.1111/j.1468-4446.2009.01247.x

Sanghi, S., Srija, A., & Vijay, S. S. (2015). Decline in Rural Female Labour Force Participation in India: A Relook into the Causes. *Vikalpa, 40*(3), 255–268. doi:10.1177/0256090915598264

Savic, S., Bedö, V., Büsse, M., Martins, Y., & Miyazaki, S. (2020). Toys for Conviviality: Situating Commoning, Computation and Modelling. *Open Cultural Studies, 4*(1), 143–153. doi:10.1515/culture-2020-0015

Sennett, R. (2018). *Building and Dwelling: Ethics for the City* (1st American Ed.). New York: Farrar, Straus and Giroux.

Sheller, M. (2018). *Mobility Justice: The Politics of Movement in an Age of Extremes*. London: Verso.

Shield, C. (2021). Seed Monopolies: Who Controls the World's Food Supply? DW, 8 April. Retrieved from www.dw.com/en/agriculture-seeds-seed-laws-agribusinesses-climate-change-food-security-seed-sovereignty-bayer/a-57118595

Shiva, V. (2019). Resources. In W. Sachs (Ed.), *The Development Dictionary: A Guide to Knowledge as Power* (pp. 263–277). London: Zed Books.

Soto Embodas, I., Barnes, A., Balafoutis, A., Beck, B., Sanchez Fernandez, B., Vangeyte, J., & Gomez-Barbero, M. (2019). *The Contribution of Precision Agriculture Technologies to Farm Productivity and the Mitigation of Greenhouse Gas Emissions in the EU*. Retrieved from https://publications.jrc.ec.europa.eu/repository/handle/JRC112505

Suarez-Villa, L. (2009). *Technocapitalism: A Critical Perspective on Technological Innovation and Corporatism* [text] (pp. 1 online resource (230 p.)).

Suarez-Villa, L. (2012). *Globalization and Technocapitalism: The Political Economy of Corporate Power and Technological Domination*. Burlington, VT: Ashgate.

Torrance, H. (2018). Data as Entanglement: New Definitions and Uses of Data in Qualitative Research, Policy, and Neoliberal Governance. *Qualitative Inquiry, 25*(8), 734–742. doi:10.1177/1077800418807239

Tsing, A. L., Deger, J., Keleman Saxena, A., & Zhou, F. (Producer). (2020). *Feral Atlas: The More-than-Human Anthropocene*. Retrieved from http://feralatlas.org/index.html

Wang, X. (2020). *Blockchain Chicken Farm: And Other Stories of Tech in China's Countryside*. New York: Farrar, Straus and Giroux.

Watts, J. (2020). 1% of Farms Operate 70% of World's Farmland. *The Guardian*, 24 November. Retrieved from www.theguardian.com/environment/2020/nov/24/farmland-inequality-is-rising-around-the-world-finds-report

Woodall, P., & Shannon, T. L. (2018). Monopoly Power Corrodes Choice and Resiliency in the Food System. *The Antitrust Bulletin, 63*(2), 198–221. doi:10.1177/0003603X18770063

Woods, D. (2014). *Scale Critique for the Anthropocene*. Durham, NC: Duke University Press.

World Economic Forum. (2020). *The Future of the Last-Mile Ecosystem: Transition Roadmaps for Public- and Private-Sector Players*. Retrieved from www3.weforum.org/docs/WEF_Future_of_the_last_mile_ecosystem.pdf

World Food Programme. (2020). *Responding to the Development Emergency Caused by COVID-19: WFP's Medium-term Programme Framework*. Retrieved from https://docs.wfp.org/api/documents/WFP-0000117124/download/

29

EMBEDDING FUTURES IN URBAN FOOD GOVERNANCE

Participatory Foresight in Eindhoven and Kyoto

Aniek Hebinck, Joost Vervoort, Astrid Mangnus and Steven R. McGreevy

Introduction

The urban food system is considered a promising site for transformative change and has gained both civil and public interest in recent years (Hebinck et al., 2021; Moragues-Faus & Morgan, 2015). Urban food systems are recognised as boundary-spanning systems and provide a starting point for integrated governance towards sustainability at the city region level (Candel & Pereira, 2017; Elmqvist et al., 2019). However, urban food systems are characterised by several challenges that need to be navigated to fulfil this promise: such as a high density of diverse food actors and activities; disparate and contesting claims, needs and perspectives on food, sustainability, and the urban system; and involvement of multiple sectors and governance departments (Moragues-Faus, 2020).

The use of participatory futuring practices to address the challenge of food systems transformations is a notable trend in food governance at various scales (Mangnus et al., 2019; Sellberg et al., 2020; Zurek et al., 2021). But using participatory futures to imagine and then effectively contribute to transformations is a challenging task that involves taking many factors into account. A key reason to engage with participatory futuring approaches is to include diverse perspectives towards desired food systems change and understandings of sustainability (Hebinck & Page, 2017). Participatory futuring practices are used to imagine and deliberate possible futures, with the express goal of guiding food systems governance. Goals often include providing concrete insights into how to shape pathways of change (Hebinck et al., 2018; Sellberg et al., 2020), and/or how to navigate the complexity and dynamism of food systems (Henrichs et al., 2010). Such strategic insights are especially salient for cities, which are faced with challenges such as climate change impacts and persistent social inequities (Elmqvist et al., 2019). Anticipatory governance practices can contribute to longer-term policy visions and decision-making and provide an impetus to new forms of social, economic, and political organisation (Boyd et al., 2015). Here,

DOI: 10.4324/9781003055907-34

we define anticipatory governance as any governance processes that attempt to take the future into account in present day decision-making (Vervoort & Gupta, 2018).

This chapter unpacks the use of participatory futuring and how such practices contribute to urban food governance. For this purpose, we interrogate case studies that featured the use of participatory foresight for urban food governance in Eindhoven, the Netherlands and in Kyoto, Japan. However, first, we explore foresight and anticipatory governance, which results in a framework of key points for reflection. We use these key points to assess the use of foresight in the two cases and reflect on their impact on urban food governance. In doing so, we explore what type of futures are developed, how they contribute to actionable knowledge and how this is taken up into governance arrangements. These provide useful insights into how participatory foresight can be utilised in urban food governance. Lastly, we discuss several points that we consider paramount for anticipatory governance in urban food governance.

Principles of participatory futures

To plan strategically in the face of uncertain futures, more and more people and organisations turn towards strategic foresight (Boyd et al., 2015; Vervoort & Gupta, 2018; Wiebe et al., 2018). Foresight is a term for a large and diverse collection of methods and practices used to explore the future in structured and consistent ways, often for the purpose of making plans, policies, strategies, and investments (Dufva & Ahlqvist, 2015; Jemala, 2010). A popular approach to foresight is the creation of multiple futures, which are considered as equally relevant, to engage with uncertainty and the plurality of societal needs and interests and to challenge currently dominant ideas about the future (Muiderman et al., 2020). In this section on principles, we map some archetypal approaches to engaging with the future, and then discuss other factors: contextual and institutional factors that shape the possibility space for urban food futures; process organisation and the who, what, and when of futures work; futures methods; and the challenge of evaluating the impacts and contributions of a futures process.

Engaging with the future: four archetypical approaches

It is important to be aware that there are fundamentally different ways to engage with the future, and what the future means for the present (Muiderman et al., 2020). Muiderman et al. (ibid.) outline four basic approaches.

1. *Probable futures*: This approach sees the future as something that should be predicted – and that any future risk should be mitigated (ibid.). It is often connected to quantitative modelling approaches to futuring that assess (im)probable futures, such as the work of the Intergovernmental Panel on Climate Change. This first approach is strongly associated with linear planning. In urban food systems contexts, where uncertainties are high and many actors are involved in creating transformative dynamics, this kind of linear, command-and-control, risk-mitigation planning is often of limited use. However, experience shows that many decision makers take this perspective on the future implicitly, so it is important to be aware of it and challenge it when necessary. In addition, carefully assigning likelihood to some aspects of the future, such as climate scenarios or population growth, may be useful, especially when uncertainties are reflexively considered.
2. *Plausible futures*: the second approach sees the future as fundamentally and deeply uncertain and thus futures as plausible, rather than probable. This approach is based on complex systems thinking, the realisation that everything is interconnected, and that all these

connected systems are always changing, often in unexpected ways. Consider, for instance, how extreme climate events may interact with political turmoil. In the face of such deep uncertainty, this approach encourages 'practicing' with different future scenarios – not to predict them, but to test the general adaptive capacities of the organisations and systems we want to maintain. 'Explorative' or 'contextual' scenarios are often core to this foresight work. Such scenarios offer different representations of what could happen in the world, whether decision makers like these developments or not. Such scenarios discuss issues like climate change, economic instability, political and cultural developments (Henrichs et al., 2010; Wilkinson & Eidinow, 2008). Contextual or explorative scenarios are often used to critique or challenge the assumptions made in plans and policies, offering ways to improve such plans (Vervoort et al., 2014).

3. *Pluralistic futures*: The third approach describes futures as fundamentally pluralistic, as different societal groups have different desires and ambitions in relation to the future. It is most interested in 'normative' or desirable futures or visions to understand the development of different desired futures as a fundamentally political activity. One popular method in this approach is to develop a vision as an end point, and then develop plans and steps to reach it, or alternatively, to 'back-cast' from this future to work out steps in reverse (Robinson et al., 2011). A more recent development is the creation of 'transformation pathways': goal-oriented scenarios that are informed by theory about transformation or transition and that describe nonlinear processes of systems change (Mangnus et al., 2019; Vervoort et al., 2014).
4. *Performative futures*: The fourth approach critically examines imaginaries and how they provide space for voices currently not included. Here, futures are considered part of the social bedrock of societies: 'social imaginaries' are collectively held and institutionally embedded images of the future (Jasanoff & Kim, 2015). An example of a social imaginary is 'the smart city', with everything that that idea entails. This approach is less often used in an active mode to create new futures – it is mostly used to investigate and unpack existing, dominant ideas about the future and their performativity, critiquing them to open new spaces for more inclusive, democratic imaginings of the future (through one of the other approaches).

Currently, foresight practitioners propose a combination of different approaches for the generation of actionable insights for governance (Henrichs et al., 2010; Kok et al., 2017; Vervoort et al., 2014). In uncertain, dynamic, multi-stakeholder urban food contexts the *probable futures* approach is not generally very useful, as this approach demands specific types of data that may not be available, while a combination of *pluralistic futures* (making desirable futures to motivate action) and *plausible futures* (making challenging contextual futures) can be very powerful, as it allows for challenging and 'stress-testing' the developed visions (Vervoort et al., 2014). This way, plural desirable futures can be imagined and then challenged in terms of their assumptions by scenarios that are solely created to offer critique. The fourth, the *performative futures* approach, is useful for critical interrogation of futures, but is less strategically oriented.

Additionally, as people tend to operate from one of these four approaches (whether they are aware or unaware themselves), recognition of this positionality is key. For instance, a foresight process is set up by people who see the future as diverse, depending on societal perspectives, and fundamentally political (the pluralistic futures approach). When they try to involve policymakers who operate in a prediction mode (probable futures), these different ideas about the future must be bridged somehow before collaboration can happen. Self-awareness and reflexivity about what approach to the future seems natural are important skills to someone who is planning to lead urban food foresight. So is an understanding of where the other participants are coming from. According to Mangnus, Oomen et al. (2021), reflexivity about our own and others' perspectives to the future is an essential to 'futures literacy' – the ability to understand, and to generate, diverse futures.

Creating societal impact: the importance of governance contexts for futures

The potential for futures work to contribute to urban food systems transformations depends on how such processes are embedded in, and connected to, their governance contexts. The notion of 'anticipatory governance' describes efforts to bring the exploration of potential futures into present-day governance processes (Vervoort & Gupta, 2018). This concept originates from the context of responsible research and innovation, connected to work around futures (Guston, 2014). Anticipatory governance has the potential to be used more widely to think critically about the use of foresight in contributing to more resilient, inclusive, reflexive, and strategic governance (Boyd et al., 2015; Vervoort & Gupta, 2018). Foresight can be understood as boundary work between the perspectives of different societal actors who exchange their ideas about the future. Key criteria for boundary work developed by Cash et al. (2003) are *credibility* (are the future scenarios or visions believable, are their sources credible?); *legitimacy* (are the future scenarios or visions supported widely by relevant stakeholders?); and *salience* (are the scenarios or visions relevant to key stakeholders? do they grab their attention?). It is important to realise that credibility, legitimacy, and salience may look different for different groups of people (Kunseler et al., 2015), especially if they have fundamentally different ideas about the future (see the four approaches).

Building on this understanding of foresight as boundary work, several contextual factors that are crucial for foresight need to be considered. Careful consideration of the context in which foresight takes place is paramount for effective and inclusive anticipatory governance. Ideally, anticipatory processes are institutionally supported and embedded, and build on social dynamics that are inclusive, ambitious and able to mobilise relevant actors (Hebinck et al., 2018; Vervoort & Gupta, 2018). However, such an ideal-type context for anticipatory governance is often difficult to achieve. Settings with less supportive or stable institutional contexts are often the ones most urgently in need of change (Pereira et al., 2020). But even if the context is 'ideal', the capacity to reflect effectively on futures work is not a given in governance: First, there is tension between the complexity of the practice of futuring and the day-to-day politics that demand knowledge in a more accessible and simpler format (Boyd et al., 2015). Second, the capacities needed to engage in meaningful anticipatory governance vary across institutional bodies operating at different scales. The use of foresight in less-than-ideal conditions is explored by Mangnus et al. (2021) who confirm that foresight interventions can be a powerful way to open seemingly difficult institutional conditions, when the institutional context, participatory culture, process design, and futures methodology are combined in strategic ways. Nevertheless, it is difficult to create these circumstances and many foresight activities are started in the middle of ongoing change processes or projects. In such conditions, it is worth considering carefully how the right approaches, process framing, and process leaders can still open unforeseen possibilities for change (Mangnus, Vervoort et al., 2021). Here, the foresight expert or researcher can even decide to take up an action-oriented and leading role (Hebinck et al., 2018), with a spectrum of possible engagements: from facilitating a foresight process in terms of methods, to helping facilitate the larger process of policy or strategy guidance, all the way to the researcher themselves becoming champions for the foresight-based strategy development (ibid.).

Analytical approach

To uncover the use of participatory futuring and how these practices contribute to urban food governance, we turn to two case studies: the case of developing an urban agriculture strategy for the Dutch city Eindhoven, and a Japanese case in Kyoto that utilised project-based futuring to establish a food policy council. These case studies are distinct in terms of geography, governance context, and culture, but have in common that they featured a participatory process with diverse futuring practices around the future of urban food. To assess how these cases differently engage with the future and how this has resulted in societal impact, we lean on several questions that surface from Vervoort and Gupta (2018) and Hebinck et al. (2018), which they argue are vital for effective foresight and anticipatory governance:

Urban food context

- Why is the foresight process undertaken?
- What is the mandate and the transformative ambition level?
- What are the contextual opportunities and barriers for using foresight for urban food transformation?

Organisation

- Who funds and leads the foresight process?
- Who among the urban food actors and stakeholders needs to be involved?
- How is the process designed in terms of timing, engagement, platforms?

Approach to urban food futuring and methods

- Which approach(es) (1 to 4) are used to engage with the future?
- What method(s) are used to engage with the future?
- How do methods connect to the governance context?

Evaluation of changes in urban food systems and governance

- What is the change in the transformative ambition level?
- How did perspectives and/or behaviours of actors change?
- What is taken up into governance in terms of arrangements or capacities?

Using data collected during the projects TRANSMANGO and FEAST (see more detail in the case descriptions), the futures developed during workshops, and the workshop reporting, we do a post-workshop evaluation of the commonalities and differences in the two case studies. Through the above-mentioned questions, we can compare the two processes, which leads us to unpacking what type of futures are developed, in what way they contribute to actionable knowledge, and how this is taken up into governance arrangements.

Case 1: A strategy for urban agriculture in Eindhoven

Urban food context

Civil activities around the themes of urban food and sustainability proliferated quickly in the city region of Eindhoven. Although ample activity took place, Eindhoven did not have an established food policy. Instead, technological innovation, design, and entrepreneurship continue to be flagship themes in Eindhoven.[1] However, to capture and better support these emerging civil activities in urban food, a participatory process of little under a year was initiated in autumn 2015 to capture the potential role of urban agriculture to shape a more sustainable city. The overall idea being that policy support for these ongoing and emerging practices would eventually help the city of Eindhoven become more sustainable and greener. Such participatory policy processes are relatively common in the Netherlands, for example in the developing of climate policy (van de Kerkhof et al., 2002) or land-use planning (de Groot et al., 2014). The belief is that this contributes to more sustainable policy dynamics that are also backed by society.

Organisation

The Eindhoven municipality commissioned a participatory process, after a member of the political party GroenLinks (associated with the European Greens) raised a motion to initiate a scoping and strategising process to uncover how to better support these civil activities, which was accepted by a majority of the local council. The municipality sought out a local knowledge network (Proeftuin040) that was connected to many civil initiatives to lead this process, considering them a legitimate leader. Collaboration with the European-funded TRANSMANGO project[2] was established after this, allowing for action-research by contributing expertise on foresight and urban agriculture and by facilitating workshops. Participants of the workshop came from a range of different sectors and institutions: the municipality, regional government, housing corporations, community centres, social welfare organisations, GGD (the regional healthy authority), urban food initiatives, retailers, local entrepreneurs, landscape architects, design studios, and (applied) universities.

Approach to urban food futuring and methods

The process was designed in a way that allowed for participation of a broad group of stakeholders over multiple workshops (Hebinck et al., 2016). The process took almost a year with eight meetings of differing sizes, with the added intention to strengthen the local network of initiatives during this process. Meetings took place in venues of associated initiatives, which also served to showcase the diversity of emerging practices. A multi-method approach consisted of (1) brainstorming innovative ideas for Eindhoven's urban agriculture by using existing, innovative 'seed' initiatives as inspiration, and mixing them to develop new innovative practices (for method see Pereira et al., 2019); (2) several steps to create a vision and back-cast[3] pathways to achieve this vision; and (3) creating explorative scenarios that were used to 'challenge and test' the normative vision and pathways and make them more robust and context-aware. Multiple thematically steered future visions were developed, as well as the creation of four challenging explorative scenarios, focusing on different socio-economic challenges for Eindhoven. While these many formats offered diverse insights, they initially made it somewhat difficult to synthesise the input to one streamlined vision. However, in the final vision, the developed futures and pathways provided inspiration for an approach that is holistic and human-nature oriented. The scenarios highlighted several points to make the developed strategy for urban agriculture in Eindhoven more robust. A key example was the recommendation to bridge technology-oriented actors and those involved in community-based urban agriculture, as this would make it easier to embed into the city's governance while building on its existing strengths. The knowledge network (Proeftuin040) used the input of the participatory workshops to draft a policy vision, which was then presented to the city in a town-hall fashion and later discussed internally within the municipal board.

Evaluation of changes in urban food systems and governance

While the municipality initiated and commissioned this process, few local government representatives participated in the anticipatory process. This meant involvement from a municipal representative who co-organised the process with the knowledge platform and the occasional interested alderman. Interestingly, they joined these meetings to merely 'watch' and when asked to participate they responded they did not want to 'bias' the process. The result was a strategy that was ambitious, multi-dimensional, and reflected various interests in urban agriculture futures, but City Council members saw the developed strategy as misaligned with the existing governance strategies and ambitions in Eindhoven. With the final product of the process guided by insights on human–nature interactions, it was difficult for the acting local council to incorporate this into their current strategy, which was more oriented towards business, innovation, and technology. The local council did not see concrete ways to carry out the strategy, given the budget for urban food-related matters. With practically only the backing of aldermen of the political party that entered the motion, there was little mandate for the produced vision and transition pathways. Nevertheless, the citizens' desire for a more sustainable urban society was made clear by the process. Eventually, this led to a compromise: the municipality created a new internal position that aimed at harnessing some of these themes for a more sustainable society. The person who had thus far been chairing the local knowledge network, took up this position – which initially focused on strengthening the 'bio-based and circular economy' of Eindhoven and later the greening of industrial areas. The loss of the person chairing also meant the demise of the local knowledge network at the end of 2018: while the twitter account of the urban agriculture knowledge network is still online, the network itself is no longer active, the main reason being a difficulty to obtain funding (public and private) to organise urban food-related activities, leading to an increasingly sluggish process in the knowledge network, resulting in its organising members dropping out.

Case 2: A food policy council in Kyoto

Urban food context

Kyoto has many food traditions, unique cooking styles, and specific vegetable varieties developed in the city over hundreds of years. It is home to the Kyoto Protocol (1997) and considers itself a bastion of environmental thought and progressive politics. The city has a history of active community organisation, especially around food issues, with many environmental non-profit organisations and the presence of universities as centres of progressive action. Kyoto City municipal government has no unified urban food policy and, as is the case everywhere in Japan and many locations internationally, urban food policy is divided over highly segregated city departments that do not have extensive experience working together. For example, urban agricultural land (dry fields, rice paddies, etc.) is not technically recognised as agricultural land but is rather defined by the municipal government as multi-purpose urban greenfield. The urban planning department has no policy orientation or plan for the 1695 hectares of urban agricultural land (as of 2017) located in the city, which continues to disappear at the present time (Oda et al., 2018). Kyoto City signed the Milan Urban Food Policy Pact in 2015 but has no reference to it on its homepage.

Contrary to the Netherlands, Japan does not have a history of strong public participation in governance and policy development. Citizens can participate in the public commentary process for major policy plans, or they may be asked to join expert panels that consult directly on policy development. However, many see this as having performative value only. Generally speaking, futures methods such as visioning and back-casting, are exceedingly rare in policy processes in Japan.

Organisation

In this context, in November 2016 the FEAST[4] research project on life worlds of sustainable food production and consumption initiated the process of exploring the potential for city-level food policy and the possibility of initiating a Kyoto food policy council (FPC). It drew inspiration from other food policy councils, especially in Canada and the United States of America. The FEAST project started the process with a series of information sessions for the civil society actors somehow connected to food and agriculture: for example, city officials, farmer–consumer co-operatives, environmental non-profits, farmers market organisers, sustainable restaurateurs, and local action groups. This was the first step in organising food systems actors: bringing them together as a group. After the information sessions, a series of futuring workshops was planned to set the agenda for this newly formed group, and to experience the workings of a food policy council.

Approach to urban food futuring and methods

The diverse group of food systems actors invited by FEAST participated in a series of futures workshops which combined the methodologies of visioning, back-casting, and simulation games to explore urban food policy issues and recruit interest in the formation of a food policy council (Mangnus et al., 2019). The methodologies chosen were used and assessed to create multiple ways of experimenting and engaging with food systems futures. The main objectives were network building and agenda setting for the Kyoto food policy council. Each of the futures methods brought its own pathway elements: first, visioning contributed to the formulation of a desirable food system in 2050; second, back-casting from the future vision in a step-by-step manner back to the present contributed a stepwise action plan; and finally, a simulation game was used to allow food systems actors to practice with the future by giving them the chance to simulate what it would be like to be in a food policy council. After the sessions, the prospective food policy council members reported that they learned about new food systems practices, extended their networks, and that their support for a future food policy council had increased.

Evaluation of changes in urban food systems and governance

The Kyoto FPC was successfully launched by a selection of the food systems actors who attended the futures workshops, and it continues to expand its membership. The futures developed in the workshops became an orienting guide to the FPC's agenda. The FEAST project, in collaboration with existing contacts in the local food system, identified key actors in the city's foodscape. Recruiting them was critical in the FPC process. It also took the members of the fledgling FPC many attempts to build bridges with the Kyoto City and Prefectural offices, as legal and regulatory structures interfere with the ability of the municipal offices to recognise and incorporate the FPC in policy discussions. Kyoto City and prefecture policy development processes are predominantly top-down. Still, the Kyoto FPC participated in public comments on Kyoto City's five-year plan and pushed their agenda.

The Kyoto FPC is included in governance arrangements in two significant ways. Firstly, Kyoto City has created a team of experts to work directly on the latest version of the municipal agriculture policy and the Kyoto FPC is consulting with the team. This a promising first step to have a seat at the table during policy discussions. Secondly, some government officials are members of the Kyoto FPC, so they can influence the closed discussions on policy happening in their departments. However, department assignments can and do change, making the establishment of long-term relationships with relevant policy departments difficult because of the continual turnover. Altogether, the FPC is still at the early stages, but the playing field is not level. The FPC will face challenges to participating in policy processes as they are closed and top-down and will continue to need to develop strategies to create in-roads to those processes.

Insights for societal impact through urban food futuring

Use of futures to strengthen and inform urban food governance is promising, but it does require significant reflection with respect to how it is aligned to the governance context, what approach to engage with the future, and how to credibly engage in such boundary work. However, the two cases presented in this chapter show that while these are valuable guidelines, foresight itself can also be instrumental for 'transformative space making', by contributing to and fostering systemic change (Marshall et al., 2018). A few insights emerge from the comparative analysis of the two cases, ranging from those directed at the design of participatory processes, to those for enhanced practice of anticipatory governance.

Awareness of approaches to engage with the future

Reflecting on the choice of approach to the future is key, as each have specific uses and perspectives with regard to the processes of change. When the approach to futuring does not align with the needs for policymaking or the expectations of the broader governance context, urban food futures work can easily be misinterpreted or simply end up not being acted on. The cases in Eindhoven and Kyoto took similar approaches to the future: aligning with the third approach in which engagement with the future is primarily in a visioning, normative mode (Muiderman et al., 2020). Here, the future is something to be imagined together so that people can work collaboratively to realise it. Through the knowledge network's leadership, the vision was aimed at mobilising the local government and other societal actors towards realising a more sustainable Eindhoven through urban agriculture. In the Kyoto case, the process was more explorative, and more focused on experimenting with a new form of collective governance and action – but it was nevertheless strongly focused on visioning and mobilisation. Both started out with more explorative, desirable shared futures and then shifted to more exploratory methods to test and challenge ideas and visioning.

Such a combined approach makes sense in processes that involve a wide range of local actors. Both cases successfully used participatory foresight to conceptualise food systems change: they yielded relevant visions of the future and pathways to lead the people involved towards that future. However, in Eindhoven, while an open and inclusive stage of visioning, it received little input from actors from the City Council, which turned out to be a key challenge for the reconnection of the commissioned process to municipal governance processes. Lacking input on the workings of policy processes, and the policy vision that was then central to City Council, participants of the workshops built on what they assumed was the role of local government. The resulting vision was deemed too radical and misaligned with ongoing governance processes. This had less to do with the general futuring approach and more with competing political agendas. There are some takeaways: the City Council expected a future vision aligned with the first approach, more towards risk mitigation. As such the Council saw mostly impossibilities in the strategy. Here, the solution would *not* have been to simply 'submit' to the first approach and to frame and organise an urban planning process purely about risk mitigation; instead, the commitments and limits of all involved in futuring approaches should have been clarified beforehand. This would have significantly increased chances of aligning expectations on the use of those futures in urban governance beforehand. Whereas in Kyoto, the approach was perfect for the context and in fact created participatory space. This was because food systems actors had clear ideas about alternative ways to organise food systems, but also because they had less experience with imagining longer-term changes or participatory governance arrangements. Indeed, it was the explorative, multi-method, open approach that created space for the imagining of such changes in governance in a participatory manner.

Going through the motions vs. a blank slate

There are several key differences between the socio-cultural and political contexts of Eindhoven and Kyoto. Whereas support for, and experience with, such participatory work is relatively high in Eindhoven, Kyoto City has little to no experience in engaging the public in policy or foresight processes. Interestingly, these starting conditions had a mixed impact on the eventual trajectories of the two processes. Misalignment of the vision and pathways with political priorities became an issue for implementation in Eindhoven, while the 'blank slate' in Kyoto enabled the foresight process to unfold freely and create connections that did not previously exist.

Several influential factors differed for the two foresight processes, such as: institutional embedding, whether or not change is prioritised, the ability to mobilise actors, and the leading change agent (Hebinck et al., 2018). In Eindhoven, there was a sense that combining public participation and foresight processes was standard practice for eliciting robust policy ideas and public ownership of any policy outcomes and part of 'going through the motions'. However, considering the outcomes, we see the need to recognise the importance of firmly embedding participatory processes in decision-making by establishing clear expectations on accountability and follow-up. While the request for futures work came from the Eindhoven local government, the resulting futures work was in no way embedded in the City Council's policy plans. This decreased the priority given to the conceptualised ideas on urban agriculture for sustainability and instead left local civil society actors as the sole remaining change agents. Interestingly, the Kyoto case is an inverse case in some ways: it started as a bottom-up initiative, with the FEAST research project as a local connector of existing initiatives. Some of the local actors were very determined change agents, who carried the plans forward and kept making the Kyoto FPC a priority. While there was no existing institutional embedding, the Kyoto FPC provided a new mode of governance in which the food systems actors could organise and present themselves at the municipal and prefectural levels.

There are various processes that play a crucial role in fulfilling the potential of participatory foresight for urban food governance. However, while these processes are beneficial, they are no guarantee for impact. In fact, the Kyoto case demonstrates that when these contextual elements are not met, these can emerge over time, mediated through participatory futuring (Mangnus, Oomen et al., 2021) and a more action-oriented role of the researcher (Hebinck et al., 2018). This demonstrates how participatory futuring can be instrumental in the making of transformative spaces. In fact, if these methods are well aligned with the context and objectives, and feed into long-term engagement, academics and knowledge brokers can use these methods as a lever for change (Marshall et al., 2018; Pereira et al., 2020).

Avoiding the illusion of inclusion

While the experience and familiarity with participatory processes is much higher in Eindhoven than in Kyoto, a drawback is that the number of participatory processes has gradually increased across the Netherlands, leading to participation-fatigue among often-called-upon institutions and (civil) organisations. As fatigue and growing unwillingness to participate will eventually undercut the essence of participatory decision-making, reflection on the processes' legitimacy, credibility, and salience is essential (Cash et al., 2003; Kunseler et al., 2015). Similarly damaging to participatory policy processes is the 'illusion of inclusion', where citizens felt they were in a participatory process for show, as they see few of their inputs, desires, and needs recognised or incorporated in policies (Few et al., 2007; Jordan & Kapoor, 2016). Or worse, when participatory processes systematically fail to include or open up to actors from marginal groups, leading to their voices not being heard or included in decision-making (Duncan, 2015).

What happened in the Eindhoven case, was an 'illusionary' participatory process that did not feed directly into either decision-making or policymaking. The City Council had outsourced the organisation of the participatory process and very few actors from the Council itself were involved in the process and remained in the background as much as possible. This is because they argued that they did not want to 'influence' the participatory process. This strongly impacted the resulting futures work, which did not sufficiently align with the municipal expectations, the Council then struggled to act on it, thus creating an illusion of inclusion. Contrary to this, Kyoto saw a much higher involvement of city officials who, together with a broad group of stakeholders, formulated the need for a food policy council. The involvement of city officials appears crucial for the embedding of lessons from futuring processes in urban food governance. In other words, having a broader governance context that is accustomed to the use of participatory processes is far from a guarantee for successful participatory policymaking. Barriers continue to exist on just use of acquired participatory knowledge in decision-making, and subsequent transparent communication of and accountability for the result (Scholte, 2011).

Nurturing futures literacy

Finally, for successful formulation and implementation of urban food futures, it becomes increasingly relevant to consider the concept of futures literacy for local governance: the capacity of people to act on, and for, the future (Miller, 2007, 2018). Various intellectual traditions and futures practices make epistemologically and ontologically distinct claims about the future and its manifestations in the present (Muiderman et al., 2020). Being futures literate depends on reflexivity about these different engagements with the future, and what different approaches can offer in terms of future-oriented action (Mangnus, Oomen et al., 2021). Such literacy and explicit reflexivity about the futures produced and the underlying power structures could have given more direction to the processes in Kyoto and Eindhoven. Especially so in Eindhoven: reflexivity about embeddedness of the futures practices in a larger governance context could have benefited the resulting food systems change (Hebinck et al., 2018). A key lesson from the two cases is the need to pay attention to building this capacity at the beginning of a futures process. Futures literacy and reflexivity about futures and power structures are important capacities for organisers and participants alike and would strengthen their ability to engage in anticipatory governance.

Conclusion

There are increasing possibilities for addressing sustainability challenges through urban food governance. Participatory futuring has the potential to contribute to more equitable and anticipatory urban food governance towards sustainability. This by helping to generate strategic insights on desired futures with diverse stakeholders; by exploring potential impacts of otherwise ignored or uncertain systems dynamics; and providing actionable pathways and leverage points for governance. However, participatory futuring is hard to do well, and dependent on many contextual factors. To make good on its promises for urban food governance, there is a need to engage with the questions we have outlined in this chapter. These questions serve to reflect on (i) the context the foresight will take place in, what its mandate, opportunities, and barriers might be; (ii) who funds, is involved, and is associated with the foresight process; (iii) what foresight methods are (planned to be) used in the process and how they align with the objectives of the process; and (iv) how the entire foresight process fed (or will feed) into the broader urban food context. These questions help illuminate the importance of aligning foresight processes to the broader governance context – and to understand what success might look like.

We recognise that positive conditions for each of these factors are rare – and that we are setting out an ideal-type situation for participatory futures work for urban food governance, useful for the design and evaluation of participatory foresight. Urban food governance realities are often far more constraining, as we have seen in our cases. However, we have demonstrated there is potential for participatory foresight to enable transformative space making, allowing for action-researchers to initiate participatory futuring to support anticipatory urban food governance towards sustainability.

Notes

1 The emergence of the tech-giant Philips in the 1890s was a major influence for the city of Eindhoven and continues to be part of the city's identity.
2 A European research project exploring processes of change in food systems. A core element of the project was a series of 18 case studies to investigate innovative food and nutrition security practices of which nine featured foresight workshops.
3 Back-casting is a futuring approach that departs from an envisioned desirable future, and from which participants reason stepwise backwards to the present. This results in a sequence of strategic steps to achieve the desired future (see e.g. Henrichs et al. 2010).
4 The FEAST Project is a five-year transdisciplinary project funded and hosted by the Research Institute for Humanity and Nature in Kyoto, Japan. The FEAST Project analysed and co-designed institutions for food systems transition in Asia with a special emphasis on local sustainable food policy.

References

Boyd, E., Nykvist, B., Borgström, S., & Stacewicz, I.A. (2015). Anticipatory governance for social-ecological resilience. *Ambio, 44*(1), 149–161.

Candel, J.J.L., & Pereira, L.M. (2017). Towards integrated food policy: Main challenges and steps ahead. *Environmental Science & Policy, 73*, 89–92.

Cash, D.W., Clark, W.C., Alcock, F., Dickson, N.M., Eckley, N., Guston, D.H., Jäger, J., & Mitchell, R.B. (2003). Knowledge systems for sustainable development. *Proceedings of the National Academy of Sciences of the United States of America, 100*(14), 8086–8091.

de Groot, M., Winnubst, M.H., van Schie, N., & van Ast, J.A. (2014). Visioning with the public: Incorporating public values in landscape planning. *European Planning Studies, 22*(6), 1165–1181.

Dufva, M., & Ahlqvist, T. (2015). Elements in the construction of future-orientation: A systems view of foresight. *Futures, 73*, 112–125.

Duncan, J. (2015). *Global Food Security Governance*. Routledge.

Elmqvist, T., Andersson, E., Frantzeskaki, N., McPhearson, T., Olsson, P., Gaffney, O., Takeuchi, K., & Folke, C. (2019). Sustainability and resilience for transformation in the urban century. *Nature Sustainability*, *2*(4), 267–273.

Few, R., Brown, K., & Tompkins, E.L. (2007). Public participation and climate change adaptation: Avoiding the illusion of inclusion. *Climate Policy*, 7(1), 46–59.

Guston, D.H. (2014). Understanding 'anticipatory governance'. *Social Studies of Science*, *44*(2), 218–242.

Hebinck, A., & Page, D. (2017). Processes of participation in the development of urban food strategies: A comparative assessment of Exeter and Eindhoven. *Sustainability*, *9*(6), 931.

Hebinck, A., Selomane, O., Veen, E., de Vrieze, A., Hasnain, S., Sellberg, M., Sovová, L., Thompson, K., Vervoort, J.M., & Wood, A. (2021). Exploring the transformative potential of urban food. *NPJ Urban Sustainability*, *1*, 38.

Hebinck, A., Vervoort, J.M., Hebinck, P., Rutting, L., & Galli, F. (2018). Imagining transformative futures: Participatory foresight for food systems. *Ecology & Society*, *23*(2), 16.

Hebinck, A., Villarreal, G., Oostindie, H., Hebinck, P., Zwart, T.A., Vervoort, J., Rutting, L., & de Vrieze, A. (2016). Urban Agriculture policy-making: Proeftuin040 – TRANSMANGO Scenario Workshop Report, The Netherlands.

Henrichs, T., Zurek, M., Eickhout, B., Kok, K., Raudsepp-Hearne, C., Ribeiro, T., van Vuuren, D., & Volkery, A. (2010). Scenario development and analysis for forward-looking ecosystem assessments. In N. Ash, H. Blanco, C. Brown, K. Garcia, T. Henrichs, N. Lucas, C. Ruadsepp-Heane, R.D. Simpson, R. Scholes, T. Tomich, B. Vira, & M. Zurek (Eds.), *Ecosystems and Human Well-being: A Manual for Assessment Practitioners*. Island Press.

Jasanoff, S., & Kim, S.-H. (2015). *Dreamscapes of Modernity: Sociotechnical Imaginaries and the Fabricationof Power*. University of Chicago Press.

Jemala, M. (2010). Evolution of foresight in the global historical context. *Foresight*, *12*(4), 65–81.

Jordan, S., & Kapoor, D. (2016). Re-politicizing participatory action research: Unmasking neoliberalism and the illusions of participation. *Educational Action Research*, *24*(1), 134–149.

Kok, M.T.J., Kok, K., Peterson, G.D., Hill, R., Agard, J., & Carpenter, S.R. (2017). Biodiversity and ecosystem services require IPBES to take novel approach to scenarios. *Sustainability Science*, *12*(1), 177–181.

Kunseler, E.M., Tuinstra, W., Vasileiadou, E., & Petersen, A.C. (2015). The reflective futures practitioner: Balancing salience, credibility and legitimacy in generating foresight knowledge with stakeholders. *Futures*, *66*, 1–12.

Mangnus, A.C., Oomen, J.J., Vervoort, J.M., & Hajer, M.A. (2021). Futures literacy and the diversity of the future. *Futures*, *132*(102793).

Mangnus, A.C., Vervoort, J.M., Mcgreevy, S.R., Ota, K., Rupprecht, C.D.D., Oga, M., & Kobayashi, M. (2019). New pathways for governing food system transformations: A pluralistic practice-based futures approach using visioning, back-casting, and serious gaming. *Ecology & Society*, *24*(2), 2.

Mangnus, A.C., Vervoort, J.M., Renger, W.J., Nakic, V., Driessen, P.P.J., Hajer, M.A., & Rebel, K.T. (2021). Too late to change the future? Envisioning alternatives in pre-structured urban sustainability transformations. *Cities*, *120*(103466).

Marshall, F., Dolley, J., & Priya, R. (2018). Transdisciplinary research as transformative space making for sustainability: Enhancing propoor transformative agency in periurban contexts. *Ecology and Society*, *23*(3), 1–13.

Miller, R. (2007). Futures literacy: A hybrid strategic scenario method. *Futures*, *39*(4), 341–362.

Miller, R. (2018). *Transforming the Future: Anticipation in the 21st Century*. Routledge.

Moragues-Faus, A. (2020). Towards a critical governance framework: Unveiling the political and justice dimensions of urban food partnerships. *Geographical Journal*, *186*, 73–86.

Moragues-Faus, A.M., & Morgan, K. (2015). Reframing the foodscape: The emergent world of urban food policy. *Environment and Planning A*, *47*(7), 1558–1573.

Muiderman, K., Gupta, A., Vervoort, J.M., & Biermann, F. (2020). Four approaches to anticipatory climate governance: Different conceptions of the future and implications for the present. *Wiley Interdisciplinary Reviews: Climate Change*, *11*(6), 1–20.

Oda, K., Rupprecht, C.D.D., Tsuchiya, K., & McGreevy, S.R. (2018). Urban agriculture as a sustainability transition strategy for shrinking cities? Land use change trajectory as an obstacle in Kyoto city, Japan. In *Sustainability*, 10(4).

Pereira, L.M., Bennett, E., Biggs, R., Mangnus, A., v. Norstrom, A., Peterson, G., Raudsepp-Hearne, C., Sellberg, M., & Vervoort, J. (2019). Seeding change by visioning good anthropocenes. *Solutions Journal, 10*(3).

Pereira, L.M., Frantzeskaki, N., Hebinck, A., Charli-joseph, L., Drimie, S., Dyer, M., Eakin, H., Galafassi, D., Karpouzoglou, T., Marshall, F., Moore, L., Olsson, P., van Zwanenberg, P., & Vervoort, J.M. (2020). Transformative spaces in the making: Key lessons from 9 cases in the Global South. *Sustainability Science, 15*, 161–178.

Robinson, J., Burch, S., Talwar, S., O'Shea, M., & Walsh, M. (2011). Envisioning sustainability: Recent progress in the use of participatory backcasting approaches for sustainability research. *Technological Forecasting and Social Change, 78*(5), 756–768.

Scholte, J.A. (2011). *Building Global Democracy? Civil Society and Accountable Global Governance*. Cambridge University Press.

Sellberg, M.M., v. Norström, A., Peterson, G.D., & Gordon, L.J. (2020). Using local initiatives to envision sustainable and resilient food systems in the Stockholm city-region. *Global Food Security, 24*, 100334.

van de Kerkhof, M., Hisschemoller, M., & Spanjersberg, M. (2002). Shaping diversity in participatory foresight studies: Experiences with interactive backcasting in a stakeholder assessment on long-term climate policy in The Netherlands. *Greener Management International, 37*, 85–99.

Vervoort, J.M., & Gupta, A. (2018). Anticipating climate futures in a 1.5°C era: The link between foresight and governance. *Current Opinion in Environmental Sustainability, 31*, 104–111.

Vervoort, J.M., Thornton, P.K., Kristjanson, P., Förch, W., Ericksen, P.J., Kok, K., Ingram, J., Herrero, M., Palazzo, A., Helfgott, A., Wilkinson, A., Havlík, P., Mason-D'Croz, D., & Jost, C. (2014). Challenges to scenario-guided adaptive action on food security under climate change. *Global Environmental Change, 28*, 383–394.

Wiebe, K., Zurek, M., Lord, S., Brzezina, N., Gabrielyan, G., Libertini, J., Loch, A., Thapa-Parajuli, R., Vervoort, J., & Westhoek, H. (2018). Scenario development and foresight analysis: Exploring options to inform choices. *Annual Review of Environment and Resources, 43*(1), 545–570.

Wilkinson, A., & Eidinow, E. (2008). Evolving practices in environmental scenarios: A new scenario typology. *Environmental Research Letters, 3*(4), 045017.

Zurek, M., Hebinck, A., & Selomane, O. (2021). Looking across diverse food system futures: Implications for climate change and the environment. *Q Open, 1*(1), 1–39.

30

MORE-THAN-HUMAN COMPUTER INTERACTION FOR URBAN FOOD GOVERNANCE

Sara Heitlinger, Lara Houston, Jaz Hee-jeong Choi, Alex Taylor and Ruth Catlow

Introduction

Networked sensing devices, cloud computing, mobile phone technology, and, more recently, artificial intelligence (AI) and blockchain (the technology underpinning cryptocurrencies such as Bitcoin), are increasingly entering all aspects of people's lives. These technologies are transforming industrial global food production and consumption into a data-driven business, at the expense of ensuring social and ecological justice, well-being, and security. Within urban contexts, computation has been central to creating visions of "eco-smart cities", where food governance is typically addressed through logics of efficiency and optimisation in supply chains, waste management, and the consumer experience (e.g. through shopping or eating experiences). Set against such visions of efficiency, governance is delegated to networked infrastructures, including algorithms and big data, which are intended to produce profit and carbon optimisations through real-time data gathering, analysis, and control (Gabrys, 2014). For example, the measurement, mapping, and sensing of soil and crops have been used to maintain and maximise yields, and algorithms have become central to logistics, helping to reduce crop losses and optimise supply chains that distribute food. Computational and algorithmic systems have also become central features of future visions for urban food production.

The digital technologies at the centre of these global transformations are being harnessed to optimise and centralise agricultural production, as well as provide urban consumers with data about food provenance and safety at a price beyond the reach of most people (Wang, 2020). They are shaping access, control, participation and benefit, across all domains of life including social, economic, political, and health for both humans and non-humans. Built and maintained by the dominant capitalist, colonial, human-centred, and patriarchal paradigms (Costanza-Chock, 2020; Zuboff, 2019), they are amplifying existing inequalities, and provide a very narrow, human-centred perspective of how urban food governance could be mediated

DOI: 10.4324/9781003055907-35

by technology. Technology here does little to address government, societal, or environmental problems that are tied up in the ways in which food is produced and consumed, such as food insecurity, mass crop species decline, or degradation of arable soils. The benefits remain in the hands of an elite few, including major shareholders of on-demand restaurant delivery companies, large supermarkets, and food brands, as well as big tech companies harvesting the data.

A technocentric, human-centred and consumer-focused solutionism (Morozov, 2013) emphasises overly simple and reductive logics for addressing the challenges of sustainability in urban food systems. Within such logics, citizens' ability to participate in food governance is reduced to either a case of individual consumer choices, or contributing as passive nodes in a network of optimisation and efficiency (Gabrys, 2014). Additionally, scholars have identified significant barriers to access and participation with these complex technologies, which inhibit work on widening civic engagement with them, because questioning how these technologies are, or should be, designed and deployed, and for whose benefit, requires a high level of technological literacy (Wolff et al., 2016), in addition to civic, environmental, and food literacies. Rather than technology providing a solution to the problems of food governance around access, control, and participation in decision-making processes, it has amplified social and environmental inequalities. Furthermore, governance is retained by a limited number of actors, wielding much of the power for their own benefits.

It is against these issues and concerns that we seek in this chapter to move beyond a human-centred, efficiency-focused approach to what we think of as algorithmic urban food governance and ask: How might we widen participation in decision-making processes around urban food production and consumption? How might emerging technologies enhance, or hinder, issues around food governance including access, control, and accounting within urban food systems? And how might we envisage an algorithmically mediated urban food governance of the future that is more sustainable and just?

To answer these questions, this chapter draws on and ties together a number of emerging strands of Human–Computer Interaction (HCI) research, a multidisciplinary field of research that seeks to understand the ways in which computation affects the lives of its (typically) human users. We build on recent HCI work that looks at the role of digital technologies, and in particular blockchain, to support more democratic governance of urban systems through the urban commons (Antoniadis et al., 2015; Baibarac & Petrescu, 2017; Balestrini et al., 2017; Parra-Agudelo et al., 2018). We also draw on recent work in HCI that has started to move beyond human-centred design, to consider the ways in which the *more-than-human* (including seeds, birds, trees and soil, but also non-living actors such as sensors and infrastructures) cohabit urban space (Clarke et al., 2019; Smith et al., 2017), and are interdependent in food systems (Dolejšová et al., 2020). We build on HCI design research into inclusive and speculative methods for engaging marginalised participants in co-designing for urban futures with emerging technologies (Nissen et al., 2018; Pschetz et al., 2019; Rankin et al., 2020). We draw these strands together by presenting a co-design research project that set out to question the role of blockchain technologies in food futures over three workshops at an urban farm in London, UK. As a case study, the project provides a means of exploring futures of algorithmic food governance that are more sustainable and just.

We begin the chapter with an overview of how blockchain is being used currently in food governance, highlighting emerging work around multispecies governance. We then present the case study, detailing the speculative and participatory engagements with diverse participants over the three workshops. We conclude with reflections on how the workshops created the conditions for considering more-than-human relations, and how they surfaced speculative futures that challenge a human-centred, efficiency-focused perspective of urban food governance, through a collective articulation of designing for more-than-human food futures, care, and the commons.

Blockchain and Food Governance

Blockchain is a general-purpose technology that offers the potential to create new types of decentralised autonomous organisations (called DAOs) and non-extractive value exchange. Blockchain facets such as tokenisation (a process by which something of value is represented by a digital token to be used in a blockchain platform) and smart contracts (pieces of code that run autonomously when certain conditions are met) provide affordances to help manage resources more fairly and transparently. For example, they allow for contributions of diverse actors to be identified and tracked within an economic system, without the need for a central authority, and they provide mechanisms for transparent voting and decision-making. For these reasons blockchain is increasingly viewed as a governance technology, including for self-organising and commons-based communities and collectives (Pazaitis et al., 2017; Rozas et al., 2021). Blockchain also offers the potential for embedding the interests of non-humans into urban systems and infrastructures (Elsden et al., 2019), providing the mechanisms for multispecies and "algorithmic creatures" (Hee-jeong Choi et al., 2020) to become agents within governance systems.

The global blockchain market has expanded from a technology used primarily in financial systems to one that has entered many different industries and application areas. This includes food systems, where it is being used to increase food traceability, safety and provenance, and in inventory management in supply chains (Feng Tian, 2016). For example, BeefLedger (Foth, 2017) is a blockchain product being developed for traceability of beef products from Australia to China, where there are consumer doubts over the product's authenticity; UK company Provenance has created a blockchain-based platform for increasing transparency, traceability, and certifiability along food supply chains for both producers and consumers (Provenance, 2015); AgriBlockIoT (Caro et al., 2018) uses the Internet of Things (e.g. networked sensing), AI and blockchain to automate data recording, verification, and execution of processes within industrial agricultural systems (Lin et al., 2018). In these examples, food governance is reduced to a logic of efficiency that seeks to optimise and centralise agricultural production. Rather than improving food access and security for communities, or repairing the ecological destruction caused by food systems, in these visions, algorithmic governance helps concentrate benefit and control in the hands of an elite few (Wang, 2020).

Elsewhere, blockchain is being developed for restorative and regenerative agriculture and more sustainable economies. For example, "Regen Network" (Regen Network, n.d.), "Nori" (Nori, n.d.) and GainForest (Dao et al., 2019) are three blockchain-based platforms that incentivise regenerative land use, carbon capture in soil, and the reversal of destructive land-use practices that contribute to CO_2 emissions, such as clearing forests for monocultural crop production. Investors can pledge money to farmers, indigenous communities, and enterprises around the world to support their endeavours to regenerate the land. The regeneration practices are measured, monitored, and verified by algorithm-driven analysis of data from satellite images and AI, with smart contracts paying out rewards to those farmers and enterprises who meet the predetermined conditions over a set amount of time. Regardless of the intentions of the stakeholders and supporters, these examples share a deterministic or techno-optimistic view of food governance, relying on technologically mediated digital marketplaces as a solution. They also take a human-centred perspective of food systems, where only human stakeholders are able to participate in accounting and economic systems.

The work we are presenting as a case study in this chapter has been inspired by terra0, a critical and speculative project using blockchain, which has emerged from participatory arts practice. In terra0, a forest becomes a DAO on a blockchain. The project "is a conceptualization of a self-owned forest; an ongoing art project and a self-utilising piece of land" (Seidler et al., 2017). When sensors report that trees have reached the level of maturity for logging, the terra0 DAO can sell its own logging rights for cryptocurrency which it spends on managing itself, eventually buying itself back from the artists. The project looks to automation not to deliver efficiencies but to give the forest autonomy and agency through the blockchain, and free it from human-centred value extraction. The project does not attempt to solve predefined or specific problems; rather, its purpose is to open a space for questioning. Blockchain provides the means for experimenting with different forms of algorithmic governance that take into account the complex ecological relations between human and more-than-human entities.

For us, the more-than-human perspective is a powerful device for thinking about how authority, agency, and values are distributed across actors and emerge through unfolding relations. Drawing on more-than-human scholars (Galloway, 2021; Haraway, 2016; Puig de la Bellacasa, 2017; Tsing, 2015) who are challenging human exceptionalism and privilege, we recognise that human survival is interwoven with that of non-human others. The analysis of indigenous epistemologies and ontologies (Lewis et al., 2018) challenges technological reductionism with a commitment to "human flourishing" which, by default, requires flourishing of other-than-humans, asserting the status of all things on the earth as beings in a network of kinship relationships, and refusing their reduction to subjects of, or vehicles for, exploitation, extraction, and depletion. More-than-human food governance, therefore, requires attending to these relations, and a recognition of the interdependencies and interconnections of more-than-human actors in the food web. In the following section, we will present a case study, Algorithmic Food Justice, a research project which aims to explore co-designing algorithmic food governance at the intersections of more-than-human perspectives, commons-based governance, and blockchain.

Algorithmic Food Justice: A Case Study

Algorithmic Food Justice was a pilot project that took place in late 2019 at Spitalfields City Farm, a 1.3-acre urban farm housed on the site of a former railway goods depot near London's financial centre, which has been running since the late 1970s. It is located in Tower Hamlets, one of the most economically deprived boroughs in the UK, characterised by high population density, large-scale immigration, ethnic diversity, poverty, and income inequality among residents. The borough has the highest rate of child poverty across the UK and its population suffers from a range of food-related illnesses, including diabetes and childhood obesity. Health inequalities are further compounded by the abundance of unhealthy eating options: 76 per cent of households are within a 10-minute walk of a supermarket, while 97 per cent are within a 10-minute walk of a fast food outlet (Caraher et al., 2009).

The site hosts varied food-growing areas and community facilities, such as a shared outdoor kitchen, and is home to farm animals such as rescue hens, rare-breed pigs, and ducks. Most of the day-to-day labour is performed by volunteers. Food is grown all-year round in rotation, with seeds being planted to replace the food that will soon be harvested. Through its community gardens, volunteering opportunities, its various educational programmes and fresh produce sales, the farm works towards improving food access, security, and sovereignty for local, marginalised communities.

The project explored co-designing more-than-human food governance futures using blockchain in three workshops that brought together a diverse group of participants, including community growers, community organisers, artists, researchers, and technologists, who we recruited from our well-established networks. Many of the participants were familiar with our participatory approach to design from prior long-term participatory research at the farm that the first author has conducted (Heitlinger et al., 2013, 2014; Heitlinger et al., 2018). We used playful and creative activities to experiment with alternative configurations of value and to open up a space where humans and non-humans, such as plants, animals and soil, as well as technologies and their infrastructures, can play a part in food governance of the future. We used mapping exercises, fictional roleplay and paper-based prototyping to create a series of visions of food futures that considered more-than-human justice, and new imaginaries for algorithmic governance. These speculative and participatory methods were used to both open up a space to explore how non-humans can play a part in food governance, as well as to better understand the affordances and implications of emerging technologies that are not yet widespread and may be beyond participants' lived experience. We considered Spitalfields City Farm as a test case for prototyping sustainable food futures, but also drew on participants' experiences of other community gardens.

Workshop 1: Mapping the Future Farm

In the first workshop, participants explored the agencies and interrelationships between multispecies members of community growing spaces. Participants drew on their expert knowledge of food growing to map human and non-human stakeholders in the city farm, now and in the future. These open-ended activities facilitated a space for experienced growers to draw on their knowledge and make visible the myriad more-than-human entities involved in small-scale regenerative agriculture, including their needs, contributions, and roles in resource flows. Participants were asked to consider resources beyond those with a financial value, such as volunteer labour, oxygen, time, and care, and to think about who manages those resources. Discussions revolved around the often invisible but important labour of care work that happens in community gardens. Participants noted how care work was not adequately recognised or compensated, for example in funding schemes, and tended to be completely elided in industrial agricultural systems. This mode of knowledge production from the grower's perspectives produced rich materials to ground the scenarios developed for the second workshop.

Following the discussion about resources, on a large piece of paper, participants also mapped interconnections between multispecies stakeholders of the farm in the present day, and in the year 2030 (as a preparatory step for the development of Workshop 2) (Figure 30.1). Rather than a managerial mapping of assets, we ended up with an expansive range of heterogeneous entities, including bacteria, local schools, parakeets, stag beetles, and natural shade, with a heterogeneous understanding of their needs and contributions across ecological, public—and often poetic—spheres. The mapping of the present-day farm also surfaced growers' own experiences of precarity and the stress they felt navigating precarious funding regimes, which often relied on their extensive volunteer (care) labour. The map of the future farm gave us a sense of desired futures of food governance, incorporating better labour conditions and expanding ecologically sound techniques, such as permaculture farming and a circular economy for materials, which were usually side projects in urban farming at present.

Figure 30.1 Workshop 1 participants mapping multispecies relations

Workshop 2: Now London is a City Farm

While the focus of the first workshop was mapping the more-than-human actors in our food systems, in the second workshop we used a type of role-playing game called a Live Action Role Play (LARP) as a research tool to open up a playful space to imagine and critically examine possibilities for more-than-human actors to take part in governing a future food commons.

Set in 2025, in the aftermath of a "Great Food Emergency", the aim of the game was to transform London from an extractive financial centre into a global city farm in which all of London's available spaces and infrastructures are turned over to creating a thriving food commons for its biodiverse inhabitants. Participants were given different roles to play within fictional scenarios and played out multispecies relationships, new economies, and radical decision-making processes for sustaining a city-wide commons. Players' actions were informed by scenarios based on what we learned in the first workshop as well as real-world events, and current facts about food and environmental injustices, as we tried to establish new decision-making systems and urban infrastructures.

Participants came from a mix of growers, organisers, researchers, and also technologists including people familiar with blockchain concepts. They were split into two groups, representing two different decision-making bodies: one role played within the Greater London City Farm Assembly (GLCFA—representing the city-wide perspective); the other role played within E1 City Farm Assembly (E1CFA—representing a local community farm like Spitalfields City Farm) (Figure 30.2). In each assembly, participants took on representative roles from committees that included: Coordination, Health, Agriculture, Security, Culture, Justice, Resources and Waste management, Education, Energy, Infrastructure, and Liaison.

Figure 30.2 Workshop 2 participants in the E1 City Farm Assembly

At the start of the game, each person filled in an official looking Identity Certificate from which they chose both a human character and a "companion species" (drawing on Haraway, 2008) to represent. Companion species included: birds, insects, farm animals, honey bees, soil, plants, trees, sensors, water, air, weather. The cast of human and non-human characters was drawn from the list of stakeholders generated in Workshop 1. The players wore a badge with a picture of their chosen companion species to remind them to account for the interests of both their human and companion species (Figure 30.3). The game began with a ritual. Participants were asked to close their eyes, imagine their human character in one hand, their companion species in the other hand, rub their hands together until they felt heat, and then to clap. They were told that after the clap they would speak (for the duration of the game) for both their chosen human character and for their companion species.

The meeting agenda revolved around questions of membership, fair shares, and conflict resolution, which are also being experimentally negotiated in blockchain commons initiatives (Pazaitis et al., 2017; Teli et al., 2018; Troncoso & Utratel, 2019) and were based loosely on economist Elinor Ostrom's 8 design principles for governing the commons (Ostrom, 1999). While the agenda items were researcher-led (based on Ostrom's design principles), the scenarios were developed from "matters of care" (Puig de la Bellacasa, 2017) that arose in discussions in the first workshop. To illustrate with an example, in Workshop 1 discussions arose around changes that could be made to the land to better support pollinating insects, including lower impact agriculture, organic measures, the creation of new habitats, and banning pesticides. This "matter of care" was used as a basis for a script for the second agenda point: *Review of the sharing policy* (based on Ostrom's design principle 2). The Chair (one of the authors) introduced the agenda item with the following script: "*The next item on the agenda is a review of how we're*

Figure 30.3 Companion species badges

managing resources, and ensuring that everyone's contributions are rewarded. ...An issue that's come up recently in the sharing policy: so the bees, as you know...have been on strike now for six months. They've stopped working." The Chair continued: "*How was the Justice Committee proposing to resolve the dispute between the bees and the gardeners?*" The representative from the committee called on then responded, representing both their human and companion species' interests at the same time. In this example, the justice representative replied, "*We are piloting various multispecies assemblies, which have representatives of all sorts of actors on the farm, to give equal voice to them all. But also working closely with infrastructure to meet the bees' demands. Which on the whole don't seem too wild and quite fair.*" Other members from other committees would then be called on to join in the discussion, and the speculative roleplay of more-than-human governance issues unfolded from there. Developing scenarios out of the previous workshop was important as it enabled participants to see their knowledge and experience put to work in the development of a future system. These scenarios helped us to imagine our emerging food commons, and work out a system of governance that would produce and distribute food for the benefit of all species.

Participants speculated on algorithms to facilitate urban food governance of the future, including an extensive digital infrastructure of control through an automated digital credits system, a food tracking app linked to a distribution centre, identity scanning on the farm gates and some (contentious) proposals to build profiles of farm members using personal data and aggregations of their social media feeds. But the proposals, which echo the intensification of today's algorithmic logics, were derailed when the EC1FA Culture representative raised the question of how these systems would apply to more-than-human members, leading to the realisation that these digital infrastructures had failed to account for more-than-human materiality or meaning. Some proposals turned towards harnessing digital technologies for interspecies communication and well-being, for example through a "very dense network of sensors across the city, which measure the health of the urban biome...through that, we could gauge the happiness of the various species...you know [the] relationship with our species" (EC1FA culture representative). This idea moves beyond governance through control, towards interspecies relationships and balance.

Many researchers have already noted the difficulties of doing future-focused work with more-than-human others, noting that this inevitably leads to researchers speaking on their behalf (Pitt, 2016). This issue is especially fraught when addressing how more-than-humans come to be included within human modes of governance, particularly in approaches that centre justice—for example in participatory design (Bastian et al., 2016). There is a risk that humanist concepts like justice or democracy collapse when considering more-than-human ontologies. As one workshop participant asked: "Is justice an anthropocentric concept though? You couldn't expect a carnivorous animal to be just to its prey—how would you mediate between a cat which has to eat rodents and things, between its things it's feeding on?" (GLCFA resources representative).

This led to a consideration of relations of interdependence more commonly found in more-than-human ontologies, where processes rather than subjectivities are foregrounded:

> If you look at soil as a model. Mostly, if you create the right conditions and the structure is right, then most organisms will exchange fairly and that usually works. And there are a few that will take and not give back, but still overall, the system works. So I think it's about...how to create a wider system that creates the right conditions for things to work. But not always, and that's ok.
>
> *GLCFA coordination representative*

What constitutes more-than-human *injustice* is easier to agree on than a shared concept of justice: "Driving other species into extinction is a no-no" (energy representative).

Workshop 3: Prototyping the Food Commons

The aims of the final workshop were to (1) co-design blockchain based conceptual prototypes for governing a more-than-human food commons and (2) critically stress-test these prototypes to better understand the implications for algorithmic food governance, including what could go wrong.

In the morning session, participants with experience of blockchain governance and local currencies created conceptual prototypes for new types of organisations to manage the more-than-human food commons. Participants were given a selection of eight scenarios, developed out of the previous workshops, on which to build new blockchain-based decentralised autonomous organisations and automated decision-making (through pieces of code called smart contracts). Each scenario highlighted conflicted and entangled relations between humans, other species and planetary systems. Each explored a different challenge for commons management, pertaining to membership, local rule making and conflict resolution. Each was assigned a speaker/role, an assembly, a companion species (from the first workshop), a quote from one of the characters in the LARP in Workshop 2, and a keyword relating to one of Ostrom's corresponding design principles. Participants used these scenarios for context and worked with paper-based prompts as design materials to define their DAOs, and deal with governance issues, such as establishing membership protocols, voting mechanisms, processes for establishing and changing the rules, and acknowledging and rewarding the contributions and value flows between multispecies members in order to sustain a food commons, as well as relations with external organisations. In three groups, participants worked to produce the following three prototypes:

(1) The first group chose Scenario 1: "*Should we expand our membership structure to include others from local city farm 'nodes'?*" This referred back to the mis-claimed salad Agenda item, played by the E1CFA Coordination Rep:

> The individual that was involved...tend[s] to a lot of the sensors that are in the park outside Bethnal Green. They built up a lot of credits within their own farm membership. And they incorrectly assumed that our farm was part of their network of food sharing...And because they weren't part of the same shared group or food node as we are—that was where the confusion came in.

The keyword was membership, and the companion species was sensors. The group devised an "umbrella" DAO, called DAO-n to Earth, that helps to coordinate the exchange of tokens (currencies) between all the farms in the London Food Network. The exchange rate is set automatically according to the soil health data of each community, as measured by networked sensors and AI, and calibrated over time. The better the quality of soil in a community, the higher the value of its local currency. Humans are incentivised to take care of the soil, by staking a currency's value to the work done to regenerate the soil in a specific local area. The DAO-n to Earth group explained that they are designing for soil health above all else, because it benefits a wider group of species (rather than the humans alone). Care for ecosystem health is woven into the dynamics of food production and exchange.

(2) The second group chose Scenario 7: "*How can we make the most of all the resources available, by using 'waste' as 'assets' to nourish other members of the farm?*" The gameplay excerpt is provided below. Here, the GLCFA Education Rep is speaking as Soil to the Resources Rep:

> E: "Can I speak as soil. With my soil hat on. The pile of waste that you're talking about. Is it just human excrement?"
> R: "It's a mix of farming manure like cattle and sheep."
> E: "So everything organic. So for me, that's food. So I wouldn't call that waste, that's wonderful."

On the card we also provided a keyword ("resources") and a related companion species ("farm animals").

This prompt triggered an interesting discussion of value. They experienced value as relational and ever-unfolding, an experience which they sought to capture in the design of a socio-technical system that nurtured multispecies relations. The Fellowshit of Dark Matter DAO consisted of an app, where humans could post waste materials and make them freely available to others within the community, thereby earning tokens that work as currency, which can be used within a broader system of value exchange. They also planned a weekly ritual, to provide a way for humans to inhabit multispecies perspectives, and spot opportunities for waste materials to be used for their own species' ends. The DAO promotes a multispecies "circular economy" with an expansive sense of value that is not only focused on material utility but the meaning of unfolding interspecies relationships as they exchange materials and tokens within a digital-physical ecosystem.

(3) The third group chose Scenario 4: "*How do we acknowledge the contributions of different species?*" which had a particular focus on plants:

> Speaking for the plants, I think there hasn't been overall enough acknowledgment of what sacrifices we make. Because principally we are generating most of the air and most of the food. So particularly as there's been a move towards vegetarianism and veganism. When this was first mooted we did originally discuss having rituals that actually thanked the plants and I don't know what's happened to that. I just know that the plants are carrying a load here that no-one is acknowledging.
>
> *GLCFA Infrastructure Rep*

The group's keywords were *contribution* and *fair share*, and the group's companion species was plants.

The Corn Council DAO seeks to repair the alienation humans experience from the conditions of food production, and proposes a system for repairing the disconnect between humans and other species. The DAO rewards humans with tokens for spending time with plants in a non-instrumental way, as well as for care-taking work such as pruning and watering. Tokens allow members to participate in voting proposals about the farm's management. Each crop in the farm has its own council and the DAOs are managed through an umbrella DAO.

In the afternoon session we invited a wider group of community growers and organisers to join in with their expertise of multispecies relations, food growing, and community governance to try and fuse these forms of knowledge in critically examining how these DAOs might serve local and wider multispecies interests, as well as all the awful things they might do by accident. Knowledgeable growers helped reconfigure tech-focused imaginings and added important depth and nuance to multispecies relationships and ecosystems by "stress testing" the DAOs, situating each DAO on a matrix with axes of dystopian/utopian, and discrete/federated.

Discussion

In the following sections we discuss how the project presented possibilities for what food governance could look like in the sustainable smart city of the future, when we include diverse, marginalised citizens and move beyond a human-centred and efficiency-focused perspective of algorithmic food governance—instead considering multispecies relations, labours of care, and notions of the commons.

Designing for More-than-Human Food Futures

Within the efficiency logics of algorithmic governance in the profit-driven global food systems, marginalised actors such as more-than-human, small-scale farmers, and low-income, immigrant communities are often overlooked and neglected. The workshops helped to make visible these actors as well as the relationships and flows between them.

Participants envisaged scenarios of food governance in a future London, where technological infrastructures, like blockchain and sensing systems, are harnessed, not to concentrate profits and intensify agricultural production for the benefit of a few human stakeholders, but rather to provide the mechanisms to facilitate ecological repair and regeneration across human and non-human communities. Rather than focus on the needs of individual actors within food systems, technology was used to help incentivise the expansion and health of mutually beneficial multispecies relations. Wider urban food systems were also transformed beyond those of individual neighbourhoods, through systems of exchange and calibration. For example, in the DAO-n to Earth prototype, the system accounted for soil health across the city. A sudden degradation of soil health, perhaps through contamination, triggers a market crash as well as a mechanism to incentivise members of other farms on the network to help clean it up.

Like with terra0, the possibility arose for an urban food system consisting of its actors, labours, and governance mechanisms, to maintain its own ecological balance, by establishing itself as an autonomous self-organising agent. For example, in the DAO-n to Earth prototype, blockchain presented possibilities for "*imagining [the system] as a collective organism and not as these individual parts that are always competing with one another*" (workshop participant). Rather than relying on efficiency logics of the "eco-smart-city", in these visions, cities are rendered smart because of the potential for them to function as self-regulating and self-repairing organisms.

Designing for Care in the Eco-Smart City

Food in the smart city typically promises convenience and efficiency, providing an end-user consumer with a perfect product at the touch of a button. In such visions, the production of food is abstracted from the labour required to maintain and care for such systems, and consumers are alienated from the lives on which our food depends, typically a devalued migrant, precariously employed labour force, as well as myriad other species, the soil in which it is grown, and the contingencies of climate. A feminist notion of care asks "who will do the work of care, as well as how to do it and for whom" (Puig de la Bellacasa, 2011). The Algorithmic Food Justice workshops surfaced visions of urban food futures where the labours of care that are typically invisible, taken for granted, or marginalised in the dominant food regimes are recognised, valued, and rewarded.

In these futures, technology has the potential to reconfigure value from something to be enclosed and extracted, into a system that hinges on care. For example, in the Fellowshit of Dark Matter DAO, organic waste is transformed from something that is devalued and erased in the dominant food system, into a valuable resource for micro-organism stakeholders, and is recognised as such. As one participant explained, "*People are incentivised to move matter from the wrong place to the place where it can have its value realised.*" Likewise, in the Corn Council DAO, the time spent caring for plants is recognised as a valuable asset and accounted for. While in the DAO-n to Earth DAO, the practices of caring for soil are made visible and brought into a socio-technical system of accounting and governance.

It is only by moving beyond a human-centred perspective of food governance to recognise the interrelations between humans and non-humans on which all life on earth depends, that we can begin to recognise the diverse value required to restore our damaged planet. A focus on care suggests a way to shift from exploitative, extractive, colonial, capitalistic paradigms of food governance, towards one in which power relations are restructured, and value redistributed more fairly and sustainably.

Designing for a Multispecies Commons

While some urban farms are profit-driven enterprises, many grassroots urban agricultural sites, such as Spitalfields City Farm and other community gardens we have worked with in the UK, prioritise the collective needs of diverse, socially marginalised inhabitants (human and otherwise) over individual profit. As researchers interested in food governance, we can learn from these communities about how cities of the future could be transformed into a food commons that benefits collective human and non-human communities, and the ways in which digital technologies could be employed for the common good.

Participants speculated on food governance for a heterogeneous set of more-than-human actors in accounting systems, as a way of addressing the inequalities and power imbalances within the current industrial food systems. Blockchain facets such as exchangeable tokens in the form of a community currency, and non-exchangeable tokens in the form of reputation, were used in the prototypes to help manage the community rules in ways that are fair for the multispecies collective. For example, in the Corn Council DAO, caring for crops is valued and incentivised with reputation tokens, which a member can then use to help the DAO evolve by proposing and voting on new proposals. In the Fellowshit of Dark Matter DAO, contributions towards furthering relations between multispecies members are collectively assessed and rewarded. Likewise, in DAO-n to Earth, reputation is allocated to individual farms according to the health of their soil over time, through a "Proof of Healthy Soil" protocol and as measured through AI-based sensor networks called "Soil Sentinels". Reputation can be used to change the algorithms of the overall DAO. The rules recognise and incentivise the work for sustaining the commons, contributing to its overall health and abundance. Rather than aiming to deliver efficiency within the commons, the projects surfaced futures in which blockchain, AI, and sensor networks are used to include multispecies stakeholders in the governance of an urban food commons.

Conclusion

In this chapter we present a case study that allows us to consider how else urban food governance might be mediated through technology in the sustainable smart city of the future, beyond top-down, efficiency-led, human-centred, and profit-driven logics. We build on recent work in HCI design research that seeks to democratise the ways in which emerging technologies, such as blockchain and AI, are shaping our urban environments, including the governance of food systems. This research works to increase participation of diverse inhabitants who are often marginalised in discussions around the design of smart cities, in order to leverage bottom-up understandings of urban sustainability and to imagine more liveable and just cities of the future.

This study raises challenges and tensions. Firstly, there are significant barriers to access to emerging technologies such as blockchain, particularly for grassroots communities who may not have the skills required. Building on prior HCI research (Clarke, 2020; Heitlinger et al., 2019), speculative and participatory activities including role play and fiction are effective ways of engaging non-technical participants in envisaging futures with unfamiliar technologies.

Secondly, as documented in other similar projects, an algorithmic approach to creating formal accounting systems of value, and introducing external rewards in what was previously informal and intrinsically motivated, risks creating perverse incentives and abuses of power (Cila et al., 2020; Pazaitis et al., 2017).

Thirdly, critical theories show that while the more-than-human may make room for multiple subjectivities, it may not serve those who have historically been excluded from the category of human in the first place, such as people of colour (Crenshaw, 1990; Forlano, 2017). A feminist ethics of care shows how we might pay attention to neglected humans as well as non-humans, in order to reconfigure value in ways that contribute to more sustainable and just urban food governance.

Finally, we recognise that despite scaffolding more-than-human autonomy through algorithmic automation, the project took place within a human frame, created by human designers and developers and played by human actors. Likewise, we recognise that grassroots urban food-growing communities and their visions for fairer food governance are not separate from the neoliberal capitalist system within which they function. But because of their values, and the inclusive practices in care time and space, working with such communities presents opportunities to lever open the totalising human-centred, efficiency-driven and profit-motivated visions of algorithmic food governance in smart cities, and see where shifts can begin to occur.

These tensions and challenges highlight the urgency of including insights of heterogeneous, marginalised actors and voices in the design of algorithmic food governance systems, in order to avoid intensifying inequalities. Without a variety of stakeholders working on these technologies, accelerationist tendencies and injustices in urban food governance will be exacerbated. It is in the combination of speculative and participatory approaches with diverse stakeholders, as well as a focus on commons-based and more-than-human values, that we see the most fruitful opportunities for computation to be used in urban food governance in the future, in ways that are more environmentally and socially just.

References

Antoniadis, P., Apostol, I., Gaved, M., Smyth, M., & Unteidig, A. (2015). DIY networking as a facilitator for interdisciplinary re-search on the hybrid city. In *Proceedings of Hybrid City 2015: Data to the People*. Athens, Greece: URIAC, University of Athens, 65–72.

Baibarac, C., & Petrescu, D. (2017). Co-design and urban resilience: Visioning tools for commoning resilience practices. *CoDesign: International Journal of CoCreation in Design and the Arts, 15*(2), 1–19. https://doi.org/10.1080/15710882.2017.1399145

Balestrini, M., Rogers, Y., Hassan, C., Creus, J., King, M., & Marshall, P. (2017). A city in common: A framework to orchestrate large-scale citizen engagement around urban issues. In *Proceedings of the 2017 CHI Conference on Human Factors in Computing Systems, ACM, New York*, pp. 2282–2294. https://doi.org/10.1145/3025453.3025915

Bastian, M., Jones, O., & Moore, N. (2016). *Participatory Research in More-than-Human Worlds, Vol. 67*. London: Routledge.

Caraher, M., Lloyd, S., & Madelin, T. (2009). *Cheap as Chicken: Fast Food Outlets in Tower Hamlets (Report No 2)*. London: Centre for Food Policy, City University.

Caro, M. P., Ali, M. S. A., Vecchio, M., & Giaffreda, R. (2018). Blockchain-based traceability in Agri-Food supply chain management: A practical implementation. In *2018 IoT Vertical and Topical Summit on Agriculture—Tuscany (IOT Tuscany)* (pp. 1–4). https://doi.org/10.1109/IOT-TUSCANY.2018.8373021

Cila, N., Ferri, G., De Waal, M., Gloerich, I., & Karpinski, T. (2020). The blockchain and the commons: Dilemmas in the design of local platforms. In *Conference on Human Factors in Computing Systems—Proceedings*, pp. 1–14. https://doi.org/10.1145/3313831.3376660

Clarke, R., Heitlinger, S., Light, A., Forlano, L., Foth, M., & DiSalvo, C. (2019). More-than-human participation: Design for sustainable smart city futures. *Interactions, 26*(3), 60–63. https://doi.org/10.1145/3319075

Clarke, R. E. (2020). Ministry of multispecies communications. In *DIS 2020 Companion—Companion Publication of the 2020 ACM Designing Interactive Systems Conference*, pp. 441–444. https://doi.org/10.1145/3393914.3395845

Costanza-Chock, S. (2020). *Design Justice: Community-led Practices to Build the Worlds We Need*. Cambridge, MA: MIT Press.

Crenshaw, K. (1990). Mapping the margins: Intersectionality, identity politics, and violence against women of color. *Stanford Law Review, 43*, 1241.

Dao, D., Cang, C., Fung, C., Zhang, M., Gonzales, R., Beglinger, N., & Zhang, C. (2019). GainForest: Scaling climate finance for forest conservation using interpretable machine learning on satellite imagery. In *ICML Climate Change Workshop at 36th International Conference on Machine Learning*, pp. 5–7.

Dolejšová, M., Wilde, D., Altarriba Bertran, F., & Davis, H. (2020). Disrupting (more-than-) human-food interaction: Experimental design, tangibles and food-tech futures. In *DIS 2020—Proceedings of the 2020 ACM Designing Interactive Systems Conference*, pp. 993–1004. https://doi.org/10.1145/3357236.3395437

Elsden, C., Gloerich, I., Spaa, A., Vines, J., & de Waal, M. (2019). Making the blockchain civic. *Interactions, 26*(2), 60–65.

Feng Tian. (2016). An agri-food supply chain traceability system for China based on RFID blockchain technology. In *2016 13th International Conference on Service Systems and Service Management (ICSSSM)*, pp. 1–6. https://doi.org/10.1109/ICSSSM.2016.7538424

Forlano, L. (2017). Posthumanism and design. She Ji: *The Journal of Design, Economics, and Innovation, 3*(1), 16–29. https://doi.org/https://doi.org/10.1016/j.sheji.2017.08.001

Foth, M. (2017). The promise of blockchain technology for interaction design. In *Proceedings of the 29th Australian Conference on Computer-Human Interaction—OZCHI '17*, pp. 513–517. https://doi.org/10.1145/3152771.3156168

Gabrys, J. (2014). Programming environments: Environmentality and citizen sensing in the smart city. *Environment and Planning D: Society and Space, 32*(1), 30–48. https://doi.org/10.1068/d16812

Galloway, A. (2021). Introduction to Part 2: More-than-human worlds. Global Discourse: An Interdisciplinary *Journal of Current Affairs, 11*(1–2), 111–114.

Haraway, D. (2008). Foreword: Companion species, mis-recognition, and queer worlding. In N. Giffney & M. J. Hird (Eds.), Queering the Non/Human. Abingdon, Oxon: Routledge.

Haraway, D. J. (2016). *Staying with the Trouble: Making Kin in the Chthulucene.* Durham, NC: Duke University Press.

Hee-jeong Choi, J., Forlano, L., & Kera, D. (2020). Situated automation: Algorithmic creatures in participatory design. In *PDC '20: Proceedings of the 16th Participatory Design Conference 2020—Participations Otherwise, Volume 2, June*, pp. 5–9. https://doi.org/10.1145/3384772.3385153

Heitlinger, S., Bryan-Kinns, N., & Comber, R. (2018). Connected seeds and sensors: Co-designing Internet of Things for sustainable smart cities with urban food-growing communities. In *Participatory Design Conference (PDC '18)*. https://doi.org/10.1145/3210604.3210620

Heitlinger, S., Bryan-Kinns, N., & Jefferies, J. (2013). Sustainable HCI for grassroots urban food-growing communities. In *Proceedings of the 25th Australian Computer–Human Interaction Conference: Augmentation, Application, Innovation, Collaboration*, pp. 255–264.

Heitlinger, S., Bryan-Kinns, N., & Jefferies, J. (2014). The talking plants: An interactive system for grassroots urban food-growing communities. In *CHI '14 Extended Abstracts on Human Factors in Computing Systems* (pp. 459–462).

Heitlinger, S., Clarke, R., Clear, A. K., Chopra, S., & Dilaver, Ö. (2019). Co-creating "smart" sustainable food futures with urban food growers. In *ACM International Conference Proceeding Series*, pp. 114–120. https://doi.org/10.1145/3328320.3328399

Lewis, J. E., Arista, N., Pechawis, A., & Kite, S. (2018). Making kin with the machines. *Journal of Design and Science, 3*(5). https://doi.org/10.21428/bfafd97b

Lin, J., Shen, Z., Zhang, A., & Chai, Y. (2018). Blockchain and IoT based food traceability for smart agriculture. In *Proceedings of the 3rd International Conference on Crowd Science and Engineering, Association for Computing Machinery, New York.* https://doi.org/10.1145/3265689.3265692

Morozov, E. (2013). *To Save Everything, Click Here: The Folly of Technological Solutionism.* London: Public Affairs.

Nissen, B., Pschetz, L., Murray-Rust, D., Mehrpouya, H., Oosthuizen, S., & Speed, C. (2018). GeoCoin: Supporting ideation and collaborative design with smart contracts. In *Conference on Human Factors in Computing Systems—Proceedings, April.* https://doi.org/10.1145/3173574.3173737

Nori. (n.d.). For further information, see https://nori.com/.

Ostrom, E. (1999). *Design Principles and Threats to Sustainable Organizations that Manage Commons.* Workshop Working Paper No. W99-6. Workshop in Political Theory and Policy Analysis, and the Center for the Study of Institutions, Population and Environmental Change, Indiana University, Bloomington, IN. http://hdl.handle.net/10535/5465

Parra-Agudelo, L., Choi, J. H., Foth, M., & Estrada, C. (2018). Creativity and design to articulate difference in the conflicted city: Collective intelligence in Bogota's grassroots organisations. *AI & SOCIETY, 33*(1), 147–158.

Pazaitis, A., De Filippi, P., & Kostakis, V. (2017). Blockchain and value systems in the sharing economy: The illustrative case of Backfeed. *Technological Forecasting and Social Change, 125*(C), 105–115. https://doi.org/10.1016/j.techfore.2017.05.025

Pitt, H. (2016). An apprenticeship in plant thinking. In M. Bastian, O. Jones, & N. Moore (Eds.), *Participatory Research in More-than-Human Worlds* (pp. 92–106). Abingdon, Oxon: Routledge.

Provenance. (2015). *Blockchain: The Solution for Transparency in Product Supply Chains.* Retrieved from www.provenance.org/whitepaper

Pschetz, L., Pothong, K., & Speed, C. (2019). Autonomous distributed energy systems: Problematising the invisible through design, drama and deliberation. In *Proceedings of the 2019 CHI Conference on Human Factors in Computing Systems. Association for Computing Machinery, New York*, pp. 1–14. https://doi.org/10.1145/3290605.3300617

Puig de la Bellacasa, M. (2011). Matters of care in technoscience: Assembling neglected things. *Social Studies of Science*, *41*(1), 85–106. doi:10.1177/0306312710380301

Puig de la Bellacasa, M. (2017). *Matters of Care: Speculative Ethics in More Than Human Worlds*. Minneapolis, MN: University of Minnesota Press.

Rankin, J., Elsden, C., Sibbald, I., Stevenson, A., Vines, J., & Speed, C. (2020). PizzaBlock: Designing artefacts and roleplay to understand decentralised identity management systems. In *DIS 2020—Proceedings of the 2020 ACM Designing Interactive Systems Conference*, pp. 1593–1606. https://doi.org/10.1145/3357236.3395568

Regen Network. (n.d.). For further information, see www.regen.network/.

Rozas, D., Tenorio-Fornés, A., Diaz-Molina, S., & Hassan, S. (2021). When Ostrom meets blockchain: Exploring the potentials of blockchain for commons governance. *Sage Open*, *11*(1), 1–14.

Seidler, P., Kolling, P., & Hampshire, M. (2017). Terra 0—Can an augmented forest own and utilize itself? In R. Catlow, M. Garrett, N. Jones, & S. Skinner (Eds.), *Artists Re:thinking the Blockchain*. United Kingdom: Torque Editions and Furtherfield.

Smith, N., Bardzell, S., & Bardzell, J. (2017). Designing for cohabitation: Naturecultures, hybrids, and decentering the human in design. In *CHI '17: Proceedings of the 2017 CHI Conference on Human Factors in Computing Systems, May*, pp. 1714–1725. http://dx.doi.org/10.1145/3025453.3025948

Teli, M., Lyle, P., & Sciannamblo, M. (2018). Institutioning the common: The case of commonfare. In *Proceedings of the 15th Participatory Design Conference: Full Papers, Volume 1, Association for Computing Machinery, New York*. https://doi.org/10.1145/3210586.3210590

Troncoso, S., & Utratel, A. M. (2019). *If Only I Had a Heart: A DisCO Manifesto*, 15 November.

Tsing, A. L. (2015). *The Mushroom at the End of the World*. Princeton, NJ: Princeton University Press.

Wang, X. (2020). Blockchain chicken farm: And other stories of tech in China's countryside. In T. Hwang, B. Tarnoff, M. Weigel, A. Daub, & X. Wang (Eds.), *FSG Originals x Logic*. New York; London: Macmillan.

Wolff, A., Gooch, D., Cavero Montaner, J. J., Rashid, U., & Kortuem, G. (2016). Creating an understanding of data literacy for a data-driven society. *Journal of Community Informatics*, *12*(3).

Zuboff, S. (2019). *The Age of Surveillance Capitalism: The Fight for a Human Future at the New Frontier of Power*. London: Profile Books.

31

A BRIEF HISTORY OF SPECULATIVE DESIGN AND URBAN FOOD GOVERNANCE

Serena Pollastri

Introduction

Food and place are inextricably linked in the way they shape each other. Settlements in all cultures around the world have always been designed around food, by either establishing them in close proximity to fertile agricultural areas, or by ensuring that produce could be easily brought into the city via infrastructures such as rivers, canals, or roads (Steel, 2008). The industrialisation of food systems has radically changed, through displacement and mediation, the relationship between urban populations and the food they eat, but it has not removed it. In a way, industrialisation has brought the importance of this relationship to the surface, by showing how the design of the city – its areas of fresh food scarcity, take away shops, out-of-town malls, car-based infrastructures, home appliances – have scripted our eating practices (Clune & Pollastri, 2020).

People need to eat; they always will. And the future of cities will also be the future of its food (and vice versa). Future city plans, visions, and imaginaries always imply strategies, visions or imaginaries for food and food systems, even if they are not always explicitly included. This chapter looks back at how speculative visions of urban food futures have changed in the last century and discusses recurring themes and ideas in relation to their contemporary culture and society.

In the broader sense, issues of food in future cities could be explored in many directions, touching upon various stages of food production, distribution, access, and consumption processes. Prototypes of future supermarkets, kitchens, and cooking appliances make frequent appearances at design and trade fairs. Science fiction films and literature are also rich in provocative representation of speculative food futures. These visions all play different roles and have different aims (e.g. to promote the adoption of specific technology in the market, test the acceptability of possible scenarios, critique emerging trends, or complement the storyline of a film). This chapter focuses specifically on visions of urban food futures in which the fabric and governance of the city and its surrounding region is shaped, directly or indirectly, by the challenge of providing food to its citizens, as will be further described in the following sections. None of the visions presented in the chapter have been developed as part of government-led planning efforts, nor were they designed to be directly implemented or built on specific sites

DOI: 10.4324/9781003055907-36

(with the exception of Soleri's Arcosanti). What all these visions have in common is that they articulate the questions of food governance that they explore, and, by doing so, articulate visually and spatially key themes and issues. A summary of the conversation threads between such themes and issues, as well as the way in which they influenced city governance practices, will be presented in the concluding section.

This study has been informed by a review of literature and archives that sought to collect and select an array of international examples that summarise and represent some dominant themes and paradigms. It is important to point out that the focus of this review is primarily on European and North American visions. Visions of futures are highly influenced by the culture, politics, and society of their historical and geographical context. They inevitably draw from histories and ideas of what a city is in order to discuss what futures might unfold. Further, "the future" is never a homogeneous entity, but rather a discreet and diverse one. Just like in the present, daily life will look differently to different people around the world (List, 2005; Savransky & Rosengarten, 2017; van der Heijden, 2005), adding further complexity to any attempt to understand what the future might be like. So, while this chapter only offers a partial peek into some of the conversations on food, futures, and urbanism that unfolded over the last century, it is also an invitation to discover and reflect on other histories, and other futures.

Building an archive of speculative visions of urban food futures

This chapter reviews speculative urban food futures that have been envisioned for different purposes: responding to "what if" questions with the aim to plan, challenge, discuss, or critique. Unlike anticipatory scenarios that are grounded on and respond to data, speculative futures are not bounded by trend forecasts, but engage with the often disruptive implications of radical choices that are made in alternative presents or near futures (Auger, 2013). As such, they have a proactive ability of worldmaking, promoting or discrediting particular agendas (Dunn & Cureton, 2020). And because future visions are never neutral, but loaded with hopes, dreams, and critiques, they can help us understand the social, cultural, and political context in which they are created (Cook, 2008). At the same time, they influence the culture in which they are disseminated, by shaping expectations, fears, and attitudes towards the future (Cook, 2012), as well as reality itself (Law & Urry, 2004). For these reasons, looking at past speculative visions when reflecting on possible urban food governance futures, may help us trace a visual history of critical cultural conversations that influenced, to different degrees, culture, policies, urban design, and societal expectations.

As no comprehensive history of speculative visions of urban food has yet been published, background research for this chapter was conducted by sifting through literature and archives in two different areas: speculative urbanism and speculative food futures, looking for intersections and common threads. It draws in part on the methodology and findings from the research that was undertaken while writing the UK Government Report: "A Visual History of the Future" (Dunn et al., 2014), which collected and analysed one hundred years of future city visions. The 20 recurrent city categories and six dominant paradigms identified in the report provided a useful map to navigate some of the key historical debates on future cities. Starting from this map, I then investigated whether and how food issues were explored in the various categories and paradigms, and how these relate to the broader discourse on food production and consumption of their time. This further research into the historical context of the visions of urban food futures derived from the report led to the (often serendipitous) discovery of additional examples. This created a growing visual archive and the foundation of a typology of sorts. But while this proved a challenging task (with categories being constantly challenged by new images added to the mix), clear conversation threads between visions of futures started to emerge.

This chapter is an attempt to reconstruct and follow some of these conversations by focusing on three main identifiable themes: *productive zoning*, *agrarian urbanism*, and *multispecies entanglements*. By using these themes as lenses, it discusses the way in which future urban food has been imagined throughout the twentieth and the first two decades of the twenty-first century.

Visions of cities shaped by food

While ensuring a reliable supply of food for the city has always been critical, large-scale food growing within the boundaries of the city has historically been a rare occurrence (Roggema, 2017; Steel, 2008). Yet, several speculative visions of urban futures do imagine productive cities providing food to their dwellers. Other visions which attempt to provide a solution to the issue of food supply and provenance do so by extending the boundaries of the city beyond its urban fabric, with material networks and infrastructures pervading peri-urban and rural productive areas. In both cases, such city visions tend to address one or more of the following concerns: food scarcity, citizen's health and well-being, and environmental concerns. While these three issues are often interrelated, they identify distinct priorities, and may lead to different urban forms and city designs. Specifically, the productive city appears to be usually articulated as *productive zoning*, *agrarian urbanism*, or *multispecies entanglements*. These three themes or paradigms describe three different types of relation between food and urban fabric:

(1) *Productive zoning* identifies situations in which one or more defined areas are dedicated to farming and food production;
(2) *Agrarian urbanism* includes visions of decline of the city in favour of decentralised models of living in productive countryside;
(3) *Multispecies entanglements* are cities where food production and multispecies relations are embedded within building and urban spaces.

Productive zoning

The planning of dedicated zones for food production within the fabric or the regional network of the city is a recurrent feature of many visions of urban food futures throughout history. A logical starting point for this review would certainly be Ebeneezer Howard's "Plan for a Garden City", first issued in 1898, which quickly became an influential predecessor of twentieth-century visions of both food grids and agrarian urbanism. Howard's plan embedded agricultural production in the city by rethinking its grid as a de-centralised network of connected small towns and functional zones surrounded by fields, forests, and water reservoirs. Howard's Garden City sought to provide a healthy alternative to polluted and overcrowded Victorian cities of Britain, by combining the vibrancy of city life with the idyllic peace of the countryside (Hardy, 1991). Socialised production of food was to be present at a different scale in the Garden City: from homes with common gardens and co-operative kitchens, to orchards and small dairy farms in common spaces, to rings of allotments marking the edge of each settlements, to a larger-scale agricultural landscape within the productive greenbelt surrounding each network of towns (Parham, 2016).

Howard was a strong proponent of keeping food networks local and saw the potential of linking food production with urban living: "every farmer now has a market close to his door. There are 30,000 townspeople to be fed... and this is a market which the rent he contributes will help to build up" (Howard, 1902, p. 12). While Howard never expected the dwellers of the Garden City to source all of their food stuff locally, he advocated for stronger local food networks, including the circular use of home food waste as compost for local agricultural land. While such radical ideas never fully materialised in the suburban landscapes of UK Garden Towns (such as Letchworth and Welwyn), which drew from Howard's models, they did contribute to the growth of the allotment movement of the twentieth century in the UK and in cities like Helsinki (Parham, 2015), as well as to a broader discourse on the importance of urban food networks.

Similarly to Howard's Garden City, Le Corbusier's unbuilt plans for the Ville Radieuse (1935) was designed as a blueprint for the metropolis of the future, and sought to bring order and social reform to the city through the use of a rational grid. But the design solutions to achieve this were radically different from the traditional English town ideals of the garden city. The plan involved a symmetrical geometry of megastructures providing high-density housing. The focus on vertical development for the built environment would allow for plenty of common green space to be enjoyed by everyone. Orchards and productive gardens were included as one of the features of the urban landscape. However, these were to be enjoyed by residents more for their aesthetic value and products rather than as an activity to be involved in. Vegetable gardens in particular were to be combined in a single area, so that it would be easy for a hired gardener to tend to them (Sadri, 2018). Le Corbusier, in fact, did not consider gardening to be an appealing activity for the urban dweller: "Some people may call all this a form of healthy exercise. On the contrary, it is a stupid ineffective and sometimes dangerous thing. The children cannot play there, for they have no room to run about in, nor can the parents indulge in games or sports there. And the result of all this is a few pears and apples, a few carrots, a little parsley and so on. The whole thing is ridiculous" (Corbusier, 1929, p. 203). Far from dismissing the importance of agricultural production, he saw it as something to be conducted through efficient methods, going as far as proposing specific plans for farms and cooperative rural villages that would mirror the rationalist methods he championed in his urban visions (Roskam, 2016).

The visions of future cities that Le Corbusier developed throughout his career all point towards a need to rethink regions as efficient networks of concentrated residential and productive areas that are connected by roads and are built for cars rather than pedestrians. In this sense, they contribute to the rise in popularity of the automobile utopias of the first half of the twentieth century (Shelton, 2011). These utopias saw in private car ownership the key to enable people to live in spacious homes in green suburbs and residential areas, with downtown office spaces located in high-rises that could be directly accessed via highways. The most influential of such models, which largely shaped the design of U.S. cities, was Futurama, a fictional diorama of a 1960s city designed by Bel Geddes for the General Motors' pavilion at the 1939 New York World's Fair. Futurama envisaged the future of not only the city, but of an entire region, including areas for farmland. These were mostly depicted as a large concentration of monocultural agriculture, designed with the intent of efficiently providing the most produce to be distributed at the national scale, rather than as an area for the enjoyment of local food and landscape. In Futurama, shopping and recreational activities were also concentrated in designated areas away from residential zones and only accessible by car. The vision of the future developed by Bel Geddes and General Motors undoubtedly contributed to justifying the need for a more pervasive car-based regional infrastructure, and in turn a design of the nation that could fit with the opportunities and requirements of the automobile, thus paving the way for the rise of out-of-town malls and food deserts, that is, areas in which people who do not drive have no access to fresh food (Clune & Pollastri, 2020).

In the 1950s, as suburban urbanism fuelled by modernist dreams of automotive utopias shaped the North American landscape, Paolo Soleri proposed the design of dense organic megastructures for communal living as a direct critique to car dependency and sprawl. Unlike the efficiently managed entirely anthropocentric urban and rural landscapes in Le Corbusier's and Bel Geddes' plans, Soleri envisioned dense settlements encapsulated by earth-casted megastructures surrounded by unspoiled nature. Such a concept is central to the design of Arcosanti, a settlement in Arizona which, almost 70 years from its original conception (1954), is still being developed by a community of permanent and temporary residents (Wainwright, 2016).

Arcosanti is the manifestation of Soleri's vision of arcologies, or ecological architectures: urban megastructures able to host all aspects of life, including work, education, culture, leisure, and health for thousands of people. Arcologies are designed as vertical multi-layered habitats with designated zones for different city and private functions (Dunn et al., 2014; Soleri, 2008). Just outside of Arcosanti, a system of greenhouses on a south-facing slope was installed both for food production and solar energy harvesting, which supplies some power to the city. Over the years, the communities who passed through Arcosanti have been experimenting with ways of improving the city's food self-reliance through various approaches and business ventures, all aimed at increasing crop efficiency while maintaining the overall organicist ethos of Soleri's approach. Crucially, arcologies were never intended to be self-sufficient, and the importance of local and interregional networks and links was never underestimated by Soleri, who saw value in increasing self-reliance, but accepted the need for certain goods to be brought in from elsewhere, particularly in Arizona, where the dry seasons and relatively poor soil make large-scale food production challenging.

The inclusion of productive zones to supply the city becomes an important feature when settlements designed as closed ecosystems are to be sent out to space. The Stanford Torus, a space colony designed by NASA in 1975, was fuelled both by environmental concerns and technological enthusiasm. Thought of as a response to unsustainable growth, it aimed to harness space-age technologies to develop a self-sufficient community, living and working in space (Johnson & Holbrow, 1977). Crucially, because of its distance from Earth, the community would have to be entirely self-sufficient in its everyday needs, including energy and food provision. For this reason, large areas within the Torus were dedicated to agriculture and food production, with gardeners and farmers to tend to mechanised plants and production facilities arranged on multiple tiers for maximised efficiency. Elsewhere in the Torus the city would have looked like a fairly dense suburb with plenty of green space availability, not too dissimilar from Howard's Garden City in look and feel. Despite the pastoral aesthetics of the living quarters, however, cutting-edge technologies would need to be implemented to achieve reliable food production, thus ensuring human survival.

While NASA's vision of a space colony may perhaps never be realised, the idea that ecosystems can be artificially generated and maintained through technologies have inspired numerous attempts to overcome Earth's limitations and support life in otherwise uninhabitable environments. Green Float, designed by Shimizu Corporation in 2014, is a concept of a self-sufficient expandable artificial island floating in the Pacific Ocean. Like Arcosanti, it is designed to fulfil all the functions of urban life, but, because of its distance from the mainland, it also seeks to respond to the challenge of providing sufficient food for its inhabitants. Each island includes a large, multi-layered "plant factory" and animal farming facilities in designated zones. Similarly to the Stanford Torus, food production in Green Float relies on fairly conventional methods of agriculture and farming (automated greenhouses, reliance on livestock, indoor growing) which are made more efficient and less reliant on external resources through the implementation of cutting-edge technologies.

The cities presented in this section are vastly different in their conceptualisation, as well as in their aesthetics and the daily life and aspirations of their inhabitants. But in their efforts to design food production zones within or outside the city limits they do help us visualise the scale of the farming operations that would be necessary to feed the city. Residential and recreational space in Howard's towns, the Stanford Torus, and Green Float are overshadowed by the scale of the areas dedicated to food production. And as to Soleri, Le Corbusier, and Bel Geddes...well, they never intended their cities to be entirely reliant on local production.

Whether based on car or communal living, the well-being of city dwellers is at the centre of these visions, and that is achieved through the re-envisioning of the city plan, starting from a more efficient and sustainable zoning. All functions are considered and arranged in designated zones, including food production. Further, there is, in all these plans, an acknowledgement of the benefits of being in close proximity to green spaces. So, what if the city itself were to become rural?

Agrarian urbanism

The examples of city visions grouped in this category all share an interest in rethinking the boundaries of *the urban* and *the rural* and propose dispersed cities in productive landscapes. In the 1920s and 1930s, as modernist approaches to urbanisation were growing in popularity, a group of town planners and architects in the Soviet Union sought to move away from the focus on rigid zoning and efficient concentration of functions, towards distributed models of living. Disurbanism, the approach theorised by Mikhail Okhitovich, was strongly opposed by the Communist party as incompatible with Stalin's collectivisation efforts, but was prolific in speculative plans and radical proposals (Lucarelli, 2012). Moisei Ginzburg's Green City plan for Moscow (1930) sought to find a "socialist medicine" for the pollution, dirt, and inequalities of the city by dismantling the idea of the city as a unit and developing a nationwide transport, energy, and communication grid connecting glass cubicles and mobile homes dispersed across the countryside, either individually or in self-sufficient settlements (Levin, 2018). Similar to Howard's Garden City, Ginzburg's idea sought to promote disperse and local access to industrial and agricultural production by integrating the rural to the urban through a grid of infrastructures. Ginzburg's visionary dismantling of the city to rearrange it as a distributed network also reverberates in later visions of integral or nomadic urbanism, such as those conceptualised a few decades later by Constant Nieuwenhuys, Luigi Pellegrin, and Archigram.

Ginzburg and Le Corbusier engaged directly in debates on the nature of the city and the countryside, with Ginzburg questioning the assumption of rural life being in itself undesirable, and stating that it might be so simply because it is often left behind in capitalist development processes focusing their resources on urban living (Lucarelli, 2012).

While Disurbanist ideas never really gained significant traction in the West, movements calling for alternatives to dense, centralised urban forms started to grow in international relevance in the twentieth century. Like Howard's Garden Cities, the alternatives proposed here called for a stronger integration of elements of the countryside in urban settlements and celebrated the benefits of rural life and green space on personal and societal well-being.

Charles Waldheim identifies clear common characteristics and connections between visions of what he calls "agrarian urbanism", that is, cities where "agricultural production [is] a formative element of city structure, rather than as an adjunct, something to be inserted into already existing structures" (2010, para. 3). In compiling a brief history of agrarian urbanism, Waldheim refers to three seminal projects, that, while developed decades apart, all directly reference each other and a desire to reconceptualise the city: Broadacre, The New Regional Pattern, and Agronica.

Both Broadacre City and The New Regional Pattern are large models intended to propose an alternative regional organisation for North America to the traditional one based on the dichotomy of city (including urban centres and suburbs) and countryside. Both plans were directly inspired by Ford's efforts to decentralise industrial production and organise it around small factories distributed in rural areas, around villages where workers would also be required to grow most of their own food on provided garden land, as self-subsistence was seen as the key out of the great depression of the late 1920s (Frampton, 2007).

Frank Lloyd Wright's plans for Broadacre City (1932–1950s) are based on his visions for Usonia: a new form of egalitarian culture for the United States based on private ownership of small but comfortable homes dispersed in a productive agricultural landscape. In "The Disappearing City" (1932), Wright drafts the initial plans for the Usonian city of Broadacre: a future city that will be "everywhere and nowhere" (Frampton, 2007, p. 190). Each resident of Broadacre would be given one modern house with a large garden and one acre of land to cultivate. This organisation of the territory would result in an extremely low-density agricultural landscape in which residents would rely on a grid-like infrastructure and private car ownership for transport and communication.

Ludwig Hilberseimer's plan for a New Regional Pattern for the United States (1944) is also based on the integration of private properties, cultivated landscape, and the infrastructure grid, to achieve a disperse model of urbanisation. Hilberseimer directly references Wright's work as well as the influence of the Garden City movement, and articulates a modular plan based on a series of "settlement units" connected by the interstate highway system. It is worth noting that both Hilberseimer's and Wright's plan for decentralised urbanisation imply a complete clearance of the landscape to be converted into agricultural land. Despite their pastoral aesthetics, these visions of the future are artificial and anthropocentric – the type of sprawling visions harshly criticised by Soleri and those who advocate for the use of technology to concentrate rather than expand the spatial impact of human activities.

Andrea Branzi offers a critical angle to the concept of the disperse city in his speculative vision for Agronica (1995), which draws on the provocation he previously offered in No-Stop City, a series of abstract city plans that he developed with Archizoom in 1969. Agronica is a vision of a dispersed productive urban landscape developed as a concept for Philips Electronics and in collaboration with Domus Academy. It responds to a question that remained open in No-Stop City: how will the nomadic, flexible city feed itself? It does so by proposing the development of a pervasive energy grid in the countryside that would connect a network of buildings and food production facilities. Neither No-Stop City nor Agronica were intended as proposals to be built, but rather as tools to instigate conversations on the nature of the contemporary city. Branzi's work offers an alternative to rigid modernist dichotomies, including those of "city" and "countryside". In this sense, it is a radical departure from the type of urbanism championed by Le Corbusier, and references Hilberseimer's grid as the basic organisational element of the landscape. However, the grid in No-Stop City and Agronica is not so much the vector for moving private vehicles, but the infrastructure onto which to "plug" light moveable structures that can be rearranged and reassembled in a continuous state of flow (Branzi, 2006). Agriculture and energy, rather than residential spaces and transport, are the forces that shape the city in Agronica (Waldheim, 2010), which is loosely configured by the network identified by the grid. As such, one could find in Agronica the same instigations to nomadism and flows proposed by the Disurbanists.

While the radical plans envisioned by Ginzburg, Wright, Hilberseimer, and Branzi may never be directly implemented, a similar interest in redesigning the countryside for the development of small residential communities strongly integrated with productive practices and landscapes, such as Aldo Cibic's "Rethinking Happiness" for the 2012 Venice Biennale or the failed plans for the Dongtan Eco-City in China. Since 2010, Andrés Duany and the New Urbanist movement have been looking at the concept of agrarian urbanism, defined here as "a society involved with the growing of food" (Haugh, 2010) as, once again, a way to counteract the ills of the sprawling North American metropolis envisioned in Futurama, and in particular its pollution, food deserts, and lack of community integration. However, unlike the speculative visions presented in this section, this version of agrarian urbanism does not seek to propose a radically new alternative, but rather looks back at the past to learn from the experience of Garden Cities to advocate for a better integration of community life and food production in cities and towns that are designed as collections of strong neighbourhood communities (Duany & Company, 2011)

Multispecies entanglements

The two paradigms of Productive Zoning and agrarian urbanism both favoured a predominantly horizontal organisation of urban fabric and regional infrastructures to address the matters of scales arising from the issues of providing food for the city.

Alongside these modes of spatial organisations of urban food, there has been in recent years a growing interest in thinking of cities in which food production is embedded within urban architecture and in private and public spaces. In general, these visions address the issue of food futures as one of coexistence of more-than-human species and their relations with artificial environments within the city. Addressing this coexistence as a resource, they propose symbiotic entanglements of technology and nature, often in unconventional places.

An early example of speculative design rethinking living spaces as spaces for food production is Vegetable Garden House, by Gruppo 9999. It was designed for the 1972 exhibition "Italy, The New Domestic Landscape" at the Museum of Modern Art in New York, which presented examples showcasing the variety of attitudes towards modernity that emerged in Italian design throughout the 1960s and early 1970s. One of such attitudes identified by the curators of the exhibition was that of "contestation" of consumerism, which used design as a method of inquiry and action (Ambasz, 1972). Gruppo 9999's work featured in this category, alongside other leading figures from the Italian Radical Design movement, including Andrea Branzi with Archizoom.

The work of Gruppo 9999 was primarily concerned with the destructive power of technology over nature, and a direct critique to modern lifestyles alienating humans from the natural world. Vegetable Garden House proposes a speculative model for a living space in which technology is at the service of nature and humans, by providing the infrastructures and means for indoor food production. In their essay for the exhibition catalogue, Gruppo 9999 proposes "returning once more to elements that have long been lost and are now forgotten: ancient and primordial things like food and water, side by side with technological inventions [...] without returning to mythical and impossible conditions" (Gruppo 9999, 1972, p. 282).

The project for Vegetable Garden House was presented as a series of drawings and photomontages, although an initial prototype was built at the Space Electronic club in Florence. It featured a bedroom with flooded floor and a series of planters for growing vegetables, as well as an "air bed" in the middle of the room for sleeping while floating on the water (Caldini & Birelli, 2008; Ornella, 2017). While drawing from broader concerns with modernity and alienation, which were characteristics of Italian Radical Design, Vegetable Garden House represented a unique example of design for multispecies coexistence, and anticipated a do-it-yourself attitude of design for personal resilience that will become more prominent in later examples of this kind.

Such an attitude is particularly evident in Mitigation of Shock, a project that Superflux first presented in 2017 at the Centre for Contemporary Culture in Barcelona, as an installation part of the After the End of the World show, and later in Singapore as part of the 2219: Future Imagined exhibition at ArtScience Museum in 2019. Mitigation of Shock transports the visitor to an apartment of 2050, in a future world of resource scarcity, food insecurity, supply network disruptions, and extreme weather events caused by climate change. The fully functioning life-sized speculative prototype of the apartment is, for Superflux, an attempt to make the complexity of climate change "tangible, relatable and specific" (Superflux, n.d.), by showing elements of daily domestic life in the "new normal" (Jain & Ardern, 2017).

In a future characterised by scarcity, all areas of the apartment, which would once have been dedicated to relaxation or leisure, are taken over by food growing devices. These include food computers and fogponics machines built from hacked IKEA furniture, components of digital devices once intended for entertainment, diffusers, as well as scavenged materials. These food computers and fogponics use optimised light and vapour to grow vegetables, herbs, and mushrooms in shelves covered in aluminium foil. Alongside newspapers reporting of food shortages, the visitor to the apartment can find recipe books on cooking with worms, pets, or urban foxes (Superflux, n.d.). The apartment is a multispecies microcosm that shows new ways of living with and through multispecies entanglements (Jain & Ardern, 2020).

Mitigation of Shock shows the degree to which human life in the Western world would have to adapt to respond to the daily threats of climate change. But despite the bleakness of the environmental models that grounded the background research for the project, Superflux resists seeing the future as solely dystopian. By telling a story of human resourcefulness and adaptability, Mitigation of Shock "deconstruct[s] the polarity of utopian and dystopian imagining to build and explore complex, heterogeneous futures which can be experienced in the present" (Jain et al., 2019, p. 56).

Many of the recent examples of multispecies entanglements seek to equip the city with ways to ensure resilient access to food during shortages or disruptions caused by climate change. Some, like the apartment designed by Superflux, envision these entanglements to be part of haphazardly retrofitted buildings. These include the Crown Heights Bodega EcoHaven, which involves a series of digital illustrations produced by Olalekan Jeyifous in 2020: a vision of a future New York where existing buildings in the Crown Heights neighbourhood are covered in aquaponic structures and imaginary self-sustaining biotechnologies (Zeiger, 2020).

Others have instead focused on structures and buildings that are specifically designed to host practices of food production to make cities resilient to the climate crisis. In 2017, Terreform ONE designed Cricket Shelter: a prototype for a modular insect farm that could also be used as an emergency shelter during extreme weather events. Individual "Bio Units" that host crickets are the building blocks of the shelter. The units are connected with tubes that crickets can use to move around and to reach "sex pods" where reproduction and birth take place (Terreform ONE, n.d.). This modular structure is designed to be easily assembled on site, and to provide easy access to a nutritious source of protein to replace meat from livestock. Cricket Shelter embodies some of the salient characteristics of the work of Terreform ONE, an architecture non-profit organisation that focuses on developing speculative plans and prototypes to tackle local environmental threats and issues. Multispecies survival and urban food provision are some of the themes that the work of Terreform ONE addresses through digital fabrication, 3D printing, and synthetic biology.

Similarly to Terreform ONE, ecoLogicStudio has been exploring how new construction techniques can be used to embed food sources into urban architecture with their Photo. Syntetica consortium, in partnership with The Urban Morphogenic Lab at Bartlett (University College London) and the Synthetic Landscape Lab at the University of Innsbruck. The consortium developed a photosynthetic urban system with live spirulina algae used in architectural cladding. The cladding is lightweight and transparent, with green micro-algae visible throughout. These algae capture solar radiation, absorb CO_2, and, when harvested and dried, can be used to produce bio-plastic, fertiliser, biofuel, and low carbon food (ecoLogicStudio, n.d.). And while this food would perhaps not fit into the culinary traditions that we are used to, it also questions (like Terreform ONE did) whether traditional food sources are still appropriate in the age of scarcity. Is now the time to rethink not just *how* we farm, but also *what* we farm?

In the last decade, new techniques of digital fabrication and processes of computational construction have inspired the design of structures and relations that could not have been achieved through traditional construction techniques (Menges, 2015). It is now possible to not only speculate, but also to prototype buildings conceived as entanglements of multiple species in symbiotic relations – living buildings that react and behave. In this new, emerging paradigm, the question of urban food planning is not only a spatial one, but also a material and relational one, which cannot be easily disentangled from the fabric and social structures of the city itself. Food production and cycles become visible and constituting matter of the city.

Conclusions

The conversations captured in this chapter are mapped and summarised in Figure 31.1. This timeline also shows threads of direct and indirect influence and oppositions, as well as the debates in which the creators of different visions have been engaged.

As already mentioned in the introduction, none of the visions presented in this chapter was developed with the purpose of being directly translated into urban plans and governance practices for specific cities, with the exception perhaps of Arcosanti, which still exists as a small-scale utopian experiment of its own kind. But, as previously mentioned in the chapter, even unbuilt visions of urban futures do influence how futures are shaped. This is also the case in the visions of urban food futures presented in this study, some of which have significantly shaped food governance practices, albeit not always in the way that was intended.

In the UK, Ebeneezer Howard directly oversaw the construction of the first garden cities (Letchworth Garden City and Welwyn Garden City), and Howard's ideas were directly incorporated into the New Towns Act of 1946, which made possible and informed the development of several New Towns in England, Scotland, and Wales, altogether housing an estimate of about 2 million people (Grindrod, 2013). But in reality, the "socialised food features" (Parham, 2015, p. 133) that constitute part of Howard's visions (including common gardens and co-operative kitchens) are rarely implemented in these New Towns, which articulate the spatial interpretation of the Garden City model without many of the social aspects of the vision. Similarly, in the U.S., the drive to leave dense and polluted cities towards idyllic countryside did not quite result in the self-sufficient networks of farms dreamt by Hilberseimer and Wright. In various iterations of Futurama, the modernist city and its individualistic society, while dreaming of agrarian utopia, disintegrated into sprawl and suburbs that swallowed up the countryside they once romanticised as a pastoral utopia.

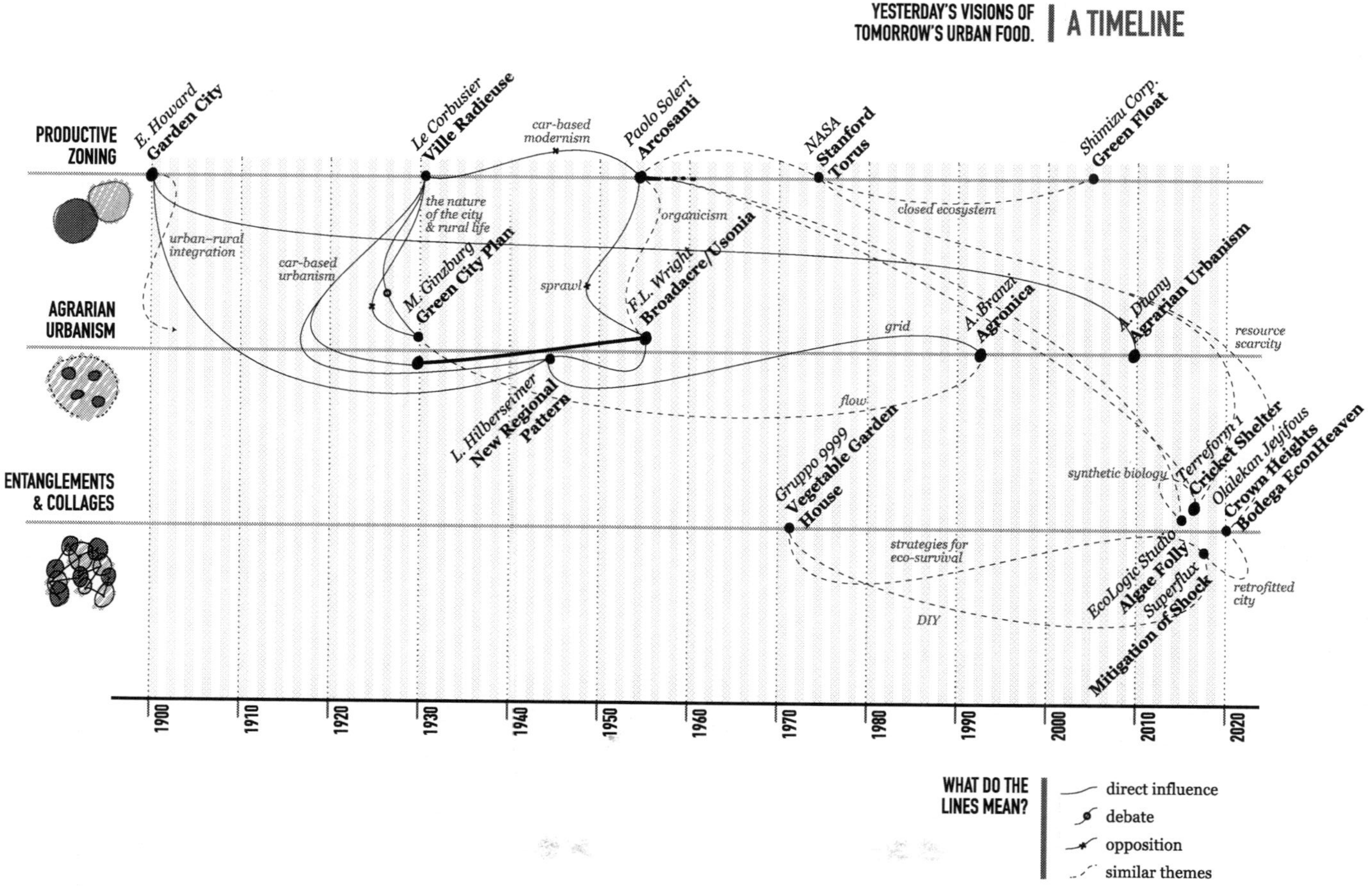

Figure 31.1 A timeline of past visions of urban food futures

In a book titled *Food and Urbanism*, Parham reflects on the evidence that relationships do not "just happen", but are affected by the design of the city, as well as by global economic and political forces (Parham, 2015, pp. 4, 7). Such complex interdependencies provide a key to understanding the failure of urban food utopias built on the self-sufficiency of cities. But at the same time, experiments in rethinking networks, creating closed ecosystems for more-than-human cooperation, and retrofitting the city for emergency food production all provide insights on how global dynamics can be rethought for resilience and preparedness (Pollastri, 2021). While technology has never been the sole answer to pressing issues of resource scarcity and climate crisis, it has provided interesting insights into how we could build (or hack) radically different relationships between us, our cities, other creatures, and our food.

The development of participatory methods that bring together diverse communities in processes of futuring is therefore essential for the development of truly sustainable pluralistic visions, as well as for questioning and understanding who may benefit from them and how (Dunn & Cureton, 2020; Pollastri et al., 2018). As we move forward to a time in which urgent action is needed to rethink the future of the world's urban food systems, looking at the plurality of futures imagined in the past should inspire us to not take monolithic solutions at face value, but engage in critical conversations on possible urban food futures, in which diverse solutions and ways of living sustainably can coexist.

References

Ambasz, E. (1972). *Italy: The New Domestic Landscape: Achievements and Problems of Italian Design*. New York Graphic Society Books. https://assets.moma.org/documents/moma_catalogue_1783_300062429.pdf?_ga=2.208116625.229098484.1614099129-119426388.1614099129

Auger, J. (2013). Speculative design: Crafting the speculation. *Digital Creativity*, *24*(1), 11–35. https://doi.org/10.1080/14626268.2013.767276

Branzi, A. (1995). Symbiotic metropolis agronica. In E. Manzini & M. Susani (Eds.), *The Solid Side: The Search for Consistency in a Changing World* (p. 103). VK Publishing.

Branzi, A. (2006). *Modernità debole e diffusa. Il mondo del progetto all'inizio del XXI secolo*. Skira.

Caldini, C., & Birelli, G. (2008). *9999* [Interview]. (E. Piccardo, Interviewer). www.youtube.com/watch?v=T5rnDhEFw1o&ab_channel=archphotochannel

Clune, S., & Pollastri, S. (2020). Design for food and wellbeing in future cities. In C. Boyko & R. F. D. Cooper (Eds.), *Designing Future Cities for Wellbeing* (pp. 91–104). Routledge.

Cook, P. (2008). *Drawing: The Motive Force of Architecture* (2nd revised edition). John Wiley & Sons.

Cook, P. (2012). Real is only halfway there. Is drawing dead? [Keynote speech], 20 March, Yale University. www.youtube.com/watch?v=Jpw3Lm8ZKOY&feature=youtube_gdata_player

Corbusier, L. (1929). *The City of Tomorrow and Its Planning*. Courier Corporation.

Corbusier, L. (1935). *La ville radieuse, éléments d'une doctrine d'urbanisme pour l'équipement de la civilisation machiniste: Paris, Genève, Rio de Janeiro, Sao Paolo, Montevideo, Buenos-Aires, Alger, Moscou, Anvers, Barcelone, Stockholm, Nemours, Piacé*. Éditions de l'architecture d'aujourd'hui.

Duany, A., & Company, D. P.-Z. (2011). *Garden Cities: Theory & Practice of Agrarian Urbanism*. The Prince's Foundation for the Built Environment.

Dunn, N., & Cureton, P. (2020). *Future Cities: A Visual Guide*. Bloomsbury Visual Arts.

Dunn, N., Cureton, P., & Pollastri, S. (2014). *A Visual History of the Future (Future Cities)*. UK Government, Office for Science. www.gov.uk/government/uploads/system/uploads/attachment_data/file/360814/14-814-future-cities-visual-history.pdf

ecoLogicStudio. (n.d.). *PhotoSynthetica*. Retrieved 1 March 2021, from www.photosynthetica.co.uk

Frampton, K. (2007). Frank Lloyd Wright and the disappearing city 1929–63. In *Modern Architecture: A Critical History* (4th edition, pp. 186–191). Thames and Hudson Ltd.

Grindrod, J. (2013). *Concretopia: A Journey around the Rebuilding of Postwar Britain*. Old Street Publishing.

Gruppo 9999. (1972). Vegetable garden house. In E. Ambasz (Ed.), *Italy: The New Domestic Landscape: Achievements and Problems of Italian Design* (p. 282). New York Graphic Society Books.

https://assets.moma.org/documents/moma_catalogue_1783_300062429.pdf?_ga=2.208116625.229098484.1614099129-119426388.1614099129

Hardy, D. (1991). *From Garden Cities to New Towns: Campaigning for Town and Country Planning 1899–1946*. Taylor & Francis Group. http://ebookcentral.proquest.com/lib/lancaster/detail.action?docID=182031

Haugh, G. (2010). A new direction for new urbanists. *Planetizen – Urban Planning News, Jobs, and Education*. www.planetizen.com/node/44662

Howard, E. (1902). *To-Morrow: A Peaceful Path to Real Reform* (1st edition). Cambridge University Press.

Jain, A., & Ardern, J. (2017). "How do you imagine your house in 2050?" Interview with the fiction design studio Superflux | Videos | CCCB. www.cccb.org/en/multimedia/videos/anaib-jain-and-jon-ardem-how-do-you-imagine-your-house-in-2050/228471

Jain, A., & Ardern, J. (2020). Feeling the future: Mitigation of shock by Anab Jain and Jon Ardern of Superflux. (Live Conversation, H. Harger, Interviewer), 23 June. www.youtube.com/watch?v=l6DLmJw4fZo&t=223s&ab_channel=ArtScienceMuseum

Jain, A., Ardern, J., & Knight, D. (2019). Mitigation of shock: Post-occupancy anthropology. *Architectural Design*, *89*(3), 54–59. https://doi.org/10.1002/ad.2435

Johnson, R. D., & Holbrow, C. H. (1977). *Space Settlements: A Design Study, Vol. 413*. Scientific and Technical Information Office, National Aeronautics and Space.

Law, J., & Urry, J. (2004). Enacting the social. *Economy and Society*, *33*(3), 390–410. https://doi.org/10.1080/0308514042000225716

Levin, A. (2018). The village within: An alternative genealogy of the urban village. *The Journal of Architecture*, *23*(3), 392–420. https://doi.org/10.1080/13602365.2018.1458045

List, D. (2005). *Scenario Network Mapping: The Development of a Methodology for Social Inquiry*. University of South Australia. www.audiencedialogue.net/snm.html

Lucarelli, F. (2012). Mikhail Okhitovich and the disurbanism. *SOCKS*, 14 July. http://socks-studio.com/2012/07/14/mikhail-okhitovich-and-the-disurbanism/

Menges, A. (Ed.). (2015). *Material Synthesis: Fusing the Physical and the Computational* (1st edition). Academy Press.

Ornella, M. (2017). Florence: The radical revolution of the 9999 group. *Domus*, 20 December. www.domusweb.it/en/architecture/2017/12/20/rivoluzione-9999-la-mostra-che-celebra-la-pratica-manuale.html

Parham, S. (2015). *Food and Urbanism*. Bloomsbury.

Parham, S. (2016). Food and garden cities in principle and practice. *The International Garden Cities Institute*, July. www.gardencitiesinstitute.com/think-piece/food-and-garden-cities-in-principle-and-practice

Pollastri, S. (2021). House of cards: Fragility and resilience of food systems in a pandemic. *Global Discourse*, *11*(1–2), 181–183. https://doi.org/10.1332/204378921X16108171282449

Pollastri, S., Dunn, N., Rogers, C. D. F., Boyko, C. T., Cooper, R., & Tyler, N. (2018). Envisioning urban futures as conversations to inform design and research. In *Proceedings of the Institution of Civil Engineers – Urban Design and Planning*, *171*(4), 146–156. https://doi.org/10.1680/jurdp.18.00006

Roggema, R. (2017). Food in spatial planning and design. In *Food Roofs of Rio de Janeiro: The Pavao-Pavaozinho and Cantagalo Case* Study (pp. 3–27). Springer.

Roskam, C. (2016). Inventing the rural: A brief history of modern architecture in the countryside. *Architectural Design*, *86*(4), 14–19. https://doi.org/10.1002/ad.2062

Sadri, H. (2018). *Neo-liberalism and the Architecture of the Post Professional Era*. Springer.

Savransky, M., & Rosengarten, M. (2017). The lure pf possible futures: On speculative research. In A. Wilkie & M. Savransky (Eds.), *Speculative Research: The Lure of Possible Futures* (1st edition, pp. 1–17). Routledge.

Shelton, T. (2011). Automobile utopias and traditional urban infrastructure: Visions of the coming conflict, 1925–1940. *Traditional Dwellings and Settlements Review*, *22*(2), 63–76.

Soleri, P. (2008). *What If? Quaderno 11 Arcosanti Genesis*. Cosanti Press.

Steel, C. (2008). *Hungry City: How Food Shapes Our Lives*. Vintage Books. www.randomhouse.co.uk/editions/9780099531685

Superflux. (n.d.). Mitigation of shock (London). *Superflux*. Retrieved 26 February 2021, from http://superflux.in/index.php/work/mitigation-of-shock/

Terreform ONE. (n.d.). *CRICKET SHELTER*. Terreform ONE. Retrieved 26 February 2021, from https://terreform.org/cricket-shelter

van der Heijden, K. (2005). *Scenarios: The Art of Strategic Conversation* (2nd edition). Wiley.

Wainwright, O. (2016). Story of cities #35: Arcosanti – the unfinished answer to suburban sprawl. *The Guardian*, 4 May. www.theguardian.com/cities/2016/may/04/story-cities-35-arcosanti-paolo-soleri-desert

Waldheim, C. (2010). Notes toward a history of agrarian urbanism. *Places Journal*, November. https://placesjournal.org/article/history-of-agrarian-urbanism/

Wright, F. L. (1932). *The Disappearing City*. W. F. Payson. www.siteations.com/courses/edgeops2014/readings/wk9/wright_disappearing.pdf

Zeiger, M. (2020). Can quarantine propel us toward planetary sanctuary? *Metropolis*, 30 June. www.metropolismag.com/ideas/quarantine-refugia-covid-19/

32

TOWARDS GOOD FOOD LANDSCAPES

The Intrinsic Links between Continuous Productive Urban Landscapes and Food Governance

Katrin Bohn and André Viljoen

Introduction

Despite environmental urgency (Rockström et al., 2020) and more than 40 years of public recognition of the importance of sustainable food provision (Bohn & Viljoen, 2014), urban food and its complex, systemic aspects are still underrepresented and just emerging in practice, planning, policy and research. This is of great concern: the recently published *Summary for Policymakers* by the UN's Intergovernmental Panel on Climate Change (IPCC) has made it clear that the negative impact of industrialised agriculture on climate change is paramount (IPCC, 2018). Loss of biodiversity, nutrition and health problems, depletion of resources, to name but a few issues, have reached a tipping point in the nexus between rural and urban (Göpel, 2020). Within this, the way urban and metropolitan agglomerations are being fed plays a crucial and currently negative role (Steel, 2008). Approaches from many directions are needed to tackle these problems in the short and long run, one of them being spatial considerations, given that land and space will always form the bases for food production and food system provision.

Urban landscapes can support future-oriented development to meet pressing needs and challenges (Waldheim, 2016). As our societies face many such challenges, including those related to food, there is not only an urgent necessity but also a great opportunity to holistically rethink the design of our cities. Examples like the British garden cities (TCPA and Parham, 2019) or, more recently, the building of *Agromere* on Dutch polders (Jansma & Wertheim-Heck, 2021) or of '*trames vertes/greenways*' in Burkina Faso (Sy et al., 2014) have shown in different ways that urban landscape can also support urban development in relation to food.

However, very little policy or research work explicitly examines the relationships between urban governance and spatial design considerations when planning for food (Tornaghi, 2014). Whilst sustainable development concepts exist in urban planning and design that include (or could include) food system activities, 'practically', there are only isolated projects and approaches – such as those presented here – that give us glimpses of what urban food

DOI: 10.4324/9781003055907-37

governance can achieve for urban spaces when proactively interacting with food-conscious urban design. The intrinsic cooperation needed between food governance and urban design to support food-productive urban landscapes currently remains under-developed and under-researched.

Using the continuous productive urban landscapes (CPULs) concept as a reference, this chapter first explores what (continuous) productive urban landscapes are and how they could shape urban food and its management in the future, as well as how they are or could be shaped by urban food governance. Two case studies from the UK and Germany will help to identify new and missing urban governance linkages between food landscapes and food policy. Aiming to support decision makers and interested citizens, the chapter will conclude by discussing the role of spatial design and planning and the challenges for urban designers engaging in urban food governance futures.

The role of productive urban landscapes in shaping sustainable urban food futures

The urban food system is closely related to urban and rural landscapes: production, processing, trading, consumption, recycling all happens in space that is under competing pressures from many stakeholders. Alongside spatial conflicts related to food, there are food activists who see urban food futures not in urban space or landscape but, for example, in large-scale public procurement (Morgan & Sonnino, 2006) and more conscious individual consumption (Ernährungsrat Berlin, 2017). Whilst it is certainly extremely important for any sustainable urban food system to get procurement, behaviour change and similar 'aspatial' activities right, there too is agreement among researchers and practitioners that the spatial side of the urban food system, especially of food production, is highly beneficial for the quality of urban life (Smit et al., 1996; Viljoen, 2005; Gorgolewski et al., 2011; Lohrberg et al., 2016). In fact, we may consider 'the spatial side', as evidenced in the urban agriculture movement, as one of the originators and inspirations of the urban food discussion as it stands today.

We can discern the growing recognition of the value of urban food spaces in parallel to the growing recognition of 'green' space as a fundamental contributor to urban life. This is exemplified by the growth of nature-based solutions (EC, n.d.) and ecosystem services (TEEB Initiative, 2010) discourses. Whilst the latter can better valorise the benefit to humans provided by the natural environment (Daily, 1997), the former fosters approaches inspired by nature that 'provide environmental, social and economic benefits and help build resilience' (EC, n.d.). Both discourses are closely connected, and nature-based solutions are explicitly tasked to 'support the delivery of a range of ecosystem services' (EC, n.d.). These discourses are also linked to various current landscape design concepts which attribute landscape – urban, rural and peri-urban – a significant role as the spatial and systemic facilitators for sustainable urban development (Viljoen & Bohn, 2020).

The broadly based green infrastructure concept, conceived in the USA around the turn of the century, has been developed in Europe as an EU planning policy instrument since about 2005 and aims at protection and improvement of ecosystem functioning for the benefit of the environment and human life. Green infrastructure here is defined as a 'network of natural and semi-natural areas, features and green spaces' (Naumann et al., 2011, p. 14). Conceptually very similar is the multifunctional landscape that focuses on 'landscapes that can provide multiple functions' and 'serve multiple planning goals/objectives or values' (Kato & Ahern, 2009, p. 799). Multifunctional green infrastructure offers 'several key benefits for designing and planning sustainable cities' (Lovell & Taylor, 2013, p. 1448). However, neither the green or multifunctional infrastructure concepts mention food production or other aspects of the urban (or any) food system (Bohn & Chu, 2019).

Among the main concepts for green (or multifunctional green) infrastructure and those for multifunctional landscape, it is only the CPUL concept that explicitly includes food (Bohn & Chu, 2019). A continuous productive urban landscape is an urban (green) infrastructure linking food-producing sites of varying scales and operating types with other (green) open spaces, right across a town or city, thereby connecting all those parcels of land to the citizens, to other food system activities and ultimately to the rural landscape (Viljoen, 2005). The infrastructural dimension of the concept is very important: We contend that, whilst urban food system activities, especially urban agriculture, could and should happen in all sorts of urban spaces (and do so globally at an unprecedented level), it is their understanding as a spatial and stakeholder network that really makes a difference for future urban development.

How can (continuous) productive urban landscapes be supported by urban food governance?

The planning for, and implementation of, any complex spatial concepts – grouped under the term Green Infrastructure – needs to be, and usually is, governed. This is especially true in the urban realm where any new infrastructures require space, both physically and metaphorically. However, we question in this chapter how such planning is, or could be, *food*-governed. Compared to other essential aspects of urban life that heavily link to urban space design and planning, such as housing, transport or water supply, the feeding of urban populations, especially in a sustainable way, still has received much less attention, as evidenced by the comparative lack of both food policies and implemented food-productive landscapes.

Urban space is always negotiated in an interplay between competing future scenarios, current interests and inherited power structures. Whilst urban food production, as well as other urban food system activities, have proven to offer multiple environmental, social and economic benefits to cities (see above), their proactive and permanent inclusion in urban planning is usually still not widely supported by policy and therefore usually only widespread in temporary, small-scale or precarious situations. One consequence is that funding opportunities, especially for larger-scale projects, have been few. However, in Europe, this is currently changing with the *European Green Deal* launched by the European Commission in 2021 (EC, 2021). Generally, though, the lack of food policy still is a 'puzzling omission' as Pothukuchi and Kaufman (2000) have pointed out in the, now seminal, *Policy Guide on Community and Regional Food Planning* of the American Planning Association (APA, 2007). Even in countries like Germany, which has one of Europe's largest market shares in organic food (BÖLW, 2021), the first food policy councils were only founded in 2016 with the one in Berlin working currently on policy recommendations that also include spaces – and landscapes – for food (Ernährungsrat Berlin, 2019).

Governance – or rather a lack of it – plays a critical role in determining how and by whom space will be used in the future (Edwards et al., 2021). Good relationships between food policy, governance and spatial planning are decisive for enabling productive urban landscapes, but in many cities they are weak (Morgan, 2014). We contend that supportive urban food governance can positively contribute to initiating, implementing and safeguarding sustainable food places and practices. We will explore this contention by focusing on three roles of urban food governance that seem to be of particular importance from a CPUL perspective:

(1) *Negotiating*: urban space as individual territories for food, including their negotiation, design and planning;

(2) *Managing*: productive urban landscapes as infrastructure designed, not only, but also for food system activities; and
(3) *Developing*: planning policy for food-focused activities for advancing urban resilience and spaces of exchange, encounter and experience.

Concepts, definitions, academic context

The CPUL concept describes an urban future based on the planned and designed introduction of networked landscapes defined by urban agriculture into existing and emerging cities. As described by Smit et al. (1996, p. 3), 'urban agriculture is an industry that produces and markets food and fuel, largely in response to the daily demand of consumers within a town, city or metropolis, on land and water dispersed throughout the urban and peri-urban metropolis. It is applying intensive production methods, using and reusing natural resources and urban waste, to yield a diversity of crops and livestock.'

The CPUL concept developed out of a body of design research instigated by the authors in the 1990s to investigate how architectural and urban design could reduce a city's Ecological Footprint (Bohn & Viljoen, 2001; Viljoen & Bohn, 2000). The food-producing elements draw on the earlier work on urban agriculture by Smit et al. (1996) and subsequent iterations by (Gorgolewski et al. (2011) and Mougeot (2001). Two books (Viljoen, 2005; Viljoen & Bohn, 2014) expanded from a theoretical case for the CPUL concept to proposals for implementation underpinned by practice-based research. Originally developed for urban contexts we were familiar with, that is, those in the Global North, the CPUL concept is also receiving attention beyond this area, for example in Burkina Faso, India, Togo, Tunisia and Uruguay.

In policy and academia dealing with city-wide spatial planning that includes urban agriculture, the CPUL concept has also started to attract attention under the term 'productive urban landscapes', although somewhat less tightly defined (SenStadt, 2012; Food Growing in the City, 2018; Detroit Future City, 2012; Greater London Authority, 2012).

It is worth considering the difference between a productive urban landscape and a *continuous* productive urban landscape. 'Continuous' refers to a spatial continuity, similar to Forman's concepts of ecological corridors connecting landscape patches (Forman, 2008), but in this case promoting and including urban agriculture patches. A connected network of open (food) spaces will give visual coherence and symbolic value to a productive urban landscape. The 'C' in CPUL extends a concept describing individual urban agriculture sites to an urban strategy for a city-wide network of many-faceted productive open urban spaces, including urban agriculture but not limited to it.

From an urban design perspective, what is urban food governance?

Urban design concepts, like CPUL, need urban design and planning mechanisms to be implemented and to function. Despite the current emergence of governance frameworks in many cities that bring together local politics, council administration and civic society around food, little has been done (or written) about food systems relationships to spatial and infrastructural design by those promoting food governance. Whilst certain spatial planning for food, for example zoning that addresses demographic or economic characteristics of an urban neighbourhood in relation to food, has received more attention in recent years, there is little governance in support of infrastructural spatial considerations, for example to where and how urban agriculture can be permanently situated. It is far easier to find examples of designers, typically architects and landscape architects, advocating for productive urban landscapes as part of wider urban food systems (Atelier d'architecture autogérée, 2019; De La Salle & Holland, 2010; Gorgolewski et al., 2011; Lohrberg et al., 2016; Sorkin, 2012; Verzone Woods Architects, 2011; Viljoen, 2005; Viljoen & Bohn, 2014). This is probably the main missing linkage, and it would be beneficial if the actors involved in advocating for more equitable and sustainable food governance explicitly recognised food-focused urban, architectural and landscape design as integral to food policy. Arguably, food-related businesses, for example restaurants, have already done this: the use and value of food markets, such as Detroit's Eastern Market (Eastern Market Partnership, n.d.) or community food gardens, such as Berlin's Prinzessinnengärten (Nomadisch Grün, n.d.) provide strong evidence that the design of food spaces has been significant for igniting conversations about the origins of urban food, participation in food system activities and support for urban (and peri-urban) food growers.

A typical approach to urban food governance can be seen in the open source material provided by the UK's Sustainable Food Places Network (Sustainable Food Places, 2020), which includes comprehensive guidance for stakeholders, cities and towns to initiate and govern transitions towards resilient and sustainable urban food systems. This network's strength is their successfully realised projects and initiatives. And yet, within its resource *Food Governance and Strategy*, which well covers action planning and collaborative goal setting, there is no explicit reference to food planning's interdependency with spatial infrastructure. So, perhaps we can reflect that, when Pothukuchi and Kaufman (2000) observed food to be a stranger to the planning system, we can add that urban design and urban food governance are strangers too?

The importance of a good relationship between CPULs and urban food governance

If urban food governance and urban design were better connected, food-sensitive urban design would benefit by gaining new advocates at decision-making levels able to challenge prevailing views about what makes for a successful city and what returns, beyond the monetary, signify success. Urban food governance can play a significant role in advancing resilient 'edible' nature-based solutions and generating traction for concepts like CPUL and their more widespread acceptance as elements of essential infrastructure. At the same time, urban food governance could benefit from including urban (food) place making as one of its objectives as an urban sustainable development goal. Currently, support in planning policy from cities for (food) place making tends to focus more on support for individual sites and less for infrastructural interventions, as we will see in our case studies.

Governance models for productive urban landscapes and individual food-growing projects cover subsistence, communal and commercial farming, the allotment movement, community gardens established by activists, market gardens and, more recently, urban and rooftop farms. All of these, apart from allotments and commercial market gardens, contribute to a legacy of productive urban landscape components where governance is highly localised, often bottom-up, radical and, at times, driven by conflict and the need for survival. By contrast, the various allotment movements in Europe are usually underpinned by formal regulatory frameworks at municipal and national levels, leading to a relatively stable governance structure. However, whilst the role of allotments within the creation of multifunctional landscapes and nature-based solutions is increasingly recognised (Cabral et al., 2017), allotment associations also need to focus on retaining rights that have been hard won and could easily be lost as urban land is sought for commercial development. Market gardens that once were common in many cities and commercially governed, have largely disappeared (Steel, 2008), and it is, in part, the reassessment of this loss, on environmental grounds, that drives the reemergence of productive urban landscapes.

Our field work and design research in Europe, the USA and Japan, indicates that the growing number of productive urban landscape initiatives are seeking out a growing number of new forms of governance. Those governance structures sit somewhere between the radical, activist-based project leads that have played such an important role in raising consciousness about urban food issues, as well as the tightly regulated policies that govern allotments and the commercial models that underpinned market gardens. As productive urban landscapes become part of a mainstream conversation, the need for more comprehensive governance is rising. In brief, this new governance requires, above all, a dialogue between urban farmer(s), planning authorities, local residents and politicians, as well as the statutory recognition for urban agriculture as a desired land use. With such high-level policy in place, not only would the leverage for farmers to negotiate space and resources grow, but the recognition of their environmental and social benefits, including employment, would also grow.

We can usefully distinguish between the governance requirements for individual food-growing projects and the more complex needs, if individual sites are to be connected to establish CPULs. The 'C' in CPUL requires the political will to plan and design at a scale that connects city centres to their peri-urban fringe and beyond. We have not found any governance models explicitly bridging CPULs and urban food governance. However, models for the governance of landscapes that are similar to the CPUL concept, including ecological networks and corridors, are emerging. For example, the International Union for the Conservation of Nature's *Guidelines for conserving connectivity through ecological networks and corridors* advocates: 'As with protected area and OECM (Other Effective Area-Based Conservation Measure) governance, ecological corridor governance has three components: how and by whom decisions are made, and who should be held accountable' (Hilty et al., 2020). Further lessons for the governance of CPULs may be drawn from other related and systematic approaches, for example to multifunctional landscape governance (CIFOR, 2020).

Common to all are recommendations for long, sustained initiatives underpinned by institutional support, including the UN and other agencies. These cross-city initiatives would involve a complex array of stakeholders with, at times, diverging agendas and interests. Perhaps the most challenging agenda is the International Union for the Conservation of Nature's suggestion that a specific individual or body is held accountable for the implementation of ecological networks. Implementing accountability may be difficult, if, for example, a policy is put in place at the municipal level and requires the support of elected councillors with limited tenure in office. The level at which policy is enacted is also critical. A national policy, for example, that obliges cities to support CPUL-like initiatives is more likely to result in action than municipal policies, especially in relation to the larger-scale and longer time frame of a CPUL.

Case studies

Embedding food in Berlin's green infrastructure planning

According to Kevin Morgan (2014, p. 23) 'one of the distinguishing features of these new urban politics [around urban food policy] is the stance of civil society organisations to mainstream political activity: where they once saw themselves as an "alternative movement" [...], they are now much more likely to forge alliances...'. In the context of Morgan's thoughts, the case of Berlin is of interest for urban food governance at an urban landscape/infrastructural scale.

In order to better cope with environmental as well as demographic challenges, the Berlin Senate adopted in 2011 an urban landscape strategy (*Strategie Stadtlandschaft*), subtitled 'natural. urban. productive', which mirrored the three main directions in which the city seeks to direct its future open space planning (SenStadt, 2012). The strategy's recommendations did not demand urban agriculture, but explicitly included it as a recognised land use under the heading 'productive'. This, in itself, can be called a defining moment in the German capital's urban food governance. Additionally, 'productive' is described by Undine Giseke as 'an urban interpretation of the cultured landscape, of open space, that is generated not only through its designers, but equally through its users' (Bohn & Giseke, 2010), thereby recognising a plurality of stakeholders. This recognition did not emerge suddenly, it was the result of community and urban agriculture advocates being active in Berlin as an 'alternative movement' for about 30 years (Meyer-Renschhausen, 2012). Around the same time, since about 2010, the city's fragmented community garden activists had started to pull their activities together in a national, and internationally much observed, network, the *Allmende Kontor* (GGAK, n.d.). One example of their capabilities was the collection of data on all communal food-growing projects and the production, in 2013, of the *Berliner Gartenkarte*, a collaboratively generated networking map of the city's, then 99, urban gardens (Richter, 2015).

Not much happened in the following years to start implementing the Senate's urban landscape strategy, though quarter-yearly round-table meetings between council administrators of the planning department and urban gardeners were established by both stakeholder groups to, basically, negotiate space. By 2018, the number of community gardens had more than doubled whilst, at the same time, urbanisation pressures, especially housing demand, suddenly increased substantially. Civil society and state/city government clashed heavily over questions of land use affecting all forms of food system activities, such as allotments, urban farms, community and school gardens, markets and small shops. The somewhat result-less urban gardening round-table meetings had lost their attraction, at least for civic society.

The slowly gathered knowledge, urgency and momentum culminated in 2019 in a third strategic document by the Senate, the *Charta für das Berliner Stadtgrün* (*Charter for Berlin's urban green*) (SenUVK, 2019). As part of the *Charta* process, the city administration embarked on the development of a new communication and knowledge tool on productive urban (green) space, the *Plattform Produktives Stadtgrün* (*Platform Productive Urban Green*). *Plattform Produktives Stadtgrün* is an interactive online communication tool that aims to engage the public and city officials in discussing the future of the German capital's open urban spaces by focusing on distinct spatial and use typologies. The first of those typologies is the community gardens, because these currently are not only the city's most prolific and successful productive urban space type, but they also command the most vocal and interested group of citizens. The platform was developed during 2019 by Berlin-based urban agriculture experts in a participatory process with the city's urban gardeners. An interactive map provides an overview of the more than 200 community gardens. The *Platform* may serve as an example for mutually beneficial urban planning and governance processes, mainly because of its:

(1) *Reciprocity*: Developing the platform *with* the community rather than *for* it was important for the gardeners and the Senate Administration. It allows the Senate to benefit from the reputation Berlin's community gardeners brought to the city and ensures at the same time prominent and official recognition of the gardeners and gardens.
(2) *Potential for space co-production*: The knowledge of Berlin's various productive green space typologies that were identified during the process will increase across all stakeholder

groups. This will not only improve the sense of local identity, but it will also open new ways into an informed and more transparent urban planning and co-design.

(3) *Large scale*: Ultimately, the platform will allow the superimposition of several productive space maps, such as those of community gardens, allotment gardens and urban farms. It will then become possible to coherently plan for a city-wide green infrastructure based on each individual component.

(4) *Economic viability*: Because the platform is held at the Senate's offices, there is a certain maintenance security. The fluctuations in funding had made it difficult for the urban gardeners to maintain previous versions of the *Berliner Gartenkarte*.

Evidently, Berlin is preparing for the implementation of a food-productive green infrastructure, but maybe due to COVID-19 delays, nothing tangible has yet improved the prospects for new and connected productive urban landscapes to be established any time soon.

Embedding food in Brighton & Hove's urban planning

Here we examine the role of Brighton & Hove City Council's *Planning Advisory Note (PAN 6) on Food Growing and Development* as an example of civic governance for productive urban landscapes. This document was, and remains, innovative and original in a number of respects. It was the first PAN in the UK specifically advocating for the inclusion of food-growing spaces in development proposals, and it came about through close cooperation between Brighton & Hove's then sustainability officers and an NGO, the Brighton & Hove Food Partnership, which led the drafting of the document, underpinned by consultation with a range of external parties, including the authors of this chapter. If CPULs are to become part of a city's essential infrastructure, we advocate for top-down initiatives like this PAN, that link with bottom-up and or development initiatives. Yet, despite its innovations, a number of challenges remain if the PAN's intentions are to be translated into active productive urban landscapes and places of exchange, encounter and experience. First adopted in 2011 and readopted as an expanded document in 2020 (BHCC, 2020), the PAN's aim is to encourage the inclusion of food-growing spaces in new urban developments and applies 'to new build commercial, residential and mixed-use developments, and if applicable, to conversions. It is intended to be used by developers and planning officers and interested members of the public as a guide to what might be achievable depending on the specific context of the development' (BHCC, 2011). In content it provides an overview of how the PAN fits within national and local planning policy, design guidance, technical guidance and a resource list. The suggestions made in a PAN are not mandatory, but they indicate approaches, that, if adopted within planning permission proposals, will be looked on favourably when planning applications are being assessed by the planning officials and elected councillors who are involved with approving them.

The 2011 edition of the PAN has been considered a success, the Brighton & Hove Food Partnership, the NGO that led its drafting, citing that between 2011 and 2015 there was 'an increase from 1% to over 38% of successful development applications incorporating food growing spaces' (BHFP, 2015, p. 27). In 2019, a systematic review of all planning applications made since 2011 revealed that 'between 1st September 2011 and 27th July 2019, thirty four of one hundred and fifty six planning applications for major housing and "other" developments in Brighton & Hove proposed at least some form of food-growing space ... almost 22% ... Thirteen of those thirty four applications (8.33% overall) were subsequently either withdrawn, had a lack of detail regarding the supposed food growing space as highlighted by the council's sustainability officer, or were to be confirmed later if deemed necessary' (Penny, 2019, p. 36).

As yet, there remains no systematic post-occupancy evaluation of the food-growing spaces that have been implemented.

With no systematic follow up or statutory requirement for minimum levels of production or social benefit from the food-growing interventions on site, it is difficult to judge the impact of the PAN. The authors' impression is that many sites are less productive than they could be, with some significantly underutilised. The following actions, linked to wider policy initiatives, are the sort that could facilitate better governance to ensure effective food growing in new developments.

Circular Economy: In December 2020, Brighton and Hove Council adopted a policy to create a circular economy framework based on a Mission and Vision outlined in a Circular Economy Route Map, with sustainable development goals set out to 2035. Food is one of the themes that the council will focus on, as part of a circular city vision. If the PAN can be formally connected to this policy, ideally in the context of a CPUL strategy, the incentive to follow up urban food-growing proposals would be strengthened.

Green Care: This is the prescription of time in gardens to undertaking therapeutic horticulture as part of a package of health and well-being treatments. The Brighton & Hove Food Partnership and the Council already collaborate on a voluntary network of local organisations under the umbrella of the 'Green Wellbeing Alliance'. Planning Advisory Note (PAN) 06 food-growing initiatives could beneficially be formally affiliated with provision of health care.

Developer commitments: PANs offer guidance to developers but are not legally binding, and so there is no comeback to developers if they have only included token food growing in a planning application. Elevating the PAN to become a Supplementary Planning Document, which provides detailed guidance on how planning policy will be implemented, could require more robust and resilient longer-term food-growing commitments from developers.

Discussion, contention, conflict

What can be achieved through good food governance for productive urban landscapes and what can productive urban landscapes offer urban food governance? We believe that a mutually beneficial relationship exists been these two; arguably urban landscape and urban governance have always been related through planning legislation, but adding urban agriculture and food systems to the mix could provide the ingredients for more food equitable and spatially desirable cities. Reflecting on current governance in relation to CPULs, we can identify three needs: Negotiation, Infrastructure and Governance.

Negotiation: Urban space as territories for food

Brighton and Hove's PAN 06 provides a good example of a planning initiative encouraging the development of urban agriculture 'patches' within an urban territory, and innovatively it is directed to developers rather than farmers. This recognises the reality that much of a city's landscape is controlled not by local authorities but by landowners, and for most an incentive will be required to convince them of implementing urban agriculture. The incentive offered by Brighton and Hove is that planning permission will be more likely if food growing is included in developments. This initiative is a success if measured by the number of planning proposals that include food growing, but after permission has been granted, there is no formal follow-up to evaluate the initiative and no penalty for failure. The lack of a formal sanction, or policy to require a robust business plan to maintain urban agriculture, means that the whole policy risks being seen as, at best, a well-intentioned, but naive policy, or an example of greenwashing.

From witnessing the development of the PAN, we are convinced that neither of these are intentional outcomes, but rather demonstrate the challenges of requiring green infrastructure to compete with market-driven development. One way to overcome this challenge would be to legislate nature-based solutions and green infrastructure into the city's binding plan for food within the circular economy. In this context, the food-productive components of a CPUL would be governed alongside those for other competing and potentially lower maintenance passive nature-based landscape solutions, such as wildflowers (aesthetic advantage) or sustainable urban drainage greenery (asset protection advantage). Experience from other pioneering cities, such as Tokyo and Heidelberg, attempting to develop CPUL-like initiatives, indicate that detailed and sophisticated negotiation between legal owners and the wider city are essential if long-term projects are to be realised (Viljoen & Bohn, 2020). In the case of the PAN 6, this negotiation is limited to the formal planning permission procedure, and the negotiation remains shallow. A deeper negotiation might, for example, require developers to identify future urban farmers who would use the space.

Infrastructure: Productive urban landscapes as infrastructure for food system activities

Landscape networks and corridors as environmentally beneficial infrastructure are accepted as good in principle, even if often not yet practised. Most urban agriculture practice and research is about individual sites – patches, not networks. So, how can cities begin to unleash the transformative potential of a productive urban landscape infrastructure and manage this?

The answer may lie in adopting a two-strand approach to urban space: one narrowly focused on gaining recognition for urban agriculture as a legally recognised land use; the other on the city-wide mapping of existing food-productive spaces and initiatives. There is evidence that both first steps are being adopted, sometimes simultaneously, in a growing number of cities worldwide.

In 2012, Berlin (SenStadt, 2012), and Detroit (Detroit Future City, 2012), explicitly named urban agriculture and productive landscapes as desired uses in their open space and landscape-planning documents. The *All London Green Grid* (Greater London Authority, 2012) planning document made a similar, but more generalised reference to productive landscapes. Defining urban agriculture as a legitimate land use has been recognised as a necessary, but often slow step in urban management, evidenced by the example of Havana's relatively late adoption of urban agriculture as a permanent urban function (Pena Diaz & Harris, 2005).

The mapping of food-productive spaces and urban agriculture initiatives in individual cities is emerging as a means to make visible, and gain an overview of, food system activities. Often online and interactive, food maps provide a framework for coordination between, if not the direct management of, individual urban agriculture sites; see, for example, maps about community gardening in London (www.capitalgrowth.org/spaces/) and Berlin (www.berlin.de/gemeinschaftsgaertnern/). These examples demonstrate how maps evolve; the London map was initiated in 2012 and Berlin's map in 2019. Both have links to websites for individual gardens and connections to a wider set of support networks.

Governance: Food-focused activities and spaces of exchange, encounter and experience

The interplay between civil society organisations and mainstream politics is evident in many cities where food urban policy is developing, and Morgan (2014) has traced much of this activity back to the emergence of civil society food policy councils in North America as an influence on activities like those described in the Berlin case study. Notwithstanding the significance of civil society organisations, mainstream municipal politics continues to play a significant role, as indicated by the Brighton & Hove case study, where policy reaches significant sectors, like property developers, who otherwise may not consider food systems or CPULs.

In facilitating exchanges between the various players advocating for productive urban landscapes, the power of experience is perhaps the best way to convince. Here we can point to The UK's Sustainable Food Cities Network, established in 2011 and re-formed in 2019 as the Sustainable Food Places programme, as a good example. It provides a platform for an exchange of evidence-based best practice. However, as yet, the urban design and landscape dimensions of food policy and governance are not covered.

The Berlin and Brighton & Hove case studies describe typical approaches to emerging governance for productive urban landscapes, both indicate the extended time scale they have required as pioneering initiatives, and both have relied on civil society organisations and city authorities to provide platforms for exchanges between stakeholders. Despite these achievements neither meet the International Union for the Conservation of Nature's (Hilty et al., 2020) call to define where responsibility lies for delivering on policy, let along wider goals such as CPULs.

Conclusion

At its most radical, the CPUL concept is a nature-based solution for the better provision of urban food in the context of climate change and rapid urbanisation. It is a concept that can also accommodate technological advances, such as protected agriculture, utilising technological innovations such as aquaponics, hydroponics and vertical farming. But beyond the fundamental desire to feed cities, it is an urban and architectural concept that asserts that, by reintroducing agriculture into cities, encounter and exchange will be encouraged – encounter and exchange between people in the spaces and by the actions associated with cultivating, sharing and distributing food, aesthetic exchange between us and cultivated landscapes and a symbolic encounter with seasonality by experiencing and observing the transformation of CPULs across a year.

The shift from where we are today to this, more or less radical, future will require significant change, which now looks like an enormous challenge. To reach it will require scenario building to describe a future which is open to all the options, from a return to subsistence to a utopian technological future in which work, as we know it, is outsourced to an Internet of Things-enabled future. This shift in relation to food may seem unrealistically optimistic, and yet we are witnessing just such a shift in energy provision away from petrochemicals to renewables. Perhaps food will witness a similarly sudden change, but however fast or slow the pace of change is, governance will have a significant role in determining how the future of food will look. Fundamental to the provision of productive urban landscapes is access to land, and governance will have a fundamental role in determining if this access is controlled by a wider public or a narrow commercial interest.

Reflecting on emerging practices that advance equitable and sustainable food futures, including productive landscapes, our challenge will be to encourage exchange and encounter through negotiation, management and development. Our case studies suggest that, whilst not perfect, supportive urban food governance can positively contribute to initiating, implementing and safeguarding sustainable food places and practices. For productive urban landscapes, this means:

(1) Recognising the significance of urban space as a site for individual productive urban landscapes, including their negotiation, design and management as food places and place makers;

2) Managing urban space as connected infrastructural landscapes designed not only, but also, for food system activities; and
3) Acknowledging spatially aware food-focused planning policy as a governance tool enabling the urban to become resilient and remain desirable.

Very likely – and hopefully, we will see in the near future an intensified discussion about the significance of food-productive urban space and green infrastructure. If we can get this right, then, in the future, we will be able to say: there is no urban food without productive urban landscapes, and there are no productive urban landscapes without good food governance!

References

APA (American Planning Association). (2007). *Policy Guide on Community and Regional Food Planning.* Retrieved from: www.planning.org/policy/guides/adopted/food.htm.

Atelier d'architecture autogérée (aaa). (2019). *L'Agrocité de Gennevilliers.* Retrieved from: www.urbantactics.org/projets/agrocite-gennevilliers/

BHCC (Brighton and Hove City Council). (2011). *Food Growing and Development* (Planning Advisory Note 06). Brighton: BHCC.

BHCC (Brighton and Hove City Council). (2020). *Food Growing and Development: Updated September 2020* (Planning Advisory Note 06). Brighton: BHCC. Retrieved from: www.brighton-hove.gov.uk/sites/default/files/2020-09/FINAL%20Food%20PAN%202020.pdf

BHFP (Brighton and Hove Food Partnership). (2015). *Brighton and Hove Sustainable Food Cities Award 2015.* (p. 27). Brighton: BHFP. Retrieved from: www.sustainablefoodplaces.org/Portals/4/Documents/Brighton%20Hove%20Food%20Partnership%20SFC%20silver%20application.pdf>

Bohn, K., & Chu, D. (2019). *Food-productive Infrastructure: Enabling Agroecological Transitions from an Urban Design Perspective.* Paper presented at the meeting of 9th International Conference of the AESOP Sustainable Food Planning Group, Universidad Politecnica de Madrid in Spain (paper in publication).

Bohn, K., & Giseke, U. (2010). Reiche Ernte für die Stadt. *Garten und Landschaft*, 12, 26–28.

Bohn, K., & Viljoen, A. (2001). Response to theme 4 – Synthesis and shape: Designs on the city. In M. Hewitt & S. Hagan (Eds.), *City Fights Debates on Urban Sustainability* (pp. 112–121). London: James and James.

Bohn, K., & Viljoen, A. (2014). Growth and challenges since 2005. In A. Viljoen & K. Bohn (Eds.), *Second Nature Urban Agriculture: Designing Productive Cities* (pp. 6–11). Oxford: Routledge.

BÖLW (Bund Ökologische Lebensmittelwirtschaft e.V). (2021). *Branchenreport 2021: Ökologische Lebensmittelwirtschaft.* Retrieved from: www.boelw.de/themen/zahlen-fakten

Cabral, I., Costa, S., Weiland, U., & Bonn, A. (2017). Urban gardens as multifunctional nature-based solutions for societal goals in a changing climate. In N. Kabisch, H. Korn, J. Stadler, & A. Bonn (Eds.), *Nature-Based Solutions to Climate Change Adaptation in Urban Areas: Linkages between Science, Policy and Practice* (pp. 237–253). Cham: Springer International Publishing.

CIFOR. (2020). About – Governing multifunctionallLandscapes. Retrieved from: www.cifor.org/gml/about/

Daily, G.C. (Ed.). (1997). *Nature's Services: Societal Dependence on Natural Ecosystems.* Washington, DC: Island Press.

De La Salle, J., & Holland, M. (Eds.). (2010). *Agricultural Urbanism: Handbook for Building Sustainable Food & Agriculture Systems in 21st Century Cities.* Faringdon, Oxfordshire: Green Frigate Books.

Detroit Future City. (2012). Detroit Strategic Framework Plan. Retrieved from: https://detroitfuturecity.com/strategic-framework/

Eastern Market Partnership. (n.d.). Eastern Market Detroit. Retrieved from: https://easternmarket.org/

EC (European Commission). (2021). *A European Green Deal: Striving to Be the First Climate-Neutral Continent.* Retrieved from: https://ec.europa.eu/info/strategy/priorities-2019-2024/european-green-deal_en

EC. (n.d.). The EU and nature-based solutions. Retrieved from: https://ec.europa.eu/info/research-and-innovation/research-area/environment/nature-based-solutions_en

Edwards, F., Pedro, S., & Rocha, S. (2021). Institutionalising degrowth: Exploring multi-level food governance. In A. Nelson & F. Edwards (Eds.), *Food for Degrowth: Perspectives and Practices.* London: Routledge.

Ernährungsrat Berlin. (2017). Ernährungsdemokratie für Berlin! Retrieved from: http://ernaehrungsrat-berlin.de/ernaehrungsdemokratie-fuer-berlin

Ernährungsrat Berlin. (2019). Unsere Sicht auf die Berliner Ernährungsstrategie. Retrieved from: https://ernaehrungsrat-berlin.de/die-berliner-ernaehrungsstrategie.

Food Growing in the City. (2018). Exploring the productive urban landscape as a new paradigm for inclusive approaches to the design and planning of future urban open spaces. [Editorial]. *Landscape and Urban Planning*, 170, 1–5.

Forman, R.T.T. (2008). *Urban Regions: Ecology and Planning Beyond the City*. Cambridge; New York: Cambridge University Press.

GGAK (Gemeinschaftsgarten Allmende-Kontor e.V). (n.d.). *Das Allmende-Kontor*. Available at: www.allmende-kontor.de/

Göpel, M. (2020). *Unsere Welt neu denken: Eine Einladung*. Berlin: Ullstein Verlag.

Gorgolewski, M., Komisar, J., & Nasr, J. (2011). *Carrot City: Creating Places for Urban Agriculture*. New York: Monacelli Press.

Greater London Authority. (2012). Green infrastructure and open environments: The all London Green Grid, supplementary planning guidance. Retrieved from: www.london.gov.uk/sites/default/files/algg_spg_mar2012.pdf

Hilty, J., Worboys, G.L., Keeley, A., Woodley, S., Lausche, B., Locke, H., Carr, M., Pulsford, I., Pittock, J., White, J.W., Theobald, D.M., Levine, J., Reuling, M., Watson, J.E.M., Ament, R., & Tabor, G.M. (2020). Guidelines for conserving connectivity through ecological networks and corridors. *Best Practice Protected Area Guidelines Series No. 30*. Gland: IUCN.

IPCC (Intergovernmental Panel on Climate Change). (2018). Global Warming of 1.5°C. An IPCC Special Report on the Impacts of Global Warming of 1.5°C above Pre-Industrial Levels and Related Global Greenhouse Gas Emission Pathways, in the Context of Strengthening the Global Response to the Threat of Climate Change, Sustainable Development, and Efforts to Eradicate Poverty. Retrieved from: www.ipcc.ch/site/assets/uploads/sites/2/2019/06/SR15_Full_Report_Low_Res.pdf

Jansma, J.E., & Wertheim-Heck, S.C.O. (2021). Thoughts for urban food: A social practice perspective on urban planning for agriculture in Almere, the Netherlands. *Landscape and Urban Planning*, 206, 103976, doi:10.1016/j.landurbplan.2020.103976.

Kato, S., & Ahern, J. (2009). Multifunctional landscapes as a basis for landscape development. Landscape *Research Japan*, 72(5), 799–804.

Lohrberg, F.L., Licka, L., Scazzosi, L., & Timpe, A. (Eds.). (2016). *Urban Agriculture Europe*. Germany: JOVIS Verlag.

Lovell, S.T., & Taylor, J.R. (2013). Supplying urban ecosystem services through multifunctional green infrastructure in the United States. *Landscape Ecology*, 28(8), 1447–1463.

Meyer-Renschhausen, E. (2012). Urban agriculture, Interkulturelle Gärten, community gardening. In K. Bohn, K. Ritzmann, & N. Awan (Eds.), *Spiel/Feld Urbane Landwirtschaft* (pp. 30–37). Berlin: Technische Universität Berlin.

Morgan, K. (2014). The new urban foodscape. In A. Viljoen & K. Bohn (Eds.), *Second Nature Urban Agriculture: Designing Productive Cities* (pp. 18–23). London and New York: Routledge.

Morgan, K., & Sonnino, R. (2006). Empowering consumers: The creative procurement of school meals in Italy and the UK. *International Journal of Consumer Studies*, 31(1), 19–25.

Mougeot, L.J.A. (2001). Urban agriculture: Definition, presence, potentials and risks. In N. Bakker, M. Dubbeling, S. Gündel, U. Sabel-Koschella, & H. de Zeeuw (Eds.), *Growing Cities, Growing Food: Urban Agriculture on the Policy Agenda: A Reader on Urban Agriculture* (pp. 1–42). Feldafing: German Foundation for International Development.

Naumann, S., Davis, M., Kaphengst, T., Pieterse, M., & Rayment, M. (2011). *Design, Implementation and Cost Elements of Green Infrastructure Projects: Final Report to the European Commission DG Environment*. Berlin: Ecologic Institute; London: GHK Consulting.

Nomadisch Grün. (n.d.). Prinzessinnengarten. Retrieved from: https://prinzessinnengarten.net/about/

Pena Diaz, J., & Harris, P. (2005). Urban agriculture in Havana: Opportunities for the future. In A. Viljoen (Ed.), *Continuous Productive Urban Landscapes (CPULs): Designing Urban Agriculture for Sustainable Cities* (pp. 135–145). Oxford: Architectural Press.

Penny, K. (2019). *Urban Food Planning Priority: A Case Study Analysis of Brighton and Hove*. Unpublished Master's thesis, University of Brighton, UK.

Pothukuchi, K., & Kaufman, J. (2000). The food system: A stranger to urban planning. *Journal of the American Planning Association*, 66(2), 113–124.

Richter, J. (2015). *Berliner Gartenkarte*. Retrieved from: https://gartenkarte.de/#!index.md

Rockström, J., Edenhofer, O., Gaertner, J., & DeClerck, F. (2020). Planet-proofing the global food system. *Nature Food*, 1, 3–5.

SenStadt Senatsverwaltung für Stadtentwicklung und Umwelt Berlin (2012). *Strategie Stadtlandschaft Berlin: natürlich – urban – produktiv*. Retrieved from: www.berlin.de/sen/uvk/natur-und-gruen/landschaftsplanung/strategie-stadtlandschaft

SenUVK Senatsverwaltung für Umwelt, Verkehr und Klimaschutz (2019). *Charta für das Berliner Stadtgrün*. Retrieved from: www.berlin.de/senuvk/umwelt/stadtgruen/charta/index.shtml

Smit, J., Ratta, A., & Nasr, J. (1996). *Urban Agriculture: Food, Jobs and Sustainable Cities*. New York: United Nations Development Program (UNDP).

Sorkin, M. (2012). New York City (steady) State. Scarcity: Architecture in an Age of Depleting Resources, *Architectural Design Special Issue*, 82(4), 102–109.

Steel, C. (2008). *Hungry City: How Food Shapes Our Lives*. London: Chatto & Windus.

Sustainable Food Places. (2020). Sustainable food places. Retrieved from: www.sustainablefoodplaces.org/

Sy, M., Baguian, H., & Gahi, N. (2014). Multiple use of green spaces in BoBo-Dioulasso, Burkina Faso. *Urban Agriculture Magazine*, March, Issue No. 27, pp. 33–36. Retrieved from: https://citeseerx.ist.psu.edu/viewdoc/download?doi=10.1.1.728.7057&rep=rep1&type=pdf

TCPA (Town and Country Planning Association) & Parham, S. (2019). Practical guides for creating successful new communities: Guide 10: Edible garden cities. Retrieved from: www.tcpa.org.uk/Handlers/Download.ashx?IDMF=633bf10c-e879-4f5b-b68f-3d03de5f19a8

TEEB Initiative. (2010). The Economics of Ecosystems and Biodiversity: Mainstreaming the Economics of Nature: A Synthesis of the Approach, Conclusions and Recommendations of TEEB. Retrieved from: http://teebweb.org/publications/teeb-for/synthesis

Tornaghi, C. (2014). Critical geography of urban agriculture. *Progress in Human Geography*, 38(4), 551–567.

Verzone Woods Architects. (2011). *Food Urbanism Typologies*. Retrieved from: www.foodurbanism.org/typologies/

Viljoen, A. (Ed.). (2005). *Continuous Productive Urban Landscapes (CPULs): Designing Urban Agriculture for Sustainable Cities*. Oxford: Architectural Press.

Viljoen, A., & Bohn, K. (2000). Urban intensification and the integration of productive landscape. *In Renewables: The Energy for the 21st Century, Part 1, World Renewable Energy Conference, VI*, pp. 483–488.

Viljoen, A., & Bohn, K. (Eds.). (2014). *Second Nature Urban Agriculture: Designing Productive Cities*. Oxford: Routledge.

Viljoen, A., & Bohn, K. (2020). Building continuous productive (peri-)urban landscapes. In J. Wiskerke (Ed.), *Achieving Sustainable Urban Agriculture* (pp. 61–100). Cambridge: Burleigh Dodds Science Publishing Limited. 10.19103/AS.2019.0063.07.

Waldheim, C. (2016). *Landscape as Urbanism*. Princeton, NJ: Princeton University Press.

INDEX

Note: Page numbers in **bold** indicate tables; those in *italics* indicate figures. Cities, towns, and states are indexed separately from their countries.

Taylor & Francis Group
an **informa** business

Taylor & Francis eBooks

www.taylorfrancis.com

A single destination for eBooks from Taylor & Francis with increased functionality and an improved user experience to meet the needs of our customers.

90,000+ eBooks of award-winning academic content in Humanities, Social Science, Science, Technology, Engineering, and Medical written by a global network of editors and authors.

TAYLOR & FRANCIS EBOOKS OFFERS:

- A streamlined experience for our library customers
- A single point of discovery for all of our eBook content
- Improved search and discovery of content at both book and chapter level

REQUEST A FREE TRIAL

support@taylorfrancis.com

Routledge
Taylor & Francis Group

CRC Press
Taylor & Francis Group

FSC
www.fsc.org
MIX
Papier | Fördert
gute Waldnutzung
FSC® C083411

Kolibri 360 GmbH
Ferdinand-Jühlke-Straße 7
99095 Erfurt, Deutschland
produktsicherheit@kolibri360.de